The Imperial
Presidency

BOOKS BY ARTHUR M. SCHLESINGER, JR.

Orestes A. Brownson: A Pilgrim's Progress

The Age of Jackson

The Vital Center

The General and the President
(*with Richard H. Rovere*)

The Age of Roosevelt
I. The Crisis of the Old Order, 1919–1933
II. The Coming of the New Deal, 1933–1935
III. The Politics of Upheaval, 1935–1936

Kennedy or Nixon: Does It Make Any Difference?

The Politics of Hope

A Thousand Days:
John F. Kennedy in the White House

The Bitter Heritage:
Vietnam and American Democracy, 1941–1966

The Crisis of Confidence:
Ideas, Power, and Violence in America

The Imperial Presidency

Robert Kennedy and His Times

The Cycles of American History

The Disuniting of America:
Reflections on a Multicultural Society

A Life in the Twentieth Century:
Innocent Beginnings, 1917–1950

War and the American Presidency

The Imperial Presidency

★

Arthur M. Schlesinger, Jr.

With a
New Introduction

A Mariner Book
Houghton Mifflin Company
Boston • New York

First Mariner Books edition 2004

Copyright © 1973 by Arthur M. Schlesinger, Jr.
Epilogue copyright © 1989 by Arthur M. Schlesinger, Jr.
Introduction copyright © 2004 by Arthur M. Schlesinger, Jr.

Visit our Web site: www.houghtonmifflinbooks.com.

Library of Congress Cataloging-in-Publication Data
Schlesinger, Arthur Meier, date.
The imperial presidency / Arthur M. Schlesinger, Jr. ; with a new
introduction by the author.
p.   cm.
Bibliography: p.
Includes index.
ISBN 0-618-42001-0 (pbk.)
1. Presidents — United States — History. 2. Executive power
— United States — History.   I. Title.
JK511.S35   1989   89-35462
353.03'13'09 — dc20   CIP

A portion of this book appeared in the *Atlantic,* copyright © 1973
by The Atlantic Monthly Company. The epilogue appeared in different form in *The Cycles of American History,* copyright © 1986
by Arthur M. Schlesinger, Jr.

For
Alexandra

★ ★

Acknowledgments

I AM INDEBTED to the kindly and searching counsel of a number of friends who read parts of this work — Benjamin V. Cohen, Joseph L. Rauh, Jr., Abraham Sofaer, Herman Kahn, and Herbert Wechsler — and I particularly absolve the lawyers in this group from responsibility for the legal and constitutional solecisms that unquestionably linger in the text. I am indebted too for many courtesies to the library staffs of the Graduate School of the City University of New York, of the Council on Foreign Relations, and of the Association of the Bar of the City of New York. I could not possibly have completed this book without the unfailingly cheerful and resourceful assistance of Gretchen Stewart, and I am endlessly grateful to her, as well as to Mary Chiffriller and Bonnie Lurer, for the long and exacting hours they spent over their typewriters. Without the patient labor of Bernice Colt there would be no index. My debt to Alexandra Emmet Schlesinger is immeasurable and inexpressible.

Arthur M. Schlesinger, Jr.

Contents

Acknowledgments		vi
Introduction to the Mariner Edition		ix
Foreword to the 1973 Edition		xxv
1.	What the Founding Fathers Intended	1
2.	Where the Founding Fathers Disagreed	13
3.	The Rise of Presidential War	35
4.	Congress Makes a Comeback	68
5.	The Presidency Resurgent: The Second World War	100
6.	The Presidency Ascendant: Korea	127
7.	The Presidency Rampant: Vietnam	177
8.	The Revolutionary Presidency: Washington	208
9.	Democracy and Foreign Policy	278
10.	The Secrecy System	331
11.	The Future of the Presidency	377
	Epilogue: After the Imperial Presidency	420
	Notes	501
	Index	551

★ ★

Back to the Imperial Presidency

A FEW YEARS BACK, the Imperial Presidency seemed to be finished. President Bill Clinton was on the ropes, facing a special prosecutor and impeachment. The presidency appeared a stricken institution in grave trouble — or so presidential scholars imagined.

In August 1998 I wrote an op-ed piece for the *New York Times* entitled "So Much for the Imperial Presidency." The presidency, I wrote, was "harried and enfeebled by an obsessed special prosecutor." Fellow presidential scholars shared in obituaries for the Imperial Presidency. "The U.S. presidency," wrote Richard E. Neustadt, "has been progressively weakened over the past three decades to the point where it is probably weaker today than at almost any time in the preceding century." Michael Beschloss chose "The End of the Imperial Presidency" as the title of his column portraying George W. Bush as "the first truly post-imperial president."

Alas, the obituaries were premature. I had written *The Imperial Presidency* in the latter days of Richard M. Nixon. The American Constitution, the book argues, envisages a strong presidency within an equally strong system of accountability. When the constitutional balance is upset in favor of presidential power and at the expense of presidential accountability, the presidency can be said to become imperial.

The perennial threat to the constitutional balance, I suggested, arises in the field of foreign affairs. Confronted by presidential initiatives in domestic policy, the countervailing branches of the national government — the legislative and the judiciary — have ample confidence in their own information and judgment. In this area they do not hesitate to challenge what they deem to be executive pretensions, nor do they lightly surrender power to the presidency. The media and public opinion, those extraconstitutional checks on the abuse of executive power, are similarly assured in dealing with domestic policy.

But confronted by presidential initiatives in foreign affairs, Congress and the courts, along with the press and the citizenry, often lack confidence in their own information and judgment and are likely to be intimidated by executive authority. The inclination in foreign policy is to let the president have the responsibility and the power — a renunciation that results from congressional pusillanimity as well as from presidential rapacity. The more acute the crisis, the more power flows to the president.

"It is chiefly in its foreign relations," Alexis de Tocqueville noted early on, "that the executive power of a nation finds occasion to exert its skill and its strength. If the existence of the American Union were perpetually threatened, if its chief interests were in daily connection with those of other powerful nations, the executive would assume an increased importance." But the young republic Tocqueville visited in the 1830s had lived, at least since the War of 1812, in happy isolation from world power struggles. So, "the President of the United States," Tocqueville observed, "possesses almost royal prerogatives which he has no opportunity of exercising."

By the twentieth century the United States itself had become a world power, its interests in daily connection with those of other powers; and the half century from Pearl Harbor to the breakup of the Soviet Union was experienced as a time of perpetual threat to the American Union. The chronic international crisis known as the Cold War at last gave presidents the opportunity for sustained exercise of those almost royal prerogatives. What began as emergency powers temporarily confided to presidents soon hardened into authority claimed by presidents as constitutionally inherent in the presidential office: thus the Imperial Presidency.

The rise of the Imperial Presidency ran against the original intent of the constitutional framers. With the war-making propensities of absolute monarchs in mind, the framers of the Constitution took care to assign the vital foreign policy powers exclusively to Congress. Article I gave Congress not only the appropriations power — itself a potent instrument of control — but also the power to declare war, to raise and support armies, to provide and maintain a navy, to regulate commerce, and to grant letters of marque and reprisal. This last provision represented the eighteenth-century equivalent of retaliatory strikes and empowered Congress to authorize limited as well as general war.

Even Alexander Hamilton, the Constitutional Convention's foremost proponent of executive energy, endorsed this allocation of powers. "The history of human conduct," he wrote in Federalist 75, "does not warrant that exalted opinion of human virtue which would make it wise to commit interests of so delicate and momentous a kind, as those which concern its intercourse with the rest of the world, to the sole disposal of . . . a President of the United States." What seemed at stake was not only the wisdom of the policy but also the freedom of the people. "Perhaps it is a universal truth," said James Madison, "that the loss of liberty at home is to be charged to provisions against danger, real or pretended, from abroad."

The specific grants of authority to the executive in foreign policy were trivial compared with the authority specifically granted to Congress. The presidency was given the power of receiving and appointing ambassadors and, by implication, of serving as the channel of communications to foreign states. The president as commander in chief was given the power to direct the armed forces once war was authorized or begun and, by implication, the power to repel sudden attacks when Congress was not in session. However, Article II vested general executive power in the presidency. And, as Federalist 64 and 75 emphasized, the structural advantages of the presidency — unity, decision, secrecy, dispatch, stability of purpose, special sources of information — made the executive the prime agent in dealings with foreign states.

Those structural advantages worked against the framers' original intent. "It is of the nature of war," Hamilton wrote in the 8th Federalist, "to increase the executive at the expense of the legislative authority." The pattern of presidential aggrandizement under the spur of international crisis was visible from the start. In opposition Thomas Jefferson had been the apostle of strict construction and the foe of executive initiative. But viewing problems from the White House, he sent a naval squadron to the Mediterranean under secret orders to fight pirates in the Barbary War, applied for congressional sanction six months later, then misled Congress as to the nature of his orders. He unilaterally authorized the seizure of armed vessels in waters extending to the Gulf Stream, engaged in rearmament without congressional appropriations, withheld information from Congress, and invoked John Locke's doctrine of emergency prerogative — the law of self-preservation — to justify action beyond congressional authorization.

Early presidents did not hesitate to engage in what later generations called covert operations against foreign states and to do so without congressional knowledge. James Madison sent Joel R. Poinsett as a secret agent to Latin America and winked at his clandestine revolutionary adventures in Argentina and Chile; the secretary of state removed Poinsett's dispatches from State Department files lest Congress request them. Both Madison and James Monroe used covert action to facilitate the annexation of Florida.

Presidential adventurism in the early republic differed in salient respects, however, from the Imperial Presidency. As Abraham D. Sofaer shows in his magisterial work, *War, Foreign Affairs, and Constitutional Power: The Origins* (1976), early presidents deliberately selected venturesome agents, deliberately failed to approve or to disapprove their constitutionally questionable plans, and deliberately denied Congress the information to determine whether aggressive acts were authorized — all precisely because the presidents wanted their men in the field to do things they knew lay beyond their constitutional right to command. "At no time," Sofaer writes of the early period, "did the executive claim 'inherent' power to initiate military action."

The early presidents thus usurped power, and usurpation creates no constitutional precedents. It is the assertion of inherent powers that defines the Imperial Presidency and creates precedents for the future. The contrast in constitutional claims between the emergency policies of Abraham Lincoln and Franklin D. Roosevelt and those of post–World War II presidents illustrates the distinction.

Both Lincoln and Roosevelt were well aware of what the Constitution said about the war-making power. In 1848 Lincoln called the Mexican War illegal and unconstitutional because it was unilaterally provoked, so he believed, by President James K. Polk. The Founding Fathers at Philadelphia, Lincoln said, had "resolved to so frame the Constitution that *no one man* should hold power of bringing this oppression [war] upon us." Similarly, Roosevelt in 1940, promising supplies to a French government under Nazi assault, carefully added: "These statements carry with them no implication of military commitments. Only Congress can make such commitments."

Yet after the attack on Fort Sumter in 1861, Lincoln, on his own, without congressional authorization, assembled the militia, enlarged the army and navy beyond their authorized strength, called out volunteers for three years' service, spent unappropriated public funds, suspended habeas corpus, arrested persons "represented" as involved in "disloyal" practices, and instituted a naval blockade of the rebel states. In the same way, in 1941, when German submarine warfare threatened to sever the lifeline of supplies to Britain, Roosevelt, on his own, without congressional authorization, dispatched troops to Iceland, instituted a convoy system, issued a "shoot on sight" order to the navy, and launched an undeclared war in the North Atlantic.

But neither president based his action on claims of inherent power. His emergency measures, Lincoln told Congress when he finally convoked a special session, "whether strictly legal or not, were ventured upon under what appeared to be a popular demand and a public necessity; trusting then as now that Congress would readily ratify them." Roosevelt, like Lincoln, relied on his sense of popular demand and public necessity. The passage of the Lend-Lease Act (1941), after uninhibited public and congressional debate, had aligned the United States with Great Britain in the European war. If Congress voted arms to Britain as national policy, then, inferentially, national policy was to make sure the arms got to Britain. Roosevelt added a murky proclamation of "unlimited national emergency." But, like Lincoln, he made no claims of inherent power to do what he believed necessary to save the nation.

Both Lincoln and Roosevelt undertook acts they knew to be

beyond the Constitution. Both did so in times of transcendent crisis when the life of the nation seemed truly at stake. Both acted, knowingly or not, on Locke's doctrine of emergency prerogative, trusting that Congress would eventually approve their actions. Both men understood and affirmed that emergency prerogative must expire with the emergency. "The Executive power itself," said Lincoln, "would be greatly diminished by the cessation of actual war." "When the war is won," said Roosevelt, "the powers under which I act automatically revert to the people — to whom they belong." Neither Lincoln nor Roosevelt claimed an inherent and routine presidential right to do what they did. That claim, the essence of the Imperial Presidency, was a product of the second half of the twentieth century.

The rarity of international crisis also delayed the emergence of the Imperial Presidency. For, while war increased presidential power, peace brought a reaction against presidential excess. The Civil War, Henry Adams wrote, "for the time obliterated Constitution." It produced what Benjamin R. Curtis, one of the two dissenting justices in *Dred Scott v. Sanford* (1857), charged was "a military despotism." But once the crisis ended, the other two branches of government lost no time in reasserting their constitutional powers. A year after Appomattox the Supreme Court held *ex parte Milligan* (1866) that Lincoln's prosecution of a proslavery conspirator under the martial law behind the lines violated the Constitution. In another two years Lincoln's successor in the White House found himself at the bar of impeachment. The republic entered the era characterized by Woodrow Wilson as one of "congressional government."

Wilson himself, writing a new preface to *Congressional Government* after the Spanish-American War, remarked on "the greatly increased power . . . given the President by the plunge into international politics." When foreign policy became the nation's dominant concern, Wilson said, the executive "must of necessity be its guide: must utter every initial judgment, take every first step of action, supply the information upon which it is to act, suggest and in large measure control its conduct." As president during the First World War, Wilson acted on his own model.

But once again the return of peace shrank presidential power, as the Senate quickly showed by rejecting the Treaty of Versailles. In the 1930s Roosevelt, a mighty domestic president, could not prevent Congress from imposing rigid neutrality legislation that put American foreign policy in a straitjacket while Germany and Japan ran amok in Europe and Asia.

The end of the Second World War brought the customary diminution of presidential power. A year after Roosevelt's death his successor was so unpopular that voters said "To err is Truman" and elected a Republican Congress. The next year Congress gained posthumous revenge against the powerful wartime president by proposing what became the Twenty-second Amendment, thereby limiting all future presidents to two terms.

But this time the diminution was brief. The Cold War, by generating a climate of sustained and indefinite crisis, aborted the customary reversion of power to the coordinate branches. The most visible sign of growing presidential imperialism was the transfer of the power to go to war from Congress to the executive. Ten years after Roosevelt told France that only Congress could make military commitments, President Harry S. Truman, confronted by the North Korean invasion of South Korea, sent American forces to war on his own.

Historically, Congress had preserved the rough balance of the Constitution because it retained three vital powers: the war-making power, the power of the purse, and the power of oversight and investigation. In 1950 it relinquished the war-making power. Truman fought in Korea, Lyndon B. Johnson in Vietnam, and Richard M. Nixon in Cambodia without believing that their dispatch of troops into combat required explicit congressional authorization (Congress provided ambiguous authorization in the case of Vietnam through the 1964 Gulf of Tonkin Resolution). In 1969 through 1974, the Nixon administration tried systematically and, until the Watergate affair, successfully to restrict the other two powers: countering the power of the purse by the doctrine of the unlimited impoundment of appropriated funds and countering the power of oversight and investigation by the doctrine of unreviewable executive privilege (a novel term, first used officially in 1958) and the extension of the executive secrecy system. Had Nixon succeeded in imposing these doctrines on top of his amplified claims for the presidential war-making power, he would have gravely weakened Congress as a serious partner in the constitutional order.

Nixon carried the Imperial Presidency still further by using against his political opponents at home — "enemies," he called them — powers that the presidency had accumulated to save the republic from foreign foes. Invoking national security as an all-purpose justification, Nixon and his attorney general, John Mitchell, set up a secret White House posse to burgle offices, forge historical documents, and wiretap officials, embassies, newspapermen, and "enemies." "When the President does it," Nixon claimed in 1977, "that means that it is not illegal." Congress eventually roused itself. Articles of impeachment charged Nixon with acting "in a manner contrary to his trust as President and subversive of constitutional government," and Nixon resigned rather than be impeached and face a trial. Mitchell was later found guilty of perjury, conspiracy, and obstruction of justice, and served a prison term.

The Imperial Presidency reached a twentieth-century climax with Nixon. The post-Watergate reaction cut back on some presidential excesses. None of Nixon's successors, for example, used emergency powers against political opponents. The presidency of Jimmy Carter even led to concerns about the impotence of the office. "We have not an imperial presidency," former president Gerald Ford said in 1980, "but an imperiled presidency." But such lamentations were soon refuted when Ronald Reagan showed that a president with only a misty understanding of issues could still dominate the government and lead the country.

Nor did the reaction constrain presidential assumption of the war-making power. Reagan in the case of Grenada and George H. W. Bush in the cases of Panama and Iraq insisted on what Bush called "the President's constitutional authority to use the armed forces to defend vital U.S. interests." In the Iraq case, Congress rescued Bush from a constitutional conflict by voting to authorize the first Gulf War. However, the end of the Cold War materially weakened the national security arguments for the Imperial Presidency.

The farewell to the Cold War and, for a moment, to international crisis meant the customary setback for presidential power. The presidency was evidently in decline once again. Such at least was the judgment of presidential scholars. But we reckoned without Osama bin Laden and al-Qaeda.

Once again, international crisis has resurrected the Imperial Presidency. Much of the impact of revitalized presidential power on American liberties is dependent on the presidential choice of attorney general. After the First World War, a sick and distracted Woodrow Wilson permitted his attorney general, A. Mitchell Palmer, "the Fighting Quaker" (a.k.a. "the Quaking Fighter"), to run wild in fomenting a Red Scare series of raids and mass arrests. During the Second World War, Franklin D. Roosevelt's selection as attorney general was Francis Biddle, a strong civil libertarian. The result was a pretty good wartime record on individual rights (with, of course, the notable exception of the internment of Japanese Americans, which Biddle opposed). During the Cold War, John Mitchell happily connived with his boss Nixon at dirty tricks and became the first attorney general to go to jail.

The situation in Washington today? President George W. Bush's attorney general, John Ashcroft, a former senator, a politician of the hard right, and a religious zealot, is on the model of A. Mitchell Palmer rather than of Francis Biddle. According to Steven Brill, the legal critic, "even some of his own deputies at Justice were surprised by how uninterested he was in the niceties of the law. One veteran staffer recalls that . . . he had never once heard Ashcroft cite a legal case and had watched him blanch when someone in the room cited a case, as if that person was discourteously speaking another language." A righteous fellow, a communicant of an evangelical sect that disapproves of drinking, dancing, going to movies, and gazing at nude statues, Ashcroft puts one in mind of Mr. Dooley's definition of a fanatic — someone who "does what he thinks th' Lord wud do if He only knew th' facts in th' case."

Ashcroft is given to early morning prayer meetings held in his office. When he was elected to the Senate, according to Judy Bachrach's sketch in *Vanity Fair,* friends anointed his head with oil in the style of the ancient kings of Israel, although in this case it was Crisco oil from the kitchen. Ashcroft, a man of pious poses, lacked when young a stern view of his patriotic duty. During the Vietnam War, he sought and received seven deferments, including an occupational deferment for teaching business law to undergraduates at a Missouri college, "an assignment," according to the *New Republic,* "he lined up with the help of a family friend." Since Ashcroft was presumably in favor of the Vietnam War, he joins the serried ranks of chickenhawks that adorn the second Bush presidency. In Vice President Cheney's famous phrase, the Bush chickenhawks had "other priorities in the '60s than military service" in Vietnam. They have shown no reluctance, however, over sending young Americans to the Iraq shooting gallery.

Ashcroft's chosen national security vehicle is the 342-page USA Patriot Act, rushed to passage without hearings or committee reports forty-five days after 9/11 by a vote of 357 to 66 in the House and 98 to 1 in the Senate. (All honor to Russ Feingold of Wisconsin, the single Senate holdout!) The Patriot Act increases the discretionary power of federal agents to collect information about individuals, to search their homes, to inspect their reading habits and their Internet queries, to view their credit reports, to conduct wiretaps without warrants, to overhear lawyer-client telephone conversations without court orders, and to reduce judicial supervision and to spy on domestic organizations and advocacy groups. In a report to Congress, the Justice Department said that federal agents had conducted hundreds of bugging and surveillance operations and visited numerous libraries and mosques.

The FBI is part of Attorney General Ashcroft's domain. On Christmas Eve 2003 the FBI sent a zany bulletin to eighteen thousand police organizations warning against people carrying almanacs. There is nothing more innocent, one would think, than to give next year's *World Almanac* for Christmas. But, according to the FBI, terrorists might use almanacs "to assist with target selection and preoperational planning." Citizens were asked to report almanac carriers to the local U.S. Joint Terrorism Task Force.

The Patriot Act alarmed libertarians on the right, such as Wil-

liam Safire of the *New York Times*, as well as the American Civil
Liberties Union crowd on the left. Bob Barr of Georgia, the
dogged impeacher of Bill Clinton, joined Grover Norquist and
David Keene, veteran right-wing leaders, in an ACLU rally
protesting the act. As Norquist said, "Some day Hillary Clinton's
going to be attorney general, and I hope conservatives keep that
in mind."

And the temper of the administration as shown by its wish lists
is even more alarming. In January 2003 there fell into the hands
of Charles Lewis, head of the invaluable Center for Public Integrity, an eighty-page draft of a presumed Patriot Act II. The
proposed amendments would authorize secret arrests, relax restrictions on wiretapping, facilitate the stripping of citizenship,
and in general limit the role of judicial oversight and give the Department of Justice looser standards to brand individuals and
groups as terrorist suspects. The libertarian, left-wing coalition
bridled, and thus far there has been no Patriot II.

The Bush Pentagon meanwhile hauled out of oblivion a discredited official, John Poindexter, convicted of five felony counts
of lying to Congress about the Iran-Contra affair (the verdict was
reversed on a technicality). Poindexter headed a so-called Total
Information Awareness Project, an electronic data bank based
on federal, state, local, and commercial records, credit card
transactions, telephone calls, travel reservations, and so on. This
Orwellian concept was too much even for Republicans, and TIA
was stopped in its tracks.

The plight of the 660 men (and boys) picked up in Afghanistan after 9/11 and transported to Guantánamo Bay, the American naval base in Cuba, excited little interest in the United
States, but a good deal abroad, especially in Great Britain. The
U.S. government declined to grant al-Qaeda jihadists prisoner-
of-war status for understandable reasons — there was no organized state behind them. Also, government lawyers denied that
Guantánamo, held under lease, was sovereign U.S. soil; so U.S.
law did not apply. The detainees were kept in ignorance of the
charges against them and were denied access to counsel, to hearings, and to their families. They existed in legal limbo.

It is difficult to find serious security reasons for presidential suspension of due process. Some detainees were unquestionably al-Qaeda or Taliban thugs, fanatics, and killers; others may have been innocent bystanders, snatched up by accident in random sweeps. The detainees included octogenarians and teenagers. They were collectively defined as "unlawful enemy combatants," a classification unknown to international law. They were subject to intensive regimens of day-and-night interrogation. A "senior defense official" told the *New York Times* that detainees would be held for many years, perhaps indefinitely. Some among them have attempted suicide.

"The question," said Lord Steyn, a judge on Britain's highest court, "is whether the quality of justice envisaged for the prisoners at Guantanamo Bay complies with the minimum international standards for the conduct of fair trials. The answer can be given quite shortly. It is a resounding 'No.'" After pleas from Prime Minister Tony Blair, five British prisoners were released, some of whom then claimed to the London press that they had been beaten by American guards. "Three of the other released British detainees," reported the *Economist*, "confirm Mr. Al-Harith's claim of frequent physical abuse and beating. They had each been subject to more than two hundred interrogations lasting up to twelve hours." American officials in turn denied the stories. The conflict in testimony invites a congressional investigation.

Meanwhile, disclosures about the American abuse of detainees at Abu Ghraib, Saddam Hussein's old torture center, appalled and disgusted the world, including the United States. Among other surprises was the amount of chatter back and forth within the Bush administration about definitions of torture, a debate not hitherto covered by the previously obsequious American media.

The second Bush presidency is indeed the most secretive administration since Nixon. John W. Dean, who knew the Nixon White House well, writes, "George W. Bush and Richard B. Cheney have created the most secretive presidency of my lifetime. Their secrecy is far worse than during Watergate." Dean should have added Ashcroft to his list of secrecy addicts.

In 1966 Congress had passed the Freedom of Information Act

based on the proposition that disclosure should be the rule, not the exception, and that the burden should be on government to justify the withholding of records. This was a most beneficial law until Ashcroft got hold of it. Rejecting the spirit of the law, the attorney general advised federal officials that when they "decide to withhold records, in whole or in part, you can be assured that the Department of Justice will defend your decisions."

Following the argument over who owned Richard Nixon's papers, Congress had passed in 1978 the Presidential Records Act based on the proposition that White House records belonged to the American people and should be made available within a dozen years. A president could restrict access to six enumerated categories, ranging from national security papers to medical files. But the 1978 act breathed the post-Watergate spirit of open government.

One of President Bush's early actions was to alter the methodology and narrow the scope of the Presidential Records Act, and to do so — i.e., amend a congressional statute — by executive order. Executive Order 13223 gave sitting presidents the right to cancel the release of papers from a previous administration, even though the previous administration had approved their release. This gave rise to the uneasy suspicion that the people behind Executive Order 13223 had secrets they wished to hide from history. President Bush's attack on the Presidential Records Act enraged historians, political scientists, archivists, and journalists, and the American Historical Association organized a lawsuit. In Congress the executive order offended Republicans as well as Democrats, and in October 2002 the House Government Reform Committee unanimously voted to overturn it. The White House moved quickly to suppress the rebellion.

"Imperial" suggests empire, and the status of the United States as the world's unchallengeable superpower headed by an Imperial Presidency rouses speculation over the future and fate of the American Empire. Comparisons are often made to the Roman Empire and to the modern British and French Empires. Is the American Empire a fitting successor?

Now Americans, unlike Romans, Britons, and the French, are not colonizers of remote and exotic places. We peopled the vacant spaces, so we whites deemed them, in continental expansion from sea to shining sea, but we did not send away our youngest sons to man the outposts of empire. Britain really created a British world in India and Africa, as the French did in equatorial Africa and Indochina. Americans, wrote James Bryce in 1888, "have none of the earth-hunger which burns in the great nations of Europe."

Some of our political leaders did. Jefferson thought Cuba "the most interesting addition which could ever be made to our system of States" and told John C. Calhoun in 1820 that the United States "ought, at the first possible opportunity, to take Cuba." John Quincy Adams agreed, considering the annexation of Cuba to be "indispensable to the continuance and integrity of the Union itself" and thinking Cuba would inexorably fall to the United States by the law of political gravitation.

As for Canada, J. Q. Adams held "our proper domain to be the continent of North America." "That the whole continent of North America and all its adjacent islands," said Henry Adams, J.Q.'s grandson, in 1869, "must at last fall under the control of the United States is a conviction absolutely ingrained in our people." "Long ere the second centennial arrives," Walt Whitman wrote in *Democratic Vistas* (1871), "there will be some forty to fifty great States, among them Canada and Cuba." As late as 1895, Henry Cabot Lodge declared, "From the Rio Grande to the Arctic Ocean there would be but one flag and one country."

These things, so authoritatively predicted, never came to pass. The American people were not much interested in empire. The United States has not annexed Cuba or Canada. There is no likelihood that we ever will. Texas waited outside the Union for a decade as an independent republic and then entered only through presidential sleight of hand, John Tyler procuring admission by joint resolution after the Senate had rejected a treaty of annexation. The movement during the Mexican War to take "all Mexico" failed. President Polk even feared that Congress would turn against the war and that he would lose California and New Mexico. The Ostend Manifesto was disclaimed, and the filibusters of the 1850s were repudiated.

After the Civil War, Secretary of State William E. Seward's

ambitious expansionist program got nowhere, except for the fly-speck of Midway Island and for Alaska, which Russia wanted to get rid of and which Congress reluctantly accepted after members were bribed, perhaps by the Russian minister. The Senate rejected the Hawaiian reciprocity treaty, the purchase of the Virgin Islands from Denmark, the annexation of Santo Domingo, and the annexation of Samoa. It took half a century of argument before we annexed Hawaii, and this might not have taken place had it not been for the Spanish-American War. Even with that war we still did not annex Cuba. The United States did annex the Philippines, but the number of Americans who lived out their lives in the archipelago was negligible, and we set the islands free forty years later. The imperial dream has encountered consistent indifference and recurrent resistance through American history. The record hardly sustains the thesis of a people red-hot for empire.

Then there is the question of control. "The term 'empire,'" writes Professor G. John Ikenberry, summing up the common understanding, "refers to the political control by a dominant country of the domestic and foreign policies of weaker countries." Rome, London, Paris, despite slow and awkward lines of communication, really ruled their empires. Today communication is instantaneous; but, despite the speed of contact, Washington, far from ruling an empire in the old sense, becomes the prisoner of its dependent states.

This was the case with South Vietnam in the 1960s, and it has been the case ever since with Israel. Governments in Saigon forty years ago and in Tel Aviv today have been sure that the United States would not pull out altogether, or even significantly reduce American aid. They therefore were enabled to defy American commands and demands with impunity. Pakistan, Taiwan, Egypt, South Korea, and the Philippines are similarly unimpressed, evasive, or defiant. For all our superhuman military strength, we cannot get our Latin American neighbors, or even the tiny Caribbean islands, to do our bidding. Americans are simply not competent imperialists, as demonstrated in Iraq in 2004. The so-called American Empire is in fact a feeble imitation of the Roman, British, and French Empires.

And yet the American presidency has come to see itself in messianic terms as the appointed savior of a world whose unpredictable dangers call for rapid and incessant deployment of men, arms, and decisions behind a wall of secrecy. This view seems hard to reconcile with the American Constitution. The impact of 9/11 and of the overhanging terrorist threat gives more power than ever to the Imperial Presidency and places the separation of powers ordained by the Constitution under unprecedented, and at times unbearable, strain.

But superhuman military power cannot solve everything, even if American presidents were free to use such power without constraints, as they are not. As a world empire, the United States is undone by its own domestic politics and its own humane, pluralistic, and tolerant ideals. The premises of our national existence undermine our imperial aspirations. So the Imperial Presidency redux is likely to continue messing things up, as we are doing so successfully in Iraq, the needless war. Then democracy's singular virtue — its capacity for self-correction — will one day swing into action.

Arthur M. Schlesinger, Jr.
April 2004

★ ★

Foreword to the
1973 Edition

THE AMERICAN CONSTITUTION was established, for better or
worse, on an idea new to the world in the eighteenth century and
still uncommon in the twentieth century — the idea of the separation of powers. This forbidding phrase represented a distinctive American contribution to the art of government. There had
been no such doctrine in medieval times. Before the eighteenth
century, everyone assumed that government required the unifi-
cation of authority.[1] But the Founding Fathers, who saw conflict
as the guarantee of freedom, grandly defied the inherited wisdom. Instead of concentrating authority in a single institution,
they chose to disperse authority among three independent
branches of government, equipping the leaders of each, in the
words of the 51st Federalist Paper, with the "necessary constitutional means and personal motives to resist encroachments of
the others." These branches, as every schoolchild used to know,
were the executive, the legislative, and the judiciary. The Constitution thus institutionalized conflict in the very heart of the
American polity.

The question has always remained — and has provided a central theme of American political history — how a government
based on the separation of powers could be made to work. The
Founding Fathers were good Newtonians, and their system of
checks and balances, conceived almost as a mechanism, contained an inherent tendency toward inertia. This was all right for
a while: the point of the system as Justice Brandeis later observed, was "not to promote efficiency but to preclude the exercise of arbitrary power."[2] Still, efficiency had its claims on government too, especially in a rapidly changing society and even
more especially in times of danger. And was government after all
a mechanism? That Founding Father *manqué* Woodrow Wilson

said it was "not a machine, but a living thing . . . shaped to its functions by the sheer pressure of life" and added, "No living thing can have its organs offset against each other as checks, and live."[3]

The metaphor of government as organism had its difficulties too. But experience did demonstrate rather quickly that the system of checks and balances would not work at all unless one of the three branches took the initiative and that it worked best in response to vigorous presidential leadership. Such leadership was necessary to overcome the tendency toward inertia. It enabled the American republic to meet the great crises of its history. It also set up a permanent tension between the Presidency and the other branches of government. And in our own time it has produced a conception of presidential power so spacious and peremptory as to imply a radical transformation of the traditional polity. In the last years presidential primacy, so indispensable to the political order, has turned into presidential supremacy. The constitutional Presidency — as events so apparently disparate as the Indochina War and the Watergate affair showed — has become the imperial Presidency and threatens to be the revolutionary Presidency.

This book does not deal systematically with all facets and issues of presidential power. A number of excellent studies already do that. Nor does it deal primarily with the shift in the *political* balance between Congress and the Presidency — as exhibited, for example, in the increasing presidential domination of the legislative process or in the increasing delegation of power by Congress to presidents. It deals essentially with the shift in the *constitutional* balance — with, that is, the appropriation by the Presidency, and particularly by the contemporary Presidency, of powers reserved by the Constitution and by long historical practice to Congress.

This process of appropriation took place in both foreign and domestic affairs. Especially in the twentieth century, the circumstances of an increasingly perilous world as well as of an increasingly interdependent economy and society seemed to compel a larger concentration of authority in the Presidency. It must be said that historians and political scientists, this writer among them, contributed to the rise of the presidential mystique. But the Imperial Presidency received its decisive impetus, I believe, from foreign policy; above all, from the capture by the Presidency of the most vital of national decisions, the decision to go to war.

This book consequently devotes special attention to the history of the war-making power. The assumption of that power by the Presidency was gradual and usually under the demand or pretext of emergency. It was as much a matter of congressional abdication as of presidential usurpation. As it took place, there dwindled away checks, both written and unwritten, that had long held the Presidency under control. The written checks were in the Constitution. The unwritten checks were in the forces and institutions a president once had to take into practical account before he made decisions of war and peace — the cabinet and the executive branch itself, the Congress, the judiciary, the press, public opinion at home and the opinion of the world. By the early 1970s the American president had become on issues of war and peace the most absolute monarch (with the possible exception of Mao Tse-tung of China) among the great powers of the world.

The Indochina War placed this problem high on the national consciousness. But the end of American military involvement in Southeast Asia would not extinguish the problem. The assertions of sweeping and unilateral presidential authority remained official doctrine in foreign affairs. And, if the president were conceded these life-and-death decisions abroad, how could he be restrained from gathering unto himself the less fateful powers of the national polity? For the claims of unilateral authority in foreign policy soon began to pervade and embolden the domestic Presidency. "Perhaps it is a universal truth," Madison had written Jefferson, "that the loss of liberty at home is to be charged to provisions against danger, real or pretended, from abroad."[4] The all-purpose invocation of "national security," the insistence on executive secrecy, the withholding of information from Congress, the refusal to spend funds appropriated by Congress, the attempted intimidation of the press, the use of the White House itself as a base for espionage and sabotage directed against the political opposition — all signified the extension of the Imperial Presidency from foreign to domestic affairs. Underneath such developments there could be discerned a revolutionary challenge to the separation of powers itself.

This book is written out of a double concern. The first concern is that the pivotal institution of the American government, the Presidency, has got out of control and badly needs new definition and restraint. The second concern is that revulsion against inordinate theories of presidential power may produce an inordinate swing against the Presidency and thereby do essential damage to our national capacity to handle the problems of the future. The answer to the runaway Presidency is not the messenger-boy Presidency. The American democracy must discover a middle ground between making the President a czar and making him a puppet. The problem is to devise means of reconciling a strong and purposeful Presidency with equally strong and purposeful forms of democratic control. Or, to put it succinctly, we need a strong Presidency — but a strong Presidency *within the Constitution.*

Scholars have long considered aspects of the problem. Much of the historical recital in these pages is at least a thrice-told tale. Yet the contemporary argument rushes along with astonishingly little exact reference to the national experience. This book is written in the hope, or faith, that an awareness of the way presidents and Congresses have struggled with past questions of national decision may impart a firmer sense of the tradition in which both the Presidency and Congress must act in the future if we are to preserve the continuities of our democracy. For, unless the American democracy figures out how to control the Presidency in war and peace without enfeebling the Presidency across the board, then our system of government will face grave troubles.

The Imperial Presidency

★ 1 ★

What the Founding Fathers
Intended

THE PLACE TO BEGIN is Philadelphia in the summer of 1787. This is not because the Founding Fathers were infallible, or because they anticipated all the perplexities of the American future, or because their original intent can be supposed to decide constitutional questions in perpetuity. The Constitution, as Chief Justice Marshall said in his most famous opinion, was "intended to endure for ages to come, and consequently, to be adapted to the various *crises* of human affairs." [1] Woodrow Wilson similarly objected to taking the Constitution as "a mere legal document, to be read as a will or contract." If composed in the spirit of Newton, it has to be construed in the spirit of Darwin. It was "a vehicle of life," and its meaning was determined "not by the original intentions of those who drew the paper, but by the exigencies and the new aspects of life itself." [2] Nor, for that matter, is the ascertainment of original intent all that easy. "No single fault has been the source of so much bad history," C. H. McIlwain reminds us, "as the reading back of later and sharper distinctions into earlier periods where they have no place." [3]

I

For all this, there is great value in consulting the Founding Fathers. Even if the search for original intent is difficult, it is not impossible. If original intent cannot settle constitutional questions, it can throw essential light on them. And it can settle related historical questions — whether or not, for example, presidential practice was indeed, as later Presidents liked to claim, what the Founding Fathers designed and desired. Above all, the Founding Fathers were exceptionally able and intelligent men, wiser on the whole than their posterity. They thought hard about these matters, and their views demand the most careful consideration.

In drafting the Constitution, they were, of course, concerned to correct the deficiencies of the Articles of Confederation, under which the rebellious colonies had been governed during the Revolution. The Articles had bestowed executive as well as legislative authority on Congress, establishing in effect parliamentary government without a prime minister. Article VI gave Congress control over the conduct of foreign affairs, and Article IX gave it "the sole and exclusive right and power of determining on peace and war." But the Constitution was founded on the opposite principle of the separation of power. The men of Philadelphia therefore had to work out a division of authority between the legislative and executive branches. In domestic policy, this division was reasonably clear. In foreign affairs, it was often cryptic, ambiguous and incomplete.

Their experience under the Articles led the Founding Fathers to favor more centralization of executive authority than they had known in the Confederation. Many of them probably agreed with Hamilton's statement in the 70th Federalist that "energy in the Executive is a leading character in the definition of good government." Those who disagreed were reassured by the expectation that Washington would be the first head of state. At the same time, their experience under the British crown led the Founding Fathers to favor less centralization of authority than they perceived in the British monarchy. As victims of what they considered a tyrannical royal prerogative, they were determined to fashion for themselves a Presidency that would be strong but still limited.

Nothing was more crucial for the new nation than the successful conduct of its external relations. There was broad agreement that national safety could best be assured through the development of equal trading relations with the states of Europe. America's "plan is commerce," Thomas Paine wrote in *Common*

Sense, "and that, well attended to, will secure us the peace and friendship of all Europe, because it is the interest of all Europe to have America as a free port." [4] Washington summed up the policy in his Farewell Address: "The great rule of conduct for us in regard to foreign nations is, in extending our commercial relations to have with them as little political connection as possible." Given the clear priority the Founding Fathers assigned to commercial over political relations, it is significant that the Constitution vested control over this primary aspect of foreign policy in Congress, assigning it the definite and unqualified power "to regulate Commerce with foreign Nations."

The Constitution also brought Congress into the treaty-making process, withholding from the President the exclusive authority enjoyed by European monarchs to make treaties. Where the British King, for example, could conclude treaties on his own, the American President was required to win the consent of two thirds of the Senate. "The one can do alone," said Hamilton, "what the other can do only with the concurrence of a branch of the legislature." [5] And Congress received other weighty powers related to the conduct of foreign affairs: the power to make appropriations, to raise and maintain the armed forces and make rules for their government and regulation, to control naturalization and immigration, to impose tariffs, to define and punish offenses against the law of nations and, above all, "to declare War, grant Letters of Marque and Reprisal, and make Rules concerning Captures on Land and Water."

II

This last clause — in Article I, Section 8, of the Constitution — was of prime importance. The Founders were determined to deny the American President what Blackstone had assigned to the British King — "the sole prerogative of making war and peace." [6] Even Hamilton, the most consistent advocate of executive centralization, proposed in the Convention that the Senate "have the sole power of declaring war" with the executive to "have the direction of war when authorized or begun." [7]

In an early draft, the Constitution gave Congress the power to "make" war. Every scholar knows the successful intervention by Madison and Gerry —

> Mr MADISON and Mr GERRY Moved to insert *"declare,"* striking out *"make"* war; leaving to the Executive the power to repel sudden attacks.

— but no one really quite knows what this exchange meant. Among the delegates, Roger Sherman of Connecticut, for example, responded to Madison and Gerry by saying he thought the original language "stood very well" and that it already permitted the executive "to repel and not to commence war." On the other hand, George Mason of Virginia, after announcing that he was "agst. giving the power of war to the Executive, because not safely to be trusted with it," then said he preferred "declare" to "make"; obviously he did not think he was thereby giving more power to the untrustworthy executive. Professor Lofgren, a most precise student of the episode, can distinguish at least four different interpretations of the Madison-Gerry amendment.[8]

What does seem clear is that no one wanted either to deny the President the power to respond to surprise attack or to give the President general power to initiate hostilities. The first aspect — the acknowledgment that Presidents must on occasion begin defensive war without recourse to Congress — represented the potential breach in the congressional position and would have the most significance in the future. But the second aspect gained the most attention and brought the most comfort at the time. James Wilson, next to Madison the most penetrating political thinker at the Convention, thus portrayed the constitutional solution: this system "will not hurry us into war; it is calculated to guard against it. It will not be in the power of a single man, or a single body of men, to involve us in such distress." [9]

The Founding Fathers did not have to give unconditional power to declare war to Congress. They might have said, in language they used elsewhere in the Constitution, that war could be declared by the President with the advice and consent of Congress, or by Congress on the recommendation of the President.[10]

But they chose not to mention the President at all in connection with the war-making power. Nor was this because they lacked realism about the problems of national security. In a famous passage in the 23rd Federalist, Hamilton said that the powers of national self-defense must "exist without limitation, *because it is impossible to foresee or define the extent and variety of national exigencies.* . . . The circumstances that endanger the safety of nations are infinite, and for this reason no constitutional shackles can wisely be imposed on the power to which the care of it is committed. This power ought to be co-extensive with all the possible combinations of such circumstances." The Founding Fathers were determined that the national government should have all the authority required to defend the nation. But Hamilton was not asserting these unlimited powers for the Presidency, as careless commentators have assumed. He was asserting them for the national government *as a whole* — for, that is, Congress and the Presidency combined.

The resistance to giving a "single man," even if he were President of the United States, the unilateral authority to decide on war pervaded the contemporaneous literature. Hamilton's observations on the treaty-making power applied all the more forcibly to the war-making power: "The history of human conduct does not warrant that exalted opinion of human virtue which would make it wise to commit interests of so delicate and momentous a kind, as those which concern its intercourse with the rest of the world, to the sole disposal of a magistrate created and circumstanced as would be a President of the United States." [11] As Madison put it in a letter to Jefferson in 1798: "The constitution supposes, what the History of all Govts demonstrates, that the Ex. is the branch of power most interested in war, & most prone to it. It has accordingly with studied care vested the question of war in the Legisl." [12]

III

At the same time, the Constitution vested the command of the Army and Navy in the President, which meant that, once Congress had authorized war, the President as Commander in Chief had full power to conduct military operations. "Of all the cares or concerns of government," said the Federalist, "the direction of war most peculiarly demands those qualities which distinguish the exercise of power by a single hand." [13] The designation of the President as Commander in Chief also sprang from a concern to assure civilian control of the military establishment. By making the Commander in Chief a civilian who would be subject to recall after four years, the Founders doubtless hoped to spare America tribulations of the sort that the unfettered command and consequent political power of a Duke of Marlborough had brought to England.

There is no evidence that anyone supposed that his office as Commander in Chief endowed the President with an independent source of authority. Even with Washington in prospect, the Founders emphasized their narrow and military definition of this presidential role. As Hamilton carefully explained in the 69th Federalist, the President's power as Commander in Chief

> would be nominally the same with that of the king of Great Britain, but in substance much inferior to it. It would amount to nothing more than the supreme command and direction of the military and naval forces . . . while that of the British king extends to the *declaring* of war and to the *raising* and *regulating* of fleets and armies, — all which, by the Constitution under consideration, would appertain to the legislature.

As Commander in Chief the President had no more authority than the first general of the army or the first admiral of the navy would have had as professional military men. The President's power as Commander in Chief, in short, was simply the power to issue orders to the armed forces within a framework established by Congress. And even Congress was denied the power to make appropriations for the support of the armed forces for a longer term than two years.

In addition to the command of the armed forces, the Constitution gave the President the power to receive foreign envoys and,

with the advice and consent of the Senate, to appoint ambassadors as well as to make treaties. Beyond this, it had nothing specific to say about his authority in foreign affairs. However, Article II gave him general executive power; and, as the 64th and
75th Federalist Papers emphasized, the structural characteristics
of the Presidency — unity, secrecy, decision, dispatch, superior
sources of information — were deemed especially advantageous
to the conduct of diplomacy.

The result was, as Madison said, "a partial mixture of powers." Madison indeed argued that such mingling was indispensable to the system, for unless the branches of government "be so
far connected and blended as to give to each a constitutional
control over the others, the degree of separation which the
maxim requires, as essential to a free government, can never in
practice be duly maintained." Particularly in the case of war and
peace — the war-making and treaty-making powers — it was
really a matter, in Hamilton's phrase, of "joint possession." [14]

In these areas the two branches had interwoven responsibilities and competing opportunities. Moreover, each had an undefined residuum of authority on which to draw — the President
through the executive power and the constitutional injunction
that "he shall take Care that the Laws be faithfully executed,"
Congress through the constitutional authorization "to make all
Laws which shall be necessary and proper for carrying into Execution . . . all . . . Powers vested by this Constitution in the
Government of the United States." In addition, the Constitution
itself was silent on certain issues of import to the conduct of foreign affairs: among them, the recognition of foreign governments, the authority to proclaim neutrality, the role of executive
agreements, the control of information essential to intelligent decision. The result, as Edward S. Corwin remarked 40 years ago,
was to make of the Constitution "an invitation to struggle for the
privilege of directing American foreign policy." [15]

IV

One further consideration lingered behind the words of the Constitution and the debates of the Convention. This was the ques-

tion of emergency. For the Founding Fathers were more influenced by Locke than by any other political philosopher; and, as students of Locke, they were well acquainted with Chapter 14, "Of Prerogative," in the *Second Treatise of Government*. Prerogative was the critical exception in Locke's rendition of the social contract. In general, the contract — the reciprocal obligation of ruler and ruled within the frame of law — was to prevail. In general, the authority of government was to be limited. But in emergency, Locke argued, responsible rulers could resort to exceptional power. Legislatures were too large, unwieldy and slow to cope with crisis; moreover, they were not able "to foresee, and so by laws to provide for, all accidents and necessities." Indeed, on occasion "a strict and rigid observation of the laws may do harm." This meant that there could be times when "the laws themselves should . . . give way to the executive power, or rather to this fundamental law of nature and government, viz., that, as much as may be, all the members of society are to be preserved."

Prerogative therefore was the exercise of the law of self-preservation. It was "the people's permitting their rulers to do several things of their own free choice, where the law was silent, and sometimes, too, against the direct letter of the law, for the public good, and their acquiescing in it when so done." The executive, Locke contended, must have the reserve power "to act according to discretion for the public good, without the prescription of law and sometimes even against it." If emergency prerogative were abused, the people would rebel; but, used for the good of the society, it would be accepted. "If there comes to be a question between the executive power and the people about a thing claimed as prerogative, the tendency of the exercise of such prerogative to the good or hurt of the people will easily decide that question." [16]

Locke's argument, restated in more democratic terms, was that, when the executive perceived what he deemed an emergency, he could initiate extralegal or even illegal action, but that he would be sustained and vindicated in that action only if his perception of the emergency were shared by the legislature and by the people. Though prerogative enabled the executive to act on his individual finding of emergency, whether or not his finding was right and this was a true emergency was to be determined not by the executive but by the community.

The idea of prerogative was *not* part of presidential power as defined in the Constitution. The Founding Fathers had lived with emergency, but they made no provision in the Constitution, except in relation to *habeas corpus,* for the suspension of law in the case of necessity (and even here they did not specify whether the power of suspension belonged to the executive). The argument of the Federalist Papers, in the words of Clinton Rossiter, was in effect that the Constitution was "equal to any emergency." [17]

Yet there is reason to believe that the doctrine that crisis might require the executive to act outside the Constitution in order to save the Constitution remained in the back of their minds. Even in the Federalist Papers Hamilton wrote of "that original right of self-defence which is paramount to all positive forms of government" and Madison thought it "vain to oppose constitutional barriers to the impulse of self-preservation." [18] The First Congress, which included sixteen members of the Constitutional Convention and many more from state ratifying conventions, has been described as almost an adjourned session of the Convention. It was here that Congressman Alexander White, who himself had led the fight for ratification in western Virginia, argued that it would be better for the President "to extend his power on some extraordinary occasion, even where he is not strictly justified by the constitution, than [that] the Legislature should grant him an improper power to be exercised at all times." In other words, the legal order would be better preserved if departures from it were frankly identified as such than if they were anointed with a factitious legality and thereby enabled to serve as constitutional precedents for future action. The doctrine of emergency prerogative carried with it two corollaries: that the official who thus acted did so at his own peril; and that, having acted, he must report at once to Congress, which would serve as the judge of his action. "That this doctrine was accepted by every single one of our early statesmen," a careful scholar, Lucius Wilmerding, Jr., has written, "can easily be shown." [19]

I am not sure how easy this showing would be. Washington, for example, made clear in his Farewell Address his rejection of "change by usurpation; for though this, in one instance, may be the instrument of good, it is the customary weapon by which free governments are destroyed." But this did not quite meet the Lockean point, for the purpose of prerogative was precisely not to establish precedents. Yet, however the Founding Fathers lined up on this question, one cannot suppose that Presidents steeped in Locke would have entirely dismissed the idea of action beyond the Constitution if necessary to save the life of the nation.

v

Congress had its weapon of last resort too — and one explicitly conferred by the Constitution. This was the power of impeachment. Here the Constitution declared that "the President, Vice President and all civil officers of the United States" could be removed from office "on Impeachment for, and Conviction of, Treason, Bribery, or other high Crimes and Misdemeanors." The House was given the sole power of impeachment, the Senate the sole power to try all impeachments, with concurrence of two thirds of the senators present necessary for conviction.

Impeachment had originated in fourteenth-century England as a means by which the House of Commons could indict high officers of the realm for a variety of offenses and call them up for trial before the Lords. It attained its English high point in the seventeenth century and, though Burke called it the "great guardian of the purity of the Constitution," was on its way out at the end of the eighteenth. The Constitutional Convention, seeking what Hamilton called in the 65th Federalist "a bridle in the hands of the legislative body upon the executive," broadly adopted the English model. The Founding Fathers, who feared despotism and had an entirely realistic view of human nature, were quite prepared to believe that Presidents might abuse their power and were therefore determined to provide the new republic with a way of removing any who did.

But they did not wish to make impeachment so easy that Congress would find it a convenient means of dominating the executive. So they made the American impeachment process somewhat more restricted than the English. In England, as Bryce wrote in 1888, an official had been "impeachable for giving bad advice to the head of the State." [20] While the Americans borrowed the operative language from English law, they specified treason, bribery and other high crimes and misdemeanors as the only grounds for impeachment, thereby denying Congress the almost unlimited power to define impeachment enjoyed by Parliament. Also, where Parliament could inflict punishment, the Founding Fathers limited Congress to the removal and disqualification from future office of persons convicted, leaving criminal penalties to subsequent indictment and judgment in the courts.

The Convention debated mainly the impeachment of Presidents. Vice Presidents and other "civil officers" were added to the impeachment clause almost as an afterthought a short time before adjournment. There was some discussion as to whether the Supreme Court should not be the tribunal to try impeachments. But, as Hamilton wrote in the Federalist, impeachment was pre-eminently a political process, likely to agitate the passions of the whole community. "As a method of NATIONAL INQUEST into the conduct of public men," it was therefore best assigned to "the representatives of the nation themselves." Only the Senate had the degree of credit and authority that could reconcile the people to decisions that must "doom to honor or to infamy" the most distinguished members of the community. Moreover, impeachment proceedings in their nature could "never be tied down by such strict rules, either in the delineation of the offence by the prosecutors, or in the construction of it by the judges, as in common cases serve to limit the discretion of courts."

The impeachment power was thus endowed with a certain flexibility. If treason and bribery were well-defined offenses, the other high crimes and misdemeanors could be construed broadly or narrowly. As Raoul Berger has pointed out, this phrase was a term of art, a category, with ascertainable English content, of crimes against the state, which the Convention meant to restrict to "great and dangerous offenses" by "great offenders." [21] But, though no one could be sure how the impeachment power would develop, it was considered, in the words of James Monroe, "the main spring of the great machine of government. It is the pivot on which it turns. . . . In this mode, the machine will be kept in motion by its own powers and on a proper balance." [22]

2

Where the Founding Fathers Disagreed

THE CONSTITUTION was an extraordinary document. But a document is only a document, and what the Constitution 'really' meant — i.e., meant in practice — only practice could disclose. It therefore fell to the daily experience of government under the Constitution to explore the document's possibilities, reconcile its contradictions and repair its omissions. This unfolding of the Constitution began, as the Convention had anticipated, under Washington who, though a man of strong private opinions, was also a chief magistrate with an exceptional sense of discipline and accountability. He agreed with Hamilton, but he valued Jefferson, and he understood that the new republic needed both. He abhorred the notion of party and truly wanted to be father of his country.

I

The application of the Constitution was shaped by Washington's desire to avoid sharp ideological division. It was shaped too by the task, beyond ideology, of making the new government work. Hamilton favored an energetic and Jefferson a limited Presidency; but there remained certain managerial necessities destined to influence Jeffersonians as well as Hamiltonians and imperceptibly to add power to the Presidency. This was especially true in foreign affairs. For the Congress could not easily stay abreast of the details of relations with foreign states. It rarely acted as a unified body. It could not conduct negotiations. It could not be relied on to preserve secrecy about matters where secrecy was indispensable. Moreover, international law itself, by requiring in every nation a single point of responsible authority, confirmed presidential primacy in foreign relations.

The power of administrative considerations was shown by the extent to which even Jefferson, as Washington's Secretary of State, was, despite doctrinal predilection, responsive to managerial need. "The transaction of business with foreign nations is Executive altogether," he emphasized in 1790. He did not take the Senate's right to confirm diplomatic appointments to mean, for example, that senators were "qualified to judge of the necessity which calls for a mission to any particular place, or of the particular grade, more or less marked, which special and secret circumstances may call for. All this is left to the President. [The senators] are only to see that no unfit person be employed." [1]

What was emerging, less from ideological prescription than from operational compulsion, was an executive perspective, a diffused feeling that the executive branch, with superior information and direct responsibility, was the source of judgments to which Congress, without abdicating its separate powers, should customarily defer. This executive perspective quickly decided, for example, the way in which the American government recognized foreign governments.

The constitutional provision empowering the President to "receive Ambassadors and other public Ministers" sounded innocuous enough, a social note from all over. But receiving an envoy implied a decision that he represented a legitimate government with which the United States should have relations — a decision that Washington rapidly appropriated for the executive. Thus by receiving Citizen Genêt he recognized the revolutionary government of France. The pro-French members of Congress, ordinarily mistrustful of executive aggrandizement, were so grateful for the result that they did not protest the means.

Subsequent Congresses, while not quite disputing the executive claim to control diplomatic recognition, never quite reconciled themselves to it. In general, Presidents freely exercised the power except in cases where recognition might have dangerous international consequences; then the power became, as a practical matter, another instance of "joint possession." Jackson noted in 1836, for example, that the recognition of new states could be "equivalent under some circumstances to a declaration of war" — as in the case of the Republic of Texas, still regarded by Mexico as no more than a province in revolt. Without expressing any opinion as to "the strict constitutional right of the Executive," Jackson was willing to leave the "expediency" of recognizing Texas to the decision of Congress.[2] For their part, members of Congress tried in various ways to force on Presidents the recognition of newly independent American republics — Argentina, for example, in 1818, Texas in 1836, Cuba in 1898. In still later years Congress sought by concurrent resolution to dissuade Presidents from recognizing the People's Republic of China.

II

Defenders of the congressional prerogative, confronted by the rise of the executive perspective, early perceived the control of information as a key issue. "The management of foreign relations," Madison said, "appears to be the most susceptible of abuse of all the trusts committed to a Government." This was because foreign relations could "be concealed or disclosed, or disclosed in such parts and at such times as will best suit particular views."[3] He was complaining to Jefferson; but Jefferson himself had on occasion in Washington's cabinet succumbed to the notion that the executive knew best what Congress should be told. "We all thought," he thus wrote about an issue with Great Britain in 1793, "that if the Senate should be consulted & consequently apprized of our line, it would become known to Hammond [the British minister]."[4]

This executive penchant for selective release of information to Congress was, however, in conflict with the prevalent assumption, inherited from and sanctioned by the history of the British Parliament, that Congress was among other things a "grand inquest" and thereby had a right to inform itself on public matters.[5] Moreover, the Constitution itself laid on the President the express duty "from time to time [to] give to the Congress Information of the State of the Union." Nor was this duty considered to be discharged by the annual presidential message. Justice Story in his famous *Commentaries* said that the Constitution required "the President to lay before Congress all facts and information which may assist their deliberation." [6]

The issue arose sharply for the first time in 1792 when the House of Representatives, investigating the failure of the expedition of General St. Clair against Indians in the northwest, called on the executive branch "for such persons, papers and records as may be necessary" to its inquiry. President Washington summoned his cabinet because this was "the first example," and "so far as it should become a precedent, it should be rightly conducted." While he did not doubt the propriety of the request, as he told his cabinet, he could readily conceive that "there might be papers of so secret a nature, as that they ought not to be given up." His colleagues, after pondering the question for a couple of days, reported back agreement on several points. The House, they said, was indeed an "inquest" and therefore might call for papers generally. The executive, they agreed, "ought to communicate such papers as the public good would permit"; then they added, "and ought to refuse those, the disclosure of which would injure the public: consequently were to exercise a discretion." Finally they agreed that in this particular case "there was not a paper which might not be properly produced." [7]

Washington therefore gave the House the papers it wanted; moreover, he sent his Secretaries of War and the Treasury to testify in person before Congress. The only precedent publicly established was thus a confirmation of congressional expectation that it would get the information it requested — and this in an inquiry, hardly calculated to benefit the administration, into a military disaster. The reservation expressed in the privacy of Washington's cabinet about the withholding of papers in the public interest, though often cited in later years, was not communicated formally either to Congress or to the people and therefore had no standing as a precedent.

A second case arose in 1796 when the House asked for copies of diplomatic instructions and other papers relating to the Jay

Treaty with Britain excepting papers that "any existing negotiation may render improper to disclose." Pointing out that "all the papers affecting the negotiation with Great Britain" had already been laid before the Senate a year earlier, Washington denied any disposition "to withhold any information which the Constitution has enjoined upon the President as a duty to give, or which could be required of him by either House of Congress as a right." But he rejected the particular request as an invasion of the treaty-making power from which the House had been specifically excluded in the Constitutional Convention. Such papers, Washington said, were irrelevant to any constitutional function of the House "except that of impeachment," and this was not the issue. In explaining why the Constitution confided the treaty power to a smaller body like the Senate, Washington offered certain *obiter dicta* about confidentiality in diplomatic negotiation: "a full disclosure of all the measures, demands, or eventual concessions which may have been proposed, or contemplated, . . . might have a pernicious influence on future negotiations, or produce immediate inconveniences, perhaps danger and mischief, in relation to other powers." [8]

Washington's refusal to give the House what he had already given the Senate produced interesting disagreement among fellow Founding Fathers. Madison, by now a political opponent, defended Washington on the floor of the House, conceding the executive "a right, under a due responsibility, . . . to withhold information, when of a nature that did not permit a disclosure at the time." But John Adams, Washington's Vice President and political ally, wrote his wife, "I cannot deny the right of the House to ask for papers. . . . My ideas are very high of the rights and powers of the House of Representatives." [9] Insofar as Washington's action set a precedent, it was only that a President could deny treaty documents to the chamber the Constitution itself had barred from the treaty process. Even this precedent did not stand long. It was undercut two years later when Adams, now President, sent the House at its request papers relating to negotiations with France. Early Presidents continued to assume that Congress, as the grand inquest of the nation, had a moral title to information, even though the executive impulse to hold things back could not always be subdued.

III

So life under the Constitution began to define the meaning of the Constitution. This process soon extended to the war-making power. In 1793 Washington proclaimed American neutrality in the war between Britain and France and thereby set off a remarkable debate. It was a debate that particularly emphasized the ambiguity of the Constitution because the antagonists were Hamilton and Madison, who six years before had served together at the Convention, had then collaborated (with John Jay) in writing the Federalist Papers and were almost uniquely qualified to say what the document 'really' meant.

Washington's declaration of neutrality was a unilateral presidential act. It involved, moreover, an interpretation and, in the eyes of some, a repudiation of obligations assumed by the United States in its treaty with France of 1778. Pro-French congressmen and newspapers promptly objected that the deed was beyond the authority of the President to do by himself and an infringement of the powers of Congress. In a series of articles signed "Pacificus" Hamilton defended both the substance of the policy and the President's unilateral right to promulgate it. Hamilton's constitutional point was that, since foreign policy was in its nature an executive function, the powers of declaring war and ratifying treaties bestowed by the Constitution on Congress were therefore "exceptions out of the general 'executive power' vested in the President" and consequently were "to be construed strictly, and ought to be extended no further than is essential to their execution." While Congress had the right to declare war, the President had the right to judge national obligations under treaties. His duty was to preserve peace till the declaration was made: "it belongs to the 'executive power' to do whatever else the law of nations, co-operating with the treaties of the country, enjoin in the intercourse of the United States with foreign powers."

Hamilton conceded that executive action might well "affect

the exercise of the power of the legislature to declare war." But
this was no reason, he felt, for the executive not to use his right-
ful authority. "The legislature is still free to perform its duties,
according to its own sense of them; though the executive, in the
exercise of its constitutional powers, may establish an antecedent
state of things, which ought to weigh in the legislative decision."
Each branch, in short, had to do its own thing. Still this need not
lead to the breakdown of government. "The division of the executive power in the Constitution," Hamilton said, "creates a concurrent authority in the cases to which it relates." This, presumably, should make both branches sensitive to the need for
forbearance and collaboration.

Though Jefferson had acquiesced in the neutrality proclamation, while stipulating that the word "neutrality" not be
used, Hamilton's enthusiastic affirmation of presidential power
alarmed him, and he secretly begged Madison to respond: "For
God's sake, my dear Sir, take up your pen, select the most striking heresies and cut him to pieces in face of the public." Without
great relish for the assignment, Madison, disguised as "Helvidius," entered the lists and attacked Pacificus's constitutional
views. He denied that the powers of making wars and treaties
were inherently executive. This "vicious" doctrine obviously
had been "borrowed" from Britain. The fact that these were
royal prerogatives in Britain did not make them presidential prerogatives in the United States. The war-declaring power, Madison contended, must include everything necessary to make that
power effective. Congress therefore had the right to judge
whether the United States was obliged to declare war or not.
This judgment could not be foreclosed by presidential decisions
about treaties and neutrality or by other executive actions creating "an antecedent state of things." As for Hamilton's theory of
a concurrent authority, this, Madison said, was "as awkward in
practice, as it is unnatural in theory." What if the two branches
judged the same situation differently? What if, each doing its own
thing, the President proclaimed neutrality and the Congress declared war? [10]

On the question that had given rise to the debate —

neutrality — Washington, with larger vision than either of the debaters and no doubt with greater faith than Hamilton himself in "concurrent authority," went along with Hamilton in theory but with Madison in spirit. Prompted by the circumstance that grand juries refused to indict violators when there was no neutrality law to violate, Washington, observing that it "rested with the wisdom of Congress to correct, improve, or enforce" the neutrality policy, soon requested the legislative branch to act.[11] Neutrality became thereafter a congressional prerogative.

But the debate had moved on to wider questions. Pacificus and Helvidius joined issue basically on the reach of the congressional power to declare war. Hamilton saw that power as rigorously limited, to be exercised jointly with and perhaps in subordination to the broad executive authority in foreign affairs. For Madison, it was a spacious power, not to be abridged by the narrowing of choices through prior presidential initiative. The Helvidius letters perhaps reflected Madison's lack of enthusiasm for his task. Though he scored some effective points, his argument did not penetrate to the heart of the administrative question: thus his sketch of the constitutional situation did not really explain how, if the executive were to be so constrained, foreign affairs were after all to be conducted. Instead of deriding Hamilton's fertile suggestion about "concurrent authority," Madison might well have turned it to congressional advantage and used it as a reason to demand procedures of consultation. Nonetheless, Madison did bring out powerfully one question — the question who was to judge the obligations of treaties; and this, after all, might be the question whether the President or Congress was to decide that war had become a necessity. The executive, in Madison's view, had "no right" to decide whether or not there was cause for war; his only right was that of convening Congress whenever such a question seemed to call for decision.

IV

By defining the issue in terms of the power to "declare" war, Hamilton and Madison, though unconfused themselves, may have helped confuse later generations about the significance of the technical act of declaration. That was not the issue. The issue was congressional *authorization* of hostilities against a foreign state. Such authorization could be made through full-dress declaration or through more limited means. There is every indication that the Founding Fathers were well aware of the gradations of warfare and meant to vest the control of limited as well as of general war in the hands of Congress.

The men who framed the Constitution knew their international law. Grotius had familiarized them with the distinction between "perfect" and "imperfect" war — between, that is, war preceded by formal declaration and involving the whole nation, and war entered without formal declaration and involving limited acts of defense and reprisal. Moreover, eighteenth-century governments had lost the habit of declaring full-dress war. "The ceremony of a formal denunciation of war," Hamilton wrote in the 25th Federalist, "has of late fallen into disuse." One study of European and American wars shows that between 1700 and 1870 hostilities began in 107 cases without declaration; in only ten cases was there declaration in advance of hostilitites.[12] And the Constitution itself, by adding the authority, in that long-forgotten clause, to "grant letters of Marque and Reprisal" to the authority to "declare" war was plainly giving Congress the power to authorize limited as well as general war.

The 'undeclared' naval war with France of 1798–1800 clarified the problem. Later commentators claimed this war as an early precedent in the cause of unilateral presidential warmaking. In fact, when trouble with France began, Adams called Congress to meet in special session "to consult and determine on such measure as in their wisdom shall be deemed meet for the safety and welfare of the said United States." In due course, Congress turned more belligerent than the President and in the spring of 1798 passed some 20 laws to encourage Adams to wage the war. Adams's Attorney General described it as "a maritime war *authorized* by both nations." [13] In 1800 the Supreme Court, called upon to define the conflict, ratified the distinction between "perfect" and "imperfect" wars. Justice Bushrod Washington, in one of the opinions for a unanimous court in *Bas v.*

Tingy, wrote that hostilities "limited as to places, persons, and things" constituted "imperfect war." Justice Samuel Chase wrote in a second opinion:

> Congress is empowered to declare a general war or Congress may wage a limited war; limited in place, in object, in time. . . . What then is the nature of the contest subsisting between America and France? In my judgment it is a limited, partial war. Congress has not declared war in general terms; but Congress has authorized hostilities on the high seas by certain persons in certain cases.[14]

Hostilities, whether general or limited, were thus presumed to require congressional sanction. In 1801 Chief Justice Marshall made the presumption explicit in a second case arising out of the "quasi-war" with France. "The whole powers of war being, by the Constitution of the United States, vested in congress," he ruled in *Talbot v. Seeman,* ". . . the congress may authorize general hostilities . . . or partial war." [15]

When Jefferson became President in 1801, he similarly acknowledged the congressional right to license hostilities by means short of a declaration of war, while at the same time affirming the right of the executive to repel sudden attack. An American naval schooner, fired on by a Tripolitanian cruiser in the Mediterranean, repulsed the assault with signal success; but, as Jefferson instructed Congress, its commander was "unauthorized by the Constitution, without the sanction of Congress, to go beyond the line of defense," so the enemy vessel, having been "disabled from committing further hostilities, was liberated with its crew." Jefferson went on to ask Congress to consider "whether, by authorizing measures of offense also, they will place our force on an equal footing with that of its adversaries." [16]

Hamilton who had actually taken this position himself in 1798 [17] now found these Jeffersonian scruples ridiculous. Pointing out that Tripoli had already declared war against the United

States, he wondered whether Jefferson was seriously proposing "that one nation can be in full war with another, and the other not in the same state." The war might be aggressive on the part of the attacker and defensive on the part of the attacked, "but the rights of both, as to the measures of hostility, are equal." When a foreign state declared war, then war existed, "and any declaration on the part of Congress is nugatory; it is at least unnecessary." [18] As for Congress, it considered the idea of formal declaration of war against a collection of pirates demeaning; but it did pass a law authorizing the Navy to wage limited war against Tripoli.

Jefferson continued to resist the temptation to enlarge the idea of defensive war. In 1805, in face of incursions into Louisiana by the Spanish in Florida, he said in a special message: "Considering that Congress alone is constitutionally invested with the power of changing our condition from peace to war, I have thought it my duty to await their authority for using force. . . . The course to be pursued will require the command of means which it belongs to Congress exclusively to yield or to deny." [19] In this case, Congress chose to deny, and the President subsided.

v

No one wrote more earnestly than Jefferson about the virtues of strict construction of the Constitution and the dangers of presidential usurpation. Yet Jefferson was a disciple of Locke and a realistic executive; and he had no doubt that national emergency might require Presidents to lay the Constitution and the law aside.

Jefferson's Louisiana Purchase of 1803 was later cited — even by such august authorities as President Truman and Chief Justice Vinson — as an example of unilateral presidential initiative exercised independently of Congress. This it definitely was not. Congress set up a clamor for Louisiana, confirmed the envoys who negotiated the purchase, appropriated the funds for the purchase, ratified the treaty consummating the purchase and passed statutes authorizing the President to receive the purchase and to establish government and law in the newly acquired territory. Jefferson's perplexity was very different. His doubts concerned the constitutional authority of the national government *as a whole,* President and Congress combined, to annex new territory. When the government *as a whole* accepted Louisiana without a constitutional amendment, Jefferson feared that this was "an act beyond the Constitution." In this act, members of Congress were his accomplices, not his adversaries. But the Louisiana Purchase was, in Jefferson's view, a national emergency justifying action beyond the Constitution. As he put it, "The legislature in casting behind them metaphysical subtleties, and risking themselves like faithful servants, must . . . throw themselves on their country for doing for them unauthorized, what we know [the people] would have done for themselves had they been in a situation to do it." [20]

Jefferson also felt that emergency might justify the exercise of presidential power beyond congressional authorization. When a British frigate attacked the *Chesapeake* in 1807, Jefferson spent unappropriated funds for munitions. "To have awaited a previous and special sanction by law," he told Congress in asking retroactive blessing, "would have lost occasions which might not be retrieved. . . . I trust that the Legislature . . . will approve, when done, what they would have seen so important to be done if then assembled." [21] And, if cases arose where Congress would not consent, emergency might still compel the executive to act on his own; for a President's final obligation was to the preservation of the country.

"On great occasions," Jefferson wrote in 1807, "every good officer must be ready to risk himself in going beyond the strict line of the law, when the public preservation requires it; his motives will be a justification." There were, he said, "extreme cases where the laws become inadequate to their own preservation, and where the universal recourse is a dictator, or martial law." This was not a passing thought. Jefferson stated the point more fully after he left the White House. "A strict observance of the written laws," he said carefully in 1810, "is doubtless *one* of the high duties of a good citizen, but it is not *the high-*

est. The laws of necessity, of self-preservation, of saving our country when in danger, are of a higher obligation. . . . To lose our country by a scrupulous adherence to written law, would be to lose the law itself, with life, liberty, property and all those who are enjoying them with us; thus absurdly sacrificing the end to the means." He understood the risks in this argument and therefore placed the emergency decisions under the judgment of history: "The line of discrimination between cases may be difficult; but the good officer is bound to draw it at his own peril, and throw himself on the justice of his country and the rectitude of his motives." [22]

Throwing oneself "on the justice of his country" was a reformulation of the standard suggested by Locke's question whether prerogative was exercised for the good or hurt of the people; and this in turn was the question whether society agreed with the executive on the definition of emergency. Most of Jefferson's reflections on emergency power were induced by the Burr conspiracy. This was a doubtful case. No one can be sure what Burr was up to. The modern scholar to look most thoroughly into the conspiracy, Professor Thomas Perkins Abernethy, had no doubt that, "next to the Confederate War it posed the greatest threat of dismemberment which the American Union has ever faced." [23] Perhaps so; and the conspiracy may well have been interrupted before it reached the stage of overt acts. Still evidence for treason as required by the Constitution was inadequate. Deeply as it troubled Jefferson, the Burr conspiracy was not regarded by courts and juries in 1807 as an emergency so imperative as to justify the laying aside of the laws.

Burr's acquittal consequently helped limit presidential invocation of emergency prerogative. It was not enough for the President personally to think the country was in danger. It was thereafter apparent that, to confirm a judgment of dire emergency, the President had to have the broad agreement of Congress and public opinion. When all three agreed that the emergency was authentic, it seemed probable that the Supreme Court would not oppose this judgment, at least not till the crisis was over.

*

VI

In 1798 Madison had argued that, since the Ex. was the branch of government most prone to war, the Constitution had solved the war problem by giving the war-making power to the Legisl. In 1812 he may well have reflected ruefully on that argument as he sat in the White House and War Hawks on Capitol Hill demanded hostilities with Britain. Madison soon acceded to their demands, and the War of 1812 represented a suitable exercise of concurrent authority — at least in the eyes of all save for the embattled Federalists of New England. These onetime champions of executive energy now proposed at the Hartford Convention that, apart from actual invasion, even Congress should not be permitted to authorize hostilities against a foreign nation unless *two thirds* of both houses concurred.[24] (This view, because the general consequences of war were so "critical and calamitous," commended itself to Justice Story, who later urged it in his *Commentaries.*[25])

Madison obtained congressional authorization for limited warfare against Algeria in 1815; but in 1817–1818, when Seminole Indians were conducting raids into American territory, President Monroe chose not to consult Congress before ordering General Andrew Jackson to chase the raiding parties back into Florida. Instead he reversed Jefferson's position of 1805 and claimed that "the United States have a right to pursue their enemy on a principle of self-defense." [26] Once in Florida, Jackson was soon fighting Spaniards and hanging Englishmen — actions that might conceivably embroil the country in serious war. In a stormy five-hour cabinet meeting, the President and most of the cabinet took the view that Jackson had indeed committed war upon Spain. Calhoun, the Secretary of War, wanted to court-martial Jackson. But John Quincy Adams, the Secretary of State, vigorously defended him.

Adams was unique among the statesmen of the first half-century of the republic in objecting to the assignment of the war power to Congress. Condemning "that error in our Constitution which confers upon the legislative assemblies the power of declaring war," he thought this power should rightly be "strictly an Executive act." The Florida problem, he confided to his diary, was "embarrassing and complicated" because it involved not only war with Spain but the right of the executive "to authorize hostilities without a declaration of war by Congress." He had, however, "no doubt that *defensive* acts of hostility may be authorized by the Executive," and he insisted that "everything [Jackson] did was defensive; that as such it was neither war against Spain nor a violation of the Constitution." "The disclaimer of power in the Executive," he added to himself, "is of dangerous example and of evil consequences." [27] His colleagues were not persuaded by this broad view of defensive war, but politics argued against the repudiation of Jackson, and Monroe took no action.

Monroe was on occasion prepared to take formidable diplomatic initiatives on his own. Though he did consult with his cabinet and with such elder statesmen as Jefferson and Madison before promulgating what in another twenty years began to be known as the Monroe Doctrine, all he did with Congress was to announce the Doctrine to it. Some members of Congress felt he was assuming an unwarrantable power. When Henry Clay drew up a joint resolution affirming Monroe's declaration, it never even came up for vote. Indeed, though other efforts were made to give the Doctrine congressional endorsement over the next three quarters of a century, it was not till the end of the century that the Senate, in accepting a reservation to the Hague Convention of 1899, implied congressional acceptance of the Doctrine as national policy. Even then the Doctrine was not mentioned by name.[28]

Still the Monroe Doctrine, if neither authorized nor ratified by Congress, was a notable and unchallenged national commitment. But Monroe did not for a moment suppose that by the act of promulgation he had empowered the executive to commit military force in support of the Doctrine. When Colombia inquired how the United States intended to go about resisting interference by the Holy Alliance in Latin American affairs, Adams replied that the Constitution confided "the ultimate decision . . . to the Legislative Department." If there were European intervention, the President would recommend to Congress "the adoption of the measures exclusively of their resort." [29] A few years later Henry Clay, now Adams's Secretary of State, reiterated the point. If the question of war arose, he told the Argentines, "Congress alone . . . is competent by our Constitution, to decide that question." [30]

Jackson himself as President meticulously respected this point. No one did more to enlarge the presidential authority in other areas. But, when it came to the war-making power, he followed not his own example of 1818 but Jefferson's of 1801. Thus in 1831, after ordering an armed vessel to South America to protect American shipping against Argentine raiders, he said, if somewhat after the fact, "I submit the case to the consideration of Congress, to the end that they may clothe the Executive with such authority and means as they deem necessary for providing a force adequate to the complete protection of our fellow citizens fishing and trading in these seas." [31]

When France persisted in her refusal to pay long-standing claims for damage to American shipping during the Napoleonic wars, Jackson, instead of moving on his own, took care to ask Congress for a law "authorizing reprisals upon French property, in case provision shall not be made for the payment of the debt." [32] The issue here was whether Congress could constitutionally give the President contingent authority to undertake reprisals — i.e., to wage limited war. The issue had arisen before. In 1799, during the undeclared war with France, Hamilton had proposed a comparable delegation of the war-making power, suggesting that Congress authorize the President, if negotiations with France proved unavailing, to "declare that a state of war exists." [33] The proposal got no farther, but in 1810 the Senate passed a resolution authorizing the President, when he deemed it expedient, to order the Navy to protect American merchant ships against British and French raiders. With almost excessive nicety, Madison objected to this as an unconstitutional delegation by Congress to the Presidency of war-making decisions. Dolley Madison's brother-in-law led the fight against the resolution in the House, asking his colleagues why, when it was the duty of Congress "to decide on our great relations with foreign nations, we shrink from the task and throw the responsibility of measures on other departments of the Government?" The House sustained the Madison family position.[34]

Jackson was not seeking a blank check but rather authorization to act in case of a formal refusal on the part of the French government to meet its obligations. John Quincy Adams spoke up for his old foe in the House of Representatives, arguing that Congress had the duty to give Jackson the authority he wanted "for the very reason that the President's measure, or some other measure which the honor of the country might require, might possibly eventuate in war." [35] But Albert Gallatin, the veteran Jeffersonian, told his friends in Congress that this "proposed transfer by Congress of its constitutional powers to the Executive, in a case which necessarily embraces the question of war or no war" was "entirely inconsistent with the letter and spirit of our Constitution." Congress declined to delegate its war-making power and turned Jackson down.[36]

In the case of Texas, as we have noted, Jackson, though he personally would have liked not only to recognize but to annex Texas, referred the question of recognition to Congress in 1836 as a question "probably leading to war" and therefore a proper subject for "previous understanding with that body by whom war can alone be declared, and by whom all the provisions for sustaining its perils must be furnished." [37] For this reason, he delayed American recognition till Congress itself proposed it in the last days of his administration.

VII

What restrained these early Presidents? It cannot be said that the fear of impeachment played much of a role. Though intended for Presidents, the power had been employed, when employed at all, against lesser officers. The first impeachment under the Constitution was an abortive attempt in 1797 to remove a senator. But the Senate on its own expelled the unfortunate William Blount of Tennessee before the House impeached him and then blandly concluded that, in any case, a senator was not a "civil officer" within the meaning of the impeachment clause. Jefferson wrote Madison sourly at the time, "I see nothing in the mode of proceeding by impeachment but the most formidable weapon for the purpose of dominant faction that was ever contrived. It would be the most effectual one of getting rid of any man whom they may consider as dangerous to their views." [38]

Once President, however, Jefferson, now enlightened by the executive perspective, himself turned to impeachment as a way of ridding the federal bench of judges whom he considered dangerous to *his* views. He succeeded in 1804 in removing a senile and alcoholic Federalist district judge from New Hampshire but failed the next year in an attempt to convict Justice Chase of the Supreme Court, author of one of the opinions in *Bas v. Tingy*. The Jeffersonian thesis, as expounded by Senator Giles of Virginia during the Chase trial, was that impeachment was "nothing more than an enquiry, by the two Houses of Congress, whether the office of any public man might not be better filled by another." Conviction and removal would not imply criminality or corruption but only "a declaration by Congress to this effect: You hold dangerous opinions, and if you are suffered to carry them into effect you will work the destruction of the nation." [39] The acquittal of Chase happily destroyed this thesis. It may well be, as Raoul Berger has persuasively argued, that Chase deserved conviction because of the clear record of prejudice and error in his judicial conduct. [40] Yet his conviction would undoubtedly have encouraged Jefferson to extend his purge of the courts, and the precedents created would have gravely threatened the independence of the judiciary.

Chief Justice Marshall, whose own seat may well have been saved by the Chase acquittal, seized an early opportunity to remind Jefferson that the President too was subject to the Constitution and the laws. Presiding on circuit over the trial of Aaron Burr for treason at Richmond, Virginia, in 1807, Marshall acceded to a defense request that Jefferson deliver certain documents from his files, especially a letter written by General James

Wilkinson, once a co-conspirator of Burr's and now a leading witness against him. Marshall accordingly directed that the President be served with a subpoena *duces tecum* — i.e., a subpoena requiring the person subpoenaed to produce specified documents. The Chief Justice observed that the Constitution and the laws made "no exception whatever" when they gave an accused person the right to invoke the compulsory process of the court. Nor did the argument that it was "incompatible" with presidential dignity for Jefferson to submit to compulsory process impress him. The English principle that the King could do no wrong, Marshall said, did not apply to the United States where the President "may be impeached and may be removed from office." At a later point in the trial Marshall put it most categorically: "That the president of the United States may be subpoenaed, and examined as a witness, and required to produce any paper in his possession, is not controverted."

Having laid down the general principle, Marshall, a realist, was not disposed to force it to the point of no return. He did not, for example, try to require Jefferson's appearance in court. The subpoena said that the delivery of the documents "will be admitted as sufficient observance of the process, without the personal attendance . . . of the persons therein named." As for Jefferson, he could hardly contest Marshall's general principle without coming close to claiming that the President could do no wrong. Moreover, he perhaps remembered how indignantly the Jeffersonians had denounced Justice Chase for refusing to subpoena President Adams during Thomas Cooper's trial under the Sedition Act in 1800. But he was incensed over the traps that his old enemies Marshall and Burr were laying for him. So, while he sent along the documents and added that he would, if desired, testify by deposition, he gave no formal answer to the subpoena and sketched out in private letters his own theory about subpoenas and Presidents.

Conceding that "all persons owe obedience to subpoenas," Jefferson contended that a President had a still higher obligation to the "particular set of duties imposed on him." The theory, in short, was not that the President was *per se* immune to subpoena, but that the courts could not command "the executive to abandon superior duties" at will. Marshall was asking him to sacrifice major duties to minor ones. If a President were obliged to honor every subpoena at the risk of imprisonment for disobedience, the courts could breach the separation of powers and "keep him constantly trudging from north and south and east and west, and withdraw him entirely from his constitutional duties." The result would be to "leave the nation without an executive branch."

The matter thus ended with Marshall asserting a constitutional right to subpoena Presidents and Jefferson standing on a practical right not to show up in court. Marshall, in other words, said that the President was subject to the same law as every other American citizen; and Jefferson said: Yes, but the President also has more solemn responsibilities than any other American citizen, and judges must take this into account. Both men were surely correct. Their collective response suggested that the answer lay in striking a balance between the President's obligation to his official duties, on the one hand, and the importance of a particular case and the indispensability of the President's testimony on the other.

As for the Wilkinson letter, the government argued that it "might contain *state secrets,* which could not be divulged without endangering the national safety." Jefferson himself wrote the federal attorney that the President, "from the nature of his case, must be the sole judge" whether "the public interests will permit publication." But this claim was not insisted upon in court. The government prosecutor gave Marshall the entire text, while indicating passages deemed immaterial. Marshall, remarking that he could "readily conceive that the president might receive a letter which it would be improper to exhibit in public," said that he could not "precisely lay down any general rule for such a case." The best he could suggest was that the President would have to make an argument for the confidentiality of the document and the defense an argument for its materiality, with the court itself presumably making the final decision.[41]

Jefferson, privately furious over Marshall's various rulings, fumed about the "error in our Constitution, which makes any branch independent of the nation." Since impeachment had become a "farce" he now favored a constitutional amendment empowering the President to remove federal judges on the joint address of both houses of Congress.[42] Removal by address — that is, by a majority vote of both houses without charges or trial — had been emphatically rejected in the Constitutional Convention. It did not seem any better as an idea two decades after.

"Experience has already shown," Jefferson concluded glumly of the Constitution in 1819, "that the impeachment it has provided is not even a scarecrow." [43] Fifteen years later the Senate, determined to chastise a President, tried another approach. An anti-Jackson majority of senators, angered by his removal of the government deposits from the Bank of the United States, passed a resolution of censure, charging that the President had "assumed upon himself authority and power not conferred by the Constitution and laws, but in derogation of both." Jackson responded with a long and forceful protest to the Senate. The President, he said, was liable to impeachment for high crimes or misdemeanors and, if convicted, to criminal prosecution and private legal redress "in the same manner and to the same extent as the humblest functionary." The Senate had accused him of having committed very high crimes indeed. The resolution of censure was "in substance an impeachment of the President." If Congress were serious, it must therefore impeach the President with all solemnity. Otherwise it was evading its own constitutional responsibility.[44] Jackson's logic was unassailable, and the idea of censure as a halfway house on the road to impeachment was eliminated.

VIII

What restrained these early Presidents was not only their respect for the Constitution. It was also that they saw constitutional principles in political context and understood that there were unwritten as well as written checks on unilateral presidential initiative in foreign affairs. The nation was young; its unity under pressure, as the War of 1812 showed, was still precarious; and responsible statesmen perceived that to lead a divided country into foreign adventure might be to risk national survival itself. Moreover, with both Washington and Hamilton dead and the Federalist party in decay, the executive prerogative had lost its champions. The Virginia dynasty governed the country in the early nineteenth century, and Jefferson and Madison, traditional advocates of the congressional role, had unequaled prestige as elder statesmen. Both, in addition, were generally zealous defenders of that free flow of information which served itself as a check on presidential adventurism as well as a means of rallying national opinion.

Nor was national opinion the only constraint. These were, after all, the men who had proclaimed that "a decent respect to the opinion of mankind" impelled them to write the Declaration of Independence. Such sentiments were not simply the rhetoric of '76. A decade later, in a far less exalted national mood, that eminently realistic document the Federalist Papers declared that "sensibility to the opinion of the world" was an indispensable characteristic of sound government. The argument so powerfully expressed in the 63rd Federalist has never sounded more to the point than on the eve of the 200th anniversary of independence:

> An attention to the judgment of other nations is important to every government for two reasons: the one is, that, independently of the merits of any particular plan or measure, it is desirable, on various accounts, that it should appear to other nations as the offspring of a wise and honorable policy; the second is, that in doubtful cases, particularly where the national councils may be warped by some strong passion or momentary interest, the presumed or known opinion of the impartial world may be the best guide that can be followed.

> What has not America lost by her want of character with foreign nations; and how many errors and follies would she not have avoided, if the justice and propriety of her measures, had, in every instance, been previously tried by the light in which they would probably appear to the unbiased part of mankind?

3

The Rise of Presidential War

THE FOUNDING FATHERS made a deliberate effort to divide the control of the war powers. They vested in Congress the authority to commence and authorize war, whether that war be declared or undeclared. At the same time they vested in the Presidency the conduct both of ongoing foreign relations and ongoing war as well as the right to respond to sudden attack when Congress was not in session. This division of powers was inherently unstable. In particular, as the Pacificus-Helvidius debate had shown, the presidential power to conduct diplomacy and the congressional power to authorize hostilities had each the potentiality of overwhelming and nullifying the other. If the President were to claim all the implications of his control of diplomacy, he could, by creating an antecedent state of things, swallow up the congressional power to authorize hostilities. If Congress were to claim all the implications of its power to authorize hostilities, it could swallow up much of the presidential power to conduct diplomacy. Still, written and unwritten checks managed to keep these two powers in rough balance in the early republic. This balance was strong enough, indeed, to survive the drastic expansion of presidential power under Andrew Jackson. Justice Story said of Jackson in 1834, "Though we live under the form of a republic we are in fact under the absolute rule of a single man." [1] But in fact even that imperious President continued to defer to Congress in situations that held out the threat of war.

I

Yet the balance remained unstable. There was, of course, the Locke-Jefferson doctrine of the law of self-preservation, though this was presumably confined to the gravest national emergencies. Short of such emergency, there were ways by which Presidents could in fact alter the original constitutional balance — and do so without appearing to lay aside the Constitution at all. For the Convention, while it gave Congress the sole power to initiate offensive war, also allowed the President to initiate defensive war. This power, limited in the original understanding, could be easily enlarged — as by J. Q. Adams when he justified Jackson's invasion of Spanish Florida in 1818 — to imply unilateral authority to conduct defense so aggressively that those on the receiving end might well be pardoned if they mistook it for aggression.

The Militia Act of 1795 had empowered the President to call forth the militia "whenever the United States shall be invaded, or be in imminent danger of invasion." But during the War of 1812 the governors of the New England states rejected the call of the Secretary of War to furnish their militia for the defense of the maritime frontier. Madison denounced this defiance, saying grimly that, if the states could thus frustrate the national authority, even in a condition of declared war, America was "not one nation for the purpose most of all requiring it," and the public safety would thereafter require "those large and permanent military establishments which are forbidden by the principles of our free government." [2] But the high courts of the New England states supported the governors, insisting that the right to determine the danger of invasion was vested in the commander in chief of the militia in each state and not in the President.[3]

In 1827 the problem reached the Supreme Court in the case of *Martin v. Mott*. Speaking through Justice Story, the Court ruled that "the authority to decide whether the exigency has arisen belongs exclusively to the President" and that "his decision is conclusive upon all other persons." [4] This power, the Court added, was to be reserved for sudden emergencies and for circumstances vital to the existence of the Union. Yet, if the President had exclusive and conclusive authority to define emergencies and circumstances, who then could gainsay his finding of "imminent" danger? And, if the Court's proposition applied to the militia, it obviously applied all the more strongly to the regular forces under the President's direct command.

The theory of defense against imminent as well as actual attack began to obliterate the distinction the Founding Fathers had tried to draw between offensive and defensive war. When the increasingly elastic theory of defensive war was added to the presidential control of diplomatic relations with foreign states, there started to accumulate within the Presidency the means to force the issue of war on the branch supposedly empowered by the Constitution to make the decision. For the President had the ability to contrive circumstances that left Congress little choice but to ratify his policy.

In 1816, Senator Rufus King, one of the last survivors of the Constitutional Convention, tried to preserve a voice for the Senate in the conduct of diplomacy. But, the Committee on Foreign Relations, making its debut as a standing committee, turned down his attempt to instruct President Monroe on future negotiations. Negotiation, the Committee said, was an executive responsibility. Because diplomacy depended on "regular and secret intelligence" which the Senate lacked the means of acquiring, the Senate was therefore in general "deficient in the information most essential to a correct decision." As for the President, he was always responsible for his conduct to the Constitution. "The committee considers this responsibility the surest pledge for the faithful discharge of his duties. They think the interference of the Senate in the direction of foreign negotiations calculated to diminish that responsibility and thereby to impair the best security for the national safety." [5]

These stately phrases were all very well. But could not presidential diplomacy raise up threats to the nation that an activist President might then claim the need to forestall by pre-emptive military action? By the time the President had got this far on his own, Congress might have little alternative but to go along. What, for example, about the Monroe Doctrine? In this case Monroe had soon made it clear that proclaiming the Doctrine did not create military commitments. But three years later J. Q. Adams, now President, proposed to send a mission to a congress of newly independent Latin American governments at Panama. This meeting was called by Simón Bolívar to discuss, among other things, the policy the new states should adopt toward Spain, whose rule they had recently overthrown. A number of leading senators, among them Martin Van Buren and Thomas Hart Benton, opposed the idea of American participation. Though their motives were partisan, they also had a serious point. The Panama mission, they contended, might lead the United States into an alliance with Latin American states and thereby into war with Spain. (Though they did not know this, the Adams administration had secret information, withheld from the Senate, that would have confirmed senatorial apprehension that Spain was still determined to regain its lost colonies.) Van Buren pretended to see in the mission "a measure by which the peace of the country is to be exposed to a contingency beyond the control of our Government — by which the great question of peace or war will be taken from the Representatives of the people." [6] At the same time, however, he did not deny that the President had the constitutional authority to send the mission whatever Congress thought. This congressional dilemma exposed a potential gap in its war-making power.

II

The prospect in the 1820s of war with Spain over Latin America was hypothetical. But the prospect in the 1830s and 1840s of war with Mexico over Texas was very real. The knowledge that public opinion was deeply divided over the idea of the annexation of Texas and the concern, after the nullification crisis and the beginnings of abolitionism, not to excite the slavery issue had constrained Jackson from employing his presidential authority to gain an objective he privately deemed desirable and necessary. In addition, as that most exacting scholar, Professor Frederick Merk, has written, Texan independence had been won with the help of Americans permitted to cross the border in blatant violation of American neutrality; "if Texas were to be annexed too soon, world opinion would be outraged." [7]

National and world opinion as well as the Constitution equally constrained Jackson's immediate successors — Van Buren and, in his moment as President, William Henry Harrison. But John Tyler, the first Vice President to claim, and succeed to, the Presidency, reversed the policy of restraint. Tyler needed an issue that would give him a political base for re-election; he also had a slaveholder's interest in extending the peculiar institution. He thereupon began secret negotiations with the Texan government looking toward annexation — secret because such negotiations would normally be secret, secret also to give time for a pro-annexation campaign to change the nation's mind.

Texans, however, were less enthusiastic about joining the United States in 1843 than they had been in 1836. Their interest now was in winning Mexican recognition of their own independence. If the Mexican government learned they were negotiating a treaty of union with the United States, it might invade Texas instead of recognizing it. The government in Austin was therefore cool to Tyler's overtures. But the Texan diplomatic agent in Washington asked on his own whether, if annexation were in prospect, the United States would be prepared to commit armed force to deter a Mexican invasion of Texas.

President Tyler had notoriously rigid views on the Constitution; that is why he had broken with Jackson a decade before. His new Secretary of State in 1843, Abel P. Upshur of Virginia, had published as recently as 1840 an unrelenting and interminable attack on the constitutional nationalism of Justice Story. The Tyler administration could not, without trampling on its own principles, commit troops in the absence of congressional authorization to a situation that might well produce war. Yet Tyler wanted Texas; so he tried to slide by the Constitution, instructing Upshur to assure the Texans orally that, once a treaty was signed, a protective force would go into place. The American chargé in Austin imprudently put this assurance in writing. Fearing that Congress might demand all papers relating to Texas, Tyler promptly disowned his man in Austin, observing piously that "the employment of the army or navy against a foreign power, with which the United States are at peace, is not within the competency of the President." [8] Senator Thomas Hart Benton, that stout Jacksonian, commented, "As to secretly lending the Army and Navy of the United States to Texas to fight Mexico while we were at peace with her, it would be a crime against God and man and our own Constitution. . . . a piece of business which belonged to Congress and should have been referred to them, and which, on the contrary, was concealed from them though in session and present." [9]

When Upshur was killed in the explosion of a cannon on the U.S.S. *Princeton,* John C. Calhoun, the strictest strict constructionist of them all, became Secretary of State. But Calhoun wanted Texas too. Early in 1844 Tyler finally ordered the deployment of force in the Gulf of Mexico and along the southwestern frontier of Texas. In notifying the Texas government, Calhoun said that, so long as the treaty was under negotiation, the President would use "all the means placed within his power by the constitution" to protect Texas from invasion. The Texans, who had studied the Constitution, did not regard this as much of a commitment. Calhoun assured them that the Americans would respond actively in case of attack — defensive war — until Congress authorized or forbade further measures. "We might, therefore," Daniel Webster exclaimed with alarm, "be in a war with Mexico at any time, with or without the authority of Congress."

With secrecy still prevailing, Tyler submitted his treaty of annexation to the Senate in 1844. The Senate, demanding and receiving information from the executive about troop deployment and other incriminating matters, rejected the treaty. Tyler, determined to have both his issue and Texas, proposed an alternative: annexation by joint resolution, to be passed by the two houses. This was another singular idea to come out of a strict constructionist administration. Albert Gallatin, the last Jeffersonian, denounced it as "an undisguised usurpation of power and violation of the constitution." The senatorial two-thirds veto, Gallatin said, was intended "to protect the weaker against the abuse of the treaty-making power, if vested in a bare majority." Tyler's proposal "transfers to a majority of both houses" what the Constitution had confided to the President and two thirds of the Senate. Senator Rives of Virginia cited Washington's refusal to send the Jay Treaty papers to the House as a reminder that the Constitutional Convention had expressly excluded the House from the treaty-making process.[10] Constitutional arguments were unavailing. Congress, by annexing Texas through joint resolution, placed another weapon in the hands of the Presidency. John Quincy Adams disgustedly called it "the apoplexy of the Constitution." [11]

III

Tyler had shown how presidential control of diplomacy and troop deployment might make gaping holes in the congressional war-making power. His successor, the tough and efficient James K. Polk, transformed possibility into fact when, in 1846, he sent American soldiers into disputed land between Texas and Mexico. Here they were, not surprisingly, attacked by Mexican units who, operating no doubt on their own theory of defensive war, supposed themselves repelling an invasion of Mexico. Polk then stampeded Congress into a recognition of a state of war.

John Quincy Adams tried to distinguish this congressional *recognition* of a state of war from the Constitution's provision for a congressional *declaration* of war. The Mexican War, he said in 1847, "has never to this day been declared by the Congress of the United States. It has [only] been recognized as existing by the Act of Mexico, in direct and notorious violation of the truth. . . . The most important conclusion from all this, in my mind," he added, "is the failure of that provision in the Constitution of the United States, that the power of declaring War is given exclusively to Congress" — an interesting reflection, given its tone of regret, from the statesman who thirty years before had regarded this same provision as the great error of the Constitution. "It is now established as an irreversible precedent," he continued — he was writing to that other old stager, Gallatin — "that the President of the United States has but to declare that War exists, with any Nation upon Earth, by the act of that Nation's Government, and the War is essentially declared." Adams concluded, "It is not difficult to foresee what its ultimate issue will be to the people of Mexico, but what it will be to the People of the United States is beyond my foresight, and I turn my eyes away from it." [12]

Many members of Congress had the uneasy feeling that the President had put something over on them. Early in 1848, with the war still on, the House doves succeeded by a narrow margin in tacking onto a resolution honoring General Taylor the declaration that the war had been "unnecessarily and unconstitutionally begun by the President of the United States." The Senate struck this thought from the bill, and the House accepted the deletion. But this was the mood that led Congressman Abraham Lincoln, a first-termer from the backwoods of Illinois, to make his celebrated and prescient attack on presidential warmaking.

Lincoln's attack was provoked by a letter from W. H. Herndon, his law partner back home. "Let me first state," Lincoln wrote Herndon, "what I understand to be your position. It is, that if it shall become *necessary, to repel invasion,* the President may, without violation of the Constitution, cross the line and *invade* the territory of another country; and that, whether such *necessity* exists in any given case, the President is to be the *sole* judge." This argument, Lincoln pointed out, went beyond any position that Polk himself had ever taken; after all, the President had obtained a declaration of war and fulfilled the constitutional proprieties; but, since it corresponded to views expressed a century and a quarter later by President Richard M. Nixon (indeed, Nixon extended it to embrace the invasion of a country on the other side of the world), it may be well to consider Lincoln's assessment of its implications.

"Allow the President," Lincoln continued, "to invade a neighboring nation, whenever *he* shall deem it necessary to repel an invasion . . . and you allow him to make war at pleasure. Study to see if you can fix *any limit* to his power in this respect." Mexico was the immediate instance; but suppose, Lincoln said, a President "should choose to say he thinks it necessary to invade Canada, to prevent the British from invading us, how could you stop him?" If the presidential power to wage defensive war on his own decision were once conceded, how could Congress hold him back? "You may say to him, 'I see no probability of the British invading us' but he will say to you 'be silent; I see it, if you dont.' " The reason why the Constitution had given the war-making power to Congress, Lincoln added, was because Kings had always been involving and impoverishing their people in wars. "This, our [constitutional] convention understood to be the most oppressive of all Kingly oppressions; and they resolved to so frame the Constitution that *no one man* should hold the power of bringing this oppression upon us. But your view destroys the whole matter, and places our President where Kings have always stood. Write soon again." [13]

Lincoln's doctrine of *"no one man"* — an unconscious restatement of James Wilson's view that it should not be in the power of "a single man" to bring the country into war — unquestionably expressed the original intent. Polk now showed that a single man, if President and if backed, as he undoubtedly was, by public opinion, could through unilateral initiative compel Congress to declare war against a foreign state. Neither written nor unwritten checks sufficed to stop a President determined to annex Texas even if it meant war with Mexico. However, it evidently did not occur to Polk to claim, in the style of contemporary Presidents, that the right of self-defense or the inherent authority of the Commander in Chief allowed him to wage war against another country without congressional authorization.

IV

As the executive branch began to develop its war-making powers, it also began to tighten its control over the transmission of information to Congress. Washington's cabinet had privately thought there might be executive papers which could not be disclosed without harm to the public interest, and Washington himself had suggested to the House of Representatives that papers involving active negotiations might fall into that category. But the presumption remained in the early republic that Congress should and would receive the information it sought.

The first Presidents were in consequence exceedingly chary about denying congressional calls. There were no incidents of denial at all under Adams. In 1807 Jefferson withheld material, "chiefly in the form of letters," he had received on the Burr conspiracy. While giving Congress an extended report on the situation, he explained that some of the material requested contained "a mixture of rumors, conjectures, and suspicions"; much of it too had come to him "under the restriction of private confidence." He therefore felt that "neither safety nor justice will permit the exposing [of] names." Jefferson thus added to Washington's concern to protect negotiations two further reasons for presidential denial — the protection of innocent persons and of confidential informants. But all this was beside the point, for the congressional request had already specifically exempted anything that Jefferson might "deem the public welfare to require not to be disclosed." [14]

There were no incidents under Madison. Monroe once withheld in 1825 when Congress asked him for documents relating to charges against naval officers in the Pacific. "It is due to their rights and to the character of Government," he said, "that they be not censured without just cause, which cannot be ascertained until, on a view of the charges, they are heard in their defense, and after a thorough and impartial investigation." But again Congress had asked for information only insofar as the President "may deem compatible with the public interest." In both the Jefferson and Monroe cases, in short, Presidents were exercising not discretion they claimed for themselves but discretion accorded them by Congress. It was not to be presumed, a House committee said in 1843, "that the exercise of the discretion by President Monroe in a case where it *was* conferred upon him, proves that he would have exercised it in a case where it *was not* conferred." [15] On the other hand, the fact that Congress itself conferred this discretion implied congressional acceptance of the principle that the President, in certain circumstances, was entitled to keep information to himself.

None of these transactions in the first forty years of the republic involved executive denial against the will of Congress. Then in 1833 the Senate asked for a copy of a paper Andrew Jackson had read to his cabinet justifying his decision to remove the government deposits from the Bank of the United States. Jackson rejected this request as an intrusion into the confidential processes of the Presidency. "I have yet to learn," he told the Senate, "under what constitutional authority that branch of the Legislature has a right to require of me an account of any communication, either verbally or in writing, made to the heads of Departments acting as a Cabinet council. As well might I be required to detail to the Senate the free and private conversations I have held with those officers on any subject relating to their duties and my own." He thus added still another reason for presidential denial — the confidentiality of the President's exchanges with his advisers in connection with official duties.

At the same time, Jackson said he was willing "upon all occasions" to explain to the American people the grounds of his conduct, "and I am willing upon all proper occasions to give to either branch of the Legislature any information in my possession that can be useful in the execution of the appropriate duties confided to them." Later he declared that cases could occur "in which it may be indispensable to the proper exercise of [the Legislature's] power that it should inquire into and decide upon the conduct of the President or other public officers, and in every case its constitutional right to do so is cheerfully conceded." Most of the time he fulfilled congressional requests for information.

But the Senate was in opposition hands, and toward the end of his second term Jackson began to feel that senatorial requisitions were a form of calculated harassment. "This is another of those calls for information made upon me by the Senate," he testily informed that body in 1835, "which have, in my judgment, either related to the subjects exclusively belonging to the executive department or otherwise encroached upon the constitutional powers of the Executive." Without conceding the right of the Senate to make such requests, he continued, he had deemed it expedient in the past to comply with them; but no more. "Their continued repetition imposes on me, as the representative and trustee of the American people, the painful but imperious duty of resisting to the utmost any further encroachment on the rights of the Executive." [16] So defense against congressional harassment — i.e., against unreasonable demands for information — was added to the list of grounds for executive withholding.

v

The developing presidential claim to control the flow of information received a comprehensive statement from President Tyler in 1843 when the House asked for Army reports on Cherokee land frauds. Tyler seized the occasion to deny that, simply because Congress called on the executive branch for "all the information in its possession relating to any subject of the deliberation of the House," the President was bound to hand it over "without the authority to exercise any discretion . . . in reference to the nature of the information required or to the interests of the country or of individuals to be affected by such compliance." He went on to add a new category to the list of grounds for presidential discretion — the protection of active investigation and litigation — and recapitulated the reasons advanced by earlier Presidents — the separation of powers; the protection of confidential informants; the protection of innocent persons. In an eloquent passage, anticipating the McCarthyism of the next century, Tyler wrote:

> Impertinence or malignity may seek to make the Executive Department the means of incalculable and irremediable injury to innocent parties by throwing into them libels most foul and atrocious. Shall there be no discretionary authority permitted to refuse to become the instruments of such malevolence?

Arguing from the analogy of private litigants in courts, Tyler said that "the general authority to compel testimony must give way in certain cases to the paramount right of individuals or of the Government." [17] He thus massed the arguments in the strongest statement thus far of presidential right to deny information sought by Congress. Still it is to be noted that Tyler spoke only of "certain cases"; he made no assertion of absolute and unchecked privilege. Moreover, in this particular case, he sent the House the papers it had requested. And the House for its part at once challenged Tyler and particularly his comparison between judicial and legislative tribunals. "The cases," the House said, "are entirely different." Where in private litigation "the public safety requires that particular evidence to be suppressed," in legislative investigation, where the object was to expose abuses in the administration itself, "the public safety requires that it should be disclosed." [18]

In 1846 still another item was added to the list of exceptions — the protection of foreign intelligence operations. The Revolution had first persuaded Americans of the utility of an intelligence function in government. The Federalist Papers commended the Constitution for enabling the President "to manage the business of intelligence in such a manner as prudence may suggest." [19] Early Congresses provided Presidents with a secret service fund; and in 1810 the Eleventh Congress regularized the procedure by passing a law providing for "contingent expenses of intercourse between the United States and foreign nations." The law required the reporting of all such expenditures except for those the President did not think it advisable to specify in detail. In such cases the President was empowered to give a certificate for the amount of the expenditure. The law made him sole judge whether expenditures should be public or secret.

Presidents did not issue many certificates, and no one raised serious questions about the use of unvouchered funds until 1846. Then the House of Representatives passed a resolution requesting an accounting of $5460 for which Tyler had given certificates five years before when Daniel Webster, as Secretary of State, was negotiating with Great Britain to settle the old dispute over the northeastern boundary of the United States. The Webster-Ashburton Treaty of 1842 was accompanied by much flimflam over maps and the use of secret funds; and an exposure of Whig peccadilloes would presumably have been of political benefit to the new Democratic administration.

But Polk decided to defend the Presidency. "The experience of every nation on earth," he told the House, "has demonstrated that emergencies may arise in which it becomes absolutely necessary for the public safety or the public good to make expenditures the very object of which would be defeated by publicity. . . . In no nation is the application of such sums ever made public." Tyler, Polk said, had "solemnly determined" that the objects and items of these particular expenditures should not be divulged. It would "certainly be a safe general rule" that a subsequent President should not in such circumstances "revise the acts of his predecessor." If a President yielded to such congressional requests, "he must answer similar calls for every expenditure of a confidential character, made under every Administration, in war and in peace, from the organization of the Government to the present period."

While thus insisting on this exemption, Polk at the same time fully conceded that the House remained "the grand inquest of the nation." If its members had any reason to believe there had been malversation in office, "all the archives and papers of the Executive Department, public or private, would be subject to the inspection and control of a committee of their body and every facility in the power of the Executive be afforded to enable them to prosecute the investigation." Above all, if the House wished to investigate executive misconduct with a view to the exercise of its power of impeachment, "the power of the House in the pursuit of this object would penetrate into the most secret recesses of the Executive Departments. It could command the attendance of any and every agent of the Government, and compel them to produce all papers, public or private, official or unofficial, and to testify on oath to all facts within their knowledge." [20]

As one of the very few presidential commentaries on impeachment (rope is rarely mentioned in the house of the man who might be hanged), Polk's statement is of particular interest. Chief Justice Marshall had said forty years before that a grand jury could compel the testimony and papers of a President through the subpoena power. Polk now said that the House of Representatives could compel the testimony and papers of a President if it were conducting an investigation with a view to impeachment.

He said this, of course, in a context that enlarged the presidential power, short of impeachment, to withhold information from Congress. In the half century since George Washington, the Presidency had materially expanded its claims to privilege in the release of executive information. Yet these claims were all put forward as exceptions to the general rule that Congress, as the grand inquest, had a right to be informed. The situation remained in rough balance. Presidents acceded to most congressional demands but sometimes asserted and once in a while insisted on their right not to do so (even while they very often did so). Congress accepted the principle of limited but not of uncontrolled presidential discretion.

A distinction too had grown up between domestic and foreign policy. Congressional resolutions now ordinarily *directed* every department except State to supply information; in the case of foreign affairs, the President was merely *requested* to supply the information "if not incompatible with the public interest." In 1848 the House of Representatives asked Polk for all the papers on his instructions to the American Minister to Mexico and did so without the familiar escape clause. Among those affirming the power of the House to make the call unconditional was John Quincy Adams, who would hardly have appreciated so peremptory a congressional requisition in the days when he was Secretary of State and President. But, as there was an executive perspective on these problems, so there was a legislative perspective; and Adams had now served in the House for seventeen years. As for Polk, who had once been Speaker of the House, he now condemned the absence of "the customary and usual reservation . . . relating to our intercourse with foreign nations" and rebuked the House for its "unconstitutional" request.[21] Doubtless he construed it as further harassment from a body that had just solemnly accused him of starting an illegal war. In any case he felt a duty to protect ongoing negotiations.

Even when the executive branch pretended to accede to congressional requests, it could, and did, deceive Congress by withholding compromising material. Thus in 1854 the House demanded a copy of the Ostend Manifesto and related expansionist documents from President Pierce. The State Department, before sending over the papers, thoughtfully deleted an inflammatory page in which the Secretary of State instructed the American Minister in Madrid to detach Cuba from Spain. Many years later an historian came upon the missing page in the files.[22] This had happened before. It would happen again.

VI

In the course of the early nineteenth century, the Presidency thus strengthened its control of information, secured its monopoly of diplomacy and enlarged its theory of defensive war. The doctrine still prevailed, however, that Congress alone could authorize hostilities against sovereign states. But what was the constitutional position when Presidents were confronted by situations calling for the armed protection of American honor, lives, law or property not against sovereign states at all but against roving bands of stateless and lawless people?

Military action against Indians — stateless and lawless by American definition — pirates, slave traders, smugglers, cattle rustlers, frontier ruffians or foreign brigands was plainly something different from warfare against organized governments. It differed both in the juridical status of the combatants under international law and in the practical fact that such fugitive hostilities would not lead to full-scale war. Moreover, a nation's use of armed force to rescue, for example, citizens endangered by the breakdown of order in a foreign land had ample sanction in international practice. Presidents therefore decided that such police actions, not directed at sovereign states, and not requiring special congressional appropriations, did not rise to the dignity of formal congressional concern.

For its part, Congress was content to leave such things to the executive — either by delegation, as in an act of 1819 authorizing the Navy to take action against pirates or an act of 1862 authorizing the Secretary of the Navy to make regulations concerning, among other things, the protection of American citizens in danger abroad, or without any congressional action at all. The result was a multitude of ephemeral military operations varying considerably in length and intensity, in the number of troops committed and in the number (if any) of casualties. Jackson in Florida was an early example; but the commitment of armed force without congressional authorization was by no means confined to North America or even to the Western Hemisphere. The American Navy in these years took military action against pirates or refractory natives in places as remote as Sumatra (1832, 1838, 1839), the Fiji Islands (1840, 1855, 1858) and Africa (1820, 1843, 1845, 1850, 1854, 1858, 1859). As early as 1836, John Quincy Adams could write in, oddly, his *Eulogy on Madison,* "However startled we may be at the idea that the Executive Chief Magistrate has the power of involving the nation in war, even without consulting Congress, an experience of fifty years has proved that in numberless cases he has and must have exercised the power." [23]

These cases make up the bulk of the lists so often compiled in recent years to show that a President, when he sends the Army or Navy into combat without benefit of Congress, does so with abundant historical precedent. Actually we know all too little about most of the incidents. To the shame of historians it has been left to a group of lawyers under the direction of Professor A. D. Sofaer of the Columbia Law School to undertake a detailed investigation, episode by episode. Professor Sofaer's preliminary findings indicate that the operations were mostly directed against nongovernmental groups, mostly concerned with the protection of American citizens and mostly trivial. A substantial number took place not only without congressional authorization but also without presidential authorization, very often the consequence of the individual initiative or short temper of lieutenants along the southern border or commodores on the high seas.

An early instance of American military action in Asia provides an example. In the first quarter of the nineteenth century American merchants came to dominate the pepper trade of northwestern Sumatra. There was no organized authority along the pepper coast, and traders made such terms as they could with local chieftains, whose own status was precarious and who sometimes contended for control in the same small port. Reports reached Washington in 1831 that the *Friendship* out of Salem had been seized and looted by a gang of Sumatrans in a town called Kuala Batu. President Jackson and his Secretary of the Navy, Levi Woodbury, sent the frigate *Potomac* to Sumatra with orders first to find out what had actually happened and then, if it developed that there had been unprovoked piracy, to demand indemnification and punishment.

Woodbury's instructions were careful and limited. But the *Potomac* was under the command of Captain John Downes, a protégé of the famous and fiery Captain David Porter. Orders from the Secretary of the Navy had never restrained Porter. During the War of 1812, while harrying British vessels in the Pacific, he had planted an American flag on an island in the Marquesas, named the island after President Madison and laid waste a valley when he encountered native resistance. In 1815 he had proposed an expedition against Japan; and in 1824, ordered to suppress piracy in the Caribbean, he had seized and terrorized a town in Puerto Rico where one of his officers had been badly treated. This last excess led to Porter's court-martial and his departure from the Navy. Downes, who had served with him in the Marquesas, remained faithful to the Porter tradition. Ignoring instructions, he made no effort to ascertain what had happened to the *Friendship* or to treat with the authorities of Kuala Batu. Instead, without advance warning, he attacked and sacked the town and, in an engagement of two and a half hours, killed around a hundred Sumatrans, including (according to a report from an observer on the *Potomac*) "several women . . . who had the hardihood to take up arms when they saw their husbands fall at their feet."

When word of this incident reached Washington in July 1832, the House of Representatives called for copies of Downes's instructions and reports. Jackson sent over the material requested the same day. But this was three days after Jackson's veto of the recharter of the Bank of the United States and on the eve of a bitter presidential campaign. The *National Intelligencer,* the anti-Jackson paper in Washington, lost no time in raising the constitutional issue. No doubt Downes had ample provocation, the newspaper said, but "the right of the *Government* to punish the Malays by indiscriminate war belonged to the government as a whole, not to the President by himself." The Constitution, "it appears to us, is of little consequence, if the *President* can *make* war without waiting for a declaration of it." The newspaper concluded sharply: "If the President can direct expeditions with fire and sword against the Malays, we do not see why he may not have the power to do the same in reference to any other power or people." Even the newspaper in Salem, the home port of the *Friendship* and center of the pepper trade, said, "Neither the President of the United States nor the Captain of a Frigate has power to make or proclaim war."

Caught in the midst of the campaign, the administration publicly defended Downes. Jackson argued that, if those who had attacked the *Friendship* had been "found to be members of a regular government," it would have been different; but, since they proved to be "a band of lawless pirates," Downes's action was justified. Privately, however, the President and the Secretary of the Navy were furious. Woodbury rebuked Downes for his failure to investigate and negotiate before he attacked, and threatened him with court-martial. By the time the *Potomac* made its slow way back to American waters in 1834, the administration showed no desire to revive a now forgotten incident by proceeding against Downes. But Downes's career was blasted. He never received sea command again and ended twenty years later as a lighthouse inspector.[24]

It was of such stuff as this that Senator Goldwater was speaking when he said in 1971, "We have only been in five declared wars out of over 150 that we have fought." The Goldwater theory that the United States had fought over 150 wars — a figure he had inflated to 204 by 1973 — wildly overstated the quality of most of these incidents. The good Senator thereby claimed an insatiable bellicosity for the United States, a war every eleven months or so throughout American history, that might astound, and would certainly gratify, our Marxist critics.[25]

VII

Though these operations were all local, mostly brief and rarely involved a challenge to sovereign states, the spreading use of armed force by unilateral decision gave Presidents new habits, whether good or bad, and promoted the erosion of the congressional control of the war-making power. Even such generally mild Presidents as Fillmore and Pierce were now emboldened to make unilateral commitment of armed force in situations that might have led to war. When Fillmore sent Commodore Perry to open up Japan in 1852, Secretary of State Daniel Webster, his 1844 worries about Tyler's provocative military deployments well behind him, assured Perry that he would be "clothed with full and discretionary powers." Perry's primary instructions were to protect shipwrecked American seamen, who, in the American view, had been treated in Japan "as if they were the most atrocious criminals." This was a legitimate executive concern. The instructions continued: "If, after having exhausted every argument and every means of persuasion, the commodore should fail to obtain from the government any relaxation of their system of exclusion, or even any assurance of humane treatment of our ship-wrecked seamen, he will then change his tone, and inform them . . . that if any acts of cruelty should hereafter be practised upon citizens of this country, whether by the government or by the inhabitants of Japan, they will be severely chastised." Then the instructions added, with due caution, "He will bear in mind that as the President has no power to declare war his mission is necessarily of a pacific character, and will not resort to force unless in self-defence." [26]

The mission of chastisement succeeded without hostilities, and Congress voted Perry thanks and $20,000. But suppose the Japanese had resisted and Perry had struck back "in self-defence"?

The line between nongovernmental organizations and sovereign states was sometimes hard to draw. In this case the executive effort to protect American citizens against "inhabitants of Japan" could have led, under presidential instruction, to "defensive" war against the government of Japan — a war that Congress had not authorized, though it doubtless would have supported.

In the spread-eagle mood of the early fifties, Americans thrilled to the idea of national self-assertion overseas. In such a mood the unwritten checks of the early century were only intermittently operative. When in 1853 Martin Koszta, a Hungarian in process of becoming an American citizen, was imprisoned on an Austrian vessel in Smyrna by order of the Austrian consul general, the captain of an American sloop-of-war, acting entirely on his own, trained his guns on the Austrians and compelled Koszta's delivery into the mediatorial hands of the French consul general. Though the American minister to Turkey, George P. Marsh, the renowned philologist and pioneer ecologist, observed that both commanders had violated the sovereignty of Turkey, diplomatic negotiation finally liberated Koszta, President Pierce took responsibility for the action and Congress voted the doughty captain a gold medal. Forty years later, the Supreme Court, celebrating inherent presidential power in *In re Neagle,* brought up Koszta and asked proudly, "Upon what act of Congress then existing can any one lay his finger in support of the action of our government in this matter?" [27]

A more spectacular case arose in Greytown, Nicaragua, in 1854 when someone in an angry crowd threw a bottle at the American Minister to Central America, who was trying to save the property of a transit company in which American citizens owned shares. The Secretary of the Navy thereupon sent in the sloop-of-war *Cyane* to demand redress and apology. The commander's orders were to teach the people of Greytown that "the United States will not tolerate these outrages" but to do so, if possible, "without a resort to violence." When Greytown remained defiant, the *Cyane* bombarded and destroyed the town.

The action roused a storm of protest. The *New York Times* condemned it as a violation of the congressional war-making power; Congress demanded a full report; and James Buchanan, the Minister to the Court of St. James's, told the British that the United States would disavow the action. But in the end the administration, though embarrassed and unhappy, felt it could not back down. Pierce finally defended the destruction of Greytown on the ground that it was "a pretended community, a heterogeneous assemblage gathered from various countries . . . not standing before the world in the attitude of an organized political society," and therefore to be treated as "a piratical resort of outlaws or a camp of savages." [28]

Later Hollins, the commander of the *Cyane,* was sued in the federal courts by an American citizen named Durand whose property had been wrecked in the shelling. Justice Nelson of the Supreme Court, sitting on circuit in the Southern District of New York, found for Hollins on the ground that "the question whether it was the duty of the president to interpose for the protection of the [American] citizens at Greytown against an irresponsible and marauding community . . . belonged to the executive to determine; and his decision is final and conclusive." [29] Actually Nelson misstated the issue. It was not a question of emergency intervention to save American citizens; it was rather calculated retaliation after the fact. Nor had such retaliation been specifically ordered by President Pierce, and both Pierce and even Nelson himself said with the utmost clarity that the action was undertaken, not against a sovereign state, but against a "piratical" and "irresponsible" group. Nevertheless this special, limited, privately disapproved and generally wretched episode was cited in later years by lawyers in desperate search of constitutional justification for presidential war against sovereign states.

Yet the debate between Congress and the executive was far from concluded. Buchanan, an inveterate strict constructionist, soon beat a retreat from the position taken by Pierce and Fillmore. The power of Congress to declare war was, he said, "without limitation." It embraced "not only what writers on the law of nations term a public or perfect war, but also an imperfect war, and, in short, every species of hostility, however confined or limited." As for the executive, "without the authority of Congress," Buchanan said, "the President cannot fire a hostile gun in any case except to repel the attacks of an enemy" — a self-denying ordinance he applied to nongovernmental organizations as well as to organized political communities.[30]

When Buchanan wanted, for example, to stop the confiscation of American cargoes in Central American harbors, he did not use the rescue authority conceded by international law and exercised by his predecessors in the White House. Instead, he asked Congress for contingency authorization to commit armed forces in cases where "local authorities do not possess the physical power, even if they possess the will, to protect our citizens." Rebuffed, he renewed his request in even more stately terms: "In the progress of a great nation many exigencies must arise imperatively requiring that Congress should authorize the President to act promptly on certain conditions which may or may not afterwards arise." Without such advance authority, he pointed out, the government could act only after the mischief had been done, could "apply the remedy only when it is too late." But Congress was unmoved. Senator William H. Seward of New York righteously condemned the proposed delegation of legislative authority as "a surrender of the war-making power." He continued in eloquent indignation:

> Could anything be more strange and preposterous than the idea of the President of the United States making hypothetical wars, conditional wars, without any designation of the nation against which war is to be declared; or the time, or place, or manner, or circumstance of the duration of it, the beginning or the end; and without limiting the number of nations with which war may be waged?

On half a dozen occasions in 1857, 1858 and 1859, Congress turned the President down.[31]

*

No doubt it was this even stricter congressional response to Buchanan's already abundantly strict constructionism that led his successor, grimly confronted by the secession of the southern states and the breakup of the American Union, to start out on his own. For Lincoln delayed the convocation of Congress from April 12, 1861, when Fort Sumter was fired upon, until July 4 lest rigid constitutionalists on the Hill try to stop him from doing what he deemed necessary to save the life of the nation. In his twelve weeks of executive grace, Lincoln ignored one law and constitutional provision after another. He assembled the militia, enlarged the Army and the Navy beyond their authorized strength, called out volunteers for three years' service, spent public money without congressional appropriation, suspended *habeas corpus,* arrested people "represented" as involved in "disloyal" practices and instituted a naval blockade of the Confederacy — measures which, he later told Congress, "whether strictly legal or not, were ventured upon under what appeared to be a popular demand and a public necessity; trusting then as now that Congress would readily ratify them."

Throughout the war, even with Congress in session, Lincoln continued to exercise wide powers independently of Congress. He asserted the right to proclaim martial law behind the lines, to arrest people without warrant, to seize property, to suppress newspapers, to prevent the use of the post office for "treasonable" correspondence, to emancipate slaves, to lay out a plan of reconstruction. His proclamations, executive orders and military regulations invaded fields previously the domain of legislative action. All this took place without a declaration of war by Congress. In such undertakings Lincoln had the enthusiastic collaboration of his Secretary of State, William H. Seward — the same Seward who had been castigating Buchanan a year or two earlier for executive usurpation. Seward, who took over responsibility for internal security, was understood to have bragged to the British Minister: "My lord, I can touch a bell on my right hand and order the imprisonment of a citizen of Ohio; I can touch a bell again and order the imprisonment of a citizen of New York; and no power on earth, except that of the President, can release them. Can the Queen of England do so much?" [32]

No President had ever undertaken such sweeping action in the absence of congressional authorization. No President had ever challenged Congress with such a massive collection of faits accomplis. Benjamin R. Curtis, who had been one of the two justices dissenting from the pro-slavery decision in the Dred Scott case, wrote that Lincoln had established "a military despotism." Wendell Phillips, the abolitionist, called him an "unlimited despot." [33] Lincoln, observed Bryce, "wielded more authority than any single Englishman has done since Oliver Cromwell." [34]

Since Lincoln's reputation as the greatest of democratic statesmen is well earned, he obviously did not become a despot lightly. He was, like Cromwell, the Protector. The nation, as he saw it, faced the most desperate of emergencies. Its very survival was at stake, and with it the survival of "free government upon the earth." This situation placed democracy in a most anguishing dilemma. Would the very principles of freedom prevent free government from defending itself? The southern rebellion, he said when he finally met Congress in 1861, "forces us to ask: 'Is there, in all republics, this inherent and fatal weakness?' 'Must a Government, of necessity, be too *strong* for the liberties of its own people, or too *weak* to maintain its own existence?' " Or, as he later put it, "Was it possible to lose the nation and yet preserve the Constitution?"

To this his answer was clear. The Constitution, he believed, was nothing without the nation. As usual, he found a homely analogy. Human beings, Lincoln noted, wished to protect both life and limb. "Yet often a limb must be amputated to save a life; but a life is never wisely given to save a limb." If the execution of the whole of the laws should require the violation of a single law, "are all the laws *but one* to go unexecuted, and the Government itself go to pieces, lest that one be violated?" And in such a case, if the government were overthrown, "would not the official oath be broken?"

In this argument the parallel was close to Jefferson's formulation of Locke's idea that "the laws of necessity, of self-preservation, of saving our country when in danger" must override written law, lest the end be absurdly sacrificed to the means. But there were important differences. Lincoln's resort to the law of necessity was provoked by the most authentic and appalling of emergencies, one so recognized by Congress and the people, and not by a phantasm like the Burr conspiracy. Moreover — and this was Lincoln's first striking innovation — where Jefferson, like Locke, saw emergency power as a weapon outside and beyond the Constitution, Lincoln suggested that crisis made it in some sense a constitutional power. His means of constitutionalizing the law of necessity was to argue that free government, if it were to surmount the crisis, had "no choice but to call out the war power." [35]

IX

The idea of the war power was not new to American constitutional discourse. In 1836 John Quincy Adams, meditating on the powers of government, had called the peace power and the war power different in nature and often incompatible. "The *peace power,*" Adams said, "is limited by regulations and restricted by provisions prescribed within the Constitution itself. The *war power* is limited only by the laws and usages of nations. This power is tremendous, it is strictly constitutional, but it breaks down every barrier so anxiously erected for the protection of liberty, of property and of life." [36] Adams, however, was talking about the war power of the national government as a whole, exercised through and with Congress, not just about presidential power.

Lincoln's second innovation was to attach this "tremendous" war power to the Presidency. This executive war power was founded first of all, he believed, in the solemn presidential oath to "preserve, protect, and defend the Constitution of the United States." Taken literally, this could be seen both as a mighty obligation and as a mighty mandate. The oath "impressed upon me the duty of preserving by every indispensable means, that government — that nation, of which the Constitution was the organic law." If the President were sworn to preserve and protect the Constitution to the best of his ability, what limits were there on his duty to act if the nation were in danger? The power of the oath, reinforced by the constitutional requirement that the President "shall take Care that the Laws be faithfully executed," was given new force, Lincoln believed, by the secession of the southern states. Here he found constitutional justification or at least consolation, by citing the provision permitting the suspension of *habeas corpus* "when in Cases of Rebellion or Invasion the public Safety may require it."

The Founding Fathers had carefully confined the "Rebellion or Invasion" exception to *habeas corpus*. This implied a rejection of the idea of a broader suspension of constitutional guarantees in the face of emergency. Nor, for that matter, did the Constitution say whether the President or Congress should have the power of suspending *habeas corpus*. But Lincoln, to Chief Justice Taney's dismay, promptly appropriated this power for the executive and then generalized the "Rebellion or Invasion" point across the board, thereby finding a broad if technically tenuous ground for the increase in executive authority. "Certain proceedings are constitutional," Lincoln said in 1863, "when, in cases of rebellion or invasion, the public safety requires them, which would not be constitutional when, in absence of rebellion or invasion, the public safety does not require them." He came very close at times to arguing that the Constitution was different in war from what it was in peace; at least, he said, it was "not in its application in all respects the same in cases of rebellion or invasion . . . as it is in times of profound peace and public security." More than this, "measures otherwise unconstitutional might become lawful by becoming indispensable to the preservation of the Constitution through the preservation of the nation." [37]

The war power flowed into the Presidency most particularly, as Lincoln saw it, in the presidential role as Commander in Chief. This marked the beginning of a fateful evolution. The

Founding Fathers had held a limited and technical conception of the President's power as Commander in Chief. Though the Constitution gave the President command of maneuvers and operations, even that command could be subject to congressional control. The Non-intercourse Act of 1799 authorized the seizure by the Navy of American vessels bound to French ports. In issuing orders to the Navy, President Adams extended this to include vessels bound *from* French ports, and a Captain Little thereupon captured a brigantine that had just left a French port in the West Indies. When the owner of the cargo complained, the Supreme Court in *Little v. Barreme* found the seizure unlawful even though ordered by the President. If Congress had been silent, Chief Justice Marshall said in his opinion, the President's authority as Commander in Chief would have sufficed. But once Congress had "prescribed . . . the manner in which this law shall be carried into execution," the Commander in Chief was obliged to respect the limitations imposed by Congress.[38] As late as 1850, the Supreme Court, reviewing "the power conferred upon the President by the declaration of war," said emphatically that, when he assumed the role of Commander in Chief, "his duty and his power are purely military." [39]

Still, as Samuel P. Huntington has pointed out, the Commander in Chief clause was "unique in the Constitution in granting authority in the form of an *office* rather than in the form of a *function*" — that is, instead of giving the President simply the function of commanding the Army and Navy, it gave him the office of Commander in Chief with functions undefined and therefore expansible.[40] Now Lincoln began to regard the Commander in Chief as the locus, if not the source, of the war power.

Thus he said, "I think the Constitution invests its commander-in-chief clause with the law of war, in time of war" — a statement that, if not altogether clear, was certainly pregnant. One letter contained an ironical echo of a phrase he had employed against Polk fifteen years before. "You ask, in substance," he wrote, "whether I really claim that I may override all the guaranteed rights of individuals, on the plea of conserving the public safety — when I may choose to say the public safety requires it." This, he continued, was really an affirmation that *no*

one should decide what the public safety required in cases of rebellion or invasion — or else a question *who* should decide.
"When rebellion or invasion comes, the decision is to be made
. . . and I think the man whom, for the time, the people have,
under the Constitution, made the commander-in-chief of their
army and navy, is the man who holds the power and bears the
responsibility of making it." [41]
So the Emancipation Proclamation began invoking "the
power in me vested as Commander-in-Chief of the Army and
Navy" and ended by justifying the act as "warranted by the Constitution upon military necessity." Lincoln later characterized the
Proclamation as without "constitutional or legal justification, except as a military measure." He added: "I conceive that I may in
an emergency do things on military grounds which cannot constitutionally be done by Congress." Or: "As commander-in-chief
. . . I suppose I have a right to take any measure which may
best subdue the enemy." [42]
An early result of the Lincoln doctrine was to uncover new
possibilities in the already flexible theory of defensive war. In
1862 William Whiting, the solicitor of the War Department, published *War Powers Under the Constitution of the United States*.
The first treatise on the subject, it achieved a 43rd edition by
1871. "Congress," Whiting conceded, "has the sole power, under
the constitution . . . to sanction or authorize the commencement of *offensive* war." But defensive war was another matter.

> If the commander-in-chief could not call out his forces
> to repel an invasion unless the Legislative department
> had previously made a formal declaration of war, a
> foreign enemy, during a recess of Congress, might
> send out its armed cruisers to sweep our commerce
> from the seas, or it might cross our borders and
> march, unopposed, from Canada to the Gulf before a
> majority of our Representatives could be convened to
> make that declaration. The constitution, made as it
> was by men of sense, never leaves the nation powerless
> for self-defence. . . .
> Nothing is clearer than this, that when such a state

of hostilities exists as justifies the President in calling
the army into actual service, without the authority of
Congress, no declaration of war is requisite, either in
form or substance, for any purpose whatsoever.[43]

Whiting's examples were straw men, and his argument, read with
care, was defensible. Its tone, however, would no doubt have disturbed the Founding Fathers.

X

Something new was happening to the Presidency under the
stress of rebellion; and the question remained whether the Supreme Court could reconcile Lincoln's extraordinary theory of
the war power to the American Constitution. The matter came
up rather quickly when persons whose ships had been seized during the first weeks of the blockade of the Confederacy in 1861
sued the government for compensation. The claimants contended
that under international law a blockade was legal only in a state
of war. Since there had been no declaration of war, Lincoln's
blockade was illegal, at least till Congress sanctioned it by legislation in July 1861. To argue that the principle of self-defense
permitted the concentration of all power in the Presidency was,
counsel said, "to assert that the Constitution contemplated and
tacitly provided that the President should be a dictator, and all
constitutional government be at an end whenever he should
think that 'the life of the nation' is in danger."

A majority of the Court categorically upheld Lincoln's actions. They did so, however, on narrow grounds. No attempt was
made to justify Lincoln's theory that the law of necessity made
otherwise unconstitutional acts constitutional. The Court simply
said that invasion or insurrection created war as a legal fact
which "the President was bound to meet . . . in the shape it presented itself, without waiting for Congress to baptize it with a
name." Moreover, the question whether the President, "in fulfill-
ing his duties as Commander-in-Chief, in suppressing an insurrection" decided to accord the rebels the status of belligerents

was "a question to be decided *by him,* and this Court must be governed by the decisions and acts" of the executive branch. Thus Lincoln's proclamation of a blockade was by itself "official and conclusive evidence" that a state of war existed "which demanded and authorized a recourse to such a measure under the circumstances peculiar to the case." If Congress ratified the act, this was gratifying but not essential.

The decision was by a 5-to-4 vote. The dissent, in which Chief Justice Taney concurred, was written by the same Justice Nelson who had so ardently defended executive power when the Pierce administration had destroyed Greytown. Rejecting the distinction between "a civil or a public war," the dissenters said that "Congress alone can determine whether war exists or should be declared." Therefore what Lincoln had done in the name of the war power was illegal until Congress acted.[44]

Common sense, and what Lincoln called the "public necessity," support the majority decision. Bagehot could not have been more mistaken when, two years after Lincoln's murder, he said that presidential government in time of sudden trouble was condemned by "the want of elasticity, the impossibility of dictatorship, the absence of a *revolutionary reserve.*" [45] Lincoln successfully demonstrated that, under indisputable crisis, temporary despotism was compatible with abiding democracy. Yet it cannot be forgotten that Lincoln's assertion of the war power took place in the context of domestic rebellion and under the color of a most desperate national emergency.

Since the majority in the Prize Cases confined its endorsement of the war power to the circumstances of ongoing domestic insurrection (or invasion), it is hard to see, as later commentators have claimed, that the decision conferred special authority on Presidents in peacetime or in relation to foreign wars. Though some of the powers exercised by Lincoln could be used against sovereign states, there is no suggestion that Lincoln himself supposed they could be thus used without congressional consent. Quite the contrary: Lincoln even believed — or so his first annual message indicates — in the need for the congressional authorization of military action against pirates on the high seas.

And, as Lincoln repeatedly emphasized, these were temporary powers, defined by the duration as well as by the size of the emergency. He said in his fourth annual message, "The Executive power itself would be greatly diminished by the cessation of actual war." Or, as he once put it more pungently, he could not believe that the American people would become reconciled to the abridgment of their freedoms "any more than I am able to believe that a man could contract so strong an appetite for emetics during temporary illness, as to persist in feeding upon them during the remainder of his healthful life." [46]

Above all, Lincoln exercised his war powers under a profound conviction of human frailty. He never pretended to the nation that these were merely the routine powers of the Presidency. Nor did he suppose that national policy was his personal prerogative, to be decided without consultation or constraint. The popular image of Lincoln is that of a lonely man brooding over insoluble problems and reaching mystical conclusions. This can be overdone. Lincoln was a shrewd and careful politician. He surrounded himself with and listened to, even if he did not always follow, strong men in his cabinet and administration. He labored to correct the excesses of his subordinates. Recognizing that the conduct of war must be in the end an area of "concurrent authority," he sought congressional ratification for executive initiative, even appearing on occasion before congressional committees. He read the newspapers, talked to an endless stream of visitors and was sensitive to the play of national and world opinion. Driven to extreme policies by unprecedented emergency, he incorporated within himself the written and unwritten checks on presidential absolutism.

His very phraseology — "measures, whether strictly legal or not," "measures otherwise unconstitutional" — revealed his sense that, when the life of the nation was at stake, Presidents might be compelled to drastic action. But the life of the nation had to be truly at stake. And Presidents undertaking such action were placing themselves under the judgment not only of history but of Providence. "In the present civil war," he once said, "it is quite possible that God's purpose is something different from the purpose of either party." As Presidents who exercised extreme powers must not pretend they were simply carrying out the peacetime Constitution, so they must not confuse their purposes with those of the Almighty. "The Almighty," as Lincoln reminded the nation in his greatest speech, "has his own purposes." [47]

4

Congress Makes a Comeback

THUS IN THE FIRST HALF of the nineteenth century the war-making power assigned by the Constitution to Congress began to drain away in opposite directions — on one side where the threat seemed too trivial to require congressional consent and on the other where the threat seemed too imperative to permit congressional consent. Through the ultimate triangularity of the system, power in both cases flowed toward the Presidency. But this did not mean that the presidential prerogative was growing by steady accretion. Nearly every President who extended the reach of the White House provoked a reaction toward a more restrictive theory of the Presidency, even if the reaction never quite cut presidential power back to its earlier level.

I

So, when Lincoln expanded presidential initiative, Congress sought means of retaliation. During the war it harassed Lincoln through the Committee on the Conduct of the War. In 1864 the House of Representatives tried to insert itself into foreign policy by voting unanimously a resolution opposing the recognition of the Maximilian regime in Mexico, "a monarchical government erected on the ruins of . . . republican government." When Secretary of State Seward encouraged the American Minister in Paris to tell the French that the House had no power in such questions and that the decision belonged constitutionally to the President, the House angrily passed a second resolution. "Congress has a constitutional right to an authoritative voice in declaring and prescribing the foreign policy of the United States," it said, "as well in the recognition of new powers as in other matters; and it is the constitutional duty of the Executive Department to respect that policy, not less in diplomatic negotiations than in the use of national forces when authorized by law; and the propriety of any declaration of foreign policy by Congress is sufficiently proved by the vote which pronounces it." [1]

The resolution never came to a vote in the Senate. While the administration did not recognize Maximilian, it ignored the House's claim to "an authoritative voice." This helped confirm the practice of regarding such resolutions, even when passed by both Houses and however peremptory or mandatory their terms, as purely advisory. Prudent Presidents, well aware that no policy could succeed without popular support, took note of the sentiments behind expressions of congressional opinion. But the force of concurrent resolutions was political, not legal.

Once the crisis was safely over, the Supreme Court enlisted in the effort to bridle the Presidency. In *ex parte Milligan* in 1866 the Court escalated a sensible decision in a case involving *habeas corpus* and martial law into a grandiloquent repudiation of Lincoln's theory of the war power. Where Lincoln had supposed that rebellion or invasion altered the application of the Constitution, the Court firmly declared that the Constitution worked "equally in war and in peace," protecting "all classes of men, at all times, and under all circumstances." In an almost explicit dismissal of the Locke-Jefferson-Lincoln idea that necessity might be a higher law than the Constitution, the Court said melodramatically:

> No doctrine involving more pernicious consequences was ever invented by the wit of man than that any of [the Constitution's] provisions can be suspended during any of the great exigencies of government. Such a doctrine leads directly to anarchy or despotism, but the theory on which it is based is false; for the government, within the Constitution, has all the powers

granted to it which are necessary to preserve its existence.

The Court, in its zeal to rebuke the Presidency, almost reversed Lincoln's analogy about giving a limb to save a life: "A country preserved at the sacrifice of all the cardinal principles of liberty, is not worth the cost of preserving." [2]

Nor did the campaign against the Presidency stop there. In 1867, the state of Mississippi sought an injunction to restrain President Andrew Johnson from enforcing the Reconstruction acts of March 1867 on the allegation of their unconstitutionality. The Court, rejecting the plea, concluded that it had no power "to enjoin the President in the performance of his official duties." *Mississippi v. Johnson* has been claimed, even by as sound a scholar as Louis Henkin, to mean that "the President is personally immune to judicial jurisdiction." [3] E. S. Corwin, I think, stated the matter with more precision when he read the Court's ruling to mean that "the President has no judicially enforcible responsibility either for nonperformance of his duties or for exceeding his powers." [4] As Attorney General Henry Stanbery observed in his argument, the charge against Johnson was not that he was about to perform illegal acts; it was that he was about to execute laws passed by Congress. In defending the President, Stanbery said he was not relying "upon any personal immunity that the individual has who happens to be President; upon any idea that he cannot do wrong; upon any idea that there is any particular sanctity belonging to him as an individual, as is the case with one who has royal blood in his veins." [5] The immunity vindicated by the Court pertained to the performance of official duties. It did not imply total presidential exemption from judicial or legislative process. Carrying out the law, for example, was an official duty; breaking the law would not be. If lawbreaking were the issue, the Court might well have agreed with Marshall and Polk that a President, unlike a King and like every other citizen of a republic, was subject to the summons of a grand jury or of a congressional committee contemplating impeachment. Whether public opinion would sustain a President in ignoring such a summons, as it certainly would in every trivial instance, depended on the Marshall-Jefferson equation that emerged from the Burr case.

It was ironic that *Mississippi v. Johnson* should have turned on the question of Johnson's enforcement of Reconstruction. In fact Johnson for some time had been setting himself against the mood and will of Congress on the question of policy toward the defeated Confederacy. He had done this through the use of his constitutional powers and without clear violation of law. But the result was to nullify much of the Reconstruction program as enacted by Congress. Johnson, moreover, was a lonely and beleaguered man, rigid, suspicious, righteous and doctrinaire, psychologically incapable of a realistic and conciliatory response to a congressional majority, especially one that was sufficiently rigid and righteous itself.

II

In defending Johnson against the state of Mississippi, Stanbery told the justices, "There is only one court or *quasi* court that he can be called upon to answer for any dereliction of duty . . . and that is not this tribunal but one that sits in another chamber of this Capitol." The tribunal on the other side of the Capitol was restive. Talk of impeachment rose, fell and rose again in 1867. Thus far the Constitution had seen five impeachments, all but the first of judges and all but one of judges from lower courts. Three of those impeached had been convicted. Even members of Congress most hostile to Johnson were at first doubtful about so crude and cumbersome a weapon, one, moreover, never before launched against a member of the executive branch and never even threatened against a President. An anti-Johnson senator wrote, "Better submit to two [more] years of misrule . . . than subject the country, its institutions, and its credit, to the shock of an impeachment." Then in August 1866 Johnson, in defiance of the Tenure of Office Act Congress had passed over his veto the preceding March, fired Edwin M. Stanton, his Secretary of War. This provided his opponents with the violation they sought, and the House voted Johnson's impeachment in February 1868.

The theory of the Tenure of Office Act was to require senato-

rial consent to the removal of government officials whose appointment required senatorial confirmation. There was serious
question, however, where the Tenure of Office Act applied to
Stanton. The act provided that cabinet members should hold
their offices "during the term of the President by whom they
may have been appointed" unless the Senate consented to their
removal. Stanton had not been appointed by Johnson but by
Lincoln. Beyond this, Johnson, with precedent going back to
the First Congress, held the denial to the President of the right
to discharge subordinates an unconstitutional invasion of presidential power. His cabinet unanimously agreed. Indeed, among
all the cabinet, it was Stanton who, Johnson later deposed,
made "the most elaborate and emphatic" condemnation of the
Act. The Supreme Court eventually agreed too, speaking
through another (if former) President, but this was nearly sixty
years later.[6]

The fact that Johnson, even if supported by his cabinet,
thought a law unconstitutional hardly entitled him to disobey it.
In his veto of the recharter of the Bank of the United States, Andrew Jackson was believed by some to have claimed the right
to ignore laws he personally considered unconstitutional; but
Taney, who had worked on the message as Attorney General,
later, and rightly, disclaimed such interpretation of Jackson's
ambiguous language.[7] The presidential obligation to take care
that the laws be faithfully executed must plainly in all usual
cases override presidential guesses about constitutionality.
But Johnson's lawyers argued that the case was different when
Congress aimed straight at the constitutional authority of the
Presidency itself. The distinction was no doubt legitimate. If,
for example, Congress passed a law divesting a President of
his power as Commander in Chief or denying him his power
to nominate officers of the government, was a President bound
to preside over the liquidation of his constitutional empire?
As Chief Justice Salmon P. Chase, who ran the trial, wrote
privately to a friend, it was a President's duty to execute a
law he believed unwarranted by the Constitution "precisely
as if he held it to be constitutional, except in the case where it

directly attacks and impairs the executive power confided to him by that instrument. In that case it appears to me to be the clear duty of the President to disregard the law, so far at least as it may be necessary to bring the question of its constitutionality before the judicial tribunals." Johnson himself claimed that he disobeyed the Tenure of Office Act in order to test its constitutionality. Historians still argue whether this claim was genuine or only something that the President thought up after impeachment became an imminent threat.

The Tenure of Office Act, however, was only the pretext. The essential congressional purpose was political: it was to bring to an end Johnson's systematic sabotage of Reconstruction. In pursuing this objective, Johnson's opponents invoked a very broad theory of impeachment. According to this view, the demonstration that abuse of power injured the public interest or subverted some fundamental principle of government would suffice for conviction, even if there had been no violation of positive law. Johnson's defenders put forward a correspondingly narrow theory, according to which impeachment was justified only if an indictable crime had been committed. The narrow theory had little historical warrant, and the broad theory, as expounded in the Congress, was exceedingly broad indeed, opening the way to congressional removal of a President for the sin, not usually mortal, of holding views which a congressional majority disliked.

Legal and political issues were inextricably mingled. Senators on each side saw great values at stake. Johnson's opponents wanted to save a Reconstruction based on racial justice — an essential objective and one commanding more respect a century later than it did in the years intervening. But his supporters had an honorable motive too. They wanted to save the Presidency. "Andrew Johnson must learn," Thaddeus Stevens had said, ". . . that as Congress shall order he must obey"; and Benjamin F. Butler, one of the prosecutors before the Senate, observed that, if the Presidency had, as Johnson claimed, the power of removal, this raised the "momentous" question whether the presidential office *ought, in fact, to exist as a part of the constitu-*

tional government of a free people." The question was indeed momentous. Some thought it the most important question of all. As Senator James Dixon of Connecticut put it, "Whether Andrew Johnson should be removed from office, justly or unjustly, was comparatively of little consequence — but whether our government should be Mexicanized, and an example set which would surely, in the end, utterly overthrow our institutions, was a matter of vast consequence." In the end, the second concern prevailed, and, eighty-one days after the House had voted to impeach him, Johnson was acquitted by a single vote. Dixon concluded presciently that this knocked out impeachment as "an ordinary means of changing the policy of the government by a violent removal of the Executive." James G. Blaine, who had voted for impeachment, wrote to similar effect nearly twenty years later, "Its success would have resulted in greater injury to free institutions than Andrew Johnson in his utmost endeavor was able to inflict." [8]

Had Johnson been found guilty, it would probably have been too late to save the original policy of Reconstruction. Johnson himself had done too much in the meantime to restore the power and reawaken the resistance of the white south. But, had Congress succeeded in destroying a President merely for honest disagreement about policy and judgment, this could well have wrought a decisive transformation of the political order.

It is interesting to speculate what directions this transformation might have taken. Benjamin F. Wade, president pro tem of the Senate, would have succeeded Johnson as President; the congressional radicals would probably have insisted on Ben Butler as Secretary of State. Grant had already been tapped as the congressional choice for the Presidency in the next election. Congress, in short, would have nominated the executive branch, as it had not done since the days of Monroe. The constitutional separation of powers would have been radically altered; and the alteration would have been protected and maintained by the overhanging threat of impeachment.

The presidential system might have become a quasi-parliamentary regime, in which the impeachment process, if it could

have been made routine, would have served as the American
equivalent of the vote of confidence. This might have answered
Bagehot's criticism of the American Constitution for its inability "at the sudden occurrence of a grave tempest, to change
the helmsman — to replace the pilot of the calm by the pilot
of the storm." [9] But the impeachment of Presidents could not
be made routine. It was by its nature convulsive. It brought
government to a stop, intensified public passions and could
hardly avoid shocking the system. Had Congress succeeded in
removing Johnson on the feeble grounds named in the indictment, the result would probably have been, not to introduce
the flexibility of the parliamentary system into American politics,
but to reduce the Presidency for a generation or more to a state
of intimidation and subservience. Johnson's acquittal made it
more certain than ever that impeachment could be used against
Presidents only in the case of major offenses and as a weapon
of last resort.

After Grant's Secretary of War escaped conviction in 1876 by
resigning two hours before the House impeached him, impeachment for the next sixty years was confined to federal district
judges, of whom two were convicted, two were acquitted and
one, following instructive precedent, avoided trial by resignation.
The narrow theory of impeachment was decisively abandoned;
but the process itself grew increasingly wearisome. As early as
1885 Woodrow Wilson saw impeachment as "little more than an
empty menace." [10] Three years later Bryce called it "the heaviest
piece of artillery in the congressional arsenal, but because it is so
heavy it is unfit for ordinary use. It is like a hundred-ton gun
which needs complex machinery to bring it into position, an
enormous charge of power to fire it, and a large mark to aim
at." [11] That acute though neglected observer of American politics Henry Jones Ford summed it up in 1904 when he said that
the American people were in the position of the Grand Turk,
"who can cut off the head of an offender, but whose affairs are
so out of control that he is robbed left and right by his
servants." [12]

By 1932, when the House submitted the case of Judge Harold

Louderback to the Senate, it was, as Hatton Summers, the chairman of the House Judiciary Committee, later said, "the greatest farce ever. . . . For ten days we presented evidence to what was practically an empty chamber." After the trial of another lower court judge in 1936, Summers concluded that impeachment took the time of the Senate "away from all of the other business of a great nation. . . . [We] know they will not try district judges, and we can hardly ask them to do so." [13] Legal scholars began to argue that the Constitution, contrary to received opinion, left room for other ways of removing federal judges and that impeachment should be reserved as a remedy for offenses at the highest level of government.

As for the highest levels of government, it was not till slightly more than a century after Andrew Johnson that impeachment of a President once again became a possibility.

III

What Congress might have done after the Civil War if impeachment had become a practical recourse is sufficiently suggested by what it succeeded in doing without impeachment. The Presidency was now on the defensive. There was not only the predictable postwar reaction against presidential power, but there were no urgent new issues in foreign affairs to encourage a revival of the Presidency. With the Presidency denied the plea of crisis and Congress determined to reclaim lost authority, the country moved into the period which Woodrow Wilson described, twenty years after Appomattox, as "congressional government." Congress, Wilson wrote in 1885, had entered "more and more into the details of administration until it has virtually taken into its own hands all the substantial powers of government." [14]

But Wilson also saw imperfections in the congressional system. In particular, he noted, "the means which Congress has of controlling the departments and of exercising the searching oversight at which it aims are limited and defective." Hostile and designing bureaucrats could always hold Congress at arm's length by dexterous evasions and concealments. Congress's "only whip," Wilson said, "is investigation"; and the chief purpose of investigation, even more than the direction of affairs, was the enlightenment of the electorate. "The inquisitiveness of such bodies as Congress is the best conceivable source of information. . . . The informing function of Congress should be preferred even to its legislative function." For "the only really self-governing people is that people which discusses and interrogates its administration." [15]

Such exhortation no doubt encouraged Congress to continue its role as the grand inquest of the nation. Post–Civil War Presidents were less militant than Jackson and Tyler had been before the war in denying congressional requests for executive information. Grant rejected one request which was a clear case of congressional impertinence and harassment; the House, resentful over his summer retreat to the cooling seaside breezes of Long Branch, New Jersey, had demanded to know how many executive acts he had performed away from the legal seat of government. When Cleveland in 1886 instructed his Attorney General to turn down a Senate request for papers relating to the removal of a federal attorney, the chairman of the Judiciary Committee, Senator George F. Edmunds of Vermont, declared that this was the first time in forty years that either House had failed "on its call to get information that it has asked for from the public departments of the Government," and the Senate censured the Attorney General.[16] However, Cleveland's nominee was confirmed.

So on the question of information a situation of give-and-take continued. Congress had a practical right to seek information, and the President a practical power to withhold it. Most congressional requests were honored; but when requests became too outrageous, public opinion — indeed, responsible congressional opinion — accepted presidential refusals. The presumption remained that, other things being equal, Congress would receive the information it sought. Disagreements were absorbed in the political process, and contention did not lead to a serious executive-legislative showdown. In the end the spirit of comity prevailed.

As for the question of the war-making power, this received an instructive test at the start of the Grant administration. The new President had the idea of annexing Santo Domingo and establishing it as an American state. After he had submitted a treaty of annexation to the Senate, war broke out between Haiti and Santo Domingo, and Grant, without congressional authorization, ordered the Navy to help resist Haitian attacks. Senator Sumner, the chairman of the Foreign Relations Committee, denounced "the employment of the Navy without the authority of Congress in acts of hostility against a friendly foreign nation" as "an infraction of the Constitution" and "a usurpation of power." The Senate rejected the treaty; and Grant canceled his order. The next time he was tempted to use military force, he politely deferred to what he now acknowledged to be "the war-making power of the country." [17]

In 1878, during the Hayes administration, Congress included a provision in the Army Appropriation Act making it a penal offense to "employ any part of the army . . . for the purpose of executing the laws, except in such cases and under such circumstances as such employment of said forces may be expressly authorized by the Constitution or by act of Congress." This provision was a by-product of the death throes of Reconstruction, and it expired with the appropriations it provided.[18] Though no one seems to have challenged this assertion of congressional power over military deployments, Presidents retained effective control of troop commitment in Indian wars, in border troubles with wandering Mexicans and in protection of American citizens elsewhere. Such presidential action generally had, however, at least implicit, and often explicit, congressional approval. Grover Cleveland was very tough, for example, in asserting the American intention to defend Venezuela against Great Britain; but his policy took the form of recommendations to Congress, not of unilateral executive decisions.

The locus of conflict between legislative and executive was shifting rather in these years to the treaty-making power. A Senate bent on self-assertion found its treaty veto a good deal more solidly embedded in the structure of the Constitution than the more impalpable right of the Congress as a whole to declare war.

IV

The Founding Fathers appeared to have envisaged the treaty-making process as a genuine exercise in concurrent authority, in which President and Senate would collaborate at all stages "in the spirit of an executive council," as Wilson once put it.[19] In this spirit Washington had made his famous effort at the start of his administration to enlist senatorial advice. But the wary senators, fearing, as one of them said, that the father of his country wished "to tread on the necks of the Senate," decided to excuse him and discuss the treaty in private among themselves.[20] The divorce the Senate thus desired in order to maintain its independence the President soon preferred in order to maintain his power. In the Jay Treaty of 1794, the executive role was to conduct the negotiations and submit the result, the senatorial role to confirm the negotiator and vote the result up or down, or swallow it with added senatorial flavoring. The practice of submitting the names of commissioners for major negotiations to the Senate continued for a time. Washington's example was followed by Adams in the negotiations with France in 1798 and 1799, by Jefferson in connection with the Louisiana Purchase and by Madison in connection with the Treaty of Ghent. But this practice lapsed after 1815. And even Washington insisted on his power to dispatch personal agents abroad without senatorial confirmation.

The Senate thus lost to Washington its claim for a voice in treaty negotiations and to later Presidents its power to confirm the negotiators. But, once the President asserted his power to negotiate without prior senatorial advice, the Senate asserted a countervailing power to modify or reject the treaty. After all, one third plus one of the senators present retained what mattered most: the power of life and death over the treaties. This power the Senate proceeded to amplify in 1868 by revising its standing rules and awarding itself the right to amend treaties by a simple majority. This enabled senators to alter the text of treaties with greater ease. It also invited parliamentary maneuvers which, by uniting opponents of a treaty with a faction of its supporters on specific amendments, might produce a document unacceptable to original supporters on the final two-thirds vote. And it facilitated the intervention of foreigners. The Russian legation, the German legation, the Clan-na-Gael — "these three forces," observed Henry Adams, "acting with the regular opposition and the natural obstructionists, could always stop action in the Senate." [21]

The Senate exercised its power in this realm with relish, freely rewriting, amending and rejecting treaties negotiated by the executive. Indeed, it ratified *no* important treaty between 1871 and 1898.[22] Then McKinley cunningly named senators to the commission to negotiate peace with Spain; even with this, the treaty passed the Senate with only two votes to spare. Noting the Senate's "irresponsible exercise" of its "semi-executive powers" in foreign affairs, Wilson feared that its actions would dangerously unbalance the federal system. When the time came to ratify treaties, he said, the President was made to approach the Senate "as a servant conferring with a master. . . . It is almost as distinctly dealing with a foreign power as were the negotiations preceding the proposed treaty. It must predispose the Senate to the temper of an overseer." Wilson acidly noted that the treaty-making power had become "the treaty-*marring* power," and a dozen years later John Hay, McKinley's Secretary of State, told Henry Adams that he did not believe "another important treaty would ever pass the Senate." [23]

Moreover, Secretaries of State in these years were themselves ordinarily ex-senators and thus well indoctrinated in the congressional perspective. Of the 24 men who headed the State Department from the appointment of Monroe in 1811 to the resignation of Blaine in 1892, all had previously served in the Senate, except for Elihu Washburne (1869), who had served in the House, W. M. Evarts (1877–1881), who became a senator later and Abel P. Upshur (1843–1844) and Jeremiah Black (1860), both of whom had very brief tenures. (Of the 28 Secretaries of State since 1892, only six — Sherman, Knox, Kellogg, Hull, Byrnes, Dulles — had previous service in the Senate.) During the nineteenth century, former senators were in charge of the State Department three quarters of the time.

The few Secretaries who lacked previous indoctrination reacted bitterly to senatorial aggression, considering it the mindless expression of institutional jealousy. As Secretary of State Richard Olney, a lawyer and former Attorney General, observed in one case, "The Treaty, in getting itself made by the sole act of the executive, without leave of the Senate first had and obtained, had committed the unpardonable sin. It must be either altogether defeated or so altered as to bear an unmistakable Senate stamp . . . and thus be the means both of humiliating the executive and of showing to the world the greatness of the Senate." John Hay, who had learned about executive power as Lincoln's private secretary, regarded the one-third veto as the Constitution's "original," "irreparable" mistake, now grown to "monstrous shape," and wrote, "The attitude of the Senate toward public affairs makes all serious negotiations impossible."

Hay took to studying the diary of John Quincy Adams when he was Secretary of State and calculated that in the three quarters of a century between their tours of duty congressional resistance had increased about ten times, measured by waste of days and increase of effort. Adams had thought himself ill-used in his day, but Hay told Adams's grandson the job was actually killing him. Adams had been, in fact, the much harder worker, but the job finally did kill Hay. Henry Adams, not only grandson but great-grandson of Presidents, summed it up from the executive perspective:

> The Secretary of State exists only to recognize the existence of a world which Congress would rather ignore; of obligations which Congress repudiates whenever it can; of bargains which Congress distrusts and tries to turn to its advantage or to reject. Since the first day the Senate existed, it has always intrigued against the Secretary of State whenever the Secretary has been obliged to extend his functions beyond the appointment of Consuls in Senators' service.[24]

*

V

Yet, as the recoil against presidential domination had produced a swing of power to Congress in the generation after the Civil War, so the recoil against congressional domination was beginning to produce a swing back to the executive. Then Congress itself, when it forced a cautious President into war with Spain in 1898, inadvertently conspired against its own authority. War, as Randolph Bourne said, was the health of the state. It was most particularly the health of the Presidency. And the Spanish-American War, by projecting the United States irrevocably into the world of great powers, strengthened the executive not just for the duration but for a long time thereafter. In 1900 Woodrow Wilson, reconsidering his earlier theory of congressional supremacy, took a postwar look at the balance of power in the federal system. When foreign affairs dominated the policy of a nation, he concluded, "its Executive must of necessity be its guide: must utter every initial judgment, take every first step of action, supply the information upon which it is to act, suggest and in large measure control its conduct. The President of the United States is now . . . at the front of affairs, as no president, except Lincoln, has been since the first quarter of the nineteenth century." [25]

The rise of foreign affairs coincided with the rise of a national economy dominated by interstate business and therefore amenable to control only through national legislation and regulation; and this brought the President to the front of affairs too. Moreover, the Supreme Court in 1890 in the case of *In re Neagle* — acting to protect one of its own members — had set forth a doctrine of inherent presidential power to defend the "peace of the United States." The President's duty, the Court said, was not limited "to the enforcement of the acts of Congress or of treaties of the United States according to their express terms" but also included "rights, duties and obligations growing out of the Constitution itself, our international relations, and all the protection implied by the nature of the government under the Constitution." [26] Such implied presidential power could be used, as in *Neagle,* to protect a Supreme Court justice from assassination, or as the Court ruled five years later in *In re Debs,* to justify presidential intervention in labor disputes. Here was the germ of an idea to which Theodore Roosevelt gave forceful expression in his New Nationalism and in his defense of what he called the Jackson-Lincoln theory of the Presidency: "that is, that occasionally great national crises arise which call for immediate and vigorous executive action, and that in such cases it is the duty of the President to act upon the theory that he is the steward of the people." Roosevelt, as he said, declined to adopt the view that "what was imperatively necessary for the Nation could not be done by the President unless he could find some specific authorization to do it. My belief was that it was not only his right but his duty to do anything that the needs of the Nation demanded unless such action was forbidden by the Constitution or by the laws." [27]

Both foreign and domestic urgencies thus worked to rehabilitate the Presidency. The Jackson-Lincoln-Roosevelt theory had an immediate impact, for example, on the old question of the power of the executive to refuse information to Congress. In the nineteenth century Presidents had occasionally withheld in cases where they could expect support and sympathy in Congress and in public opinion. Conceding the idea of Congress as the grand inquest of the nation, Presidents only claimed particular exceptions to the general rule of unlimited executive disclosure — Washington, the protection of the exclusive constitutional jurisdiction of one house of Congress against invasion by the other house; Jefferson, the protection of innocent persons and of confidential informants; Jackson, the protection of presidential relationships within the executive branch and the defense of that branch against congressional harassment; Tyler, the protection of ongoing investigation and litigation; Polk, the protection of state secrets in intelligence and negotiation. While exceptions might accumulate, no President had claimed a general and absolute prerogative to withhold.

Then congressional power began to suffer attrition after the Spanish-American War. The notion began thereafter to arise that the formula by which Congress was accustomed to request information about foreign affairs — "if not incompatible with the public interest" — was less a matter of congressional courtesy than of executive right. In the famous debate in 1906 between Senator J. C. Spooner of Wisconsin and Senator Augustus O. Bacon of Georgia, Spooner, defending Theodore Roosevelt's activism in foreign policy, said that the Senate had "no right to demand that he shall unfold to the world or to it, even in executive session, his instructions or the prospect or progress of the negotiation." Save for the Senate's treaty veto, the President had "absolute and uncontrolled and uncontrollable authority" in the conduct of foreign relations. Bacon disagreed; but when Spooner asked him whether he believed the President had "the legal duty" to send over all information requested by the Senate, even Bacon was constrained to reply, "I do not dispute the fact that there may be occasions when the President would not." Spooner: "Who is the judge?" Bacon: "The President, undoubtedly." [28]

Theodore Roosevelt extended this view to domestic policy, refusing a Senate request that the Attorney General explain why certain legal proceedings had not been instituted against United States Steel. When the Senate threatened to imprison the head of the Bureau of Corporations for contempt if he did not deliver the desired information, T.R. with great relish ordered the papers to the White House and challenged the Senate to come and get them. "The only way the Senate or the committee can get those papers now," he happily told a friend, "is through my impeachment, and I so informed Senator Clark last night." [29]

William Howard Taft, who became President a few weeks later, quickly generalized Roosevelt's example in an executive order directing heads of departments to refer the request to the President when they deemed it incompatible with the public interest to supply information called for by House or Senate resolutions.[30] After his Presidency Taft contended that the constitutional provision requiring the President to give Congress information on the state of the union did not authorize Congress "to elicit from him confidential information which he has acquired for the purpose of enabling him to discharge his constitutional duties, if he does not deem the disclosure of such information prudent or in the public interest." [31]

VI

Another expression of the presidential revival was the increased resort to ways around the Senate's treaty veto. One route was the joint congressional resolution — that is, the substitution of a majority of both houses for two thirds of the Senate. Texas had provided the precedent; and now in 1898, after the Senate Democrats had blocked the acquisition of Hawaii by treaty, Congress as a whole annexed it by joint resolution.

But the device to which McKinley and the first Roosevelt gave particular new force was the international compact entered into by the President on his own motion and authority. The executive agreement is one of the mysteries of the constitutional order. Its constitutional warrant lay in a distinction, drawn but not defined in Article I, section 10, between treaties, which states of the union were forbidden to make, and agreements or compacts, which they could make with the consent of Congress. Hamilton later wrote that the intent of the treaty-making provision "was understood by *all*" as giving that power "the most ample latitude," rendering it competent to the making of every "species of convention usual among nations." [32] Despite this, the Founding Fathers, who were well acquainted with international law, undoubtedly accepted the distinction made by Vattel (Hamilton himself described Vattel in the third Pacificus as "one of the best writers on the laws of nations") between treaties, in which "the acts called for must continue as long as the treaty exists," and agreements, in which obligations were "fulfilled by a single act." [33] As Chief Justice Taney, citing Vattel, put the distinction in 1840, a treaty was a compact made "for perpetuity, or for a considerable time" requiring "repeated acts"; agreements had "temporary matters for their object" and were "accomplished by one single act." [34]

Gradually, in a way that neither historians nor legal scholars have made altogether clear, the executive agreement began to emerge in the early republic. The executive found this form of compact a practical convenience in making once-and-for-all international arrangements, at first of minor consequence. The Senate accepted the device if only to spare itself the tedium of having to give formal consideration to a multitude of technical transactions. International law saw no distinction between treaties and executive agreements. The status of the agreement under the Constitution was, however, a separate question. In general, three types of executive agreement developed. Those made pursuant to existing treaties involved no challenge to Congress, nor did those that had prior or subsequent legislative authorization. But there was a third category: agreements made by Presidents in areas where they possessed constitutional authority to act without consent of Congress. Thus the President as organ of foreign relations could recognize foreign governments and settle foreign claims without congressional intervention; as Commander in Chief he could arrange cease-fire or armistice agreements. He could in addition make what were not quite agreements but rather unilateral commitments on the order of the Monroe Doctrine.

As early as 1817, the executive agreement became an instrument of major foreign policy when Monroe arranged with Great Britain for the limitation of naval forces on the Great Lakes. The presidential initiative had a color of legislative sanction in an act of 1815 authorizing the President to lay up armed vessels on the lakes. The intention to do this in concert with the British was written down in an exchange of notes between Richard Rush, the acting Secretary of State, and Charles Bagot, the British minister in Washington. Monroe promptly put the agreement into operation. Some time later Bagot, who was evidently a student of the American Constitution, observed to John Quincy Adams, the Secretary of State, that the agreement constituted "a sort of treaty" and asked whether Monroe intended to communicate it to Congress. Adams spoke to Monroe, who said he did not think this necessary.

Nearly a year after the exchange of notes Monroe changed his mind and sent the agreement to the Hill, inquiring particularly of the Senate whether in its judgment "this is such an arrangement as the Executive is competent to enter into, by the powers vested in it by the Constitution, or is such an one as requires the advice and consent of the Senate." It was an interesting question. Since the Rush-Bagot agreement involved continuing obligations, it clearly fell into the category Vattel had reserved for treaties. Moreover, an arms-control compact with a nation with which the United States had fought two wars in forty years would certainly seem of sufficient consequence to call for formal ratification. Monroe himself, though he had not been at the Constitutional Convention, was in every other respect a vintage Founding Father. An intimate of Madison and Jefferson, he was presumably well aware of original intentions. He was, in addition, no mean strict constructionist in his own right. Nevertheless he had succumbed sufficiently to the executive perspective to assign himself the power to make the agreement; and the Senate acquiesced sufficiently not to return a specific answer to his question. It endorsed what it agreed in calling the "arrangement" by a two-thirds vote but not in the form of a treaty ratification, nor were ratifications ever exchanged with Great Britain.[35]

The Rush-Bagot agreement showed that the executive agreement could do the work of a treaty, especially when blessed by the Senate after the fact. But the executive agreement at first made its way slowly. During the first half century after independence, of 87 international compacts, 60, and most of the significant ones, were handled through the treaty process. In the next half century there were 215 treaties and 238 executive agreements, but treaties were still used for major matters.[36]

McKinley, however, used the executive agreement to lay down the terms by which the Spanish-American War was concluded — terms confirmed in subsequent and more formal negotiations. The executive agreement was the means too by which McKinley and Hay developed the Open Door policy in the Far East. Then, when Theodore Roosevelt became President in 1901, the executive agreement rushed into its own. Thus in 1905, when the Senate declined to ratify a treaty with Santo Domingo placing its customhouses under American control, Roosevelt, as he himself described it, "put the agreement into effect, and I continued its execution for two years before the Senate acted; and I would have continued it until the end of my term, if necessary, without any action by Congress." [37]

In the same year he made a secret executive agreement with Japan bestowing American approval on the Japanese military protectorate in Korea — an agreement that remained unknown until the historian Tyler Dennett unearthed it nearly twenty years later in the Roosevelt papers. Roosevelt even made personal démarches of a drastic sort to foreign governments. Determined to stop European intervention in the Russo-Japanese War, "As soon as the war broke out, I notified Germany and France in the most polite and discreet fashion that, in the event of a combination against Japan to try to do what Russia, Germany, and France did to her in 1894, I should promptly side with Japan . . . to whatever length was necessary on her behalf." [38] Where this left Congress and the Constitution was not immediately clear.

There were other notable executive agreements in these years especially with Japan: the Gentlemen's Agreement of 1907, restricting Japanese immigration into the United States; the Root-Takahiri Agreement of 1908, upholding the Open Door policy in China; the Lansing-Ishii Agreement of 1917, recognizing Japan's "special interests" in China. In the years 1889 to 1939, of 1441 international compacts 917 were executive agreements and only 524 treaties.

VII

The rise of the executive agreement was accompanied by new presidential exuberance in the commitment of armed force to combat. Victory over Spain made the United States a world power; and in 1900 McKinley set the tone for the new century by sending 5000 American troops to China. The pretext was the protection of American lives and property. In fact, it was a spectacular case of military intervention for political purposes. Americans joined an international force, besieged Peking and helped to suppress the Boxer Rebellion. The Chinese government even declared war against the United States. Though the United States declined to declare war back, the Courts later ruled that a state of war had existed.[39] But at no point was Congress consulted. Nor did it object. Later, again without reference to Congress, the President accepted the Boxer indemnity from the government of China.

The intervention in China marked the start of a crucial shift in the presidential employment of armed force overseas. In the nineteenth century, military force committed without congressional authorization had been typically used against nongovernmental organizations. Now it was beginning to be used against sovereign states, and, in the case of Theodore Roosevelt, with less consultation than ever. As T.R. wrote a few days before he left the White House in 1909 in a ringing statement of the executive outlook, "The biggest matters, such as the Portsmouth peace, the acquisition of Panama, and sending the fleet around the world, I managed without consultation with anyone; for when a matter is of capital importance, it is well to have it handled by one man only." [40]

In this spirit Roosevelt sent American forces into Caribbean countries and, in some cases, even installed provisional governments — all without prior congressional sanction. Though protection of American citizens and property remained the pretext, the result in the Roosevelt and Taft administrations was a series of challenges to sovereign states. In an effort to minimize this result, J. Reuben Clark, the solicitor of the State Department, proposed in 1912 (or took over from John Bassett Moore) a distinction between "interposition" and "intervention." Interposition meant simply the limited insertion of troops to protect lives and property; it implied neutrality toward the government or toward contesting forces within the country; and, since it was a normal exercise of international law, it did not, Clark argued, require congressional approval. The power to interpose he derived from the President's executive power; nothing special was claimed for the President in his role as Commander in Chief. Intervention, on the other hand, meant interference in sovereign affairs; it implied an act of war and required congressional authorization. The United States, except for Cuba and Samoa, had, Clark thought, confined itself to interposition.[41]

Whatever merit this distinction might have had in the nineteenth century when the United States was a small power, by the twentieth century a great power could hardly interpose anywhere without intervening in sovereign affairs. On the other hand, it could be argued that the superior force of the United States was now so great relative to the Caribbean states that intrusion, whether interposition or intervention, did not invite the risk of war and therefore did not require congressional consent. Still, whatever the nuances of arguments, limitations were evaporating. The executive was becoming habituated to the unconstrained deployment of American forces around the world, and Congress chose not to say him nay.

In an effort to restore congressional control over troop deployment, Senator Bacon proposed in 1912 to deny military appropriations for forces sent without congressional consent beyond the jurisdiction of the United States, except in cases of emergency when Congress was not in session. Going back to the Boxer expedition, Bacon complained that Presidents now deemed themselves free to order the Army into foreign countries without congressional authorization even when Congress was in session and to do so without reporting the fact to Congress.

Elihu Root, the eminent lawyer who had been Secretary of War during the Boxer affair and Secretary of State under Roosevelt and was now a senator from New York, opposed the Bacon amendment. There was, Root said, no law that forbade the President to send troops "into any country where he considers it to be his duty as Commander-in-Chief of the Army to send them, unless it be for the purpose of making war, which of course, he cannot do." No doubt, Root conceded, "Congress could by law forbid the troops' being sent out of the country." But any Congress that attempted to deprive the Commander in Chief of the power to protect American citizens would hear from the American people. "I say there is no law, and I do not believe there ever was a law, and I do not believe there ever will be a law to pre-

vent the Commander-in-Chief of the Army and Navy of the
United States from . . . giving them the protection required by
self-respect." [42] The statement was strong, and the Senate rejected the Bacon amendment. Still Root in his fine print not only
agreed that Congress could control troop deployment if it wished
to do so but denied that the President could commit troops to
combat on his own authority.

Four years later William Howard Taft, in midcourse between
the Presidency of the United States and the Chief Justiceship of
the Supreme Court, addressed himself to the question. The President as Commander in Chief, Taft said, could "order the Army
and Navy anywhere he will, if the appropriations furnish the
means of transportation." Taft conceded that this gave the President "opportunity to do things which involve consequences that
it would be quite beyond his power under the Constitution directly to effect." He could, for example, get the country into war
and "leave Congress no option but to declare it or to recognize
its existence." Taft elsewhere said that such a use of the Army
and Navy would be "a usurpation of power" on the President's
part; but still, there it was. Moreover, recalling the Prize Cases,
Taft added that it was "only in the case of a war of our aggression against a foreign country that the power of Congress must
be affirmatively asserted to establish its legal existence." [43] Taft's
analysis implied that Congress might be able to restrict the sending about of the Army and Navy by cutting down on transportation, but, beyond that, he appeared to see few practical limits on
presidential power over troop deployment.

By now Woodrow Wilson was President. He had already written
in 1908 that "one of the greatest of the President's powers" was
"his control, which is very absolute, of the foreign relations of
the nation. The initiative in foreign affairs, which the President
possesses without any restriction whatever, is virtually the power
to control them absolutely." [44] Still, as President five years later,
Wilson proceeded with due respect for congressional prerogative
on the question of troop deployment. When he sent troops to protect American citizens against the Huerta regime in Mexico in
1914, he felt additionally justified in doing so because the

United States did not recognize Huerta, which made his regime in Wilson's eyes a nongovernmental organization. After the blood-shed at Tampico, Wilson immediately applied to Congress. "No doubt I could do what is necessary in the circumstances to en-force respect for our Government without recourse to the Con-gress and yet not exceed my constitutional powers as President," he said, "but I do not wish to act in a matter of so grave conse-quence except in close conference and cooperation with both Senate and House." [45] Though some members of Congress doubted whether the provocation justified Wilson's reaction, they were entrapped by what Hamilton had called the "ante-cedent state of things" and were constrained to vote approval. American troops occupied Vera Cruz for the next seven months. Two years later, when Pancho Villa was murdering American citizens in Mexico and sending raiding parties into New Mexico and Texas, the Senate approved armed intervention, though in this case the President would surely have been justified in unilat-eral action to repel invasion. Wilsonian intervention elsewhere in Central America and the Caribbean was based on the need to protect American citizens or on requests by local governments or on treaty provisions.[46]

During the First World War, Wilson relied much less on the exec-utive war power and much more on congressional authorization — on "delegated war power," in Corwin's phrase [47] — than Lin-coln had done three quarters of a century before. His determina-tion to bring in Congress — a determination deriving perhaps from his conception of the President as a sort of prime minister — was nobly expressed before American entry into the war in his message requesting congressional support in the policy of arming American merchantmen. No doubt, Wilson said, echoing his statement after Tampico, he already had the authority to do this "by the plain implication of my constitutional duties and powers; but I prefer, in the present circumstances, not to act upon general implication. I wish to feel that the authority and the power of the Congress are behind me in whatever it may be-come necessary for me to do. We are jointly the servants of the people and must act together and in their spirit, so far as we can divine and interpret it." [48]

Nonetheless, in spite of Wilson's predilections, war was once again the health of the Presidency. The Fourteen Points were of critical significance to the war and peace, but this was entirely a presidential initiative, without congressional consultation or clearance. It is notable that, when Wilson reinforced an American expeditionary force in Siberia after the war, he did not go to Congress. Some members of Congress were unhappy, but their resolutions died in committee. "We may well wonder," Charles Evans Hughes said in 1920, "in view of the precedents now established whether constitutional government as hitherto maintained in this Republic could survive another great war even victoriously waged." [49]

VIII

The revival of presidential initiative under Theodore Roosevelt and Wilson provoked the inevitable reaction. In spite of the rise of the executive agreement, the Senate had by no means lost interest in the control of foreign policy through the treaty power. Arbitration treaties were a particular target of senatorial concern. Roosevelt, complaining privately to Sir Edward Grey, the British Foreign Secretary, about "the great difficulty of getting the Senate to allow the President anything like a free hand in such matters," refused to refer amended arbitration treaties negotiated by Hay in 1904 and 1905 back to the signatory states.[50] Similar fate befell an effort by Taft and Knox in 1911. A majority report of the Committee on Foreign Relations that year said, "To take from the Senate, in any degree or by any measure, the power of saying whether a given question is one for arbitration or not is to destroy the power of the Senate on the most important point to be decided in connection with differences arising with any other nation." [51]

Before his Presidency Wilson thought he knew how to handle the treaty problem. Instead of wrangling with the Senate, he said, the President should be "less stiff and offish." He should act "in the true spirit of the Constitution . . . keeping himself in confidential communication with the leaders of the Senate while his plans are on course, when their advice will be of service to

him and his information of the greatest service to them." Instead
of laying the completed result before the Senate for a final contest of acceptance or rejection, the President should seek "verita-
ble counsel and a real accommodation of views." [52] But as President, Wilson, now transformed by the executive perspective,
forgot this wisdom. He ignored the Senate while he labored in
Versailles; and the Senate, invoking its treaty power, struck back
at him as, after the Civil War, it had used other devices to strike
back at Lincoln's successor.

Defenders of the two-thirds veto have pointed out that actually very few treaties defeated by the Senate have carried a majority of senators. But the Versailles Treaty did win a majority in
1920. The debate canvassed issues of executive-legislative tension if in a vehement and sometimes murky way. It should be
noted that, when the elder Henry Cabot Lodge claimed in his
second reservation that Congress had the "sole power" to "authorize the employment of the military or naval forces," his fellow isolationist William E. Borah disagreed, calling this "a recital
which is not true." [53] After the failure of the Treaty, Congress
terminated the war by joint resolution.

Despite the revival of Congress on other matters, Borah's view
rather than Lodge's continued to prevail on questions of overseas
troop deployment. When Senator Reed of Missouri contended in
1922 that Congress could order the President to bring back
troops from abroad, Borah said, "We could not make the President do it." If the President in the discharge of his duty as Commander in Chief wanted to send troops anywhere, "I do not
know of any power that we can exert to compel him to bring
them home. We may refuse to create an Army, but when it is created he is the commander." [54] This seemed particularly true in
the western hemisphere. In 1927 Coolidge, otherwise a strict-constructionist President, sent 5000 men to Nicaragua. There was
much criticism in Congress, but it went more to the substance
rather than to the constitutionality of the American intervention.
In 1928 Senator Blaine, raising the constitutional issue, proposed to cut off funds for the Marines, and Senator Norris said
that, if Congress remained silent, "the power of declaring war

. . . will be entirely taken away by the executive." But Senator Hiram Bingham said that the presidential war was constitutional, and Senator Borah questioned the constitutionality of the Blaine amendment. The amendment was defeated.[55]

Still, and especially in conducting foreign policy beyond the hemisphere, the Presidency was increasingly an object of congressional mistrust. Historians and publicists unfolded the theory of the First World War as the malign consequence of excessive presidential discretion in foreign affairs. By the 1930s the reputations of Theodore Roosevelt and Wilson were at their nadir. Congress, determined that no one man should again seize control of foreign policy, proceeded to assert itself on all issues of external relations that might involve the nation in war. It pursued this course with astonishing success in face of the fact that the domestic crisis of depression was producing an unprecedented delegation of powers to a new President and that the President himself not only was masterful in the use of these powers but enjoyed exceptional public confidence.

The second Roosevelt, for all his popularity, preferred — certainly in his first two terms — to base his actions on congressional legislation rather than on executive prerogative. In this respect he was more the heir of Wilson, whom he had served as Assistant Secretary of the Navy, than of the first Roosevelt, his kinsman and the idol of his youth. "In the event that the national emergency is still critical," as he said in his first inaugural, "I shall not evade the clear course of duty that will then confront me. *I shall ask the Congress* for the one remaining instrument to meet the crisis — broad Executive power to wage a war against the emergency" (emphasis added). In domestic policy Congress gave him the power he wanted. In foreign policy it stubbornly declined to do so. The power flowing to the Presidency to enable the national government to meet domestic problems thus failed to enlarge presidential authority in foreign affairs.

In one of his first external initiatives, Roosevelt in the spring of 1933 authorized the American representative in Geneva to say that, if international agreement could bring about a substantial reduction in armaments, the United States was prepared to consult with other states in case of a threat to the peace. When the other states identified an aggressor and took steps to halt his aggression, the United States, if it concurred in their judgment, would "refrain from any action tending to defeat such collective effort which these states may thus make to restore peace." Qualified as this pledge was, it was a bold move, the first since the rejection of the League of Nations, to align the United States with international attempts to keep the peace.

But when Roosevelt asked the Senate to pass a resolution authorizing the President at his discretion to embargo arms shipments to aggressor nations, a resolution that had already cleared the House, the chairman of the Foreign Relations Committee said that a discriminatory embargo "would have a strong tendency to involve the United States to such an extent that a condition of war might arise." The Committee then amended the resolution to compel the President to embargo shipments to *all* nations involved in a war. This amendment destroyed the original purpose of the resolution, which was precisely to discriminate against aggressors. Its effect would be to strengthen the nations that had arms already and to abandon those that had none. Its result was to wreck the attempt to coordinate American policy with collective security.[56]

IX

Roosevelt, preoccupied with the depression at home and realistic about the national mood of isolationism, let the Senate have its way. After the defeat of the World Court treaty in 1935 — an innocuous proposal that had received endorsement in both Democratic and Republican platforms and now carried a majority of the Senate — Roosevelt wrote to Elihu Root, who had proposed a world court at The Hague a generation before, "Today, quite frankly, the wind everywhere blows against us." [57] Congress, stimulated by success and unmoved by the prospect of German or Japanese aggression, proceeded to work out its own neutrality policy. Roosevelt acquiesced in a number of neutrality stipulations; indeed, he probably welcomed them, so long as he could choose when and where they would be applied. The House gave him the discretionary bill he wanted. But the senators, with the image of the perfidious Wilson in their minds, passed a mandatory program, designed to go into automatic effect against all belligerents.

The resulting compromise contained both mandatory and discretionary features. Roosevelt, fearing that a veto would exacerbate isolationist sentiment, decided that he could live with the bill. Secretary of State Hull, while not recommending a veto, advised Roosevelt that the mandatory provisions were "an invasion of the constitutional and traditional power of the Executive" and would "tend to deprive this Government of a great measure of its influence in promoting and preserving peace." He also sent Roosevelt a cautionary statement, to which the President himself added further cautions before he put it out. In a lucid expression of the executive perspective, Roosevelt said:

> It is the policy of this Government to avoid being drawn into war between other nations, but it is a fact that no Congress and no Executive can foresee all possible future situations. History is filled with unforeseeable situations that call for some flexibility of action. It is conceivable that situations may arise in which the wholly inflexible provision of Section I of this act might have exactly the opposite effect from that which was intended. In other words, the inflexible provisions might drag us into war instead of keeping us out.[58]

Congress thus used neutrality legislation as a means of reining in the executive in foreign affairs. Some wondered, however, whether even Congress could be trusted with the war-making power. In 1924 both the Democratic and Progressive platforms had endorsed the idea of a popular referendum of war "except in case of actual or threatened attack" (Democrats) or "except in cases of actual invasion" (Progressives). Congressman Louis Ludlow of Indiana revived the idea in 1935, and by 1937, according to a Gallup poll, three quarters of the country was in favor of a so-called Peace Amendment, which provided that, except in the event of invasion, "the authority of Congress to declare war shall not become effective until confirmed by a majority of all votes cast in a Nation-wide referendum." "To declare war," said Ludlow, "is the highest act of sovereignty . . . and should not be delegated to any man or body of men."

The administration tried to keep the bill in committee, but at the end of 1937 Ludlow got enough support from his colleagues, including the signatures of nearly half the Democrats in the House, to force it onto the floor. Roosevelt wrote the Speaker of the House that the Ludlow Amendment "would cripple any President in his conduct of our foreign relations, and it would encourage other nations to believe that they could violate American rights with impunity." Walter Lippmann pointed out that the Amendment would make "preventive diplomacy" impossible and would insure "that finally, when the provocation has become intolerable, there would be no remedy except a total war fought when we were at the greatest possible disadvantage." With all this, the proposal failed in the House only by a vote of 209 to 188.[59] Despite the appearance of support in the polls, however, most people accepted Roosevelt's judgment on the issue; and the war referendum movement died away.

Congress successfully defended its own prerogative against the total democratization of the war-making power. At the same time, it used its control over neutrality policy — the control Washington had conceded to it in 1794 — to remove a crucial area of foreign relations from executive control and to place American foreign policy in a straitjacket during the critical years before the Second World War. It was able to do this because it accurately reflected inchoate emotions in the electorate, but, as the instrument of these emotions, it could not escape responsibility for the result. The Roosevelt administration struggled to the very eve of Pearl Harbor to untie the knots in which Congress had bound it.

In retrospect, the verdict of history — indeed, the verdict of Congress itself — has been that the congressional policy was a failure. Walter Lippmann, writing about the interventions of the

Senate Committee on Foreign Relations in the summer of 1939, said, "It was then that the emasculation of American foreign policy reached its extreme limit — the limit of total absurdity and total bankruptcy." [60] No one for a long time after would trust Congress with basic foreign policy. Congress did not even trust itself. The grand revival of the presidential prerogative after Pearl Harbor must be understood as a direct reaction to what happened when Congress tried to seize the guiding reins of foreign policy in the years 1919 to 1939.

5

The Presidency Resurgent:
The Second World War

THE OUTBREAK of the Second World War found the American President constrained by Congress from doing what he deemed necessary to save the life of the nation — constrained by the neutrality laws and, more fundamentally, by an invincible faith on the part of leading members of Congress that they knew better than he did whether the country was in danger. When the administration, seeking repeal of the arms embargo, informed the Senate in 1939 that war was imminent, Senator Borah confidently replied, "We are not going to have a war. Germany isn't ready for it. . . . I have my own sources of information." [1] But the most popular and most inventive President of the century was not without weapons of his own. Some, ironically, were placed in his hand by the same Supreme Court that had so sternly condemned his New Deal.

I

In 1936 the Nine Old Men of the Supreme Court were, it was supposed, hell-bent on confining the power of Presidents, and especially the power of the second Roosevelt. Yet in December of that year the Court, speaking almost unanimously and through one of its most conservative members, quietly bestowed greater power on Franklin D. Roosevelt than it had denied him in the previous eighteen months when it had much more dramatically vetoed such New Deal experiments as the NRA and the AAA.

The case of *U.S. v. Curtiss-Wright Corporation et al.* [2] arose because Congress in 1934 had passed a joint resolution authorizing the President to stop the sale of arms to Bolivia and Paraguay, then engaged in bitter war in the Chaco jungles. Roosevelt immediately imposed an arms embargo by executive proclamation. Subsequently the Curtiss-Wright Corporation was discovered in a conspiracy to violate the embargo. Brought into court, Curtiss-Wright contended that Congress, when it gave discretionary power to the President, had made an unlawful delegation of its authority. The district court accepted this argument, pronounced the resolution an "attempted abdication of legislative responsibility" and dismissed the charges. The government then appealed the case to the Supreme Court.

Here the corporation might well have expected a sympathetic hearing. The old Court, after all, was notoriously disposed both to favor property against government and to question congressional delegations of power to the executive. Even its most liberal member, Benjamin N. Cardozo, had condemned NRA the year before as "delegation running riot." But NRA was a question of domestic policy. The case at hand involved foreign policy. Two members of the Court had a particular background in foreign affairs — Charles Evans Hughes, Chief Justice and former Secretary of State, and the man he asked to write the opinion for the Court, George Sutherland, a robust conservative, a former member of the Senate Committee on Foreign Relations and author seventeen years before of a book entitled *Constitutional Power and World Affairs.*

With only the cantankerous McReynolds dissenting (and not bothering to explain why), the Court drew a "fundamental" distinction between the President's powers in domestic and foreign matters. The two classes of power, Sutherland said, were different both in origin and in nature. The proposition that the "federal government," by which Sutherland meant the executive branch, could exercise "no powers except those specifically enumerated in the Constitution, and such implied powers as are necessary and proper to carry into effect the enumerated powers, is categorically true only in respect of our internal affairs." For the powers of external sovereignty did not rest, the Court contended, on the affirmative grants of the Constitution. They predated the

Constitution and were the "necessary concomitants of sovereignty." Sutherland even advanced the highly dubious historical argument that with the Declaration of Independence the powers of external sovereignty passed from the British King to the United States of America as a collective entity. From this recital Sutherland deduced "the very delicate, plenary and exclusive power of the President as the sole organ of the federal government in the field of international relations — a power which does not require as a basis for its exercise an act of Congress."

The inherent authority of the President in foreign affairs, the Court continued, found sanction not only in past history but in present necessity. The President, "not Congress, has the better opportunity of knowing the conditions which prevail in foreign countries. . . . He has his confidential sources of information. . . . Secrecy in respect of information gathered by them may be highly necessary." Nor could Congress demand information from the President when "premature disclosure" might be "productive of harmful results." Misconstruing the grounds for Washington's refusal to send the Jay Treaty papers to the House of Representatives, the Court opined that the wisdom of Washington's decision "has never since been doubted" and offered it as a general precedent for presidential secrecy in foreign affairs.

Constitutional, historical and practical reasons therefore joined in requiring that congressional participation in the exercise of power over foreign policy be "significantly limited." For "in this vast external realm, with its important, complicated, delicate and manifold problems, the President alone has the power to speak or listen as a representative of the nation. . . . Into the field of negotiation the Senate cannot intrude; and Congress itself is powerless to invade it." All this, Sutherland concluded, disclosed "the unwisdom of requiring Congress in this field of governmental power to lay down narrowly defined standards by which the President is to be governed." Legislation in foreign affairs "must often accord to the President a degree of discretion and freedom from statutory restriction which would not be admissible were domestic affairs alone involved."

The Court thus did in foreign policy what it had been reluctant to do in domestic policy: it affirmed the existence of an *inherent,* independent and superior presidential power, not derived from the Constitution and not requiring legislation as the basis for its exercise.

Several points must be made about this decision. The case itself involved the power to act under congressional authorization, not the power to act independently of Congress. Moreover, it involved the power over foreign commerce, not the power over war. Its actual holding was restricted. Its expansive contentions were in the nature of *obiter dicta.* And, as Thomas Reed Powell used to tell his students at the Harvard Law School, "Just because Mr. Justice Sutherland writes clearly, you must not suppose that he thinks clearly." [3] Still the Court, in a year when most of its crucial decisions were bitterly divided, spoke here with a single voice, placing its imprimatur on the doctrine of inherent presidential authority in foreign affairs. For this doctrine it claimed "overwhelming support in the unbroken legislative practice which had prevailed almost from the inception of the national government." The mood thus registered by an anti-presidential Supreme Court, thereafter strengthened by thirty years of world crisis and confirmed by a succession of Congresses, encouraged a series of Presidents in the conviction that there were few, if any, limits to executive initiative in the making of foreign policy.

Nor did the Court stop with *Curtiss-Wright.* The next year, speaking again through Justice Sutherland, the Court in the case of *United States v. Belmont* laid to rest major doubts about the constitutional validity of the executive agreement.

The *Belmont* case arose in connection with the series of agreements accompanying the American recognition of the Soviet Union in 1933. Sutherland gave it as the verdict of the Court that international compacts did not always have to be treaties requiring the participation of the Senate. "There are many such compacts, of which a protocol, a modus vivendi, a postal convention, and agreements like that now under consideration are illustrations." [4] While he could have argued that the executive agreement under consideration derived its force from the presidential power to recognize foreign governments, Sutherland did not thus limit the range of his approval. Instead he blessed the executive agreement in general as an instrument legal in power and not clearly limited in applicability.

The mystery remained. One is compelled to agree with Professor Louis Henkin's summation of the *Belmont* result: "There are agreements which the President can make on his sole authority and others which he can make only with the consent of the Senate, but neither Justice Sutherland nor any one else had told us which are which." [5] When Senator Gillette of Iowa asked the State Department in 1954 to make everything perfectly clear, the Department (or so Gillette informed the Senate) replied "that a treaty was something they had to send to the Senate to get approval by two-thirds vote. An executive agreement was something they did not have to send to the Senate." This reminded Gillette of the time when as a boy on the farm he asked the hired man how to tell the difference between male and female pigeons. The answer was: "You put a corn in front of the pigeon. If he picks it up, it is a he; if she picks it up, it is a she." [6] Still, if all mysteries were not dispelled, the *Belmont* decision unquestionably confirmed the President in his unilateral authority in appropriate situations to make agreements with foreign governments.

Both *Curtiss-Wright* and *Belmont* represented extraordinary vindications of presidential power in foreign policy — a field to which the Supreme Court had paid little attention for a century and a half. If Congress and the public ignored these decisions in their concern over the fate of Roosevelt's domestic program, lawyers were well aware of their implications. The *Belmont* decision, said a commentator in the *California Law Review,* was "without doubt . . . one of the most extreme extensions which could be accorded to the power of the President" in international relations.[7] The *Curtiss-Wright* decision, said a commentator in the *Yale Law Journal,* "represents the most extreme interpretation of the powers of the national government. It is the farthest departure from the theory that the United States is a constitutionally limited democracy." [8]

*

II

The executive agreement became the means employed when Roosevelt exchanged American destroyers for the lease of British bases after the fall of France in 1940. Thirty years later the destroyer deal was often cited as an instance of indefensible presidential activism. Senators Church and Fulbright said that Roosevelt in sending the destroyers through executive agreement "usurped the treaty power of the Senate." [9] It may therefore be useful to consider in detail what Roosevelt in fact did.

The United States in 1940 faced what could be convincingly seen as a genuine national emergency. The British were standing alone against Hitler. Their situation could hardly have been more desperate. The Nazi armies controlled France and were poised for an invasion of Britain. If Britain fell, Hitler's conquest of western Europe would be complete and the danger to the United States extreme. Of the hundred or so British destroyers in home waters, almost half had been destroyed or damaged when Churchill in May 1940 asked for "the loan of forty or fifty of your older destroyers" to help the Royal Navy hold the Channel. A month later, as more destroyers were put out of action, he renewed the request: "Nothing is so important for us. . . . We must ask therefore as a matter of life and death to be reinforced with these destroyers." Soon the British King sent a personal letter to Roosevelt on the subject. In July Churchill said, "Mr. President, with great respect I must tell you that in the long history of the world this is a thing to do NOW." In August: "The worth of every destroyer that you can spare to us is measured in rubies."

Roosevelt had responded to Churchill's first request by saying that "a step of that kind could not be taken except with the specific authorization of the Congress, and I am not certain that it would be wise for that suggestion to be made to the Congress at this moment." His assessment of Congress was accurate. In June the Senate amended the Naval Appropriations bill to deny the President authority to send military materiel to a foreign country unless the Chief of Staff or the Chief of Naval Operations certified that it was "not essential to" the defense of the United States. (The original language added "and cannot be used in the defense of the United States" until Senator Lister Hill of Alabama, seeing that this would end all aid to the opponents of Hitler, had it struck out.) The consequence of this congressional action was a certainly peculiar and arguably unconstitutional arrangement conferring on military and naval officers the authority to overrule their Commander in Chief. How in face of all this was Roosevelt to get destroyers to Britain in time to stop the triumph of Hitler?

He did not in more recent fashion go off to the Catoctin Mountain, brood in solitude and then, without talking to anybody, announce that he was sending the destroyers under his authority as Commander in Chief. Contrary to the latter-day view that a strong President is one who acts without consultation and without notice, Roosevelt proceeded with careful concern for the process of consent. He consulted with his cabinet. He consulted with congressional leaders. He consulted through intermediaries with the Republican candidates for President and Vice President.

For some time Roosevelt's view remained that he could not send destroyers to Britain without legislation. When Benjamin V. Cohen argued that executive action would be legal if it could be shown that this would strengthen rather than weaken American defense, the President dissented, adding, "I fear Congress is in no mood at the present time to allow any form of sale." On August 2, nearly three months after Churchill's first urgent request, a cabinet meeting conducted an intensive review of the question. The President himself, in a rare recourse to the record, wrote down the conclusions: "It was the general opinion, without any dissenting voice, that the survival of the British Isles under German attack might very possibly depend on their getting these destroyers. It was agreed that legislation to accomplish this is necessary."

Then Senator McNary, both the Republican Senate leader and the Republican candidate for Vice President, told Senator Pepper, a Democratic hawk, that, while it would be hard for him to support the transfer of destroyers if it required formal Senate consent, he would make no objection if persuasive grounds could be found for going ahead without resort to the Senate. This bulletin, along with the idea that the destroyers might be traded for bases and with Roosevelt's growing reluctance to have Congress debate the fate of Britain in the erratic atmosphere of an American presidential election, led him to take a fresh look at Ben Cohen's constitutional argument. This impulse was strengthened by the growing pressure of interventionist groups and, in particular, by a letter to the *New York Times*, based on the Cohen memorandum and signed by Dean Acheson and other eminent lawyers, arguing that the executive had the authority to make the transfer. In the meantime, Wendell Willkie, the Republican presidential candidate, had indicated through William Allen White, the chairman of the Committee to Defend America by Aiding the Allies, that he would not make trouble. (Later in the campaign, while not criticizing the transaction, Willkie called it "regrettable" that Roosevelt had not gone to Congress. After the election he told Cohen that this was the campaign utterance he was sorriest about.)

Having informed the Republican candidates, Roosevelt obtained from his Attorney General, Robert H. Jackson, an opinion telling him he could exchange destroyers for bases through executive action. Jackson mentioned *Curtiss-Wright* but added that presidential power over foreign relations was "not unlimited." When negotiations involved commitments requiring future congressional action, such arrangements, he said, were customarily submitted to the Senate as treaties. But — here he reverted to the old distinction of Vattel's — the destroyer deal would be a completed, not a continuing transaction, containing "no promises or undertakings by the United States that might raise the question of the propriety of inclusion in a treaty." Hence in this case an executive agreement was an appropriate instrument. Jackson also mentioned the Commander in Chief clause but observed, "Happily, there has been little occasion in our history for the interpretation of the powers of the President as Commander in Chief. . . . I do not find it necessary to rest upon that power alone to sustain the present proposal."

Instead of relying exclusively upon the "constitutional power" of the Presidency, Jackson claimed "ample statutory authority to support the acquisition of these bases" — authority derived from his construction of laws passed by Congress with particular emphasis on the point that new bases would contribute more than over-age destroyers to American defense. His refusal to find a case for the transfer of mosquito boats as well as destroyers gave evidence that his statutory construction had at least a measure of discrimination.[10]

When Roosevelt announced the destroyer deal, he said, "Preparation for defense is an inalienable prerogative of a sovereign state. Under present circumstances this exercise of sovereign right is essential to the maintenance of our peace and safety." He added that this was the most important action in the reinforcement of national defense since the Louisiana Purchase: "Then as now, considerations of safety from overseas attack were fundamental." Not everyone agreed: Professor Edward S. Corwin, whose glosses on the Constitution have been much cited in this work, called the deal "an endorsement of unrestrained autocracy in the field of our foreign relations," adding that "no such dangerous opinion was ever before penned by an Attorney General of the United States." Yet was Corwin right? were my friends Fulbright and Church right in later years in condemning the transaction as presidential usurpation?

The destroyer deal was compelled by a threat to the nation surpassed only by the emergency which led Lincoln to take his actions after Sumter. In working it out, Roosevelt paid due respect to the written checks of the Constitution and displayed an unusual concern for the unwritten checks on presidential initiative. Though the transaction was unilateral in form, it was accompanied by extensive and vigilant consultation — within the executive branch, between the executive and legislative branches, among leaders of both parties and with the press. To have tried to get destroyers to Britain by the treaty route was an alternative only for those who did not want Britain to get destroyers at all. Congress, by voting money to build the bases, soon gave the deal its implicit sanction. The public reception, despite dissonant

notes, was predominantly favorable. It is difficult to quarrel with
the conclusion of Professors Langer and Gleason: "The destroyer deal was at least as much the achievement of private effort as of official action and it should be viewed as a truly popular, national commitment to share in the conflict against Hitler
to the extent required by American security." [11] In retrospect,
this all seems less a flagrant exercise in presidential usurpation
than a rather circumspect application of the Locke-Jefferson-
Lincoln doctrine.

III

Later generations remember Roosevelt's taste for bold strokes
and a certain unscrupulous relish in the exercise of power. But
he was also a cautious man, deeply sensitive to the ebb and flow
of public opinion, deeply aware that democratic government was
a process of consent and accountability. When the Nazi Blitzkrieg
was overrunning France in June 1940, Roosevelt, while assuring
Prime Minister Reynaud that the United States would send supplies so long as the French continued their resistance, added, "I
know that you will understand that these statements carry with
them no implication of military commitments. Only the Congress can make such commitments." [12] During the anxious
months thereafter, when Britain was fighting alone, a group
waited one day on Henry L. Stimson, the Secretary of War, and
asked why, when the future of the world hung in balance, the
United States was holding back. Stimson indicated sympathy
with their view; then, waving his hand in the direction of the
White House, said that they should take their question over there
to the greatest isolationist of them all. When they went on to the
White House, Roosevelt told them that he could see Harry's
[Stimson's] point; he had felt the same urgency in 1914 to 1917
that they felt now; but one thing that Woodrow Wilson had taught
him was the terrible responsibility of bringing a divided nation
into war. He was going to be sure, very sure, that, if the United
States had to enter the war, it would enter as far as humanly possible a united nation.[13]

Once the 1940 election was over, Roosevelt submitted the policy of aid to Britain — that is to say, the policy of taking sides against Hitler — to full congressional consideration. The debate over the Lend-Lease bill could hardly have been more arduous, exacting and uninhibited. The enactment of Lend-Lease in March 1941 represented congressional ratification of the Roosevelt policy, much as the Civil War Congress had ratified Lincoln's acts of executive initiative. This is not to say that in voting for Lend-Lease Congress was voting for war. The Administration defended the policy of aid to Britain as a means of staving off war, not of getting into it. Very likely Roosevelt believed this himself; certainly he regarded war as a last resort. Nonetheless, every one voting for Lend-Lease knew that he was voting to align the United States with Great Britain and against Nazi Germany. Moreover, attached to the Lend-Lease Act (as well as to the First War Powers Act, the Emergency Price Control Act, the Stabilization Act and the War Labor Disputes Act) was a proviso that Congress could repeal the measure and reclaim its powers at any point by the passage of a concurrent resolution, which, unlike a joint resolution, was not subject to veto. Roosevelt thought this proviso unconstitutional, but signed the bills anyway.[14]

The British situation in 1941 was more critical than ever. Britain was still standing alone against Germany, now the master of Europe. If Congress had authorized the loan and lease of goods in order to keep Britain in the war, did this not imply at least an effort to make sure that the goods actually arrived? As German submarines and destroyers sank increasing numbers of British ships, Roosevelt cast about for means both of protecting the Atlantic lifeline and of strengthening the defenses of the western hemisphere. In April 1941 he made an executive agreement with the Danish Minister to send American troops to Greenland. There was little objection. Greenland was part of the western hemisphere.

Then at the end of May Roosevelt issued a presidential proclamation declaring a state of "unlimited national emergency." This presumably deepened the state of "limited" emergency he had declared after war broke out in Europe in 1939. The idea of "limited" national emergency seems to have been Roosevelt's own; at least it had no warrant in statutes or precedent. It was probably intended to ease the nation into a new and perilous situation and meant only that the President planned to limit himself in the application of emergency powers. These powers were derived, not from claims of inherent presidential authority, but from clauses written by Congress into statutes providing for delegation of certain powers to the executive in conditions of emergency. When the Senate had formally inquired about emergency powers in 1939, the Attorney General passed along a list of 99 statutes, eleven of which went back to the nineteenth century and one to 1798, containing emergency provisions. (He added enigmatically that the President had in addition "powers not enumerated in the statutes — powers derived not from statutory grants but from the Constitution," but these constitutional powers could not be specifically defined, since the executive right to take action "might not exist under one state of facts, while under another it might be the absolute duty of the Executive to take such action.") [15]

The proclamation of "unlimited emergency" went on to say that American defenses must be put in readiness "to repel any and all acts or threats of aggression directed against any part of the Western Hemisphere." [16] Under this proposition Roosevelt proceeded to move further into the North Atlantic. In July an executive agreement with the government of Iceland resulted in the dispatch of American troops to an island that was not, like Greenland, part of the hemisphere. Had the Nazis got there first, Roosevelt said, this would have constituted a grave threat to "the steady flow of munitions to Britain — which is a matter of broad policy clearly approved by Congress."

Senator Robert A. Taft of Ohio, diverging from his father's views of a quarter century before, protested that Roosevelt had "no legal or constitutional right to send American troops to Iceland" without congressional authorization. There had been, he said, no attack on the United States, and there was no threat of attack. If the Senate acquiesced in such presidential initiatives, it might "nullify for all time the constitutional authority distinctly reserved to Congress to declare war." Only one senator supported Taft's protest.[17]

In proceeding in the summer and autumn of 1941 to institute a convoy system and issue the "shoot-at-sight" order to the Navy in the North Atlantic, Roosevelt was ordering the Navy, without express congressional consent, to protect American convoys on the high seas. Senator Fulbright has latterly charged that he "circumvented the war powers of the Congress." [18] But the poignant character of Roosevelt's dilemma was made clear when in August 1941 the House of Representatives renewed the Selective Service Act by a single vote. If Congress came that close to disbanding the Army at home, how could Roosevelt, when time was of the essence, have reasonably expected prompt congressional action in support of his forward policy in the North Atlantic? His choice was to go to Congress and risk the fall of Britain to Hitler or to proceed on his own with measures which, "whether strictly legal or not, were ventured upon under what appeared to be a popular demand and a public necessity; trusting then as now that Congress would readily ratify them."

He did not claim authority independent of Congress. After his Atlantic Charter conference with Churchill in August, he reported, if perfunctorily, to Congress, justifying the "military and naval conversations at these meetings" on the ground that "the Congress and the President" had "heretofore determined through the Lend-Lease Act on the national policy of American aid to the democracies." In September he told his press conference that the idea was to defend the Americas against Hitler. "Congress has made it perfectly clear that a part of that defense is to try to help, in every way we can, those people who are conducting active war against this attempted domination. . . . That is why we have got American troops in Iceland today. That is why we are keeping the [sea] lanes open." In October he requested the revision of the neutrality laws and authorization to arm merchant ships: "I ask for Congressional action to implement Congressional policy." [19]

Such gestures toward Congress were no doubt shrewd politics.

Nor can it be said that Roosevelt made much effort to offer Congress a real, as contrasted to a symbolic, role, or that he even told it fully and candidly what was going on in the North Atlantic. Still even a symbolic concern for Congress expressed a lurking sensitivity to constitutional issues. Though the threat to the United States from Nazi Germany could be persuasively deemed somewhat greater than that emanating thirty years later from North Vietnamese troops in Cambodia, and though his commitment of American forces to combat was far more conditional, Roosevelt made no general claims to inherent presidential power. In particular, he did not assert in the later royal manner that there was no need to consider Congress because his role as Commander in Chief gave him all the authority he needed. Indeed, the pre–Pearl Harbor documents are notable for the singular lack of reference to the office of Commander in Chief. Jackson's opinion on the destroyer deal showed how undeveloped Commander in Chief theory was in 1940; and in 83 press conferences in 1941 up to Pearl Harbor, Roosevelt never once alleged special powers in foreign affairs as Commander in Chief. When the title was mentioned in his speeches and messages, it generally signified only the narrow and traditional view of the Commander in Chief as the one who gave orders to the armed forces.[20]

Nevertheless 1941 marked a significant change in Roosevelt's approach to presidential power. "There is Presidential initiative *and* Presidential initiative," E. S. Corwin wrote after the war, "— that type which, recognizing that Congress has powers — great powers — in the premises, seeks to win its collaboration; and that type which, invoking the 'Commander-in-Chief' clause or some even vaguer theory of 'executive power,' proceeds to stake out Congress's course by a series of *faits accomplis.*" Roosevelt, in Corwin's view, had generally employed the first type in constructing his New Deal. But, after the enactment of Lend-Lease, he shifted to the second, "a course that must in the end have produced a serious constitutional crisis had not the Japanese obligingly come to the rescue." [21]

We are back again to John Locke. Jefferson had been a student of Locke; if the only Locke we know Lincoln read as President was the lesser one who wrote under the name of Petroleum V. Nasby, Lincoln was nonetheless steeped in Lockeanism. Franklin Roosevelt had probably never looked at the *Second Treatise on Civil Government* since Harvard, if he had ever looked at it then. But the Lockean doctrine of emergency prerogative had endured because it expressed a real, if rare, necessity in a free state. FDR was a Lockean without knowing it, as Monsieur Jourdain spoke prose without knowing it. Confronted by Hitler, Roosevelt supposed, as Jefferson and Lincoln had supposed in the crises of their Presidencies, that the life of the nation was at stake and that this justified extreme measures. Unlike Jefferson's case of the Burr conspiracy but like Lincoln's case of the Civil War, Roosevelt's case had substantial public backing, and the electorate (and therefore the courts) sustained his use of emergency power. Roosevelt knew where he wanted to go and where he believed the nation had to go. But he did not want — and this was why he was one of the greatest of Presidents — to go there alone.

IV

Pearl Harbor solved the President's constitutional dilemma. Once Congress had declared war, Roosevelt seized on the role of Commander in Chief with relish. Cordell Hull later said that during the war FDR preferred the title Commander in Chief to that of President. One result was to charge that formerly technical office with new potentiality. Even then, the Supreme Court tried to remind the Commander in Chief that, though he was in full charge of military operations, he was still in significant ways subject to Congress. The Constitution, said Chief Justice Stone in the case of the Nazi saboteurs in 1942, "invests the President as Commander in Chief with power to wage war which Congress has declared, and to carry into effect all laws passed by Congress for the conduct of war and for the government and regulation of the Armed Forces." [22] The Court thus still urged a restricted view of the powers of Commander in Chief. Roosevelt's view was less restricted.

War accelerated the change in Roosevelt's approach to presidential power. He had built his New Deal government on the basis of authority directly granted by Congress through specific statutes. One of his first actions after Pearl Harbor — the submission of the omnibus Second War Powers Act — showed a desire to continue in this fashion. He wanted, in the manner of Wilson, to get his powers from Congress. But the urgencies of war led him to turn increasingly to less particularized authority — in part on the powers he asserted as "Commander in Chief in wartime" and even more on the emergency powers released by his proclamations of 1939 and 1941 and stuffed into an all-purpose agency, the Office of Emergency Management, which in turn provided the legal base for the great agencies directing war production, manpower, information, transportation, collective bargaining, economic warfare and so on. Of the agencies in control of the wartime economy, only one, the Office of Price Administration, had its legal base in a specific statute, the Emergency Price Control Act. This was the agency that most touched the daily lives of the citizens and therefore depended most on popular consent. Congress did not vote to establish the others but rather acquiesced in their establishment by the President in response to manifest public necessity.

Roosevelt's most notorious claim to unilateral authority came on September 7, 1942, when he told Congress that, if it did not repeal a farm parity provision in the Emergency Price Control Act in the next three weeks, he would refuse to carry it out. "The President has the powers, under the Constitution and under Congressional acts," Roosevelt said, "to take measures necessary to avert a disaster which would interfere with the winning of the war." He added that the people could be sure he would use these powers "with a full sense of my responsibility to the Constitution" and that — in his version of the Locke-Jefferson-Lincoln doctrine of prerogative — "when the war is won, the powers under which I act automatically revert to the people — to whom they belong." Congress repealed the provision, and a showdown was averted.[23]

Even if his thesis was not put to test — and Roosevelt, being Roosevelt, no doubt knew he had the votes before he made the challenge — it was still an extraordinary assertion of presidential power. But these were genuinely tough times. Next to the Civil War, the Second World War was the greatest crisis in American history. Powers thus claimed in a war for survival on issues on which Congress and public opinion supported the President provided only strained and meager precedents for powers claimed without equivalent crisis or consensus. Nor did Roosevelt suggest that such powers were part of the routine equipment of the Presidency.

The most shameful abuse of power within the United States during the Second World War — the removal of the Japanese Americans — was not a unilateral presidential act. It was quickly ratified by Congress and, regrettably, upheld by the Supreme Court in a series of cases. Dissenting in one of these cases, Robert H. Jackson, whom Roosevelt had advanced to the Court in 1941, came close to judicial notice of Lockean prerogative. Locke had said in essence, not that emergency created power, but that authentic emergency created exceptions; Jackson's point now was to prevent emergency action from turning into constitutional precedent. If a military commander, Jackson said, overstepped the bounds of constitutionality, that was an incident. "But if we review and approve, that passing incident becomes the doctrine of the Constitution. There it has a generative power of its own, and all that it creates will be in its own image." By legalizing the evacuation policy, the majority had left a "loaded weapon ready for the hand of any new authority that can bring forward a plausible claim of an urgent need." Jackson did not feel that the Court should challenge the military expediency of removal in the midst of a war for survival. But "if we cannot confine military expedients by the Constitution, neither would I distort the Constitution to approve all that the military may prove expedient." [24]

*

v

The Second World War also brought in its wake a new and ominous development in American life — the establishment on a scale larger than ever before of a government internal security system, compiling dossiers on government employees. This development raised the perennial issue of congressional access to executive information. Despite the bravura claims of the first Roosevelt, the issue of congressional requisition and presidential refusal was still contained within the spirit of comity. That issue does not seem to have arisen at all in the Wilson administration. Coolidge had one case of withholding, and Hoover a couple. Franklin Roosevelt, who, for all his expansion of presidential power, tried to stay close to Congress, appears to have rejected no calls for information during his first two terms.

The creation of security files, however, presented a different problem. Some members of Congress, not always the most admirable, liked nothing better than to rummage around in personnel records in search of ammunition against the New Dealers. Roosevelt was reluctant to indulge inquisitive congressmen for much the reasons advanced a century before by Jefferson and Monroe — such files were too often a mixture of rumor, conjecture and suspicion, and their disclosure might do damage to innocent persons and impede the investigative process. He also no doubt had in mind one of Andrew Jackson's reasons: the defense of the executive branch against congressional harassment. So in 1941 Attorney General Robert Jackson, acting, he said, "with the approval and at the direction of the President," declined a dragnet request by the House Naval Affairs Committee for "all" FBI reports over the two preceding years bearing on labor disturbances and subversive activity in plants under naval contract and "all" future reports in this area.

In defending this refusal, Jackson contributed to historical confusion by offering a list of questionable precedents. He invoked the cases of Washington, Monroe and Jackson without precise analysis, found half a dozen twentieth-century Attorneys

General who had engaged in similar denials and, again without precision, brought in the judiciary. "The courts," he said, "have repeatedly held" that they would not require the executive to produce papers "when in the opinion of the executive their production is contrary to the public interest." The cases cited, however, dealt either in general terms with the separation of powers or else with the use of executive information in trials. None dealt with the transmission of information from the executive branch to Congress.[25]

As for the military and diplomatic reins of war, Roosevelt kept them very much in his own hands, and Congress was generally content that he should do so. But on many questions he displayed concern for the congressional prerogative. A few days after Pearl Harbor, Senator Arthur H. Vandenberg, a leading Republican isolationist, proposed to Roosevelt the creation of a Joint Congressional Committee on War Cooperation. It would, he said, be "highly useful to both the Executive and the Legislature if a more intimate connecting link should be created between us for the duration." Roosevelt replied, "If the Congress believes greater cooperation can be had by the appointment of such a Committee, I will be only too happy to consult with and seek the advice of the members of the Committee." Roosevelt, as he told Vandenberg, saw some difficulties with the idea; and Vandenberg eventually developed doubts about it himself.[26] But Roosevelt did consult constantly with congressional leaders. He paid careful attention to the recommendations of Senator Truman's War Investigating Committee. He sought, and gained, congressional authorization to send military missions to friendly nations. When Vandenberg objected to the notion that American participation in the United Nations Relief and Rehabilitation Administration should be by executive agreement, the administration agreed to submit the plan to approval by both houses through joint resolution. Above all Roosevelt was determined to give Congress a role in the making of peace. Recalling the fate of Wilson when he neglected to take senators or Republicans to Versailles, Roosevelt made elaborate and unprecedented efforts to bring members of Congress from both parties into the discussion of postwar policy. He did this through the State Department's Advisory Committee on Postwar Foreign Policy and through congressional representation at Bretton Woods and San Francisco — precedents followed by his successors in the selection of annual delegations to the United Nations General Assembly.

VI

For its part, Congress, perhaps in penance for the years in which it had repudiated the League of Nations and passed ill-considered neutrality laws, showed a particular interest in promoting the American role in postwar international organization. In 1943 senators like Joseph Ball of Minnesota, Harold Burton of Ohio, Lister Hill of Alabama and Carl Hatch of New Mexico, congressmen like J. W. Fulbright of Arkansas, went out ahead of the administration on this issue. One result of their pressure was the passage that year by the Senate of the Connally Resolution and by the House of the Fulbright Resolution, both endorsing the participation of the United States "through its constitutional processes" in an international authority with power to prevent aggression. Both resolutions, however, as well as the American presentation to the Dumbarton Oaks conference of 1944, dodged what seemed to militant internationalists as well as to militant isolationists the crucial issue: whether, if the international authority decided through *its* constitutional processes to take military action against aggression, the President had the power to commit American force without seeking congressional authorization in each separate case.

The insistence on case-by-case congressional authorization had been the second of Lodge's reservations in 1919. Isolationists treasured it a quarter century later, while internationalist senators like Ball felt that, unless the new world organization could take automatic military action against aggressor states, it would collapse as the League had collapsed. Secretary of State Hull privately agreed that the American President must be able on his own motion to contribute American troops to collective-security actions. John W. Davis advised him that, while the President probably had such authority under the Constitution, it would be better to ask Congress to make a formal delegation of war-making power when it voted for American membership in the international organization. But Vandenberg, as a member of the bipartisan senatorial committee consulting with Hull on post-war organization, opposed total renunciation of congressional power. It would be all right, he thought, for Presidents to act in lesser crises, as Presidents had long done in Latin America, without consulting Congress. Other great powers should assume the same responsibility for peace-keeping in their regions of special interest. But "I would never consent that our delegate on the new 'League' Council should have the power to vote us into a *major* military operation (tantamount to declaring war) without a vote of Congress as required by the Constitution." The Vandenberg position implied a congressional veto on American military participation in collective security outside the hemisphere. Still, as Vandenberg sensibly added, it was hard to believe that the effort to stop a clear case of worldwide aggression would not win immediate congressional consent, or that any President would dare take the country into major war "without the clear and obvious support of the American people." 27

The Vandenberg view nonetheless alarmed Joe Ball. "If we make that kind of crippling reservation," he said, "so will every other nation . . . and we will have no more certainty of international law enforcement than we had in the twenties and thirties." He now tried to force the issue into the 1944 presidential campaign. Though a Republican, Ball said that, before he decided how to vote, he had to know how the two candidates, Roosevelt and Thomas E. Dewey, stood on the question whether the United States representative on the United Nations Security Council could commit American force "to action ordered by the council to maintain peace without requiring further congressional approval." If Congress insisted on passing on each particular case, the UN "will be simply a debating society, without power to act, and future aggressors will sneer at it just as Hitler sneered at the League of Nations." 28

Dewey's first reaction in a speech on October 18 was evasive. As for Roosevelt, he felt privately (Judge Rosenman tells us) that Congress should give the President general authority to provide military support to the United Nations so that it would not have to pass on the question each time force had to be used. But his first public reaction — a press conference remark that Ball's question was "a little bit ahead of time," [29] — was evasive too. Still, he was hard pressed in the campaign and wanted Ball's endorsement. So, speaking before the Foreign Policy Association on October 21, Roosevelt said, "If the world organization is to have any reality at all, our American representative must be endowed in advance by the people themselves, by constitutional means through their representatives in the Congress, with authority to act." The American people "want their Government to act, and not merely to talk, whenever and wherever there is a threat to world peace." A policeman, Roosevelt added, would not be very effective if, when he saw a felon break into a house, he had to "call a town meeting to issue a warrant before the felon could be arrested.[30] Ball promptly came out for Roosevelt. (Dewey, having lost the horse, thereupon locked the barn door, saying that he too would not expect to apply to Congress in each separate case in order to use American force in a collective-security crisis.)

Ball's question and Roosevelt's answer turned out to make less difference than could have been expected at the time. Roosevelt's thesis presupposed action under the theory later expressed in Article 43 of the United Nations Charter that military contributions by member nations should be based on special agreements negotiated by the Security Council and ratified by the various nations "in accordance with their respective constitutional processes." Section 6 of the United Nations Participation Act subsequently empowered the President to negotiate, subject to the approval of Congress, agreements of the sort described in Article 43, specifying that the President should not be deemed "to require authorization of the Congress" to make armed force available to the Security Council on its call pursuant to such special agreement. Section 6 also made clear that the Act could not be construed as an authorization by Congress to make armed assistance available in numbers and types beyond the limits laid down in the agreement. It has been argued that the procedure represented a doubtfully constitutional delegation by Congress of its war-making power, the first in American history.[31] But would American participation in a duly constituted United Nations security force be equivalent to an American national war? In any case, no special agreements were negotiated under Article 43, so Section 6 never came into play. The Act was silent on whether the President in the absence of Article 43 agreements could provide armed assistance to the United Nations.

Nevertheless Ball's success in getting both Roosevelt and Dewey to endorse his thesis showed how far even members of Congress were prepared to go in limiting congressional control over the employment of armed force for collective security. No change was more symptomatic than Senator Vandenberg's. As late as 1944 he was insisting on the congressional veto. Then in 1945 he announced his conversion to internationalism and toured the country arguing the necessity of the "automatic availability of force." "The unlimited Presidential use of force to implement a disarmament treaty," he wrote, ". . . is the exercise of that same constitutional prerogative in behalf of the 'national defense,' which he has used (I believe seventy-one times) without challenge for 150 years." [32] When Vandenberg asked Chief Justice Charles Evans Hughes, now retired, whether the President had the authority to commit troops without congressional approval, Hughes replied, "Our Presidents have used our armed forces repeatedly without authorization by Congress, when they thought the interests of the country required it." [33]

VII

War once again nourished the Presidency. The towering figure of Franklin Roosevelt, the generally accepted wisdom of his initiatives of 1940 and 1941, his undisputed authority as Commander in Chief after Pearl Harbor, the thundering international pronouncements emanating from wartime summits of the Big Two

or the Big Three — all these gave Americans in the postwar
years an exalted conception of presidential power. This conception was strengthened by the vivid memory of the poor congressional performance in the years between Versailles and Pearl
Harbor — a performance generally regarded as compounded of
presumption, ignorance and folly. Willkie in 1943 had spoken of
devoting the rest of his life "to saving America from the
Senate." [34] Roosevelt himself evidently saw little prospect of congressional improvement. On the boat back from Yalta, he
shocked the young Charles E. Bohlen by the "bitterness" with
which he denounced the Senate "as a bunch of incompetent obstructionists." Roosevelt named no senators but gave the impression "that the only way to do anything in the American government was to bypass the Senate." [35]

War had accustomed those in charge of foreign policy to a
complacent faith in the superior intelligence and disinterest-
edness of the executive branch. Dean Acheson of the Department of State observed that members of Congress by definition
represented narrow constituencies. The Secretary of State came
to them "bearing words of troubles about which Congress does
not want to hear." Foreign policy was a "troublesome intrusion"
into their consuming concern, which was domestic affairs. The
characteristic congressional mood was consequently one of "exasperated frustration" and "sulky opposition." Of his experience
in the mid forties as Assistant Secretary of State for Congressional Relations, Acheson observed that "those who assert that I
do not suffer fools gladly . . . do me less than justice for these
anguishing hours." Nothing pleased the Hill. Members of Congress were "indignant at either inclusion or exclusion — at either
'putting Congress on the spot' or 'bypassing' it." Acheson calculated that one sixth of his working days as Secretary of State
after 1949 was spent in preparing for or attending meetings with
Congress. In all those hours and days, "the moments of positive
accomplishment, of forward movement, are disappointingly few.
Much of the time is spent in what Secretary Stimson used to call
'stopping rat holes.' " [36]

George Kennan, that most brilliant of diplomat-historians,

spoke in similar vein for colleagues in the Foreign Service when he acknowledged a "distaste amounting almost to horror for the chaotic disorder of the American political process." The subordination of foreign policy to domestic politics seemed to him a hopeless flaw in the system. "In a sensitive matter, where its own ignorance could scarcely have been greater, Congress would have been better advised to leave the conduct of foreign policy in the hands of those who had been constitutionally charged with it; because external interference of this nature, separating the power to shape policy from the power to discuss it with a foreign government, could only paralyze the process of diplomacy." [37] On this principle Kennan declined in 1954 to judge the American policy toward Indochina. "There is little to be gained at this moment by any attempt to master-mind our government's activities, day by day, from the outside. . . . The time has passed when any back seat driving can do any good. . . . Having elected a government, we will be best advised to let it govern and to let it speak for us as it will in the councils of the nations." [38]

American historians and political scientists, this writer among them, labored to give the expansive theory of the Presidency historical sanction. Overgeneralizing from the prewar contrast between a President who was right and a Congress which was wrong, scholars developed an uncritical cult of the activist Presidency. Some carried the point very far indeed. "Deception of the people may in fact become increasingly necessary," wrote the diplomatic historian Thomas A. Bailey in 1948, "unless we are willing to give our leaders in Washington a freer hand. . . . Just as the yielding of some of our national sovereignty is the price that we must pay for effective international organization, so the yielding of some of our democratic control of foreign affairs is the price that we may have to pay for greater physical security." [39] The image of the Presidency as "the great engine of democracy," the "American people's one authentic trumpet," "the central instrument of democracy" soon passed, as Thomas E. Cronin has shown, into the textbooks and helped shape the views of a new generation. [40]

Thoughtful commentators in the press shared the prevailing

disdain for the legislative branch. "When the Senate of the United States tries to direct the nation's foreign policy," wrote James Reston of the *New York Times,* "it almost always gets into trouble." [41] In 1955 the most thoughtful commentator of them all, Walter Lippmann, delivered himself in *The Public Philosophy* of a gloomy inquiry into what he conceived as the decline of liberal democracy. Strategic and diplomatic decisions, he said, called for professional knowledge and seasoned judgment. But representative assemblies and mass opinion had "converged upon the modern democracies to devitalize, to enfeeble, and to eviscerate the executive powers." When hard issues of war and peace were up for decisions, "the executive and judicial departments, with their civil servants and technicians, have lost their power to decide." Mass opinion, the new ruler, had one supreme instinct: always to oppose changes in the existing policy, whatever that policy might be. Mass democracy could not prepare for war in time of peace, nor negotiate peace in the midst of war.

> The unhappy truth is that the prevailing public opinion has been destructively wrong at the critical junctures. The people have imposed a veto upon the judgments of informed and responsible officials. They have compelled the governments, which usually knew what would have been wiser, or was necessary, or was more expedient, to be too late with too little, or too long with too much, too pacifist in peace and too bellicose in war, too neutralist or appeasing in negotiation or too intransigent. Mass opinion has acquired mounting power in this century. It has shown itself to be a dangerous master of decisions when the stakes are life and death. [42]

This was a devastating proposition. Could it be that the Founding Fathers had failed in their allocation of the war-making power because of innate disabilities in popular government itself? Tocqueville had raised this question long before, in the first half century of the republic. "Foreign politics," he then observed, "demand scarcely any of those qualities which are peculiar to a democracy; they require, on the contrary, the perfect use of almost all those in which it is deficient." The indispensable qualities, Tocqueville said, were steadfastness in a course, perseverance against difficulties, efficiency in the execution of policy, prudence, patience, secrecy — all qualities, he thought, more likely to prevail when power was concentrated in the executive.[43] This was the ultimate doubt that haunted the minds of Americans when the United States passed from the Second World War into the Cold War — the doubt that democracy was designed for the conduct of foreign affairs. It was against this doubt that the postwar Presidency developed its pretensions and its powers.

6

The Presidency Ascendant:
Korea

THERE REMAINED the postwar congressional impulse to strike back at the war-magnified Presidency. This impulse pretty much had its way in internal affairs after the Second World War. Congress derided President Truman's domestic program, passed significant legislation over his veto and generally dismissed his hope of extending the Roosevelt New Deal into the Truman Fair Deal. Nor did Congress stop with Truman. As Congress after the Civil War had repudiated the Lincolnian Presidency by impeaching Andrew Johnson, as Congress after the First World War had repudiated the Wilsonian Presidency by endorsing Harding and normalcy, so Congress after the Second World War repudiated Franklin D. Roosevelt by recommending the 22nd Amendment and restricting all future Presidents to two terms.

But congressional retaliation had its limits. Where the Civil War and the First World War had been followed by times of quiescence in foreign relations, the years after the Second World War were a time of international peril. This situation of external danger restrained the post-Roosevelt Congress from attempting the moral equivalent of rejecting Lincoln's Reconstruction or Wilson's League. In consequence, the postwar congressional revival, for all its success in humiliating the domestic Presidency, did not usher in a general age of congressional government. In foreign affairs Congress was forced onto a terrain where many of its more thoughtful members now confessed to a sense of institutional inferiority, if not of institutional guilt. The Cold War, moreover, with its uncertain definitions and its shifting boundaries, appeared to create unprecedented problems for foreign policy. The menace of unexpected crisis hung over the world, demanding, it was supposed, the concentration within government of the means of instant decision and response. All this, reinforcing the intellectual doubt about democratic control of foreign relations, appeared to argue more strongly than ever for the centralization of foreign policy in the Presidency.

I

Such centralization came in stages. The new President had been a senator himself. This was less of an advantage in dealing with Congress than sometimes supposed. In addition Truman was a Democrat, and the Congress elected in 1946 was controlled by Republicans. Still, when Truman required congressional consent in foreign policy either because of the need for appropriations (the British loan, the Greek-Turkish aid program, the Marshall Plan) or for treaty ratification (NATO), he succeeded in rallying the necessary support. He also paid a price: to get the policy he had to overcolor the crisis. Thus Senator Vandenberg told him that, if he wanted to enlist Congress behind aid to Greece and Turkey, he would have to scare hell out of the country. Truman therefore elevated a reasonable and limited program into a transcendent principle. The result was the Truman Doctrine: "it must be the policy of the United States to support free peoples who are resisting attempted subjugation by armed minorities or outside pressures." Truman himself did not construe his Doctrine in any crusading way, applying it neither to China nor to eastern Europe, for example, as he applied it to Greece and Turkey. But the sweeping language remained, as did the technique of scaring hell out of the country.

Truman's relative success with Congress on foreign policy was facilitated by the invention of the "bipartisan foreign policy," in which Vandenberg, who preferred to call it a nonpartisan foreign policy, was the indispensable partner. Bipartisanship had essentially begun with Roosevelt's appointment of Republicans as Secretaries of War and of the Navy in 1940. It grew in the Hull-

Dulles consultations during the 1944 presidential campaign and rushed to the fore in the years after the war. Not everyone thought it a good idea to take foreign policy out of politics. "There are some who say that politics should stop at the water's edge," Senator Robert A. Taft had said in 1939. ". . . I do not at all agree. . . . There is no principle of subjection to the Executive in foreign policy. Only Hitler or Stalin would assert that." [1] Taft retained that belief after the war. In January 1951 he called the bipartisan foreign policy "a very dangerous fallacy threatening the very existence of the Nation." [2] Nor did the bipartisan foreign policy — as Vandenberg, the keystone of bipartisanship, occasionally protested — cover all aspects of foreign relations. Vandenberg agreed with, and soon appropriated, the suggestion made in 1946 by Harold Stassen, a promising young Republican politician of the period, that "the Republicans would like to be co-pilots in the foreign policy take-offs as well as in the crash landings." [3]

Still, for the Truman administration bipartisanship was the only solution once the 1946 election presented it with a Republican Congress. Even the 80th Congress, as it hacked away at Truman's domestic program, would not oppose his foreign policy when the President could persuade Vandenberg to go along. Vandenberg usefully reminded the executive that Congress had constitutional responsibilities too and often improved the legislation. Against Taft and other Republican skeptics he argued that bipartisanship, far from eliminating discussion, required that foreign policy "be *totally* debated." This was optimistic. Once debate was over, bipartisanship became the means, as Vandenberg liked to put it, of placing "national security ahead of partisan advantage." [4]

The bipartisan foreign policy was not a good idea. It was only a necessity. At least it was a necessity for those who believed that the American national interest enjoined resistance to the Stalinization of western Europe. But it encouraged crisis diplomacy, and therefore escalated public emotion. Despite Vandenberg, it had the effect, the longer it ran, of stifling debate. And it gave the Presidency a powerful new peacetime weapon by refurbishing the wartime theory of 'national security' as the end to which other values could be properly sacrificed in times of crisis.

Presidential prestige in foreign policy was strengthened by the fact that the postwar congressional impulse to cut the Presidency down to size so often produced aberrant results. On the question of China, for example, Congress generally criticized Truman's effort to compose the Chinese civil war by bringing Mao Tse-tung into a coalition government and denounced him for his failure to send sufficient assistance to Chiang Kai-shek. In 1948 Congress even voted more aid to Nationalist China than the administration wished to give. As late as March 1950 Truman wrote Vandenberg that "the Chinese, as you know, are fundamentally anti-foreign, and we must be exceedingly careful to see that this anti-foreign sentiment is not turned in our direction," and that "the Chinese and Far Eastern situation eventually will be rescued from the totalitarian regime in Moscow." [5] In retrospect no one can doubt that Truman had a more intelligent China policy than his congressional critics.

Nor was congressional performance on the defense budget more persuasive. In 1948 Congress voted funds for a 70-group Air Force. When Truman by presidential directive cut the Air Force back to 48 groups, Congress the next year voted an increase to 58 groups, though with the qualification, insisted upon by the Senate in conference, that the President need not spend all the money. Truman thereupon impounded $615 million. Whether Congress was trying to force the presidential hand on China or the defense budget, whether it was trying to cut Marshall Plan appropriations by more than a quarter (1948) or imposing, over vigorous presidential objection, a mandatory loan to Franco Spain (1950) or questioning the loyalty of government officials (*passim*), its independent initiatives reawakened dismal memories of the years between the wars.

II

Truman worked hard at congressional relations. But he was also a man of doughty temperament who regarded his office, in the words of his last Secretary of State, as "a sacred and temporary trust, which he was determined to pass on unimpaired by the slightest loss of power or prestige." [6] Secretary Acheson himself, though an eminent lawyer, was impatient with what he saw as constitutional hairsplitting and encouraged the President in his stout defense of prerogative. Vandenberg agreed that the President had to have leeway in the use of troops for peace-keeping purposes. In April 1948, for example, when Truman claimed the power to send American soldiers to Palestine without congressional consent as part of a United Nations force, he received Vandenberg's support.[7] No troops were sent then; but the issue burst forth in decisive form when news reached Washington on June 24, 1950, that the North Korean Army had invaded South Korea.

Truman and Acheson saw this as a challenge, possibly crucial, to the whole postwar structure. If North Korea succeeded in its attack, the peace system would collapse, and communist aggression would be encouraged at every soft point along the periphery of the free states. Since this was above all a test of collective security, their first resort was to the United Nations. On June 25 the UN Security Council pronounced North Korean aggression "a breach of the peace," called for the withdrawal of the invading forces and directed member states in general terms "to render every assistance" to the UN in the execution of the resolution. That evening Truman, convening his top foreign policy and defense officials and asking each for his views, decided to commit American air and sea forces to the support of South Korea. Not until June 27, two days after the decision and three after the attack, did the President meet with congressional leaders. He then told a bipartisan group of his decision and received their support. When he announced the decision publicly the same day, he cited the UN resolution as his authorization. Actually the resolution had not specified military intervention; but that evening the Security Council passed a second resolution, this time calling for "urgent military measures . . . to repel the armed attack." When Truman was thereafter criticized for having acted in advance of the more explicit resolution, Trygve

Lie, the Secretary-General of the UN, defended him on the ground that there was no time to be lost and diplomatic soundings had shown that the call to arms would pass.

On June 28 Taft, while supporting Truman's decision to respond by force in Korea, gave it as his opinion that there was "no legal authority" for what Truman had done. He added that he would vote for a joint resolution authorizing American intervention. Acheson thought this was "typical senatorial legalistic ground." On June 29 Truman decided to make a commitment of ground forces south of the combat zone. On June 30 he decided to increase that commitment. At a new meeting with congressional leaders, Senator H. Alexander Smith of New Jersey suggested that the President request a joint resolution approving his action. Truman said he would consider this and instructed Acheson to prepare a recommendation on it. In the meantime, the debate spilled over to the Senate. Kenneth Wherry of Nebraska said that the President should not have acted without congressional authorization, adding that there was "no doubt" he would have obtained it. William Knowland of California, another conservative Republican, replied that the President had the necessary authority under the UN Charter and under his power as Commander in Chief.[8]

This was a fateful moment. Truman had evidently not yet fully made up his mind about the scope of presidential authority. Nor did he pretend to legal skills. But he had a most eminent lawyer at his right hand. His Secretary of State had been law clerk for Justice Brandeis, whom Truman had known and revered as a majestic expositor of the Constitution. Acheson, moreover, had been a senior member of Washington's leading law firm and was still a daily walking companion of Justice Frankfurter. On July 3 Acheson recommended that Truman *not* ask for a resolution but instead rely on his constitutional powers as President and Commander in Chief. On the same day the State Department churned out a memorandum listing 87 instances (an improvement over Vandenberg's 71) in which Presidents had sent American forces into combat on their own initiative. Truman, impressed by the appearance of precedent and concerned not to squander the power of his office, accepted his Secretary of State's recommendation.[9]

The State Department argument was that "the President, as Commander in Chief of the Armed Forces of the United States, has full control over the use thereof," that there was a "traditional power of the President to use the armed forces of the United States without consulting Congress," and that this had often been done in "the broad interests of American foreign policy." [10] In the Senate Paul H. Douglas, the much respected liberal Democrat from Illinois, amplified the defense of Truman's unilateral action. Douglas rested his case particularly on the need for swift presidential action in emergencies. "With tanks, airplanes and the atom bomb, war can become instantaneous and disaster can occur while Congress is assembling and debating." Citing the UN resolutions, he contended that the introduction of armed force to drive the invaders back to the 38th parallel "was not an act of war, but, instead, merely the exercise of police power under international sanction." (He could have added that the resolutions were pursuant to the UN Charter, a treaty ratified by the Senate and that the UN Participation Act was a statute enacted by the Congress.[11]) Though Congress had the power to declare general war, situations calling for "the retail use of force," Douglas suggested, ought to be left to the President, as they had been left throughout American history. There might be "grave dangers" in thus giving the Presidency discretionary power to commit troops to battle, but Douglas found consolation in "the sobering and terrible responsibilities of the office of President itself" and in the fact that action grossly offensive to the national interest and public will could lead to impeachment.[12]

The constitutional case was far from conclusive. The precedents invoked by Acheson, the State Department and Douglas were precedents for limited action to suppress pirates or to protect American citizens in conditions of local disorder. They were not precedents for sustained and major war against a sovereign state. As for the United Nations resolutions, while they justified American military action under international law, they could not serve as a substitute for the congressional authorization required in national law by the Constitution.

Yet in fairness to Truman it was not at all clear at the moment of first intervention that the United States was entering the grim and protracted war eventually produced by the later decision to go beyond the 38th parallel. Truman's initial decision may well have seemed to those involved less likely to risk serious war than Roosevelt's decision nine years before — also taken without reference to Congress — to send convoys into the North Atlantic. And the appeal to emergency was powerful. Even if the attack on South Korea carried no immediate and direct threat to the United States of the sort that had justified Lincoln and the second Roosevelt in their assertions of independent presidential authority, it nonetheless did demand an extremely quick decision with great potential import for American security. Nor did Truman make his decision in royal seclusion. He consulted fully and candidly with his executive colleagues. If he told rather than asked the congressional leaders, Congress soon confirmed and, in a sense, ratified American intervention by voting military appropriations and extending selective service.

For all this, it is hard not to agree with the judgment some months later of Senator Vandenberg, now gravely sick in Michigan. "The President's great mistake," Vandenberg wrote, "was in not bringing his Korea decision to the immediate attention of Congress (as Wilson did at Vera Cruz)." [13] Truman might even, like Wilson at Vera Cruz, have requested congressional sanction without implying any surrender of presidential power by saying that he did not wish to act in a matter of such grave consequence except in close cooperation with the Senate and House. The argument against this course would have been Acheson's, that congressional debate was not "calculated to support the shaken morale of the troops or the unity that, for the moment, prevailed at home." [14] But this argument was hardly persuasive. If even Taft had said he would vote for a resolution, it is hard to see who would have opposed it. The passage of a resolution would have preserved the congressional role in the decision to go to war. For that matter, a resolution would have spared troop morale and national unity, not to mention the administration itself, at least one damaging form of attack after the war became unpopular. Few wars are unpopular in their first thirty days.

Korea beguiled the American government first into an unprecedented claim for inherent presidential power to go to war and then into ill-advised resentment against those who dared bring up the constitutional issue. "The circumstances of the present crisis," an executive document sourly said in 1951, "make any debate over prerogatives and power essentially sterile, if not dangerous to the success of our foreign policy." [15] By insisting that the presidential prerogative alone sufficed to meet the requirements of the Constitution, Truman did a good deal more than pass on his sacred trust unimpaired. He dramatically and dangerously enlarged the power of future Presidents to take the nation into major war.

III

Truman did not at first receive much constitutional criticism over Korea. American troops after all were defending international virtue against the communist hordes and doing so at the behest and with the blessing of the United Nations. But, especially as the war began to go badly, conservative congressmen began to realize, as one of them, Frederic R. Coudert, Jr., of New York, put it, "how devastating a precedent they have set in remaining silent while the President took over the powers specifically reserved for Congress in the Constitution." The President meanwhile increased their alarm by indicating his intention to send, without reference to Congress, four more divisions to reinforce the American Army in Europe. Never before had a President claimed constitutional authority to commit so many troops to a theater of potential war against a major foe. Sending Marines to Latin America in the old style was a radically different thing in terms of national commitment and danger. Coudert accordingly, on January 3, 1951, introduced a resolution declaring it the sense of the Congress that "no additional military forces" could be sent abroad "without the prior authorization of the Congress in each instance." The resolution also provided, in an anticipation of devices later proposed to stop the war in Indochina, that no funds appropriated for the armed forces could be used for sending troops abroad (except to help extricate Americans from Korea).[16]

Truman told his press conference the next day that he certainly did not need the approval of Congress to send more troops to Europe. A week later he expanded his case, claiming that "under the President's constitutional powers as Commander in Chief of the Armed Forces" he had the authority to send troops anywhere in the world, that this power had been "repeatedly recognized by Congress and the courts," and that his administration would "continue to send troops wherever it is necessary to uphold" its obligations to the United Nations. When asked about constitutional precedents, he said, "I haven't got it with me just now, but you will find decisions by at least three Chief Justices on that very subject." Did the opinion of the Court require him to consult Congress? "No, it did not," Truman answered with characteristic briskness, ". . . and I do not have to unless I want to. But of course I am polite, and I usually always consult them. . . . The opinions are all in favor of the President's exercise of the Presidential power when in his judgment it is necessary." [17]

The purpose of his resolution, Coudert now rejoined in reply both to Truman and to a disapproving editorial in the *New York Herald Tribune,* was "to prevent the commitment of armed forces abroad in advance of aggression solely by executive decision." (Actually his resolution was poorly drafted; it did not include the phrase "in advance of aggression" and thereby would have prevented presidential commitment of armed forces abroad even in cases of aggression.) The President, Coudert continued, "asserts precisely such power. I say that he does not and should not have it. If the President alone is allowed to send anywhere abroad, at any time, hundreds of thousands of American troops without a declaration of war . . . then, indeed, there is little left of American constitutional government." If this is what the people wanted, they might as well, Coudert said, dismiss Congress and accept government by presidential decree.[18]

The issue was now sharply drawn. For the first time in American history the Presidency and the Congress were moving toward a showdown on the question of which branch of government should control the commitment of troops abroad. Nearly forty years before, Elihu Root, while conceding to Congress the power to forbid troop commitment abroad, had doubted whether any Congress would dare exercise that power. Thirty-five years before, Robert Taft's father, perhaps one of Truman's trio of Chief Justices, had said that the President could order the Army and Navy wherever he wished as long as he had the funds to do so and if war was not his purpose. Eleven years before, Professor Edward S. Corwin, that formidable guardian of the Constitution, had raised the question "whether the President may, without authorization by Congress, take measures which are technically acts of war in protection of American rights and interests abroad," and had replied, "The answer returned both by practice and by judicial doctrine is yes." As little as eighteen months before, Corwin had described the power "to employ without congressional authorization the armed forces in protection of American rights and interests abroad wherever necessary" as "almost unchallenged from the first and occasionally sanctified judicially." [19]

Two days after the introduction of the Coudert resolution Taft opened what came to be known as a "great debate" with an elaborate speech in the Senate. He dealt quickly with an argument much heard in later years — that "basic elements of foreign policy" should not be publicly argued lest argument give aid and comfort to enemies. "I think," Taft sensibly said, "that the value of such aid and comfort is grossly exaggerated. The only thing that can give real aid and comfort to the enemy is the adoption of a policy which plays into their hands." Much of the rest of the speech was a confused ramble into the substance of foreign policy, in which Taft simultaneously denounced and minimized the communist threat and, while calling for the limitation of American commitments, went on to propose the American defense of such remote places as the Suez Canal, northern Africa, Formosa, Singapore, the Malay peninsula, Australia and New Zealand. On the constitutional point Taft renewed the argument he had made against Roosevelt ten years earlier. "The President," he said, "simply usurped authority, in violation of the laws and the Constitution, when he sent troops to Korea to carry out the resolution of the United Nations in an undeclared war." Now "without authority he apparently is now attempting to adopt a similar policy in Europe." This was a matter, Taft insisted, to be debated and determined by Congress.[20]

A number of senators — Douglas, J. W. Fulbright, Herbert Lehman, Wayne Morse — challenged Taft. Fulbright observed that, if the President thought the defense of America required the sending of troops to Europe, "he has the power and the duty to do so." [21] Morse inserted the full text of the *Curtiss-Wright* decision into the *Congressional Record* in vindication of "a discretionary power which I believe is inherent in the President of the United States in the field of foreign policy." [22] Tom Connally, the chairman of the Senate Committee on Foreign Relations, was peremptory. "The authority of the President as Commander in Chief to send the Armed Forces to any place required by the security interests of the United States," he said, "has often been questioned, but never denied by authoritative opinion." Secretary of State Acheson claimed the President's authority as not only inherent but exclusive:

> Not only has the President the authority to use the Armed Forces in carrying out the broad foreign policy of the United States and implementing treaties, but it is equally clear that this authority may not be interfered with by the Congress in the exercise of powers which it has under the Constitution.[23]

Acheson added irritably: "We are in a position in the world today where the argument as to who has the power to do this, that, or the other thing, is not exactly what is called for from America in this very critical hour." [24]

Arthur Vandenberg, dying of cancer in Grand Rapids, watched the great debate with deeply troubled spirit. He did not like "the idea of complete Presidential freedom, without a reference to Congress, to send American troops abroad." But the President was, after all, Commander in Chief, and the idea of congressional approval of overseas troop deployment was a challenge to the President's general constitutional power "which I do not believe can be successfully sustained." Indeed, it seemed "dangerous and futile" to try to keep the country out of war "by any one such Presidential limitation." In the end, Vandenberg decided, two constitutional powers were in collision — the constitutional prerogative of the President to defend the United States and the constitutional prerogative of the Congress to declare war. This "twilight zone" had existed for 150 years; but "the law of self-preservation . . . has always resulted in sustaining the President's prerogative." When there was time, the President should consult with Congress; if time did not permit, Congress "should frankly recognize the President's ultimate prerogative as Commander-in-Chief," though the President "should immediately notify the Congress whenever an emergency requires the summary use of his personal responsibility." [25]

Scholars rushed into the fray. Henry Steele Commager wrote, "Whatever may be said of the expediency of the Taft-Coudert program, this at least can be said of the principles involved — that they have no support in law or in history." [26] The present writer, with a flourish of historical documentation and, alas, hyperbole, called Taft's statements "demonstrably irresponsible." [27] Commager and Schlesinger, who had learned much of what they knew about the constitutional powers of the Presidency from Professor Corwin, were accordingly astonished when Corwin denounced them, with some justice, as "high-flying prerogative men" who ascribed to the President "a truly royal prerogative in the field of foreign relations . . . without indicating any correlative legal or constitutional control to which he is answerable."

Corwin now argued that the fact Congress had not exercised power over troop deployment abroad did not mean that it did not have that power to exercise, and that when it chose to intervene (here he cited Marshall's decision in *Little v. Barreme*) the President must follow its directions. In any case the answer, he said with a wisdom this embattled writer did not then appreciate, lay not in "embittered debate between the holders of powers that must be exercised in close co-operation if at all" but in "a decent consultation and accommodation of views." Therefore something like the Coudert resolution should be adopted. It would be paradoxical, Corwin observed with permissible irony, to reduce Congress to the role of a rubber stamp of policies the professed purpose of which was the preservation of free institutions.[28]

The great debate of 1951 ended inconclusively with the passage of a "sense-of-the-Senate" resolution in which the Senate approved the sending of Truman's four divisions but said no additional ground troops should be sent to Western Europe "without further congressional approval" — the last provision carrying over administration opposition by the close vote of 49 to 43. Senator Richard M. Nixon of California was among those voting against inherent presidential authority and for the principle of congressional control of troop deployment. Taft applauded the resolution as "a clear statement by the Senate that it has the right to pass on any question of sending troops to Europe to implement the Atlantic Pact, that it is unconstitutional for the President to send troops abroad to implement that pact without congressional approval, at least until war comes." [29] Acheson, on the other hand, said it was "without force of law" and "had in it a present for everybody." [30] Both were right. Since no subsequent President has tried to increase the permanent (if that is the word) American Army in Europe, the resolution has not been tested.

IV

This inconclusive outcome left the Truman administration generally unperturbed about its theory of presidential power. Nor had the Supreme Court done much to challenge this complacency.

In cases involving the postwar use of powers asserted during the Second World War it generally upheld the government. "The war power does not necessarily end with the cessation of hostilities," as Justice William O. Douglas put it for the Court in *Woods v. Miller* in 1948. Still, Justice Jackson, while agreeing with the result in this case, expressed foreboding over the future of "this vague, undefined and undefinable 'war power.' " It was, he said, a power invoked in haste and excitement, applied in patriotic fervor, interpreted by judges under the influence of passion and pressure. "Always, as in this case, the Government urges hasty decision to forestall some emergency or serve some purpose and pleads that paralysis will result if its claims to power are denied." He added, "No one will question that this power is the most dangerous one to free government in the whole catalogue of powers." [31]

Two years later the Korean War brought about a new national emergency, formally proclaimed by Truman in December 1950, and thereby injected new life into the war power and its personification, the Commander in Chief. By bringing the nation into war without congressional authorization and by then successfully defending his exercise of independent presidential initiative, Truman enormously expanded assumptions of presidential prerogative. "The acquisition of a dozen bases and gift of fifty destroyers that President Roosevelt moved on so cautiously less than fifteen years ago," Harold Stein, an eminent government-official-turned-political-scientist, wrote in the wake of Korea, "would be a routine, indeed a minor transaction today." [32] And, where independent power exercised in domestic affairs did not necessarily produce equivalent power in foreign affairs, as the case of Roosevelt in the 1930s had shown, independent power exercised in foreign affairs was very likely to strengthen and embolden the Presidency at home.

In April 1952, fearing that a nationwide strike would shut down the steel industry and stop the flow of military material to the troops in Korea, Truman directed the Secretary of Commerce to seize and operate the steel mills. This was not done with particular relish or sweep. Truman emphasized his "distaste" for government operation of the steel industry. Presidential intervention was announced as temporary. Assurance was given that the mills would return as soon as possible to private ownership. Truman reported his action without delay to Congress and conceded its power to supersede his policy if it wished to do so. Subsequently he wrote the Senate requesting that Congress act, preferably in support of the seizure but, if it so judged, in rejection of "the course of action that I have followed." Truman's own summary was accurate enough: "I have twice sent messages to the Congress asking it to prescribe a course . . . if the Congress disagreed with the action I was taking. The Congress has not done so." [33] In short, there was an emergency of a sort, the President's action was neither unreasonable nor irreversible, and Congress declined repeated invitations to veto the President's policy and enact one of its own.

Yet behind the moderate action lay an immoderate theory. Truman set forth the theory with typical bluntness. "The President of the United States," he said, "has very great inherent powers to meet great national emergencies"; indeed, "it was the duty of the President under the Constitution to act to preserve the safety of the Nation." In a somewhat garbled historical excursion he lectured to a press conference about "a gentleman by the name of Jefferson" who had used such powers to buy Louisiana ("they tried to impeach him for that, if I remember correctly"), "a gentleman by the name of Tyler . . . a gentleman by the name of Polk . . . Mr. Lincoln . . . President Roosevelt." As for the present situation, "We are in one of the greatest emergencies the country has ever been in." It would be "unthinkable" to let a steel strike block "our efforts to support our armed forces and to protect our national security." "I feel sure," the President said, "that the Constitution does not require me to endanger our national safety by letting all the steel mills shut down." In the name of emergency, in short, Truman was asserting the power to rule by decree in a field — industrial seizure — customarily controlled by Congress. Nor was it clear what he thought the limits on his emergency authority were. If he could seize steel mills under his inherent powers, could he also seize newspapers and radio stations? Asked this question, Truman made a direct, imprudent and characteristic response, "Under similar circumstances the President of the United States has to act for whatever is for the best of the country. That's the answer." [34]

This was Lockean prerogative with a vengeance. The steel companies promptly sued to get their property back, and the Truman thesis thereupon underwent judicial scrutiny. In the lower court an Assistant Attorney General defended the seizure in Trumanesque terms, claiming that the President had inherent and independent power, limited only by impeachment or by defeat in the next election, to save the nation from catastrophe. The district judge denied this spacious claim; and, when the case moved up to the Supreme Court, the government offered a more circumspect argument. It now said that the acuteness of the emergency required the President to act, and "the aggregate of his constitutional powers" as President and Commander in Chief authorized him to act, until Congress was prepared to act for itself. Both sides thus acknowledged ultimate legislative supremacy. The difference was that, where the government contended that the President had the right to act in an emergency unless or until Congress expressly denied his power to take the action, the steel companies contended the President had no power to act without prior congressional authorization or against earlier congressional instruction.

The Court delivered its judgment eight weeks after the President's intervention.[35] It pronounced the seizure unconstitutional by a 6 to 3 vote. The nine justices, however, elaborated their views in seven separate opinions. The result was a confusing, if intermittently dazzling, examination of the presidential claim to emergency prerogative. The import of the verdict must be divined (to borrow the phrase Justice Jackson applied in his own opinion to the mystery of the Founding Fathers and the war-making power) from materials almost as enigmatic as the dreams Joseph was called on to interpret for Pharaoh.

There is no question that the idea of independent presidential power received a severe rebuke. But the rebuke was by no means total. It was confined, in the first place, to domestic abuse of presidential power. Neither the majority nor even the minority saw the case as involving in any primary sense the President's authority in foreign affairs. Jackson scouted the government's suggestion that, because Truman had sent troops to Korea in an exercise of "the President's constitutional powers," he was therefore justified in taking over the steel plants. "No doctrine that the Court could promulgate would seem to me more sinister and alarming," Jackson said,

> than that a President whose conduct of foreign affairs is so largely uncontrolled, and often even is unknown, can vastly enlarge his mastery over the internal affairs of the country by his own commitment of the Nation's armed forces to some foreign venture.

Justices were particularly caustic about the notion that the Commander in Chief clause conferred domestic powers on the Presidency. "Even though 'theater of war' be an expanding concept," Justice Black said dryly for the Court, "we cannot with faithfulness to our constitutional system hold that the Commander in Chief . . . has the ultimate power as such to take possession of private property in order to keep labor disputes from stopping production. This is a job for the Nation's lawmakers, not for its military authorities." Jackson dismissed the Commander in Chief thesis as a "loose appellation" unjustifiably advanced as support for any presidential action, internal or external, involving the use of force, "the idea being that it vests power to do anything, anywhere, that can be done with an army or navy." The Constitution, Jackson said, in making the President Commander in Chief of the Army and Navy, did not also constitute him "Commander in Chief of the country, its industries and its inhabitants." His powers as Commander in Chief were to be "measured by the command functions usual to the topmost officer of the army and navy." He added, "No penance would ever expiate the sin against free government of holding that a President can escape control of executive powers by law through assuming his military role."

The Court's rebuke to independent presidential power was further narrowed by the argument, advanced more carefully by some justices than others, that the steel seizure was invalid because undertaken in disregard of remedies already laid down by Congress for industrial emergencies. In this connection Jackson set forth an analysis, brilliant then and classic now, of the American separation of powers. Speaking for the Court, Black had given a rigid and rather unrealistic account of the equal and coordinate branches of government. Jackson, while agreeing that the Constitution had divided power in order to secure liberty, added that it had also supposed that practice would unite the divided powers into a workable government. The Constitution, he said, therefore enjoined upon the branches of government "separateness but interdependence, autonomy but reciprocity."

As for the Presidency and Congress, the two branches in contention over the steel seizure, they, Jackson continued, had three distinguishable levels of interdependence. The first was when the President acted in accordance with the express or implied authorization of Congress. Then, Jackson said, "his authority is at its maximum." Only in such a case could the President be said "to personify the federal sovereignty." When the Presidency and Congress acted together, they would be supported "by the strongest of presumptions and the widest latitude of judicial interpretation." The second level was a "zone of twilight" where the Presidency and Congress shared authority or where the distribution of authority was uncertain. In the twilight zone "congressional inertia, indifference or quiescence may sometimes, at least as a practical matter, enable, if not invite, measures on independent presidential responsibility." Acceptance of such presidential initiative would depend "on the imperatives of events and contemporary imponderables" rather than on abstract theories of law.

The third level, in which Jackson included the case at hand, was when the Presidency took measures "incompatible with the expressed or implied will of Congress." In this case presidential power was "at its lowest ebb," and the Court could sustain exclusive presidential control only by disqualifying Congress from acting upon the subject. "Presidential claim to a power at once so conclusive and preclusive must be scrutinized with caution, for what is at stake is the equilibrium established by our constitutional system." The steel seizure was therefore illegal because Congress had already covered the situation in statutes inconsistent with the President's action. Had Congress not pre-empted the field, then presumably the seizure would have fallen in the "zone of twilight" and would be validated or not by contemporary imperatives and imponderables rather than by abstract theories of law.

v

Jackson's twilight zone thus seemed to admit a possibility of presidential emergency power. On the other hand, Jackson also took care to attack "the unarticulated assumption . . . that necessity knows no law." The Founding Fathers, he said, had known emergencies; they were children of revolution. But they had known too that emergency might be the pretext for usurpation. That was why, aside from a single exception, the suspension of *habeas corpus* in time of rebellion or invasion, they had made no express provision for exercise of extraordinary authority. "I do not think," Jackson said with a certain force, "we rightfully may so amend their work." Here Jackson disagreed with Lincoln, who, less convincingly, had claimed the *habeas corpus* clause as a precedent for broad suspension of constitutional rights in the presidential interest in time of rebellion or invasion.

In any case, Jackson felt that presidential claims to act beyond Congress required the most suspicious examination. For one thing, Congress itself had long since evolved a technique by which normal executive powers could be enlarged to embrace an emergency; "under this procedure we retain Government by law — special, temporary law, perhaps, but law none the less." Jackson pointed out that Franklin Roosevelt, though confronted by no less a catastrophe than the imminent collapse of the economic system, had not taken this as a justification for rule by decree;

the New Deal had been founded on delegated congressional power, not on inherent presidential power. So too Frankfurter: "The fact that power exists in the Government does not vest it in the President. The need for new legislation does not enact it." It was an illuminating commentary on the changes in the Presidency since the Second World War that the four justices who had been closest to Roosevelt—Frankfurter, Douglas, Black, Jackson, fervent New Dealers all fifteen years before—saw no precedent in the New Deal for the steel seizure and united in voting against Truman's enlargement of independent presidential authority.

Where did all this leave Locke, Jefferson and Lincoln? Here the materials for divination grow more enigmatic than ever. Jackson was evidently against the law of necessity, except when Congress was silent and contemporary imperatives and imponderables might sustain presidential initiative. This was quite an exception. Justice Douglas said, "What a President may do as a matter of expediency or extremity may never reach a definitive constitutional decision" Justice Burton said, "The present situation is not comparable to that of an imminent invasion or threatened attack. We do not face the issue of what might be the President's constitutional power to meet such catastrophic situations." Justice Clark, who agreed with the majority in result but not in argument, went even farther. The Constitution in his view *did* "grant to the President extensive authority in time of grave and imperative national emergency. In fact, to my thinking such a grant may well be necessary to the very existence of the Constitution itself." In describing this authority, Clark said he did not care whether it was called "inherent," "residual," "implied," "emergency," "aggregate" or whatever; it existed, and had to exist. But having gone so far toward Lockean prerogative, Clark pulled back. In the case of the steel seizure, he said, Congress had laid down specific procedures, and Truman should have followed them. Yet "in the absence of such action by Congress, the President's independent power to act depends upon the gravity of the situation confronting the nation."

Clark's concern with the gravity of the particular emergency made the essential point. Truman claimed the strike as one of the greatest emergencies the country had ever faced, and Chief Justice Vinson wrote in his dissent that "the survival of the Republic itself might be at stake." But the opinions of the Court majority registered the sense of Congress and the nation, volubly expressed in the two months since the seizure, that Truman and Vinson had it wrong, and that this was simply not an emergency calling for drastic recourse to inherent presidential power. Had Congress not pre-empted the field and had the nation seen the necessity as truly imperious, a majority of justices — perhaps, as one counts the escape clauses in their opinions, all save Black — would probably have upheld the President.

The decision thus by no means excluded presidential initiative in authentic and indisputable crisis. But the Court made it clear that such initiative could not be exerted every time a President proclaimed a crisis not readily visible to the rest of the nation. In 1807 the judicial and public response to Jefferson's overreaction to the Burr conspiracy had disclosed certain practical limits on presidential claims of emergency power. In 1952 the judicial and public response to Truman's overreaction to the steel strike helped further define the conditions in which Presidents might persuasively invoke the Lockean prerogative.

The case contributed one further clarification to the problem of prerogative, or rather revived a distinction recognized in the early republic but blurred during the Civil War and forgotten thereafter. Popular comment on the steel seizure, as Lucius Wilmerding, Jr., noted in an acute article, revolved around two antagonistic doctrines: the view that the President had legal authority, inherent in the Constitution, to act on his own for the nation in cases of imperious necessity; and the view that no necessity, however dire, could excuse the President from exact obedience to the Constitution and the law. Wilmerding found these doctrines "equally fallacious and equally dangerous," and the Founding Fathers, he thought, would have rejected both. Their view, he said, was that grave emergency might sometimes require high officers of government to act outside the law in order to save the nation; but, when they had done so, they were not to pretend that the act was legal but were rather to confess the illegal act to Congress, state the reasons for it and throw themselves, as Jefferson had said, upon the rectitude of their motives and the justice of their country.

Wilmerding drew here an important distinction between the *abuse* of power and the *usurpation* of power. Usurpation seemed to him the less dangerous, both because it was less likely to happen and, when it did happen, it created no constitutional precedents. The President who usurped power in an emergency would be "careful to see that the necessity which he pleads to excuse his act (not to justify his power) is indeed invincible." But the President who could claim *legal* sanction for extreme acts would move with less caution, would be less scrupulous about weighing the necessity and would set dangerous precedents for the future. Let extreme actions, in short, stand or fall as they related to particular national crises rather than incorporate them into a legal system, where they could be applied thereafter without regard to the gravity of the crisis. Would such actions, even when not permitted by the Constitution, be in a real sense faithful to its spirit when necessary to its preservation? This had been Lincoln's point. But Wilmerding did not discuss Lincoln and concluded ambiguously that, while the Constitution conferred no legal power to act outside the law in emergencies, none the less emergency action outside the law was a "constitutional doctrine."

If the Court did not deny the Presidency the resort to emergency power in all circumstances, it did valuably challenge the presidential mystique in vogue among historians and political scientists. Executive power, as Jackson observed, had the advantage of concentration in a single person chosen by the whole nation, who became in consequence the unique focus of public hope and expectation. "In drama, magnitude and finality his decisions so far overshadow any other that almost alone he fills the public eye and ear." His prestige as chief of state and his command of public opinion blotted out those supposed to check and balance his power. "I cannot be brought to believe," Jackson said, "that this country will suffer if the Court refuses further to aggrandize the presidential office, already so potent and so relatively immune from judicial review, at the expense of Congress."

The Presidency, in short, was not the only source of wisdom in government. This very proposition, however, sent Congress an urgent message — a most solemn judicial reminder that congressional default was a large cause of presidential aggrandizement and that Congress, not the Court, had the key role to play in restoring the constitutional balance. Again Jackson made the point most vividly. "I have no illusion," he wrote, "that any decision by this Court can keep power in the hands of Congress if it is not wise and timely in meeting its problems." When a crisis challenged the President, it challenged Congress equally, or perhaps primarily. Recalling Napoleon's maxim that the tools belonged to the man who could use them, Jackson issued his own challenge to Congress: "We [the Court] may say that power to legislate for emergencies belongs in the hands of Congress, but only Congress itself can prevent power from slipping through its fingers." [36] As for Truman, he yielded at once to the Court and ordered the government out of the mills.

VI

For its part, Congress was beginning to thresh around to find ways to reclaim abandoned authority. Having lost control of its war-making power, it turned now to the constitutional powers it still possessed — notably the power of the purse, the treaty-making power and the power of investigation.

In foreign affairs Congress asserted itself most successfully in the area of foreign aid, where executive policy was entirely dependent on annual legislative appropriations. Here Congress neither then nor later hesitated to tie up executive programs with all manner of hortatory prescriptions, rigid stipulations and detailed specifications, often over presidential opposition. Where economic assistance became a major part of the substance of policy — in Latin America, for example — the Presidency therefore lost substantive power to Congress. When Monroe had announced his Doctrine, Theodore Roosevelt his Corollary, Franklin Roosevelt his Good Neighbor Policy, they did not seek or need congressional assent. But when Kennedy called for the Alliance for Progress, he was at the mercy of Congress at every step along the way.

The problem of the treaty power was more complicated. For several years, conservatives had been whipping themselves into a rage over the agreements, some of which they supposed had yet to be disclosed, negotiated by Roosevelt, Churchill and Stalin at Yalta. Prime Minister Attlee's visit to Washington in December 1950 excited new fears of summit hanky-panky; and 24 senators put in a resolution declaring it the sense of the Senate that the President not only report in full on his talks but refrain from entering into any agreements with Attlee that might bind the United States. Acheson regarded this as "an infringement of the constitutional prerogative of the President to conduct negotiations." [37] So it probably was, but the resolution, while failing, received 30 votes. Among the senators voting to deny the President authority to make agreements with visiting heads of state was Nixon of California. (A kindly Congress failed to remind Nixon of this vote when Brezhnev came to the White House 23 years later.)

Congressional agitation over presidential agreements soon flowed into the movement for the Bricker Amendment. This Amendment, extensively pressed in the early 1950s and at one time claiming the support of 57 senators, went through a succession of orchestrations, but the pervading theme was that treaties and executive agreements should have no domestic standing without internal legislation. This meant that positive action by Congress as a whole, and in many cases by state legislatures as well, would be necessary to put international compacts into effect. An early version of the Amendment specified that "executive agreements shall not be made in lieu of treaties." But, since Bricker was no more successful in 1952 in defining the distinction between the two than Monroe had been in 1818 or Sutherland in 1936, he soon turned to a more general clause empowering Congress "to regulate all executive and other agreements with any foreign power or international organization."

By 1954 he dropped this too in favor of a still more general reference to "a treaty or other international agreement" as requiring legislation valid in the absence of international agreement in order to become effective as internal law in the United States. The Bricker Amendment, despite successive dilutions, was opposed by the Eisenhower administration and finally beaten in the Senate.

In the meantime, a more deadly attack had been launched on the executive. This was the movement so gaudily incarnated by Senator Joseph McCarthy of Wisconsin. Many Americans of the time no doubt agreed with William F. Buckley, Jr., who wrote, as late as 1954, "As long as McCarthyism fixes its goal with its present precision, it is a movement around which men of good will and stern morality can close ranks." [38] But others, conceivably of even better will and sterner morality, regarded the havoc wrought by McCarthy as the ultimate consequence of congressional intrusion into the executive conduct of foreign affairs — and regarded too the prolonged complaisance of President Eisenhower in face of the McCarthy assault as evidence that congressional aggression had placed the Presidency in serious danger. "The current gravitation of power into the hands of Congress at the expense of the executive," the political scientist Wilfred E. Binkley, author of a standard work on *President and Congress,* wrote in 1953, "is a phenomenon so fatuous as to be incredible if the facts were not so patent." [39] "What the President has not yet faced up to," another political scientist, Clinton Rossiter, wrote the same year, "is the blunt truth that Congress is now completely unable — technically, politically, spiritually — to give the American people the kind of leadership essential to survival. . . . His experiment in co-operation has failed miserably. He must reassert the legitimate prerogatives of the Presidential office." [40]

But Eisenhower had come to the White House as a Whig (in the American sense) — that is, as one opposed to presidential usurpation. He believed that Roosevelt and Truman had gathered too much power into the executive branch, and he hoped to restore what he saw as the constitutional balance between the Presidency and Congress. He was therefore reluctant by definition to get into contention with the legislative branch. Yet McCarthyism finally provoked Eisenhower, against his Whig principles, into an astonishingly militant assertion of presidential prerogative.

The issue was the old one of congressional access to executive information. It now took, with McCarthy, the more modern and less defensible form of congressional insistence on access to the security files of government employees. The Second World War, as we have seen, had introduced loyalty investigations and dossiers, and the Cold War brought with it an extension and institutionalization of the government security system. This system was relatively immune to outside control, whether executive or legislative. Security men could easily intimidate their presumed superiors in the executive departments; few officials wished the reputation of inadequate devotion to the protection of state secrets. As for Congress, its interest in this period was not in tempering the security system but in denouncing it for its moments of restraint and scruple. The problem of Stalinist penetration and espionage was perfectly real and sufficiently serious. But uncontrolled reaction to this problem was a problem too. In the long run it may have been a worse problem.

Truman had established a security system partly to make sure that Soviet espionage of the sort uncovered in Ottawa immediately after the war would not escape discovery in Washington, partly to head off congressional (and Republican) criticism of executive (and Democratic) indifference to the Red menace. The House Committee on Un-American Activities, that self-appointed guardian of American political purity, decided in early 1948 that a blameless physicist, then serving as director of the National Bureau of Standards in the Commerce Department, was the weakest link in American security. The Committee thereupon served a subpoena on the Department of Commerce Loyalty Board, directing it to hand over Dr. Condon's security files to the Committee. Averell Harriman, the Secretary of Commerce, commented acidly that he had seen nothing like this since he had left the Soviet Union, where he had served as wartime ambassador, and ignored the subpoena. This seems to have been in conformity with precedent; there apparently had been no instance in history when a head of department had gone before a congressional committee in response to a subpoena or had been held in contempt for refusal to do so.[41] A few days later Truman issued a general order to the executive branch to refer future congressional requests for employee loyalty records to the office of the President, where determination would be made according to "the public interest in the particular case." The House retaliated by adopting a resolution requiring executive disclosure to House committees of all information necessary "to enable them to properly perform the duties delegated to them by the Congress." The vote was 219 to 152. An especially ardent supporter of the resolution was Congressman Richard M. Nixon of California. Truman's contention that the President should judge what information could be released to Congress, Nixon said, "cannot stand from a constitutional standpoint." It would mean that "the President could have arbitrarily issued an Executive order in the Meyers case, the Teapot Dome case, or any other case denying the Congress of the United States information it needed to conduct an investigation of the executive department and the Congress would have no right to question his decision." [42]

The resolution died in the Senate, to the general applause of enlightened opinion. The right of the executive "to withhold certain kinds of information from Congress, and the public interest in having such information withheld," observed the *St. Louis Post-Dispatch* in a typical comment, "has been successfully defended since the time of President Jefferson." [43] Truman continued to withhold security files throughout his administration. In 1952 he extended this protection even to those already dismissed as security risks: "The reputations of these persons should not be besmirched unnecessarily by making their names public." Determined as ever to pass on his sacred trust unimpaired, he argued that no President had "ever complied with an order of the Legislative Branch directing the Executive Branch to produce confidential documents, the disclosure of which was considered by the President contrary to the public interest." He would not accept, he stoutly said, "any act of the Congress which would threaten or diminish so preeminently necessary a right of the Chief Executive." [44]

But Truman's withholding was confined to matters related to the performance of official duties. When it came to criminal questions, he withheld nothing. As Clark Mollenhoff, the mid-century scourge of official secrecy, later wrote, "The tax scandals of the Truman administration could have been concealed by a claim that all papers except final decisions were confidential executive communications." Instead, these preliminary communications — 'working papers' in a later usage — became the basis of criminal charges on which a White House aide and the Assistant Attorney General in charge of the tax division were sent to prison.[45]

VII

The Truman administration never produced an organized theory about the range of presidential power to deny information to Congress. However, in 1949 a Department of Justice attorney named Herman Wolkinson, writing on his own, published a detailed historical recital in the *Federal Bar Journal*. For more than 150 years, Wolkinson claimed, "Our Presidents have established, by precedent, that they and members of their Cabinet have an undoubted privilege and discretion to keep confidential, in the public interest, papers and information which require secrecy." The judgment was entirely the President's to make. "Courts have uniformly held that the Presidents and the heads of departments have an *uncontrolled discretion* to withhold the information and papers in the public interest" (emphasis added). When Presidents had fulfilled congressional requests, they had done so "only in a spirit of comity and good will, and not because there has been an effective means to compel them to do so." Wolkinson did not distinguish particularly between presidential power and presidential right but concluded in the end that power created right. He did not consider it likely that "the Supreme Court will ignore more than 150 years of legislative acquiescence in the assertion of that power." [46]

This never became the official doctrine of the Truman administration. According to Mollenhoff, the Department of Justice examined the memorandum, found it unsupported by law and by court cases and discarded it as of no value.[47] But when by 1954 the McCarthy inquisition had reached a degree of squalor that exhausted even Eisenhower's forbearance, the administration turned to Wolkinson as ultimate authority. Eisenhower might have confined executive denial to such specific and traditional categories as the protection of state secrets and of innocent persons. Instead, in a letter to the Secretary of Defense on May 17, 1954, he made the most absolute assertion of presidential right to withhold information from Congress ever uttered to that day in American history.

To the list of limited exceptions advanced by Presidents from Washington to Polk, Eisenhower added a new and virtually unlimited category of information which he declared deniable at presidential will: material generated by the internal deliberative processes of government. "It is essential to efficient and effective administration," Eisenhower wrote, "that employees of the Executive Branch be in a position to be completely candid in advising with each other on official matters." Therefore "it is not in the public interest that *any* of their conversations or communications, or *any* documents or reproductions, concerning such advice be disclosed." [48] The Attorney General in due course supplied a partial list of items to be withheld: "Interdepartmental memoranda, advisory opinions, recommendations of subordinates, informal working papers, material in personnel files, and the like, cannot be subject to disclosure if there is to be any orderly system of government." Disclosure, it was explained, would inhibit free debate within the executive branch and dry up the flow of candid analysis and recommendation necessary to wise decisions.[49]

Presidents since Jackson had claimed their own conversations and communications with their aides and with cabinet members as privileged, nor had Congress seriously disputed this. What was new was the idea that this privilege extended to everybody in the executive branch. The general diffusion throughout the bureaucracy of the personal immunity heretofore confined to the President himself represented a claim of boundless and unreviewable executive control of information in which the Whig Eisenhower outdid all his activist predecessors, including such renowned exponents of presidential power as Jackson, Lincoln and the two Roosevelts. The historic rule had been disclosure, with exceptions; the new rule was denial, with exceptions.

An accompanying memorandum by Attorney General Herbert Brownell sought to give the new rule legal color. This memorandum, plagiarizing shamefully and shamelessly from Herman Wolkinson, now made official what Wolkinson had written on his own authority and in identical language: that for over 150 years "our Presidents have established, by precedent, that they and members of their Cabinet and other heads of executive departments have an undoubted privilege and discretion to keep confidential, in the public interest, papers and information which require secrecy." Sticking faithfully to the original script, Brownell continued, "Courts have uniformly held that the President and the heads of departments have an uncontrolled discretion to withhold the information and papers in the public interest." Attorney General Jackson's "repeatedly" of 1941 had now become Attorney General Brownell's (and Herman Wolkinson's) "uniformly" in 1954; but Eisenhower's Attorney General was no more successful than Roosevelt's in citing a single court case involving executive denial of information to Congress, and for the same reason — that there was not a single case to cite. Then, like Jackson and Wolkinson, Brownell went through the litany of alleged executive precedent — the same cases as Wolkinson and often the same words.[50]

"Uncontrolled discretion" was now official doctrine, and presidential immunity covered all exchanges within the executive branch. Yet the detestation of McCarthy was by this time so universal that few noted the absolute sweep of Eisenhower's claim. "The committee has no more right to know the details of

what went on in these inner Administration councils," said the
New York Times, "than the Administration would have the right
to know what went on in an executive session of a Committee of
Congress." "President Eisenhower was abundantly right," said
the *Washington Post,* "in protecting the confidential nature of executive conversations in this instance." [51] An exception to the
general enthusiasm was Telford Taylor, who wrote in 1955 that,
if Eisenhower's directive were applied generally and literally,
Congress "would frequently be shut off from access to documents to which they are clearly entitled by tradition, common
sense, and good governmental practice." For this reason he considered it unlikely that the ruling would endure beyond the particular controversy that precipitated it.[52]

Taylor was right in his analysis but wrong in his prediction.
The Eisenhower directive ushered in the greatest orgy of executive denial in American history. From June 1955 to June 1960
there were at least 44 instances when officials in the executive
branch refused information to Congress on the basis of the Eisenhower directive — more cases in those five years than in the
first century of American history. By 1956 the Department of
the Interior, in rejecting a congressional request, even explained
that while the documents "did not contain any information
which the Department would be unwilling to make available to
Congress, it, nevertheless, considered itself bound to 'honor the
principle which has been followed from the beginning of our
Government.'" How quickly Americans establish traditions! The
principle by that time was two years old.[53] Not only were officials at some distance from the White House turning down congressional requests on their own motion, but in 1955 the Attorney General bestowed the power of refusal on independent
regulatory agencies. In 1958 the Secretary of the Air Force even
turned down a request from the Comptroller General for a report on the management of the ballistic missile program — an
act in patent violation of the Budget and Accounting Act of
1921, which assured the Comptroller General access to all relevant records.

That same year, when William P. Rogers, the new Attorney

General, attempted a comprehensive justification of the spreading practice (an exercise in which, like his predecessor, he freely appropriated language as well as doctrine from the now forgotten Herman Wolkinson), he made the first official use I have encountered of the term "executive privilege." [54] Executive privilege had the advantage of sounding like a very old term. It passed rapidly political discourse and very soon (though, so far as I have been able to discover, no President or Attorney General used it before the Eisenhower administration) acquired the patina of ancient and hallowed doctrine. What had been for a century and a half sporadic executive practice employed in very unusual circumstances was now in a brief decade hypostatized into sacred constitutional principle.

The casual adoption by Eisenhower of the doctrine of absolute executive privilege showed how the combination of congressional delinquency with the executive perspective could lead even a Whig administration to aggrandize the Presidency. "The Teapot Dome scandals of the Harding Administration," Clark Mollenhoff wrote, "could have been covered up if government officials had then applied even the mildest form of executive privilege as laid down by President Eisenhower." [55] Nor was the process of aggrandizement confined to domestic matters. It was equally marked in foreign affairs.

VIII

Here the Eisenhower administration began by doing what Truman had neglected to do after the invasion of South Korea; that is, it asked Congress to pass joint resolutions at moments when the government faced the possibility of military engagement overseas.

So in 1955 Eisenhower requested a joint resolution to cover possible American military action around Formosa. The President's message was ambiguous, probably inescapably so, in its constitutional argument. He said that "authority for some of the actions which might be required would be inherent in the authority of the Commander in Chief" but that congressional ratification would publicly "establish" that authority; he also spoke cryptically of "the authority that may be accorded by Congress." In any case, Congress overwhelmingly voted a resolution by which the President was "authorized to employ the Armed Forces of the United States *as he deems necessary*" in defense of Formosa, the Pescadores and "related positions and territories of that area." [56]

What kind of congressional authorization was thereby implied? Unlike, say, the resolutions by which Congress had authorized war against Tripoli in 1802 and Algeria in 1815, the Formosa Resolution ordered no action and named no enemy, except as the President might thereafter decide. Rather it committed Congress to the approval of hostilities without knowledge of the specific situation in which the hostilities would begin. It was therefore a contingency authorization of the sort that Hamilton had unavailingly proposed in 1799, that Madison had declined in 1810 as an unconstitutional delegation of the war-making power and that Congress, for the same reason, had subsequently refused to Jackson and to Buchanan.

Still the very process of consideration offered Congress a chance to deal with the ambiguities and contingencies. It lacked any inclination to do so. The Old Guard of the "great debate" fell silent. Taft had died in 1953; Coudert was replaced by John V. Lindsay in 1956; others felt less strongly about presidential war now that a Republican was in the White House. As for the Democrats, they remained loyal to the theory of presidential power Truman had expounded over Korea. While voting for the resolution, they rejected the opportunity to affirm a congressional claim. Lyndon B. Johnson, the Senate leader, said, "We are not going to take the responsibility out of the hands of the constitutional leader and try to arrogate it to ourselves." Sam Rayburn, veteran of forty years in the House, now Speaker, old Mr. Congress himself, said that he did not think that "any one who has ever studied our Constitution" could deny that the President already had the power the resolution purported to confer on him. "If the President had done what is proposed here without consulting with the Congress," Rayburn said, "he would have had no criticism from me." Indeed, Eisenhower might be setting a "dangerous" precedent if he, "as Commander in Chief of our Armed Forces, under any and all circumstances, should feel it his duty to come before the Congress and ask for a resolution such as this." This exercise in congressional self-immolation was generally commended. Mr. Justice Krock of the *New York Times* wrote, "Not a scrap in the Constitution or the statutes required [the President] to consult Congress in the circumstances." Many historians, this writer included, agreed. Even Walter Lippmann felt that the President's authority plainly extended to the commitment of armed forces without congressional approval to combat in defense of Formosa and the Pescadores, though he regretted the phrase about "related positions and territories." [57]

Two years later Eisenhower asked Congress for a resolution that would authorize him to use American force to help Middle Eastern governments "against overt armed aggression from any nation controlled by International Communism." Former President Truman, faithful to the precepts of the President's Club, promptly said, "Only the President is in possession of all the facts. . . . Congress has no alternative but to go along." [58] But Senator Fulbright, who had reflected on the experience of the Formosa Resolution, was not so sure. The 1955 resolution had purported to be — perhaps could have become, had Congress so willed — a sharing of the war-making power. But in fact it had been nothing of the sort. The President had shared the responsibility but monopolized the power. The new resolution seemed more of the same — "no real prior consultation with Congress" but rather a contrived atmosphere of "suspense and urgency . . . designed to manage the Congress, to coerce it into signing this blank check." Why should Congress thus "abdicate its constitutional powers"?

Fulbright, citing Jefferson on the law of necessity and self-preservation, did not doubt that a President had inherent power to use armed forces in an emergency without congressional authorization. But, if this were so, then a resolution of the kind proposed was "entirely superfluous and positively bad" —

superfluous because the President already had emergency power; bad because, if Congress established a practice of formally granting such authority, Presidents might come to believe they could not act without a congressional resolution, and this might "jeopardize the life of the Republic in a true emergency."

If the last possibility seemed fanciful, Fulbright nonetheless made a fruitful application of the distinction between the abuse and the usurpation of power. If there were a crisis in the Middle East, let Eisenhower act on his own and then justify his action to Congress rather than have Congress implicate itself in advance by awarding the President power that, because it was undefined, invited abuse. "Here we are asked for only $200 million without restrictions or safeguards. If we grant this," he asked with a prescience that would have been better applied to the Tonkin Gulf resolution seven years later, "how can we deny a similar request for 2 billion next year?" [59]

Fulbright was making two points. The first was that the resolution process was meaningless in the absence of serious consultation. All it did, especially when put in the form of contingency authorization, was to hand the executive a blank check. The second was that, if a real emergency left no time for congressional consultation, the President should act on his own judgment and at his own peril. He would be more likely in such circumstances to be careful in what he did than if he were granted contingency authority to start hostilities for which he could hold Congress equally responsible.

The Senate Foreign Relations Committee went along with Fulbright to the extent of striking out the idea of congressional authorization, leaving the Middle East resolution as a mere declaration of United States policy. The effect on Eisenhower, however, was to convince him less of the need for serious consultation with Congress than of his inherent authority to employ armed force at presidential will. When in 1958, in what seems in retrospect a mysterious and hazardous adventure, he sent 14,000 American troops into Lebanon, he invoked not his own Middle East resolution but the ever more capacious presidential prerogative.

The congressional dilemma was acute. The Eisenhower administration had no doubt gone into resolutions out of Whig principle. But, as the years had passed, it had seemed to seek resolutions less because it really thought Congress had authority or wisdom in the premises than because a resolution, by involving Congress in the takeoff, might incriminate it in a crash landing. The process had become a means by which the executive, in Fulbright's later phrase, sought not advice and consent but "consent without advice." [60] It was a rite of propitiation in which Presidents yielded no claims and Congress made none but which provided a metaphor of partnership; it was in domestic terms what someone had said of the Kellogg Pact—"an international kiss." On the other hand, the idea that Congress should intervene in foreign policy by, for example, demanding control over troop deployment was still regarded as isolationism and thus to be abhorred by right-thinking men. The result of the impasse was a congressional disposition to throw up hands and let the Presidency proceed on its own.

IX

The executive branch thus continued, it seemed inexorably, to accumulate power at the expense of Congress—and this in spite of the postwar reaction against the Presidency, in spite of an intermittently, if often irresponsibly, aggressive legislature, in spite of a whistle-blowing Supreme Court, in spite of Eisenhower's own Whig predilections. The fact that a President who had started out so deeply opposed to executive aggrandizement should have ended by accelerating the transfer of power to the Presidency suggested that deeper forces were at work.

Two things had happened: the belief that the world was greatly endangered by the spread of communism had generated a profound conviction of crisis in the United States; and the conviction of crisis had generated a foreign policy that placed the separation of powers prescribed by the American Constitution under unprecedented, and at times unbearable, strain. It is not necessary here to argue whether crisis was real or imagined and the foreign policy decent or imperialistic. Surely all those adjectives applied at one time or another. I personally have no doubt that the United States was everlastingly right to do its best to prevent the Stalinization of western Europe, and that without the Marshall Plan and NATO this would have been a most serious prospect. But I have no doubt that the Soviet Union felt endangered too, and that each side undertook on defensive grounds actions which the other side saw as aggressive and intolerable. The Cold War therefore involved a wide measure of reciprocal misperception as well as perfectly genuine differences in principle and clashes of interest. Each side corroborated the fears of the other and thereby heightened the interlocking delusions bred by crisis. On the American side, I believe that the policy of containment was initially correct and necessary, but that it came under the hypnosis of crisis to confuse political and military threats, to lose a sense of limit and discrimination and to engender a mystique that poorly served its original aims. But, whatever the motives and merits of American foreign policy in these years, our present analysis requires us only to assess the impact of that policy on American political institutions.

For in the 1950s American foreign policy called on the American government to do things no American government had ever tried to do before. The new American approach to world affairs, nurtured in the sense of omnipresent crisis, set new political objectives, developed new military capabilities, devised new diplomatic techniques, invented new instruments of foreign operations and instituted a new hierarchy of values. Every one of these innovations encouraged the displacement of power, both practical and constitutional, from an increasingly acquiescent Congress into an increasingly imperial Presidency.

The new political objective was to preserve noncommunist nations (or the Free World as it was known in those heady days) from communist subversion or conquest. Washington appointed itself the savior of human freedom and endowed itself with worldwide responsibility and a worldwide charter. Moscow did the same thing on behalf, as it claimed with equal validity, of Marxist revolution. The guardianship of world freedom required, first of all, an enormous military establishment. In the forties Truman had substantially demobilized the wartime Army and then held national-security expenditures down to an average of $13 billion a year in 1947 through 1950. But Korea changed all that by defining communism as a military as well as a political threat. Two years after the invasion of South Korea, the United States had 3.6 million men under arms. This fact by itself vastly increased presidential power. Before the Second World War, Presidents, no matter how martial their fantasies, were restricted in their use of armed force by the number of soldiers and sailors, happily limited, available to them. Only Lincoln had dared increase the Army without congressional consent, and his necessity was unique. After Korea, the availability of great standing armies and navies placed extraordinary and unprecedented resources in presidential hands.

At the same time, the United States in the Eisenhower years vastly expanded its international commitments, moving far beyond its historic interests in western Europe, the western hemisphere and the maritime Pacific to establish a far-flung network of treaties embracing nearly fifty nations and stretching to remote corners of the planet. The 'pactomania' of the 1950s made it more difficult than ever for Congress to prevent Presidents from deploying troops as treaty commitments and the national security were deemed to require (and the President was the judge of both). Presidents therefore acquired the habit of moving the armed forces as if they were institutional, if not personal, property.

Moreover, the problem of dealing with an unscrupulous and unpredictable enemy, always pressing on and always capable of striking without warning, was held in the fifties to call for a diplomacy of brinkmanship — that is, for constant readiness to go to the brink of war if it were necessary to force an enemy to back down. This, John Foster Dulles believed, was the essence of peace-keeping. Such a policy, dependent on secrecy of intention and rapidity of decision, was hardly amenable to congressional control or even accessible to congressional knowledge. It was for the sake of brinkmanship that the joint resolutions of the Eisenhower era asked Congress to delegate its war-making authority and leave the event to presidential discretion.

The revolution in the technology of war increased the premium placed on the capacity for swift and secret action residing uniquely in the Presidency. Nor did the President or Congress or public opinion see this as executive usurpation. It appeared rather the ineluctable conclusion imposed on the American government by the age of nuclear weapons. "As Commander-in-Chief of the armed forces," Fulbright wrote in 1961, "the President has full responsibility, which cannot be shared, for military decisions in a world in which the difference between safety and cataclysm can be a matter of hours or even minutes." [61] The political scientist Richard Neustadt told a Senate committee in 1963 that, while the Constitution had contemplated that judgments on peace and war should come from the President and Congress combined, this could no longer work in the nuclear age: "When it comes to action risking war, technology has modified the Constitution." The President, perforce, became the only man in the system capable of exercising judgment under the extraordinary limits now imposed by secrecy, complexity and time.[62] "Is there really a way," Eric Goldman, a historian who served in Lyndon Johnson's White House, asked as late as 1970, "to restrict the powers of the Commander in Chief . . . when one man's swiftly pressing the button may be necessary for some degree of national survival, or his prompt decision to use non-nuclear armed forces could be essential to achieving a purpose generally agreed upon by the country?" [63]

Only the President could take the nation to the brink, and only he (He?) could press the ultimate button. He had to be entrusted with these responsibilities because he was the only officer of government elected by all the people. And he could be trusted with them because he knew better than anyone else what the problems were. Where Congress had to rely on what it could spell out in the *Washington Post* and *New York Times,* the President received every day a flood of authoritative intelligence from his diplomatic, military and economic experts all over the world.

Intelligence was more than ever a crucial issue, made so by the extent of commitment as well as by the pressure of decision. It was therefore imperative that the information flowing in to the President be complete and accurate. So the National Security Act of 1947 set up the Central Intelligence Agency. For the first time in its peacetime history the United States cast out a worldwide net of intelligence collection and analysis. Secret intelligence implied agents; and agents could be used for political as well as for intelligence purposes. So intelligence led on to covert political and military operations — rendered all the more necessary, it was argued, because the United States had no choice but to employ clandestine tactics in order to counter the dirty tricks of an infinitely wily and unprincipled foe.

Though President Eisenhower displayed prudent skepticism about conventional war waged by regular forces, this did not mean that he was skeptical about intervention *per se*. Instead he made the CIA the primary instrument of American intervention in other countries. The CIA helped to overthrow governments in Iran (1953) and Guatemala (1954), failed to do so in Indonesia (1958), helped to install governments in Egypt (1954) and Laos (1959), organized an expedition of Cuban refugees against the Castro regime (1960–1961) and engaged in a multitude of lesser experiments in subvention and subversion. In no way perhaps did the old Whig more effectively deprive the Congress of a voice in foreign policy than by confiding so much power to an agency so securely out of congressional reach. Congress, it is true, had set up the CIA; but through the years successive National Security Councils had, in effect, amended the National Security and Central Intelligence Acts by a long series of Top Secret NSC directives, thereby creating a 'secret charter' to which the Agency became far more responsive than to the statutes themselves. Though the CIA was persistently, ingeniously and sometimes irresponsibly engaged in undertakings that confronted the nation with the possibility of war, Congress had no effective means of control or of oversight or even of finding out what the Agency was up to (and has none to this day).

The new American approach to world affairs, the obsession

with crisis, the illusion of 'world leadership,' the obligations of duty so cunningly intertwined with the opportunities of power, carried forward the process, begun during the Second World War, of elevating 'national security' into a supreme value. No sensible person would reject national security, realistically construed, as a self-evident necessity of state. But, under the stimulus of the Cold War, a mystique of national security, increasingly defined in short-run military terms, emerged as the decisive criterion of right and wrong. If Chiang Kai-shek, Batista, Diem or Franco were sufficiently anticommunist, national security demanded their support, whatever the ultimate consequence for their own people or, indeed, for longer-run American influence in the world. National security demanded opposition to a nuclear test ban and other forms of arms limitation. And national security became the overriding value at home as well as abroad. A presidential system of internal security was unleashed to achieve such dubious triumphs as the withdrawal in 1953 of the security clearance of the physicist J. Robert Oppenheimer, the father of the atomic bomb. A government review board even declared in a frightening phrase that the Oppenheimer case "demonstrated that the Government can search . . . the soul of an individual whose relationship to his Government is in question." It added ominously that national security "in times of peril must be absolute." [64]

Everything seemed both to compel and to license the increasing centralization of foreign policy in the Presidency, and everything therefore undermined the constitutional separation of powers. This was not to say that the American Constitution was a mandate for isolationism. It could easily have sustained the weight of a responsible and selective internationalism, addressed to the historic interests of the United States, committed only to regions of the world where American security was directly and vitally involved and where American intervention was locally sought and could be locally effective. The separation of powers was in no trouble before the Korean War, nor need it have been in trouble during that war.

But the Constitution could not easily sustain the weight of the indiscriminate globalism to which the Korean War gave birth. It was hard to reconcile the separation of powers with a foreign policy animated by an indignant ideology and marked by a readiness to intervene speedily and unilaterally in the affairs of other states, nor with an executive branch that saw everywhere on earth interests and threats demanding immediate, and often secret, American commitment and action. This vision of the American role in the world unbalanced and overwhelmed the Constitution.

In the decade after Korea Congress receded not alone from the effort to control the war-making power but almost from the effort to participate in it, except on occasions when national-security zealots on the Hill condemned the executive branch for inadequate bellicosity. Mesmerized by the supposed need for instant response to constant crisis, overawed by what the Senate Foreign Relations Committee later called "the cult of executive expertise," [65] confused in its own mind as to what wise policy should be, delighted to relinquish responsibility, Congress readily capitulated to what Corwin at the start of the fifties had called "high-flying" theses of presidential prerogative.

At the same time, the national-security consensus swallowed up unwritten as well as written checks on executive supremacy in foreign affairs. The *Washington Post* and the *New York Times* were as ardent defenders of the Presidency as anyone in the White House. The academic community harbored few doubters. Liberals and conservatives agreed on the presidential mystique if on nothing else. Consider liberal comment in the year 1960. Early in the year Senator John F. Kennedy observed that, however large the congressional role in domestic policy, "it is the President alone who must make the major decisions of our foreign policy." [66] In the spring Dean Rusk of the Rockefeller Foundation pronounced the Commander in Chief clause "an independent source of constitutional authority." "As Commander-in-Chief the President can deploy the Armed Forces and order them into active operation. In an age of missiles and hydrogen warheads, his powers are as large as the situation requires." [67] Early the next year Fulbright even said that "for the existing requirements of American foreign policy we have hobbled the President by too niggardly a grant of power." While it was "distasteful and dangerous to vest the executive with powers unchecked and unbalanced," the question was "whether we have any choice but to do so. . . . The price of democratic survival in a world of aggressive totalitarianism is to give up some of the democratic luxuries of the past." [68] As late as 1965, on the eve of President Johnson's inauguration, the political scientist Louis W. Koenig published an article concisely entitled "More Power To the President (Not Less)." [69]

Conservatives were no less eager to transfer war-making power to the executive. "It is a rather interesting thing," Senator Dirksen, then Republican leader, told the Senate in 1967, " — I have run down many legal cases before the Supreme Court — that I have found as yet no delimitation on the power of the Commander in Chief under the Constitution." [70] "The Constitution," said Senator Goldwater, the right-wing Republican presidential candidate in 1964, "gives the President, not the Congress, the primary war-making powers." "There is no question," he added, "that the President can take military action at any time he feels danger for the country or, stretching a point, for its position in the world." [71] In this state of intellectual and moral intimidation, Congress forgot even the claim for foreign policy consultation and was thrilled when the executive bothered to tell what he planned to do. And overburdened Presidents, who already, God knows, had enough problems and worries without taking off long hours to inform and propitiate Congress, gratefully accepted the royal prerogative.

X

This was the prevailing atmosphere when Kennedy became President in 1961. One felt then more than ever the difference between the domestic-policy Presidency and the foreign-policy Presidency. Kennedy was elected by an exceedingly small margin. Democratic control of Congress was more nominal than real because of the number of southern Democrats, especially in the

House, who voted with Republicans on domestic issues. Congress itself, denied a voice in basic foreign policy and struggling for institutional survival, fought back where it could — on foreign aid, on the defense budget and in domestic affairs generally. In domestic affairs Kennedy was a somewhat beleaguered President.

He was sensitive to his political problems. Also, he had served in both House and Senate. Though Eisenhower had wished to redress the imbalance between the executive and Congress while Kennedy proposed to be a "strong" President, Kennedy did not see presidential strength simply in terms of the independent exercise of authority. Eight years in the Senate under Eisenhower, for example, had left him greatly irritated by the abuse of executive privilege. His Attorney General, and brother, who had been counsel to congressional committees, shared this irritation. Neither was inclined to change now that they were in the executive branch. The issue arose at once when Congressman Porter Hardy of Virginia demanded certain foreign aid documents. The new State Department, operating on the old directives, asserted executive privilege on its own initiative and in the sweeping Eisenhower manner. When the question came to Kennedy's attention, he intervened, and 48 hours later the documents were released.

Kennedy invoked executive privilege only once — in February 1962 when a Senate committee, on an expedition of harassment, demanded to know by name which of Secretary McNamara's subordinates had deleted unduly warlike passages from speeches by fire-eating generals and admirals. The Secretary of Defense, Kennedy said, had laid down the guidelines and accepted the responsibility; it would not be possible to maintain an orderly department, he instructed McNamara, if your subordinates "instead of you and your senior associates, are to be individually answerable to the Congress, as well as to you, for their internal acts and advice." When the claim of privilege came before the committee, Senator Stennis, its chairman, said, "The chair sustains the plea" [72] — a careful congressional reservation, conceding no right to the executive.

Kennedy's ground sounded a bit like Eisenhower's theory that executive privilege could be invoked to protect the internal administrative process. But Kennedy disclaimed any general principle of denial: "each case must be judged on its merits." Congressman John Moss, chairman of the Government Information subcommittee of the House, promptly asked the President to amplify his disclaimer in order to "prevent the rash of restrictions on government information" that had followed the Eisenhower statement. Kennedy replied that his instruction to McNamara had been "limited to that specific request." His policy, he said, was that "executive privilege can be invoked only by the President and will not be used without specific Presidential approval." He thus both rejected the sweeping Eisenhower claim to uncontrolled discretion in the withholding of executive information and ended the Eisenhower practice of delegating such discretion to lower government officials. Kennedy's "Draconian edict," as Raoul Berger has called it, halted the Eisenhower splurge of executive privilege. As Secretary of State Rusk observed, "When your President tells you that he is very reluctant to invoke executive privilege you try to avoid the situation as much as you can." [73] Still, as Congressman Moss reflected a year later, "The powerful genie of executive privilege is momentarily confined but can be uncorked by future Presidents." [74]

But in foreign affairs Congress and the executive alike, as if under hypnosis, unquestionably accepted the thesis of executive supremacy — a thesis reinforced, as we have seen, by Eisenhower's decision to place so much unvouchered power in the hands of the CIA. At a last meeting before the inauguration, Eisenhower told Kennedy that it was "the policy of this government" to aid anti-Castro guerrilla forces "to the utmost." Mentioning the anti-Castro legion he had put under CIA training in Guatemala, Eisenhower recommended that "this effort be continued and accelerated." [75] In the nature of things the Bay of Pigs operation was not to be disclosed to Congress. It never occurred to Eisenhower even to discuss informally with senior members of Congress the project of an attack organized by the United States against a neighboring state with which Washington (till January

1961) had diplomatic relations. Kennedy did solicit the opinion of Senator Fulbright, who had become chairman of the Foreign Relations Committee in 1959, and asked him to a meeting with the planners of that misbegotten undertaking, where Fulbright made, to no avail, the most sensible series of remarks uttered in any of those dismal sessions. But Kennedy did this more or less by accident and out of personal regard for Fulbright's intelligence rather than in official recognition of his status.

After the Bay of Pigs Kennedy took some steps to rein in the CIA and established the so-called 303 Committee as a mechanism for executive control. But CIA secrecy continued to shelter clandestine operations in Southeast Asia and further confirmed presidential domination of the war-making power. In other situations containing the threat of war, the Berlin problem was in the phase of negotiations and remained properly in the hands of the executive, with Congress acting when appropriations were required (as in the increase of the defense budget after Kennedy's meeting with Khrushchev in 1961). And the management of the great foreign policy crisis of the Kennedy years — the Soviet attempt to install nuclear missiles in Cuba — came as if in proof of the proposition that the nuclear age left no alternative to unilateral presidential decision.

XI

Here was the most authentic national emergency since the Second World War.[76] The Soviet nuclearization of Cuba was a far more direct threat to the security of the United States than the North Korean attack on South Korea had been; and the involvement of nuclear weapons made it far more ominous in its import for the planet. Time was short, because something had to be done before the bases became operational. Secrecy was imperative. Kennedy took the decision into his own hands, but it is to be noted that he did not make it in imperial solitude. The celebrated Executive Committee became a forum for exceedingly vigorous and intensive debate. Major alternatives received strong, even vehement, expression. Though there was no legislative consultation, there was most effective executive consultation.

There was also a form of consultation with the press and an acknowledgment therefore of the existence of unwritten checks on presidential action. For very soon the press caught on to the existence, though not to the location, of the crisis. Kennedy, who had no illusion that any secret, even this one, could be kept for very long in Washington, asked the *New York Times* to give him a chance to comment if it found out where the trouble was. Twenty-four hours before the time set for Kennedy's speech to the nation the *Times* staff decided on Cuba. The President, when notified, explained the problems of premature disclosure and suggested that the *Times* forgo its scoop. The *Times,* consulting with itself, recalled that Kennedy had admitted error in asking the *Times* to suppress stories that might have stopped the Bay of Pigs. It therefore asked the President, as Max Frankel of the *Times* remembers it, to "give his word that he will shed no blood and start no war during the period of our silence." Kennedy agreed, and the story was postponed. He had no intention of shedding blood and starting war in the next 24 hours in any case. Still, he evidently did not take the bargain as an insult to presidential dignity; according to Frankel, he perceived "no affront in this arrogant demand from the sidelines." [77] I imagine he felt that the *Times* bureau stood a chance of being blown up too and therefore was entitled to add its bit to the decision.

But Congress played no role at all. It is true that some weeks before Congress had passed a resolution designed to strengthen the President's hand in dealing with Cuba. The administration, while not seeking such a resolution, was not averse to an affirmation of congressional support. In its original draft, as recommended by the State Department, the resolution said that the executive "possesses all necessary authority" to use armed force to stop the establishment of any "externally supported offensive military base" in Cuba. A number of senators objected to this language. Russell of Georgia called the resolution "a clear delegation of the congressional power to declare war." Morse of Oregon said it was "a predated declaration of war." The offending language was dropped, and the resolution ended as a simple statement of national policy. Kennedy attached no great importance to the exercise and did not refer to the resolution when it came time to act.

It was only after he had made his decision that Kennedy called in the congressional leaders. The object was not to consult them but to inform them. They gave him a rough time, but this was because of the decision itself, not because they had been excluded from it. Russell and Fulbright even advocated the invasion of Cuba by American forces. Fulbright reflected afterward, "Had I been able to formulate my views on the basis of facts since made public rather than on a guess as to the nature of the situation, I might have made a different recommendation." [78] Should Kennedy have included members of the Congress on his ExCom? This might have made a marginal political difference if the policy had not worked, but it would have made no constitutional difference, since the presence of selected members of Congress on an executive council was no substitute for formal congressional action. The serious argument for informal congressional participation would have been if members of Congress might have urged views that the executive branch had not adequately considered. In many cases, especially in the later cases of the Dominican Republic and Vietnam, this might well have been so. But in this particular case Kennedy had already made provision for the forceful representation of a diversity of views. Congressional participation in the discussions, as Fulbright's reflection suggests, would probably have changed the members of Congress more than the policy.

Was a congressional role possible in the missile crisis? Kennedy, his counsel, Theodore Sorensen, has written, acted "by Executive Order, Presidential proclamation and inherent powers, not under any resolution or act of Congress." [79] He also had the approval of the Organization of American States, and he carefully waited for this before making the formal proclamation of quarantine; but he would certainly have gone ahead without OAS endorsement. Had the crisis exploded into war, Congress would no doubt have acted at once. But, even in retrospect, the missile crisis seems an emergency so acute in its nature and so peculiar in its structure that it did in fact require unilateral executive decision.

Yet this very acuteness and peculiarity disabled Kennedy's action in October 1962 as a precedent for future Presidents in situations less acute and less peculiar. For the missile crisis was unique in the postwar years in that it *really* combined all those pressures of threat, secrecy and time that the foreign policy establishment had claimed as characteristic of decisions in the nuclear age. Where the threat was less grave, the need for secrecy less urgent, the time for debate less restricted — i.e., in all other cases — the argument for independent and unilateral presidential action was notably less compelling.

Alas, Kennedy's action, which should have been celebrated as an exception, was instead enshrined as a rule. This was in great part because it so beautifully fulfilled both the romantic ideal of the strong President and the prophecy of split-second presidential decision in the nuclear age. The very brilliance of Kennedy's performance appeared to vindicate the idea that the President must take unto himself the final judgments of war and peace. The missile crisis, I believe, was superbly handled, and could not have been handled so well in any other way. But one of its legacies was the imperial conception of the Presidency that brought the republic so low in Vietnam.

★ 7 ★

The Presidency Rampant: Vietnam

AMERICAN MILITARY INTERVENTION in Vietnam thus began when the presidential mystique was in full glory. In the Kennedy years that intervention was limited and provoked no constitutional questions. The dispatch of "advisers" — 16,000 by the time of Kennedy's death — took place under familiar arrangements for military assistance based on congressional legislation and appropriation. When advisers participated, as some occasionally did, in combat, or when American helicopters ferried South Vietnamese troops to the field of battle, this was plainly beyond express congressional authorization. But there were few American deaths — fewer than 100 during the Kennedy Presidency — and Congress agreed with the policy anyway; so American involvement in actual fighting drew little notice, except on the part of Senators Ernest Gruening, Wayne Morse and George S. McGovern. The rest of the American commitment in this period was covert and thus, under the Eisenhower precedent and with tacit congressional consent, immune to legislative scrutiny.

I

Lyndon Johnson came to the Presidency with an old and honest belief in spacious presidential authority to deploy force abroad in the service of American foreign policy. He had defended Truman's decision of 1950; and, while he had come to believe that Truman made a mistake in not asking for a congressional resolution, he saw this as political, not constitutional, error. A resolution could protect an administration's flanks, but the President already had the legal power. In 1954, with Eisenhower in the White House, Johnson had disclaimed any desire to take the responsibility out of the hands of "the constitutional leader." Now that he was the constitutional leader himself, it could not be supposed that he would take a narrower view of presidential prerogative. "There are many, many, who can recommend, advise and sometimes a few of them consent," he said in a speech in 1966. "But there is only one that has been chosen by the American people to decide." [1] American history had traveled a long distance from Lincoln's proposition that *"no one man* should hold the power" of bringing the nation into war.

So in the spring of 1965 Johnson ordered 22,000 American troops to the Dominican Republic without seeking congressional authorization. His pretext was the protection of American lives. This was a traditional usage of executive power and did not require congressional consent. But 22,000 troops were about a hundred times more than were necessary for the specified purpose. Johnson's real reason, as he soon revealed, was that "we don't propose to sit here in our rocking chair with our hands folded and let the Communists set up any government in the Western Hemisphere." [2] Armed intervention for political purposes clearly raised questions which under the Constitution, if not in the mind of the President, called for congressional participation.

With the same confidence in exclusive presidential prerogative, Johnson in early 1965 decreed the Americanization of the war in Vietnam, sending American combat units for the first time to the south and American bombers for the first time on a continuing basis to the north. This brought about a major change in the nature of the American involvement. What Kennedy on September 3, 1963, had called "their war" ("They are the ones who have to win it or lose it") [3] had become, and remained for many years thereafter, "our war." It was a momentous decision — one that brought the United States into a war lasting longer than any other in American history, a war causing more American deaths in combat than any except the Civil War and the two World Wars, a war costing more money than any except the Second

World War. "If this decision was not for Congress under the Constitution," Alexander Bickel of the Yale Law School has well said, "then no decision of any consequence in matters of war and peace is left to Congress." [4]

There were no serious precedents for this decision. Unlike Roosevelt's Atlantic policy in 1941, Johnson was ordering American troops into immediate and calculated combat. Unlike Truman's decision in Korea, there were no UN resolutions to confer international legality, nor had there been clear-cut invasion across frontiers. Unlike the Cuban missile crisis, there was no emergency threat to the United States itself to compel secret and unilateral presidential decision. Unlike the Dominican Republic, there were no American civilians to be rescued.

There was of course the Tonkin Gulf resolution (officially the Southeast Asia resolution), rushed through Congress in August 1964 in a stampede of misinformation and misconception, if not of deliberate deception. After the alleged attacks on American destroyers off the coast of North Vietnam, Johnson called in the congressional leaders. Reminding himself, and them, of Taft's criticism of Truman for not seeking congressional ratification of the Korea decision, he asked their judgment about getting something this time that, as he cautiously put it, "would give us the opinion of Congress." [5] The leaders thought it a fine idea, and the administration pulled out a draft resolution, prepared months before and awaiting the occasion.

The resolution passed the House unanimously. In the Senate only Wayne Morse and Ernest Gruening voted no, though Gaylord Nelson and others raised penetrating questions. The constitutional import of the resolution was by no means clear. The main reference to Congress held that Congress "approves and supports the determination of the President, as Commander in Chief, to take all necessary measures to repel any armed attack against the forces of the United States and to prevent further aggression." Did this last phrase mean further aggression against American forces or further aggression anywhere in Southeast Asia? Was Congress delegating *its* war-making authority to the President or was it acknowledging *his* pre-existing authority to do whatever he found necessary? Another section said that "the United States" — the United States government, Congress and President together? the United States as a whole, all 193,-526,000 people? — was "prepared, as the President determines, to take all necessary steps, including the use of armed force, to assist any member or protocol state of the Southeast Asia Collective Defense Treaty requesting assistance in defense of its freedom."

Whatever the exact significance, the language on its face gave the President remarkable scope. When Senator John Sherman Cooper asked whether, "if the President decided that it was necessary to use such force as could lead into war, we will give that authority by this resolution?" Senator Fulbright, who was managing the bill, responded, "That is the way I would interpret it." He added optimistically, "I have no doubt that the President will consult with Congress in case a major change in present policy becomes necessary." [6]

A resolution giving the President authority to use force as he saw fit in vague future contingencies was precisely the sort of resolution rejected as unacceptable in the early republic. The vagueness created a variety of congressional views as to what, in fact, Congress had authorized. Senator Sam Ervin, the North Carolina constitutionalist, observed in 1970 that the resolution was "clearly a declaration of war," and a good thing too.[7] The legislative history leaves little doubt, however, that others who voted for it did *not* suppose they were authorizing a large and protracted war on the Asian mainland — "the last thing we would want to do," as Fulbright said in the debate. Indeed, President Johnson's defenders assert that, when he requested the resolution in August 1964, he did not himself suppose he would Americanize the war six months later, though some students of the Pentagon Papers dispute this assertion.

But there can be no doubt at all what Johnson thought Congress was doing. He had not used the phrase "the opinion of Congress" lightly. In his view, the Tonkin Gulf resolution was that, and nothing more. "We stated then," he said in 1967 of his conference with the leaders, "and we repeat now, we did not think the resolution was necessary to what we did and what we're doing." [8] The significance of the resolution in Johnson's view was exclusively political. "Part of being ready, to me," he wrote in his memoirs, "was having the advance support of Congress for anything that might prove to be necessary. It was better to have a firm congressional resolution, and not need it, than some day to need it and not have it." [9] Though it amused him to taunt members of Congress by pulling the Tonkin Gulf resolution out of his pocket and flourishing it as proof that Congress had authorized the escalation of American involvement, he did not believe for a moment that the resolution provided the legal basis for his action.

The role of Congress under the Johnson theory of the war-making power was not to sanction but to support the war — a role that nearly all of Congress, except for the indomitable Morse and Gruening, accepted till 1966, and that most accepted for a long time afterward. In practice, Johnson could certainly have obtained congressional authorization beyond the Tonkin Gulf resolution for a limited war in Vietnam in 1965. He might even, had he wished (but no one wished), have obtained a declaration of war. Neither he nor most of Congress thought formal congressional action necessary.

Johnson's conception of presidential prerogative was somewhat overlaid by his protestations of an inexhaustible desire to "consult" with his old friends on Capitol Hill. But presidential consultation had become something of a mirage. If ordinary mortals fell into confused silence in any presidential presence, even senators, constrained less perhaps by awe than by a concern for future benefits, tended to repress their innermost thoughts, especially when confronted by so demanding and unrelenting a President as Lyndon Johnson. "The wise senator," George Reedy, who served as Johnson's press secretary, has written, ". . . enters cautiously, dressed in his Sunday best and with a respectful, almost pious, look on his face." If for any reason, he must express a dissent, "it is most deferential, almost apologetic." The aura of reverence surrounding a President, Reedy observed, was "so universal that the slightest hint of criticism automatically labels a man as a colossal lout." [10]

Nor was consultation between lesser officials of the executive branch and members of Congress much more satisfactory. Such consultation usually meant, in effect, for one side to give and the other to receive a briefing; it was a form of political cajolery, serving no constitutional or substantive purpose. "The distinction between solicitation of advice in advance of a decision and the provision of information in the wake of a decision would seem to be a significant one," the Senate Foreign Relations Committee finally commented in 1969. Pointing out that in the cases of the Cuban missile crisis and the Dominican intervention congressional leaders were informed what was to be done only a few hours before the decisions were carried out, the Committee added dryly, "Such acts of courtesy are always to be welcomed; the Constitution, however, envisages something more." [11] As for Vietnam, one searches in vain through the Pentagon Papers for mention of Congress except, in Fulbright's bitter remark, "as an appropriate object of manipulation, or as a troublesome nuisance to be disposed of." [12] In the consciousness of the executive branch, the legislative branch existed as an irrational force, to be ignored as long as possible, then to be humored, managed or circumvented, never to be sought out as a possible source of intelligent advice.

II

If Johnson did not think the Tonkin Gulf resolution was necessary to what he had done and continued to do, the State Department appeared less convinced on this point, no doubt because it did not want to abandon any scrap of constitutional justification. Thus Under Secretary of State Nicholas Katzenbach, a distinguished lawyer, who had been Attorney General and, before that, professor of law at Yale and Chicago, described the resolution as constituting, along with SEATO, the "functional equivalent" of a declaration of war. Congress had voted for both; and the President had therefore "fully" met his obligation "to give the Congress a full and effective voice." The resolution, Katzenbach continued, was "an authorization to the President" and "as broad an authorization of war so-called as could be in terms of

our internal constitutional process." But Katzenbach added that
the President had the constitutional authority anyway, with or
without the resolution.[13]

The SEATO Treaty was itself a late, and unconvincing,
starter in the constitutional sweepstakes. It had never been invoked in the Kennedy administration. Though the Gulf of Tonkin resolution mentioned SEATO, Rusk, testifying at the time,
called it only "a substantiating basis for our presence," adding,
"We are not acting specifically under the SEATO Treaty." [14]
Johnson did not cite it in his elaborate defense of American involvement at Johns Hopkins University in April 1965, nor did
Rusk when he discoursed a few days later before the American
Society of International Law. The State Department Legal Adviser said the same month, "It has been true at all times that we
have not had *legal* obligations toward Vietnam." Henry Cabot
Lodge, Jr., then Ambassador to Saigon, said that the American
intervention was "not under the aegis of the United Nations or
the South East Asia Treaty Organization." When Rusk unexpect-
edly said in March 1966 that "a fundamental SEATO obligation
. . . has from the onset guided our actions," this provoked a sardonic column by Arthur Krock called "The Sudden Rediscovery
of SEATO." [15] SEATO was indeed a frail reed, because no previous administration, and no other signatory, had interpreted the
pact the way the Johnson administration now chose to interpret
it.

In the most systematic official justification of the constitutionality of the war, the State Department Legal Adviser in a 1966
memorandum invoked both the resolution and SEATO but, like
Johnson himself, rested his essential argument on "the constitutional powers of the President." Never had these powers been
stated so expansively. "There can be no question," the State Department said, ". . . of the President's authority to commit
United States forces to the defense of South Viet-Nam." It cited
the usual list of historical precedents — this time "at least
125" — but based its case in the main on an extraordinary restatement of the old theory of defensive war.

In 1787, when the Founding Fathers reserved for the Presi-

dent the power to repel sudden attacks, "the world was a far
larger place, and the framers probably had in mind attacks upon
the United States." Now the world had grown much smaller. In
the twentieth century, "an attack on a country far from our
shores can impinge directly on the nation's security. . . . The
Constitution leaves to the President the judgment to determine
whether the circumstances of a particular armed attack are so
urgent and the potential consequences so threatening to the security of the United States that he should act without formally consulting the Congress." [16] In short, warfare anywhere on earth
could, if the President so judged, constitute an attack on the
United States and thereby authorize him to wage 'defensive' war
without congressional consent. Under this theory it was hard to
see why any future President would ever see any legal need to go
to Congress before leading the nation into war.

The presidential mystique had now burst all traditional bonds.
The idea that a situation in any corner of the broad world might
so threaten the United States that the President could go to war
on his own enlarged the doctrine of defensive war to the point
where it brought to mind Schumpeter's classic account of the
state of mind of the Roman Empire:

> There was no corner of the known world where some
> interest was not alleged to be in danger or under ac-
> tual attack. If the interests were not Roman, they were
> those of Rome's allies; and if Rome had no allies, then
> allies would be invented. When it was utterly impossible
> to contrive such an interest — why, then it was the na-
> tional honor that had been insulted. Rome was always
> being attacked by evil-minded neighbors, always fight-
> ing for a breathing-space. The whole world was
> pervaded by a host of enemies, and it was manifestly
> Rome's duty to guard against their indubitably aggres-
> sive designs.[17]

Defensive war had always been the doctrine of empire. The
Johnson shrunken-world theory of defensive war could hardly

have been what the Founding Fathers had intended in reserving
for the executive the right to repel sudden attack on the United
States when Congress was not in session.

III

As the Johnson theory thus overrode the written checks of the
Constitution, so the Johnson practice began to liquidate unwritten checks, especially those operating at other times within
the executive branch itself.

During the Cuban missile crisis, for example, Kennedy had
organized the most searching canvass of possible alternatives,
from doing nothing about the missile bases to pulverizing them
in a Pearl Harbor attack. To make sure that the presidential
presence would not constrain the debate he had even absented
himself on occasion from sessions of his Executive Committee.
Johnson, however, not only abandoned serious legislative consultation but very much reduced the meaning of executive consultation. His well-known demand for 'consensus' was a matter of
psychological need as well as of political strategy. Arthur Goldberg who, as Ambassador to the United Nations, tried unavailingly to restrain the Vietnam policy, remembers a cabinet colleague pleading with him not to carry his opposition to a new
measure of escalation into the National Security Council. The
colleague, who had served with Goldberg in Kennedy's cabinet,
said, "Kennedy didn't mind disagreement. It didn't bother him.
But disagreement really bothers this President. He is going to do
what you dislike anyway; so let's not upset him by having an
argument in front of him."

It is true that George Ball, the Under Secretary of State, continued to deliver cool and reasoned dissents in the presidential
presence; but his role was complacently discounted as soon as he
was labeled the "devil's advocate" — a misnomer, for Ball was
arguing a case in which he deeply believed. In any case, dissent
unaccompanied by the threat of resignation and of thereafter
going public could be easily absorbed. Too few in the American
government, then or ever, had the attitude of Joseph P. Kennedy:

"Home holds no terrors for me." George Reedy has left a splendid account of what he saw in the National Security Council

> where everything is very gentlemanly, or where whatever dissent takes place is a sort of official dissent that can always be anticipated. You know, the sort of thing where we finally reach the man who is supposed to dissent and you know who he is going to be, because he is the one who always dissents anyway. . . . And he will make some remark such as, "well, all I can say, Mr. President, is that I really do not think we know where we are going." That makes everyone in the room feel happy because they assume they have heard both sides of the issue.
>
> Well, Senator, I submit this is not genuine debate. I do not believe that men with any sincerity or any passion or any conviction really argue things out that way. Debate over issues of that size, debate over issues that decide whether our sons are going to go out and wade through a rice paddy in Vietnam with somebody shooting at them — I do not think people are gentlemanly about things like that.

Discussions around the President, Reedy concluded, were "really monologues in which one man is getting reflections of what he sends out." [18] So insistent were Johnson's demands for conformity, and so deeply did they penetrate his administration, that middle-level officials, increasingly unhappy about the war, dared not admit their reservations even among themselves. "In the Pentagon," Townsend Hoopes, who was then Deputy Assistant Secretary for International Affairs, has written, "the Tet offensive [of February 1968] performed the curious service of fully revealing the doubters and dissenters to each other, in a lightning flash." [19]

Shortly afterward, when Clark Clifford came to the Pentagon, he received indispensable assistance from these closet dissenters in his drive to stop the further escalation of the war. And in spite of Johnson's own angry resistance to bad news, his own complex antennae kept him, in the end, in unwilling and indignant touch with reality. The rising protest in the executive branch, in Congress, in the press and on the streets — above all, probably, the prospective loss of the impending Wisconsin primary to Senator Eugene McCarthy — eventually persuaded him that he could go down the road no farther. The unwritten checks, though hated and condemned, had their belated effect.

IV

Lincoln had said that the view that one man had the power of bringing the nation into war placed our Presidents where Kings had always stood. If Johnson construed the high prerogative more in the eighteenth-century style of the British monarch than of the republican executive envisaged by the Constitution, his successor carried the inflation of presidential authority even further. For President Nixon stripped away the fig leaves which his predecessor had draped over his assertion of unilateral presidential power. The SEATO treaty was returned to the oblivion from which the State Department had plucked it in 1966. The Tonkin Gulf resolution was disowned by the administration in 1970 [20] and revoked by Congress in January 1971; strict constructionists like Sam Ervin even voted against repeal on the ground that it deprived the President of his legal right to carry on the war. The claim of exclusive presidential authority now rested squarely on the powers of the Commander in Chief, especially his power to do whatever he thought necessary to protect American troops.

"I shall meet my responsibility as Commander in Chief of our Armed Forces," Nixon said in his announcement of the invasion of Cambodia in 1970, "to take the action necessary to defend the security of our American men." "The legal justification," he later explained, ". . . is the right of the President of the United States under the Constitution to protect the lives of American men." "As Commander in Chief, I had no choice but to act to defend those men. And as Commander in Chief, if I am faced with that decision again, I will exercise that power to defend those men." [21]

The repeated use of the term Commander in Chief, as if it were an incantation, would have confounded the Founding Fathers. As we have seen, the office through most of American history had a strictly technical connotation: it meant no more than the topmost officer in the armed forces. Lincoln in special circumstances had used it as a source of extra authority; but the Civil War could serve as precedent only for another civil war. Then the Second World War had given the title new glamor; and, beginning with the Truman Presidency, the Commander in Chief clause began to serve a variety of secular purposes. A President facing an unpopular decision, whether firing General MacArthur or seizing the steel plants, no doubt felt he could get away with it better if he wrapped himself in his military robe. For Truman's successor, donning the military robe was doing what came naturally. In any case, the growing militarization of American life under both the realities and the delusions of the Cold War increased the resonance of the office.

By the 1970s the title Commander in Chief had acquired almost a sacramental aura, translating its holder from worldly matters into an ineffable realm of higher duty. A dithyramb by Senator Goldwater in 1971 evokes the process of transfiguration. "We come," Goldwater said, "to the President's power as Commander in Chief. . . . Just why the founding fathers saw fit to confer this title on him and to invest him with these powers, I've never quite been able to understand; but I have a growing feeling that with the recognized and infinite wisdom of the founding fathers, they realized that a single man with these powers who would not be disturbed by the politics of the moment would use them more wisely than a Congress which is constantly looking toward the political results." The Founding Fathers, he continued, foreseeing the day when a divided Congress could not agree on a "single American course," must in their wisdom have arranged that "the power of war and peace might better be vested in a single man. . . . I believe it would offer an explanation of a means by which our forefathers and we ourselves were meant to become a single people with a single purpose." [22]

For Nixon his authority as Commander in Chief, conjoined with the principle of troop protection and the model of the missile crisis, was all he needed. In his announcement of the incursion into Cambodia, he compared himself to Kennedy who, "in his finest hour," had sat in the identical room in the White House and made "the great decision" that removed the missiles from Cuba. Later Nixon used the missile crisis to justify his failure to consult Congress over Cambodia. "I trust we don't have another Cuban missile crisis. I trust we don't have another situation like Cambodia, but I do know that in the modern world, there are times when the Commander in Chief . . . will have to act quickly. I can assure the American people that this President is going to bend over backward to consult the Senate and consult the House whenever he feels it can be done without jeopardizing the lives of American men. But when it is a question of the lives of American men or the attitudes of people in the Senate, I am coming down hard on the side of defending the lives of American men." [23]

One can only wonder whether Nixon seriously believed that Cuba and Cambodia were equal situations — equal in their danger to the security of the United States, equal in their need for secrecy, equal in their lack of time for congressional consideration. The enemy bases and the threat to American forces had existed in Cambodia for years; there was no sudden emergency in April 1970; indeed the enemy had already largely evacuated the sanctuary areas by the time the invasion began. There was ample time for congressional consultation. There was even more time within the executive branch for a canvass of the sort Kennedy had conducted in the infinitely more imperious case of the missiles in Cuba.

Indeed, so astute a student of the Presidency as Richard Neustadt had just argued that debate within the executive branch could replace Congress as the means of check and balance in the nuclear age. "Any modern President," Neustadt had written in a discussion of the missile crisis, "stands at the center of a watchful circle with whose members he cannot help but consult. . . . He is no freer than he would have been with Congress to ignore them." [24] But Nixon did ignore them. He had already cut the

State Department out of serious policy, looking instead to a mini–State Department in the White House under the direction of his Assistant for National Security Affairs, Henry A. Kissinger. And in the case of Cambodia, Nixon, instead of exposing himself to a candid discussion among even his closest colleagues, seems to have withdrawn into solitude and sprung his unilateral decision on them as well as on the world.

V

As for the Constitution, Nixon showed no more interest in the location of the war-making power than his immediate predecessors, though, as the first lawyer to sit in the White House since Franklin Roosevelt, he might have had at least a professional curiosity about the subject. But his own public remarks on the question have already been reproduced nearly in their entirety; and the matter weighed so little on his mind that, according to the *New York Times,* he did not ask the State Department lawyers to prepare the legal case for the invasion of Cambodia until four days after it began.[25] For a systematic constitutional defense of his actions in Cambodia, Nixon relied on an Assistant Attorney General, William Rehnquist.

Rehnquist's argument was that the Commander in Chief clause was "a grant of substantive authority" which had enabled Presidents throughout American history to send troops "into conflict with foreign powers on their own initiative" and even to deploy "armed forces outside of the United States on occasion in a way which invited hostile retaliation." Congress had acquiesced in such presidential initiative, and the courts, he claimed, had repeatedly approved it. As for Indochina, war there had been authorized by the Tonkin Gulf resolution. (It is interesting that, in Nixon's case as in Johnson's, their lawyers clung to documents the principals had thrown overboard.) In carrying the war into Cambodia as a means of assuring the safety of American armed forces in the field, Nixon had made "precisely the sort of tactical decision traditionally confided to the commander-in-chief in the conduct of armed conflict."

Whatever merits Rehnquist possessed as a President's lawyer, he displayed few, in this instance at least, as a legal scholar. The Commander in Chief clause gave a President only the substantive powers that the officer in top command of the armed forces would have had if he were not President. The idea that the clause gave a President authority beyond this was a product not of the Constitutional Convention but of the years after the Second World War. Rehnquist's judicial precedents were marked by a comparable indifference to history. Thus he cited the case of *Durand v. Hollins,* where Justice Nelson had upheld the bombardment of a Nicaraguan town by an American naval vessel. Rehnquist, who oddly thought the case was called *Durand v. Hollis* and even more oddly thought Nelson was "later a Justice of the Supreme Court" (Nelson had been on the Supreme Court for fifteen years at the time of *Durand v. Hollins*), now tried to transform unilateral executive action against what President Pierce had carefully defined as "not . . . an organized political society" into a precedent for President Nixon's invasion of the sovereign state of Cambodia. With the same disdain for context, he even cited the Prize Cases, as if Cambodia were a Confederate state in rebellion against the Union.

Most of the Rehnquist case was persiflage. His serious argument derived from the proposition, which no one disputed, that the Commander in Chief has full power to conduct a war once begun. But did this wartime power of command authorize a Commander in Chief, as Rehnquist contended, to invade neutral countries on his personal finding that they housed a potential danger to American forces? As a claim under international law, this was not impressive. The Nixon administration itself might not have been deeply moved if Brezhnev had said that the Red Army was perfectly justified in invading a neutral country in order to secure the safety of Russian forces. In such a case Americans would have denounced the argument as self-serving and specious. Was the same argument less self-serving on American lips? A century and a half before the incursion into Cambodia, Chief Justice Marshall had laid down the rule: "An army marching into the dominions of another sovereign may justly be considered as committing an act of hostility; and, if not opposed by force, acquires no privilege by its irregular and improper conduct." [26] This was the position the American government had taken in 1957 when French forces in Algeria, acting on the troop-protection principle, attacked a guerrilla sanctuary in Tripoli, as it was the continuing American position when Israeli forces attacked Arab guerrilla sanctuaries beyond the frontier of Israel.

As a claim under American law, the Nixon-Rehnquist proposition was even more troubling. Cambodia was not a threat to the security of the United States. Since the danger to American forces in South Vietnam had become less great than it had been for several years, it was hard to claim a sudden emergency. It was not a case of hot pursuit; nor could Rehnquist cite any previous occasion when a President ordered a massive attack on a neutral country to protect American troops in a third country. And what were the limits on this theory of presidential war? If Nixon could invade Cambodia and later bomb Laos without congressional consent on this principle, could he not also on the same principle attack China and Russia without congressional consent? Herndon had written to Lincoln that, if it should become necessary to repel invasion, the President could cross the line and invade a neighboring country, and that the President was the sole judge of the. necessity. If this were so, Lincoln had replied, "Study to see if you can fix *any limit* to his power in this respect, after you have given him so much as you propose." Now Nixon claimed this power, not just in the case of a neighboring country or an imminent invasion of the United States, but in the case of a country on the other side of the world. He thereby equipped himself with so expansive a theory of the power of the Commander in Chief and so elastic a theory of defensive war that he could freely, on his own initiative, without a national emergency, without reference to Congress, as a routine employment of unilateral executive authority, go to war against any country containing any troops that might in any conceivable circumstance be used in an attack on American forces. And Rehnquist (whom Nixon soon elevated to the Supreme Court in

what he hilariously called a strict-constructionist appointment)
even contended ominously that the invasion of Cambodia was
only the mildest exertion of presidential prerogative: "one need
not approach anything like the outer limits of his power, as defined by judicial decision and historical practice, in order to conclude that it supports the action he took in Cambodia." [27]

Both Johnson and Nixon had indulged in presidential war-
making beyond the boldest dreams of their predecessors. Those
who had stretched the executive war power to what had seemed
its "outer limits" in the past had done so in the face of visible
and dire threat to national survival: Lincoln confronted by rebellion, Roosevelt by Hitler. Neither had pretended to be exercising routine powers of the Commander in Chief. Johnson
and Nixon had surpassed all their predecessors in claiming that
inherent and exclusive presidential authority, unaccompanied
by emergencies threatening the life of the nation, unaccompanied
by the authorization of Congress or the blessing of an international organization, permitted a President to order troops
into battle at his unilateral pleasure.

VI

There were interesting differences, however, between the Johnson and Nixon theories of the presidential war power. Johnson's
theory was more sweeping in principle but more confined in
practice. His administration had argued that an attack on a
country far from American shores could impinge "directly" on
the nation's security and thereby sanction unilateral presidential
action, where Nixon made his case on the presumably narrower
ground of potential attack on American forces. But Johnson had
restricted his unilateral action to a country with which the
United States was in a state of *de facto* war. He had rejected recommendations from his military leaders that he carry the war
into the neutral states of Cambodia and Laos.

Now in justifying the commitment of American troops to battle in neutral states with no gesture at all toward (in the words of
Andrew Jackson) previous understanding with that body by

whom war could alone be declared and by whom all the provisions for sustaining its perils must be furnished — in doing this, Nixon cited no emergency that denied time for congressional action, expressed no doubt about the perfect legality of his personal extension of the war into two new countries, and showed no interest even in retrospective congressional ratification. The authority claimed by Nixon appeared indefinitely extensible so long as a President could declare American forces anywhere in the world in danger of attack. It appeared extinguishable only when an American military withdrawal ended the hazard of such attack.

Though Congress was reluctant to use the power of the purse to stop the war in Vietnam, it did in 1969 and 1970 vote to deny funds for American ground combat troops in Laos, Thailand and, after the fact, Cambodia. In 1971 it added an amendment to the Defense Procurement Authorization Act declaring it "the policy of the United States to terminate at the earliest practicable date all military operations of the United States in Indochina." This declaration, especially in conjunction with the repeal of the Tonkin Gulf resolution, could be considered a cancellation by Congress of its implicit authorization of further war in Indochina. But, since the amendment contained nothing, such as a fund cutoff, to give it substance, Nixon, on signing the bill, could say with impunity that the congressional declaration did "not represent the policies of the Administration," that it was "without binding force or effect" and that "my signing of the bill that contains this section . . . will not change the policies I have pursued." There was ample precedent for this disavowal of hortatory congressional resolutions, even if the tone seemed unnecessarily contemptuous. But Senator Church also had a point when he commented, "A century ago, it is inconceivable that a chief executive would have disregarded a statute, let alone dismiss its provisions in such an abrupt and peremptory way. That Mr. Nixon felt no compunction in doing so is a reflection of the low estate to which the Congress has fallen." [28]

Nixon's troop-protection doctrine hinged, however, on one factual requirement: there had to be American troops to protect. It was on this premise, and this premise alone, that the Nixon administration, having abandoned SEATO and the Tonkin Gulf resolution and the Johnson shrunken-world theory of defensive war, had rested its constitutional justification for the continuation of warfare in Indochina. Nixon repeated in 1971 that he would "use American airpower any place in North Vietnam, or in Southeast Asia, where I found that it would be necessary for the purpose of protecting American forces. . . . The justification was, and *must always be,* the defense of American forces in South Vietnam." [29] If this thesis was not very convincing, at least it was a thesis. But what would happen once American forces were withdrawn? On March 28, 1973, this was the situation. Yet the Nixon administration, unperturbed, began to bomb Cambodia more intensively than ever and on occasion threatened renewed bombing in Vietnam. By what authority did it now claim to send Americans into battle?

When Henry Kissinger was asked, after the conclusion in January 1973 of the Paris Agreement on Ending the War and Restoring Peace in Vietnam, if there were "no inhibitions" on the renewal of American bombing in Vietnam, he replied, "That is legally correct. We have the right to do this." [30] Presumably he meant that the American government had a unilateral right under international law to resume bombing in case of violations of the Paris Agreement. If so, that right was short-lived. On March 2 the Declaration of the International Conference on Vietnam, signed by, among others, the American Secretary of State, pledged the signatories, if the Agreement were violated, to consult "either individually or jointly . . . with the other parties to this Act with a view to determining necessary remedial measures."

It is hard to believe that Kissinger, who after all was once a professor of government at Harvard, could have meant in addition that the President of the United States had the unilateral right under the American Constitution to resume warfare in Indochina. For powers conferred by international law on the government as a whole, President and Congress together, were not necessarily powers at the independent disposal of the President.

In Washington members of Congress pressed the constitutional issue for some weeks in vain. One rather sympathized with the administration. The problem of finding legal grounds for the bombing of Cambodia was not easy. Not only were there no troops left to defend, but Cambodia had long since rejected any claim to protection under SEATO, as the administration had conceded to Congress in 1970.[31] Moreover, Congress itself had prohibited the sending of American military advisers or ground troops into Cambodia and had stipulated that other forms of aid to Cambodia could "not be construed as a commitment by the United States to Cambodia for its defense." [32]

Nevertheless the new Secretary of Defense in 1973 (this was Elliot Richardson, who had once served as Justice Frankfurter's law clerk and later as Attorney General of the state in whose constitution John Adams had inserted the phrase "a government of laws, and not of men"; soon he became Attorney General of the United States) now spoke of the Lon Nol government in Cambodia as an "ally." This perplexed members of Congress. It was, Senator McGovern commented, "a fascinating question of law how a country which has refused protection under a treaty, a country whose defense by the United States is prohibited by law, none the less qualifies as an 'ally.' " Indeed, McGovern continued, Cambodia was evidently more than an ally, since Richardson seemed to feel that Lon Nol's "request" for American air strikes gave the President authority to mount those strikes. The Lon Nol regime would therefore seem "a kind of super-ally, with an active role, superseding that of Congress . . . in our constitutional processes." [33]

VII

Richardson, who was an able lawyer, had obviously had an off day. But the administration did not vouchsafe a considered explanation until April 30, 1973, when Secretary of State Rogers presented a memorandum to the Senate Foreign Relations Committee. The Secretary now denied that the withdrawal of American forces had "created a fundamentally new situation in which new authority must be sought by the President from Congress to carry out air strikes in Cambodia." The Paris Agreement, Rogers said, not only provided for a cease-fire in Vietnam but in Article 20 contemplated a cease-fire in Cambodia. Article 20 in consequence legalized the continuation of air strikes in Cambodia "until such time as a cease-fire could be brought into effect." If it were said that the Constitution required the "immediate cessation" of air strikes in Cambodia, this would imply "a Constitution that contains an automatic self-destruct mechanism designed to destroy what has been so painfully achieved." Rogers therefore concluded that the President's executive powers were adequate "to prevent such a self-defeating result." [34]

This was a feeble argument.[35] Article 20 of the Paris Agreement did not call for a cease-fire in Cambodia. By bringing this up three months later, Rogers seemed to be stating a new condition for the end of American warfare in Indochina. Nor did Article 20 give any of the signatories unilateral authority to enforce the settlement in Cambodia. Nor did Rogers say anything about the consultation required by the Declaration of the International Conference on Vietnam that he himself had signed eight weeks earlier. Nor, indeed, had the Paris Agreement ever been submitted by the President to the Senate as a treaty or to Congress as a joint resolution. When the Geneva Accords of 1954 brought the French war in Indochina to an end, Premier Pierre Mendès-France did submit the Accords to the National Assembly, even though French constitutional practice did not clearly oblige him to do so. The Assembly approved the Accords and commended the government. Mendès-France also promised that, if violation should necessitate a reintroduction of force, he would consult with the Assembly before sending French troops into battle.[36] It was a measure of the difference between the Fourth Republic of 1954 and the American republic of 1973 that the American President, unlike the French Premier, saw no need to include the American Congress in these decisions. (There was less difference, perhaps, between the American republic of 1973 and the Fifth Republic of General de Gaulle.) And, even if the Paris Agreement had been submitted to Congress, the congressional war-making power could hardly be transferred to the executive by an international compact.

All this fiddling, one feels, was by the way. The Deputy Assistant Secretary of State for Far Eastern Affairs probably put the administration view more bluntly when he was asked about the President's legal authority at a congressional briefing. "It is interesting you should ask me about that," he said. "I have got a couple of lawyers working on it." After a moment he added, "The justification is the re-election of President Nixon." "By that theory," the *Washington Post* commented, "he could level Boston." [37]

The Nixon theory of presidential war, above all in its post-troop-protection version, had effectively liquidated the constitutional command that the power to authorize war belonged to the Congress. Nixon had thereby erased the most solemn written check on presidential war. He had not, like Lincoln, confessed to the slightest misgiving about the legality of his course; nor, like Franklin Roosevelt, had he sought to involve Congress, if not in the decisions of war, then at least in the decisions of peace. He had aimed to establish as normal presidential power what previous Presidents had regarded as power justified only by extreme emergencies and employable only at their own peril.

With Nixon as with Johnson, the central role for Congress in foreign affairs was to provide aid and comfort to the Commander in Chief. He never sought its advice before major initiatives, and acknowledged its existence afterward mainly by inviting members of Congress to hear Henry Kissinger tell them in mass briefings what they had already read, if less stylishly expressed, in the newspapers.

VIII

Nor was this all. The imperial Presidency required one further instrument: the unimpeded and secure control of the armed forces. The Commander in Chief clause gave every President nominal command of the Army and Navy. But it could not guarantee him, as Johnson and Nixon had discovered in Vietnam, the loyalty of the soldiers in the field, nor the support of their families back home. When a citizen army had a war it believed in, like the Second World War, it fought with unsurpassed courage; but, thrown into a war it could not understand, it could become sullen and disaffected. Nixon now tried to solve the problem of the undependable army, and thereby eliminate one more check on presidential war, by replacing the army made up of civilians by an army made up of professional soldiers.

Had such an army existed in the 1960s, public criticism of the Indochina War would have been much slower to emerge. Even as it was, so long as the Americans killing and dying in Vietnam were sons of poor whites and poor blacks, the American middle class remained generally uninvolved. It was only when the contraction of educational deferments in 1967 and 1968 exposed their own sons to the draft that they (and, in many cases, their sons too) first began to wonder whether the American interest was after all worth the sacrifice of American lives. It was then that opinion began to change. Had conscription been on an egalitarian basis, the middle class would undoubtedly have swung against the war much earlier.

A citizen army is a projection of the whole nation and therefore has the capacity to find means of resisting a President who wants to fight wars in which the nation does not believe. A professional army is by definition a much more compliant and reliable instrument of presidential war. Its members are in the army by their own free choice. Because they believe in their career, they do not have to believe in a particular war. This would not matter if the United States needed only a very small army — say the 189,839 of the Army of 1939. But Nixon planned a very large professional army — 2,233,000 men. The establishment of a vast professional army could only liberate Presidents for a wider range of foreign adventure.

A vast professional army, in addition, could provide dangerous temptations to the imperial Presidency at home. Tocqueville had long since pointed out the different consequences a citizen army and a professional army had for a democracy. When men were conscripted into an army, a few might acquire a taste for military life, "but the majority, being enlisted against their will and ever ready to go back to their homes," found military service not a chosen vocation but a vexatious duty. "They do not therefore imbibe the spirit of the army, or rather they infuse the spirit of the community at large into the army and retain it there." But a professional army "forms a small nation by itself, where the mind is less enlarged and habits are more rude than in the nation at large." Its officers in particular "contract tastes and wants wholly distinct from those of the nation." In consequence, "military revolutions, which are scarcely ever to be apprehended in aristocracies, are always to be dreaded among democratic nations." [38]

It was not unknown for professional officers in the citizen army to complain about a want of discipline and patriotism in the nation. Nor was it inconceivable that the existence of an army professional in all its ranks might suggest things to a President who regarded dissent as a form of subversion or anarchy and wished to restore law and order in the name of national security. *Seven Days in May* might seem melodramatic fantasy; but President Kennedy, who knew the military, wanted it filmed as a warning to the nation.[39] In any case, there seemed no advantage in compounding the problems of an already volatile political society by introducing into it a "small nation by itself," united by professional prejudices, resentments and ambitions and possessing a monopoly of the weapons of war. Here, it would appear, was precisely the large and permanent military establishment which, as Hamilton had written in the Eighth Federalist, tended to destroy the civil and political rights of the people and which, as Madison had said in 1812, was forbidden by the principles of our free government.

IX

Not only had the war-making power passed from Congress, not only had Congress now placed a professional army at presidential disposal, but the Presidency in these years asserted as never before an authority to make international commitments without the consent and, on occasion, without the knowledge of Congress.

In time the Indochina War forced this situation on congressional attention. When the Secretary of State listed for the benefit of the Senate Foreign Relations Committee the grounds for the American commitment to the Saigon regime, he mentioned that, in addition to SEATO and the Tonkin Gulf resolution, there were bilateral assistance agreements with South Vietnam. "So far as I know," Fulbright said later, "none of the bilateral assistance agreements referred to has ever been submitted to the Congress." Could unknown agreements of this sort really be deemed national commitments requiring the use of armed force in Southeast Asia? [40] And every time a high member of the administration went to Asia, it seemed, there were new commitments. Vice President Humphrey, after the Honolulu conference between President Johnson and Marshal Ky in 1966, described the Honolulu Declaration, a rapidly forgotten document, as "a pledge to ourselves and to posterity to defeat aggression, to defeat social misery, to build viable, free political institutions. Now, those are broad terms, but these are great commitments." [41] Commitments? The Vice President's usage was doubtless metaphorical, except that recent history had shown how general statements could become national obligations without the collaboration of Congress. The case of Israel was to the point. Here a succession of executive declarations through five administrations had produced an apparently indestructible commitment without the pretense of a treaty or even an executive agreement.[42]

Increasingly disturbed, the Senate Foreign Relations Committee in February 1969 set up, under the chairmanship of Stuart Symington of Missouri, a special committee to inquire into United States security agreements and commitments abroad.[43] Symington was a man of notable experience in the field of national security. He had been Surplus Property Administrator during the Second World War and Secretary of the Air Force under Truman. He was now the only senator to sit on the three vital national security committees — Foreign Relations, Armed Services and Atomic Energy — and therefore had access to more secret intelligence than anyone else in the Senate. But even Symington, as he said after his committee completed its work, found himself "often in ignorance" of what the United States had promised to foreign countries because of the way international agreements had come to be "handled by a very very few people." [44]

Once again, Congress had primarily itself to blame. In 1953, when the Eisenhower administration was organizing its world-wide system of military bases, Secretary of State Dulles asked congressional leaders whether base agreements had to be in the form of treaties. The congressional view, he told Eisenhower, was that "such agreements may be concluded by the President without further authority, particularly as future commitments for funds are subject to Congressional appropriation." [45] A pattern was thereby established. The appropriations process did indeed enable Congress to know roughly what the money was being paid for. But it did not enable Congress to know what else the United States might be giving in exchange.

The Symington Committee now learned how executive initiative had deepened American involvement in Southeast Asia. In 1962 Secretary of State Rusk and the Thai Foreign Minister made a joint declaration expressing "the firm intention of the United States to aid Thailand . . . in resisting Communist aggression and subversion." While this was a public statement and intended as no more than a specification of SEATO obligations, it led to the authorization by Johnson in 1964 of joint Thai-American contingency planning — an exercise that carried with it the plain implication that, if Thailand were in trouble, the United States would rush to its defense. On a visit to Thailand in 1966, Vice President Humphrey emphasized "the determination of the United States to provide all necessary assistance to enable Thailand and the other countries of Southeast Asia threatened by Communist aggression to defend themselves." As the Thai Prime Minister interpreted the joint contingency plan in 1969, "The United States asserts it will not desert us, that it will help prevent Communist aggression." President Nixon said the same year, "The United States will stand proudly with Thailand against those who might threaten it from abroad or from within." In 1971 the United States had seven air bases, seven generals and 32,000 soldiers in Thailand. Whatever its merits, all this was done without specific congressional authorization and, until the Symington Committee came along, without detailed congressional knowledge.[46]

In the case of Laos, the executive branch had led Congress to believe that American bombing over Laos was directed against North Vietnamese troops passing along the Ho Chi Minh trails in southeastern Laos. To its astonishment the Symington Committee discovered, largely by sending men of its own to the spot, that the executive branch had been waging a separate and secret war in support of the Vientiane government against the Pathet Lao in northern Laos since 1964. "When our initial Congressional effort was made to get the truth about Laos," the Committee grimly reported, "we were either blocked [by the executive branch], or the responses were misleading." After the administration was finally forced to confirm the story in closed session, it then opposed the Committee's efforts to put it on the public record, predicting all manner of dire consequence if the facts were known. The Committee persisted, however, and got the story out. As the Committee counsel later observed, "None of the parade of horrors which the State Department imagined did in fact occur." [47]

Nor were mysterious military agreements confined to Southeast Asia. Since 1953 the United States had been subsidizing the Ethiopian army in payment for an electronic communications base at Kagnew. But Congress did not know, until the Symington Committee dug it up in 1969, that in 1960, when Haile Selassie felt himself endangered by the formation of the Somali Republic, the Eisenhower administration had secretly assured him of the "continuing interest" of the United States "in the security of Ethiopia and its opposition to any activities threatening the territorial integrity of Ethiopia." In the next years, the Committee reported, the United States became deeply involved "in the military structure and activities of the Ethiopian Army." That army, with American aid, grew to the size of 40,000. Somali, the alleged threat, only had an army of 2000, whereupon it turned for military assistance to the Russians, who thereby gained a foothold in East Africa. In 1969 the State Department denied to Symington that the 1960 assurance had been a commitment to defend Haile Selassie. But, whatever it was, it sounded like a decision in which Congress might have expected a voice.[48]

Similarly it had been known since 1953 that the United States was paying for bases in Spain. It was known too that the Kennedy administration, extending the agreement in order to add on a Polaris base, had declared in 1963 (to the dismay of some of its members) that "a threat to either country . . . would be a matter of common concern to both." This language was astutely borrowed by the Spanish Ambassador in Washington from the SEATO Treaty, and the statement had every aspect of being a military commitment. The Under Secretary of State acknowledged as much in 1970 to the Senate Foreign Relations Committee. The Spanish plainly thought so, judging by their indignation when they understood it was not to be reaffirmed. It should therefore have been submitted to the Senate for ratification. But the Kennedy administration did not do so in 1963, and the Senate did not protest.

In the next years, however, senators grew increasingly uncomfortable over the implied guarantee of the Franco regime, especially when they discovered that several thousand American paratroopers had been flown down from Germany to take part with the Spanish Army in joint maneuvers directed not against a foreign invasion but against a hypothetical internal uprising of anti-Franco Spaniards. When the 1963 agreement expired in 1968, the Foreign Relations Committee made clear its opposition to any renewal of the 1963 pledge.

The State Department now, for some reason, entrusted General Wheeler, the chairman of the Joint Chiefs of Staff, with the opening phase of a new negotiation. Wheeler handed the Spanish a document in which he promised American assistance to protect Spain against a Soviet attempt to gain "a foothold in Western Europe through limited aggression." Wheeler added grandly, "Together we can frustrate such efforts in Iberia. . . . By the presence of U.S. forces in Spain, the U.S. gives Spain a far more visible and credible security guarantee than any written documents."

These singular assurances were unknown to Congress until Flora Lewis wrote a story about them for the *Washington Post*. The Foreign Relations Committee thereupon summoned Wheeler. When Fulbright asked whether he did not think so important an obligation should have been submitted to the Senate as a treaty, the general modestly replied, "I am not competent to respond to your comment." But he had felt entirely competent, as Merlo Pusey justly observed, to make the United States a guarantor of the regime of General Franco. Senatorial protest now killed the defense commitment. And, in dragging forth the peculiar story, the Symington Committee discovered that the original 1953 agreement had secret annexes — something kept from the Congress for nearly twenty years.[49]

Beyond all this lay the most difficult problem of all: the placement of nuclear weapons in foreign countries. In 1967 the Secretary of Defense said there were 7000 nuclear warheads in Europe alone. The host governments knew where they were. Moscow had undoubtedly found out where they were. But the American Congress did not know. The Foreign Relations and Armed Services Committees of the Senate had been told nothing, not even in closed session. The Symington Committee at first received cooperation in this field from American representatives overseas, but the executive branch subsequently forbade all discussion of the nuclear question in the hearings in Washington. Most of the weapons had been deployed years before in a different world. The political implications of nuclear deployment demanded review in the changed context. But Congress was systematically denied the information that might have enabled it to contribute to such review. "As long as this excessive secrecy is allowed to continue," Symington observed in 1972 with understandable irritation, "the most important single component of our defense posture cannot even be discussed in the Congress, let alone be understood by most of its members or the American people."[50]

The idea that the appropriations process would secure congressional control of the military base program had failed. Moreover, as the Symington Committee said, "Once an American overseas base is established, it takes on a life of its own." Changing technologies — the intercontinental ballistic missile and the Polaris submarine — rendered original functions obsolete, but the Pentagon was adept at thinking up new functions to keep its facilities going. And, as General Wheeler had suggested to the Spanish, an American base was a splendid way to involve American troops, create American interests and entrap American foreign policy. The Symington Committee tersely summarized what it believed executive practice had come to be: "Maximize commitment in secret discussions with foreign governments; then minimize the risk of commitments in statements made to the American public." [51]

x

The presumed requirements of a global and messianic foreign policy had thus begun to swallow up the congressional power to oversee international agreements as well as the congressional power to send armed force into battle against sovereign states. As the American Presidency came to conceive itself the appointed savior of a world whose interests and dangers demanded rapid and incessant deployment of men, arms and decisions, new power, reverence and awe flowed into the White House. Few Presidents had so much rejoiced in the exercise of power as Franklin D. Roosevelt; but even FDR had preferred, when possible, to act in concert and partnership with Congress. The presidential breakaway really came after the Second World War. The postwar Presidents, though Eisenhower and Kennedy markedly less than Truman, Johnson and Nixon, almost came to see the sharing of power with Congress in foreign policy as a derogation of the Presidency. Congress, in increasing self-abasement, almost came to love its impotence. The image of the President acting by himself in foreign affairs, imposing his own sense of reality and necessity on a waiting government and people, became the new orthodoxy.

As the Presidency pursued its independent course in foreign affairs, the constitutional separation of powers began to disappear in the middle distance. In 1967 an apprehensive Senate Judiciary Committee established a Subcommittee on Separation of Powers under the redoubtable chairmanship of Sam Ervin. Six years later the Ervin Subcommittee concluded that "the movement of the United States into the forefront of balance-of-power realpolitik in international matters has been accomplished at the cost of the internal balance of power painstakingly established by the Constitution." Whether this was a necessary cost, the Subcommittee did not say. It would be excessively gloomy, however, to suppose that a moderate balance-of-power foreign policy was irreconcilable with the separation of powers. An immoderate balance-of-power foreign policy, however, involving the United States in useless wars and grandiose dreams, was another matter.

Certainly American foreign policy in the age of global intervention had steadily reduced the importance of Congress in the field of national security. Old Carl Vinson of Georgia, who first came to the House of Representatives in 1914, and who served as chairman of the Naval Affairs Committee under the second Roosevelt and as chairman of the Armed Services Committee thereafter, had had an intimate view of this process. The role of Congress, Vinson at last said, "has come to be that of a sometimes querulous but essentially kindly uncle who complains while furiously puffing on his pipe but who finally, as everyone expects, gives in and hands over the allowance, grants the permission, or raises his hand in blessing, and then returns to his rocking chair for another year of somnolence broken only by an occasional anxious glance down the avenue and a muttered doubt as to whether he had done the right thing." [52]

★ 8 ★

The Revolutionary Presidency: Washington

THE IMPERIAL PRESIDENCY was essentially the creation of foreign policy. A combination of doctrines and emotions — belief in permanent and universal crisis, fear of communism, faith in the duty and the right of the United States to intervene swiftly in every part of the world — had brought about the unprecedented centralization of decisions over war and peace in the Presidency. With this there came an unprecedented exclusion of the rest of the executive branch, of Congress, of the press and of public opinion in general from these decisions. Prolonged war in Vietnam strengthened the tendencies toward both centralization and exclusion. So the imperial Presidency grew at the expense of the constitutional order. Like the cowbird, it hatched its own eggs and pushed the others out of the nest. And, as it overwhelmed the traditional separation of powers in foreign affairs, it began to aspire toward an equivalent centralization of power in the domestic polity.

I

We saw in the case of Franklin D. Roosevelt and the New Deal that extraordinary power flowing into the Presidency to meet domestic problems by no means enlarged presidential authority in foreign affairs. But we also saw in the case of FDR and the Second World War and Harry S. Truman and the steel seizure that extraordinary power flowing into the Presidency to meet international problems could easily encourage Presidents to extend their unilateral claims at home. Now, twenty years later, the spillover effect from Vietnam coincided with indigenous developments that were quite separately carrying new power to the Presidency. For domestic as well as for international reasons, the imperial Presidency was sinking roots deep into the national society itself.

One such development was the decay of the traditional party system. For much of American history the party has been the ultimate vehicle of political expression. Voters inherited their politics as they did their religion. It was as painful to desert one's party as to desert one's church. But this had begun to change. The Eisenhower period, marked by a President who considered himself above party and by an electorate which decided to balance the Republican President with a Democratic Congress, ushered in a time of decline in the parties. By the 1970s ticket-splitting had become common. Independent voting was spreading everywhere, especially among the young. Never had party loyalties been so weak, party affiliations so fluid, party organizations so irrelevant.

Many factors contributed to the decline of parties. The old political organizations had lost many of their functions. The waning of immigration, for example, had deprived the city machine of its classical clientele. The rise of civil service had cut off the machine's patronage. The New Deal had taken over the machine's social welfare role. Above all, the electronic revolution was drastically modifying the political environment. Two electronic devices had a particularly devastating impact on the traditional structure of politics — television and the computer. That structure had, in effect, three tiers: the politicians; the voters; and, in between, a cluster of intermediate agencies — the political machine, the trade union, the chamber of commerce, the farm organization, the ethnic brotherhood — mediating between politician and voter, interpreting each to the other and providing the links that held the structure together. The electronic innovations were changing all this. Television now presented the politicians directly to the voters; computerized public opinion polls now presented the voters directly to the politicians; and the mediating agencies, the traditional brokers of politics, were left to wither on the vine.

As the parties wasted away, the Presidency stood out in solitary majesty as the central focus of political emotion, the ever more potent symbol of national community. When parties were strong and media weak, Presidents were objects of respect but not of veneration. There were no great personal cults of Rutherford B. Hayes and Benjamin Harrison. Now voters wanted not only to respect but to adore their Presidents, even when, as in the cases of Johnson and Nixon, they found the effort difficult and unrewarding. For their part, historians and political scientists discovered in the images of the two Roosevelts and Wilson, strong Presidents using power for enlightened ends, the model of the Presidency to teach their students and hold up before aspiring politicians. The electronic revolution, having helped dissolve the parties, also helped exalt the Presidency by giving the man in the White House powerful means, first through radio and then through television, to bring his presence and message into every home in the land. Almost alone, Justice Jackson had said in the steel case, the President filled the public eye and ear.

At the same time, the economic changes of the twentieth century had conferred vast new powers not just on the national government but more particularly on the Presidency. The depression of the 1930s had left little doubt that government must thereafter underwrite economic activity and regulate the excesses of business. But the New Deal had been limited by the fact that the levers of private economic power remained in the hands of the political opposition. Then the Second World War strengthened both the techniques and the habits of centralized control. The combination of the New Deal and the war, E. S. Corwin wrote in 1947, had begun to transform a Constitution of Rights into a Constitution of Powers: "the Constitution of peacetime and the Constitution of wartime have become, thanks to the New Deal, very much the same Constitution." [1] But if a Constitution of powers, it was still a Constitution of limited powers — limited during the Second World War by standards of equity written into legislation and sustained in administration; limited in Truman's case by his own instinct and, on the occasion his instinct failed, by the Supreme Court; limited in Eisenhower's case by his disbelief in government; limited in Kennedy's case by instinct and narrow political margins; limited in all these cases by the capacity of corporate managers to resist government control employed for purposes they disliked.

But the trend toward the managed economy had set in. As Keynes himself had once dealt with the economic consequences of Versailles, Americans were now required to deal, in Samuel Lubell's phrase, with the political consequences of Keynes.[2] For Keynesianism made the federal budget the center of economic control and thereby gave presidential government the means, tempered only by what slight modification Congress might force through its taxing and appropriation powers, of deciding the levels of spending and the allocation of government outlays, which meant deciding the social priorities and, to an unprecedented degree, the economic pattern of American society.

There was, alas, no alternative to centralized economic responsibility. History had demonstrated beyond any social interest in further experiment that a high-technology economy would not, left alone, necessarily, or even probably, balance out at levels of high employment. It had demonstrated further that unregulated private ownership generated excessive inequality in the distribution of income, wealth and power and could not restrain greed from exploiting human labor or from despoiling the natural environment. No one, not even those businessmen who eulogized free enterprise at every public banquet, really wanted to get back on the roller coaster of boom and bust, or return to the bucket shop and the sweatshop. National control was the only way to civilize industrial society. But national control without firm mechanisms of equality could quickly degenerate into a system of favoritism, of injustice and of graft.

The Keynesian instrumentalities of government were an intelligent response to public necessity. But they were instrumentalities designed for executive use. Congress showed no capacity to organize across-the-board control of spending or to alter the aggregates of spending in response to the needs of the economy. But, if the President could control employment and investment through the manipulation of the budget, he could do this for the benefit of the industries and regions that gave him steadiest support. And his power to create new economic situations through executive action enabled him to foreclose both decisions by other bodies — Congress, for example — and movement in other directions. The managed economy, in short, offered new forms of unilateral power to the President who was bold enough to take action on his own. "The drive for presidential power," Lubell wrote in 1973, "has been a drive to commit the future. . . . Once the fishhook of commitment becomes lodged in a nation's throat, voter opinion will thrash about furiously, like a powerful but helpless sailfish." [3] The combination of exasperation and impotence increasingly characterized American politics in domestic as well as in foreign affairs.

II

The imperial Presidency, born in the 1940s and 1950s to save the outer world from perdition, thus began in the 1960s and 1970s to find nurture at home. Foreign policy had given the President the command of peace and war. Now the decay of the parties left him in command of the political scene, and the Keynesian revelation placed him in command of the economy. At this extraordinary historical moment, when foreign and domestic lines of force converged, much depended on whether the occupant of the White House was moved to ride the new tendencies of power or to resist them.

For the American Presidency was a peculiarly personal institution. It remained, of course, an agency of government, subject to unvarying demands and duties no matter who was President. But, more than most agencies of government, it changed shape, intensity and ethos according to the man in charge. Each President's distinctive temperament and character, his values, standards, style, his habits, expectations, idiosyncrasies, compulsions, phobias recast the White House and pervaded the entire government beyond. The executive branch, said Clark Clifford, was a chameleon, taking its color from the character and personality of the President.[4] The thrust of the office, its impact on the constitutional order, therefore altered from President to President. Above all, the way each President understood it as his personal obligation to inform and involve the Congress, to earn and hold the confidence of the electorate and to render an accounting to the nation and posterity determined whether he strengthened or weakened the constitutional order.

Historically most Presidents had felt it a duty to keep close to the people. They characteristically exposed themselves, for example, to a wide range of national opinion. They appointed political chieftains of substance and following to their cabinet. They stayed in constant touch with the leadership of their party in Congress and in the states. They engaged in far-flung correspondence. They read the newspapers; McKinley spent two hours every morning at it. For a good deal of the first century of the republic, they held weekly *levées* and were accessible even to casual visitors to Washington. They deemed it a basic requirement of the job, in a phrase Garfield once quoted from Lincoln, "to take a bath in public opinion." [5]

Even as the nation grew more populous and public business more complicated, Presidents like the two Roosevelts and Wilson found their own ways of taking baths in public opinion. All of them had their monarchical moments. It has latterly become fashionable to say that the imperial Presidency began with FDR. But FDR, though he delighted in power, did not in the later royal style frown on argument and dissent in the presidential presence. Quite the contrary: he valued obstinate and opinionated men (who else could have put up for a dozen years with Harold Ickes?) and made debate a fundamental method of government. Even during the Second World War, Roosevelt continued to believe, as he showed when he began to plan for the peace, that a strong President had to be, when possible, strong *with* the Congress, not strong *against* the Congress.

It was in the years after the Second World War that the Presidency, first with Truman and then more vehemently with Johnson and Nixon, acquired pretensions to powers construed not only as inherent but as exclusive. Personality continued to modify the evolution of the office. In the case of Truman his exceptional directness, openness and lack of affectation considerably offset the impact his unilateral exercise of power might have had on the institution. He declined to remove the Presidency from the people and was far too spontaneous an American democrat to fit comfortably into the imperial Presidency. No doubt there were royal elements in Eisenhower's occupancy of the White House, but his Whiggishness confined them largely to the ceremonial side of the office. Kennedy's Presidency was too short to permit confident generalization; but his ironic and skeptical intelligence customarily kept the Presidency in healthy perspective. Johnson, however, poured an insatiable personality, a greed for consensus and an obsession with secrecy into the institution. The office now began to swell to imperial proportions.

The Johnson Presidency provoked George Reedy's brilliant and influential book *The Twilight of the Presidency*, the first sustained analysis of the office in its imperial phase. Seeing everything through the Johnsonian prism, Reedy may have failed to distinguish the psychological requirements of a particular President from the structural requirements of the Presidency. But his account was filled with insight and prophecy. The analysis was based on what might be called Reedy's Law: "Isolation from reality is inseparable from the exercise of power." [6] His portrait of the White House as a court was not unduly exaggerated. I am not sure, though, that even a court need aid and abet presidential isolation. And I am quite sure that the White House need not necessarily be, as Reedy at times suggested, a Byzantine court.[7] That was not one's experience in the Kennedy years nor particularly one's reading of the Roosevelt, or Jackson, years. Most of all, I think he may have understated the capacity Presidents have to overcome isolation if they wish to do so. Reedy's Law was penetrating but not absolute.

One of the great myths of American political folklore was that the Presidency, with its 'awesome' responsibilities, was the loneliest job in the world.[8] This was nonsense. "No one in the country," said John F. Kennedy, "is more assailed by divergent advice and clamorous counsel." [9] Any President who accepted the obligation of accountability and the discipline of consent knew he must incorporate within himself a nation of diverse values and discrepant objectives. The fact that the decision he made was technically his own did not mean that a sensitivity to what his associates and Congress and the country thought could possibly be excluded from the inscrutable processes of decision. These things played more intensively on conscientious Presidents than anyone outside could possibly imagine.

No one, if he wished it, could see a greater variety of people than the President or consult a wider range of opinion or tap more diversified sources of knowledge. Reedy well described how every White House assistant in New Deal days recalled the experience of bringing a report to FDR and "discovering, in the course of the conversation, that the president had gained from some mysterious, outside source knowledge of aspects of the project of which the assistant himself was not aware." When a President used all his manifold resources to gather information, it became both risky and futile for a member of his staff to hold out on him.[10] I was always astonished at how much more President Kennedy seemed to know about what was going on, including the adverse items, than members of his staff did. In Kennedy's case the Bay of Pigs had provided a salutary if costly lesson in the perils of presidential isolation. One reason for the difference between the Bay of Pigs and the missile crisis was that fiasco had instructed Kennedy in the importance of uninhibited debate in advance of major decision.

But, if the White House provided unparalleled facilities to enable a President to find out everything that was going on, it also, if a President wanted to be shielded from bad news and vexatious argument, gave him unparalleled facilities to fulfill that ambition too. Reedy's book was an illuminating generalization from Reedy's own President projected less persuasively on the Presidency in general. Ironically his thesis applied more precisely to Johnson's successor than to Johnson himself. For Johnson, after all, had his three television sets and three wire service tickers in the Oval Office. He made his angry morning dash through the newspapers and the *Congressional Record*. He could not abide being alone. Even the company of courtiers could tell an intelligent and curious man a good deal; and Johnson's court was brighter than most. In addition, Johnson talked to, even if he too seldom listened to, an endless stream of members of Congress and the press. He unquestionably denied himself reality for a long time, especially when it came to Vietnam. But in the end reality broke through, forcing him to accept unpleasant truths he did not wish to hear. Johnson's personality was far closer than Truman's to imperial specifications. But the fit was by no means perfect.

III

With Nixon there came, whether by weird historical accident or by unconscious national response to historical pressure and possibility, a singular confluence of the job with the man. The Presidency, as enlarged by international delusions and domestic propulsions, found a President whose inner mix of vulnerability and ambition impelled him to push the historical logic to its extremity.

A more traditional politician like Hubert Humphrey, if he had been elected in 1968, a more conscientious politican like George McGovern, if he had made it in 1972, would doubtless have tempered the tendency to gather everything into the White House. But Nixon, underneath a conventional exterior, was a man with revolutionary dreams. The structural forces tending to transfer power to the Presidency were now reinforced by compulsive internal drives — a sense of life as a battlefield, a belief that the nation was swarming with personal enemies, a flinching from face-to-face argument, an addiction to seclusion, a preoccupation with response to crisis, an insistence on a controlled environment for decision. For a man so constituted, the imperial Presidency was the perfect shield and refuge. But Nixon not only had an urgent psychological need for exemption from the democratic process. He also boldly sensed an historical opportunity to transform the Presidency — to consolidate within the White House all the powers, as against Congress, as against the electorate, as against the rest of the executive branch itself, that a generation of foreign and domestic turbulence had chaotically delivered to the Presidency.

Speculation about motivation is ordinarily unprofitable, and psychobiography is a notoriously underdeveloped science. Nonetheless, because the Presidency is so peculiarly personal an institution, and because the psychic drives of the man who sits in the Oval Office so fundamentally affect the impact of each particular Presidency, and because Nixon's destiny was to carry the logic of the imperial Presidency to the point of no return, one cannot avoid pondering why he did things it never occurred to Truman or Eisenhower or Kennedy or even Johnson to attempt.

In *Six Crises,* itself a revealing title, Nixon had written in a revealing phrase about the "warfare of politics." [11] Politics was indeed for him a succession of battles *à toute outrance,* to be fought against cunning and vicious foes with every weapon at hand. "He is the only major American politician in our history," an observer wrote in 1960, "who came to prominence by techniques which, if generally adopted, would destroy the whole fabric of mutual confidence on which our democracy rests." [12] As the observer in question, I took care to make the point subjunctively. People change in politics and life; and one could not hold forever against Nixon what he said about Jerry Voorhis in 1946 or Helen Gahagan Douglas in 1950 or Adlai Stevenson in 1952 ("Adlai the appeaser . . . who got a Ph.D. from Dean Acheson's College of Cowardly Communist Containment") or Dean Acheson thereafter, especially in contrast to Dulles ("Isn't it wonderful finally to have a Secretary of State who isn't taken in by the Communists, who stands up to them?"). There was always the possibility of the new Nixon. Indeed, after his trips to Peking and Moscow in 1972, he seemed an honors graduate of the College of Cowardly Communist Containment himself.

Yet it was easier to alter policies than sets of mind.[13] "I believe in the battle," Nixon told an interviewer during his high after his victory in 1972, "whether it's the battle of a campaign or the battle of this office. . . . It's always there wherever you go. I, perhaps, carry it more than others because that's my way." It was indeed his way. His concern through life had been to master the panic stirred within him by crisis, to be, when the moment arrived, calm, balanced, objective. He told his post-election interviewer proudly, "I have a reputation for being the coolest person in the room."

To assure coolness in the clutch, he believed, it was essential above all to simplify the arena of decision. This meant withdrawal from the provocations of criticism and argument. The President, said Tom Charles Huston, who served for a year as domestic security planner in the White House, "abhors confrontations, most particularly those based on philosophical convictions." [14] Nixon himself observed, "The [presidential] office as presently furnished probably would drive President Johnson up the wall. He liked things going on. He kept three TV sets here. . . . I could go up the wall watching TV commentators. I don't. I get my news from the news summary the staff prepares every day." The White House itself evidently drove him up the wall too. He deserted the light and lovely Oval Office for a small working room in the Executive Office Building; Joseph Alsop, an admirer, called him an agoraphobe. Even more soothing was Camp David, the old Shangri-La of FDR, high on the Catoctin Mountain of Maryland. Nixon now transformed FDR's rural retreat into an armed fortress, where he sought shelter behind a triple fence and a forest overflowing with Marines. [15] "I find that up there on top of a mountain," he said, "it is easier for me to get on top of the job." [16]

Every President reconstructs the Presidency to meet his own psychological needs. Nixon displayed more monarchical yearnings than any of his predecessors. He plainly reveled in the ritual of the office, only regretting that it could not be more elaborate. What previous President, for example, would have dreamed of ceremonial trumpets or of putting the White House security force in costumes to rival the Guards at Buckingham Palace? Public ridicule stopped this. But Nixon saw no problem about using federal money, under the pretext of national security, to adorn his California and Florida estates with redwood fences, golf carts, heaters and wind screens for the swimming pool, beach cabanas, roof tiling, carpets, furniture, trees and shrubbery. [17]

IV

Comic opera dress for White House guards and heaters for the San Clemente swimming pool were unimportant except as the expression of a regal state of mind. What mattered much more was the extent to which the same state of mind led Nixon, far more even than Johnson, to banish challenge from the presidential environment.

"The first impression that one gets of a ruler and his brains," we are told in *The Prince,* "is from seeing the men that he has about him." A prudent prince, Machiavelli said, chose wise men for his council and gave these alone full liberty to speak the truth to him. The prince, moreover, must so comport himself that each adviser "may see that the more freely he speaks, the more he will be acceptable." Machiavelli added that a ruler "ought to be a great asker, and a patient hearer of the truth about those things of which he has inquired; indeed, if he finds that anyone has scruples in telling him the truth he should be angry." [18]

It cannot be said that many American Presidents have lived up to Machiavelli's standard. Bad news is always an irritant; and a consistent bearer of bad news is likely to find himself exiled from any presidential presence. Nevertheless genuinely strong Presidents had never been afraid to surround themselves with genuinely strong-minded men. Historically the American cabinet, though never a responsible unit in the British sense, had characteristically contained men with independent views, reputations and constituencies — men to whom even a strong President was compelled, often to his annoyance, to listen and with whom he had in some fashion to come to terms. Jackson had to deal with Van Buren, Taney, Livingston, Woodbury, Cass, Kendall and Butler; Lincoln with Seward, Chase, Stanton, Blair, Welles; Wilson with Bryan, McAdoo, Baker, Daniels, Glass, Garrison, Palmer, Houston; Roosevelt with Hull, Stimson, Ickes, Morgenthau, Wallace, Hopkins, Biddle, Jackson, Perkins, Jones, Knox; Truman with Marshall, Acheson, Byrnes, Vinson, Harriman,

Johnson, Forrestal, Patterson; Kennedy and Johnson with Rusk, McNamara, Clifford, Robert Kennedy, Dillon, Goldberg, Udall, Katzenbach, Clark, Freeman, Wirtz, Ribicoff, Gardner, not to speak of subcabinet men of the stature and force of Harriman and Ball.

Nixon, running for the Presidency, had promised "a Cabinet made up of the ablest men in America, leaders in their own right and not merely by virtue of appointment." [19] But, once he was in the White House, who in his cabinet talked back to him — assuming, that is, they could get past H. R. Haldeman and into the Oval Office? The fate of those who tried was instructive. Messrs. Hickel, Romney, Laird, Connally, Peterson, Finch had vanished from the cabinet by inaugural day 1973. In his first term Nixon kept his cabinet at arm's length. In his second he began with the most anonymous cabinet within memory, a cabinet, with one or two exceptions, of clerks, of compliant and faceless men who stood for nothing, had no national identity of their own and were certified not to defy presidential whim. More than this, he even tried, in his drive for presidential supremacy, to abolish the cabinet in the traditional sense, superseding it by a small super-cabinet to which the lesser cabinet members would report. When events forced him to abandon this idea, he allowed that henceforth he would have "a direct line of communication" with his cabinet members [20] — a concession which would have astounded all previous Presidents, who assumed such direct lines as a matter of course, and which showed how sadly the cabinet had been demoted. Probably many Americans could name more members of the Kennedy cabinet of a decade before, or of the Roosevelt cabinet of thirty years before, than they could of the Nixon cabinet in the first year of his second term.

Nixon was engaged in a drastic reorganization of national authority; and, in place of the cabinet, he began to centralize the powers of government in the White House. Until rather recently Presidents had made do with very little in the way of personal staff. When Hoover persuaded Congress to give him a third secretary, it was, Franklin Roosevelt used to say, the most positive accomplishment of his administration. In 1939 the Government

Reorganization Act gave the President the authority for the first time to hire administrative assistants. There was excellent reason for this: a personal staff was increasingly necessary if a President were to have any hope of controlling the decisions and operations of an increasingly uncontrollable executive bureaucracy. The White House entourage could give the President essential support in the inevitable tug of war between the Presidency and the permanent government.[21] But the original idea was that the White House staff should be no more than the eyes and ears of the President. The committee in making the recommendation to Roosevelt firmly stipulated that presidential assistants "would have no power to make decisions or issue instructions in their own right." [22]

For a generation the White House staff was, as envisaged, a personal extension of the President. It remained small enough for its members to have easy access to their chief. They saw their job as channels — both ways — between the President and the operating departments and agencies. The Second World War no doubt heaped more burdens on the President of the United States than anything in the thirty years thereafter. But during the entire course of the war Franklin Roosevelt never had more than eleven White House assistants. Truman's largest number was thirteen. With Eisenhower the roster leaped by 1959 to 37. Kennedy had 23 when he died. Johnson averaged hardly more than 20 during his five years in the White House.

In 1972 Nixon had 48 personal assistants. How many of these ever saw the President? The total of those on the White House payroll had grown from 266 in 1954 to 600 in 1971. An undisclosed number, in addition, served at the White House while remaining on departmental payrolls. The Executive Office staff had grown from 1175 in 1954 to 1664 in Kennedy's last year to a stupefying 5395 under Nixon in 1971. In the first Nixon term the operating cost of the Executive Office rose from $31 million to $71 million.[23]

What all this signified, and what was far more crucial than the increase in numbers and budget, was the centralization in the White House of substantive operations. By Nixon's time White

House aides were no longer channels of communication. They were powerful figures in themselves, making decisions and issuing instructions in their own right, more powerful than members of the cabinet — Kissinger more powerful than the Secretary of State or Defense, Haldeman and Ehrlichman more powerful than the forgotten men who headed the domestic departments. But they were not, like members of the cabinet, subject to confirmation by the Senate or (pre-Watergate) to interrogation by committees of the Congress.

No one who had witnessed the capacity of established bureaucracies to frustrate presidential purposes could fail to sympathize with Nixon's effort to annex the permanent government to the Presidency. But such an effort could work only with an open White House and a President accessible to people and to ideas. Nixon's fatal error was to institute within the White House itself a centralization even more total than that he contemplated for the executive branch. He rarely saw most of his so-called personal assistants. If an aide telephoned the President on a domestic matter, his call was switched to Haldeman's office. If he sent the President a memorandum, Haldeman decided whether or not the President would see it. "Rather than the President telling someone to do something," Haldeman explained in 1971, "I'll tell the guy. If he wants to find out something from somebody, I'll do it." [24]

Presidents like Roosevelt and Kennedy understood that, if the man at the top confined himself to a single information system, he became the prisoner of that system. Therefore they pitted sources of their own against the information delivered to them through official channels. They understood that contention was an indispensable means of government. But Nixon, instead of exposing himself to the chastening influence of debate, organized the executive branch and the White House in order to shield himself as far as humanly possible from direct question or challenge — i.e., from reality.

The result was the enthronement of unreality. "The more a President sits surrounded only by his own views and those of his personal advisers," said Senator Charles Mathias, "the more he lives in a house of mirrors in which all views and ideas tend to reflect and reinforce his own." [25] It was a fine phrase, and all too exact. Remembering the ease of access to the President in other White Houses — Roosevelt's and Kennedy's, for example — one could only wonder at the intense psychic compulsions that led Nixon to establish so rigid and, in the end, so predictably self-deceiving and self-defeating a procedure. The White House became a world of its own, cut off from Washington and the nation. "There is a myth and unreality about the place," said John Dean, who served for a time as counsel to the President, "and when I worked there I was subject to the same feelings." [26] It all reminded an English journalist of Abdul the Damned, who immured himself in the Yildiz Kiosk, "reduced his ministers, whom he rarely saw, to executive officers, transmitted orders to them through the Mabeyn, his intimate secretaries, and left the Chief Eunuch to deal with other matters. Like Mr. Nixon he lived in the midst of alarms which were largely due to his own temperament and isolation." [27] With Nixon, withdrawal from external reality allowed him to impose his private sense of what was real on the government and, if he could, on the nation. America was entering the age of the solipsistic Presidency.

v

There had long been means outside the government to recall Presidents to reality. Through history the media of mass opinion — newspapers and, in more recent years, radio and television — had provided an unwritten check on Caesarism.[28] One way this had played particularly upon Presidents, at least since the days of the second Roosevelt, was through the presidential press conference.

Franklin Roosevelt did not invent the presidential press conference. Theodore Roosevelt was the first President to give the press a bridgehead in the White House, Wilson the first to hold regular press conferences. Suspended during the First World War, the presidential press conference made a limited comeback in the twenties, but under highly circumscribed conditions. Hoover, for example, insisted that all questions be submitted in advance and answered only those he felt like answering. Newspapermen were forbidden to ask follow-up questions; they were even forbidden to report the questions the President declined to answer.

But it was FDR who transformed the press conference into a potent instrument of government. On his fourth day in office, he invited reporters to join in regular sessions of give-and-take along the lines of the "very delightful family conferences I have been holding in Albany for the last four years." Written questions were abolished; and, while there could be no direct quotation except when specifically authorized, there was no limit on indirect citation except for occasional remarks defined as "background," which could be used without attribution to the White House, and for very occasional passages put entirely off the record. "I am told that what I am about to do will be impossible," FDR said, "but I am going to try it." [29]

Roosevelt held 1011 press conferences during his twelve years and one month in the White House — an average of almost two a week. Some ran forty minutes or even an hour in length. As the President became a major and steady source of news, the number of reporters attending his conferences increased, and the "very delightful family conferences" gradually turned into mob scenes around the presidential desk. Roosevelt met the press in the Oval Office to the end. But in 1950 Truman, who held conferences only once a week, transferred them to the Indian Treaty Room in the old State Department. Here the President, instead of chatting while seated at his desk, looked down at the reporters from a podium. Under Truman too reporters were permitted to make transcripts, though their stories still had to be couched in indirect discourse. Under Eisenhower the White House began to issue the transcripts itself. Eisenhower in time permitted his conferences to be taped for television, and Kennedy both issued exact transcripts and went on television live.

The press conference was by now well known as a means by which the President could influence the country. It was less well known as a means by which the country could influence the President. For the press conference, as most Presidents rapidly discovered, was a forum in which they not only told things but learned things. Preparation for the conference required the President to acquaint himself with matters of public business that might be far from his own immediate concern. And the questions asked at the conference often disclosed to him things about the government and the country that his own executive establishment, consciously or not, had been keeping from him. The press conference, in short, was not a one-way but a two-way form of communication. "When I was President," wrote Truman, "I felt that I always learned more about what was on the minds of the people from the reporters' questions than they could possibly learn from me." [30]

By mid-century the presidential press conference seemed well established as an integral part of the political process. Arthur Krock called it "the American counterpart of the question period in the House of Commons" — a not quite precise analogy, since the ground rules of the press conference were far more flexible. Erwin D. Canham spoke of "the fifth wheel of democracy." [31] Political scientists agreed with newspapermen about both the value of the conference and its permanence. Clinton Rossiter saw it as "a completely accepted institution . . . a fixed custom in our system of government." Louis Brownlow, that sagacious student of the American polity, even wrote, "It would be almost impossible, in my opinion, for any President now to change this pattern or to interfere in any material way with this institution, set up without the authority of the law, required by no Constitutional mandate, embodying no rights enforceable in a court of law, but nevertheless an institution of prime importance in the political life of the American people." [32] As late as 1965 James MacGregor Burns could say, "The press conference is as much a White House fixture as the cabinet meeting." [33]

Burns was prescient in a way he could not have realized. Under Nixon both cabinet meeting and press conference practically disappeared. In his first four years Nixon held as many press conferences (28) as FDR had held in his first three months. In a way it was odd that Nixon should have thus renounced so powerful an instrument of government — one, moreover, that he employed with reasonable proficiency. In 1959 Clinton Rossiter had thought it would be "altogether imbecile" for any President to surrender "the power he draws from this unique institution." [34] But the whole process of exposure, scrutiny, challenge and accountability evidently exacted too heavy a psychic toll. "I believe you should be able to have a press conference," Vice President Agnew said, "without having reporters key in on certain divisive issues." [35] Alas, this was hard to arrange, unless one was General de Gaulle.

Not being General de Gaulle, Nixon, when he had to appear in public, preferred the most controlled circumstances. He was protected from reporters on trips and liked best to display himself to the nation in television addresses, where no one could talk back, except impotently to the home screen. He was the supreme prime-time President. In his first eighteen months Nixon was on television at prime time more than Eisenhower, Kennedy and Johnson combined in their first eighteen months. Returning from China, he lay over at Anchorage in Alaska for nine hours simply so that he could descend on Washington at 9 P.M., the primest of prime hours.

But all this denied the country the opportunity to hear the President respond in a continuous way to questions on national policy. It is hard, for example, to imagine any other President, confronted by the Indochina negotiations, not seeing it as his obvious personal responsibility to inform the people what was going on. When Roosevelt went to summit conferences, he did not send out Harry Hopkins or Admiral Leahy to explain it all to the press, nor did Johnson, confronted by Vietnam, consider for a moment letting Walt Rostow do the talking. But the American people got so quickly inured to Nixon's flight from public interrogation that no one expressed surprise when he kept trotting out Henry Kissinger to do what he should have been doing himself. Or, to take another example, one of FDR's most impressive exercises was his annual budgetary press conference. "We go over the Budget message that is going up to Congress the following day," as Roosevelt described it, "and take it apart. Anybody can ask any question he wants about it." [36] Nixon never dared attempt anything of the sort, and the electorate was therefore deprived of his personal views about the way priorities were set and taxes spent.

Since presidential press conferences had no great value unless held regularly and frequently — otherwise the pent-up flood of questions made it impossible to pursue any single topic very far — Nixon gravely enfeebled the institution that Louis Brownlow thought it impossible for any President to change. This was a disservice not only to the country but to himself. For all its abundant vanities and vagaries, the press in the American system served as the champion of the reality principle against the presidential capacity for self-delusion. Reading FDR's press conferences makes it evident how much meeting the press twice a week contributed to the singular vitality and responsiveness of his Presidency. Nixon instead shut himself off from the press, and from the country. If he had, for example, been exposed to constant questioning by the press over the long months after the agents for the Committee for the Re-election of the President were discovered in the Democratic headquarters at the Watergate, he could hardly have remained in his professed state of invincible ignorance over the misdeeds of the men he described ten months later as "my closest friends and most trusted aides." [37]

VI

Nixon's disdain for the presidential press conference was part of a larger suspicion and dislike of the press. This attitude diverged a good deal from the national tradition. Nothing had been more solidly imbedded in American political literature than belief in freedom of the press. The Founding Fathers had recognized that a sprawling country like the United States required a strong national government, which is why they abandoned the Articles of Confederation and drafted the Constitution. At the same time, all of them had a fear of despotism, and some of them had a fear of democracy. The best antidote to despotism, they reasoned, was the guarantee of freedom of speech and the press; and the best safeguard for democracy was the wide diffusion of information. Few themes were more insistently repeated by the statesmen of the early republic. "The freedom of the press," Jefferson wrote in Article XIV of the Virginia Declaration of Rights, "is one of the great bulwarks of liberty, and can never be restrained but by despotic governments." "None of the means of information are more sacred, or have been cherished with more tenderness and care by the settlers of America," wrote John Adams,

> than the press. . . . Be not intimidated, therefore, by any terrors, from publishing with the utmost freedom whatever can be warranted by the laws of your country; nor suffer yourselves to be wheedled out of your liberty by any pretenses of politeness, delicacy, or decency. These, as they are often used, are but three different names for hypocrisy, chicanery, and cowardice.[38]

This had been the theory of the republic. Tocqueville, visiting America in the 1830s, quickly seized the point. "The more I consider the independence of the press in its principal consequences," he wrote, "the more am I convinced that in the modern world it is the chief and, so to speak, the constitutive element of liberty." [39] I do not suggest that the Founding Fathers enjoyed criticism any more than their descendants, but they did ultimately recognize the free press as essential to enable the people to combat the pretensions of government. Even the sainted Jefferson had moments of bad temper when he recommended that state governments prosecute editors for seditious libel, but this was not his abiding view. Lincoln suppressed newspapers but regretted having to do it. The first Roosevelt invented the Ananias Club and denounced investigative reporters as "muckrakers." But in his *Autobiography* he described the Washington correspondents as "a singularly able, trustworthy and public-spirited body of men, and the most useful of all agents on the fight for efficient and decent government." [40] The second Roosevelt gave John O'Donnell an Iron Cross but held press conferences twice a week. Kennedy canceled the White House subscriptions to the *New York Herald Tribune* but called the press "an invaluable arm of the Presidency, as a check really on what is going on in the administration. . . . Even though we never like it, and even though we wish they didn't write it, and even though we disapprove, there isn't any doubt at all that we could not do the job at all in a free society without a very, very active press." [41]

For its part, the press has welcomed this role. It did not always discharge it with the utmost intelligence or responsibility, but it did understand that the press was not a part of government and had no duty to support the government. The creed was well stated by the great Delane of the London *Times* in 1852 when the *Times* outraged the Prime Minister by breaking a story about negotiations between Britain and Louis Napoleon. "We cannot," Delane told Lord Derby, "admit that a newspaper's purpose is to share the labors of statesmanship or that it is bound by the same limitations, the same duties, the same liabilities as that of Ministers. The purpose and duties of the two powers are constantly separate, generally independent, sometimes diametrically opposite. The dignity and freedom of the press are trammeled from the moment it accepts an ancillary position." [42]

The personal attitude of any President toward the press and television inescapably governed the reaction of his associates. Kennedy, however wrathful he could briefly become over the latest newspaper excess, encouraged the rest of us at the White House to a policy of the open door. The press, never satisfied (and properly insatiable), complained about news management, but it could not complain about a closed administration. Nixon, on the other hand, regarded newspapers and newspapermen, indeed public debate in general, with thinly disguised impatience and resentment. In October 1972 he extemporaneously castigated "the so-called opinion leaders of this country" on the ground that they did not understand "the necessity to stand by the President of the United States when he makes a terribly difficult, potentially unpopular decision." [43] And in his interview with Garnett Horner of the *Washington Star-News,* he made his celebrated observation that "the average American is just like a child in the family." [44] He may have been trying only to say that, like a child, the average American grew through the acceptance of responsibility; but it was still a curious and revealing, way to make the point — curious too that this atrocious remark survived White House editing of the text of the interview, which suggests that everyone around the White House took the proposition as self-evident. Nixon inevitably created an administration determined to put the press in its place — "the most 'closed' administration in recent decades," according to the National Press Club report. [45]

The President, it could only be supposed, suffered from delusions of persecution. In three presidential elections Nixon had the support of eighty percent of the press. Truman, who endured far more savage and unrelenting criticism than Nixon had before 1973, took it as part of political life, which he correctly understood to be a high-risk occupation: "If you can't stand the heat, stay out of the kitchen." In 1972, as the Press Club report had it, "the national press corps was tougher on George McGovern than it was on Richard Nixon." Nevertheless Nixon after the election complained bitterly to the head of the Associated Press bureau in Washington about "four years of the most devastating attacks on TV, in much of the media, in editorials and columns." [46] He saw himself as the pitiful and helpless victim of a media conspiracy — as someone who existed, in his famous phrase of 1962, for the press to kick around.

There is little need now to recall in detail the diversity of ways in which the Nixon administration in its first term and for a season in its second waged war against the media. For the first time in American history the government, in the case of the Pentagon Papers, tried to impose prior restraint on the publication of news. The President ordered the phones of offending newspapermen to be wiretapped. His press secretary deceived newspapermen for many months and then blandly declared his deceptions "inoperative." The Vice President went around the country in a jihad against disloyal newspapers and newspapermen. The Department of Justice tried for a while to subpoena reporters' notebooks and tapes. The acting head of the FBI complained that

American journalists were "too much a part of the culture of disparagement which threatens to destroy all respect for established institutions." A White House assistant warned networks that they might be subject to antitrust prosecution if they did not "move conservatives and people with a viewpoint of Middle America onto the networks." The head of the White House Office of Telecommunications denounced "ideological plugola" and added ominously, "Station managers and network officials who fail to correct imbalance or consistent bias from the networks — or who acquiesce by silence — can only be considered willing participants, to be held fully accountable . . . at license-renewal time." [47]

Nixon's president of the Corporation for Public Broadcasting cut down public-affairs shows. Nixon's Supreme Court appointees made possible the 5 to 4 decision in *Branzburg v. Hayes* which confirmed the practice of jailing newspapermen who declined to disclose confidential sources to grand juries, a decision which Justice Stewart, a Republican appointed by Eisenhower, called a "crabbed view of the First Amendment" reflecting "a disturbing insensitivity to the critical role of an independent press in our society." The decision, Stewart continued, invited "state and federal authorities to undermine the historic independence of the press by attempting to annex the journalistic profession as an investigative arm of government." [48] If the logic of the decision were carried further, it implied the death of investigative reporting in America. Senator Ervin summed up the record: "The Administration assaulted the very integrity of the press and called into question its right to disagree with official views." [49]

Nor was the campaign cast only in general terms. When the *Washington Post* threatened lèse majesté by pursuing the Watergate story, persons associated with the Nixon 1972 campaign promptly challenged the renewal of licenses for two Florida television stations owned by the *Post,* thereby producing a loss of 25 percent of the market value of the *Post* stocks in a fortnight. When John Mitchell, the former Attorney General, was asked about a *Post* story connecting him with Watergate, he replied, inelegantly and imprudently, "All that crap, you're puttin' in the paper? It's all been denied. . . . Katie Graham is gonna get her tit caught in a big fat wringer if that's published." [50] But Mrs. Graham, the owner of the *Post,* courageously backed her staff in the pursuit of the story. In the end it was Mitchell who got caught in the big fat wringer.

It is hard to imagine an idea that would have more astounded the framers of the Constitution than that of the obligation of American newspapers and American citizens, in peacetime and outside the government, to give automatic approval to whatever the President wanted to do. In the past it had been supposed that the American system worked best when American citizens spoke their minds and consciences. But, if Nixon dismissed public opinion in the United States as refractory and pernicious when it dared dissent from the President, he was even more scornful of what in the past had served as another check on presidential power — that is, the opinion of foreign nations. Where the Federalist Papers had recommended that American policies be tried in the light in which they might appear to the unbiased part of mankind, Nixon declined to listen to any form of foreign criticism. He thus treated the United Nations with studied contempt and evidently considered the post of United States Ambassador to the United Nations as less important than that of the chairman of the Republican National Committee; at least one imagines that he thought he was promoting, not demoting, George Bush when he shifted him from one job to the other. Perhaps the triumph of presidential petulance came in the case of Sweden where Nixon did everything short of breaking off diplomatic relations because the Swedish government dared criticize American policy in Vietnam. In 1973 Senator Humphrey, condemning "this infantile game of diplomatic wrist-slapping," introduced a resolution calling for the normalization of relations.[51]

VII

This psychological background, this dislike of challenge and scrutiny, explained in part Nixon's desire to centralize governmental power within the White House itself. His predecessors had already done this to a considerable degree with regard to questions of war and peace. But, more than his predecessors, Nixon perceived that the imperial Presidency was now acquiring a base in domestic policy. He had a constituency to defend and a set of values to vindicate, and he planned to make Congress as impotent in domestic affairs as it had come to be in foreign affairs.

He understood, first of all, the political possibilities of the managed economy. The budget was the main instrument of executive action. Stop-and-go fiscal policy, for example, could produce a boom in time for the 1972 election. Price controls, tax relief, subsidies, tariffs, import quotas provided other levers for presidential manipulation. So did the setting of milk prices and the negotiation of grain deals with the Soviet Union and the activities of multinational corporations like the International Telephone and Telegraph Corporation. The idea was to make as many interests as possible dependent on government favor; then to use this favor to reward politically sympathetic sectors of the economy and to punish the unregenerate. If armament corporations and hard-hats supported the administration and professors and the poor did not, the budget could send more money to defense and less to education and social welfare. Beneficiaries could demonstrate their gratitude by contributions to the Republican party or, in 1972, to the Committee for the Re-election of the President. But it was more than a matter of individual arrangements; it went to the future structure of the economy. Nixon, as Lubell wrote, "set his own priorities, which favored defense, manufacturing, and business quite heavily, and restricted funds for fields like ecology, teaching, social services, and public employment generally." [52] By establishing through arms contracts a durable pattern of military spending and by transferring the major competition for remaining funds to the states through revenue sharing, Nixon hoped to secure presidential control over the economy for some time to come.

Of course the economic management of the Nixon administration was notoriously incompetent. But, far from discrediting the presidential quest for power, failure, as Lubell pointed out, became rather "the means of gaining additional power." [53] Thus the predictable collapse of the hopeless anti-inflation program of 1969–1971 enabled Nixon to impose a system of price and wage controls in August 1971 and thereby gain even more power. Similarly the steady decline in foreign trade balances led Nixon in April 1973 to ask Congress to delegate to the Presidency more discretionary authority than any previous President had ever had to change tariffs and other trade barriers. Strong arguments could be made on their merits both for the system of controls and for the trade bill; but problems remained when a President used economic powers for political ends.

The essence of politics in a managed economy, Lubell justly said, was "not verbal debate but actions taken and resistance provoked. Ineffective resistance becomes tantamount to ratification of the action by the voters." [54] But what was effective resistance? In earlier years the conditioned reflexes of a business community dominated by Republicans had set limits on the ability of Democratic Presidents to make economic changes. But now government and the private economy worshiped at the same church. Once the President was one of their own, leaders of business no longer sprang to arms when White House decisions modified the economy. After all, they had given more money to Nixon's election and re-election than any presidential candidate had ever received in American history. As for organized labor, it had now largely settled for a junior partnership with business. Unions were too dependent on government patterns of spending to offer militant or united opposition. Within the public community, mayors and governors could inveigh against budgetary cutbacks and from time to time stir enough fuss and receive a few bones. On occasion courts could veto presidential usurpation. But the critical question under the Constitution was the nature of resistance proposed by Congress to the control of national priorities by the President.

Neither the Presidency nor the Congress had the exclusive right to decide priorities. The Constitution enjoined them to make such decisions together. When a President tried to pull all authority into the White House, Congress had in its appropriations power a constitutional means of defense and self-assertion.

If Nixon were to complete his campaign for presidential supremacy, he had therefore to find ways to circumvent the powers
given Congress by the Constitution to indicate priorities through
the control of appropriations. His solution was simple and direct.
It was, when laws passed by Congress conflicted with his own
conception of national priorities, to refuse to spend the funds
Congress had solemnly voted.

VIII

Impoundment, as it was called, had a minor status in law
and custom. Presidents had withheld small amounts for limited periods since the now celebrated occasion when Jefferson
declined to spend money appropriated for gunboats in 1803.
Actually the Jefferson gunboat case, though fervently invoked as
a precedent 170 years later, hardly bore the weight placed on it
by the Nixon administration. All that happened in 1803 was, as
Jefferson explained to Congress, that "the favorable and peace-
able turn of affairs on the Mississippi" — that is, the acquisition
of Louisiana — had rendered unnecessary the "immediate" expenditure of $50,000 voted by Congress the preceding February
for fifteen gunboats to patrol the river. "Time," Jefferson added,
"was desirable in order that the institution of that branch of our
force might begin on models the most approved by experience."
A year later he reported to Congress, "The act of Congress of
February 28, 1803, for building and employing a number of
gunboats, is now in a course of execution to the extent there
provided for." [55]
In short, Jefferson did not decline to spend appropriated
money in 1803 because he objected to the gunboat program. On
the contrary, he adored gunboats and wanted to make them the
basis of American defense. When he left office, about 180 gunboats were stationed in American ports. "If he had had his way,"
his latest biographer tells us, "there would have been at least
three hundred." [56] Jefferson simply *deferred* spending on gunboats for a few months in 1803 both because an emergency had
disappeared and because he wanted to wait for later and better

models. This was an entirely different form of impoundment from that practiced in Jefferson's name in the 1970s.

Impoundment was exceedingly rare in the nineteenth century. The only other conspicuous case was the withholding by Grant of river and harbor funds in 1876 on the ground that such expenditure was not "obligatory" and that, in view of the need for retrenchment in depression, "under no circumstances will I allow expenditures upon works not clearly national." [57] But presidential impounding remained an inconsequential issue till 1941, when Franklin Roosevelt began to lay aside money appropriated for public works not directly related to the war effort. Such impoundment, Roosevelt emphasized, was "not a substitute" for an item veto — that is, the power to veto specific items in appropriations bills without vetoing the entire bill — "and should not be used to set aside or nullify the expressed will of Congress." [58] Truman's famous impoundment of Air Force funds in 1949 was the exercise of an option expressly granted by Congress. When Johnson, anxious to avoid adding to inflationary pressure during the Vietnam War, decided to postpone the spending of some $5 billion appropriated by Congress, he explained the situation to congressional leaders and obtained their tacit consent. It could be contended, in addition, that military impoundment — Jefferson's in 1803, Roosevelt's in 1941 and thereafter, Truman's in 1949, Kennedy's refusal in 1961 to spend an extra $180 million voted by Congress for the B-70 bomber, even arguably Johnson's in 1967 — fell within the legitimate powers of the Commander in Chief.

There was also a measure of legal authority to withhold funds for domestic programs. The Anti-Deficiency Acts of 1905 and 1906, with amendments in 1951, authorized impoundment to effect savings and to establish reserves for contingencies so long as the funds impounded were not needed to fulfill the purposes of the original appropriations.[59] The Civil Rights Act of 1964 required the denial of federal aid to education when districts failed to integrate their schools. It was claimed too that the Employment Act of 1946 authorized impoundment when government spending might increase inflationary pressures, though this was reaching rather high since the Act mentioned neither inflation nor impoundment and was concerned with the adequacy rather than the reduction of government spending. It was further pointed out that most appropriations bills were permissive rather than mandatory in form — that is, that they authorized rather than commanded the President to spend the funds appropriated. This distinction gained a certain recognition in 1962 when the House Armed Services Committee tried to force the hand of the Kennedy administration on the B-70 bomber, but Kennedy persuaded Chairman Carl Vinson to substitute permissive for mandatory language and then did not spend the appropriation.

Presidential impoundment in these years remained, however, within the framework of predominant congressional intent and was controlled by the give-and-take of the political process. If Congress made enough of an outcry, Presidents released the funds. Moreover, such impoundment was rooted in statutes or in the President's military authority; it was not based on a general claim to constitutional power. In 1963, when the Civil Rights Commission proposed that federal aid be denied Mississippi because of local violation of desegregation orders, Kennedy said, "I don't have the power to cut off the aid in a general way." "What they were suggesting," he later explained, "was . . . a blanket withdrawal of Federal expenditures. . . . I said that I didn't have the power to do so, and I do not think the President should be given that power, because it could be used in other ways differently." [60] Indeed, William Rehnquist of the Department of Justice actually advised the White House in 1969, before the Nixon administration had embarked on its free-swinging impoundment policy, "With respect to the suggestion that the President has a *constitutional* power to decline to spend appropriated funds, we must conclude that the existence of such a broad power is supported by neither reason nor precedent." He found it difficult, he added, "to formulate a *constitutional* theory to justify a refusal by the President to comply with a Congressional directive to spend." [61]

Rehnquist's doubts did not, however, deter Nixon, who midway in his first term embarked on an impoundment trip unprecedented in American history. Nixon's distinctive contribution was what Senator Humphrey called "policy impoundment" [62]: that is, impoundment employed precisely as FDR had said it should not be employed — to set aside or nullify the expressed will of Congress. He also impounded far more money than any of his predecessors. A good deal came out of defense, space and highway appropriations, but a good deal too came out of health, manpower, housing, urban, educational and environmental appropriations. Of the $7 billion appropriated to conserve natural resources and to clean up air and water, for example, nearly $1 billion was impounded.[63] By 1973 Nixon's impoundments had affected more than a hundred federal programs and reached the level of about $15 billion, which meant about 17 to 20 percent of controllable funds. Jefferson's $50,000 in 1803, though now often cited, was no precedent for Nixon's preposterous sum, any more than Jefferson's postponement of spending could stand as a precedent for Nixon's evisceration or abolition of programs.

Nixon administration officials flourished charts purporting to prove that their own impoundment represented no larger a share of total outlays than the impoundment in the three preceding administrations. The figures were misleading. Previous impoundment was very largely the deferment of immediate expenditure, with funds simply stretched out over a longer period. Such impounding did not carry with it the rejection of legislated policies. "Past actions," the Library of Congress reported in 1973, "tended to be more for routine financial management while current impoundments often are for the purpose of terminating or curtailing programs." [64] Impoundment, said Senator Ervin, had become "a means whereby the White House can give effect to social goals of its own choosing by reallocating national resources in contravention of congressional dictates." Impoundment enabled the President "to modify, reshape, or nullify completely laws passed by the legislative branch, thereby making legislative policy — a power reserved exclusively to the Congress.[65]

Nor did Nixon, like Johnson, consult with congressional leaders on impoundment questions. In asserting his independent authority to decide not only whether money appropriated by Con-

gress should be spent or withheld but whether programs
authorized by Congress should be continued or killed, Nixon
now claimed precisely the constitutional authority that Rehnquist had disclaimed in 1969. In 1973 a new Deputy Attorney
General derived a "substantial latitude to refuse to spend" from
the "executive power" itself.[66] Asked in a press conference to answer the contention that his impoundment policy abrogated authority the Constitution had given to Congress, Nixon, whether
ignorant himself or relying on the ignorance of his listeners, replied, "The same way that Jefferson did and Jackson did and
Truman did. . . . The constitutional right for the President of
the United States to impound funds . . . when the spending of
money would mean either increasing prices or increasing taxes
. . . is absolutely clear." [67] This was an astonishing venture in
constitutional interpretation. It would be hard to find in the
Constitution the command that the President must hold down either prices or taxes; and, since Nixon invariably asserted that all
expenditures he disliked increased prices and taxes, he seemed to
be claiming unlimited constitutional power to nullify appropriation laws.

For Nixon impoundment had become not an instrument of
economy but of policy. Convinced that the electorate was behind
him in his determination to hold down nondefense spending, persuaded that Congress was incapable of keeping public spending
under control, exhilarated by the margin of his re-election in
1972, he saw the Presidency as the judge of last resort. Impoundment now became what Franklin Roosevelt had said thirty
years before it should not be — a substitute for the item veto.
Certainly a case could be made for the item veto. It existed in
over forty states; it was embodied in Article I, Section 7 of the
Confederate Constitution; it had been requested by Grant in
1873, by Roosevelt in 1938 and Eisenhower in 1957; and it was
a reform long advocated by political scientists (though enthusiasm now slackened when they saw what use Nixon made of it).
But, whatever the merits of the item veto, the Constitution authorized the President to veto only entire bills. The item veto
was simply not a legal power of the Presidency.

Nixon's exercise of an item veto through policy impoundment was not only an instance of real executive usurpation; it meant not only a rejection of priorities set constitutionally and, it was to be presumed, authoritatively by Congress; but it involved the President himself in the anomalous situation of selective enforcement of laws passed by Congress. Selective enforcement meant, among other things, an evasion of the President's constitutional responsibility to veto laws which he thought were bad for the country. Nixon's situation was all the more offensive when, as in the case of the Water Pollution Control Act, Congress made its priorities unequivocally clear by passing the law over a presidential veto — and the President, allocating himself an unconstitutional double veto, still refused to carry out the law.

Congress, the 58th Federalist had said, held the purse; and "this power over the purse may, in fact, be regarded as the most complete and effectual weapon with which any constitution can arm the immediate representatives of the people, for obtaining a redress of every grievance, and for carrying into effect every just and salutary measure." If Nixon could establish the idea of policy impoundment at presidential pleasure, he would divest Congress of this "most . . . effectual weapon" and significantly alter the theory of the Constitution. Policy impoundment was an essential instrumentality of the imperial Presidency.

IX

The Nixon theory of impoundment was a central attack on the role of Congress in the American polity. But it by no means exhausted the President's resources in his drive for presidential supremacy. At an early point he extended the idea of the selective enforcement of the law to other statutes besides appropriations.

Thus on July 3, 1969, the Attorney General and the Secretary of Health, Education and Welfare put out a long and impenetrable joint statement, the effect of which was to say that the administration had decided not to enforce Title VI of the Civil Rights Act of 1964 — a title requiring the government to cut off federal funds to school districts or other recipients which continued to practice discrimination. Taken to court, the government argued that the language of Title VI was permissive. But a district judge and a unanimous Court of Appeals ruled in the case of *Adams v. Richardson* that the language was mandatory and ordered the Secretary of Health, Education and Welfare to carry out the law.

Selective enforcement of the law was, needless to say, illegal; and here again Nixon was outdoing all his predecessors. During the Second World War, in what E. S. Corwin called "the most exorbitant claim for Presidential power ever made by a President," Roosevelt had warned Congress, that if it did not repeal a law, he would disobey it. But Roosevelt did after all go to Congress; if disobedience were to become a necessity, he was ready to assume the responsibility himself; and, as Corwin also said, "the circumstances of total war" might well render drastic action necessary.[68] Twenty-five years later there was no emergency to justify extreme policies, no request to Congress to repeal the offending law, not even the President himself to make the announcement. Though Roosevelt's message in 1942 had become a textbook case of presidential aggrandizement, Nixon's far more arbitrary edict in 1969 passed almost without comment — a measure of how much power the Presidency had gained in a generation. Nixon did not bother, as Roosevelt had, to assert a claim or make an argument. He simply acted, or had his subordinates act — until the action produced effective resistance.

In the case of the Office of Economic Opportunity, Nixon's purpose was to destroy a government agency that Congress had voted to continue. The OEO, originally invented to conduct Lyndon Johnson's war against poverty, passed on in diminished status into the Nixon administration. Then, in January 1973, the Nixon budget for 1974 simply omitted funds for OEO programs; and a newly appointed Acting Director of OEO, arguing that Nixon's budget message superseded congressional authorization, set to work dismantling the agency. This argument, the courts soon found, "would in effect give the President a veto power through the use of his budget message," a veto power not granted him by the Constitution. The executive budget, the decision continued, did not have, when submitted, the force of law; it was "nothing more than a proposal to the Congress for the Congress to act upon as it may please." The government, the court said, "really argues that the Constitution confers the discretionary power upon the President to refuse to execute laws passed by Congress with which he disagrees." If its case were sustained, "no barrier would remain to the executive ignoring any and all Congressional authorizations, if he deemed them . . . contrary to the needs of the nation.[69]

The courts thus repulsed the Nixon revolution on two fronts. But the revolution went on elsewhere. Another way by which Nixon sought to move the constitutional balance toward permanent presidential supremacy was through a new use of the pocket veto. The Constitution of course provided that every bill passed by Congress should go to the President for acceptance or rejection. The President could sign the bill. Or he could return it to Congress with a statement of disapproval, in which case Congress had the power to override the veto by a two-thirds vote in each House. The Constitution added:

> If any Bill shall not be returned by the President within ten Days (Sundays excepted) after it shall have been presented to him, the Same shall be a Law, in like Manner as if he had signed it, *unless the Congress by their Adjournment prevent its Return,* in which Case it shall not be a Law. [Emphasis added]

This last was the pocket veto. It was infrequently exercised in the early republic. There were only eighteen pocket vetoes before the Civil War, of which seven were by Jackson. All took place after the final adjournment of Congress or after the adjournment of a session of Congress.

Until about 1943 the practice of the adjournment *within* a session was itself most unusual. Of the five instances of intra-session adjournment before the Second World War, three occurred in 1867 and provided the first pocket vetoes within a session. Andrew Johnson used the pocket veto then, however, under what the Supreme Court thirty years later declared to be the misap-

prehension that the President had no power to sign bills when
Congress was not meeting. Between Johnson and Franklin Roosevelt there were only three cases of pocket vetoes within sessions; and in the whole course of American history before Nixon
there had been but 64 such vetoes, of which more than half took
place in the Truman administration. Nearly two thirds of these
64 pocket vetoes were of private bills. Of the 25 public bills
none had been of importance. More than 84 percent of these
pocket vetoes, moreover, came during adjournments of at least
one month, characteristically over the summer. There was only
one case of a pocket veto during an adjournment of less than ten
days — when Lyndon Johnson pocket vetoed a private relief bill
during a nine-day adjournment in 1964. It should be added that
Congress never formally agreed to the principle of pocket vetoes
within a session, though, as a matter of comity and since the bills
involved were of small consequence, it rarely quarreled with the
results in particular cases.

The Supreme Court had spoken twice on the subject of pocket
vetoes. In the Pocket Veto case of 1929,[70] it resolved a constitutional ambiguity and ruled that a pocket veto was valid at the
end of a session of Congress as well as at the end of a Congress.
The finding was based in part on the idea that, if Congress was
in adjournment, no officer or agent was authorized to receive on
behalf of Congress a bill rejected by the President. A few years
later, Franklin Roosevelt vetoed a bill and sent it back with appropriate explanation to the Secretary of the Senate at a time
when the Senate was in three-day recess. The beneficiary of the
bill then applied to the courts, claiming the bill had become law
because the President had returned it when the Senate was not in
session and therefore incapable of receiving it. In 1938 the
Court, modifying the earlier decision, held in *Wright v. United
States* [71] that in these circumstances (which it carefully distinguished) the Secretary of the Senate did have the authority to receive the President's message. There was some indication in
Chief Justice Hughes's decision that the pocket veto might be
valid in the case of a prolonged intra-session adjournment but
certainly not in the case of a three-day adjournment.

On December 14, 1970, Congress sent President Nixon the

Family Practice of Medicine Act, authorizing grants of $225 million to hospitals and medical schools in the field of family medicine. The Senate had passed the bill by 64 to 1, the House by 345 to 2. On December 22 — two days before the President's ten days of consideration were up — Congress went home for Christmas. The Senate took care to authorize the Secretary of the Senate to receive messages from the President during the five-day adjournment. On December 24, in the face of these precautions, Nixon announced a pocket veto. In declining to return the bill to Congress, he avoided the virtual certainty that a bill which only three out of 412 members of Congress had opposed would be passed over his veto.

By treating the Christmas break as if it were a *sine die* adjournment at the end of a session, Nixon could employ, not the conditional veto prescribed by the Constitution, but an absolute veto — i.e., one against which Congress had no recourse. No President had ever done this before. Moreover, he used this veto against a bill that had not only been passed overwhelmingly by Congress but involved far more money and far more weighty considerations of national policy than any bill previously pocket-vetoed within a session. And, as Senator Edward M. Kennedy, who argued a civil action on behalf of the bill in federal district court in 1973, observed in his brief, "If the pocket veto clause applies to a five-day adjournment, why should it not also apply to an adjournment of three days, or a weekend, or one day, or even overnight?" Senator Jacob Javits, a Republican, said the bill had been "illegally vetoed." In 1971 and again in 1972 the Senate actually voted appropriations to effectuate the bill.

Up to this time a state of comity between the President and Congress had controlled the use of the pocket veto. Now Nixon, fearing that a bill he did not like would be passed over a constitutional veto, had engaged in gross violation of the traditional comity. His action, though again largely ignored by the press, raised serious political and constitutional issues. "A disregard on either side of what it owes to the other," Madison had written long before in a discussion of the veto power, "must be an abuse, for which it would be responsible under the forms of the Constitution. An abuse on the part of the President, with a view sufficiently manifest, in a case of sufficient magnitude to deprive Congress of the opportunity of overruling objections to their bills, might doubtless be a ground for impeachment." [72]

There were other revealing expressions, each perhaps minor in itself, of Nixon's revolutionary drive toward presidential supremacy. Thus, in the midst of his misguided effort to put G. Harrold Carswell on the Supreme Court, Nixon wrote a letter to Senator Saxbe of Ohio in which he spoke of himself as "the one person entrusted by the Constitution with the power of appointment" of Supreme Court justices, a claim repeated twice more in the course of the letter.[73] Had the President bothered to consult the Constitution, he would have discovered that this document said, with customary precision, that the President "shall nominate, and by and with the Advice and Consent of the Senate, shall appoint" judges of the Supreme Court. The difference between nomination and appointment was something that Presidents of the United States before Nixon had had no difficulty grasping. "I was only one-half the appointing power," Theodore Roosevelt wrote in his *Autobiography;* "I nominated; but the Senate confirmed." [74] But Nixon was evidently trying to transform that shared constitutional power into, as he instructed Saxbe, the exclusive "constitutional responsibility" of the President, with Congress assigned the duty of endorsing the presidential choice.

Another curious case arose in connection with an old project of Nixon's, the Subversive Activities Control Board, established in 1950 under a law derived from the Mundt-Nixon bill of 1948. No agency of the federal government had done less or, indeed, had had less to do. In 1971, the Board held hearings on 111 cases, disposing of each, according to Senator Ervin in 1972, in an average of forty-eight seconds; "that is all they did last year, except draw their breaths and their salaries." With understandable loyalty to the agency he had helped father, Nixon on July 2, 1971, conferred new powers on the Board by executive order. Even conservative members of Congress were outraged. "I do not see," said Senator McClellan of Arkansas, "how the President, by executive order, can give to a board created for one purpose by the Congress a function which the Congress did not authorize." The Senate promptly voted to forbid the use of appropriated funds to carry out the executive order; and the House, though balking at first, agreed in 1972 on a stipulation that no funds voted to the Board could be used to carry out the executive order.[75]

X

The Nixon revolution thus aimed at reducing the power of Congress at every point along the line and moving toward rule by presidential decree. To perfect his design he had to control the use of information by Congress and the flow of information to Congress. To do this his administration mounted an unprecedented attack on legislative privilege and made unprecedented claims of executive privilege.

Unlike executive privilege, legislative privilege had explicit basis in the Constitution — in Article I, Section 6, providing that "for any Speech or Debate in either House, they [Senators and Representatives] shall not be questioned in any other Place." Through the years the Supreme Court had construed "Speech or Debate" as embracing every form of legislative activity and "any other Place" as including the other two branches of government. But the Nixon administration now proceeded against sitting senators in two very dissimilar cases — against Senator Mike Gravel of Alaska, whose assistant had declined to testify about the Pentagon Papers before a grand jury, and against Senator Daniel Brewster of Maryland, who had been charged with accepting a bribe. The Supreme Court, in decisions handed down the same day and made possible by the Nixon justices, ruled, in effect, that the Constitution did not immunize senators from proceedings involving third-party crimes and only casually related to legislative affairs. The result, according to Senator Ervin, was "the first broad-scale restriction in the scope of protection provided members of Congress by the [speech or debate] clause since the adoption of the Constitution." The decisions, Ervin said, so limited legislative immunity that members of Congress could no longer acquire information on the activity of the executive branch nor inform their constituents of their findings "without risking criminal prosecution." [76]

As the Nixon administration succeeded in contracting legislative privilege, despite its specific constitutional sanction, so it tried to expand executive privilege, despite its total lack of such sanction. President Kennedy, as Congressman Moss had said, had put the genie of executive privilege back into the bottle, and his successor in the main followed Kennedy's example. Johnson did not formally invoke executive privilege once, though his Associate Special Counsel declined to testify on one occasion, and there were two or three other instances of executive withholding during his administration. Nixon, on coming to office, assured Moss that his administration too would never invoke executive privilege "without specific Presidential approval." But if his principle was Kennedy's, his practice was Eisenhower's, and he uncorked the genie with a vengeance.

During his first term he personally invoked executive privilege four times. Members of his administration rejected formal congressional requests for testimony or documents in 15 additional instances. Members of the White House staff refused testimony or documents in 8 further instances. [77] The General Accounting Office, for all its statutory authorization, found it far more difficult even than in the Eisenhower years to gain access to pertinent government records. [78] In addition, there were innumerable instances when tactics of delay and evasion permitted the administration, in Senator Fulbright's words, "to exercise executive privilege without actually invoking it." "More often than not," said Senator Symington,

> it has been the implied threat of executive privilege, rather than its actual exercise, that has hovered over negotiations to obtain the release of information, even in executive session; information which we considered so crucial to the Senatorial responsibility that it belonged to the Committee as a matter of right; and therefore information which should have been volunteered.

The Nixon promise that only the President personally would claim executive privilege, said Fulbright, had become a meaningless technicality: "Only the President may invoke executive privilege but just about any of his subordinates may exercise it — they simply do not employ the forbidden words." [79]

To justify this program of denial Nixon resurrected the Eisenhower-Brownell-Wolkinson thesis, quietly interred in the Kennedy-Johnson years, that the President had "uncontrolled discretion" to keep executive information from Congress. Thus Attorney General Kleindienst assured the Ervin Subcommittee in April 1973 of "the constitutional authority of the President in his discretion" to withhold information in his possession *"or in the possession of the Executive branch"* (emphasis added) if he believed disclosure "would impair the proper exercise of his constitutional functions." When incredulous senators asked whether the Attorney General was saying that Congress had no power to compel testimony over presidential objection from any one of the 2.5 million employees of the executive branch. Kleindienst replied that that was exactly what he was saying. The President's judgment, he continued, was final; and, if Congress did not like it, it could cut off appropriations or impeach the President. The last was said with more than a hint of sarcasm, and the senators were not pleased. Ten weeks later Kleindienst himself had gone; but his successor, Elliot Richardson, repeated to the Senate that there were no limits on executive privilege, adding that, if Congress tried to regulate the use of executive privilege through a statute, it would be unconstitutional.[80]

When Eisenhower had laid down his sweeping principle in 1954, Joe McCarthy and his friends were in full cry after middle-level public officials, including Foreign Service officers who had proffered what a conspicuous McCarthyite fellow traveler, Richard Nixon, might later agree to have been perspicacious advice about Communist China. It was not unreasonable in 1954 to suppose that the prospect of immediate disclosure might well incline officials to see little future in candor. There was much appeal indeed in the British idea that the head of a government department should take final responsibility and that the legislature should not seek out victims among his subordinates. The cabinet member who made the decision, wrote Professor Bishop of the Yale Law School in 1957, "should be answerable to Congress for its wisdom. But the subordinate civil servants who advise him should be answerable only to him — i.e., they should be able to present unpalatable facts and make unpopular arguments without fear of being dragooned by the first Congressman who needs a headline. . . . The Secretary's own responsibility to Congress for wrong decisions is a sufficient guarantee that he will not long tolerate incompetent or disloyal advisors." [81]

But was the British analogy really all that convincing? The British civil service was a notably compact and disciplined body, broadly responsive to its political masters. Yet even in Britain doubts had arisen as to whether the civil service should be exempt from parliamentary concern. "Whoever is in office," Harold Wilson had said from the wilderness in the 1950s, "the Whigs are in power." [82] When Wilson himself became Prime Minister in the sixties, the Whigs remained in power. Not only were the English themselves questioning the idea of total civil service immunity, but the American civil service was in any case very different in character. It was notably sprawling and undisciplined, neither especially responsive to its political chiefs nor especially dependent on their protection. No American President before Eisenhower had felt it necessary to claim that congressional access to internal deliberations would be, as a general rule, destructive of government. The suspension of the Eisenhower rule in the Kennedy-Johnson years caused no trouble. On the other hand, this rule had played a demonstrable role, as in the Dixon-Yates case under Eisenhower, in covering up executive malfeasance that surely lay within the congressional power to investigate. "If Congress is to expose corruption and waste," wrote Raoul Berger, "it cannot stop with pinning the mistakes on the head [of the department] who more often than not is totally unaware of their presence." Recalling the peculations of Billie Sol Estes, of which "an upright Secretary of Agriculture, Orville Freeman, was quite unaware," Berger suggested that "the price of misdoing by some obscure employee should not be Orville Freeman's head. . . . Perhaps the sheer bulk of our administrative establishment argues for a different rule." [83]

Certainly the blanket withholding of internal communications to Congress, as defended by Eisenhower and Nixon, could easily become a shield for folly and crookedness in the executive branch. There remained the problem that prompted Eisenhower to make his original assertion of unreviewable privilege — the problem posed by McCarthys, past and to come. Here the proper answer would lie in Andrew Jackson's assertion of the right to defend the executive against congressional harassment; and the definition of harassment, though made initially by the President, would be sustained or rejected by the reaction of responsible members of Congress and of national opinion. The answer lay, in short, not in absolute privilege but in constitutional comity.

Nixon not only took over the Eisenhower claim of unreviewable privilege for the entire executive branch but made the privilege even more absolute, if possible, for the White House itself — and did so at the very time he was giving the White House staff unprecedented power. The cloak of invisibility could reasonably cover White House advisers in other days when they constituted an intimate personal staff and concentrated mainly on advice. Then they had little to testify about beyond their chats with the President. "I believe executive privilege should protect the President's conversations with his key aides," former Justice Goldberg said. ". . . But on substantive matters of concern I do not believe that the privilege ought to exist." [84] In those years, the occasional White House man with an operating job saw no problem about testifying on substantive matters before congressional committees. Former Justice James F. Byrnes, who supervised the home front from his office in the White House during the Second World War, often went to the Hill. When Averell Harriman served as Truman's assistant for national security, he was, as he told the Subcommittee on the Separation of Powers, "glad to respond to a call by the Senate." [85] But in the main Congress had not needed testimony from the White House. When the Department of State had a serious role in American foreign policy, for example, the Secretary of State was able to answer congressional questions about foreign affairs.

In Nixon's first term, however, a *de facto* Secretary of State ran foreign policy in the basement of the White House. Haldeman and Ehrlichman counted a good deal more than the domestic cabinet. John Dean, counsel to the President, observed correctly in 1972 that "no recent President has ever claimed a 'blanket immunity' that would prevent his assistants from testifying before Congress on any subject," [86] but this was precisely what his own President claimed. By denying Kissinger, Haldeman and Ehrlichman to Congress even on substantive matters, he was transferring immunity from the information to the job. Congress felt understandably aggrieved — especially when Kissinger, for example, answered questions from foreign journalists that Nixon forbade him to take from the Senate Foreign Relations Committee. After the 1972 election Nixon proceeded to deepen the White House privilege. In March 12, 1973, in an unprecedented claim, he said that past as well as present membership on the White House staff conferred immunity against appearances before congressional committees, thereby enunciating what Senators Ervin and Muskie promptly called the doctrine of "eternal privilege." On May 3, 1973, in another first, he extended the doctrine of executive privilege, heretofore applied only to Congress, to questions asked by grand juries and even by the FBI, and extended it also to "presidential papers," defined as "*all* documents, produced or received by the President or *any member of the White House staff* in connection with his official duties." [87]

President Nixon thus tried to make executive privilege a far more effective instrument of presidential domination than ever before. When a White House staff had gathered to itself so many powers traditionally exercised by officials freely available to Congress, and when immunity was claimed for presidential assistants without regard to the topic of congressional inquiry and by the fact of their position and for the duration of their lives, Congress could properly believe that it was denied things to which for nearly two centuries of American history it had enjoyed fairly unimpeded access. If President Nixon's interpretation of executive privilege survived, it would, far more even than the sufficiently extravagant Eisenhower interpretation, deprive Congress of information necessary for its own survival as a partner in the constitutional order.

XI

As one examined the impressive range of Nixon's initiatives — from his appropriation of the war-making power to his interpretation of the appointing power, from his unilateral determination of social priorities to his unilateral abolition of statutory programs, from his attack on legislative privilege to his enlargement of executive privilege, from his theory of impoundment to his theory of the pocket veto, from his calculated disparagement of the cabinet and his calculated discrediting of the press to his carefully organized concentration of federal management in the White House — from all this a larger design ineluctably emerged. It was hard to know whether Nixon, whose style was banality, understood consciously where he was heading. He was not a man given to political philosophizing. But he was heading toward a new balance of constitutional powers, an audacious and imaginative reconstruction of the American Constitution. He did indeed contemplate, as he said in his 1971 State of the Union message, a New American Revolution. But the essence of this revolution was not, as he said at the time, power to the people. The essence was power to the Presidency.

For Nixon these well may have seemed the same thing. No one could doubt that he was infinitely sincere in seeing himself the tribune of what he called in a speech of November 3, 1969, "the great silent majority." It may be that he was the first President in American history to conclude that the separation of powers had so frustrated government on behalf of the majority that the constitutional system had become finally intolerable — and to move boldly to change the system. For Congress, it could be argued, had failed majority government in the high-technology society.[88] It had proved itself incapable of the swift decisions demanded by the twentieth century. It could not make intelligent use of its war-making authority. It had no ordered means of setting national priorities or of controlling aggregate spending. It was not to be trusted with secrets. It was fragmented, parochial, selfish, cowardly, without dignity, discipline or purpose. The Presidency had not stolen its power; rather Congress had surrendered it out of fear of responsibility and recognition of incapacity. Congress was even without pride and, if ignored or disdained, waited humbly by the White House and licked the hand of its oppressor.

Was such a system worth preserving? No other working democracy in the world, it could be observed, was based on the principle of the separation of powers. Institutionalized checks and balances might have been all right for an isolated nation of four million farmers 200 years ago; but had they not become first a nuisance and now a positive danger to a mighty industrial power destined to world leadership? These were legitimate and searching questions. Nixon faced them. He continued to invoke the separation of powers when he wanted to protect the executive branch from congressional intrusion; but on all other matters his conclusion evidently was that presidential supremacy was the only salvation.

Kevin Phillips, an early Nixon brain-truster and author of *The Emerging Republican Majority*, expounded the implicit logic of the Nixon revolution. The separation of powers, he wrote, was an eighteenth-century idea, now obsolete. "Congress's separate power is an obstacle to modern policymaking." That separate power was itself further separated among the multitude of congressional committees. "One has to go back to the Ottoman Empire for a similar array of pompous, uncoordinated satrapies." Moreover, with its "rubber-chicken circuitry and local-ombudsman mentality," Congress could not hope to exert national leadership. The separation of powers was "distorting the logical evolution of technology-era government." The answer, Phillips said, lay in "a *fusion of powers* tying Congress and the executive together, eliminating checks and balances and creating a new system." [89]

The President, if one judges by his actions, agreed with the diagnosis but disagreed with the prescription. For Phillips was advocating a parliamentary solution. In a parliamentary regime the chief executive was not only a member of and, to some degree, accountable to his parliamentary party but was regularly exposed to face-to-face interrogations on equal terms by his political opposition. Quite apart from the other arguments against transplanting an alien growth to American soil, the personal accountability and exposure involved would obviously be unbearable to a man of Nixon's psychic constitution.

What Nixon was moving toward was something different: it was not a parliamentary regime but a plebiscitary Presidency. His model lay not in Britain but in France — in the France of Louis Napoleon and Charles de Gaulle. A plebiscitary Presidency, unlike a parliamentary regime, would not require a new Constitution; presidential acts, confirmed by a Supreme Court of his own appointment, could put a new gloss on the old one. And a plebiscitary Presidency could be seen as the fulfillment of constitutional democracy. Michels explained in *Political Parties* the rationale of the "personal dictatorship conferred by the people in accordance with constitutional rules." By the plebiscitary logic, "once elected, the chosen of the people can no longer be opposed in any way. He personifies the majority and all resistance to his will is antidemocratic. . . . He is, moreover, infallible, for 'he who is elected by six million votes, carries out the will of the people; he does not betray them.' " How much more infallible if elected by 46 million votes! If opposition became irksome, it was the voters themselves, "we are assured, who demand from the chosen of the people that he should use severe repressive measures, should employ force, should concentrate all authority in his own hands." The chief executive would be, as Laboulaye said of Napoleon III, "democracy personified, the nation made man." [90]

The plebiscitary conception, construed in the most personal terms, dominated the 1972 election. Nixon cut loose from his party, ran his campaign through the Committee for the Re-election of the President rather than through the Republican National Committee, abandoned Republican governors, senators and congressmen to their fate and concentrated on collecting the largest possible majority for himself. Once he had gained that majority, his associates propagated the mystique of the 'mandate.' The mandate, it was alleged, justified the President in doing anything that he believed the interests of the nation required him to do. Since the Democrats won Congress by a considerable majority, they thought they had a mandate too — one to carry out the Democratic platform. But the White House defined the presidential mandate as definitive and overriding and declared it the duty of Congress to support the President.

Nixon, it was said, admired no contemporary statesman so much as de Gaulle. Certainly after his re-election he began what can be profitably seen as an attempt to establish a quasi-Gaullist regime in the United States. Instead of conciliating the defeated minority, he was cold and unforgiving. Instead of placating Congress, he confronted it with executive faits accomplis taken without explanation. The mandate became the source of wider power than any President had ever claimed before. Whether a conscious or unconscious revolutionary, Nixon was carrying the imperial Presidency toward its ultimate form in the plebiscitary Presidency — with the President accountable only once every four years, shielded in the years between elections from congressional and public harassment, empowered by his mandate to make war or to make peace, to spend or to impound, to give out information or to hold it back, superseding congressional legislation by executive order, all in the name of a majority whose choice must prevail till it made another choice four years later — unless it wished to embark on the drastic and improbable course of impeachment. Here at last was the "elective kingship" that Henry Jones Ford had foreseen three quarters of a century earlier.[91]

XII

Nor was this the limit of the revolutionary Presidency. Nixon was pressing his conception of the Presidency still further, if in ways required less perhaps by a critique of the separation of powers than by the compulsions of his own personality. For the Presidency *is* a peculiarly personal institution; and Nixon's view of the world, we have noted, was one of unrelenting crisis, in which the United States, personified in its President, was assailed by a host of remorseless enemies. His own election to the Presidency, far from increasing his sense of security, seemed only to intensify his anxiety.

He thus became seriously disturbed, according to his own account, by leaks of government information in the spring of 1969. The most important leak resulted in a *New York Times* story about "secret" B-52 raids over Cambodia. In fact, the raids were hardly secret to the Cambodians, or to the North Vietnamese, or to the Chinese, or to the Russians; but the administration wished to hide from the American Congress and people the fact that it was carrying on a war in Cambodia unauthorized by one and unknown to both. In 1973 Melvin Laird, who had been Secretary of Defense in 1969, said that keeping the raids secret "was not of great concern to the Defense Department, but to the State Department." But it appeared to have been of no great concern to the State Department either, which could find no record that it had ever asked anyone to keep them secret. It *was* of great concern, however, to the President who, according to the chairman of the Joint Chiefs of Staff, made the secrecy of the raids his personal, repeated and "very emphatic" command.[92] This presidential insistence was plainly not, as later alleged, to avoid embarrassing the Cambodian government — which resumed diplomatic relations with the United States a few weeks after the *Times* story — but to avoid reawakening the antiwar movement at home. In any case, Nixon, claiming that leaks were endangering national security, ordered the tapping of the telephones of at least 13 members of the National Security Council staff and of at least four newspapermen. The program continued till February 1971. "I authorized the entire program," Nixon said in 1973, adding that the wiretaps were "legal at the time." [93]

The taps were undertaken without judicial clearance in spite of the procedures laid down in Title III of the Crime Control and Safe Streets Act of 1968. But Attorney General John Mitchell, then renowned as a champion of law and order, shared Nixon's vision of crisis. "Never in our history," he said, "has this country been confronted with so many revolutionary elements determined to destroy by force the government and the society it stands for." [94] In this extremity he therefore claimed "inherent" presidential power to tap without warrants in the interests of domestic security. When the Senate Subcommittee on Constitutional Rights wondered in March 1971 whether this doctrine did not place undue power in executive hands, Assistant Attorney General William Rehnquist reassured them: "I think it quite likely that self-discipline on the part of the Executive branch will provide an answer to virtually all of the legitimate complaints." [95]

Many authorities doubted Mitchell's law as well as his self-discipline; several lower courts rejected his doctrine; and in June 1972 the Supreme Court (Justice Rehnquist abstaining) ruled unanimously that the government had no power to eavesdrop without prior judicial approval unless it could show evidence of foreign intelligence links. Justice Douglas, concurring, had unkind things to say about "the omnipresent electronic ear of the Government" and "another national seizure of paranoia." [96] This decision made Nixon's subsequent claim that his tapes were "legal at the time" hard to fathom, especially coming, as it did, from a lawyer. For, as former Justice Goldberg said, "The Supreme Court, when it decides a new question such as the status of these wiretaps, does not make illegal what was previously legal; it gives a final authoritative determination of whether an action was legal when it took place." [97]

The leaks were the first crisis. Then, as Nixon recalled it in 1973, "in the spring and summer of 1970, another security problem reached critical proportions." This was the time when the campuses exploded over the American invasion of Cambodia. It was also the heyday of the Weathermen and the Black Panthers. It was unquestionably a time of protest, much of it shrill and ugly. But was it really a "security problem" of "critical proportions"? Was the republic itself in danger? So, from all indications, the White House thought. John Dean later described the atmosphere he found when he became counsel to the President in July 1970 — "a climate of excessive concern over the political impact of demonstrators, excessive concern over leaks, an insatiable appetite for political intelligence, all coupled with a do-it-yourself White House staff, regardless of the law." [98]

Whether the Nixon White House actually regarded the riots, burnings and bombings of 1970 as the primary danger to the republic was doubtful. Certainly the famous Enemies List of 1971 suggested otherwise. The question, John Dean had written to his White House colleagues, was "how we can maximize the fact of our incumbency in dealing with persons known to be active in their opposition to our Administration"; then, switching from the patois of the bureaucracy to the patois of the locker room: "Stated a bit more bluntly — how we can use the available Federal machinery to screw our political enemies." [99] The List itself pretty much ignored the bomb-throwers of the New Left and concentrated on what the White House plainly saw as the real Enemies — the eastern 'establishment' with its attendant politicians, lawyers, journalists, television commentators, professors and preachers. Nixon had long perceived this crowd as a self-appointed elite who did not know or understand or represent the real America, who had opposed him all his life and who were now using their domination of the media of communications to destroy his Presidency.

The middle-class fear of left-wing militancy could be easily channeled into an attack on the eastern establishment. This was no doubt why the Nixon people did so much to feed this fear — by sending agents, who not seldom became *agents provocateurs*, into students' and veterans' groups and even by giving money to far-left outfits like the Peace and Freedom party of California.[100] The more sharply the issue was drawn on the question of civil liberties, the more the establishment would compromise itself by appearing to defend the militants. Could even more direct connections be shown? In 1970 Nixon's own Commission on Campus Unrest rejected the thesis that student militancy was the product of "outside agitators and subversive propagandists" and saw it as the reflection of "a more profound crisis in the nation as a whole." [101] But the Commission itself could easily be dismissed as an establishment plot — its chairman was former Governor William Scranton of Pennsylvania, its executive director W. Matthew Byrne, Jr., who later became the judge in the Ellsberg case — and the President himself refused to believe that the militants were acting on their own. He insistently demanded proof that their activities were sponsored or financed by a foreign enemy. "Some of the disruptive activities," he said as late as 1973, "were receiving foreign support" — a charge which the CIA, after extensive investigations in 1969 and again in 1970, had pronounced groundless [102] and for which no evidence was ever subsequently produced. We need, Haldeman told Dean after the 1972 election, "to put out the story on the foreign or Communist money that was used in support of demonstrations against the President in 1972. We should tie all 1972 demonstrations to McGovern." [103] "We never found," Dean later testified, "a scintilla of viable evidence indicating that these demonstrators were part of a master plan; nor that they were funded by the Democratic funds; nor that they had any direct connection with the McGovern campaign. This was explained to Mr. Haldeman, but the President believed that the opposite was, in fact, true." [104]

When investigation failed to turn up any ties between the agitators and either foreign governments or opposition leaders, the White House staff, according to Dean, was "disbelieving and complaining" and thereupon decided that "the entire system for gathering such intelligence was worthless." Much more had to be done to save the republic. Some things were already under way. The Department of Justice had begun a series of political trials, mostly on grounds so tenuous that the defendants were eventually acquitted or the charges against them were dismissed. Agents of the Treasury Department visited public libraries to take down the names of persons who borrowed books on guerrilla warfare, explosives and other dangerous subjects. The Post Office Department proposed that it be allowed to open sealed first-class letters from abroad without notice to the writer or to the recipient.[105]

Even this was not enough. On June 5, 1970, President Nixon

summoned the heads of the FBI, the CIA, the Defense Intelligence Agency and the National Security Agency to discuss what Nixon called "the urgent need for better [domestic] intelligence operations." The involvement of the Director of Central Intelligence was singular. The law setting up the CIA had, in the words of Allen Dulles, "made it expressly mandatory that he shall exercise no internal security function." The interagency committee subsequently came up with a set of recommendations, some of which T. C. Huston, the White House man on the committee, warned the President were illegal. Nevertheless Nixon in July 1970 instructed the intelligence community in a formal Decision Memorandum that surreptitious entry — breaking and entering — was now presidentially authorized ("use of this technique is clearly illegal; it amounts to burglary. . . . However, it is also the most fruitful tool" — Huston); that undercover agents were to be planted in the universities; that the CIA was to spy on students and other itinerant Americans abroad; that the electronic surveillance of Americans "who pose a major threat to the internal security" as well as of foreign embassies in Washington was to be intensified; that the National Security Agency was to listen in on Americans making international telephone calls; and that restrictions were to be removed on legal mail coverage — that is, opening and copying letters — and relaxed on covert coverage ("illegal . . . however, the advantages . . . outweigh the risk" — Huston).[106]

XIII

No President in peacetime had ever requested and approved such a scheme of lawless action. J. Edgar Hoover's opposition compelled Nixon to rescind the plan. But a few months later Nixon set up an Intelligence Evaluation Committee to coordinate domestic intelligence. It is not clear what this committee did; but there can be no doubt concern over national security remained high at the White House and took, in John Dean's description, "a quantum jump" when the *New York Times* received the Pentagon Papers from Daniel Ellsberg and began

printing them on June 13, 1971. Nixon himself called this publication of the interminable historical study compiled in 1967 as
"a security leak of unprecedented proportions" creating — this
he still insisted in 1973, after two years in which the documents
had full opportunity to wreak their havoc — "a threat so grave
as to require extraordinary actions."

One extraordinary action was his establishment within the
White House of a special investigations unit whimsically known
as the "plumbers" because one of their assignments was to stop
leaks. Nixon set the unit up, as John Ehrlichman, whom he
placed in charge, later testified, because he did not trust Hoover
to conduct an adequate investigation of Ellsberg. In its agitation
the White House had the theory that Hoover and Ellsberg's
father-in-law were intimate friends; in fact, they had met only
once some thirty years before. Nevertheless this supposition on
top of Hoover's resistance to the 1970 plan persuaded Nixon
that the FBI was no longer to be relied upon to protect the nation's security. The result was his decision to rely on Egil Krogh,
E. Howard Hunt and G. Gordon Liddy.

Up to this point in American history, all government investigative agencies — the Secret Service, the FBI, the CIA and the
rest — had been set up by Congress under law and with a sem-
blance, however vague, of accountability. Nixon, following his
usual practice of replacing statutory by personal institutions,
now invented an extralegal investigative force, subsidized by the
taxpayer but unknown to Congress and accountable to no one
but himself. And he immediately sent his personal posse into action, telling Krogh, the head plumber, "that as a matter of
first priority the unit should find out all it could about Mr. Ellsberg's associates and motives. . . . I did impress on Mr. Krogh
the vital importance to the national security of his assignment."
Having been rousingly charged by the leader of the free world,
Krogh, acting along the lines of the Decision Memorandum
Nixon had briefly approved the year before, arranged to bur-
glarize Ellsberg's psychiatrist. This may well not have been
anything the President intended. But the more serious question
was whether the President of the United States was making much

sense when he said that finding out everything possible about Ellsberg's associates and motives was of "vital importance to the national security" and supposed that, in any case, Egil Krogh could do a better job of it than the FBI.

Nixon, by his own testimony, had other jobs for his special investigations unit. One was to compile "an accurate record of events related to the Vietnam war." This was a mysterious assignment. An accurate record of events related to the Vietnam War? If the Pentagon Papers did not suffice, there were excellent professional historical offices in the State Department and the Pentagon. Nor, it must be said, would the writing of history seem the sort of thing Hunt and Liddy were good at. One had known nothing about Liddy, except for the lunacy of his later proposals, but I had known Howie Hunt since we worked together in the first days of the Marshall Plan in Paris in 1948. He was an amiable writer of cheap thrillers, a *fantaisiste* now suddenly empowered by a President of the United States to live out his fantasies. His contribution to an accurate record of events in Vietnam was to forge a cable designed to prove the direct involvement of John F. Kennedy in the assassination of Ngo Dinh Diem in South Vietnam in November 1963.

It is evident that the American government was cognizant of the conspiracy to overthrow Diem.[107] But there is no evidence that anyone in the government contemplated the murder of Diem; indeed, plans had been made to fly him safely out of the country. Yet, in the same week that Hunt concocted his Top Secret message, Nixon said in a press conference, "I would remind all concerned that the way we got into Vietnam was through overthrowing Diem, and the complicity in the murder of Diem." [108] Was this pure coincidence? Or was Nixon helping Charles Colson of the White House staff to palm off the forged cable on *Life* magazine, as Colson later tried to do? Or did the President really believe it, and was his belief the source of the assignment and of Hunt's effort to make history live up to presidential fantasy? Nor was this all the plumbers did. Between the burglary of the psychiatrist's office and the forgery of the Vietnam cables in 1971 and the Watergate break-in in 1972, they apparently did many other things. "It was and is important," said Nixon in August 1973, "that many of the matters worked on by the special investigations unit not be publicly disclosed because disclosure would unquestionably damage the national security." [109] Presumably, had the other matters not already come out, they too would have been withheld in the name of national security.

XIV

On March 11, 1972, midway between the domestic intelligence plan of July 1970 and the construction of the Enemies List, Nixon, addressing the National Conference on the Judiciary, said, "The only way that justice can truly be done in any society, is for each member of that society to subject himself to the rule of law — neither to set himself above the law in the name of justice nor to set himself outside the law in the name of justice." [110] One can easily imagine the earnestness with which the President spoke those righteous sentiments. How then is one to understand that the same man, by his own confession, directed members of his administration to set themselves above and outside the law?

His answer would be in effect: the emergency required it. We are back again to John Locke and the question of prerogative. This was not the first time in American history that Presidents had claimed that emergency required them to act beyond or even against the Constitution. Lincoln and the second Roosevelt had been sustained in such claims. The nation had agreed with them that the emergencies they confronted were real. Jefferson, in the Burr case, and Truman, in the steel-seizure case, had been turned down because the emergencies so clear to them remained dim to most of the country. History had shown that an emergency had to be genuinely imperious and its identification widely shared if a President were to be upheld in his invocation of prerogatives.

Even in the cases not sustained, certain extenuating points could be made. Jefferson, for example, did after all face a plot by a former Vice President of the United States who was in confidential communication with the Spanish and British ministers, who controlled a personal army, who had clandestine support among disaffected officers in the regular forces and who, whether he meant it or not, liked to boast after dinner that he could drive the President and Congress into the Potomac.[111] Moreover, Jefferson set forth his theory of the emergency in a special message to Congress. And, if he overreacted, as he undoubtedly did, he confined his overreaction to Burr and his fellow conspirators. He did not call for a general surveillance of all his political enemies. As for Truman, he directed his Secretary of Commerce to take over the steel mills because the emergency of Korea required it, as he believed, in order to keep up production for the troops.[112] No more than Jefferson did he conceal his conception of the emergency from the nation. He took his action without dissembling, in light of day and with full reports to Congress. Even if the republic rejected their contentions, both Jefferson and Truman publicly explained the threats that in their view justified an extreme response.

In this case, as in so many others, Nixon exceeded all his predecessors. He evidently perceived an emergency so urgent and authentic that he, though head of an administration fervently pledged to law and order, felt justified in setting his government on a lawless course. Yet he made no case to the nation. Perhaps his plebiscitary conception of the Presidency relieved him of the obligation felt by Lincoln and Roosevelt, Jefferson and Truman, to define the emergency. "The plebiscite," as Michels said of Napoleon III, "was a purifying bath which gave legitimate sanction to every illegality." [113] In any case, there was no message to Congress saying the republic was about to be overthrown by angry college students, the Weathermen, the Black Panthers and Daniel Ellsberg; no proclamation of national emergency, limited or unlimited, in response to the internal threat. Instead, on the basis of personal theories of national danger, theories unexplained to the people, unshared with Congress, sketchily checked within the executive branch (and apparently rejected by J. Edgar Hoover, who up to that time had let no one surpass him in the paranoid guardianship of the republic), he authorized a system of burglary, wiretapping, bugging, mail covers, secret agents and political blackmail in defiance of the laws and the Constitution. And, when Hoover forced him to cancel this government-wide plan, he then set up his own private outfit which acted faithfully in the plan's spirit.

Nixon never set forth publicly the constitutional theory on which he justified such actions. In July 1973, however, Ehrlichman, after observing that he found the burglarization of the office of Ellsberg's psychiatrist "well within the President's inherent constitutional powers," added that the President himself in March had expressed to him "essentially the view that I have just stated, that this was an important, a vital national security inquiry, and that he considered it to be well within the constitutional both obligation and function of the Presidency." [114] How far, Ehrlichman was asked, would he press this point? Would national security warrant a President's ordering not just a burglary but a murder? Ehrlichman replied judiciously that he would not want to say just where the line was to be drawn. But the suggestion did not appear to outrage him. (What did outrage him was the thought of drunken legislators tottering onto the floors of Congress. *This* was really a moral issue. One was reminded of those religious denominations before the Civil War that sternly condemned dancing and card-playing but could not find it in their hearts to oppose slavery.)

Ehrlichman went on to try and give this thesis statutory basis. He cited a provision in the Crime Control and Safe Streets Act of 1968 affirming the constitutional power of the President to protect national security against foreign espionage; and cited also the reminder by the Supreme Court in its decision requiring judicial approval for wiretapping in domestic security cases that it was not addressing itself to the problem of foreign intelligence activities. But both the Court's decision and the section of the Crime Control Act referred to wiretapping, not to burglary; and in any case there was no evidence of foreign intelligence involvement in the Ellsberg affair. Ehrlichman said that the Pentagon Papers had been delivered to the Soviet embassy, but there was no proof that this was true nor did the government so charge when it brought Ellsberg to trial. The Ehrlichman argument was entirely far-fetched, a contemptible version of Lockean prerogative. Still it unquestionably expressed the White House mood.

Richard M. Nixon, for all his conventionality of utterance and mind, was a genuine revolutionary. Who can say why? No doubt it was partly out of inner need: he had to create for himself a Presidency he could handle psychologically. Partly it may have been out of honest ignorance of American traditions: few Presidents seem to have had such limited acquaintance with the history of the republic. It was partly, one must hope, out of a considered judgment that the old separation of powers had outlived its time: nothing else could confer dignity on what constitutional historians will otherwise regard as a piratical administration.[115] Whatever, the explanation, the theory of the Presidency he embodied and propagated meant that the President of the United States, on his own personal and secret finding of emergency, had the right to nullify the Constitution and the law. No President had ever made such a claim before.

"If Government becomes the lawbreaker," said Brandeis, "it breeds contempt for law; it invites every man to become a law unto himself; it invites anarchy. . . . To declare that the Government may commit crimes in order to secure the conviction of a private criminal . . . would bring terrible retribution." [116]

XV

Retribution came, and its name was Watergate. But it came almost by accident. Watergate was a probable, but by no means a necessary, consequence of the effort to change the nature of the Presidency. Had Nixon confined executive aggrandizement to such visible fields as the war-making and treaty-making powers, impoundment and executive privilege and the pocket veto, he might have carried his revolution against the separation of powers very far indeed. Given the chicken-heartedness of Congress, the acquiescence of most of the press and the predilections of the American lower middle class — all things Nixon well understood and exploited — he could have traveled a good deal further down the road to a plebiscitary Presidency without encountering effective resistance.

But his purpose was probably more unconscious than conscious; and his revolution took direction and color not just from the external circumstances pressing new powers on the Presidency but from the needs and drives of his own agitated psyche. This was the fatal flaw in the revolutionary design. For everywhere he looked he saw around him hideous threats to the national security — threats that, even though he would not describe them to Congress or the people, kept his White House in constant uproar and warranted in his own mind a clandestine presidential response of spectacular and historic illegality. If his public actions led toward a scheme of presidential supremacy under a considerably debilitated Constitution, his private obsessions pushed him toward the view that the Presidency could set itself, at will, *above* the Constitution. It was this theory that led straight to Watergate.

In the early months of 1972 Nixon had slipped badly in the polls. In January Gallup showed him one point ahead of Senator Edmund Muskie; Harris showed them tied at 42 percent.[117] It was this situation that shifted the attention of the special investigations unit from the national security to the security of Nixon's re-election. The techniques set forth in the secret plan of 1970 and practiced by the plumbers in 1971 were now put to use in domestic politics. What Watergate meant was the introduction into presidential elections of methods devised by the Office of Strategic Services and the Central Intelligence Agency for use against foreign enemies.[118] There was no inevitability about this. The British, from whom OSS and CIA learned most of their dirty tricks, had used them abroad for generations without applying them at home. "The Americans," wrote Richard Crossman, "adored subversion, but . . . they never learned from us to play it as a game and give it up when the war was over." [119] Still, it required an explicit will to import subversion into domestic politics. This the Nixon administration was the first to do. Not only did most of the men involved in Watergate have past CIA connections; but Nixon had forced the CIA against its better judgment to mix in domestic matters, and the White House staff even ordered CIA to furnish the White House spooks with wigs, voice modifiers, forged papers and psychographs of Daniel Ellsberg.

It was this that made Watergate new in the long and gaudy history of American political corruption. Stewart Alsop stated the issue with precision: "To transfer such secret-service techniques, on an obviously planned and organized basis, to the internal American political process is a genuinely terrifying innovation. . . . The Watergate scandal, it is clear by now, is different — truly different, different in kind — from all the scandals that have preceded it in American history. It is this difference that makes it so frightening." [120] There was one other salient difference; that this was not the local adventure of a courthouse boss but a national conspiracy by the White House itself. Malcolm Moos, the political scientist who had served in Eisenhower's White House, wrote, "We were the victims of a coup d'état or an attempted coup. I weigh my words carefully." [121]

There had been scandals in the White House before; in fact, they came every half century — the Grant scandals of 1873, the Harding scandals of 1923, the Nixon scandals of 1973. But crookedness in the simple days of Grant and of Harding was old-fashioned graft. It was politics as defined by Ambrose Bierce in *The Devil's Dictionary* — "the conduct of public affairs for private advantage." Repellent as it might be, stealing money for oneself was in an old American tradition. What distinguished the Nixon crowd was, in a sense, the purity of their motives. Far from being jolly rogues like the cronies of Grant and Harding, they tended to be thin-lipped, hard-eyed, crew-cut pharisaical types who did not drink or smoke or visit call girls and spent a lot of time in sanctimonious complaint about the permissive society. They were not thieves, except by the way; rather they were moralistic opportunists who had been led to understand that the Presidency was above the law and that the end justified the means. "What they were seeking to steal," said Senator Ervin, "was not the jewels, money or other property of American citizens, but something much more valuable — their most precious heritage, the right to vote in a free election." [122] Fanaticism could be a greater danger than graft to a free state.

Locke himself, for all his defense of prerogative in times of emergency, sharply condemned the executive who in normal times "set up his own arbitrary will as the law of society" or who employed "the force, treasure, and offices" of society to gain his purposes through interference in the political process. "Thus to regulate candidates and electors, and new model the ways of election," Locke said, "what is it but to cut up the government by the roots, and poison the very foundation of public security?" [123] What indeed?

XVI

It was a very near thing. In the months after the exposure, Americans tended to preen themselves on the virtues of the American form of government: "the system worked." But it came terribly close to not working. If, for example, that forgotten hero Frank Wills, the twenty-four-year-old security guard, had not noticed tape over the latches of two doors on the bottom level of the Watergate on June 17, 1972, the burglary would have remained undetected. Even when Wills called police and the burglars were arrested, nothing much happened. Public opinion could hardly have been less concerned. Despite Senator McGovern's efforts to rouse the conscience of the electorate, most Americans regarded "the Watergate caper" with indifference if not with complacency till well into 1973, and then began to react only after the issue had changed from the original depredation to the subsequent obstruction of justice.

As for President Nixon, he responded to growing congressional and public curiosity by enlarging his claims of presidential prerogative. Thus he wholly rejected any idea of personal appearance before a congressional committee or grand jury as incompatible with presidential dignity and the separation of powers. Actually Presidents more dignified than Nixon had failed to perceive so vast a barrier. Washington went to Congress to ask its advice about a treaty. Lincoln appeared before the House

Judiciary Committee in 1862 to discuss the leak of his State of the Union message to the *New York Herald* and before the Committee on the Conduct of the War on other occasions, once, according to legend, to deny that his wife was a Confederate spy. Numerous Presidents, among them Lincoln, Wilson and Franklin Roosevelt, invited committees of Congress to meet them at the White House. Truman, as Nixon pointed out, did after his Presidency turn back a subpoena from the House Un-American Activities Committee; but the subpoena did not even specify the matter on which the Committee sought the former President's testimony, and the newspapers had indicated that it was in an area — his reasons for making executive appointments — that was exclusively a presidential responsibility.[124] Ulysses S. Grant even thought it would be appropriate for himself, as President, to appear in a courtroom as a witness for the defense when his private secretary, General Orville Babcock, was under prosecution by his own Department of Justice.

Nixon, in short, wanted to make absolute what some of his predecessors had plainly regarded as less than absolute. It is true that, as he mentioned several times to Ervin, he was prepared to waive the lawyer-client privilege and let his former White House counsels testify. But here he was waiving something none of his predecessors had ever claimed; no previous President seems to have supposed that the White House counsel, whose job was to deal with public issues and whose salary was paid by the taxpayer, was equivalent to the President's personal attorney. As for papers, Nixon had contended that executive privilege covered everything that went in, through or out of the White House in connection with official duties. Then it developed that he himself had systematically taped conversations and meetings at the White House over a considerable time. Much of the discussion on the tapes unquestionably had to do with official business; but some of the tapes no doubt contained evidence pertinent to both judicial and congressional inquiries into the Watergate affair. Accordingly both Professor Archibald Cox, the Special Prosecutor, and the Senate Select Committee on the Watergate case chaired by Sam Ervin of North Carolina requested release of specified tapes.

These requests raised tangled constitutional problems. Nixon's first reaction was to tell Ervin that even controlled and selective disclosure would "inevitably" result in the destruction of "the indispensable principle of confidentiality." In a second letter to Ervin, however, he seemed to retreat for a moment from the claim of absolute privilege. If the release of the tapes would settle the question at issue, he now said, "then their disclosure might serve a substantial public interest," but, since he himself found the evidence on the tapes inconclusive, he would keep them under his "sole personal control." A few days later, he returned to the idea of absolute privilege. The issue, he wrote Judge John Sirica, who had presided over the trial of the Watergate burglars and who now, at the Special Prosecutor's behest, was seeking the tapes, went to the independence of the three branches of government: "It would be wholly inadmissible for the President to seek to compel some particular action by the courts. It is equally inadmissible for the courts to seek to compel some particular action from the President." [125] This was a peculiar statement. From the time of *Marbury v. Madison* the other branches had conceded to the courts the power to construe the Constitution; and, pursuant to that power, the Supreme Court had repeatedly compelled particular actions from Presidents, such as requiring Truman to divest himself of the steel industry and Franklin Roosevelt to divest himself of much of the early New Deal.

In any case, the court served a subpoena *duces tecum* on the President — the first since Marshall's to Jefferson 166 years before. Nixon's lawyers now claimed the issue as "starkly simple: will the Presidency be allowed to continue to function?" If the courts could command the disclosure of presidential conversations, the damage to the Presidency would be "severe and irreparable." Nor did executive privilege vanish simply because the grand jury was looking into charges of criminal conduct. Executive privilege "would be meaningless if it were to give way whenever there is reason to suspect that disclosure might reveal criminal acts." The decision about the tapes was the President's. "He — and he alone — must weigh the interest in prosecuting a wrongdoer against the interest in keeping all Presidential conversations confidential." He had "absolute power to decide what may be disclosed to others." [126]

Cox pointed out in response that he was not asking to rummage through presidential files but only for the tapes of particular conversations identified in sworn testimony as relating to the Watergate cover-up. He scouted the idea that their disclosure would destroy the Presidency. After all, the involvement of the White House in criminal conduct was "virtually unique. Because it is unlikely to recur, production of White House documents *in this investigation* will establish no precedent." The issue was whether the President had the "absolute prerogative" to withhold evidence of crime, especially if he had a personal and private interest in the outcome of the case. How could Nixon be a disinterested judge when his "highest and closest associates" had been accused? He was bound to them not only by natural emotions of loyalty and gratitude "but also by the risk that his present political power and future place in history will be linked to the effect of disclosure." The issue, in short, was whether the President was above the law. "Unlike a monarch," said Cox, "the President is not the Sovereign." [127]

Nixon continued thereafter to insist that "the principle of confidentiality of Presidential conversations" was at stake.[128] Yet some wondered why, if he cared so much about the principle of confidentiality, he had taped everything in the first place. "The way to insure the confidentiality of future presidential conversations," as the *Wall Street Journal* sensibly said, "is to stop recording them on tape." [129] While no one doubted the right to protect presidential conversations connected with the performance of official duties, the cover-up of crimes hardly rated as an official duty, and the claim that the President in discussing the cover-up was seeing that the laws were faithfully executed could only be substantiated if he had taken strong action against the lawbreakers. In any case, as Nixon's own lawyers conceded in their brief, "Quite commonly Presidents have voluntarily made available information for which a claim of privilege could have been made. That happens very often." [130] Why did it not happen this time? Nixon, in the manner of his predecessors, could easily have affirmed the sacred principle while waiving it in this particular case. The answer, as murkily indicated in the presidential brief, was evidently that in this particular case Nixon felt that disclosure would do concrete harm to the public interest. The *public* interest?

The profounder question was whether any President could place himself beyond the process of law in a case involving not, like the case of *Mississippi v. Johnson,* the performance of official duties but criminal conduct as well as the President's own personal and political fortunes. "The privilege," as Justice Cardozo had said in another connection, "takes flight when abused." [131] Woodrow Wilson surely stated the common sense of the Constitution when he said that "no peculiar dignity or sanctity attaches amongst us to any officer of government. The theory of our law is that an officer is an officer only so long as he acts within his powers; that when he transcends his authority he ceases to be an officer and is only a private individual, subject to be sued and punished for his offense." [132]

Nixon's series of claims represented a last fling of the revolutionary Presidency. His conceded ability to make a one-time waiver without abandoning the principle led some to wonder whether his action was a defense of principle or of himself. If his claims were sustained by the courts, it would have the effect of confirming the President as judge in his own case and thereby giving him an immunity denied all other American citizens. The result could come close to establishing what Chief Justice Marshall had rejected so long ago — the view that the American President, like the English King, could do no wrong.

XVII

Whatever the future of the tapes, it could be said, I suppose, that the runaway Presidency had been checked by the recalcitrance of institutions — the independent judiciary, the free press, the investigative power of Congress. Still, these institutions would not have been effective had they not happened to be manned, at the critical conjunctions, by courageous individuals, ready to accept the risk and obloquy of becoming Enemies of the

President. Another judge than John Sirica might have played the cover-up game and stopped the judicial inquiry once the men caught in the burglary had pleaded guilty. Another publisher than Katharine Graham might have succumbed to pressure and taken her reporters and editorial writers off the story. Another Senator than Sam Ervin might have lacked the prestige and perseverance to conduct an authoritative investigation.

Within the executive branch the major institutional decision to resist came not, as one might have expected, from the CIA, which sulked and went along, but from the FBI.[133] In the discussions leading up to the domestic security plan of 1970, T. C. Huston complained to Nixon about J. Edgar Hoover's "concern that the civil liberties people may become upset." [134] The civil liberties people had not known that J. Edgar Hoover cared, and it may well be that he did not care all that much about civil liberties; but he did care supremely about the professional reputation of the FBI. Thus caring, he slew the plan. Within ten days of the Watergate arrests, Nixon asked the CIA to ask the FBI to limit its investigation on the phony national-security pretext that "an unrelated covert operation of the CIA" might be exposed.[135] Both L. Patrick Gray, the acting director of the FBI, and General Vernon Walters, the deputy director of the CIA, were old friends of Nixon's and wanted to do what they could to help. But Gray, after holding things up for a few days, finally told Walters (as Walters reported their conversation in a memorandum for the files) that he "could not possibly suppress the investigation. . . . He did not see why he or I should jeopardize the integrity of our organizations to protect some mid-level White House figures." Walters himself said, "I did not believe a letter from the Agency asking the FBI to lay off this investigation on spurious grounds that it would uncover covert operations would serve the President. . . . I said quite frankly that I wouldn't write such a letter." [136] White House pressure was hard to resist, and both Gray and Walters yielded too much to it, but there were things they knew they could not get their organizations to do. And, after the administration had succeeded in putting off the Watergate trial till after the election, frustrated

FBI agents, whose loyalty to their organization and to the truth was deeper than their loyalty to the President, began to leak the facts to the newspapers.

Had it not been for Wills and Sirica, for Mrs. Graham and Ervin and the FBI, Haldeman and Ehrlichman would have served a second term at the White House; the special investigations unit, conscripting the Internal Revenue Service and the rest of the federal machinery, would have happily screwed the Enemies; and the revolutionary Presidency would have been in full swing. "Watergate," Walter Lippmann observed in the summer of the Ervin committee hearings, "shows how very *vulnerable* our constitutional system is. If the national government falls into the hands of sufficiently unprincipled and unscrupulous men, they can do terrible things before any one can stop them." [137] He could have added that another time it might be too late.

God, it has been well said, looks after drunks, children and the United States of America. However, given the number, the brazen presumption and the clownish ineptitude of the conspirators, if it had not been Watergate, it would surely have been something else. For Watergate was a symptom, not a cause. Nixon's supporters complained that his critics were blowing up a petty incident out of all proportion to its importance. No doubt a burglary at Democratic headquarters was trivial next to a mission to Peking. But Watergate's importance was not simply in itself. Its importance was in the way it brought to the surface, symbolized and made politically accessible the great question posed by the Nixon administration in every sector — the question of presidential power. The unwarranted and unprecedented expansion of presidential power, because it ran through the whole Nixon system, was bound, if repressed at one point, to break out at another. This, not Watergate, was the central issue.

Hugh Trevor-Roper, explaining Watergate to an English audience, drew an illuminating comparison with the revolt against royal prerogative in seventeenth-century England. When Hampden refused to pay ship-money in 1636, the apologists for Charles I asked why there was so much fuss over so trivial a matter. But ship-money was no more the central issue in England in 1635–1640 than Watergate was in America in 1973. "The central issue then was royal power: the evident determination of the Crown to rule absolutely, and its evident success in building up the means of so doing. Those who opposed the king's aims, and disliked his ministers, saw well enough that unless they could halt this process, the whole system of English government might be permanently changed." Ship-money "was seen as the Achilles heel of an otherwise invulnerable enemy."

I cannot do better than to keep on quoting Trevor-Roper's brilliant essay:

> Like Charles I, President Nixon found himself the ruler of a nation at a time when governments everywhere were gaining strength at the expense of parliamentary institutions. Like Charles I, he used methods which, though politically irritant, seemed legally unassailable; and he used them with indiscreet reliance on sheer power and mere law. Like Charles I, he found means to raise money and make war without the consent of the 'political nation.' Instead, he surrounded himself with new men whom that 'political nation' came to dislike. Like Charles I, he also made matters worse by convincing his people that he was not to be trusted.
>
> By these methods Charles I alienated many men who, fundamentally, preferred his rule to that of his opponents; but he kept to his course, confident that, in the last resort, respect for his office would always prevail: if he stood firm, his enemies, having no alternative tradition, and no desire for extreme courses, would surely crumble.

Trevor-Roper noted the argument of those who would isolate and trivialize Watergate because they so much admired the Nixon foreign policy. Similarly, he observed, the foreign policy of Charles I was probably preferable to that of his critics. "No doubt, in the 1630s, foreigners thought the English very foolish to make such a fuss about ship-money when a firm and unhampered English government might have been effective in Europe. But the English thought first of their own liberties; and who shall say that they were wrong?" Historians, Trevor-Roper concluded, do not judge the opposition to Charles I on the merits and demerits of ship-money but on the broad issue of royal absolutism vs. parliamentary rights. "So we should not measure the importance of the American constitutional crisis by the trivialities of Watergate, but should look at the struggle as a whole; a struggle which was already looming up, in vague, intangible form, before it was suddenly made real on this accidental battleground." [138]

Made real it was; and, whatever the ultimate outcome, Watergate did stop the revolutionary Presidency in its tracks. It blew away the mystique of the mandate and reinvigorated the constitutional separation of powers. If the independent judiciary, the free press, Congress and the executive agencies could not really claim too much credit as institutions for work performed within them by brave individuals, nonetheless they all drew new confidence as institutions from the exercise of power they had forgotten they possessed. The result could only be to brace and strengthen the inner balance of American democracy.

★ 9 ★

Democracy and Foreign Policy

WATERGATE ended the most serious effort in American history to change the nature of the Presidency. But it did not end the conditions that made this effort possible and even plausible. The question remained how a government based on the principle of the *separation* of powers could be made to work. This question never ceased to fascinate foreigners, to whom the American form of government seemed an attempt to defy the laws of gravity. Bagehot could explain the survival of the United States only as the triumph of innate political genius over the Constitution: "Sensible shareholders, I have heard a shrewd attorney say, can work *any* deed of settlement; and so the men of Massachusetts could, I believe, work *any* Constitution." [1]

A century after Bagehot, men of Massachusetts had less power (though the tradition endured: Massachusetts was the only state [2] to vote against the revolutionary Presidency in 1972), and public affairs had acquired a new urgency and complexity. The question seemed more insistent than ever whether the constitutional separation of powers was compatible with the requirements imposed on the American government in the nuclear age. Was there really a way to give Congress as an independent branch a serious role in the making of national decisions? Or was the Nixon assault on the separation of powers simply the crude and corrupt first approximation of a solution to a perfectly real problem?

*

I

The question posed itself most sharply in the area of foreign relations. For it was from foreign policy that the imperial Presidency drew its initial momentum. And it was in foreign policy that the reversal of original intentions was most dramatic.

The Constitution had conferred the power to go to war on Congress. The Founding Fathers were determined to insure that *"no one man,"* in Lincoln's phrase, "should hold the power of bringing this oppression upon us." Two centuries after independence the congressional role had evaporated. In matters of war and peace the American President was supreme. Certainly Brezhnev in the Soviet Union,[3] even probably Mao Tse-tung in China, had to consult more people and secure more institutional clearances before sending armies into battle. Was the American situation beyond remedy?

Some political philosophers would have regarded the failure of the constitutional solution as inevitable. A most respectable line of thought, from Tocqueville to Lippmann, had contended that legislatures and mass opinion were simply unqualified for a serious role in the conduct of foreign affairs. In Great Britain, the declaration of war and the signing of treaties remained, in form at least, almost as much a matter of executive prerogative in the 1970s as they had been in the time of George III. "Under the British Constitution," wrote Churchill, "the Crown declares war on the advice of Ministers, and Parliament is confronted with the fact." [4] In practice the situation was not so drastic. Any British government that declared war against the predominant sentiment of the country, and certainly against the majority sentiment of the House of Commons, would be turned out as a result. Still the government ordinarily controlled the House; and in any case, the theory remained that Parliament had no independent role in the decision to go to war or in the making of commitments that might lead to war.[5]

This theory was natural enough where there was no separation of powers, where the executive itself, in other words, sprang from the bosom of Parliament and commanded an automatic majority until it lost a vote of confidence. For its part, Parliament seemed content to confide to the executive the right not only to make foreign policy decisions but to keep the decisions to itself. Efforts to change the system proved unavailing. In 1924 the first Labour government, in a Wilsonian mood, promised to inform the House of Commons "of all agreements, commitments, and understandings which may in any way bind the nation to specific action in certain circumstances." But the Conservative government that came to office at the end of 1924 declined to renew this pledge. Labour, now in opposition, moved a resolution demanding that Parliament be informed before the government made undertakings to foreign states involving national obligations; no military cooperation pursuant to such undertakings would otherwise be legal. The government replied that foreign policy was an executive responsibility and that (as Max Beloff summarized its case) the democratic element in the British system was "enshrined in the right of the House of Commons to dismiss a ministry with whose policies it disagreed, and ultimately in the dependence of the House itself upon the electorate." The member for Cambridge University even noted how embarrassing congressional intervention had been for the United States. The House rejected the resolution by a vote of 255 to 133. This was, Beloff wrote in 1954, "in some respects the high-water mark of the democratic protest" in Great Britain.[6] Thereafter even Labour governments lost their pristine belief in a parliamentary role. To this day the House of Commons has no equivalent of the Senate Foreign Relations Committee and has no general power to confirm ambassadors, advise on and consent to treaties or declare war.

It was the separation of powers which thus compelled the United States, more than any other democracy, to confront the question of the relationship of the legislature to the control of foreign affairs. And, though a miserable congressional performance, especially in the years between the wars, lent substance to the Tocqueville-Lippmann thesis, an opposing line of political thought offered hope for the idea of democratic control.

This was best expounded by Lord Bryce, who stood next to Tocqueville as the classic foreign interpreter of American institutions.

Writing toward the end of the First World War, Bryce had no doubt that the demand for the abolition of secret diplomacy and for the popular control of foreign policy appealed to an "incontestable principle, because a nation has every right to deliver its opinion on matters of such supreme importance as the issues of peace and war." Nor for that matter did the record, as he read it, show that the management of foreign affairs by a small elite produced such brilliant results. In recent English history, for example, there had been three notable occasions when mass opinion had disagreed with the foreign policy establishment — during the American Civil War, during the Russo-Turkish troubles of 1876 to 1880 and during the Boer War. Everybody, wrote Bryce, now admitted that it was a gain for the world that the North won the Civil War; Disraeli's pro-Turkish policy had been condemned by its failure; the South African war was generally accepted as a blunder. "It is interesting to note that in all three cases the 'classes' would appear to have been less wise than the 'masses.' " As for the United States, the record persuaded Bryce that "public opinion, which is there omnipotent, is generally right in its aims, and has tended to become wiser and more moderate with the march of the years." And what of those ideal countries from the viewpoint of the foreign policy elite, Russia, Germany and Austria-Hungary, in which "no popular clamour disturbed the Olympian heights where sat the monarch and his group of military and civil advisers, controlling foreign policy as respects both ends and means"? The answer, as Bryce looked out at the wreckage of the three great empires, was self-evident.

On the other hand, Bryce readily acknowledged limits to democratic control. Large assemblies could not handle international relations from day to day; these must be determined "by administrators who are incessantly watching the foreign sky." Ministers had to be allowed a measure of discretion and secrecy in the conduct of negotiations. The answer, Bryce thought, was to distinguish between means and ends. The distinction was hard to draw, because most ends were means to a larger end. Yet, "while Foreign Offices and diplomatic envoys may be the proper persons to choose and apply Means, the general principles which should guide and the spirit which should inspire a nation's foreign policy are a different matter, too wide in scope, too grave in consequence, to be determined by any authority lower than that of the people." He summed up his argument in cogent aphorisms:

> In a democracy the People are entitled to determine the Ends or general aims of foreign policy.
>
> History shows that they do this at least as wisely as monarchs or oligarchies, or the small groups to whom, in democratic countries, the conduct of foreign relations has been left, and that they have evinced more respect for moral principles.
>
> The Means to be used for attaining the Ends sought cannot be adequately determined by legislatures so long as international relations continue to be what they have heretofore been, because secrecy is sometimes, and expert knowledge is always required. . . .
>
> Whatever faults modern democracies may have committed in this field of administration, the faults chargeable on monarchs and oligarchies have been less pardonable and more harmful to the peace and progress of mankind.[7]

II

The theory, so dominant and so persuasive in the years after the Second World War, that a foreign policy must be trusted to the executive, went down in flames in Vietnam. Who could say, for example, that the National Security Council had been all that much wiser in this melancholy period than the Senate Foreign Relations Committee? One after another the traditional arguments in favor of presidential supremacy — unity, secrecy, superior expertise, superior sources of information, decision, dispatch — turned out to be immensely overrated. Vietnam discredited executive control of foreign relations as profoundly as Versailles and mandatory neutrality had discredited congressional control.

Unity? This had been a strong argument in the 1790s when the State Department consisted of Thomas Jefferson and half a dozen clerks. But unity was an illusion in the vast and refractory executive branch of the 1970s, where a cluster of quarreling departments and bureaus and hundreds of people contended (generally in vain) for a share in the making of foreign policy. Secrecy? The very condition of disunity rendered the executive branch incapable of secrecy. The best way to frustrate a rival agency was often through a well-placed leak. Expertise? The test of expertise was in the judgments it produced; and no episode in American history had been more accompanied by misjudgment, misconception and miscalculation than the war in Vietnam.[8] Information? The newspapers and magazines provided far more accurate information about the progress of the war in Indochina than Top Secret cables from Saigon. Decision and dispatch? No doubt the executive could decide faster, but the need for fast decisions, as we have seen, was enormously exaggerated; apart from Korea and the Cuban missile crisis no postwar emergency had demanded instant response. There had been far stronger reason for exclusive presidential decision in the 1790s, when it took a month for Congress to convene, than in the age of the telephone and the jet airplane. Every argument that Jay and Hamilton had made in the 64th and 75th Federalist Papers applied, apart from the narrow question of negotiation, a good deal more to their own time than to the nuclear age.

What remained was the mystical assumption that the Presidency was more likely to be right than the Congress. But no one could argue this with much conviction after Vietnam. Presidential supremacy in foreign affairs had worked well enough when the electoral process sent men of intelligence, restraint and constitutional sensitivity to the White House. But, as Americans understood in the 1970s more vividly than ever before in their history, the electoral process was not infallible. And, as they understood too, when a President got the bit between his teeth, it was impossible for a foreign-policy bureaucracy, however expert, to stop him and improbable that Congress, given its disabilities, would choose to do so.

Moreover, since Americans had not found angels in the form of Presidents to govern them, the principle that one man could decide better than many was, as Jefferson pointed out in his first inaugural, philosophically defective. It was also incompatible with the democratic idea. Indeed, if decisions of war and peace were not subject to popular control, how much scope and substance did democracy really have? In the nineteenth century, when war had relatively limited destructive consequence, this had not been perhaps a terribly pressing issue. But in the nuclear age the power to go to war could mean the power to blow up the planet. Was this dread power, this ultimate power, to be bestowed upon a single fallible man — above all a man systematically withdrawn from reality by the bewitchments of the imperial Presidency?

Both history and philosophy led, I think, to an irresistible conclusion: the constitutional goal — that no one man should hold the power of committing the nation to war or of keeping it at war — was still valid and must prevail. But the Constitution had manifestly failed to provide the machinery by which that goal could be surely attained. The problem for the future was how power was to be divided between the Presidency and the Congress in order to restrain presidential war without at the same time impairing the safety of the republic.

III

A people with a weakness, as Tocqueville had remarked, for resolving political into judicial questions might look to the courts for an answer. This was not so easy as it sounded. No doubt practice with regard to the war-making clause had departed very far indeed from original intent. But this fact was not conclusive on questions of constitutionality. As problems unforeseen in 1787 had emerged, judicial interpretation had unfolded new possibilities in the Constitution, which was after all, as Holmes said, a document to be read "in the light of our whole experience

and not merely in that of what was said a hundred years ago." [9]
In the instance of the commerce clause, for example, the failure
of fundamentalist standards in the face of new social imperatives
made it necessary to revise constitutional interpretations in order
to attain constitutional objectives. Could not this be just as true
for the war-making power?

History spoke on this point with its customary inscrutability.
Throughout the life of the nation each side of the argument over
the location of the war-making power — the congressional side
and the presidential side — had won the support of illustrious
men. This would be by itself sufficient to discourage a rush to
final judgment. But what was even more admonitory was the remarkable extent to which the *same* men, in different circumstances and at different points in their careers, had argued first
one side and then the other of the issue.

The Abraham Lincoln who challenged the presidential prerogative of Polk during the Mexican War was the same Abraham
Lincoln who a dozen years later gave the Presidency greater
powers over war and peace than ever before, as the Andrew
Jackson who showed such deference to Congress in the 1830s
was the same Andrew Jackson who had charged without congressional authorization into Spanish Florida in 1817. The Federalists who had defended presidential war-making in the 1790s
were the champions of the congressional prerogative in 1814.
Webster and Seward saw the powers of Congress in one light
when they were senators and in quite another light when they became Secretaries of State. Justice Nelson offered one constitutional view of presidential war in *Durand v. Hollins* and a very
different view three years later in the Prize Cases.

Nor was such vacillation confined to the nineteenth century.
Richard M. Nixon had one set of opinions in 1951 on the question whether Congress could control troop deployments and executive agreements. In 1971 he had a diametrically opposite set
of opinions. Senator Fulbright, moving in the reverse direction,
repented his earlier belief that the President needed more authority in foreign affairs. Professor Corwin's "high-flying prerogative
men" of 1951 subsequently parachuted safely back to earth.

Professor Commager in effect accepted the Taft-Coudert case; and this writer freely concedes that Senator Taft had a much more substantial point than he supposed twenty years ago. But to make that point, Taft in 1951 had to explain away the views of his father, the Chief Justice; and, while the younger Senator Taft in 1971 followed his father rather than his grandfather, other heirs of Taft, like Goldwater and Rehnquist, became the very model of Corwin's high-flying prerogative men. For that matter Corwin himself took one position on the President's power to use force abroad without congressional authorization in 1940 and 1949 and the opposite position in 1951. It is little wonder that John Quincy Adams, one of the most conscientious of American statesmen, who himself moved from a most latitudinarian theory of presidential war-making authority in 1816 to an equally latitudinarian theory of congressional war-making authority in 1846, wrote in 1836, "The respective powers of the President and Congress of the United States, in the case of war with foreign powers are yet undetermined. Perhaps they can never be defined." [10]

There were obvious reasons for this chronicle of contradiction. For one thing, the issues involved were ones of genuine intellectual difficulty, about which reasonable men might well find themselves changing their mind. For another, power always looked more responsible from within than from without. For another, general questions often assumed different shapes in different lights. "I remember," Professor Hans Morgenthau wrote with admirable frankness, "how I used to implore a succession of Presidents to assert their constitutional powers against Congress as long as I disagreed with the foreign policies to which Congress appeared to be committed." [11] Similarly I. F. Stone: "To be honest about it, how one feels about the 'inherent' powers of the Presidency has been generally determined throughout our history by how one feels about the use to which they are put and the pressing needs of the time." [12] Though the less clear-eyed sometimes found it gratifying to claim constitutionality for policies they thought necessary and to denounce as unconstitutional policies they thought dangerous, this more often expressed a need to turn relative into absolute judgments than a definitive reading of the Constitution.

All this pointed to a single conclusion: that the argument was not, save at its outer fringes, primarily constitutional. It was primarily political. History offered statesman, lawyer or historian almost any precedent needed to give legal color to almost any policy. People generally raised constitutional questions when they disagreed with the policy, and few of these questions had precise or absolute constitutional answers. Because the Supreme Court saw this as the case, it prudently refrained from serious intervention in the problem. In a long and voluble history — 400 thick volumes of judicial reports — the Court's decisions bearing even marginally on the location of the war-making power could be numbered on the fingers of two hands. The illumination thus provided was, at best, flickering if not dim. As Justice Jackson wrote in 1948, Presidents took action in foreign affairs on the basis of information that courts did not have. Even if courts could require full disclosure, "the very nature of executive decisions as to foreign policy is political, not judicial. Such decisions are wholly confided by our Constitution to the political departments of the government, Executive and Legislative. They are delicate, complex, and involve large elements of prophecy. They are and should be undertaken only by those directly responsible to the people whose welfare they advance or imperil. They are decisions of a kind for which the Judiciary has neither aptitude, facilities nor responsibility and which has long been held to belong in the domain of political power not subject to judicial intrusion or inquiry." [13] Jackson could well have added that the Court, in entering the field, ran the risk no such institution could afford to run very often — that the executive would simply ignore its command. Never in American history had the Court tried in any significant way to interfere with a war in progress, whatever its afterthoughts, as in *ex parte Milligan*, when the killing had come to a stop.

*

IV

The doctrine expounded by Justice Jackson was the old one of "political questions." Marshall had first set forth this idea in *Marbury v. Madison* in 1803 when he placed beyond the reach of judicial examination the application of those powers vested by the Constitution in the President "in the exercise of which he is to use his own discretion, and is accountable only to his country in his political character, and to his own conscience"; a quarter-century later he extended the doctrine to embrace similar actions on the part of Congress.[14] For most of American history the nature and scope of this doctrine were exceedingly unclear. It was not applied, for example, in the steel seizure case, which involved a conflict of claims between the Presidency and Congress. Judge Learned Hand called it in 1958 a term that the Court had "never tried to define — although this feature of the doctrine has been a stench in the nostrils of strict constructionists." [15]

Finally in 1962 the Court offered, if not a definition, at least a series of tests by which political questions could be identified. In his opinion in *Baker v. Carr,* Justice Brennan said, among other things, that there had to be both a "textually demonstrable constitutional commitment of the issue to a coordinate political department" and "a lack of judicially discoverable and manageable standards" for settling the issue. In addition, he said, the Court should not intervene if the initial policy decision was of a kind "clearly for nonjudicial discretion" or if its intervention expressed disrespect for other branches of government or created undue problems for political decisions already made, "embarrassment of our government abroad, or grave disturbance at home." If a question did not meet one or more of these tests, then it became, as lawyers say, justiciable. The Court, though it was considering a domestic issue, added that it was "error" to suppose that "every case or controversy which touches on foreign relations lies beyond judicial cognizance." [16]

This explanation still left unresolved the problem whether the political-questions doctrine gave the Supreme Court a discretion not to take up cases when judicial intervention would be futile and might well, as Justice Frankfurter said in his dissent in *Baker v. Carr,* damage "the Court's position" and "the Court's authority." [17] Here the experts disagreed. Professor Alexander Bickel defended the prudential argument; Professor Herbert Wechsler said that abstention was proper only when the Constitution had "committed the determination of the issue to another agency of government than the courts." [18] In any case, the Indochina War raised the issue of the justiciability of presidential war as it had never before been raised in American history.

At the start lower courts denied jurisdiction to war cases on the political-questions thesis. The Court of Appeals for the District of Columbia, Warren E. Burger joining in the opinion, said in 1967 that it was difficult to imagine "an area less suited for judicial action" and warned future petitioners that resort to the courts would be "futile" as well as "wasteful of judicial time." [19] The Supreme Court itself declined to take war cases on appeal. But in November 1967 Justices Stewart and Douglas, dissenting from a denial of *certiorari* by their brethren, insisted that such cases involved "questions of great magnitude" (Stewart) and raised "a host of problems" (Douglas).[20] In the next years, lower courts, perhaps responding to these signals, began to find war cases justiciable, at least up to a point. Instead of throwing them out at once, judges recalled the principle of the steel-seizure case, curiously overlooked by Judge Burger and his colleagues in 1967, and acknowledged a judicial role in case of conflict between the two other coordinate branches of government. The question where the power to decide on war lay was clearly a constitutional and therefore a judicial question, even if the question of the wisdom of particular decisions was not. The duty of the judiciary, one judge said, was to "insist upon compliance with the required constitutional components" of any such decision. What then was the constitutional scheme? The Constitution, said another judge, envisaged "the joint participation of the Congress and the executive in determining the scale and duration of hostilities." [21] But the manner in which Congress chose to express this participation — whether by declaration of war or by other means — remained a political question, beyond judicial control.

V

It was on this ground that courts continued to uphold the legality of the Vietnam War. They did not do so, it should be noted, on the grand theories of presidential prerogative advanced by Presidents Johnson and Nixon. No judge sustained the war on the theory of the inherent power of the Presidency.[22] Judges even disagreed among themselves as to whether the Tonkin Gulf resolution had constitutional significance.[23] But in two cases in 1970 — *Orlando v. Laird* and *Berk v. Laird* — District Court judges John Dooling and Orrin Judd agreed that there was a "discoverable and manageable" test of constitutionality. This was whether "the reality of the collaborative action of the executive and the legislative required by the Constitution" had been present from the earliest stages. Even if Congress had not explicitly authorized the Americanization of the war in 1965, it might thereafter have ratified the new war by its votes on military appropriations, on selective service and on other measures sustaining the escalation policy. Such "joint action" or "mutual participation," the judges independently contended, would satisfy the requirements of the Constitution.[24]

On May 4, 1965, Johnson, requesting special funds to meet the mounting costs of the new war, told Congress that this was "not a routine appropriation. For every member of Congress who supports this request is also voting to persist in our effort to halt Communist aggression in South Vietnam." But he also said, "I do not ask complete approval for every phase and action of your Government." The House passed the appropriation by 408 to 7, the Senate by 83 to 3. The State Department argument for the legality of the war, citing the first statement and omitting the second, briskly but doubtfully claimed the vote as "a clear congressional endorsement and approval of the actions taken by the President." [25] To what extent could the government justifiably contend that appropriations to enable the armed forces to fight an unauthorized war constituted an implicit authorization of that war?

The Supreme Court had accepted the idea of retroactive legislative ratification of executive initiative on certain conditions. "Ratification may be effected through appropriation acts," Justice Douglas said for the Court in 1944. ". . . but the appropriation must plainly show a purpose to bestow the precise authority which is claimed." [26] The Vietnam appropriations did not qualify as ratification by this standard. Moreover, appropriations to support men in battle presented a special problem. During the Mexican War, for example, Joshua Giddings of Ohio challenged his antiwar colleagues in the House of Representatives by reminding them that British Whigs had refused to vote supplies for the British troops in America.[27] But Abraham Lincoln, at the height of his opposition to the war, said, "I have always intended, and still intend, to vote supplies." [28] Even John Quincy Adams, though he drew the line at voting decorations to generals, always voted money for the troops.[29] In the case of Vietnam, though many senators were against the war by 1968, only Morse, Gruening and Nelson were voting against appropriations. Gruening later recalled Johnson saying to the antiwar minority, "I don't care what kind of speeches you make as long as you don't vote against the appropriations." [30] The point was repeatedly made in both houses, however, that, as the chairman of the House Appropriations Committee, George Mahon of Texas, put it in 1968, voting money for the troops "does not involve a test as to one's basic views with respect to the war in Vietnam. The question here is that they are entitled to our support as long as they are there, regardless of our views otherwise." [31]

Judges argued among themselves as to the significance of votes on appropriations. Congressional claims that there was no choice but to vote supplies were, Dooling said, simply a confession of "Congressional pusillanimity"; such evidence "could only disclose the motive and could not disprove the fact of authorization." "That some members of Congress talked like doves before voting with the hawks," said Judd, "is an inadequate basis for a charge that the President was violating the Constitution in doing what Congress by its words had told him he might do." [32] On the other hand, Judge Charles Wyzanski, who had taken this position in 1968, changed his view on further reflection. "The court cannot be unmindful of what every schoolboy knows," he wrote five years later in *Mitchell v. Laird*, "that an honorable, decent, compassionate act of aiding those already in peril is no proof of consent to the actions that placed and continued them in that dangerous posture. We should not construe votes cast in pity and piety as though they were votes freely given to express consent." [33]

Still, if too much could not be inferred from the refusal of a legislator to punish fighting men for the sins of those who sent them into the line, might there not come a point where legislative acquiescence in presidential war became so systematic, pervasive and comprehensive that it amounted in every practical sense to ratification? Listing 24 statutes facilitating the fighting in Vietnam, Senator Goldwater said with some justice in 1971, "Congress is and has been involved up to its ears with the war. . . . No one can now claim innocence of what he was voting about." [34] Throughout these years Congress retained the power to limit or end the war. Indeed, it had the power, specifically embodied in Section 3 of the Tonkin Gulf resolution itself, to terminate that resolution by a concurrent resolution (i.e., a resolution of both houses not subject to presidential veto).

Given the length and weight of congressional complaisance, there was persuasiveness in the opinion of Judge Frank Coffin, a former member of the House of Representatives, sitting on the Court of Appeals in the First Circuit, in the case of *Massachusetts v. Laird*. Here a three-man court ruled unanimously in 1971 that in a situation of prolonged but undeclared hostilities, where the President "continues to act not only in the absence of any conflicting Congressional claim of authority but with steady Congressional support, the Constitution has not been breached." Congress had it within its power to assert a conflicting claim. It might presumably, as the House briefly did in 1848, have declared the war unnecessarily and unconstitutionally begun by the

President. In the case of Vietnam, it had not done anything like this. "Because the branches are not in opposition, there is no necessity of determining boundaries [between them]. Should either branch be opposed to the continuance of hostilities, however, and present the issue in clear terms, a court might well take a different view." [35]

In the summer of 1973, some courts, contemplating the presidential air war against Cambodia, did indeed take a different view. The same Judge Judd who had declared the Vietnam War legal in *Berk v. Laird* in 1970 now applied his mutual-participation test to the bombing of Cambodia. But he could not discover the same evidence of executive-congressional collaboration in support of the war. Quite the contrary: in this case the legislative branch was clearly opposed to the continuance of hostilities. Every military appropriation bill from October 1970 on contained a proviso expressly forbidding military support for the government of Cambodia except in connection with the withdrawal of American troops from Southeast Asia and the release of the prisoners of war — conditions fulfilled by March 1973. Nor, Judd added, had Congress authorized the bombing of Cambodia thereafter for the purposes cited by the administration in defense of the policy — to protect the cease-fire in Vietnam and to achieve a cease-fire in Cambodia. More than that, it had eliminated any possible doubt about its opposition when it voted in June 1973 to prohibit the use of funds for further war in Cambodia. It was true that, after Nixon vetoed the fund cut-off, Congress accepted a compromise by which bombing continued until August 15, 1973. But Judd endorsed the contention of Fulbright, who had sponsored the compromise, that this was the only practical way, given the presidential determination to veto anti-bombing amendments, to bring the bombing to an end and did not imply congressional recognition of a presidential right to bomb. If the courts, Judd said, were to rule that Congress, in order to terminate hostilities it had not authorized, had to override presidential vetoes, this would mean that a President could keep a war going so long as he had the support of no more than one third (plus one) of either House. Judd therefore held the presidential war in Cambodia unconstitutional and issued an injunction against further bombing.[36]

Judd's decision loosed the cat among the judicial pigeons. The Second Circuit Court ordered a stay of the injunction, a ruling immediately appealed to Justice Thurgood Marshall of the Supreme Court. Marshall said that he "might well conclude on the merits that continued American operations in Cambodia are unconstitutional." But the Supreme Court as a whole, he continued, had never considered the issue, and he did not see how he could take on himself the responsibility for reinstating the injunction.[37] His brother Justice Douglas did not hesitate, however. Recalling the Court's decision in the steel seizure case, Douglas observed, "Property is important, but, if Truman could not seize it in violation of the Constitution, I do not see how any President can take 'life' in violation of the Constitution." [38] He thereupon vacated the stay ordered by the Court of Appeals. Marshall, polling the other seven brothers by phone, promptly issued a new stay with their united support. Chief Justice Burger then denied a request that the Court interrupt its holidays to hear the case; and the Second Circuit Court reached the comfortable conclusion — though by a split vote and in apparent contradiction of earlier rulings by the same court — that the issue was, after all, political "and thus beyond the competence" of courts to determine.[39] In the meantime, the American Air Force proceeded during the stay of the injunction to kill a large number of Cambodian villagers who had supposed up to the moment the bombs dropped that the Americans were fighting in their defense.

The flight of the courts from responsibility was at once ludicrous, tragic and understandable. It clearly showed limits of judicial control of the war-making power. The mutual-participation test, as Marshall conceded, made great sense. The Department of Justice itself had used it when it served its purposes. But what if the Supreme Court were to adopt that test and then confront a President determined to conduct a war without congressional consent, as Nixon had conducted the bombing of Cambodia after March 1973? This was precisely the showdown a cautious judiciary felt that it must avoid in its own institutional self-interest — at least until the war was safely over. As Justice Jackson had written in 1944, explaining why he thought the forced evacuation of the Japanese-Americans unconstitutional but why he also thought the Court could do nothing about it in wartime, "If the people ever let command of the war power fall into irresponsible and unscrupulous hands, the courts wield no power equal to its restraint. The chief restraint upon those who command the physical forces of the country, in the future as in the past, must be their responsibility to the political judgments of their contemporaries and to the moral judgments of history." [40]

VI

Though the courts could patrol the far frontiers and outlaw outrageous transgressions by the Presidency or by Congress, they did not intend to stop wars in progress or to settle the precise allocation of powers of foreign policy. Such restraint was probably sound. The problem in its nature called for solution, within constitutional limits, through the representation and balancing of political forces in a specific context under the pressure of desperate possibilities. Possibly this is what the Founding Fathers, consciously or unconsciously, had intended through their ambiguous formulas. For, at any concrete historical point, the constitutional balance was too much at the mercy of fluctuating intangibles of circumstance, judgment, opinion and prophecy to permit the Court to lay down a mechanical standard. The test of power depended, in Justice Jackson's phrase, on the imperatives of events and contemporary imponderables rather than on abstract theories of the law.

If this were so, then the lesson for American politicians and scholars was to suppress their natural propensity to cast relative questions in absolute terms. Some of them had gone too far in the 1940s in devising theories of exclusive presidential power in foreign affairs because they agreed with the way one set of Presidents had used that power. Now in the 1970s others (and sometimes the same ones) showed signs of moving too far in the opposite direction and devising theories of exclusive congressional power because they disagreed with the international projects of another set of Presidents. One form of the common fallacy was that of converting political into constitutional questions. Another was that of converting political into institutional questions.

The habit of assuming the superior virtue of one or the other of the institutions of government was an old one, with virtue generally assigned to the branch where one's own power lay. In the 1790s Jefferson and Madison had argued that Congress was the more democratic body and therefore the safer depository of national decision. A string of victories in presidential elections disabused the Jeffersonians of this notion. By 1848 Polk, the political heir of the Jeffersonian tradition, could inform Congress that "the President represents . . . the whole people of the United States" while each member of Congress only represented "portions of them" and that "the mere passage of a bill by Congress is no conclusive evidence that those who passed it represent the majority of the people of the United States or truly reflect their will." [41]

So too Jefferson and Madison had begun by supposing Congress inherently the peace-loving branch. That impression was cured by the War Hawks of 1812. The subsequent congressional record in this regard was, to put it mildly, mixed. Congress was bellicose in 1898 and 1962 when it might better have been restrained; it was complacent in 1916 and 1938 when it might better have been concerned. By 1952 Adolf Berle could argue plausibly on the basis of twenty years' history that Congress tended "to lag behind the facts in an international case to which the President must address himself. . . . The President's estimates of what will happen have usually been better than those of the men who do not live with the problem." [42] Twenty years after that, with a considerably less plausible historical case, Barry Goldwater could still say, "I would put more faith in the judgment of the Office of President in the matter of warmaking at this time than I would of Congress." [43]

Congress no doubt had manifest defects as an instrumentality for the making of foreign policy. It lacked continuity of purpose

and interest in foreign affairs. It lacked information and expertise. It lacked the power to command national attention. It
lacked the capacity to make clear and quick decisions. It lacked
guts. It was dominated, Senator Fulbright said in 1961, by "lo-
calism and parochialism. . . . Only the President can provide
the guidance that is necessary, while legislators display a distressing tendency to adhere to the dictates of public opinion, or at
least to its vocal and organized segments." [44] A "distressing tendency"? All this assumed unwisdom in public opinion and wisdom in the Presidency. Then Vietnam showed that Presidents
could be unwise too. "The collective judgment of the Congress,
with all its faults," Fulbright concluded after Vietnam, "could be
superior to that of one man who makes the final decision, in the
executive." [45]

Both Goldwater and Fulbright prudently preserved their escape hatches — Goldwater's "at this time," Fulbright's "could
be." Prudence was advisable, for history did not support the assignment of superior virtue to either branch. Congress could be
peace-loving, even at times when the safety of the nation might
require preparations for war; it could be war-loving when the
Presidency was the force for restraint. Those of us who hated the
Indochina War might see more hope in Congress than in the Presidency, just as those who grew up in the days when Congress rejected Versailles and demanded mandatory neutrality legislation
saw more hope in the Presidency. But it would be folly to regard
either presidential or congressional wisdom as a permanent condition; worse folly to try and build final answers on transient situations. There was no great gain in replacing high-flying presidential men by high-flying congressional men. Nor was James
Buchanan, who would hardly cross the street without congressional approval, necessarily the beau ideal of Presidents.

The problem was not to vest power in one or the other
branch. It was rather to distribute power between them in accordance with what Herbert Wechsler in another context had called
"neutral principles" — principles, that is, that were not shaped
in response to a particular situation but worked all the time,
transcending any immediate result involved.[46] The indispensable
neutral principle was surely that no one man should have the

power to send the nation into war. This was the principle that
the age of the imperial Presidency had forgotten. To restore the
constitutional balance in the 1970s, it was now necessary to rebuke presidential pretensions, as it had been necessary in other
times to rebuke congressional pretensions. But in demythologiz-
ing the Presidency it was essential not to remythologize the Congress. For history had shown that neither the Presidency nor the
Congress was infallible, and that each needed the other — which
may well be what the Founding Fathers were trying to tell us.

VII

The problem then was how to set up the machinery of government to make sure that decisions on war, and on foreign policies
likely to invite or provoke war, rested on full and *real* congressional participation.

Fundamentally the answer lay not in machinery but in policy.
For the constitutional crisis had arisen in the first instance from
the belief that the United States must serve as the guardian of
freedom everywhere on the planet. The globalist policy called
for an impassioned sense of ideological mission, a readiness to
intervene unilaterally in the affairs of other states and a capacity
to dispatch armed forces at will to the far corners of the world.
It called, in consequence, for the concentration of authority, secrecy, speed and discretion in the Presidency. Fulbright put the
situation well in 1969. Americans were trying to do by themselves, he told the Senate, "all of the things that Wilson and Roosevelt hoped to accomplish through the collective power of a
world organization but never even conceived of the United
States undertaking alone." Such a course, Fulbright continued,
could only lead to endless foreign exertions, chronic warfare,
burgeoning expense and the militarization of American life. In
the imperial setting independent congressional authority could
not long survive.

> Whatever lip service might be paid to traditional forms,
> our Government would soon become what it is al-

ready a long way toward becoming, an elective dictatorship, more or less complete over foreign policy and
over those vast and expanding areas of our domestic
life which in one way or another are related to or dependent upon the military establishment. If, in short,
America is to become an empire, there is very little
chance that it can avoid becoming a virtual dictatorship as well.[47]

The weight of messianic globalism was indeed proving too
much for the American Constitution. If this policy were vital
to American survival, then a way would have to be found to
make it constitutional; perhaps the Constitution itself would
have to be revised. In fact, the policy of indiscriminate global
intervention, far from strengthening American security, seemed
rather to weaken it by involving the United States in remote,
costly and mysterious wars, fought in ways that shamed the nation before the world and, even when thus fought, demonstrating
only the inability of the most powerful nation on earth to subdue
bands of guerrillas in black pajamas. When the grandiose policy
did not promote national security and could not succeed in its
own terms, would it not be better to pursue policies that did not
deform and disable the Constitution?

Statesmen of the early republic had foreseen the imperial illusion. In the late 1960s people began to rediscover a July Fourth
address delivered a century and a half before by John Quincy
Adams. "Wherever the standard of freedom and independence has
been or shall be unfurled," Adams had said of the young republic, "there will her heart, her benedictions and her prayers be.
But she goes not abroad, in search of monsters to destroy." If
America were to become involved in all the wars "which assume
the colors and usurp the standard of freedom . . . the fundamental maxims of her policy would insensibly change from *liberty* to *force*." He added solemnly, "She might become the dictatress of the world. She would no longer be the ruler of her own
spirit." [48]

A first step toward reclaiming the American spirit and restoring the constitutional balance would be to hold down the objectives of foreign policy — "elevate them guns a little lower," as folklore reports Jackson saying at New Orleans.[49] To make this stick, it would be necessary to deplete the authority and resources of the main prop and beneficiary of that policy, the military establishment. For, as the Indochina War had shown, the military establishment had become the most powerful pressure for military intervention and escalation. *"Created by wars that required it,"* Schumpeter had written of the war machines of ancient times, *"the machine now created the wars it required."* [50] A redefinition of American interests abroad would make possible a contraction of American military deployments, a marked reduction in the defense budget and containment of the Pentagon and CIA through executive control and congressional oversight. If such things took place, then the imperial heat would be off, and Congress would have the opportunity (the desire and will were another matter) to reassert its role in the constitutional scheme.

The Nixon administration had an unparalleled chance to accomplish precisely this revision of American foreign policy. For developments within the communist world had transformed the international position of the United States. By the late 1960s the antagonism between Moscow and Peking became so sharp that each great communist state began an ardent courtship of Washington in order to block any possibility of an American alliance with its deadly communist rival. The Cold War in its original form — the dominating Soviet-American hostility — had come to an end. Russia and China were now obsessed with each other; and the security of the United States no longer required, as it had been held to require in the fifties, the will to unlimited global intervention.

Yet the Nixon administration, proffered this extraordinary opportunity, did not essay a systematic redefinition of American interests. The so-called Nixon Doctrine meant, as the administration repeatedly said, not a revaluation of commitments but merely a contraction of the American force on hand to meet those commitments, with the gap to be filled by local force. Far from cutting the defense budget, the Nixon administration provided for its steady increase, even after arms-limitation agreements had been concluded with the Soviet Union. Far from containing the military, the administration organized an enormous professional army. Far from containing the CIA, the administration even demanded its participation, in violation of its original charter, in questions of domestic security.

VIII

Given these circumstances, Congress had to seek other means of restraining presidential war. Oddly enough, there was little interest in the popular solution of thirty-five years earlier — the transfer of the war-making power to the people as envisaged by the Ludlow Amendment. The only one in Congress to revive this proposal was the most right-wing member of the House, John Rarick of Louisiana. Rarick's People Power Over War Amendment provided that, except in case of actual or threatened attack on the country or the hemisphere, "the people shall have the sole power by a national referendum to declare war or to engage in warfare overseas." Rarick could find only two colleagues to cosponsor the resolution.[51] Marcus Raskin of the Institute for Policy Studies, a New Left think-tank, subsequently gave the idea an opaque endorsement.[52] Nothing was heard of it thereafter.

There was much more interest in war-powers legislation as a means of restraint. In 1972 and again in 1973 the Senate, with the support of most of its liberals and many of its conservatives, overwhelmingly passed a war-powers bill conceived and indefatigably promoted by Senator Javits of New York. The bill's declared purpose — to insure that future decisions to go to war would express the collective judgment of Congress and the President — could not have been more laudable. But, when one moved from preamble to text, the bill raised serious questions.

The heart of the Senate bill was, first, an enumeration of four conditions — the *only* four conditions — in which, in the absence of a declaration of war, a President could legally send troops into battle, and, second, a stipulation that presidential hostilities started under these conditions must be stopped in thirty days unless Congress specifically authorized their continuation.[53] Now any attempt to reduce to four static categories the contingencies that would alone warrant presidential emergency response must strike an historian as both hazardous and presumptuous. Who among us would be wise enough to succeed in something the Founding Fathers themselves were too wise to attempt — that is, in Hamilton's words, *"to foresee or define the extent and variety of national exigencies"?*

But the Senate bill had the peculiar character of being too expansive as well as too restrictive. For, at the same time that it proposed to limit presidential discretion in face of future dangers, it also proposed to grant the Presidency new statutory authority to begin wars without congressional consent. A President always had to act in emergencies so imperious as to preclude resort to Congress, and he always had the power — reaffirmed in the bill — to defend American territory, forces and citizens against sudden attack. (These were the first three categories of permitted presidential action; the fourth would empower Presidents to defend American treaty partners when Congress had previously voted a contingency authorization of the use of force on the model of the Formosa or Middle East resolutions.) But the Senate bill would now confer on him the added authority to commit force within the four categories "to forestall the direct and imminent threat of such attack," thereby making legal what Presidents hitherto, if they had done at all, had to do at their own risk. This language thus conferred unprecedented congressional sanction, in advance of any specific emergency, on that most elastic of theories, so often invoked in the past to justify presidential military adventures, the theory of pre-emptive war. What the Senate bill would do, in short, was to offer a President blanket legal authority to send American troops into battle whenever he found, in his own, personal, independent and unchecked judgment, a "direct and imminent threat" of attack against American forces and citizens.

As for the 30-day deadline after which Congress had to give the President authority to continue the war, this, in so far as it pretended to be a check on the Presidency, was plainly a hoax. Most wars are popular in their first thirty days. In these thirty days the President who ordered the action would overwhelm Congress, the press and television with his own rendition of the facts and his own interpretation of the crisis. It generally took much longer than thirty days for other facts to emerge and other interpretations to win a hearing. With the President's immense advantage in his ability to define the emergency, in his control of information, in his capacity to rouse the nation, it would require an unwontedly hardhearted Congress to veto his request for the continuation of hostilities — except in those infrequent cases where profound differences in policy had already crystallized well in advance of the emergency. The 30-day provision, in short, would virtually compel Congress to support the President. And the Senate bill made its own deadline even more of a hoax by empowering the President to keep the war going beyond thirty days if he would only certify in writing that he was doing so because of "unavoidable military necessity" connected with the disengagement of American troops. President Nixon had kept the Indochina War going four years on that theory.

Nor measured by the historical test — by a consideration of its probable impact had it been on the statute book during past crises — did the Senate bill inspire confidence. The actions undertaken by Franklin Roosevelt in the North Atlantic in 1941, for example, would not have fallen within the four categories of presidential initiative legalized by the bill. Even if they had, it was inconceivable that the 1941 Congress, which had extended the draft by a single vote in the House, would have authorized the President to continue an undeclared naval war in the Atlantic after the deadline. For this was one of those cases where the deepest policy differences had crystallized well in advance of the commitment of force. On the other hand, and in a more usual case, Lyndon Johnson could unquestionably have got all the congressional blessing he wanted for war in Vietnam. The Senate bill would only have dug Congress more deeply into the escalation policy. In short, the Senate bill would have prevented Roosevelt from protecting the British lifeline but would not have prevented Johnson from intensifying the war in Vietnam nor Nixon from carrying that war into Cambodia and Laos. Such a bill would hardly serve either the purpose for which it was drafted or the national interest of the United States.

The mystery was that supporters of the Senate bill supposed they were restraining the Presidency, while some of its opponents, like Senator Goldwater, worked themselves into a state of panic over what they thought the bill would do to the presidential prerogative. Plainly its practical effect would be to delegate short-term war-making power to the President. As Senator Javits himself said, his bill would give "the President more authority to do what is necessary and proper in an emergency than he now possesses" and would assure "ample play to the need of the Commander in Chief to have 'discretionary' as well as 'emergency' authority." [54] And it would delegate this war-making power under conditions that would leave Congress in most cases little choice but to ratify executive initiative. The Senate bill seemed far less likely to become a means of preventing warlike presidential actions than a means of inducing formal congressional approval of such actions.

A few senators saw the point. The bill, said Abourezk of South Dakota, was "a blank check which will implicate Congress in whatever aggressive war-making a President judges to be necessary." The only difference it would make, he added, was that it would enable future Presidents when they sent troops into combat to tell the people that Congress had given them authority to do so. Fulbright similarly condemned the bill's "de facto grant of expanded Presidential authority." A President, he observed, could easily construe the bill as sanctioning a nuclear first-strike on his own unilateral judgment. Fulbright, returning to the point he had made fifteen years before in connection with the Middle East resolution, rejected the whole effort to codify presidential emergency power: far better to require a President in an emergency to act entirely on his own responsibility, with no advance assurance of congressional support. "A prudent and conscientious President, under those circumstances, would hesitate to take action that he did not feel confident he could defend to the Congress. He would remain accountable to Congress for his action to a greater extent than he would if he had specific authorizing language to fall back upon. Congress, for its part, would retain its uncompromised right to pass judgment upon any military initiative taken without its advance approval." [55]

The fact that the Senate, after its years in the wilderness, should have chosen this pretentious and ill-considered measure as the vehicle for its constitutional comeback in foreign affairs could only depress those who hoped it might play a responsible role in the making of foreign policy. In the meantime the House in 1973 came up with a war-powers bill of its own that represented in most ways a sizable improvement. The House bill made no attempt, for example, to codify the President's powers and therefore placed no restriction on his capacity to meet emergencies. Unlike the Senate bill, it provided for the convening of Congress if hostilities began when it was not in session. Unlike the Senate bill, it gave Congress authority to recall substantial changes in overseas troop deployment as well as force actually committed to battle. Unlike the Senate bill, it did not invite the President to circumvent the whole process by claiming that "unavoidable military necessity" required him to keep going.

The House bill, in addition, had much more effective procedures for the termination of hostilities. The Senate would give Congress power to stop the fighting within the 30-day emergency period only by joint resolution, which a President, of course, could veto. This would in effect devolve the war-making power, confided by the Constitution to two thirds of both houses, to one third plus one of one house. The House bill provided much more sensibly for termination in the emergency period through concurrent resolution, which could not be vetoed. The House bill did, unfortunately, not only retain the idea of an emergency period during which Congress would delegate war-making authority to the President but extended the period to 120 days. This had the advantage of giving Congress time to get over the first thrill of combat but the disadvantage of giving the President four legal months to lock the country into war.

The Vietnam experience persuaded many Americans that something had to be done to discourage Presidents from regarding the war-making power as their private property, to be exercised at presidential will. If a President's own commitment to the Constitution was too feeble to lead him to involve Congress in the decisions, then war-powers legislation of some sort might usefully remind him of his constitutional duty. But there was no reason to make everything so complicated. All that was necessary was a statute with two main elements: an obligation laid upon the President to report at once to Congress, with full information and justification, whenever he sent troops into battle and to keep on reporting so long as the hostilities continued; and a declaration by Congress of its right at any point to terminate such military action by concurrent resolution. There was ample precedent for this. The Lend-Lease Act and other wartime laws as well as various government reorganization acts and even the Gulf of Tonkin resolution had all contained provisions for repeal through concurrent resolution. This had become, E. S. Corwin wrote as long ago as 1958, an indispensable means by which Congress could control or recover powers it had delegated to the Presidency; "that Congress may qualify in this way its delegation of powers which it might withhold altogether would seem to be obvious." [56] An even stricter bill might, on the model of the Reorganization Act of 1949, give a single house of Congress power to veto the continuation of presidential war. There was evident logic in this. If one house of Congress could prevent the declaration or authorization of war, why should not a single house be able to prevent the continuation of undeclared or unauthorized war?

A war-powers bill requiring the executive branch to testify before Congress on the reasons for and status of presidentially initiated hostilities and giving Congress the right to terminate such hostilities through concurrent or simple resolution would serve a valuable purpose. To this might be added a positive and absolute statutory obligation on Presidents to seek congressional consent when hostilities seemed likely to pass beyond a certain degree of magnitude. John Norton Moore and Quincy Wright, for example, proposed that congressional approval be required in all cases where regular combat units were committed to sustained hostilities or where military action would require congressional action, as by appropriations, before it was completed.[57]

Such a bill could accomplish everything that needed to be accomplished without opening up a series of gratuitous questions — without the impossible attempt to codify all future contingencies, without the delegation of congressional war-making power to the President, without bestowing congressional approval on pre-emptive war, without the 30-day or 120-day rigmarole. Moreover, Presidents not deluded by false conceptions of the Presidency would surely welcome a rational war-powers law. After the Vietnam experience, it was hard to see why any future President would ever wish to go to war without Congress beside him as a genuine and definite partner in the decision. But a war-powers law would not stop presidential war in the future any more than (if it had been law) it would have stopped presidential war in Indochina unless Congress for its part were prepared to display the capacity both for wisdom and for responsibility.

IX

If Congress were really serious about reclaiming its war-making authority, it had other possibilities. One conceivable way to get a grip on the problem, for example, was through an exertion of congressional control over the deployment of armed force outside the United States.

It is true that the constitutional status of this question was obscure. While no one could dispute the exclusive power of the President as Commander in Chief to deploy American forces overseas in wartime, the question where the power lay in peacetime was by no means so clear. Statesmen, as usual, were divided. Elihu Root, the elder Henry Cabot Lodge, Robert A. Taft and Stuart Symington thought Congress had the power to forbid the sending of at least the Army outside the country. William Howard Taft, William E. Borah, Calvin Coolidge, Dean Acheson and Barry Goldwater thought not. Legal scholars were equally at odds. W. W. Willoughby believed that the President's power to send troops outside the country was a "discretionary right vested in him, and, therefore, not subject to congressional control." [58] Alexander Bickel believed that the power of Congress "to govern the international deployment of forces is really beyond question." [59] Quincy Wright agreed with Willoughby, Raoul Berger with Bickel and E. S. Corwin argued one side at one time, the opposite side at another.

Nor did history clarify the issue. Congress generally let Presidents employ the armed forces, but occasionally asserted, as in 1878, its power to govern such employment itself. Presidents had the advantage of being able to create faits accomplis. In 1907, when Theodore Roosevelt decided to send the fleet around the world, the chairman of the Senate Naval Affairs Committee, fearing to leave his Atlantic seaboard state defenseless, said Congress would not appropriate the money. T.R. replied that he had enough money to take the fleet around to the Pacific; "if Congress did not choose to appropriate enough money to get the fleet back, why, it would stay in the Pacific." [60] During the 1920s members of Congress tried at various times to amend appropriations bills to keep American forces out of Haiti, the Dominican Republic and Nicaragua. Such efforts were voted down but on grounds of policy rather than constitutionality. In the Selective Service Act of 1940 Congress succeeded in stipulating that draftees could not be used outside the western hemisphere (except in American possessions); but the younger Henry Cabot Lodge, who sponsored this provision, described it as "a pious hope." [61] The next year Roosevelt ignored the provision and sent draftees to Iceland, but this was after a proclamation of unlimited national emergency. When Truman sent troops to Europe in 1951, the Senate resolution was ambiguous and, in any case, hortatory. It has been noted that Richard M. Nixon was among those then affirming the principle that Congress could control overseas military deployments. The courts, it need hardly be said, preserved a judicial, and doubtless judicious, silence on the issue.

All this suggested that, like the war-making power itself, this was a shared power. Certainly there seemed meager constitutional justification for the high-flying presidential contention that Congress was on principle excluded from any voice on troop deployment. The Constitution, after all, gave Congress the power to "provide for the common Defence," to "raise and support Armies" (with no appropriation to last for longer than two years) and to "make Rules for the Government and Regulation of the land and naval Forces." Hamilton in the 26th Federalist added with emphasis that the limitation on army appropriations *"obliged"* Congress "once at least in every two years, to deliberate upon the propriety of keeping a military force on foot; to come to a new resolution on the point; and to declare their sense of the matter, by a formal vote in the face of their constituents." All this implied a congressional interest in the question where the military forces Congress had the exclusive power to raise, maintain and regulate were to be kept "on foot." Jefferson, in his first state-of-the-union message, had called on Congress to appropriate "specific sums to every specific purpose susceptible of definition." [62] And, as Raoul Berger has cogently argued, British practice had established as early as the mid-seventeenth century that the power of appropriation embraced the right to specify the purposes for which appropriations should be spent.[63]

The proper conclusion, it would seem to me, was that the question of the control of deployment fell into Justice Jackson's "zone of twilight." In this zone Marshall's rule in *Little v. Barreme* customarily prevailed: the President could act until Congress acted; but, if Congress acted, its legislation would supersede an otherwise valid order of the President. The zone of twilight, in other words, was something Congress could enter at will. Whether Congress should, as a matter of prudence, try to exert detailed control over peacetime deployments was another question. The movement of ships, planes and men could be a valuable adjunct to diplomacy; and, so long as Presidents did not move force provocatively or in the service of policies disapproved by Congress, there was the strongest argument for preserving a measure of presidential discretion. When it came to large-scale and long-term troop dispositions, there was an equally strong argument, in terms of presidential self-interest, for getting explicit congressional approval. Like so many aspects of the relationship between Congress and the Presidency, the question of overseas deployments had been resolved through most of American history by comity.

But by the 1960s and 1970s, Presidents began to claim the power to send troops at will around the world as a sacred and exclusive presidential right. The Senate beat back Fulbright's effort to amend the Senate war-powers bill in order to challenge this claim. But the House bill proposed congressional authorization (after 120 days) for any commitment of or substantial increase in American forces "equipped for combat" in foreign nations. Had this provision been on the books, Kennedy, for example, would have had to secure congressional approval before sending 16,000 American military advisers to Vietnam. The Symington Committee recommended even more sternly that "no United States forces should be stationed abroad without specific prior authority of the Congress in each case." [64]

Perhaps such rigidity was a necessary congressional defense against the imperial Presidency. It was probably not to be recommended on its merits. A more manageable approach might be found in the defense budget itself. No one denied Congress the power to review the procurement of military weapons. Why should it not, in its annual encounter with the defense budget, review military manpower in the same way, especially as manpower began to consume more than half of the budget? In 1972 the Research and Policy Committee of the Committee for Economic Development set forth a procedure by which Congress might, among other things, regularly authorize by major overseas areas the number of troops to be deployed each year outside the United States. [65] Under this proposal Congress would legislate not a rigid pattern of deployment but rather a base line from which to measure departures. If emergency compelled a President to act outside the pattern, he had a positive requirement to report at once the reasons for his action and, if his departure from the program was expected to last beyond thirty days, to submit to Congress a request for legislative revision of the troop ceilings. A President who denied the constitutionality of such congressional control ran the risk of inviting congressional retaliation on parts of the defense budget where congressional power was clearly beyond challenge. In any case, the question of overseas deployment under this procedure would become a routine part of annual debate rather than an occasion for angry confrontation and *ad hoc* action.

X

This approach, no doubt for excellent if undisclosed reasons, did not commend itself. Instead Congress decided in the early 1970s to tackle the question at an angle. The most serious attempt to assert control over the stationing of the armed forces abroad consequently came through a campaign against the executive agreement — a campaign that fitted in with a larger effort to regain congressional control over American commitments to foreign states.

The old concern about the treaty-making process *per se* had largely evaporated. Immediately after the Second World War, liberal reformers, recalling the rejection of the League of Nations and the earlier frustrations of Olney and Hay, had proposed that treaties be ratified by a majority of both houses rather than by two thirds of one. But the Cold War consensus solved, or at least suspended, the one-third Senate veto. It also encouraged resort to the executive agreement, which, given the consensus, Congress saw little reason to protest. In the early fifties conservative reformers tried to regulate supposed abuses of treaties and executive agreements through the Bricker Amendment. But subsequent decisions of the Supreme Court made clear what no one should ever have doubted — that the treaty power was subordinate to the Constitution.[66] With Vietnam, however, the spirit behind the Bricker Amendment — the mistrust of executive control of international agreements — flared up again, though with drastic reversals in the congressional line-up. By the early 1970s liberal Democrats assumed positions once cherished by conservative Republicans — another warning against stating relative issues in absolute terms. The Bricker Amendment, Senator Claiborne Pell of Rhode Island even mused at one hearing, "if put up today, I think, would be voted overwhelmingly by all of us." [67] Fortunately no one put it up, thereby sparing the Senate and nation the resumption of an exceptionally tedious debate.

But in 1954 two conservative Republicans, Knowland of California and Ferguson of Michigan, had plucked out of the rubble of the Bricker fight a proposal requiring all executive agreements to be transmitted to the Senate within sixty days of their negotiation; agreements deemed too sensitive for public disclosure would go to the Foreign Relations Committee only and not to the whole body. The Eisenhower administration regarded the bill with indifference, and the Senate passed it in 1956. But the House, seeing no institutional gain for itself, failed to act. Fourteen years later, Senator Clifford Case of New Jersey, a liberal Republican, revived and broadened the bill, prudently applying its benefits to the House as well as to the Senate. Though the Nixon administration disapproved, the Senate passed the bill unanimously; the House passed it too; and it became law in August 1972.

The revulsion against executive agreements drew emotional support from a couple of misconceptions: that most executive agreements were made on the claim of independent presidential authority; and that the executive agreement had become a primary means of American military and thus political commitment abroad. In fact, most executive agreements — 97 percent, according to the State Department [68] — were made pursuant to treaties approved by the Senate or statutes passed, before or after the fact, by Congress as a whole. And the vast majority of the 384 major and 3000 minor military installations around the world had resulted from the fit of pactomania that involved the United States through 8 security treaties in the defense of 43 countries. That Congress had had little to say about these bases was the result of its own voluntary subservience to the Pentagon and could hardly be laid to the President's power to enter into executive agreements. In only four countries — Spain, Ethiopia, Morocco and Cuba (Guantanamo) — did major bases exist outside the treaty framework.

Yet, if the executive agreement *per se* was not the villain, there was plausible reason to suppose that, if not reined in, it could become a central means of commitment under the imperial Presidency. Senators noted that in the year 1930 the United States made 25 treaties and only 9 executive agreements; in 1971, 214 executive agreements and only 17 treaties. The Nixon administration, up to May 1, 1972, had concluded 71 treaties and 608 executive agreements.[69] These agreements covered a vast range of subjects — military missions and bases, affiliation with international organizations, communication satellites, stationing of nuclear weapons, atomic energy, economic and military assistance. The executive agreement, Fulbright said in 1972, had "virtually become a sorcerer's apprentice." And treaties, at least to senatorial eyes, seemed increasingly confined to matters of majestic inconsequence. "The Senate is asked to convene solemnly to approve by a two-thirds vote a treaty to preserve cultural artifacts in a friendly neighboring country," Fulbright said a little bitterly. "At the same time, the Chief Executive is moving American military men and materiel around the globe like so many pawns in a chess game." [70] "We are not put in the Senate," said Case, "to deal only with treaties on copyrights, extradition, stamp collections and minor questions of protocol. If that is the meaning of the Constitution, then I think the Founding Fathers wasted their time." [71] Senator Church showed understandable irritation when in 1972 the Senate, having been studiously ignored on momentous questions of foreign policy, was asked to ratify a treaty with Brazil concerning shrimp.[72]

The senatorial view was that treaties were the appropriate means of making significant political commitments and the executive agreement the appropriate device for routine, nonpolitical arrangements. "We have come close," the Foreign Relations Committee declared in 1969, "to reversing the traditional distinction between the treaty as the instrument of a major commitment and the executive agreement as the instrument of a minor one." [73]

This distinction was hardly traditional. But, if it had little basis in history, it had much in reason. "We have no choice," said Case, "but to specify clearly that executive agreements can no longer be used to settle matters which are vital to our national security. . . . The stationing of U.S. troops abroad on a permanent basis in foreign military installations is the kind of thing which ought not to be done without the approval of the Senate." [74]

Such presidential deployment, Case argued, tended to create quasi-commitments; and he followed his successful bill requiring the registration of all executive agreements with Congress by submitting a second bill proposing that all agreements for military bases be sent to the Senate as treaties. When the Nixon administration made agreements on its own with Portugal and Bahrain in 1971, the Senate voted by 50 to 6 that these particular arrangements must be submitted as treaties; and, when the administration rejected the senatorial request, Case offered an amendment to the foreign aid bill to block the assistance promised the two countries until the Senate ratified the agreements. In the meantime, Ervin proposed to give Congress the general power to veto all executive agreements within sixty days by concurrent resolution; and Fulbright, who felt this did not go far enough, wanted to amend the bill to make the disapproval of one house sufficient.

Once again willful use of presidential power had caused excessive congressional reaction. The Ervin bill would have enabled Congress to nullify agreements based on the independent and exclusive authority of the President, such as, for example, the recognition of foreign governments. As for the second Case bill, the executive agreements with Portugal and Bahrain did not involve defense commitments on the part of the United States (though who could tell what might result from building up an American base in the Persian Gulf?), and putting these agreements in the form of treaties might well give them wholly disproportionate weight and permanence. The treaty and the executive agreement had equal legal effect in international relations, but they conveyed different political messages. A rational compromise would certainly be to request that all military base agreements be confirmed by joint resolution. But, since this would have meant sharing power with the House, it evidently did not occur to the Senate.

While the effort to bring executive agreements within congressional knowledge and purview was long overdue, the notion that all important international undertakings must be subject to congressional veto could soon return the republic to the frustrations of Olney and Hay. Was Congress seriously suggesting that every time a President met another head of state their understandings could be extinguished by one third of the Senate? Would even high-flying congressional men contend that the Monroe Doctrine, the Emancipation Proclamation, the Fourteen Points and the Atlantic Charter — or for that matter Roosevelt at Yalta and Nixon in China — were cases of presidential usurpation? The senatorial initiatives, though understandable in terms of presidential provocation, would hardly pass the historical test.

Most fundamentally, if executive agreements were to require congressional ratification, Presidents would only resort to something else. For it was impossible to stop Presidents from making assurances to other nations, and assurances could take other forms than formal agreements; Israel was a notable case. A President could make a speech, for example, or write a personal letter to the head of another government, or whisper something in his ear at a state banquet. If Congress tried to police the field of executive agreements in too minute and absolute a way, it would simply drive Presidents into finding other, and less controllable, means of transacting international business.

The answer lay less in the establishment of rigid procedures than in the re-establishment of comity. What Congress had to do — what the Case and Ervin bills unquestionably did — was to raise the consciousness of the executive branch so that Presidents, instead of regarding executive agreements as their divine right, would understand that no agreement could be effective for long without substantial congressional assent to the basic policy. Secrecy, so beloved to Presidents in the short run, could easily damage the Presidency itself in the longer run. "Secret agreements," as former Under Secretary of State Katzenbach told a

Senate committee, "don't really have the base of popular support they ought to have if you are going to have a commitment." [75] Congressional understanding and confidence remained the essential condition for a strong foreign policy, above all for a foreign policy that might take the nation to war. This should have been evident to Presidents; after Vietnam, it should certainly be evident to foreign states to which Presidents might offer secret assurances on their own responsibility. No doubt presidential declarations on which other nations had acted or which, like the Monroe Doctrine, had come to be sanctioned by our own tradition, could not be lightly cast aside. But the doctrine of the imperial Presidency that Congress and the American people were under an obligation to treat improvident presidential declarations as sacred commitments had no basis in the Constitution.

XI

Still another question, if Congress were serious in wishing to recover a voice in war-making, was what it proposed to do about secret military and political operations organized and paid for by the CIA. For Congress, through its own deliberate actions, had made — and kept — the CIA an agency uniquely immune to congressional control. The Central Intelligence Agency Act of 1949, for example, exempted the Agency from laws and regulations on spending, giving its director the power to cover the spending of unvouchered funds through the issue of certificates — a power enjoyed in the early republic only by Presidents. Congress also released CIA from compliance with federal laws requiring the disclosure of the number, names, titles, functions and salaries of public employees.

As early as 1953 Senator Mansfield had questioned the wisdom of allowing "almost complete independence" to so powerful an agency. Obviously intelligence operations required secrecy, but secrecy could easily be carried too far. "Secrecy now beclouds everything about CIA — its cost, its efficiency, its successes, and its failures," said Mansfield, returning to the subject in 1954. ". . . once secrecy becomes sacrosanct, it invites abuse." The CIA, moreover, was becoming a means by which the executive was excluding Congress from the field of foreign affairs. The need was for "regular and responsible congressional scrutiny"; this "would reduce the threat to our democratic processes which this uncontrolled agency by its very nature now possesses." Mansfield's proposal was for a Joint Committee on Central Intelligence; the Joint Committee on Atomic Energy after all had dealt very successfully with a subject requiring at least as much secrecy.[76] It was not till 1956 that Mansfield could get his bill onto the floor, where it was voted down 59–27 (John F. Kennedy for, Lyndon B. Johnson against). The proposal never reached the floor again.[77]

In 1963 Harry S. Truman, forgetting that secret operations had started in his own administration, said that CIA should be "restored to its original assignment as the intelligence arm of the President" and that "peacetime cloak-and-dagger operations" be terminated.[78] But Congress continued to prefer not to know what the Agency was up to. "There is no Federal agency of our Government whose activities receive less scrutiny and control," said Senator Symington bitterly in 1971.[79] "I can safely say," said Representative Findley in 1973, "that fewer than a dozen Members of Congress have any idea how much money the CIA spends each year, and probably none of them has much of an idea what the Agency actually does with that money." [80]

So long as the CIA behaved responsibly, there was an argument for congressional ignorance. "Spying is spying," as Senator Stennis comfortably put it in 1971. If the country were going to have an intelligence agency, it had to be run as an intelligence agency and not as if it were the Department of Health, Education and Welfare. "You have to . . . protect it as such, and shut your eyes some and take what is coming." [81] But it was increasingly hard to take what was coming. While the intelligence branch of CIA had shown considerable perception and responsibility, the operations branch had compiled a notable record for impudent and provocative clandestine adventure in foreign countries. When in 1970 the leadership of the CIA collaborated with the Nixon domestic intelligence plan (and in 1973 denied having done so), when in 1971 CIA lent its technical facilities to advance the criminal career of the White House plumbers, it had plainly forfeited any further claim to immunity from congressional oversight.[82]

The various war-powers bills ignored the CIA problem. Indeed, by confining their restrictions to the regular armed forces, they could have encouraged future Presidents to recall the Eisenhower example and make the CIA the main instrument of American intervention abroad. Eagleton of Missouri made a vigorous effort in 1973 to amend the Senate bill in order to cover the CIA. He doubted, he said, whether America had learned the lesson of Southeast Asia "unless we plug this loophole and unless we treat all Americans in military situations alike, whether they are wearing a green uniform, red-white-and-blue, or a seersucker suit. . . . From little involvements — little CIA wars — big wars grow." [83] Javits, however, succeeded in defeating the Eagleton amendment. Other senators discussed versions of the old Mansfield proposal, all less comprehensive than the original; and Stennis, opening his eyes a little, promised a review of the CIA Act by the Armed Services Committee. It was not clear, though, that Congress intended to do much about CIA beyond wringing its hands.

What it might do was to return to Truman's recommendation of 1963. Intelligence about other countries — even intelligence secretly obtained inside other countries — remained a necessity in a world of antagonistic national states. But clandestine operations organized by one state to overthrow the government of another state with which it was not at war were neither necessary nor, in American hands, particularly productive. Why not let CIA concentrate on intelligence collection and analysis, which it did well, and forgo the cloak-and-dagger life? It was ironic that, despite the high reputation of the CIA intelligence branch and the wayward record of the CIA operations branch, it was the operators rather than the analysts who had impact on high circles of government. When Presidents chose CIA career officers to become directors of Central Intelligence, they always came from operations. No doubt imprisoned in every President there was a James Bond signaling to be let out.

Perhaps Congress, instead of further indulging the mystique, fundamentally adolescent, of special operations might better deny the use of CIA appropriations at least for paramilitary purposes except in time of war and, as Senator John Sherman Cooper proposed, arrange for its own regular access to CIA intelligence estimates.

XII

Whatever the logical plausibility of the Tocqueville-Lippmann argument against the intrusion of legislatures into the making of foreign policy, the ghastly war in Indochina furnished powerful evidence in support of Bryce. This was a war the national security establishment had run every step of the way, and it was hard to argue that Congress could have made a worse botch of things. But Congress had had its bad seasons too, some not so long before; and the transfer of predominant authority from the executive to the legislative branches hardly seemed the solution. Nor did recent congressional proposals inspire all that much confidence in the capacity of Congress to use the levers of foreign policy already in its constitutional possession. The neutral principle — that *no one man* should have the power to take the nation to war — must be extended to read no one *institution*.

Whatever tragedy the imperial Presidency had brought to the nation, a pogrom against the Presidency was not the answer. Abuse of presidential power was not an argument against presidential power *per se*. Stripping the President of all his independent authority was no more advisable from the viewpoint of the national interest than it was possible constitutionally or functionally. The Founding Fathers had been right to repose wide powers in the executive branch. Only the President could administer the processes of foreign relations, and the very first Presidents, Washington, Adams, Jefferson, had correctly taken this to imply broad executive scope in the definition of foreign policy. Only the President could serve as Commander in Chief of the armed forces. He could initiate the use of force to repel sudden attack or, within limits, to rescue American citizens; he had absolute control over the use of force in war; and again it was undoubtedly sound that this should be so. And, if one defined emergencies as threats so imperious as to preclude resort to Congress, obviously only the President was left to take the lead in emergency situations.[84]

To some degree Congress could provide in advance for certain emergency actions and thereby give them legal status. *Ex parte Milligan* had laid down the rule that "emergency may not create power," but the Court amended this during the First World War to say that "it may afford a reason for exerting a power already enjoyed.[85] In any case, Congress had passed laws as early as 1798 containing dormant provisions which the President could activate by declaring a national emergency. By the 1970s this had grown into an uncoordinated, uncodified, crazy-quilt collection of powers, many of them relics of previous and forgotten emergencies, many of them (like the Trading with the Enemy Act of 1917) applied for purposes never dreamed of by the Congress that passed the original statute. In 1947 Congress had passed a joint resolution terminating the national emergencies proclaimed by Roosevelt in 1939 and 1941. But Roosevelt's national emergency proclamation at the time of the bank holiday in 1933 and Truman's Korean War proclamation of 1950 were still in effect in 1973; and during the financial crisis of August 1971 Nixon superimposed still another national emergency on top of them. Some experts were not even sure that Grover Cleveland's proclamation during the Pullman strike of 1894 had ever been formally terminated.

Each extant proclamation gave the Presidency access to a bewildering diversity of powers scattered among 580 separate sections of the United States Code. The President was thereby authorized, or could authorize himself, to do a great many drastic things — to take over industrial plants and radio stations, to stockpile and allocate strategic materials, to seize real estate and personal property, to freeze prices and wages, to restrict overseas investments and regulate external financial transactions, to call up reservists and forbid citizens to leave the country.

On the whole, Presidents had used these powers with discretion. Still the situation was a mess. There were no standards by

which to define national emergencies, nor was there any prescribed procedure by which to invoke, review or end them. In
1973 a Special Senate Committee on the Termination of the National Emergency began an arduous expedition into the thickets
of statutory emergency powers. This committee had the opportunity to weed out careless and obsolete statutory provisions and
present a sensible design for emergency legislation. Most important of all, it could recommend means of involving Congress
in the declaration, control and termination of emergencies, perhaps by giving the President provisional authority to proclaim
emergencies subject to congressional ratification within thirty
days and by giving Congress the power to oversee the use of emergency authority as well as the power to bring the emergency to an
end through concurrent resolution.[86]

XIII

These were emergency powers within the constitutional order
— government by special, temporary law, Justice Jackson had
called it, but by law nonetheless. The harder but inescapable
question was that of emergency prerogative — whether desperate occasions gave the President the right to suspend or trans-
gress the law and the Constitution. On earlier pages we have discussed the question of emergency prerogative in terms of the
specific tradition that shaped American political thought — the
tradition of Locke, as it was interpreted by Jefferson and Lincoln
and as it created the climate in which two Roosevelts, Truman
and Nixon acted. But consideration of the question was by no
means confined to Locke. It was an inevitable issue for anyone
trying to work out the theory of a free republic. To judge
whether emergency prerogative had a role in the American
scheme, it may be well to enlarge our inquiry and see how other
great republican political philosophers dealt with the issue.

Machiavelli, the first modern political theorist, had no doubt
that all republics required an institution like the Roman dictatorship. He also believed that it was better to provide such an institution by law than to invoke it against the law. "Those republics," he said, "which in time of danger cannot resort to a

dictatorship, or some similar authority, will generally be ruined when grave occasions occur." Machiavelli was sure that law could supply "a remedy for every emergency." But Rousseau argued two and a half centuries later that a thousand emergencies would arise which legislation could not hope to anticipate. "The ability to foresee that some things cannot be foreseen," he said, "is a very necessary quality." He felt that "the sacrosanct nature of the laws" never should be interfered with "save when the safety of the State is in question." But at that point "the People's first concern must be to see that the State shall not perish," and, if the law became an impediment to meeting the danger, "a single ruler must be appointed who can reduce all law to silence." Machiavelli and Rousseau were hardly civil liberties democrats. But even the great liberal philosopher John Stuart Mill, writing in the first year of Lincoln's Presidency, made it clear that he was "far from condemning, in cases of extreme exigency, the assumption of absolute power in the form of temporary dictatorship" [87]; and Bagehot, as we have seen, criticized presidential government because of the impossibility of dictatorship.

Salus populi suprema lex: the essential logic was irresistible. No one, save possibly the majority in *ex parte Milligan,* ever said it would be better to lose the nation than to break the law. Even William Howard Taft, after making his case for limiting the Presidency, was constrained to add: "so far as it is possible to limit such a power consistent with that discretion and promptness of action that are essential to preserve the interests of the public in times of emergency, or legislative neglect or inaction." [88] Unquestionably, in some sense, Machiavelli and Locke, Rousseau and Mill, Jefferson and Lincoln were right. The President had to be conceded reserve powers to meet authentic emergencies. And yet, and yet . . . no argument was more depressing to constitutionalists, and no argument more appealing to usurpers. Milton, after recording some remarks of Satan, observed:

So spake the Fiend, and with necessitie,
The Tyrants plea, excus'd his devilish deeds.[89]

Through the ages necessity has indeed been the tyrant's plea, which is why it would seem that Rousseau had the better of it over Machiavelli in resisting the idea of incorporating temporary dictatorship into the legal order. The Weimar Republic had done just that in the famous Article 48 of the German Constitution; the result was to simplify things for Hitler. If the American Constitution had had an Article 48, what might not Nixon have been able to do legally in the name of national security! It may be indispensable on desperate occasions for the American President to become the Protector of the nation, but it should not be easy for him to do so. He must not be encouraged to treat every trouble as if it were a crisis or be led to suppose that everything he does in response to crisis thereby becomes constitutional.

Yet the question of necessity cannot be burked. Crises threatening the life of the nation have been happily rare. But, if such a crisis comes, a President must act. The Founding Fathers did not limit the President's right to use force when necessary to repel attack. They also, at least the wisest among them, wished the Constitution to be capable of life and growth in order to meet changing and unforeseeable exigencies. So they left to future generations to determine whether there were not situations analogous to the repelling of attack where time was of the essence and the preservation of the nation was at stake — situations in which the President would be justified in acting without formal congressional approval. In such cases, as in the periods before Sumter and Pearl Harbor, the failure of the President to act might have constituted the greater danger to national survival. The prerogative is not unqualified. It is not a mandate to the President to do as he pleases or to act against the expressed will of Congress. The criteria are clear: the threat must be unquestionably dire; time must unquestionably be of the essence; Congress must be unable or unwilling to prescribe a national course; the problem must be one that can be met in no other way; and the President must do everything he can to explain himself to Congress and the people.[90]

Only major threat creates this level of emergency — in American history only the Civil War, the Second World War, possibly the

Cuban missile crisis. Precedents thus created apply only to equal emergencies, which mean that they cannot be cited to justify the increase of routine presidential power. Presidential actions — those, for example, of Jefferson, Truman, Nixon — which pretended to prerogative in situations well below the threshold of danger have suffered deserved national repudiation. The rigorous defense of the Constitution in normal times is the best insurance against the abuse of presidential power in abnormal times.

XIV

Presidents had never quite dangled on the leading strings of Congress, even in the placid era of "congressional government," and the shifting and unpredictable world of the last quarter of the twentieth century hardly seemed a propitious time for such an experiment to begin. Yet by the 1970s the Constitution was out of balance, and the balance had to be restored or the republic would lose its original point. Recent Presidents had claimed — had been permitted by Congress and the people to claim — exclusive powers far beyond those assigned by the Constitution and had employed those powers against the national interest in a wicked and wanton war. A way had to be found to end presidential war. Yet this had to be done without so disabling the conduct of foreign affairs as to prove the case of those who called the separation of powers an eighteenth-century principle at odds with a twentieth-century world.

The problem was surely not insoluble. The solution, as Wilson wrote in 1908, lay in finding "the right accommodation of parts in this complex system of ours." Wilson added, "No one can play the leading part in such a matter with more influence and propriety than the President." [91]

The men who became Presidents in the last quarter of the twentieth century would have to begin by ridding themselves of honest misconceptions about the nature and power of the office, misconceptions arising in the wake of the New Nationalism, the New Deal and the Second World War, enlarged and hardened by the Cold War, propagated by a generation of scholars, sustained thereafter by the myth-making of the press and the acclaim of sycophants. They would have to understand that, though the President had day-to-day control of American foreign relations, he was not king of the world and that foreign policy was not his personal property.

Future Presidents would have to do something to revive the Department of State. This would not necessarily be easy. Past Presidents had wanted to do it, had become frustrated with automatic bureaucratic resistance to new departures and had ended by turning the problems over to their own White House staff. But there was no ineluctable necessity about the decline of the State Department, and there was also a sure way to restore its primacy in the field of foreign affairs. When a strong man, confident by temperament and secure in his relationship to the President, became Secretary of State — a Marshall, Acheson, Dulles, Kissinger — the rest of the government, even the White House itself, was not inclined to fool around with his Department. The President would continue to need a resident national security staff so that he could find out for himself what was going on, but that staff should be small and wise rather than, as in the earlier Nixon-Kissinger manner, large and greedy.

The even more important task of future Presidents would be to admit Congress to genuine, if only junior, partnership in the foreign policy process. Presidential monopolization of foreign policy was as self-defeating politically as it was erroneous constitutionally. "No foreign policy will stick unless the American people are behind it," the American of the century most experienced and sagacious in international affairs, Averell Harriman, told a Senate committee. "And unless Congress understands it the American people aren't going to understand it." [92] The presidential monopoly was never more self-defeating than when foreign policy involved the risk of war. For the war-making authority not only rested on express and complex interdependence of constitutional powers [93] but required for its exercise the widest and deepest base of popular consent. The decision to go to war must above all be made by Congress and the President together. Only if Congress and the President agreed on the necessity could the people be expected to pay the cost, anguish and sacrifice.

The acceptance of a larger accountability should not be taken by future Presidents as a vexatious and wasteful interruption of their serious work. It is rather a resource to be developed, an indispensable means of gaining counsel as well as consent. We know now that neither Presidents nor their executive establishments are infallible. Both can benefit, if not always from congressional wisdom, at least from the systematic exposure of executive views to debate and criticism. The Senate Foreign Relations Committee, which in the past included such men as Clay and Webster, Seward and Sumner, Lodge and Root, Borah, Vandenberg, Cooper and Morse, is not necessarily a collection of imbeciles.[94] Moreover, Congress is a necessary proving-ground for national policies. "Recalcitrance in the Congress," Ben Cohen has observed, "may represent recalcitrance of important segments of public opinion"; and congressional pressure can revise executive projects to make them less offensive to deeply rooted public sentiments and less vulnerable to popular attack.[95]

The prospect of debate, especially face to face, may well dismay a weak man in the White House. Even a strong President, it must be said, grows more impatient of contradiction the longer he stays in office. But he knows all the same that it is good for him; this is why the only President to serve for more than two terms retained a disputatious cabinet and kept up his press conferences, even with the excuse and pressure of total war. "If [the President] have character, modesty, devotion, and insight as well as force," Wilson put it, "he can bring the contending elements of the system together into a great and efficient body of common counsel." [96] The truly strong President is not the one who relies on his power to command but the one who recognizes his responsibility, and opportunity, to enlighten and persuade; not the one who wants to transcend the Constitution but the one who sees that the disciplines of the Constitution are indispensable to his own success as a democratic leader and to the survival of democratic government.

XV

The accommodation may start with the President, but it must end with the Congress. In the years after the Second World War

Congress (if one may pretend that so disparate and disunited a body has an institutional identity) had given off the impression that it was the helpless victim of the insensate power drive of a succession of Presidents. The sad fact was that it had been, a good deal of the time, the enthusiastic creator of its own impotence. The Presidency had become the great alibi for members of Congress who preferred to avoid accountability for national decisions lest they lose the support of one or another faction of true believers back home. Moreover, Congress tended to be an assembly of loners if not of prima donnas, concerned with shoring up individual power bases and carving out individual reputations and susceptible only under the most extreme provocation to a sense of institutional responsibility.

Congress had a special inferiority complex in the arena of foreign policy. Not only did it want to disclaim responsibility most of all for decisions affecting national security, but it often lacked clear signals from its constituencies and, in any case, was sure it did not have the facts. If Congress were to attain a place of dignified partnership in the determination of foreign policy, how was it to go about it? Here one may perhaps recur to Bryce's distinction between means and ends. Not only must the executive branch display a serious wish for consultation but Congress must develop a clear sense of priorities as to what it wanted to be consulted about. When congressional resentment over exclusion from the large decisions had become unbearable, it had tended to erupt in a disproportionate and querulous concern with the petty detail of administration. Even the most conscientious members of the executive branch were likely to regard such congressional attention as calculated harassment.

Senator Fulbright once distinguished between two kinds of power involved in the shaping of foreign policy — that pertaining to its direction, purpose and philosophy; and that pertaining to the day-to-day conduct of foreign relations. The first, he suggested, belonged peculiarly to Congress, the second to the executive. The trouble was that Congress had reversed the order. "We have tended to snoop and pry in matters of detail, interfering in the handling of specific problems in specific places which we happen to chance upon. . . . At the same time we have resigned from our responsibility in the shaping of policy and the defining of its purposes, submitting too easily to the pressures of crisis, giving away things that are not ours to give: the war power of the Congress, the treaty power of the Senate and the broader advice and consent power." [97]

The distinction between means and ends, as Fulbright readily acknowledged, was not all that simple. If Congress yielded too much in the field of day-to-day conduct of foreign relations, it could well discover that it has lost control over policy too. In 1969 the Senate Foreign Relations Committee described the elusive process by which operations determined policy as "commitment by accretion." [98] Yet there could be no doubt that Congress was too often busy in the sideshows while the big parade marched down Main Street. And the more the discussion moved from means to ends, from technical detail to general policy, the more it called for those practical judgments of politics and priorities at which members of Congress were usually more competent than the specialists of the national security establishment. By concentrating on major purposes rather than on minor errors, Congress could re-create itself as a factor in the making of foreign policy — as a force the Presidency could no longer ignore without serious political risk to itself. Even if Congress was internally divided over the substance of policy, it still might have a united institutional interest in gaining a voice in the decisions.

XVI

If there was an institutional interest, was there also an institutional remedy? Consultation was the key; but consultation became meaningless when, as in 1966, the State Department insisted on talking to the Senate Foreign Relations Committee on tuna fishing but declined to talk about the American military involvement in Thailand or when, conversely, State Department officials found it hard to catch the ear of overscheduled members of Congress in order to discuss parts of the world currently off the front pages.[99] Was there some institutional device that might make consultation regular and real?

Suggestions took two main forms: the establishment of a Joint Committee on National Security within Congress to provide Congress with its own moral equivalent of the National Security Council (Hubert Humphrey [100]); or the establishment of an executive-congressional commission, half the members appointed by Congress, half by the President, empowered to receive the most secret information and charged with exchanging the most candid views on emerging as well as existing international problems (Dean Rusk, Benjamin V. Cohen, Francis O. Wilcox [101]).

Of the two approaches, the second seemed more likely to compel serious consultation. Yet the formation of such a commission was unlikely. Too many members of Congress might feel they were delegating the foreign-affairs responsibility to a small elite, even though an elite composed of their own colleagues. And, if formed, it could hardly help including the most respectable members of Congress — precisely the ones most likely to feel that their overriding responsibility was to support the President (the only one we have).

Still another possibility would be to draw members of Congress into the executive foreign-policy process. Secretary of State Byrnes used to take Senators Connally and Vandenberg along to meetings of the Council of Foreign Ministers. Congressional service on delegations to the United Nations General Assembly has been invaluable for both branches. We have seen that Kennedy invited Fulbright to a secret session on the Bay of Pigs. Should he have invited, say, Fulbright and Russell to sit on the Executive Committee during the Cuban missile crisis? But how is the President to decide whom to anoint for special consultation among members of a body notorious for its personal and jurisdictional jealousies?

Institutional devices could make a contribution to the task of accommodation. But they would not work unless there were a will on both sides to make them work. If that existed, the particular devices might not be all that necessary. The Presidency must have the will to share power, but Congress must also have the will to take responsibility. For a major part of Congress's trouble came not from lack of power but from lack of courage to use the power it had. The great powers of the American government resided in the area of joint possession. They therefore demanded the active self-assertion of each branch, but always within a pervading frame of good faith, mutual respect and self-restraint. The Constitution assumed that democratic control of foreign policy was a possibility. The Indochina War proved it to be a necessity. The ultimate answer lay in the restoration of the constitutional comity so badly breached by the imperial Presidency and so nearly destroyed by the revolutionary Presidency.

The restoration of comity need not weaken the nation in the face of danger. History has shown that the American Constitution is a spacious document within which very strong men indeed have been able to direct the affairs of state and guard the interests of the republic.

10

The Secrecy System

THE RESTORATION of constitutional comity and the hope of democratic control over foreign policy required one further development: the loosening of the executive monopoly of information. Few doubted that government had to keep some things secret, at least for a while. But nothing had done more to sanctify the national security establishment than the rise of a religion of secrecy after the Second World War. The high priests had only to utter their incantation — 'national security' — and international actions and policies of the United States were supposed to vanish into some *sanctum sanctorum*. Consecrated by crisis, the secrecy system overawed Congress and nation, producing the doctrine so commonly voiced in the 1950s and 1960s, so commonly voiced and so profoundly anti-democratic, "We must trust the President because only he [He?] knows the facts."

The question of the secrecy system was related to but distinct from that of executive privilege. These two modes of official withholding shared an absence of statutory basis and a commitment to unchecked executive judgment, and they often covered similar subjects. But executive privilege was properly invoked only by Presidents personally; it was directed against Congress; and it was not institutionalized. The secrecy system was, so to speak, the privilege of the permanent government. It was a radiation from the national security establishment; it was directed against the public and most of all against the press, only incidentally (and not necessarily) against Congress; and it was gloriously institutionalized in the vast and intricate machinery of security classification. If a less personal instrument than executive privilege, the secrecy system was just as essential a weapon of the imperial Presidency.

I

Ironically the republic was conceived in secrecy. The Constitutional Convention was closed to press and citizenry. On the last day Benjamin Franklin observed that during the deliberations he, like the others, may have expressed doubts, but "within these walls they were born, and here they shall die." Rufus King even wondered whether the Convention's journals should not be destroyed lest a "bad use" be made of them by the Constitution's opponents.[1] Madison denied his indispensable record of the proceedings to Congress and the people for another half century.[2]

Such presumption of secrecy in the affairs of state was natural in what was in many respects, despite the Revolution, a deferential society. "So often and so essentially have we heretofore suffered from the want of secrecy and despatch," John Jay observed in the 64th Federalist, "that the Constitution would have been inexcusably defective, if no attention had been paid to those objects." Actually the only specific attention the Constitution paid to secrecy was a provision granting Congress the authority, if it wished, to keep its own proceedings secret. But the Federalist interpreted the Constitution as a command to executive secrecy in two vital areas — in diplomatic negotiation, where "perfect *secrecy* and immediate *despatch* are sometimes requisite"; and in "the business of intelligence," where "the most useful intelligence may be obtained if the persons possessing it can be relieved of the apprehensions of discovery."

The rising democratic society, however, nourished the opposite principle — the principle of disclosure. Even those Founding Fathers who feared democracy thought that the wide diffusion of information was the best remedy for whatever troubles democracy might create. "A popular Government, without popular information, or the means of acquiring it," Madison himself said, "is but a Prologue to a Farce or a Tragedy; or, perhaps both. Knowledge will forever govern ignorance: And a peo-

ple who mean to be their own Governors must arm themselves
with the power which knowledge gives." [3] When patriotic men felt
that information had to be withheld from the people in the interests of national safety, no less patriotic men might feel with equal
righteousness that the people, in the phrase now stale through incessant repetition, had a right to know. The conflict between the
principles of secrecy and of disclosure broke out very early in
the republic. In 1795 President Washington laid before the Senate
in secret session the text of the treaty Jay had just negotiated
with Great Britain. Senator Stevens Thomson Mason of Virginia
thought it essential to arm the people with the power given
by knowledge. Accordingly he sent the document to Benjamin
Franklin Bache of the Philadelphia *Aurora,* who promptly published it.

This transaction was the first of what became, if not a common, at least a recurrent, pattern in American history. When the
republic faced a hard decision in foreign policy and the executive branch had not revealed facts that would enable the
people to reach their own judgment, aggrieved citizens felt themselves morally warranted in violating a system of secrecy exploited (as they earnestly believed) by government against the
national interest. In seeking to disclose what the Presidency preferred to suppress, they found their means in the free press and
their allies in editors, or at least in the unintimidated minority
among them.

Bache was the first of a line of bold American newspapermen
to specialize in secret documents. His greatest coup came in
1798 when, during the undeclared war with France, he published a secret dispatch from Talleyrand — a document that the
Secretary of State, who had only just received it himself, had not
even had time to show President John Adams. Bache used the
letter as proof that France wanted peace while the Adams administration wanted war. The administration, sure that the
French government had put it in his hands in order to turn opinion against the war, thereupon had him arrested for seditious
libel under the common law. Stimulated by this revelation of
danger to the republic, Congress a fortnight later passed the fa-

mous Sedition Act to provide statutory basis for future action against errant editors.[4]

Neither the common law of seditious libel nor the Sedition Act, odious as they were, went so far as to impose prior restraint on publication. But in their protest against the Sedition Act the Jeffersonian Republicans, led by Madison and Gallatin, formulated the first broad libertarian theory of the freedom of the press.[5] The rapid victory of this theory coincided with the spreading democratization of American life. Social attitudes toward secrecy underwent change, and the balance moved decisively toward disclosure. Half a century after independence there even appeared the first political party in the history of the world dedicated to the abolition of secrecy. Secrecy, the Anti-Masonic party declared in 1830, was "corroding and wearing away the very basis of all public and private virtue in our country; and eradicating that mutual confidence, upon which the business of life, its peace, and its enjoyments essentially depend." [6] Even John Quincy Adams was soon scouring around trying to remove the stigma of secrecy from the Phi Beta Kappa Society.

The executive, of course, did not and, in its nature, could not surrender the claim to secrecy on certain matters. The markings Secret, Confidential and Private, for example, were used in the War of 1812.[7] So long as government handled secrecy responsibly, there was no responsible objection. But the claim to secrecy was not absolute. In 1844 the Tyler administration, determined to avoid public debate over the acquisition of Texas, tried to sneak a treaty of annexation through the Senate in executive session. Senator Benjamin Tappan of Ohio, irate at this procedure, wrote his brother Lewis, the New York abolitionist: "Suppose I send you the Treaty & Correspondence, will you have it published in the Evening Post in such a way that it cannot be traced back?" Lewis Tappan, a little apprehensive, consulted with Gallatin, now eighty-three years old. The veteran of the battle against the Sedition Act told him to go ahead.[8] William Cullen Bryant, the editor of the *Evening Post,* rushed out an extra, and Tyler's stratagem was defeated. The Tappan papers, like the Mason papers before and the Ellsberg papers after, raised a fundamental question. Was the word of the President final — as Jefferson himself had asserted during the Burr trial — on matters of official secrecy? Were the Tappans, Gallatin and Bryant — all illustrious patriots of unquestioned probity — to be condemned because their judgment differed from the President's? Or did Tyler's abuse of secrecy leave them no recourse but to do what they did? History has vindicated Tappan. Two years later, Polk, refusing to disclose secret intelligence operations undertaken by the Tyler administration, said ruefully, "I am fully aware of the strong and correct public feeling which exists throughout the country against secrecy of any kind in the administration of government." [9]

II

Even the Civil War was fought to a remarkable degree in the open. Lincoln's government, it is true, suspended *habeas corpus*, intercepted the mail, suppressed newspapers and so on; but there was no effective censorship, no Sedition Act, no Espionage Act. The Confederates got more information from northern reporters than they did from southern spies. "The location of Grant's guns secretly placed against Vicksburg in 1863 was published," J. G. Randall writes; "his proposed concentration upon City Point in July, 1864, was revealed; Sherman's objectives in his Georgia march and the disposition of his various corps were proclaimed; full details concerning the land and sea expedition against Wilmington, North Carolina, in December, 1864, were supplied." It is little wonder that Lee was a faithful reader of the northern press or that Sherman threatened to treat correspondents as if they were spies.[10] Lincoln himself wrily said in his Second Inaugural, "The progress of our arms, upon which all else chiefly depends, is as well known to the public as to myself."

Matters were almost equally open on the diplomatic front. In 1861 the Department of State began the publication of the series called (after 1870) *Foreign Relations of the United States*. The 1861 volume actually contained dispatches of that very year describing the campaign to prevent European states from recognizing the Confederacy — documents that under contemporary standards, as William M. Franklin, the director of the State Department Historical Office, noted in 1973, could easily warrant a Top Secret stamp.[11] Their publication wrought no demonstrable harm to national security. Indeed, until nearly the end of the century, each new volume of *Foreign Relations* published official secrets only a few months old. The 1870 volume, for example, ran a dispatch of the same year from the Minister to Italy, George P. Marsh (the same Marsh who had figured in the Koszta affair), in which he condemned the Italian government for its "vacillation, tergiversation and duplicity." An Italian newspaper reprinted the dispatch on a day when Marsh was dining with the Minister of Foreign Affairs. "Was Mr. Marsh handed his passport?" Franklin has written. ". . . No, as Mr. Marsh had to admit, the only result was that the Italians treated him better than ever. He continued happily and successfully in his Italian post until his death twelve years later." [12] John Bassett Moore, the great authority on international law in the first half of the twentieth century, who himself had served as Assistant Secretary of State, said that the State Department before the First World War had no secrets whatever, except for personnel reports.[13]

"Light is the only thing that can sweeten our political atmosphere," the young Woodrow Wilson wrote in 1884," — light thrown upon every detail of administration in the departments; light diffused through every passage of policy; light blazed full upon every feature of legislation; light that can penetrate every recess or corner in which any intrigue might hide; light that will open to view the innermost chambers of government." [14] He was writing as a scholar, but, running for the Presidency more than a quarter century later, he returned to the theme more forcibly than ever. "Government," he said, "ought to be all outside and no inside. I, for my part, believe there ought to be no place where anything can be done that everybody does not know about. . . . Secrecy means impropriety." [15] It was the shortest possible step to the first of the Fourteen Points and "open covenants of peace, openly arrived at," with diplomacy to "proceed always frankly and in the public view."

*

III

But events were conspiring against the ideal. As society grew more complex, government grew more powerful. The instinct of bureaucracy, as Max Weber pointed out, was "to increase the superiority of the professionally informed by keeping their knowledge and intentions secret." The concept of the 'official secret' was "the specific invention of bureaucracy," and officials defended nothing so "fanatically" as their secrets.[16] Involvement in foreign affairs strengthened the addiction. "In proportion as the nation's statecraft is increasingly devoted to the gainful pursuit of international intrigue," Thorstein Veblen wrote shortly after the First World War, "it will necessarily take on a more furtive character, and will conduct a larger proportion of its ordinary work by night and cloud." Splendid phrase! The people, Veblen predicted, would tend to accept this in a complaisant, even grateful, spirit on the growing conviction that night and cloud best provided for national security.[17]

Wilson found much of this out for himself when he went to Versailles. The prophet of open diplomacy ended by shutting himself up in a room with Lloyd George and Clemenceau while one Marine stood with fixed bayonet at the door and another paced up and down on the garden terrace outside.[18] When he used the word "diplomacy" in his First Point, Wilson, whatever he meant in Washington, meant in Paris the results of negotiation, not the process. His "new diplomacy" was aimed not at secret talks but at secret treaties. If his rhetorical taste had been for paradox rather than for parallelism, he would have written "open covenants, secretly arrived at" — and would have been more accurate. Before the war, for example, the French Assembly had not known of certain clauses in their government's alliance with Russia, nor had the British Foreign Secretary informed even his own cabinet, not to speak of Parliament, of military understandings between the British and French General Staffs. This was what Wilson, quite rightly, wanted to stop. But in doing so he was, also quite rightly, no more ready than John Jay to abandon secrecy in negotiation.

War also fastened secrecy more firmly than ever before on the military. Admirals and generals had long locked up their war plans. But for 130 years the military establishment had managed without a formal and permanent system of security classification. It was not till 1867 that the War Department issued orders to protect seacoast defenses against foreign surveillance, not till 1907 that a War Department circular called for the use of security markings, not till 1912 that a general order provided for the security of military plans and deployments. Then in 1917 a general order from Pershing's headquarters in France instituted, in imitation of his British and French allies, the markings of Secret, Confidential and For Official Circulation Only. This system was adopted at home and extended to peacetime in a regulation of 1921.[19]

War, in addition, led to the passage of an Espionage Act. But even under the stress of war Congress rejected a provision that would have made it a crime to communicate and publish national defense information that "might" be useful to the enemy.[20] Instead the Act required proof that a person disclosing such information had "reason to believe" it could be used "to the injury of the United States or to the advantage of any foreign nation." It was aimed at spies, not at Masons and Baches, Tappans and Bryants. Moreover, the Espionage Act and the military classification system were wholly unrelated. When the Supreme Court construed the Act in 1941 (this was the case of a Soviet spy named Gorin who made the unfortunate mistake of leaving secret documents in a suit he sent to the cleaners), it did not mention the classification system and left it to the jury to decide whether the information involved related to the national defense.[21] The marking on the document, in other words, was not sufficient by itself to settle the question.

The classification system thus remained on a separate track and existed as a military hobby in a legal limbo. So unimportant did the protection of secrets seem to the State Department by the end of the twenties that Henry L. Stimson, as Hoover's Secretary of State, disbanded the code-breaking section on the celebrated ground that gentlemen did not read other gentlemen's mail. As the diplomat Robert Murphy wrote in his memoirs, there were "practically no security precautions in the State Department prior to the war." [22]

War brought this placid condition to an end. The United States was on the brink of the second greatest crisis in its history; the Germans and the Russians (these were the days of the Hitler-Stalin pact) were masters, or at least zealous practitioners, of espionage; and it was entirely reasonable to take measures of self-defense. On March 22, 1940, Franklin D. Roosevelt by executive order conferred presidential recognition for the first time on the military classification system. For statutory authority, Roosevelt cited a 1938 law empowering the President to prohibit the making of photographs, maps or sketches of vital "installations or equipment." [23] While Congress had hardly intended that this law apply to documents, Roosevelt, as usual, preferred to cite statutory authority, however tenuous, rather than invoke inherent presidential power. The system was still confined to military intelligence. "The test," Roosevelt told a press conference early in 1941, "is what the Commander in Chief of the Army and Navy thinks it would be harmful to the defense of this country to give out." And "give out" meant give out publicly; committees of Congress, Roosevelt continued, were receiving much of this information in executive session.[24]

But national defense was an elastic concept; and total war made security a total concern. The classification system rapidly spread to the State Department and soon infected other parts of the government. War also encouraged the inflation inevitable in security systems: thus Top Secret now made its debut in response to the British marking of Most Secret. And, as hot war gave way to cold war, secrecy became more obsessive than ever. Since communists were thought to be far wilier spies than the now discredited Nazis had been, the need for precaution seemed even more intense. "Germany was a pipe dream," Allen Dulles of the CIA said, "compared with what we have to meet now." [25] Popular anxiety over communist espionage, heightened by the discovery of Soviet spy rings in a number of countries and dramatized in the United States by the Hiss case, prepared public opinion for a security system that would cover information as well as personnel. In 1950 Truman issued a new executive order for military secrets, superseding Roosevelt's order of a decade earlier, and in 1951, in still another executive order, he extended the system to non-military agencies, authorizing *any* executive department or agency to classify information when it seemed "necessary in the interest of national security." Unlike Roosevelt, Truman made no effort to cite statutory authority; and the remarkable breadth and vagueness of the order roused much criticism.[26]

Eisenhower consequently replaced it in 1953 by Executive Order 10501. Like Truman's order, this rested on a general claim of presidential authority. Though the new order narrowed the classification standard from "national security" to "national defense" and reduced the number of agencies authorized to wield the stamp, it provided no effective control over the stampers and no workable method for the declassification of documents once they had passed into the system. Moreover, the executive orders brought security bureaus into existence across the government; and an army of professional security men, speaking through the little-known but powerful Interagency Committee on Internal Security (ICIS), became one of the strongest vested interests in the bureaucracy, well protected against administrative control by alliances with right-wing congressional committees.

IV

The new system had legitimate objectives. It was hard to dispute the necessity for preserving some secrecy in the areas mentioned by the Federalist — negotiations and intelligence; or in the area of military plans, movements and weaponry; or in regard to information that might compromise foreign governments or leaders or American friends or agents in foreign lands. There were, in addition, self-evident categories in domestic affairs (though these were not usually marked for security classification): personal data given the government on the presumption it would be kept confidential — tax returns, personnel investigations and the like, and official plans or decisions that, if prematurely disclosed, would lead to speculation in land or commodities, pre-emptive buying, higher governmental costs and private enrichment. Even the most ardent opponent of official secrecy might hesitate before demanding that government at once throw open its files in these categories.

Yet no one could doubt that a legitimate system of restriction grew after the Second World War into an extravagant and indefensible system of denial. This was able to take place because the only control over the secrecy system was exercised by the executive branch itself. And it took place in spite of the fact that classification had no standing in law. The secrecy system was no more than a collection of internal rules for government employees; violators were liable only to administrative discipline or discharge, not to criminal prosecution (unless defense information was involved and there was reason to believe that its disclosure might injure the United States or help a foreign nation). But the legal limitations of the system were not widely understood. The religion of secrecy was sanctified and sustained by unquestioning popular faith in the Presidency and unquestioning popular fear of communism.

There was an uneasy feeling almost from the start, even on the part of those who liked secrecy, that the system was getting out of control. A Commission on Government Security under the chairmanship of Loyd Wright reported in 1957 that some 1.5 million government employees were empowered to wield the stamp of classification. A Defense Department committee under the chairmanship of Charles A. Coolidge warned that overclassification "inevitably resulted in a casual attitude toward classified information" within government and encouraged newspapermen to regard official markings "with feelings that vary from indifference to active contempt." [27]

Such admonitions had little effect. In Congress, two unsung heroes in the middle fifties reopened the historic battle between secrecy and disclosure — Thomas C. Hennings, Jr., of Missouri [28] and his Constitutional Rights Subcommittee in the Senate and John E. Moss and his Government Information Subcommittee in the House. Their investigations exposed one imbecility after another: the security classification, for example, of reports on bows and arrows (in Pentagonese, "silent flashless weapons") and shark repellents. When Moss dared wonder why the Defense Department had classified the fact that monkeys were being sent into outer space, one loyal Republican congressman angrily charged that Moss's subcommittee wanted to make vital technical information available to the enemy; "we might just as well install a Communist in every executive department." The general counsel of the Defense Department accused the Moss Subcommittee of inciting "disrespect" for the system; "the only real beneficiaries can be the Communist propagandists." [29]

Presidents themselves found such absurdities exasperating. James Hagerty, Eisenhower's press secretary, later told how, when wildly overclassified documents arrived at the White House, he had the President declassify them on the spot. "Believe me, the only thing that was 'Top Secret' about that was what he would say when he was talking to me and had to go through such nonsense." [30] Yet Eisenhower, though his instinct was good,[31] did nothing to moderate the system. The sense of crisis was too great; Congress, except for Moss and Hennings, was too docile; the power secrecy conferred on Presidents was too irresistible.

Even John F. Kennedy, in the worst and most inexplicable speech of his Presidency, weighed in on the side of secrecy. Addressing the American Newspaper Publishers Association a few days after the Bay of Pigs, he said that newspapers must ask not just the question, "Is it news?" but the question, "Is it in the interest of the national security?" Our way of life, Kennedy said, was under attack; the enemy boasted of reading in American newspapers information their agents would otherwise have to acquire through theft, bribery or espionage. "If the press is awaiting a declaration of war before it imposes the self-discipline of combat conditions, then I can only say that no war ever imposed a greater threat to our security. . . . The danger has never been more clear and its presence has never been more imminent." [32]

A group of editors and publishers soon called on Kennedy to discuss what might be done. So astute a correspondent as Douglass Cater wrote that the solution lay "in stimulating a sense of realization among reporters, and more particularly among editors, that the decision to publish news affecting national security should be based on a higher standard than what is referred to as 'news judgment.' " [33] One voice of sanity cut through the nonsense. "The whole concept of a return to secrecy in peacetime demonstrates a profound misunderstanding of the role of a free press. . . . The plea for security could well become a cloak for errors, misjudgments and other failings of government." The speaker, not, alas, always so wise, was Richard M. Nixon.[34]

Kennedy gave no further speeches of this sort. Indeed at the meeting with the newspaper delegation after the speech, Kennedy, mentioning the Bay of Pigs, told Turner Catledge of the *New York Times* in an aside, "If you had printed more about the operation you would have saved us from a colossal mistake." [35] Four months later he amended the Eisenhower executive order on security classifications to set up an automatic downgrading and declassification procedure.[36] Unfortunately government security officers, fearing that reform of the system would weaken their own power, sabotaged the effort, interpreting the Kennedy order to mean that automatic downgrading did not apply to documents classified before the date of the order. And, though Robert McNamara enjoined his legion of security-stampers in the Pentagon, "When in doubt, underclassify," this exhortation proved ineffective too, since no penalty was set for overclassification. "Throughout the 180 years of our Government," a candid admiral once told the Moss Committee, ". . . I have never known a man to be court-martialed for overclassifying a paper, and that is the reason, I am afraid, we are in the mess we are today." [37]

Kennedy was the only President after the Second World War to show any interest in slowing down the secrecy machine, and his interest was desultory. His successors and their administrations thrived on secrecy. In the 1968 hearings on the Tonkin Gulf incident McNamara casually revealed to a startled Senate Foreign

Relations Committee that the government had by now achieved classifications "above Top Secret" — classifications unknown to Executive Order 10501 and themselves classified.[38] As civilized a general as Maxwell Taylor could say as late as 1971 when asked about the people's right to know, "I don't believe in that as a general principle. . . . A citizen should know those things he needs to know to be a good citizen and discharge his functions." [39]

But by the 1970s the principle of disclosure was gathering increasing support, especially on Capitol Hill. Congressman William Moorhead of Pennsylvania, who succeeded Moss as chairman of the House Government Information Subcommittee, carried the battle forward in a series of hearings. The mess was now greater than ever. By 1972, the General Accounting Office told the Moorhead committee, the cost of protective measures for classified material in Defense, State, the Atomic Energy Commission and the National Aeronautics and Space Administration amounted to more than $60 million a year.[40] A former Pentagon security officer, William G. Florence, testified that there were 20 million classified documents (including copies) in the defense security system, of which "less than one-half of 1 per cent . . . actually contain information qualifying even for the lowest defense classification under Executive Order 10501. In other words, the disclosure of information in at least 99½ per cent of those classified documents could not be prejudicial to the defense interests of the Nation." Newspaper clippings were classified; information in the public domain was classified; and, when one member of the Joint Chiefs of Staff wrote another saying that too many undeserving papers were being stamped Top Secret, his note itself was stamped Top Secret. Classification had become "a way of life," and the Pentagon view, Florence wearily concluded, was that "information is born classified" and should be declassified only if it could be proven to be of no interest to foreigners.[41]

Because the secrecy system was controlled by those on whom it bestowed prestige and protection, it had long since overridden its legitimate objectives. In certain areas, secrecy unquestionably remained a necessity. But by the 1960s and 1970s the religion of secrecy had become an all-purpose means by which the American Presidency sought to dissemble its purposes, bury its mistakes, manipulate its citizens and maximize its power.

v

A system at once so dangerous and so absurd was bound to invite defiance. Like the Masons and Tappans of the past, conscientious citizens believed that the classification process was wrongfully denying necessary information to Congress and the people. Some resistants, like Senator Mike Gravel of Alaska, were themselves members of Congress. Others, like Otto Otepka or Daniel Ellsberg, were officials or former officials of the executive branch. All felt morally justified in giving out documents that still bore government stamps of secrecy. Otepka gave them to the counsel for the Senate Internal Security Committee; Ellsberg gave them first to the Senate Foreign Relations Committee and then to the *New York Times;* Gravel read them into the record of the Senate Subcommittee on Buildings and Grounds. All engaged in selective declassification to serve a cause — Otepka the cause of saving the nation from procommunist softies like Walt W. Rostow; Ellsberg and Gravel the cause of saving the nation from anticommunist fanatics like Walt W. Rostow.

The nature of the cause tended to determine the nature of the reaction. Kennedy regarded Otepka as an abomination and fired him from the government. Nixon called him back, appointed him to the Subversive Activities Control Board and instead regarded Ellsberg as the abomination.[42] Ellsberg's Pentagon Papers had been classified Top Secret; and, unless newspapers stopped serializing them, the government solemnly said, "the nation's security will suffer immediate and irreparable harm." [43]

Immediate and irreparable harm? The passage of time soon tested these dire words. Executive Order 10501 had reserved the Top Secret stamp "only to that information or material the defense aspect of which is paramount, and the unauthorized disclo-

sure of which could result in exceptionally grave damage to the
Nation such as leading to a definite break in diplomatic relations
affecting the defense of the United States, an armed attack
against the United States or its allies, a war, or the compromise
of military or defense plans or intelligence operations, or scientific or technological developments vital to the national defense."
In the third year after the publication of the Pentagon Papers
not a single one of these calamities had taken place.[44] In 1973
Nixon still claimed that the publication had created a situation
"in which the ability of Government to carry on foreign relations
even in the best of circumstances could have been severely
compromised." [45] But this standard would not have justified a
Top Secret marking; and, in any case, the President himself in
other moods portrayed these same years as the most glorious in
the history of American diplomacy. All this suggested that the
Pentagon history was overclassified and the Nixon group over-
agitated.

But the agitation, if excessive, was unquestionably real. The
publication by a man long out of government of an historical
study commissioned by an earlier administration and dealing
with events from three to twenty-five years old had traumatic impact on an administration that had already placed itself in a state
of psychological siege.[46] Nixon's response was to act on all
fronts to establish sterner control of official secrets. While the
White House plumbers investigated leaks by night and cloud, the
government moved in more formal ways to get an American
equivalent of the British Official Secrets Act — that is, a law
making it a crime to disclose classified information to unauthorized Americans as well as to foreign spies. If this could be done,
then the government could punish newspapers for the simple act
of publishing classified documents and, better still, punish those
who delivered the documents to the newspapers, even when no
reason to believe it would help a foreign nation or harm the
United States could be shown.

The Nixon administration sought first to obtain an Official Secrets Act through judicial construction. Its suit against the *New
York Times* and the *Washington Post* outdid even the Sedition

Act of 1798 in the attempt — the first in the history of the republic — to impose prior restraint on newspapers. The Supreme
Court on June 30, 1971, saved the press by a vote of 6 to 3. But,
as in the steel seizure case nearly twenty years before, the justices
delivered themselves of a diversity of opinions — in this case
nine — and the meaning of the verdict was again enigmatic.
Only three justices — Black, Douglas and Brennan — claimed
the First Amendment as an absolute bar to action, whether presidential or congressional, against the press. Marshall, pointing
out that Congress had declined in 1917 and 1957 to pass legislation that would have justified the prosecution, seemed to say that,
if Congress were to act in the future, the situation might be different, though, until it did, the President could not legislate in
the place of Congress. White and Stewart said that, while newspapers were, alas, free to publish classified material, they had
better understand that they did so at their own risk. If the case
had emerged in a different context, the vote might have been 6 to
3 in the opposite direction.[47]

Nevertheless, the effort failed. But, if the receiver of stolen
goods thus escaped, might it still not be possible to punish the
thief? This too presented difficulties. As a secret CIA memorandum complained in 1966, anyone who revealed classified data
was for all practical purposes "immune from prosecution since
his defense, of course, would be that he thought the American
public had a right to know." [48] But, if Ellsberg could be found
guilty, then giving secrets to the American public, up to now
only an internal administrative offense, would become a federal
crime. The Espionage Act, as Justice Harlan had remarked in
his dissent in the Pentagon Papers case, was "a singularly opaque
statute." The government now argued that the espionage
standard — injury to the United States and benefit to a foreign
nation — was limited to the transmission of "information"; in
the case of the transmission of artifacts — pieces of paper, photographs, maps and so on — it was sufficient, in the government's reading of the act, to prove only that the items related to
national defense and were delivered into unauthorized hands.
The semantic argument hinged on the interpretation of the punc-

tuation of the statute. But no court for more than half a century had construed the act in this sense, and in 1957, at the height of the Cold War, Congress had declined to pass a bill recommended by the Loyd Wright Commission making the unauthorized disclosure of classified data *per se* a crime.

Doubtless it was the desperate desire to convert the Espionage Act into an Official Secrets Act that led Nixon to expend more energy in trying to convict Ellsberg than any President had devoted to a criminal case since Jefferson had tried to convict Aaron Burr. The government withheld from the court for many months an exculpatory Defense Department analysis indicating that national security had suffered negligible damage from the publication of the Pentagon Papers. Nixon personally suppressed for six weeks the fact of the burglarization of the office of Ellsberg's psychiatrist. A brigadier general was assigned full-time to the prosecution; and, in the midst of the trial, Nixon even solicited Judge Matthew Byrne's interest in the directorship of the FBI. Executive interference in the process of justice finally became so intolerable that the judge brought the trial to an end.

VI

In the meantime, the administration tried another approach to the problem. This was through a replacement of Eisenhower's Executive Order 10501 on the security classification system. The Pentagon Papers controversy had led to much public criticism over the abuse of secrecy; and in 1971 Nixon appointed a committee, headed first by William H. Rehnquist and then wonderfully by David Young of the plumbers, to recommend reforms. Early in 1972 the committee circulated a draft of a new order within the executive branch, while refusing congressional requests for consultation; and on March 8, 1972, Nixon issued Executive Order 11652. Two months later, when the Moorhead Committee asked Young to testify on the new order, the White House invoked executive privilege.[49]

On its face Executive Order 11652 called for a liberalization of the secrecy system. It purported to reduce the number both of agencies and of officials empowered to stamp documents, and to set up an improved procedure for automatic declassification. At the same time, however, it quietly extended the reach of the system, replacing the Eisenhower "national defense" standard by the far more spacious standard of the "interest of the national defense or foreign relations of the United States (hereinafter collectively termed 'national security')." An assistant attorney general informed the Moorhead Committee that the "national security" standard covered not only international matters but domestic intelligence surveillance relating to national defense or foreign relations.[50] Moreover, the Nixon order expanded the definition of Top Secret, which Executive Order 10501 had confined in the main to defense information, to apply to information that, if disclosed, could lead to the "disruption of foreign relations vitally affecting the national security" — an exceedingly vague category and one that in the form of "jeopardizing the international relations of the United States" had been considered in the Eisenhower order to rate no higher classification than Secret. By upgrading this category, the administration could justify Top Secret markings for future Pentagon Papers and more easily deter Congress from inquiring into essentially diplomatic questions.

In addition, the Nixon order pretended to supply a basis for criminal prosecution in cases of unauthorized disclosure. In 1966 Congress, after years of effort by John Moss, had passed the Freedom of Information Act. This law was based on the proposition that disclosure should be the rule, not the exception and that the burden should be on the government to justify the withholding of a document, not on the person who requested it. It further provided for judicial review if the request were denied. However, it also allowed certain exemptions, the first of which was for matters "specifically required by Executive order to be kept secret in the interest of the national defense or foreign policy." This exemption was permissive in the statute, but it did imply congressional recognition of the executive classification system.

The Nixon order now tried to incorporate the Freedom of Information Act but replaced the term "foreign policy" as used in the Act by the considerably more elastic term "foreign relations" and asserted that the Act had "expressly exempted" such information from disclosure, thereby suggesting falsely that exemption was mandatory. It concluded: "Wrongful disclosure of such information or material is recognized in the Federal Criminal Code as providing a basis for prosecution." But, since an executive order could not amend a statute, the threat of prosecution could apply only to the types of information specifically described in the Criminal Code and not to the types mentioned in Executive Order 11652. "There is no basis in law," the Moorhead Committee staff analysis concluded, "for an Executive Order, in effect, to threaten Members of Congress, newsmen, or anyone else for what the Order refers to as a 'wrongful disclosure.' " [51]

"It is time," President Nixon cried out amidst the wreckage of Watergate, "for . . . a new sense of dedication of everybody in the bureaucracy that if a document is classified, keep it classified. . . . It is time in this country to quit making national heroes out of those who steal secrets and publish them in newspapers." [52] But his effort to consolidate the legal control of the secrecy system through the courts had failed; his effort to do it through executive decree was minatory, not statutory. If there were to be an American Official Secrets Act, if, in other words, any unauthorized disclosure of classified information were to be a crime, there could be no escape from congressional action. An opportunity now lay at hand in a proposed massive revision of the Federal Criminal Code. On March 22, 1973, the Nixon administration submitted a 600-page bill which contained, along with the revival of the death penalty and the attenuation of the insanity defense, a proposal on official secrecy far more drastic than anything thought necessary during the First World War, the Second World War, the Cold War, the Korean War or the Vietnam War.

The point of the new Nixon proposal was to overcome the problems raised by the *Gorin* decision when it gave the jury the power to decide whether information communicated to unauthorized persons truly pertained to the national defense. This requirement, the Department of Justice complained, made it "necessary to disclose the very information which the law seeks to protect"; the government therefore had had to forgo prosecutions when security prevented the exposure of information to a jury. Yet the nation had lived with the *Gorin* standard through the Second World War, the Cold War, the Korean War and the Vietnam War. With an age of negotiation succeeding an age of confrontation, it was not clear what emergency required a stricter standard in 1973. To get around the *Gorin* requirement, the Nixon administration now tried to introduce a scheme, novel in American law, according to which knowing disclosure by present or former government officials of classified information to unauthorized persons would be *per se* a crime and in which the claim of improper classification would be no defense. Whether a document had been marked to protect a legitimate state secret or to conceal error, stupidity, waste or fraud, no judge or jury would be entitled to go behind the marking. Though one section of the bill excluded those who received the information from prosecution, another section, designed to repair what the administration had seen in the Ellsberg case as a defect in the Espionage Act, proposed to remove national defense "information" as well as artifacts from the espionage standard and to provide that recipients — reporters, for example, and their publishers — could be prosecuted if they published such information or even failed to turn it over to the government (that is, if the government were prepared to have the information examined in court).[53]

Widespread opposition, powerfully expressed by Senator Edmund Muskie of Maine with fervent support from most of the press, made enactment of the bill improbable, especially when the Watergate testimony soon illustrated the specialized uses to which the Nixon administration had put its theory of national security. The proposal itself remained as evidence of the extraordinary lengths to which the administration wished to go — in a time not of international storm but, by its own proud claim, of unprecedented serenity — to complete the design of the revolutionary Presidency.

*

VII

Ironically, at the very moment when the President urged the American Congress to adopt an Official Secrets Act, the British Parliament, after sixty years' experience with such an act, was contemplating revision and liberalization.

The British had wrestled with the problem of state secrets ever since the Foreign Office in 1837 tried to stop a newspaper from publishing dispatches sent by the Duke of Wellington from Spain nearly thirty years before, when he was still Sir Arthur Wellesley. Ten years later the *Times* defied the government and published Castlereagh's correspondence at the Congress of Vienna, held more than a generation earlier. A succession of such horrid infractions led the Permanent Secretary of the Treasury to write in 1873, "The unauthorised use of official information is the worst fault a civil servant can commit. It is on the same footing as cowardice by a soldier. It is unprofessional." [54]

This bracing spirit led to an Official Secrets Act in 1889 and to a more conclusive version enacted by the House of Commons in a brisk half-hour in 1911. The first section of both acts dealt with foreign espionage and created no serious problems. Section 2, so much envied by the Wright Commission, the CIA and the Nixon administration, dealt with the transmission of government information to British subjects. It said flatly that the communication of *any* information picked up by *any* official in the line of duty to *any* unauthorized person was an absolute offense, both for the communicator and (if he understood what he was getting) for the recipient.

A libertarian nation suffered under this preposterous law for more than half a century. It did this through a marvelously British process of selective enforcement. In 1916, for example, Asquith, the Prime Minister, solemnly told the House of Commons that the Official Secrets Act applied to Ministers of the Crown at the very time he was sending daily communiqués filled with official secrets to his mistress.[55] The law was never applied seriously to prime ministers — to Lloyd George, to Churchill, to

Avon, to Macmillan, to Wilson — but, when Compton Mackenzie in 1932 published a memoir in which he named some intelligence officers with whom he had worked in Greece during the
First World War, he was fined £100. The Official Secrets Act was
invoked to prevent the press from reporting the location of possible infected cans of corned beef, the contents of the Services'
Manual for Survival, the number of trees blown down in a park
during a gale and other momentous matters.[56]

Eventually, in 1971, when the *Sunday Telegraph* published a
dispatch from Jonathan Aitken about Biafra, the dike broke.
The dispatch included a confidential government report, which,
while it raised questions about policy, had no bearing on questions of security. When Aitken and his co-conspirators were
brought to trial at Old Bailey, the Crown counsel summed up
the spirit of the Official Secrets Act in the style of the Nixon
prosecution of Ellsberg: "The whole structure of government
would fall down if people had complete freedom to communicate any document that was not a document useful to an
enemy." [57] But Mr. Justice Caulfield in an historic decision concluded that Section 2, having had its 60th birthday, had reached
retirement age and should be pensioned off. This encouraged the
Heath government to appoint a commission to review Section 2
under the chairmanship of Lord Franks, whom Americans remembered with admiration from the time when, as Sir Oliver
Franks, he served as British Ambassador to Washington in the
great days of the Marshall Plan.

The Commission's report was remarkably circumspect. While it
proposed to replace the "catch-all" Section 2 by more narrowly
defined provisions, this simply meant, as Lord Franks said, "a
highly selective attack in depth" instead of "an attack on all
fronts." At the same time, the Commission proposed to tie the
government classification system into the Official Secrets Act
and thereby give criminal sanctions to what had been up to this
point, as in the United States, an administrative system uncon-
nected with the criminal law. It opposed any interference by Parliament or the courts with the presumably divine right of the executive to make final decisions on classification. It rejected the

heretical idea that publication in good faith and in the public interest might serve as a defense. Yet the Heath government, in spite of the pledge in its own election manifesto to "review the operations of the Official Secrets Act so that government is more open and more accountable," regarded even so timorous a report as dangerously permissive.[58]

VIII

The temptations of secrecy were too great for all save the most conscientious or confident leaders to resist, even in nations as ostensibly devoted to openness and accountability as Great Britain and the United States. The reason for this was obvious. Secrecy seemed to promise government three inestimable advantages: the power to withhold, the power to leak and the power to lie. In fact, these advantages were often illusory. Few things could be kept really secret in a democracy. But every government always hoped that it would be able to make secrecy effective.

The power to withhold held out the hope of denying the public the knowledge that would make possible an independent judgment on executive policy. The mystique of inside information — "if you only knew what we know" — was a most effective way to defend the national-security monopoly and prevent democratic control of foreign policy. Even as good a Senate man as Arthur H. Vandenberg once warned his colleagues that the habit of senatorial intervention in foreign affairs should not become "too contagious" because, unless the Senate could be sure "of a complete command of all the essential information prerequisite to an intelligent decision," it should not take "the terrific chance of muddying the international waters by some sort of premature and ill-advised expression of its advice to the Executive." [59] Robert A. Taft put the same point in a manner less solicitous of the Presidency. "The result of a general practice of secrecy," he told the Senate in 1951, ". . . has been to deprive the Senate and Congress of the substance of the powers conferred on them by the Constitution." [60]

Vandenberg and Taft were speaking at the start of the postwar period when the secrecy system was still relatively unsophisticated. This was the time when Harold Nicolson was writing, "I am confident that, in the Free World at least, the age of secret treaties is behind us." [61] Who could have anticipated that secret covenants secretly arrived at would soon enjoy so rich and rank a growth in Woodrow Wilson's native land? But under the power to withhold it was easy for Wilson's successors to make commitments unknown to Congress and the people. The so-called Hyde Park Aide-Memoire on atomic energy, signed by Roosevelt and Churchill on September 18, 1944, was not known in the United States until it was found among FDR's papers and published by the State Department in a documentary volume in 1960. When the Symington Committee set to work in 1969–1970, it unearthed, as we have seen, one secret deal after another. The Senate Foreign Relations Committee first learned of a secret agreement with Korea concerning the Indochina War *from a Korean* and then spent months trying to persuade the State Department to let the Senate see it.[62] The imperial Presidency thrived in the culture of secrecy.

The power to leak meant the power to tell the people what it served the government's purpose that they should know. Government itself put out more classified information in these years than members of Congress, newspapermen and foreign spies put together. "What good does it do to spend millions to protect ourselves against espionage if our secrets just leak away?" Allen Dulles once mused. "Basically, I feel that government is one of the worst offenders." [63] He was right, but he should have addressed the question to his brother. When Daniel Ellsberg gave the *New York Times* the Top Secret Pentagon Papers, it was, in the eyes of all God-fearing men, reprehensible, but when John Foster Dulles gave the *New York Times* the Top Secret Yalta Papers, it was presumably very different. Government was the leakiest of all ships; and, as the Washington joke had it, it differed from other ships in leaking most at the top.

Officials, Max Frankel said, freely leaked what they thought would promote a "political, personal, bureaucratic or even commercial interest." [64] Frankel as the *New York Times*'s diplomatic correspondent had been the recipient of many leaks; indeed, without leaks, he said, diplomatic reporting could hardly exist. This, he added in an affidavit in the Pentagon Papers case, was why it seemed so hypocritical when the party that had leaked so long suddenly decided that the unauthorized release of classified information was intolerable. Frankel plainly had a point. Why was it fine to hand out secrets when they served the political purposes of the men in power and damnable to hand out secrets when they enabled Congress and the public to assess national policy and performance? Richard M. Nixon had stated the issue during the MacArthur controversy of 1951. "If classified documents are now to be made public," he said, "the committees of Congress and the American people should be entitled to see not only those documents which might reflect against MacArthur, but also those which reflect in his favor. . . . The new test for classifying secret documents now seems to be not whether the publication of a document would affect the security of the nation but whether it would affect the political security of the Administration." [65] An interesting thought in the decade of Watergate.

The power to withhold and the power to leak led on inexorably to the power to lie. The secrecy system instilled in the executive branch the idea that foreign policy was no one's business save its own, and uncontrolled secrecy made it easy for lying to become routine. It was in this spirit that the Eisenhower administration concealed the CIA operations it was mounting against governments around the world. It was in this spirit that the Kennedy administration stealthily sent the Cuban brigade to the Bay of Pigs and stealthily enlarged American involvement in Vietnam. It was in this spirit that the Johnson administration Americanized the Vietnam War, misrepresenting one episode after another to Congress and the people — Tonkin Gulf, the first American ground force commitment, the bombing of North Vietnam, My Lai and the rest.

The longer the secrecy system dominated government, the more government assumed the *right* to lie. The secret air war waged by the Nixon administration against Cambodia in 1969–1970 involved some 3600 B-52 raids over fourteen months.

One result was the devaluation of the secrecy system itself, for an obedient Defense Department now falsified the classified bombing reports it sent to the Senate Armed Services Committee and an obedient Secretary of State told the Senate Foreign Relations Committee in secret session, "Cambodia is one country where we can say with complete assurance that our hands are clean and our hearts are pure." The bombing campaign turned out to be a failure, in consequence of which Nixon decided to order a ground invasion of Cambodia. Announcing this invasion, he incredibly assured the American people that the United States, with splendid forbearance, had not previously "moved against these enemy sanctuaries because we did not wish to violate the territory of a neutral nation." [66]

The only people for whom the air war against Cambodia was a secret were the Americans. In retrospect, had it really been worthwhile to wage a murderous and ineffectual war, unauthorized by Congress, unsuccessful against the enemy and damaging chiefly to the Constitution and to the credibility of the American government? Yet such a war was the inevitable consequence of the mentality created and the facilities provided by the secrecy system. And the perfect bureaucratic rationalization was at hand. General George S. Brown, the Air Force's gift to the Joint Chiefs of Staff, simply denied that it was illegal to give false classified statistics to Congress. "For falsification to constitute an offense," he said, "there must be proof of 'intent to deceive.' This is a legally prescribed element of the offense and is negated when the report is submitted in conformity with orders from a higher authority in possession of the true facts." [67] If one may translate: lies to Congress, even classified lies to Congress, were all right so long as higher authority, who alone had the 'need to know,' had the facts.

It was in this same spirit that, while the State Department proclaimed American policy during the India-Pakistan War of 1971 as one of "absolute neutrality," Henry Kissinger secretly instructed the government that "the President does not want to be even-handed" and called for programs that would "tilt" American power in favor of Pakistan.[68] The Indochina deceptions, the

India-Pakistan deceptions, were only the episodes that came to light. No one could know how many other lies had succeeded, how many policies and projects still lay out of Jack Anderson's reach within the *sanctum sanctorum*.

Yet, though secrecy conferred a measure of power, it also exacted a psychic price. When government fell into the habit of falsification, how could anyone, especially at the top, be sure what was true? In the middle and late 1960s information making the long trajectory from a field post in Vietnam to 1600 Pennsylvania Avenue underwent successive improvement as each echelon endeavored to please the next higher till truth drained away in the process. Who could tell what was real any longer? "In our office, the Secretary's office or the White House," wrote Phil Goulding, Assistant Secretary of Defense for Public Affairs in the Johnson years, "we never knew how much we did not know." [69]

In such conditions wish tended to rule fact and, in George McGovern's phrase, government fell prey "to its own delusions and fantasies." [70] At the far end of this road lay the madness of totalitarian government, where leaders tried to remold reality by force of personality and terror. But democracies, even plebiscitary democracies, required a relationship to the reality principle. Secrecy, however convenient in the short run, could not hide blunders and lies forever if a resourceful opposition and an uninhibited press had their own means of challenging the claims of government. Secrecy, moreover, selected and fostered traits of personality that democracy was bound in time to abhor. It rejected openness, generosity, candor and mutual respect and favored duplicity, insolence and its twin, sycophancy, the cold mouth, the sneering or trembling lip, the hard and wary eye.[71] Government by night and cloud after a while eroded its own basis of consent. Government by lies, especially by clumsy little lies, was peculiarly self-defeating.

Up to the year 1965 most Americans most of the time had believed the word of their government. Within a decade thereafter, the proportion of Americans who assumed as a matter of course that their government was lying was greater than it had ever be-

fore been in the nation's history.[72] Of all the prices exacted by
the secrecy system, this was the most terrible.

IX

By the 1970s Americans had begun to lose confidence in the integrity of the secrecy system. Illegitimate secrecy had corrupted
the conduct of foreign affairs and had on occasion deprived voters
of information necessary for democratic control of foreign policy.
The Nixon solution — the attempt to make secrecy an even
more absolute presidential weapon — was bound to perish along
with the rest of his effort to revolutionize the Presidency. The serious question remained, however, of striking a balance between
the relative claims of secrecy and disclosure. In the steel seizure
case of 1952 the Supreme Court had offered the nation a brilliant inquiry into the theory of emergency prerogative. In 1971
the Court had the equivalent opportunity in the Pentagon Papers
case to inquire into the principles involved in the presidential
claims to control national security information. Each Court had
been under intense pressure of time; but the opinions in the second case were, for whatever reason, far inferior to those in the
first.

Justice Stewart was almost alone in reflecting on the fundamental question. In the area of basic national defense, he said,
the need for "absolute secrecy" was self-evident. The responsibility for maintaining this secrecy "must be where the power is" —
that is, in the Presidency. Such a responsibility required wisdom
of a high order, and "moral, political, and practical considerations would dictate that a very first principle of such wisdom
would be an insistence upon avoiding secrecy for its own sake.
For when everything is classified, then nothing is classified, and
the system becomes one to be disregarded by the cynical or the
careless, and to be manipulated by those intent on self-protection
or self-promotion." The hallmark of a truly effective secrecy system, Stewart concluded, "would be the maximum possible disclosure, recognizing that *secrecy can best be preserved only
when credibility is truly maintained.*" [73]

Even Stewart, it would seem, had hardly thought the problem through. For, if the Presidency had exclusive control over the secrecy system, was not the system foredoomed to end up in secrecy for secrecy's sake? Yet Stewart's idea of a balance between secrecy and credibility, if inconsistent with the rest of the argument, got to the heart of the matter. This proposition clearly affirmed government's right to protect secrecy essential to the discharge of continuing responsibilities in international relations and national defense. At the same time, the proposition implied that such control of information was not an unconditional right of the Presidency. In exchange for the power to preserve secrecy, government took on the obligation to maintain credibility.

This must mean not only the negative obligation to make sure that only information demonstrably vital to security was withheld but the affirmative obligation to speak truth to the people and supply Congress the information necessary to responsible debate. This is, one would think, exactly what an intelligent President would be doing anyway. No President could succeed for long unless his policies were founded on consent; and secrecy, by definition, meant policies undertaken without consent. It would therefore be to the interest of Presidents to reopen the Presidency. But recent Presidents either became so enamored of the short-run conveniences of secrecy, or else had enough to conceal, that they forgot the long-run necessity, above all for the Presidency itself, of open government.

Once again we are back to the question of constitutional comity. Democracy required some rough but rational balance between official control of information and public need for it. When the Presidency upset that balance by deceiving Congress and the public or by holding back information essential for intelligent decision, a healthy democracy was likely to move to re-establish the balance, whether through the agency of dissenting officials, indignant legislators or unintimidated newspapermen. And, just as official abuse of secrecy would lead newspapers to publish forbidden matter, so newspaper abuse of disclosure would turn public opinion against the press. The principle of re-establishing the balance was confessedly elusive. Anyone rejecting secrecy on that principle was taking a chance. Only the aftermath could prove him right or wrong in deciding that government had already violated its part of the contract.

Yet this principle registered historical practice. When government had withheld information from Congress and the people, as in the cases of the Jay Treaty and the annexation of Texas, or when it lied to Congress and the people, as in the days of Johnson and Nixon, the only recourse under the existing system was defiance. So long as Congress did not care, or dare, to assert itself, the rebellious collaboration between anonymous and disgusted officials and the press seemed the only means of getting the American democracy back into working equilibrium.

But might it not be better to maintain the balance between secrecy and disclosure in a less nerve-racking way? A rational approach to the problem was long overdue. Such an approach required some redressment of perspective. It required perhaps a return to the relaxed attitude toward official secrecy that characterized the republic till the Second World War. For nothing had confused the situation more in later years than the self-serving overestimate the executive had placed on the value of classified information. There were few greater frauds than the idea that only those with access to classified information had a right to a judgment on foreign affairs. "I really don't know of any secrets," Dean Rusk said after he left office, "which have a significant bearing upon the ability of the public to make their judgments about major issues of policy." [74] My own experience is a good deal more limited; but, after spending various periods of my life looking at classified cables, I can attest to the fact that, war aside, 99 percent of the information necessary for intelligent political judgment is available to any careful reader of the *New York Times,* the *Washington Post* or the *Congressional Record.* The country would have been far better off during the Kennedy years had the White House confined itself to reading newspaper dispatches about Vietnam and never opened a Top Secret cable from Saigon.

Just as classified information was not all that essential, keeping it classified was not always that essential either. "Though secrecy in diplomacy is occasionally unavoidable," wrote Lord Bryce, himself a distinguished diplomat, "it has its perils. . . . Publicity may cause some losses, but may avert some misfortunes." [75] In recent American experience the misfortunes averted by publicity were clearer than the losses entailed. After all the years of the American obsession with secrecy, could anyone name a case where a leak did serious damage to the national security? Espionage was a different matter; but even there it was hard to argue any longer that, without espionage, Russia or France or China would never have achieved the atomic bomb. Conceivably the nation might have been better off had there been more rather than fewer leaks. Unauthorized disclosure of the CIA political action operations of the fifties, of the Bay of Pigs expedition, of war crimes in Vietnam, of secret wars in Laos and Cambodia, far from harming the republic, could well have saved it from some of its more notable disasters. Certainly one of Richard M. Nixon's best leaks, when he told an 'off-the-record' meeting of a thousand editors in 1954 that the United States might put troops into Vietnam, had the highly beneficial consequence of alerting congressional and public opinion and killing the idea, at least for 1954.[76]

X

If all this were so, why not abolish secrecy altogether? This idea, inconceivable in the 1950s, acquired champions twenty years later. What was even more inconceivable was that foremost among these champions was the same Edward Teller who twenty years earlier was directing the development of the hydrogen bomb and hounding Robert Oppenheimer as a security risk. "Secrecy, once accepted," he wrote in 1973, "becomes an addiction." But he had at last kicked the habit, and now he urged the United States to move toward "unilaterally abandoning all forms of scientific and technical secrecy." If people insist on classifying information, "let's only classify things for one year and then make them public." [77]

Teller may have received this revelation as a member of a

Task Force on Secrecy set up by the Defense Science Board in the Pentagon in 1970 under the chairmanship of Frederick Seitz, another physicist and former president of the National Academy of Science. The Task Force was refreshingly skeptical about classified information. It doubted whether vital matters could be kept secret for more than a year and suggested that classification was "more effective in withholding information from our friends than from potential enemies." Moreover, classification impeded the flow of information within the United States and could "easily do far more harm than good by stifling critical discussion or by engendering frustration." Had it not been for timely declassification, the United States would not have its lead in microwave electronics and in computer technology. The Task Force advanced the proposition that "more might be gained than lost if our nation were to adopt — unilaterally, if necessary — a policy of complete openness in all areas of information" but reluctantly concluded that "in spite of the great advantages that might accrue from such a policy, it is not a practical proposal at the present time." Instead it recommended a 90 percent decrease in the amount of scientific and technical information under classification.[78]

The idea of no secrets at all was arresting. It was undoubtedly true that the secrecy system had been a fertile source of folly and scandal in foreign policy, that it had kept more things from the American people than it had from the enemy, that it had wasted time, cost money and bred the unappealing profession of security men. Moreover, the abolition of official secrecy might even diminish international tension by making it harder for one power to place the most sinister possible interpretation on the intentions of another. Ignorance made it easy to suppose the worst, but the worst might not always be the most accurate. We begin to understand today that both America and Russia did things in the early Cold War that each government saw as modestly defensive and that the other government saw as intolerably aggressive. If a series of Pentagon Papers and Kremlin Papers recording in detail what the two governments were actually saying and planning in their inner councils had been published, say, in 1949, each side might have reconsidered its view that the other was fanatically bent on world conquest. Herbert Feis, who spent nearly twenty years in the Department of State before he turned to the writing of history and was therefore not unaware of the diplomatic interest in secrecy, put it correctly, I think, when he said that "earlier publication of the American record would, on the whole, dispel suspicion and mistrust of our policies rather than nourish them." [79]

Still the abolition of secrecy presupposed a different world. Dr. Seitz and his colleagues were right in regretfully concluding it to be impractical. If rigorously carried out, it would make international negotiation difficult, candid counsel and personal privacy impossible. Yet its error was surely no greater than the opposite error of claiming secrecy as a national imperative so overwhelming that it must override the First Amendment. Experience had shown that the Presidency could not be trusted with exclusive control of the secrecy system. Experience also strongly suggested that some things had to be kept secret. Rational reform would therefore lie in sharing the control of the system, which meant bringing Congress into the picture.

Congress would not enter, it must be said, with particularly clean hands. Secrecy pervaded the legislative as well as the executive process, and it was as liable to abuse at one end of Pennsylvania Avenue as at the other. While congressional committees piously condemned the closed executive branch, they were determined to preserve their own power to 'mark up' appropriations, tax and other special-interest legislation behind locked doors. The House in 1973 finally voted to open all committee sessions unless a majority of the committee decided otherwise, but this was a considerable exception, and even this was too much for the Senate. In 1973 the Senate Foreign Relations Committee was only beginning an invaluable but belated publication of hearings held in secret session in 1947–1950.

Congress had in a sense already entered the field when it passed the Freedom of Information Act. But the national security exemption made that Act useless as a means of breaking the secrecy barrier in foreign affairs — a fact emphasized when in

1971 thirty-three members of the House, led by Patsy Mink of Hawaii, requested classified documents relating to the environmental impact of Project Cannikin, the underground nuclear test on Amchitka Island in Alaska. When the executive branch turned them down, they applied to the courts as provided in the Act. Eighteen months later the Supreme Court in the *Mink* case ruled that the fact the documents were classified was all it needed to know under the Freedom of Information Act. Justice Douglas, dissenting, observed that the majority had made the classification stamp "sacrosanct," without caring whether or not the information thereby denied had any defensible relationship to national defense or foreign policy. Justice Stewart, concurring, blamed Congress itself for having inserted into the act an exemption that provided no means "to question an Executive decision to stamp a document 'secret,' however cynical, myopic, or even corrupt that decision might have been." [80]

This argued all the more strongly for a congressional effort to prescribe the principles of security classification by statute. "I have no doubts," former Justice Goldberg assured the Moorhead Committee, "that Congress is authorized to enact such legislation." [81] Indeed, Congress had already done so when it established a statutory classification system for the Atomic Energy Commission in the Atomic Energy Act of 1954.

A classification statute could begin by stating as its purpose the reduction of the amount of classified material to the absolute minimum necessary to protect national security. It could assert that the government's right to keep things secret must be balanced against the people's interest in the democratic control of foreign policy. It could carefully define the sorts of information qualifying for classification — information relating to active national defense (so long as it did not conceal cost overruns, industrial incompetence and graft), information relating to active diplomatic negotiations and plans (so long as the underlying policy had been clearly stated), information relating to intelligence collection (so long as the methods employed would not, if discovered, have catastrophic political potentialities). It could require that every classified document bear the name of the classifier and the date on which automatic declassification would be complete. It could lay an affirmative obligation on the executive, with penalties in case of violation, to make full disclosure regarding the commitment to combat of American troops (including the Air Force, as in Cambodia) and regarding any promises to foreign states or groups likely to result in such commitment. It could expressly restrict the Espionage Act to espionage — the clandestine delivery of state secrets to foreign nations — and forbid its application if classified information is divulged to the American people. It could even, as proposed in various forms by Muskie and by Moorhead, establish a full-time independent Classification Review Commission empowered to make sure that classification decisions met standards of reason.

It was unfortunate that presidential abuse of the secrecy system had to lead to some of these recommendations. An independent Classification Review Commission would be a cumbersome and possibly a dangerous mechanism. Some newspapermen feared that the courts might decide that documents published without clearance by the Commission were published unlawfully, even that Congress itself might endow the Commission's decisions with criminal sanctions.[82] Still the Presidency had proved it could not be trusted to run a rational secrecy system; and, if the people did not want to leave corrective therapy to the Andersons and Ellsbergs, there seemed no alternative to prudent congressional intervention.

The people, in addition, could themselves take steps to disavow the religion of secrecy. They could make it clear through their representatives, their newspapers and their actions that, if they would on occasion accept secrecy in method, they would not accept secrecy in policy, above all when policy meant commitment. On this point Wilson was everlastingly right. Few secret undertakings ever did any nation any good. Nor should any government expect to commit a nation to hostilities by engagements of which they were unaware and which their representatives had not approved. Harold Nicolson put the democratic view on this matter in memorable language: "I feel it to be the duty of every citizen in a free country to proclaim that he will not consider himself bound by any treaty entered into by the Administration behind his back." [83]

XI

If all hands (except Dr. Teller) agreed that some secrets had to be locked up for a while, the next question was: for how long — a question of obvious and particular interest to historians. In this regard the record of the American government compared favorably to that of any other government in the world. Even though the publication of the State Department's *Foreign Relations of the United States* kept falling farther behind — five years behind the year of origination by 1914, fifteen years behind by 1940, twenty-six years behind by 1972 — the United States was still ahead of every other country in the release of its diplomatic documents. Presidents tried occasionally to reduce the lag, even though neither they nor Congress seemed able to come up with enough money to enable the Department's first-rate historical office to do the job. In 1961 President Kennedy wrote the Secretary of State: "In my view, any official should have a clear and precise case involving the national interest before seeking to withhold from publication documents or papers fifteen or more years old." [84] Eleven years later President Nixon directed his Secretary of State to cut the ever-lengthening gap to twenty years.[85]

Practice abroad varied widely. When Denis Mack Smith, the leading English historian of Italy, wrote his *Victor Emmanuel, Cavour and the Risorgimento* (1971) dealing with the period from 1840 to 1870, he was denied access both to the royal archives and to Cavour's papers. Cavour had died in 1861, Victor Emmanuel in 1878. Such caution seemed excessive. In the Soviet Union and other communist countries, though the Bolsheviks threw open the czarist files with great flourishes of self-congratulation, a scholar too curious about recent history ran the risk of arrest as a subversive or expulsion as a spy. For a long time the French required clearance for the inspection of every official document after 1871; then in a burst of liberalization the

Archives Diplomatiques accepted a 30-year rule *en principe.*

In Great Britain Parliament in 1958 established a 50-year rule for Foreign Office papers and a 100-year rule for Home Office papers. Sir Alec Douglas-Home remarked as Prime Minister a few years later that his inclination "would be rather to tighten up the 50-year rule than to relax it." [86] But Harold Wilson's Labour government, with inclinations less aristocratic, reduced the closed period for the Foreign Office to thirty years. Historians of the underside of British history, denied access to records of police surveillance of radical movements, bitterly protested the continuation of the 100-year rule for the Home Office; this meant also, for example, that the dossier on Sir Roger Casement would be closed till 2016, a century after his death, even though his famous diaries were now available to scholars. In 1971 the Heath government carried the liberalization policy an important stride further by opening the cabinet records and other departmental papers for the Second World War, putting Britain in this area ahead of the United States.

In the United States, though the establishment, beginning with Franklin Roosevelt, of the system of presidential libraries enormously facilitated research in recent history,[87] and though the State Department did its best to speed up the publication of *Foreign Relations,* the historian's problem grew more complex. New and relatively impenetrable bodies — the National Security Council, the Joint Chiefs of Staff, the Central Intelligence Agency — were now playing larger and larger roles in the formation of foreign policy. The JCS and the CIA, in particular, detested the idea that independent historians might look at their operations. The raw material for history seemed increasingly inaccessible, nor did the voluminous writings of former Special Assistants to Presidents, however glittering, quite fill the gap.[88]

Historians became increasingly restless under the restrictions. Herbert Feis, whose years in the State Department gave his arguments as a scholar special weight, spoke eloquently about "the shackled historian." In a sardonic reference to the formation of NATO, he wrote in one book that "perhaps it is now possible for historians of diligence to be as well informed as the Soviet authorities in Moscow presumably were at the time." A footnote recalled that during the crucial periods of negotiation Guy Burgess was private secretary to the British Under Secretary for Foreign Affairs and Donald MacLean was First Secretary of the Embassy in Washington.[89]

Another historian, Julius Epstein of the Hoover Institution on War, Peace and Revolution, invoked the Freedom of Information Act in an attempt to gain access to Top Secret Army files on Operation Keelhaul, a shameful undertaking in which Britain and America tried to force the repatriation of displaced Soviet citizens to the Soviet Union after the Second World War. But lower courts rejected his plea on the ground, later adopted by the Supreme Court in the *Mink* case, that they could not go behind the official classification; and the Supreme Court refused *certiorari,* Justice Douglas dissenting. Eventually the American government declassified the documents but still denied them to Epstein on the ground that they were of joint origin and British concurrence had not been received.[90] The Freedom of Information Act was in any case ill-adapted for the historian since it required specific identification of required documents in advance while the scholar's habit was to roam through files and discover documents he did not know existed. Historians called this requirement Catch-22.

After the British opened their Second World War papers in 1971, the State Department was soon enabled to follow suit. In the meantime, Nixon, spurred on by discontent over the now admitted overclassification of the Pentagon Papers,[91] authorized the declassification of Second World War papers throughout the government, though this was to be done on a page-by-page basis and would take, it was estimated, 110 people, five years and $6 million. Six months later Executive Order 11652 set up an elaborate declassification schedule, ostensibly intended to declassify everything after ten years. A number of exemptions, however, could delay declassification in many cases for as long as thirty years and in some cases indefinitely. Moreover, the order incorporated Catch-22 by specifying that the historian must describe a document "with sufficient particularity" to enable the Department to identify and discover it "with only a reasonable amount of effort." The result, as Felix Belair, Jr., wrote in the *New York Times* was that the Nixon order made "access to classified information more difficult rather than the reverse." [92]

The question remained: how long should secret materials be locked up? Moss and Gravel said two years; Moorhead and Muskie said three. George Ball, an ex-Under Secretary of State, said five years — a significant concession from a notably astute veteran of the executive branch. His former boss Dean Rusk said twenty years, and Rusk's former boss Dean Acheson said twenty-five. Historians tended to come in between. They were concerned, first of all, that precipitate declassification might dilute the research quality of documentary records. Robert J. Donovan's book of 1956 *Eisenhower: The Inside Story* drew largely from minutes of cabinet meetings made available to that excellent reporter by the White House; there was great protest over Donovan's revelations, and the keeping of cabinet minutes came to an end with the Eisenhower administration. Justice Black's will called for the destruction of his "bench notes" — working papers in advance of decision — because he disapproved of the way A. T. Mason had used comparable notes in his life of Harlan Stone; Black's command, alas, was carried out. As Herman Kahn of Yale, the historian whose services as head of the Franklin D. Roosevelt Library and later of the presidential libraries system have benefited a generation of scholars, has well said, "Scholars who push most forcefully for early access to papers run the danger of . . . drying up some sources of documentation upon which the successful accomplishment of their own work depends." [93] It was paradoxical that newspapermen, so righteous about the protection of their own sources that they clamored for a shield law, should also clamor for the immediate disclosure of all internal government documentation. A moment's reflection might suggest that this, for precisely the same reasons, would have the same 'chilling effect' on sources on which they and, even more, the historian must depend.

Some scholars, in addition, especially those venerable enough to remember the days of Joe McCarthy, were not anxious to make disclosures so instantaneous as to discourage government officials from candor or heterodoxy. The McCarthy period had a dismal enough effect on the public service; think what that effect could have been if members of the foreign service had known that everything they put on paper would be submitted to Roy Cohn in the next three years. "I don't mind particularly people being embarrassed in later life," said Dean Acheson in arguing for a longer closed period; "but I should regret their being cagey and over-cautious when young." [94] This was the serious argument, though not an overriding one, against the publication of the Pentagon Papers — not that publication did any immediate damage to national security, which was nonsense, but that it might discourage frank and honest writing in the bureaucracy.

For such reasons most historians would be content to lock things up for more than three or five years but would definitely unlock them well before twenty or twenty-five. William L. Langer thus suggested that classified documents be opened "to qualified scholars" after five or ten years.[95] Langer's testimony carried particular authority; not only was he the leading American historian of European diplomacy, but he had served in important posts in the OSS and the CIA and as a member of the President's Foreign Intelligence Advisory Board. James MacGregor Burns, the author of two notable volumes on Franklin Roosevelt, proposed eight years.[96] Herbert Feis in 1967 and the American Historical Association in 1971 voted for ten years. That period — two and a half administrations — would seem about right to me.

All these rules contemplated some form of appellate procedure so that government, if it wanted to hold back specific documents, could make a case to a review board. A longer period — probably a very much longer period — should apply to documents that described intelligence operations, compromised foreigners or invaded the privacy of American citizens. Exempted documents, however, should be listed, and the lists should be available. On the other hand, codes, that old bogeyman, no longer served as a bar to blanket declassification; computers had transformed cryptography and produced ciphers that, in the words of David Kahn, "can withstand massive disclosures and that are, in all practical senses, unbreakable." [97] What historians rejected most strongly was the old method of page-by-page declassification still required by the Nixon Executive Order of 1972. Systematic declassification on this principle, Langer correctly said, "was patently impossible."

No doubt blanket declassification would let some dubious items slip through. But there were fewer sensations and scandals in those musty files than laymen imagined. Langer and Gleason wrote their two superb books on American foreign policy just before the Second World War with full access to State Department documents and published them within a dozen years or so of the events, and the republic did not come to an end. Nor did it come to an end when the MacArthur hearings of 1951 placed on the public record the inner quarrels of American policy in the two preceding years, or when Robert Donovan described the Eisenhower cabinet meetings in 1956, or when Theodore Sorensen and I in 1965 published verbatim accounts of the Kennedy-Khrushchev meeting of 1961, or when Ellsberg in 1971 gave out the Pentagon Papers.

Laymen, and government officials, grew far too excited over the idea of revealing documents of another day. The past was really not all that much a danger to the present. Surely the stronger argument ran in the opposite direction: that the republic would benefit from a more detailed knowledge of recent triumphs and follies. "I believe," Herbert Feis well said, "the American nation could stand the shock of being adequately informed about its past in time for possible improvement and correction." [98]

XII

Restraining the secrecy system would not automatically restore a congressional voice in foreign policy. But it would at least deprive Congress of a favorite alibi: that, because it did not have the facts, it had no choice but to let Presidents make the decisions. This plea of ignorance was not entirely disingenuous. Neither normal legislative processes nor personal experience brought members of Congress the sort of intelligence on foreign affairs they received every day on domestic affairs. Constituents, committee hearings, newspapers, wives and children kept them well informed on the impact of internal policies; in any case they considered themselves in this field fully the intellectual equals of the executive branch. But in foreign affairs, with little in the way of experience, confidence or independent sources of information, they were undoubtedly far more at the mercy of what the executive chose to tell them.

But this was not, alas, the whole story. When Congress had ridden high on foreign policy in the 1930s, its members rejected information from the executive simply, so far as one can see, because they did not like to disturb their own preconceptions. Like Borah in 1939, they supposed they had better sources of information; or like Vandenberg in 1939–1941 they denounced the "pressure and propaganda" of the Roosevelt administration, only to complain a week after Pearl Harbor that the executive had not told them enough about the aggressive Japanese.[99] The demonstration that Congress did not after all know best helped explain the subsequent congressional determination to avoid responsibility for national security decisions. "I have had the experience of giving information to some Members of Congress," Dean Rusk observed in 1971, "who have said to me, gee, I wish you hadn't told me that. I really don't want to know that kind of thing." [100] When Gravel sent fellow senators classified documents relating to Project Cannikin, one wrote back, "As soon as I opened this up I immediately saw it was classified information. I closed it and I am sending it back to you, Mike, because I won't read it until somebody gives me the authority to read it." [101] To a considerable degree Congress over the last generation has remained ignorant about foreign policy because it has preferred to be ignorant. It was better not to be accountable. Few votes were lost by backing the President in foreign affairs, many were gained; and, if things went wrong, it was the President's responsibility.

In later years the myth arose that the secrecy system kept

from Congress and the people the crucial facts about the deepening American involvement in Vietnam. It was simply not true, however, that successive administrations lied the republic into that fatal war. Smaller lies along the way made it hard to believe the word of government, but the larger truth was never concealed, even in spite of the government. Examination of the newspapers of the time showed, as Henry Fairlie concluded after his study of the years 1961–1963, that "there was always sufficient knowledge within the public realm on which to form a political judgment." The press thus told the people in 1961 of the presumed urgency of the situation, of the decision to strengthen the American commitment, of the plans to develop counter-insurgency operations. "Every effort should be made to save the situation," said the *New York Times* in one editorial that year, and in another: "To accept it as a matter of course is to hand the Communists half a victory without a fight." In 1963 the *Times* criticized Kennedy for calling Vietnam "their war"; it was, the *Times* said, "our war — a war from which we cannot retreat and which we dare not lose." "From its correspondents at home and abroad," Fairlie wrote in 1973, *"The New York Times* was receiving and publishing the clearest evidence of what was being done. If it failed 10 years ago to understand the significance of what its own reporters were saying, it seems unjust for it to turn around now and say it was deceived by the politicians." [102]

The Pentagon Papers came to many Americans with the shock of revelation. Yet again, as Richard Harwood wrote in the *Washington Post,* "The substance and in some cases the precise details of virtually everything the *Washington Post* and the *New York Times* have printed from the Pentagon papers is ancient history. It was nearly all published while it was happening." The 'options,' the contingency plans, the widening American combat role, the commitment of American helicopters to the battlefields, the role of the Special Forces, the guerrilla raids into North Vietnam, the use of napalm — all were reported "repeatedly and accurately." Peter Arnett, who covered the war in Vietnam for the Associated Press for nearly a decade, reached the same conclusion: "Through leaks and reporters' observations in Vietnam, the press told much of the story, including matters now mistakenly thought to have been revealed to the American public for the first time in the Pentagon Papers." It was all, or nearly all, in the newspapers; but, as Harwood said, it was a futile enterprise; "neither the public nor the congressional politicians were listening." [103]

It may be said, of course, that many conflicting stories appeared in the press and that the public and Congress had no means for deciding which among them were accurate. That was true enough of the public. But it was not true of Congress. For, unlike the public in general, Congress always had the means, if it wished to use them, to discover the truth. Congress has in fact the power to learn almost anything it really wants to know. But it must *want* to know — and accept the risk that knowledge means an acceptance of responsibility.

Wilson said long ago that the "informing function" of Congress was even to be preferred to its legislative function.[104] If Congress were determined to inform the people, there were a great many things it could do. It could, for example, build up the professional staffs of its committees. It could, like the Symington Committee, send staff members to 23 countries to dig out what the executive branch had declined to tell. It could relieve the Congressional Research Service of its obligation to do short-term research for congressmen and their constituents and transform it into a policy-research institute for Congress. It could enact the bill introduced in 1971 by one of the wisest of senators, John Sherman Cooper of Kentucky, to establish as a matter of law that CIA intelligence analyses be made available to relevant committees in the same manner that the Atomic Energy Commission was required under law to give information to the Joint Atomic Energy Committee.[105] It could avail itself of the vast resources in the public domain and summon newspapermen, academics and informed citizens to serve as consultants for committees or witnesses in hearings.

The attainment of democratic control over American foreign policy depended in the end, and in the field of information as in every other field, on congressional will. The events of the sixties had exploded the notion of presidential infallibility, as the events of the thirties had ended the idea that Congress knew best. The time had come when a chastened Presidency and a responsible Congress had the chance to re-establish the partnership envisaged by the Constitution.

11

The Future of the Presidency

"THE TYRANNY of the legislature is really the danger most to be feared, and will continue to be so for many years to come," Jefferson wrote Madison six weeks before Washington's first inauguration. "The tyranny of the executive power will come in its turn, but at a more distant period." [1] On the eve of the second centennial of independence Jefferson's prophecy appeared on the verge of fulfillment. The imperial Presidency, created by wars abroad, was making a bold bid for power at home. The belief of the Nixon administration in its own mandate and in its own virtue, compounded by its conviction that the republic was in mortal danger from internal enemies, had produced an unprecedented concentration of power in the White House and an unprecedented attempt to transform the Presidency of the Constitution into a plebiscitary Presidency. If this transformation were carried through, the President, instead of being accountable every day to Congress and public opinion, would be accountable every four years to the electorate. Between elections, the President would be accountable only through impeachment and would govern, as much as he could, by decree. The expansion and abuse of presidential power constituted the underlying issue, the issue that, as we have seen, Watergate raised to the surface, dramatized and made politically accessible. Watergate was the by-product of a larger revolutionary purpose. At the same time, it was the fatal mistake that provoked and legitimized resistance to the revolutionary Presidency.

*

I

In giving great power to Presidents, Americans had declared their faith in the winnowing processes of politics. They assumed that these processes, whether operating through the Electoral College or later through the congressional caucus or still later through the party conventions, would eliminate aspirants to the Presidency who rejected the written restraints of the Constitution and the unwritten restraints of the republican ethos.

Through most of American history that assumption had been justified. "Not many Presidents have been brilliant," Bryce observed in 1921, "some have not risen to the full moral height of the position. But none has been base or unfaithful to his trust, none has tarnished the honour of the nation." [2] Even as Bryce wrote, however, his observation was falling out of date — Warren G. Harding had just been inaugurated — and half a century later his optimism appeared as much the function of luck as of any necessity in the constitutional order. At this point the pessimism of the Supreme Court in *ex parte Milligan* seemed a good deal more prescient. The nation, as Justice Davis had written for the Court, had "no right to expect that it will always have wise and humane rulers, sincerely attached to the principles of the Constitution. Wicked men, ambitious of power, with hatred of liberty and contempt of law, may fill the place once occupied by Washington and Lincoln." [3]

The Presidency had been in crisis before; but the constitutional offense that led to the impeachment of Andrew Johnson was trivial compared to the charges now accumulating around the Nixon administration. There were, indeed, constitutional offenses here too — the abuse of impoundment and executive privilege, for example; or the secret air war against Cambodia in 1969–1970, unauthorized by and unknown to Congress; or the prosecution of the war in Vietnam after the repeal of the Tonkin Gulf Resolution; or the air war against Cambodia after the total withdrawal of American troops from Vietnam. But these, like Johnson's defiance of the Tenure of Office Act, were questions that a President might contend — till the Supreme Court decided otherwise — lay within a range of executive discretion. The Johnson case had discredited impeachment as a means of resolving arguable disagreements over the interpretation of the Constitution.

What was unique in the history of the Presidency was the long list of potential *criminal* charges against the Nixon administration. Even before the various investigations were concluded, it seemed probable that Nixon's appointees had engaged in a multitude of indictable activities: at the very least, in burglary; in forgery; in illegal wiretapping; in illegal electronic surveillance; in perjury; in subornation of perjury; in obstruction of justice; in destruction of evidence; in tampering with witnesses; in misprision of felony; in bribery (of the Watergate defendants); in acceptance of bribes (from Vesco and the ITT); in conspiracy to involve government agencies (the FBI, the CIA, the Secret Service, the Internal Revenue Service, the Securities and Exchange Commission) in illegal action.

As for the President himself, he consistently denied that he had known either about the warfare of espionage and sabotage waged by his agents against his opponents or about the subsequent cover-up. If Nixon had known about these things, he had himself conspired against the basic processes of democracy. If he really had not known and for nine months had not bothered to find out, he was evidently an irresponsible and incompetent executive. For, if he did not know, it could only have been because he did not want to know. He had all the facilities in the world for discovering the facts. The courts and posterity would have to decide whether the *Spectator* of London was right in its harsh judgment that in two centuries American history had come full circle "from George Washington, who could not tell a lie, to Richard Nixon, who cannot tell the truth." [4]

Whether Nixon himself was witting or unwitting, what was clearly beyond dispute was his responsibility for the moral atmosphere within his official family. White House aides do not often do things they know their principal would not wish them to do — a proposition to which I and dozens of other former White House aides can attest from experience. It is the President who both sets the example and picks the men. What standards did Nixon establish for his White House? He himself admitted that in 1970, till J. Edgar Hoover forced him to change his mind, he authorized a series of criminal actions in knowing violation of the laws and the Constitution — authorization that would appear to be in transgression both of his presidential oath to preserve the Constitution and of his constitutional duty to see that the laws were faithfully executed. In 1971, as he also admitted, he commissioned the White House plumbers, who set out so soon thereafter on their career of burglary, wiretapping and forgery. "From the time when the break-in occurred," he said of the Watergate affair in August 1973, "I pressed repeatedly to know the facts, and particularly whether there was any involvement of anyone in the White House" [5]; but two obvious authorities — John Mitchell, his intimate friend, former law partner, former Attorney General, head of the Committee for the Re-election of the President, and Patrick Gray, acting director of the FBI itself — both testified under oath that he never got around to pressing them. He even, through John Ehrlichman, asked the Ellsberg judge in the midst of the trial whether he would not like to be head of the FBI. And he continued to hold up Ehrlichman and Haldeman as models to the nation — "two of the finest public servants it has been my privilege to know." [6]

Nixon, in short, created the Nixon White House. "There was no independent sense of morality there," said Hugh Sloan, who served in the Nixon White House for two years. ". . . If you worked for someone, he was God, and whatever the orders were, you did it. . . . It was all so narrow, so closed. . . . There emerged some kind of separate morality about things." [7] "Because of a certain atmosphere that had developed in my working at the White House," said Jeb Stuart Magruder, "I was not as concerned about its illegality as I should have been." And again: "You are living in an unreal world when you work there." [8] "The White House is another world," said John Dean. "Expediency is everything." [9] "No one who had been in the White House," said Tom Charles Huston, "could help but feel he was in a state of siege." [10] "On my first or second day in the White House," said Herbert Porter, "Dwight Chapin [the President's appointments secretary] said to me, 'One thing you should realize early on, we are practically an island here.' That was the way the world was viewed." The highest calling, said Porter, was to "protect the President" from the hostile forces surrounding that "island." The "original sin," Porter felt, was the "misuse" of young people "through the whole White House system. They were not criminals by birth or design. Left to their own devices, they wouldn't engage in this sort of thing. Someone had to be telling them to do it." [11] Gordon Strachan told of his excitement at "being 27 years old and walking into the White House and seeing the President"; but, when asked what word he had for young men or women who wanted to come to Washington and enter the public service, he said grimly, "My advice would be to stay away." [12]

This was not the White House we had known — those of us, Democrats or Republicans, who had served other Presidents in other years. An appointment to the White House of Roosevelt or Truman or Eisenhower or Kennedy or Johnson seemed the highest responsibility one could expect and called for the highest standards of behavior. And most of us looked back at our White House experience, not with shame and incredulity, as the Nixon young men did, not as the "White House horrors," but as the most splendid time in one's life. Government, as Clark Clifford said, was a chameleon, taking its color from the character and personality of the President.

Nixon's responsibility for the White House ethos went beyond strictly moral considerations. In the First Congress Madison, arguing that the power to remove government officials must belong to the President, had added, "We have in him the security for the good behavior of the officer." This made "the President responsible to the public for the conduct of the person he has nominated and appointed." If the President suffered executive officials to perpetrate crimes or neglected to superintend their conduct so as to check excesses, he himself, Madison said, would be subject to "the decisive engine of impeachment." [13]

II

The crisis of the Presidency led some critics to advocate a reconstruction of the institution itself. For a long time people had felt that the job was becoming too much for one man to handle. "Men of ordinary physique and discretion," Woodrow Wilson wrote as long ago as 1908, "cannot be President and live, if the strain be not somehow relieved. We shall be obliged always to be picking our chief magistrate from among wise and prudent athletes, — a small class." [14]

But what had been seen until the late 1950s as too exhausting physically was now seen, after Vietnam and Watergate, as too dizzying psychologically. In 1968 Eugene McCarthy, the first liberal presidential aspirant in the century to run against the Presidency, called for the depersonalization and decentralization of the office. The White House, he thought, should be turned into a museum. Instead of trying to lead the nation, the President should become "a kind of channel" for popular desires and aspirations.[15] Watergate made the point irresistible. "The office has become too complex and its reach too extended," wrote Barbara Tuchman, "to be trusted to the fallible judgment of any one individual." "A man with poor judgment, an impetuous man, a sick man, a power-mad man," wrote Max Lerner, "each would be dangerous in the post. Even an able, sensitive man needs stronger safeguards around him than exist today." [16]

The result was a new wave of proposals to transform the Presidency into a collegial institution. Mrs. Tuchman suggested a six-man directorate with a rotating chairman, each member to serve for a year, as in Switzerland. Lerner wanted to give the President a Council of State, a body that he would be bound by law to consult and that, because half its members would be from Congress and some from the opposite party, would presumably give him independent advice. Both proposals had, in fact, been considered and rejected in the Constitutional Convention.[17] That was no argument against considering them again.

Still, the reasons why the Founding Fathers turned them down were worth noting. When James Wilson first moved in the Convention that the executive consist of a single person, there ensued, as Madison put it in his notes, "a considerable pause." Finally Benjamin Franklin observed that this was an important point and he would like to hear some discussion. Wilson said that a single magistrate would impart "most energy, dispatch and responsibility" to the office. Edmund Randolph of Virginia then strenuously opposed the idea as "the foetus of monarchy," proposing instead a three-man magistracy. Eventually the Convention agreed with Wilson, though not before it gave serious thought to surrounding the President with a Council of State, which might include the Chief Justice, the President of the Senate and the Speaker of the House as well as the heads of the executive departments. George Mason of Virginia said that, if the Convention did not establish a Council of State, the new republic would embark on "an experiment on which the most despotic Governments had never ventured. The Grand Signor himself had his Divan." Franklin thought a Council "would not only be a check on a bad President but be a relief to a good one." But the Convention rejected the idea, not, it should be noted, because it considered such a Council in violation of the separation of powers, but because, as Charles Pinckney of South Carolina put it, the President ought to be authorized to call for advice or not as he might choose. "Give him an able Council and it will thwart him; a weak one and he will shelter himself under their sanction." [18]

Hamilton and Jefferson disagreed on many things, but they agreed that the Convention had been right in deciding on a one-man Presidency. A plural executive, Hamilton contended, if divided within itself, would lead the country into factionalism and anarchy and, if united, could lead it into tyranny. When power was placed in the hands of a group small enough to admit "of their interests and views being easily combined in a common enterprise, by an artful leader," Hamilton thought, "it becomes more liable to abuse, and more dangerous when abused, than if it be lodged in the hands of one man, who, from the very circumstances of his being alone, will be more narrowly watched and more readily suspected. . . . From such a combination

America would have more to fear, than from the ambition of any single individual." With a single executive it was possible to fix accountability. But a directorate "would serve to destroy, or would greatly diminish, the intended and necessary responsibility of the Chief Magistrate himself." [19]

Jefferson had favored a plural executive under the Articles of Confederation, and, as an American in Paris, he had watched with sympathy the *Directoire* of the French Revolution. But these experiments left him no doubt that plurality was a mistake. As he later observed, if Washington's cabinet, in which he had served with Hamilton, had been a directorate, "the opposing wills would have balanced each other and produced a state of absolute inaction." But Washington, after listening to both sides, acted on his own, providing the "regulating power which would keep the machine in steady movement." History, moreover, furnished "as many examples of a single usurper arising out of a government by a plurality, as of temporary trusts of power in a single hand rendered permanent by usurpation." [20]

The question remained whether the world had changed enough in two centuries to make these objections obsolete. There was, of course, the burden-of-the-Presidency argument. But had the presidential burden become so much heavier than ever before? The scope of the national government had expanded beyond imagination, but so too had the facilities for presidential management. The only President who clearly died of overwork was Polk, and that was a long time ago. Hoover, who worked intensely and humorlessly as President, lived for more than thirty years after the White House; Truman, who worked intensely and gaily, lived for twenty. The contemporary President was really not all that overworked. Eisenhower managed more golf than most corporation officials or college presidents; Kennedy always seemed unhurried and relaxed; Nixon spent almost as much time in Florida and California as in Washington, or so it appeared. Johnson's former press secretary, George Reedy, dealt with the myth of the presidential workload in terms that rejoiced anyone who had ever served in the White House. "There is far less to the presidency, in terms of essential activity," Reedy correctly said, "than meets the eye." The President could fill his hours with as much motion as he desired; but he also could delegate as much "work" as he desired. "A president moves through his days surrounded by literally hundreds of people whose relationship to him is that of a doting mother to a spoiled child. Whatever he wants is brought to him immediately — food, drink, helicopters, airplanes, people, in fact, everything but relief from his political problems." [21]

As for the moral and psychological weight of these political problems, this was real enough. All major presidential decisions were taken in conditions of what General Marshall, speaking of battle, used to call "chronic obscurity" — that is, on the basis of incomplete and probably inaccurate intelligence, with no sure knowledge where the enemy was or even where one's own men were. This could be profoundly anguishing for reasonably sensitive Presidents, especially when decisions determined people's livelihoods or ended their lives. It was this, and not the workload, that did in Wilson and the second Roosevelt. But was the sheer moral weight of decision greater today than ever before? greater for Johnson and Nixon than for Washington and Lincoln or Wilson or FDR? One doubted it very much.

If there was an argument for a plural executive, it was not the alleged burden of the Presidency. The serious argument was simply to keep one man from wielding too much power. But here the points of Hamilton and Jefferson still had validity. The Council of Ten in Venice was surely as cruel as any doge. One wonders whether a six-man Presidency would have prevented the war in Vietnam. It might well, however, have prevented the New Deal. The single-man Presidency, with the right man as President, had its uses; and historically Americans had as often as not chosen the right man.

The idea of a Council of State had more plausibility. But it would work better for foreign than for domestic policy. A prudent President would be well advised to convoke *ad hoc* Councils of State on issues of war and peace. Kennedy added outsiders to his Executive Committee during the Cuban missile crisis; and it was an *ad hoc* Council of State in March 1968 that persuaded Johnson to cease and desist in Vietnam. But, as an institutionalized body, with membership the *ex officio* perquisite of the senior leadership of House and Senate — that is, of the men in Congress who in the past had always been more inclined to go along with Presidents — it could easily become simply one more weapon for a strong President. As Gouverneur Morris said at the Convention, the President "by persuading his Council . . . to concur in his wrong measures would acquire their protection for them." [22]

Above all, both the plural executive and the Council of State were open to the objection that most concerned the Founding Fathers — the problem of fixing accountability. In the case of high crimes and misdemeanors, who, to put it bluntly, was to be impeached? James Wilson once compared the situations in this regard of England and the United States. There the King's counselors interposed an "impenetrable barrier" between power and responsibility. But "in the United States, our first executive magistrate is not onubilated behind the mysterious obscurity of counsellors. Power is communicated to him with liberality, though with ascertained limitations. To him [alone] the provident or improvident use of it is to be ascribed." [23] The more convincing solution surely lay not in diffusing and blurring responsibility for the actions of the executive but in making that responsibility categorical and in finding ways of holding Presidents to it.

III

The other change in the institution of the Presidency under discussion in the early 1970s ran in the opposite direction. The idea of a single six-year presidential term was obviously designed not to reduce but to increase the independence of the Presidency. This idea naturally appealed to the imperial ethos. Lyndon Johnson advocated it; Nixon commended it to his Commission on Federal Election Reform for particular study. What was more puzzling was that it also had the support of two eminent senators, both unsympathetic to the imperial Presidency, Mike Mansfield of Montana and George Aiken of Vermont — support that gave it a hearing it would not otherwise have had.

It was not a new idea. Andrew Jackson had recommended to Congress an amendment limiting Presidents to a single term of four or six years; Andrew Johnson had done the same; the Confederate Constitution provided for a single six-year term; Hayes proposed a single six-year term and Taft a single term of six or seven years. Mansfield and Aiken now pressed their version on the ground, as Mansfield said, that a six-year term would "place the Office of the Presidency in a position that transcends as much as possible partisan political considerations." The amendment, said Aiken, "would allow a president to devote himself entirely to the problems of the Nation and would free him from the millstone of partisan politics." [24]

This argument had a certain old-fashioned good-government plausibility. How nice it would be if Presidents could be liberated from politics for six years and set free to do only what was best for the country! But the argument assumed that Presidents knew better than anyone else what was best for the country and that the democratic process was an obstacle to wise decisions. It assumed that Presidents were so generally right and the people so generally wrong that the President had to be protected against political pressures. It was, in short, a profoundly anti-democratic position. It was also profoundly unrealistic to think that any constitutional amendment could transport a President to some higher and more immaculate realm and still leave the United States a democracy. As Thomas Corcoran told the Senate Judiciary Committee during hearings on the Mansfield-Aiken amendment, "It is impossible to take politics out of politics." [25]

But, even if it were possible to take the Presidency out of politics, was there reason to suppose this desirable? The electorate often knew things that Presidents did not know; and the nation had already paid a considerable price for presidential isolation and ignorance. Few things were more likely to make Presidents sensitive to public opinion than worries about their own political future. Even if public opinion was at times a baneful influence, what else was democracy all about? The need to persuade the nation of the soundness of a proposed policy was the heart of democracy. "A President immunized from political considerations," Clark Clifford told the Senate Judiciary Committee, "is a President who need not listen to the people, respond to majority sentiment, or pay attention to views that may be diverse, intense and perhaps at variance with his own." [26] To release the President from the discipline of consent would be to create irresponsible Presidents. The idea of a President 'above politics' was plainly hostile to the genius of democracy.

The six-year concept, moreover, had marked disadvantages. In the eighteenth century, when the pace of change was relatively slow, the country could afford a six-year Presidency. Still, Jefferson, who began by favoring a seven-year term, decided that "service for eight years, with a power to remove at the end of the first four" was better. [27] In the nineteenth century, as President Kennedy used to point out, a politician had to know only three or four issues, and these issues dominated political life for a generation. But in the twentieth century, with the enormous acceleration in the rate of change, new problems piled up on government in unprecedented variety and with unprecedented rapidity. Six years in the second half of the twentieth century were equivalent in terms of change to a generation in the first half of the nineteenth century; and, given the onward rush of contemporary life, the nation could hardly afford to place in power for so long a time an administration that might lack the capacity or the will to meet fresh problems with fresh solutions. A four-year term gave both the President and the voters a fair test. If they approved his general course, they could then re-elect him for four years more.

The Mansfield-Aiken amendment expressed distrust of the democratic process in still another way — by its bar against re-eligibility. If anything was of the essence of democracy, it was surely that the voters should have an unconstrained choice of their leaders. "I can see no propriety," George Washington wrote the year after the adoption of the Constitution, "in precluding ourselves from the service of any man, who on some great emergency shall be deemed universally most capable of serving the public." [28] Hamilton brilliantly amplified this argument in the 72nd Federalist. The ban against indefinite re-eligibility, he said, would result in "the banishing men from stations in which, in certain emergencies of the state, their presence might be of the greatest moment to the public interest or safety . . . perhaps it would not be too strong to say, to the preservation of [the nation's] political existence."

There was a great deal to be said for the two-term principle as a tradition; in all normal circumstances it should be controlling. But it had proved itself sufficiently effective as a tradition. The only time the tradition was violated was in precisely the circumstances envisaged by Washington and Hamilton. And there was nothing to be said for setting the two-term tradition in concrete via the 22nd Amendment. Except for the 18th and the 22nd, constitutional amendments had invariably enlarged rather than restricted the rights of the people; and the 18th was in due course repealed. In 1912 when Congress had an equivalent of the Mansfield-Aiken amendment under consideration, Wilson observed that the nation appeared to be going in two opposite directions at the same time: "We are seeking in every way to extend the power of the people, but in the matter of the presidency we fear and distrust the people and seek to bind them hand and foot by rigid constitutional provision. My own mind is not agile enough to be both ways." He concluded, "We singularly belie our own principles by seeking to determine by fixed constitutional provision what the people shall determine for themselves and are perfectly competent to determine for themselves. We cast a doubt upon the whole theory of popular government." [29]

If the 22nd Amendment seemed on its face a restraint on the imperial Presidency, events had shown it totally ineffective. Though its retention or repeal was not one of the momentous issues of the age, it remained an anomaly in a generally democratic Constitution.

IV

Oddly the crisis of the imperial Presidency did not elicit much support for what at other times had been a favored theory of constitutional reform: movement in the direction of the British parliamentary system. This was particularly odd because, whatever the general balance of advantage between the parliamentary and presidential modes, the parliamentary system had one feature the presidential system badly needed in the 1970s — the requirement that the head of government be compelled at regular intervals to explain and defend his policies in face-to-face sessions with the political opposition. Few devices, it would seem, would be better calculated both to break down the real isolation of the latter-day Presidency and to dispel the spurious reverence that had come to envelop the office.

In a diminished version, applying only to members of the cabinet, the idea was nearly as old as the republic itself. The proposal that cabinet members should go on to the floor of Congress to answer questions and take part in debate, "far from raising any constitutional difficulties," as E. S. Corwin once observed, "has the countenance of early practice under the Constitution." [30] Justice Story contended for it in his *Commentaries* because it would require the President to appoint strong men to his cabinet and require the cabinet to justify the administration's program before the Congress, thereby making for openness and responsibility in government. The Confederate Constitution authorized Congress to grant the head of each executive department "a seat upon the floor of either House, with the privilege of discussing any measures appertaining to his department," and Congressman George H. Pendleton of Ohio, with the support of Congressman James A. Garfield, argued for a similar proposal in the Union Congress in 1864. In 1881 Pendleton, now a senator and the champion of civil service reform, renewed the proposal in a rather impressive report supported, among others, by James G. Blaine. In his last State of the Union message Taft suggested that cabinet members be given access to the floor in order, as he later put it, "to introduce measures, to advocate their passage, to answer questions, and to enter into debate as if they were members, without of course the right to vote. . . . The time lost in Congress over useless discussion of issues that might be disposed of by a single statement from the head of a department, no one can appreciate unless he has filled such a place." [31]

In the meantime, the young Woodrow Wilson had carried the idea a good deal further toward the British model, arguing that cabinet members should not just sit voteless in Congress but should be actually chosen "from the ranks of the legislative majority." Instead of the chaotic and irresponsible system of government by congressional committees, the republic would then have cabinet government and ministerial responsibility.[32] Though Wilson did not renew this specific proposal in later years, it very likely lingered in the back of his mind. On the eve of his first inauguration he noted that the position of the Presidency was "quite abnormal, and must lead eventually to something very different." "Sooner or later," the President must be made "answerable to opinion in a somewhat more informal and intimate fashion — answerable, it may be, to the Houses whom he seeks to lead, either personally or through a cabinet, as well as to the people for whom they speak. But that is a matter to be worked out." [33]

Wilson never found time to work it out. Those who followed in his footsteps moved from his concern with the President's personal answerability back to the more general problem of the accountability of the cabinet. Before the Second World War Corwin proposed that the President construct his cabinet from a joint legislative council created by the two houses of Congress.[34] Representative Estes Kefauver of Tennessee soon revived the Story-Pendleton-Taft idea to the applause of Walter Lippmann. After the war Thomas K. Finletter set forth a well-argued and ingenious scheme of collaboration between the two branches in his book *Can Representative Government Do the Job?* Finletter saw a joint executive-legislative cabinet as the keystone of a system in which the President could, if faced by legislative stalemate, dissolve the government and call for new elections. Congress obviously had the power to force dissolution itself by rejecting the proposals of the joint cabinet. Finletter distinguished this process from the parliamentary model because it preserved the direct election of the President, the independence of the executive branch, decentralized parties, the federal system, judicial review and, at least in the form contemplated by the Founding Fathers, the separation of powers.[35]

But in the 1970s there appeared little interest in reforms that squinted at parliamentarianism. This may have been in part because the parliamentary regimes best known in America — the British and French — had themselves moved in the direction of prime-ministerial or presidential government [36] and offered few guarantees against the Vietnam-Watergate effect. Kevin Phillips did not elaborate on his proposal of a "new system" tying Congress and the executive together. In 1973, however, Senator Walter Mondale of Minnesota offered a version of the Story-Pendleton-Taft-Kefauver idea, proposing that heads of executive departments be required to appear before the Senate for a weekly question hour on live television.[37]

If enacted, such a question hour, though it still excluded Presidents, hedged more than ever now with divinity, might well force them to appoint stronger and therefore more independent men to their cabinets; and it would certainly increase the flow of information and counsel between the two branches. But it would also threaten the vested prerogatives of congressional committees. As for the President, a question hour could subtly alter the balance of his personal power both as against his cabinet, whose members would have the chance to acquire new visibility and develop their own relationships with Congress and the electorate, and as against Congress, which would have the opportunity of playing off his own cabinet against him. Most of all, the fear of plunging into the unknown operated on both sides as a barrier to a change that might have unforseen and quite extensive consequences for the traditional system.[38]

v

The problem of reining in the runaway Presidency, as it was conceived in the 1970s, centered a good deal more on substantive than on structural solutions. Congress, in other words, decided it could best restrain the Presidency by enacting specific legislation in the conspicuous fields of presidential abuse. The main author of this comprehensive congressional attack on presidential supremacy was, well before Watergate, Senator Sam Ervin of North Carolina.

The republic owed a great deal to Sam Ervin. No one for a long time had done so much to educate the American people in the meaning and majesty of the Constitution (though his Constitution seemed to stop with the ten amendments adopted in 1791; at least he never showed the same zeal for the 14th and 15th Amendments). For most Americans the Constitution had become a hazy document, cited like the Bible on ceremonial occasions but forgotten in the daily transactions of life. For Ervin the Constitution of 1787, like the Bible, was superbly alive and fresh. He quoted it as if it had been written the day before; the Founding Fathers seemed his contemporaries; it was almost as if he had ambled over himself from the Convention at Philadelphia. He was a true believer who endowed his faith with abundant charm, decency, sagacity and toughness. The old-fashioned Constitution — "the very finest document ever to come from the mind of men" [39] — could have had no more fitting champion in the battle against the revolutionary Presidency.

But Ervin was concerned with more than the vindication of the Constitution. His larger design was to establish a new balance of constitutional power. Congress itself, Ervin thought, had negligently become "the chief aggrandizer of the Executive." [40] The restoration of the Constitution, he believed, required the systematic recovery by Congress of powers appropriated by the Presidency. The war powers bills were, in his view, a confused and sloppy application of this strategy; he had little use for them. His own approach, direct and unequivocal, was expressed in the bill in which he proposed to give Congress absolute authority to veto executive agreements within sixty days. [41] Congress had never had, or even seriously sought, such authority before. While the provocation was real enough, the bill if enacted would give Congress unprecedented control over the presidential conduct of foreign affairs.

A leading item on Ervin's domestic agenda was executive privilege. This question, as we have seen, had been historically one of conflicting and unresolved constitutional claims. In the nineteenth century, while insisting on a general congressional right to executive information, Congress had acknowledged a right, or at least a power, of presidential denial in specific areas. It acquiesced in these reservations because they seemed reasonable and because responsible opinion outside Congress saw them as reasonable. But what Congress had seen as an expression of comity the Presidency in the later twentieth century came to see as its inherent and unreviewable right. Still both Congress and the Presidency had taken care to avoid a constitutional showdown.

The Nixon administration, with its extravagant theory of an absolute privilege covering everything, whether related or not to the performance of official duties, made a showdown almost inevitable. Some legal scholars — Raoul Berger, for example — remembering Madison's injunction in the 49th Federalist that neither branch could "pretend to an exclusive or superior right of settling the boundaries between their respective powers," argued that the question should be bucked over to the courts. Nixon himself said in early 1973 that, if the Senate wanted a court test, "we would welcome it. Perhaps this is the time to have the highest court of the land make a definitive decision with regard to the matter." [42] But the judiciary had traditionally steered clear of this question. "The federal courts," as Justice Douglas said in another connection in 1972, "do not sit as an *ombudsman,* refereeing the disputes between the other two branches." [43]

But could not courts handle the denial of executive information to Congress as they were coming to handle denial of such information to the courts themselves — that is, by judicial inspection of the documents *in camera* to determine whether the executive had a case for withholding them? In 1953, the Supreme Court had reserved for judges the power to "determine whether circumstances are appropriate for the claim of privilege" and added, "Judicial control over the evidence in a case cannot be subordinated to the caprice of executive officers." [44] In this case, the documents involved national security; and the Court did not order their inspection. But the trend of lower court decisions in the early 1970s was plainly to favor judicial examination of documents, even those allegedly concerned with national security, in order to decide whether or not they were admissible as evidence. "No executive official or agency," the Court of Appeals for the District of Columbia said in 1971, "can be given absolute authority to determine what documents in his possession may be considered by the court. . . . Otherwise the head of any executive department would have the power on his own say so to cover up all evidence of fraud and corruption when a federal court or grand jury was investigating malfeasance in office, and this is not the law." [45] The lower courts made similar rulings in the case of the Nixon tapes. A district judge proposed the same solution when the Nixon White House, in an even more sweeping claim of privilege, asserted absolute power to withhold documents that it admitted had no bearing on national security. This was a case arising from Nixon's decision to increase government price supports for milk after the dairy industry contributed $422,500 to his re-election campaign.[46]

Still, the willingness of judges to assert control over evidence in trials by no means assured an equivalent willingness to assert control over the communication of information between the Presidency and Congress. On the other hand, in other critical controversies like the steel seizure case of 1952, the Court had indeed sat as an *ombudsman* and settled disputes between the other two branches. Should the Court rule on the invocation of executive privilege against Congress, one trusts that the Justices will respond in the spirit of Felix Frankfurter, who somewhere said: "Democratic government may indeed be defined as the government which accepts in the fullest sense responsibility to explain itself."

Congress, in any case, was in no mood to wait. The Senate Foreign Relations Committee, for example, felt it had been denied too much information too long and for too little reason. The Presidency and the State Department thus had only themselves to blame if, when the Senate, after its years of docility, struck back, it overdestroyed the target. In ultimate frustration, Congress passed a bill in 1973 saying that, if the State Department, the United States Information Agency, the Agency for International Development, the Arms Control and Disarmament Agency and other agencies involved in international affairs did not furnish information requested by Congress within 35 days, their funds would be cut off. This was a draconian solution produced by an hubristic policy. The State Department complained that diplomats could not do their job if every cable was turned over to Congress; but the fear was fanciful, and in any case the Nixon administration should have thought of this before it contemptuously denied committees of Congress — committees to which Franklin Roosevelt and George C. Marshall had confided the most secret intelligence in the midst of a rather more considerable national crisis — such things as the Pentagon's five-year program for foreign military aid and, heaven help us, the country program memoranda from the USIA.[47]

Appropriations provided one handle on the problem of executive privilege. Another, and the one favored by Sam Ervin, was to meet the problem head-on. The Ervin bill, based on an earlier bill introduced by Senator Fulbright, required members of the executive branch summoned by a committee of Congress to appear in person, even if they were intending to claim executive privilege. Only a personal letter from the President could warrant the claim; and the Fulbright-Ervin bill gave the committee the power to decide whether the presidential plea was justified. As Fulbright said, it placed "the final responsibility for judging the validity of a claim of executive privilege in the Congress, where it belongs." [48]

A presidential thesis in violation of the traditional comity between the two branches thus produced a congressional answer that would itself do away with what had been not only an historic but an healthy ambiguity. For 180 years the arbiter in this question had been neither Congress nor the President nor the courts but the political context and process, with responsible opinion considering each case more or less on merit and turning against whichever side appeared to be overreaching itself. The system was not tidy, but it encouraged a measure of restraint on both sides and avoided the constitutional showdown. Now absolute presidential claims provoked an absolute congressional response.

Would this really be an improvement? Would Fulbright and Ervin themselves twenty years earlier have wanted to give Joe McCarthy and his committee "the final responsibility" to judge whether executive testimony could be properly withheld? In the area of executive privilege as well as of executive agreements, Nixon's revolutionary conception of the Presidency finally forced Congress into sweeping and dramatic proposals of self-defense.

VI

Next in the Ervin agenda to the achievement of congressional control over executive information stood the restoration of congressional control over something Congress thought peculiarly its own — the power of the purse. This meant a solution of the problem of presidential impoundment. Impoundment had existed before Nixon, but no previous President had used it to overturn statutes and abolish programs against congressional will. For Nixon impoundment had become a means of taking from Congress the determination of national priorities.

The courts were by no means so diffident about impoundment as they had initially been about executive privilege. In decision after decision in 1973, judges declared one aspect after another of the impoundment policy illegal. No judge accepted Nixon's claim that he had a "constitutional right" not to spend money voted by Congress. One judge called his use of impoundment "a flagrant abuse of executive discretion." "It is not within the discretion of the Executive," said another, "to refuse to execute laws passed by Congress but with which the Executive presently disagrees." [49] The decisions were, however, as they should have been, constructions of specific statutes and stopped short of proposing a general solution to the impoundment controversy.

Though the courts had rallied splendidly, it was not really very satisfactory to have to sue the executive branch in every case in order to make it carry out programs duly enacted by Congress. But Congress itself found it hard to make a stand on the Constitution. For Nixon had changed the issue with some success from a constitutional to a budgetary question. Impound-ment, in other words, was alleged as the only answer a fiscally responsible President could make to insensate congressional ex-travagance. Sam Ervin derided this proposition. "Congress," he said, "is not composed of wild-eyed spenders, nor is the Presi-dent the embattled crusader against wasteful spending that he would have you believe." The figures bore Ervin out. Congress, for example, had cut more than $20 billion from administration appropriation requests in Nixon's first term. Congress and the Presidency roughly agreed on the amount of money government should spend but disagreed, as Ervin put it, "over spending priorities and [the President's] authority to pick and choose what programs he will fund." Impoundment, said Ervin, had to do not with the budget but with the separation of powers. "I have voted against many of the programs for which the Presi-dent has impounded funds, but I do not believe that we should allow him to nullify acts of Congress by executive fiat. There is not one syllable in the Constitution which authorizes the Presi-dent to exercise such power." [50]

Many members of Congress, however, accepted the view that Congress could not reclaim the appropriation power granted it by the Constitution until it first established its own system of fiscal discipline. Orderly-minded members of Congress, indeed, had long liked the idea of a congressional budget to serve as a baseline from which to criticize the executive budget. Congress might even, it was thought, regain the role in budget-making it had enjoyed in the early republic. For the Presidency had not al-ways been in firm command of the budget. Until the Civil War the Senate Finance Committee and the House Ways and Means Committee had each a comprehensive view of national spending while the Presidency was without any sort of central budget con-trol. The United States, as Woodrow Wilson wrote in 1885, had "a financial policy directed by the representative body itself, with only clerical aid from the executive." [51] However, this had al-ready begun to change. The Senate Finance Committee doled out some of its powers to the Appropriations Committee (estab-lished in 1867) and the Banking and Currency Committee

(1913). The House Ways and Means Committee similarly delegated a share of its powers to the Appropriations Committee
(1865) and a diversity of particular committees. As responsibility was thus scattered among committees, Congress increasingly
regarded each spending bill as a separate entity and lost any
ability it might once have had to decide among competing priorities. Then the Presidency obtained a unified budget office
through the passage of the Budget and Accounting Act in 1921,
and the balance of control shifted decisively toward the executive.

As early as 1939 Roosevelt's Secretary of the Treasury, Henry
Morgenthau, Jr., proposed that the appropriations and tax committees of both houses constitute themselves as a single joint
committee on the federal budget.[52] Congress remained indiffer-
ent to the idea till 1973 when a Joint Study Committee recommended a somewhat similar process designed to produce a unified congressional budget.[53] This vision, however, really ran
against the grain of Congress, a body capable under extreme
provocation of uniting against a constitutionally insensitive and
aggressive President but normally divided within itself by
deeply rooted differences of party, section and ideology. While the
Nixon Presidency induced a momentary sense of congressional
unity, a more skillful President could readily restore the customary situation where members of Congress felt more solidarity
with a President of their own party than with colleagues of the
opposite party. In that more usual situation, a unified budgetary
process would not be likely to produce a unified result. Indeed, it
could be argued that Congress should build on its strength,
which lay precisely in its responsiveness to a diversity of particular pressures, and try to identify choices rather than to seek an
institutional position.

It was a political fact, however, fully recognized by Ervin,
that anti-impoundment legislation would have to be accompanied by evidences of congressional self-control in spending. He
was personally a budget-balancer anyway. So his impoundment
bill included a spending ceiling. The bill, as passed by the Senate
in 1973, also had certain eccentricities for a constitutional fun-

damentalist. After a clear statement in Section 1 that impoundment was unconstitutional, subsequent sections said that nevertheless the President was authorized to commit this unconstitutional act for periods up to seventy days. Thereafter impoundments not covered by the anti-deficiency laws must cease unless Congress specifically approved them by concurrent resolution. The House, on the other hand, was quite willing to let impoundments stand unless specifically disapproved by one house of Congress. Both bills legitimized impoundment; but, where the House would place the burden on Congress in each case to stop impoundment, Ervin would place the burden on the President in each case to justify impoundment.

A strong argument could be made for conceding Presidents leeway in the spending and transfer of appropriated funds, so long as they were not thwarting the intent of Congress when it made the appropriations. But this assumed Presidents whom Congress could trust; it assumed, in short, comity. Here as elsewhere presidential abuse produced extreme counterclaims of congressional authority. The revolutionary Presidency had tried to abolish the congressional power of the purse and make spending a matter of executive decree. The congressional reaction was to stop the President by measures that introduced rigidity into a political process which had always prospered by flexibility.

VII

There were other elements in Ervin's design. He had, for example, a bill to prevent presidential abuse of the pocket veto by defining adjournment, as used in the Constitution, to mean adjournment *sine die* and not just over the weekend or the Christmas holidays.[54] (In the meantime, a federal judge pronounced Nixon's pocket veto of the Family Practice of Medicine Act unconstitutional in response to the suit brought by Senator Edward Kennedy.) In one area after another, with the concealed passion and will of a deceptively relaxed personality, Ervin moved to restore the balance of the Constitution by cutting the Presidency down to constitutional size. But his was the "Con-

stitution not of Abraham Lincoln but of *ex parte Milligan*.
"What the framers intended," he said, "was that the President
. . . should be merely the executor of a power of decision
that rests elsewhere; that is, in the Congress. This was the
balance of power between the President and Congress intended
by the Constitution." The "ultimate power," Ervin said, was
"legislative." [55]

The Ervin scheme, in short, was a scheme of presidential subordination. Where presidential abuse of particular powers had
harmed the country, those powers were now to be vested in Congress. The authority and discretion of the Presidency were to be
held to their constitutional minimum. All this was entirely
understandable as a response to the Nixon scheme of presidential supremacy. It had great value both in checking a deluded
President and in raising the consciousness of Congress and the
people on constitutional issues. But, pursued to the end, it
could produce a national polity which, if it had many more
roots in the Constitution than the Nixon scheme, would be
almost as overbalanced in the direction of congressional supremacy as the Nixon scheme was in the direction of presidential supremacy.

The Ervin counterattack envisaged a general limitation of the
Presidency with all functions reconsidered and all powers diminished. It saw presidential power as unitary and indivisible, and
therefore to be reduced across the board. Yet the dilemma of
the Presidency was surely that presidential power was not unitary. It could well be argued that while the Presidency had come
to have too much discretion in foreign affairs, where error was
sometimes irreversible, it had too little in domestic affairs,
where error could usually be corrected. As President Kennedy
used to say, "Domestic policy can only defeat us; foreign policy
can kill us." The revolt against the Presidency had begun in reaction against extravagant assertions of unilateral presidential
power to go to war. It would be ironic if it were to end in more
binding restraints on the Presidency as an instrument of the general welfare at home.[56]

In domestic affairs the President could not claim superior information and wisdom, nor could he easily allege life-and-death

crisis and invoke patriotism and national unity, nor could he even cite the *Curtiss-Wright* case. His authority was challenged and harassed by Congress, by the permanent government establishment, by state and local governments, by reporters, by disc jockeys, by every wiseacre down the block. Where the Prime Minister in a parliamentary regime could be pretty sure that anything he proposed would become law in short order, the President of the United States could not even be sure that *his* proposals would reach the floor of Congress for debate and vote (though there was no reason why this could not be arranged by agreement with the congressional leadership).

While the American President possessed vast powers over the pattern and level of economic activity, no chief executive in any other democratic state had so little discretion in economic management. The President could reasonably be given standby authority to adjust tax rates in response to economic fluctuations, cutting taxes against recession and increasing them against inflation. But, when Kennedy asked Congress for this authority, he did not succeed even in getting a bill onto the floor. Eisenhower denounced the idea in 1962 as an example of the "thirst for more and more power centered in the Federal government . . . one-man government . . . unconscionable grab of power . . . What is Congress for?" [57] There was a strong argument also for standby spending authority, under which the President, if unemployment increased at a specified rate, would have power to release funds for public works. This was another Kennedy proposal, and it too got nowhere.

Congress resisted these eminently sensible ideas on the ground that they meant a delegation of power to the President. But, since Congress had displayed no capacity for quick action in these fields, and since the standards for delegation could be set in part by the indexes of production and employment, such delegation hardly seemed unreasonable. When, thirty years before, Franklin Roosevelt asked Congress for authority to negotiate reciprocal trade agreements and to revise tariff rates up to 50 percent either way in accordance with such agreements, there was similar congressional complaint. "This proposal," said Arthur

Vandenberg, "is Fascist in its philosophy, Fascist in its objective
. . . palpably unconstitutional . . . economic dictatorship come
to America." "We are," said Warren Austin of Vermont, "at the
parting of the ways." [58]

Both Vandenberg and Austin, as their subsequent careers
showed, came to know better. But both succumbed to facile
constitutional sophistries of the moment. If Congress had been
able to handle the tariff question in a rational way, it would
have been one thing; but a century of American history had
proved that it could not. Forty years later no one regretted this
delegation to the Presidency. I have no doubt that in time the republic will accept standby presidential authority to vary tax rates
and initiate public works, as people now accept reciprocal
trade agreements, and wonder why any serious person would
ever have objected.

VIII

It was hard to know how literally to take the Ervin scheme. If
it sounded at times like an effort to replace presidential government by congressional government, it must be remembered that
the proposals were provoked by an unprecedented attempt to
alter the political order. Ervin and his colleagues were fighting
not to frustrate the leadership of a President who recognized
his accountability to Congress and the Constitution but to
protect Congress and the Constitution from the revolutionary
Presidency. Yet, if taken literally, the Ervin scheme ran the risk
of creating a generation of weak Presidents in an age when the
turbulence of race, poverty, inflation, crime and urban decay
was straining the delicate bonds of national cohesion and demanding, quite as much as in the 1930s, a strong domestic
Presidency to hold the country together. For Sam Ervin was
of the pure Jeffersonian school, like the old Tertium Quids who
felt that Jefferson and Madison, in strengthening the Presidency
and seeing national government as an instrument of the general
welfare, had deserted the true faith. It has been noted that Ervin,
the eloquent expositor of the 1st and 4th Amendments, rarely

mentioned the 14th and 15th, and that the great constitutional champion of civil liberties had also been the great constitutional opponent of civil rights.

The pure Jeffersonian doctrine had been a witness rather than a policy, which is why Jefferson and Madison themselves abandoned it. The pure Jeffersonian idea of decentralized power receded in the course of American history because local government simply did not offer the means to attain Jeffersonian ends. In practice, pure Jeffersonianism meant a system under which the strongest local interests, whether planters, landlords, merchants, bankers or industrialists, consolidated their control and oppressed the rest; it meant all power to the neighborhood oligarchs. Theodore Roosevelt explained at the start of the twentieth century why Hamiltonian means had become necessary to achieve Jeffersonian ends, how national authority was the only effective means of correcting injustice in a national society. "If Jefferson were living in our day," said Wilson in 1912, "he would see what we see: that the individual is caught in a great confused nexus of complicated circumstances, and that . . . without the watchful interference, the resolute interference, of the government there can be no fair play." [59] And, for the first Roosevelt and for Wilson, as for their joint heir, the second Roosevelt, national authority was embodied in the Presidency.

This had not been a bad thing for the republic. It was presidential leadership, after all, that brought the country into the twentieth century, that civilized American industry, secured the rights of labor organization, defended the livelihood of the farmer. It was presidential leadership that protected the Bill of Rights against local vigilantism and natural resources against local greed. It was presidential leadership, spurred on by the Supreme Court, that sought to vindicate racial justice against local bigotry. Congress would have done few of these things on its own; local government even fewer. It would be a mistake to cripple the Presidency at home because of presidential excesses abroad. History had shown the Presidency to be the most effective instrumentality of government for justice and progress. Even Calvin Coolidge, hardly one of the more assertive of Presidents, said, "It is because in their hours of timidity the Congress becomes subservient to the importunities of organized minorities that the President comes more and more to stand as the champion of the rights of the whole country." [60]

The scheme of presidential subordination could easily be pressed to the point of national folly. But it was important to contend, not for a strong Presidency in general, but for a strong Presidency within the Constitution. The Presidency deserved to be defended on serious and not on stupid points. In 1973 Watergate produced flurries of near hysteria about the life expectancy of the institution. Thus Charles L. Black, Jr., Luce Professor of Jurisprudence at the Yale Law School, argued that, if Nixon turned over his White House tapes to Congress or the courts, it would mean the "danger of degrading or even destroying the Presidency" and constitute a betrayal of his "successors for all time to come." The republic, Professor Black said, could not even risk diluting the "symbolism" of the office lest that disturb "in the most dangerous way the balance of the best government yet devised on earth"; and it almost seemed that he would rather suppress the truth than jeopardize the symbolism.[61]

Executive privilege was not the issue. No Presidents cherished the Presidency more than, say, Jackson or Polk; but both readily conceded to Congress the right in cases of malversation to penetrate into the most secret recesses of the executive department. Nor, in the longer run, did either Ervin's hope of presidential subordination or Black's fantasy of presidential collapse have real substance. For the Presidency, though its wings could be clipped for a time, was an exceedingly tough institution. Its primacy was founded in the necessities of the American political order. It had endured many challenges and survived many vicissitudes. It was nonsense to suppose that its fate as an institution was bound up with the fate of the particular man who happened to be President at any given time. In the end power in the American order was bound to flow back to the Presidency.

Congress had a marvelous, if generally unfulfilled, capacity for oversight, for advice, for constraint, for chastening the Presidency and informing the people. When it really wanted to say No to a President, it had ample means of doing so; and in due course the President would have no choice but to acquiesce. But its purpose was, as Wilson said, "watchful criticism, talk that should bring to light the whole intention of the government and apprise those who conducted it of the real feeling and desire of the nation . . . in order that nothing which contravened the common understanding should be let pass without comment or structure, in order that measures should be insisted on which the nation needed, and measures resisted which the nation did not need or might take harm from." [62] It was inherently incapable of conducting government and providing national leadership. Its fragmentation, its chronic fear of responsibility, its habitual dependence on the executive for ideas, information and favors — this was life insurance for the Presidency.

Both Nixon and Ervin were wrong in supposing that the matter could be settled by shifting the balance of power in a decisive way to one branch or the other. The answer lay rather in preserving fluidity and re-establishing comity. Indeed, for most people — here Ervin was a distinguished exception — the constitutional and institutional issues were make-believe. It was largely a matter, as Averell Harriman said, "of whose ox is getting gored: who is in or out of power, and what actions either side may want." [63] When Nixon was in the opposition, there had been no more earnest critic of presidential presumption. Each side dressed its arguments in grand constitutional and institutional terms, but their contention was like that of the two drunken men described long ago by Lincoln who got into a fight with their greatcoats on until each fought himself out of his own coat and into the coat of the other.[64] To aficionados of constitutional controversy, this doubtless seemed reductionism; but history, in this case as in the case of the war-making power, sustained the proposition. Neutral principles! Neutral principles!

The supreme neutral principle, as vital in domestic policy as in foreign policy, was that all great decisions of the government must be shared decisions. The subsidiary principle was that, if the Presidency tried to transform what the Constitution saw as concurrent into exclusive authority, it must be stopped; and, if Congress tried to transform concurrent into exclusive authority, it must be stopped too. If either the Presidency or Congress turned against the complex balance of constitutional powers that had left room over many generations for mutual accommodation, then the ensuing collision would harm both branches of government and the republic as well. Even together Congress and the Presidency were by no means infallible; but their shared decisions, wise or foolish, at least met the standards of democracy. And, shared, the decisions were more likely to be wise than foolish. "I never came out of a committee meeting or a conference," Wilson once said, "without seeing more of the question that was under discussion than I had seen when I went in. And that to my mind is an image of government." He summed up the essential spirit of the constitutional republic: "The whole purpose of democracy is that we may hold counsel with one another, so as not to depend upon the understanding of one man, but to depend upon the counsel of all." [65]

Easier to say than to do, of course, as Wilson's subsequent career attested. All Presidents affected a belief in common counsel, but most after a time preferred to make other arrangements. Still, the idea was right, and the process of accountability had to begin inside the President himself. A constitutional President could do many things, but he had to believe in the discipline of consent. It was not enough that he personally thought the country in trouble and genuinely believed he alone knew how to save it. In all but the most extreme cases, action had to be accompanied by public explanation and tested by public acceptance. A constitutional President had to be aware of what Whitman called "the never-ending audacity of elected persons" [66] and had to understand the legitimacy of challenges to his own judgment and authority. He had to be sensitive directly to the diversity of concern and conviction in the nation, sensitive prospectively to the verdict of history, sensitive always to the decent respect pledged in the Declaration of Independence to the opinions of mankind.

Yet Presidents chosen as open and modest men were not sure

to remain so amid the intoxications of the office; and the office grew steadily more intoxicating in the later twentieth century. A wise President, having read George Reedy and observed the fates of Johnson and Nixon, would take care to provide himself, while there still was time, with passports to reality. Presidents in the last quarter of the twentieth century might, as a beginning, plan to rehabilitate (I use the word in almost the Soviet sense) the executive branch of government. This does not mean the capitulation of the Presidency to the permanent government; nor should anyone forget that it was the unresponsiveness of the permanent government that gave rise to the aggressive White House of the twentieth century. But it does mean a reduction in the size and power of the White House staff and the restoration of the access and prestige of the executive departments. The President will always need a small and alert personal staff to serve as his eyes and ears and one lobe of his brain, but he must avoid a vast and possessive staff ambitious to make all the decisions of government. Above all, he must not make himself the prisoner of a single information system. No sensible President should give one man control of all the channels of communication; any man sufficiently wise to exercise such control properly ought to be President himself.[67]

As for the cabinet, while no President in American history has found it a very satisfactory instrument of government, it has served Presidents best when it has contained men strong and independent in their own right, strong enough to make the permanent government responsive to presidential policy and independent enough to carry honest dissents into the Oval Office, even on questions apart from their departmental jurisdictions. Here again, Franklin Roosevelt, instead of being the cause of it all, was really a model of how a strong President fitted the cabinet into the constitutional order. In his first term he recognized that his reform program needed support from the progressive wings of both parties. Accordingly he brought two progressive Republicans, Wallace and Ickes, into his cabinet and took special care to work with progressive Republicans in Congress. Toward the end of his second term Roosevelt saw that foreign

policy posed a different set of political problems. He now re-
organized his cabinet to include internationalist Republicans
like Stimson and Knox. In this way FDR gained some of the
objectives and advantages of cabinet government, using the
cabinet both to broaden his base of support and to reassure
the people that there was no risk of his taking momentous decisions without the counsel of men in whom the nation reposed
trust. His idea of government was to gather round him independent and opinionated men and, up to a point, give them
their head.

While no President wants to create the impression that his
administration is out of control, FDR showed how a masterful
President could maintain the most divergent range of contacts,
surround himself with the most articulate and positive colleagues
and use debate within the executive branch as a means of clarify-
ing issues and trying out people and policies. Or perhaps FDR
was in a way the cause of it all, because he alone had the vitality,
flair and cunning to be clearly on top without repressing everything underneath. In a joke Henry Wallace, not usually a humor-
ous man, told in my hearing in 1943, FDR could keep all the
balls in the air without losing his own. Some of his successors
tried to imitate his mastery without understanding the sources of
his strength.[68]

But not every President is an FDR, and FDR himself, though
his better instincts generally won out in the end, was a flawed,
willful and, with time, increasingly arbitrary man. When Presidents begin to succumb to delusions of grandeur, when the
checks and balances inside themselves stop operating, external
checks and balances may well become necessary to save the
republic. The nature of an activist President in any case, in
Sam Lubell's phrase, was to run with the ball until he was
tackled.[69] As conditions abroad and at home nourished the imperial Presidency, tacklers had to be more than usually sturdy
and intrepid.

How to make external checks effective? Congress could tie the
Presidency down by a thousand small legal strings, but, like Gulliver and the Lilliputians, the President could always break

loose. The effective means of controlling the Presidency lay less in law than in politics. For the American President ruled by influence; and the withdrawal of consent, by Congress, by the press, by public opinion, could bring any President down. The great Presidents understood this. The President, said Andrew Jackson, must be "accountable at the bar of public opinion for every act of his Administration." [70] "I have a very definite philosophy about the Presidency," said Theodore Roosevelt. "I think it should be a very powerful office, and I think the President should be a very strong man who uses without hesitation every power that the position yields; but because of this fact I believe that he should be sharply watched by the people [and] held to a strict accountability by them." [71]

Holding a President to strict accountability required, first of all, a new attitude on the part of the American people toward their Presidents, or rather a return to the more skeptical attitude of earlier times: it required, specifically, a decline in reverence. An insistent theme in Nixon's public discourse was the necessity of maintaining due respect for the Presidency. The possibility that such respect might be achieved simply by being a good President evidently did not reassure him. He was preoccupied with 'respect for the office' as an entity in itself. Can one imagine Washington or Lincoln or the Roosevelts or Truman or Kennedy going on in public, as Nixon repeatedly did, about how important it was to do this or that in order to maintain 'respect for the office'? But the age of the imperial Presidency had in time produced the idea that run-of-the-mill politicians, brought by fortuity to the White House, must be treated thereafter as if they had become superior and perhaps godlike beings.

The Nixon theoreticians even tried to transform reverence into an ideology, propagating the doctrine, rather novel in the United States, that institutions of authority were entitled to respect *per se,* whether or not they had done anything to earn respect. If authority were denied respect, the syllogism ran, the whole social order would be in danger. "Your task, then, is clear," my friend Pat Moynihan charged his President in 1969: "To restore the authority of American institutions." But should insti-

tutions expect obedience they do not, on their record of performance, deserve? To this question the Nixon ideologues apparently answered yes.[72] An older American tradition would say
no, incredulous that anyone would see this as a question. In that
spirit I would argue that what the country needs today is a little
serious disrespect for the office of the Presidency; a refusal to give
any more weight to a President's words than the intelligence of
the utterance, if spoken by anyone else, would command; an understanding of the point made so aptly by Montaigne: "Sit he on
never so high a throne, a man still sits on his own bottom."

And what if men not open and modest, even at the start, but
from the start ambitious of power and contemptuous of law
reached the place once occupied by Washington and Lincoln?
What if neither personal character, nor the play of politics, nor
the Constitution itself availed to hold a President to strict accountability? In the end, the way to control the Presidency might
have to be not in many little ways but in one large way. In the
end, there remained, as Madison said, the decisive engine of impeachment.

IX

This was, of course, the instrument provided by the Constitution.
But it was an exceedingly blunt instrument. Only once had a
President been impeached, and there was no great national desire to go through the experience again. Yet, for the first time
in a century, Americans in the 1970s had to think hard about
impeachment, which meant that, because most of them flinched
from the prospect, they began to think hard about alternatives to
impeachment.

One alternative was the censure of the President by the Congress. That had been tried in 1834 when the Senate censured
Andrew Jackson on the ground that, in removing the government deposits from the Second Bank of the United States, he
had assumed illegal and unconstitutional powers.[73] Jackson's
protest to the Senate had been eloquent and conclusive. If
Congress really meant what the Senate said, Jackson replied, let

the House impeach him and the Senate try him. Jackson was plainly right. If a President committed high crimes and misdemeanors, censure was not enough. The slap-on-the-wrist approach to presidential delinquency made little sense, constitutional or otherwise. The continuation of a lawbreaker as chief magistrate would be a strange way to exemplify law and order at home or to demonstrate American probity before the world. This did not mean, of course, that a fainthearted Congress might not censure a lawless President and pretend to have done its duty. But unless the terms of the resolution made it clear why the President was merely censurable and not impeachable, the action would be a cop-out and a betrayal of Congress's constitutional responsibility.

Were there other halfway houses? Another proposal seemed worth consideration: that is, the removal of an offending President by some means short of impeachment. A joint resolution calling on the President to resign and passed by an overwhelming two thirds of each house (and therefore immune to veto) could have a powerful effect on a President who cared about the Constitution and the country. If either the President or the Vice President then resigned, the President, old or new, could, under the 25th Amendment, nominate a new Vice President who would take office upon confirmation by both houses of Congress. This would enable a constitutionally responsible President, as Clark Clifford suggested in 1973, to ask Congress for a list of, say, three persons, from which he would select a new Vice President; after which the President, knowing that he had lost national confidence, would resign and the Vice President would become President.[74] This plan would re-establish relations between Congress and the Presidency and, presumably, revive popular confidence in the government.

"Admirable," said Cardinal Fleury after he read the Abbé de St. Pierre's *Projet de Paix Perpetuelle,* "save for one omission: I find no provision for sending missionaries to convert the hearts of princes." [75] Alas, a President who had succeeded in provoking a long-suffering Congress into a resolution calling for his resignation was not likely to be deeply moved by congressional disapproval nor inclined to cooperate in his own liquidation.

If Presidents would not resign of their own volition, could they be forced out without the personal and national ordeal of impeachment and conviction? A proposal advanced in various forms by leading members of the House of Representatives in 1973 contemplated giving Congress authority by constitutional amendment to call for a new presidential election when it found that the President had so lost popular confidence he could no longer effectively perform his responsibilities (Jonathan Bingham) or that the President had violated the Constitution (Edith Green and Morris Udall).[76] A new election would clear the slate and restore a mandate to govern, while impeachment would, at best, replace a discredited President by a Vice President of the President's own choice, elected under the same auspices and by the same methods and inescapably part of the moral climate that caused the President to be impeached. This consideration acquired particular force with the disclosure in the summer of 1973 that Vice President Agnew was under criminal investigation.

The idea of introducing the power of dissolution was not new. But in its previous incarnations it had generally been conceived as giving the President the power to dissolve the Congress.[77] Now members of Congress proposed to give Congress the power to dissolve the Presidency. Each of these proposals was punitive in relation to the other branch and self-serving in relation to itself. Thomas K. Finletter alone advocated simultaneous dissolution of both Congress and the Presidency. This plainly was the clean way as well as the best means of getting a genuinely fresh mandate. But it was difficult to work special elections into the staggered terms of senators and representatives. The best solution would be to provide that a congressional term expired at the end of six (or two) years, or at the next presidential election, whichever came first. Finletter's solution — to have Presidents, senators and congressmen all serve six-year terms [78] — moved the American polity quite far toward plebiscitary if not parliamentary government.

The possibility of dissolution and new elections at times of hopeless stalemate or blasted confidence had serious appeal. Dissolution would give a rigid electoral system flexibility and responsiveness. It would permit the timely replacement of the pilot of the calm by the pilot of the storm, thereby pleasing the ghost of Bagehot. It would remind intractable Congresses that they could not block Presidents with immunity, as it would remind high-flying Presidents that there were other ways of being shot down besides impeachment. But one's instinct was somehow against it. A congressman observed of the Green-Udall amendment that it "would, in effect, take one-half of the parliamentary processes and not the entire parliamentary process." [79] This was certainly the direction and logic of dissolution. The result might well be to alter the balance of the Constitution in unforeseeable and perilous ways. It might, in particular, strengthen the movement against the separation of powers and toward a plebiscitary Presidency. "The republican principle," said the 71st Federalist, "demands that the deliberate sense of the community should govern the conduct of those to whom they intrust the management of their affairs; but it does not require an unqualified complaisance to every sudden breeze of passion, or to every transient impulse which the people may receive from the arts of men, who flatter their prejudices to betray their interests."

I think that the possibility of inserting dissolution into the American system is worth careful examination. But digging into the foundations of the state, as Burke said, is always a dangerous adventure.

x

Impeachment, on the other hand, was part of the original foundation of the American state. The Founding Fathers had placed the blunt instrument in the Constitution with every expectation that it would be used, and used most especially against Presidents. "No point is of more importance," George Mason told the Convention, "than that the right of impeachment should be continued. Shall any man be above Justice? Above all shall that man be above it, who [as President] can commit the most extensive injustice?" Benjamin Franklin pointed out that, if there were no provision for impeachment, the only recourse would be assassination, in which case a President would be "not only deprived of his life but of the opportunity of vindicating his character." Corruption or loss of capacity in a President, said Madison, was "within the compass of probable events. . . . Either of them might be fatal to the Republic." [80]

The genius of impeachment lay in the fact that it could punish the man without punishing the office. For, in the Presidency as elsewhere, power was ambiguous: the power to do good meant also the power to do harm, the power to serve the republic also the power to demean and defile it. The trick was to preserve presidential power but to deter Presidents from abusing that power. Shall any man be above Justice? George Mason had asked. Obviously not; not even a President of the United States. But bringing Presidents to justice was not all that simple.

History had turned impeachment into a weapon of last resort — more so probably than the Founding Fathers would have anticipated. Still, it was possible to exaggerate its impact on the country. It had taken less than three months to impeach and try Andrew Johnson, nor was the nation — in a favorite apprehension of 1868 as well as of 1974 — torn apart in the process. Three months of surgery might be better than three years of paralysis. Yet impeachment presented legal as well as political problems. There was broad agreement, among scholars at least, on doctrine. Impeachment was a proceeding of a political nature, by no means restricted to indictable crimes. On the other hand, it plainly was not to be applied to cases of honest disagreement over national policy or over constitutional interpretation, especially when a President refused to obey a law that he believed struck directly at the presidential prerogative. Impeachment was to be reserved, in Mason's phrase at the Constitutional Convention, for "great and dangerous offenses." [81]

The Senate, in trying impeachment cases, was better equipped to be the judge of the law than of the facts. When Johnson was impeached, there had been no dispute about the fact that he had removed Stanton. When Jackson was censured, there had been no dispute about the fact that he had removed the deposits. The issue was not whether they had done something but whether what they had done constituted a transgression of the laws and the Constitution. But in the Nixon case the facts themselves remained at issue — the facts, that is, of presidential complicity — and the effort of a hundred senators to determine those facts might well lead to chaos. The record here was one of negligence, irresponsibility and even deception, but it had not yet been proven one of knowing violation of the Constitution or of knowing involvement in the obstruction of justice. While impeachment was in the Constitution to be used, there was no point in lowering the threshold so that it would be used casually. All this argued for the determination of facts before the consideration of impeachment. There were two obvious ways to determine the facts. One was through the House of Representatives, which had the sole power to initiate impeachment. The House could, for example, instruct the Judiciary Committee to ascertain whether there were grounds for impeachment, or it could establish a select committee to conduct such an inquiry. The other road was through the courts. If the Special Prosecutor established incriminating facts, these could serve as the basis for impeachment.

But what if a President himself withheld evidence — as, for example, Nixon's tapes — deemed essential to the ascertainment of facts? If a President said "the time has come to turn Watergate over to the courts, where the questions of guilt and innocence belong," [82] and then denied the courts the evidence they needed to decide on innocence or guilt, what recourse remained to the republic except impeachment? Apart from the courts, Polk had said quite explicitly that the House, if it were looking into impeachment, could command testimony and papers, public and private, official or unofficial, of every agent of the government.[83] If a President declined for whatever reason to yield material evidence in his possession, whether to the courts or to the House, this itself might provide clear grounds for impeachment.

All these things were obscure in the early autumn of 1973. It was even possible that Nixon might conclude that the Watergate problems were not after all (as he had told the Prime Minister of Japan) "murky, small, unimportant, vicious little things" [84] but were rather evidence of a profound and grievous imbalance between the Presidency and the Constitution. Perhaps he might by an honest display of candor and contrition regain a measure of popular confidence, re-establish constitutional comity and recover presidential effectiveness. But full recovery seemed unlikely unless the President himself recognized why his Presidency had fallen into such difficulties. Nixon's continued invocation, after Watergate, of national security as the excuse for presidential excess, his defense to the end of unreviewable executive privilege, his defiant assertion that, if he had it to do over again, he would still deceive Congress and the people about the secret air war in Cambodia — such unrepentant reactions suggested that he still had no clue as to what his trouble was, still failed to understand that the sickness of his Presidency had been caused, not by the overzealousness of his friends nor by the malice of his enemies, but by the expansion and abuse of presidential power itself.

For the issue was more than whether Congress and the people wished to deal with the particular iniquities of the Nixon administration. It was whether they wished to rein in the runaway Presidency. Nixon's Presidency was not an aberration but a culmination. It carried to reckless extremes a compulsion toward presidential power rising out of deep-running changes in the foundations of society. In a time of the acceleration of history and the decay of traditional institutions and values, a strong Presidency was both a greater necessity than ever before and a greater risk — necessary to hold a spinning and distracted society together, necessary to make the separation of powers work,[85] risky because of the awful temptation held out to override the separation of powers and burst the bonds of the Constitution. The nation required both a strong Presidency for leadership *and* the separation of powers for liberty. It could well be that, if continuing structural compulsions were likely to propel future Presidents in the direction of government by decree, the rehabilitation of impeachment would be essential to contain the Presidency and preserve the Constitution.

Watergate was potentially the best thing to have happened to the Presidency in a long time. If the trails were followed to their end, many, many years would pass before another White House staff would dare take the liberties with the Constitution and the laws the Nixon White House had taken. And if the nation wanted to work its way back to a constitutional Presidency, there was only one way to begin. That was by showing Presidents that, when their closest associates placed themselves above the law and the Constitution, such transgressions would be, not forgiven or forgotten for the sake of the Presidency, but exposed and punished for the sake of the Presidency.

If the Nixon White House escaped the legal consequences of its illegal behavior, why would future Presidents and their associates not suppose themselves entitled to do what the Nixon White House had done? Only condign punishment would restore popular faith in the Presidency and deter future Presidents from illegal conduct — so long, at least, as Watergate remained a vivid memory.[86] We have noted that corruption appears to visit the White House in fifty-year cycles. This suggests that exposure and retribution inoculate the Presidency against its latent criminal impulses for about half a century. Around the year 2023 the American people would be well advised to go on the alert and start nailing down everything in sight.

A constitutional Presidency, as the great Presidents had shown, could be a very strong Presidency indeed. But what kept a strong President constitutional, in addition to checks and balances incorporated within his own breast, was the vigilance of the nation. Neither impeachment nor repentance would make much difference if the people themselves had come to an unconscious acceptance of the imperial Presidency. The Constitution could not hold the nation to ideals it was determined to betray.[87] The reinvigoration of the written checks in the American Constitution depended on the reinvigoration of the unwritten checks in American society. The great institutions — Congress, the courts, the executive establishment, the press, the universities, public opinion — had to reclaim their own dignity and meet their own responsibilities. As Madison said long ago, the country could not trust to "parchment barriers" to halt the encroaching spirit of power.[88] In the end, the Constitution would live only if it embodied the spirit of the American people.

"There is no week nor day nor hour," wrote Walt Whitman, "when tyranny may not enter upon this country, if the people lose their supreme confidence in themselves, — and lose their roughness and spirit of defiance — Tyranny may always enter — there is no charm, no bar against it — the only bar against it is a large resolute breed of men." [89]

★ Epilogue ★

After the Imperial Presidency

THE IMPERIAL PRESIDENCY was written in the latter days, hectic
and ominous, of the Presidency of Richard M. Nixon. The book
argues that the Constitution intends a strong Presidency within
an equally strong system of accountability. The title refers to the
condition that ensues when the constitutional balance between
presidential power and presidential accountability is upset in favor
of presidential power.

The perennial threat to the constitutional balance, I suggested,
comes in the field of foreign policy. Confronted by presidential
initiatives at home, Congress and the courts — the countervailing
branches of government under the constitutional separation of
powers — have ample confidence in their own information and
judgment. They do not lightly surrender power to the executive.
In domestic policy, the republic is all Missouri: it has to be shown.
But confronted by presidential initiatives abroad, Congress and
the courts, along with the press and the citizenry too, generally
lack confidence in their own information and judgment. In foreign
policy the inclination is to let the Presidency have the responsibility — and the power.

"It is chiefly in its foreign relations," as Tocqueville noted
long ago, "that the executive power of a nation finds occasion
to exert its skill and its strength. If the existence of the American
Union were perpetually threatened, if its chief interests were in
daily connection with those of other powerful nations, the executive would assume an increased importance." But the nation
that Tocqueville inspected in the 1830s lived in happy isolation
from world power conflicts. In consequence, he wrote, "the Pres-

ident of the United States possesses almost royal prerogatives which he has no opportunity of exercising." [1] In the last half century, international crisis, genuine, contrived or imagined, has at last given Presidents the opportunity to exercise these almost royal prerogatives — with the results Tocqueville predicted. This is the story of the imperial Presidency.

I

Richard Nixon came along in ironic fulfillment of Tocqueville's prophecy. Seizing the possibilities created by forty years of international crisis, the 37th President became the first to profess the monarchical doctrine that the sovereign can do no wrong. As he put it unrepentantly three years after he resigned to escape impeachment, "When the President does it, that means that it is not illegal." [2]

This novel doctrine of the divine right of Presidents lay behind both Nixon's Watergate cover-up and his drive to transform the nature of the American polity. "I felt," he wrote in his memoirs, "that we were at a historical turning point. My reading of history taught me that when all the leadership institutions of a nation become paralyzed by self-doubt and second thoughts, that nation cannot long survive unless those institutions are either reformed, replaced, or circumvented. In my second term I was prepared to adopt whichever of these three methods — or whichever combination of them — was necessary." [3]

Historically Congress had maintained the rough balance of the Constitution because it retained three vital powers: the war-making power; the power of the purse; and the power of oversight and investigation. By 1950 it had relinquished the war-making power. Truman fought in Korea, Johnson in Vietnam and Nixon in Cambodia without the explicit congressional authorization required by the Constitution. In 1969–1974 the Nixon administration tried systematically and, until Watergate, successfully to nullify the other two powers: countering the power of the purse by the doctrine of unlimited impoundment of appropriated funds; countering the power of oversight and investigation by the doctrine of unreviewable executive privilege and the extension of the presidential secrecy system. Had Nixon succeeded in imposing these doctrines on top of his amplified claims for the presidential war-making power, he would have effectively ended Congress as a serious partner in the constitutional order.

His further contribution to the imperial Presidency was to take emergency powers the Presidency had accumulated in order to save the republic from foreign adversaries and to turn these powers against his political opponents — "enemies," he called them — at home. Invoking "national security" as an all-purpose justification for presidential criminality, he set up a secret White House posse to burgle offices, forge historical documents and wiretap officials, embassies, newspapermen and "enemies." The Presidency was above the law, and national crisis justified extreme methods.

Whether a conscious or unconscious revolutionary, Nixon was carrying the imperial Presidency toward its ultimate form in the plebiscitary Presidency (see pages 254–255). Events frustrated Nixon's revolution. The press and the courts exposed his methods as furtive and lawless. Congress, at last bestirring itself, acted to save the Constitution. The House of Representatives prepared articles of impeachment, charging Nixon, in words too quickly forgotten, with acting "in a manner contrary to his trust as President and subversive of constitutional government, to the great prejudice of the cause of law and justice and to the manifest injury of the people of the United States."

II

Nixon's attempt to institutionalize the imperial Presidency failed. By the mid-1970s, Vietnam and Watergate had shattered public trust in the Presidency. In 1959, when pollsters asked which knew best, the President or Congress, 61 percent of respondents had voted for the President, only 17 percent for Congress. A comparable question in 1977 almost reversed the proportions, favoring Congress by 58 to 26 percent.[4]

Congress, seized by a temporary passion to prevent future

Vietnams and Watergates, enacted laws designed to reclaim lost powers, to dismantle the executive secrecy system and to ensure future presidential accountability. The War Powers Resolution of 1973 was supposed to restrain the presidential inclination to go to war. A variety of laws limited presidential resort to paramilitary and covert action. Congress set up select committees to monitor the Central Intelligence Agency. It gave the Freedom of Information Act new vitality. It imposed its own priorities — human rights and nuclear nonproliferation, for example — on the executive foreign policy. The Congressional Budget Act of 1974 restricted presidential impoundment. The National Emergencies Act of 1976 terminated existing presidential emergency authority and established congressional review for future national-emergency declarations. Legislative vetoes and reporting requirements curtailed presidential freedom of action in a diversity of fields.

A few scholars had feared during the Watergate crisis that too zealous an investigation might cripple the presidential office. After Congress began its mild post-Watergate effort to restore the constitutional balance, scholarly pessimism intensified. Some saw the once mighty Presidency tied down, like Gulliver, by a web of debilitating statutory restraints. A theory arose about the fragility of the American Presidency. Not only Congress but history itself seemed, as political scientists saw it, to be conspiring against Presidents. The job was overwhelmed by insuperable problems — inflation, energy shortages, urban decay, the nuclear arms race, the Communists. The national consensus on which Presidents had relied since the war for domestic as well as foreign policy was disintegrating. The party system, which had long supplied the connective sinews of government, was in decay. Lobbies were importunate. Single-issue fanaticisms were distorting the political process.

Presidents, scholars added, had compounded their problems by personifying the government in themselves, promising miracles they could not work and exciting hopes they could not fulfill. "The president," said Theodore Lowi, "is the Wizard of Oz." [5] The inevitable gap between popular expectation and presidential delivery guaranteed, in this view, both presidential failure and popular resentment. Vice President Walter Mondale, defending Jimmy Carter in 1979, cited an observation John Steinbeck had made in the previous decade in defense of Lyndon Johnson: "We give the President more work than a man can do, more responsibility than a man should take, more pressure than a man can bear. . . . We wear him out, use him up, eat him up. . . . He is ours and we exercise the right to destroy him." [6]

The Presidency appeared in rout. Vietnam drove Johnson from the White House. Nixon drove himself. Nixon's successors — the hapless Gerald Ford and the hapless Jimmy Carter — proved incapable of mastering the discordant frustrations of the day. Failure, it seemed, had passed the point of coincidence. These recent Presidents, a veteran political reporter noted in a book on the Presidency, came from a variety of political backgrounds and from all sections of the country; they ran the spectrum in personal temperament and social philosophy. "Their combined experience suggests that the chronic failings of the presidency" sprang not from personal characteristics but from "the political and governing system to which presidents must respond." [7] "When five consecutive men . . . all fail to operate an office, when their tasks seem to get progressively more and more difficult with the passing of time," wrote an intelligent English journalist in his own book on the subject, "then the fault can hardly be in the individuals. It must be in the institution." [8]

"Never has so powerful a leader," the English commentator added, "been so impotent to do what he wants to do, what he is pledged to do, what he is expected to do." [9] Columnists wrote of "the Presidency in decline." Scholars mobilized their colleagues to join in producing books under such titles as *The Tethered Presidency*, *The Post-Imperial Presidency*, *The Impossible Presidency*. Pundits confidently predicted an age of one-term Presidents. The impression arose at the end of the 1970s of a beleaguered and pathetic fellow sitting forlornly in the Oval Office, assailed by unprecedentedly intractable problems, paralyzed by the constitutional separation of powers, hemmed in by congressional and bureaucratic constraints, pushed one way and another by exigent interest groups, seduced, betrayed and abandoned by the mass media. "Presidential government is an illusion," proclaimed one political scientist in 1980, "—an illusion that misleads presidents no less than the media and the American public, an illusion that often brings about the destruction of the very men who hold the office. Presidential government is the idea that the president, backed by the people, is or can be in charge of governing the country. . . . Far from being in charge or running the government, the president must struggle even to comprehend what is going on." [10] In 1980 ex-President Ford said to general applause, "We have not an imperial presidency but an imperiled presidency." [11]

III

There is a sense in which the Presidency has always been weak. The President's power over policy is great; for the power to set the nation's course derives from the constitutional prerogatives of the office. But the President's power over execution is incomplete; for the power to manage the vast, whirring machinery of government derives from individual skills as persuader, bargainer and leader. Even Franklin D. Roosevelt, who possessed all those skills to a high degree, had his problems. "Half a President's suggestions, which theoretically carry the weight of orders," one of his assistants, Jonathan Daniels, later recalled, "can be safely forgotten by a Cabinet member." [12] "He'll sit here," Harry Truman said in contemplation of Eisenhower, "and he'll say, 'Do this! Do that!' *And nothing will happen*." [13] Even when the imperial Presidency culminated in Nixon, the President lived in a state of chronic and profane frustration, unable to command Congress, the judiciary, the press, the universities, unable even to get the FBI, the CIA and the Internal Revenue Service to do his bidding.

There is obviously nothing new, therefore, about this form of presidential frustration; nor, indeed, about the political irritations allegedly imperiling the Presidency in the 1970s. Refractory Congresses, greedy lobbies, wild-eyed single-issue movements, even excessive expectations—all were old hat in American history.

Contemporary pundits sometimes write, for example, as if fractiousness in Congress represents a lamentable lapse from better times when legislators obeyed their whips and voted the straight party line. But when were those better times? Even Franklin Roosevelt, in the epoch of rubber-stamp Congresses, had to fight hard for every New Deal bill after the first hundred days. Congresses controlled by his own party defeated some of his most cherished initiatives, such as discretionary neutrality legislation and the Supreme Court plan.

Nor was legislative indiscipline new in the days of FDR. Half a century earlier, Woodrow Wilson, writing in the golden age of party regularity, called his book *Congressional Government*. But Wilson did not portray a well-ordered Congress. "Our parties marshal their adherents with the strictest possible discipline for the purpose of carrying elections," he wrote, "but their discipline is very slack and indefinite in dealing with legislation. . . . There are in Congress no authoritative leaders who are the recognized spokesmen of their parties. Power is nowhere concentrated; it is rather deliberately and of set policy scattered amongst many small chiefs." [14]

Legislative indiscipline is inherent in the American Constitution. The separation of powers denies the executive branch organic means of controlling the legislative majority. Federalism turns national parties into loose coalitions of state parties. Between the commands of the Constitution and the sprawl of the country, strict party discipline has always been alien to Congress. Tocqueville made the point a century and a half ago. In the American democracy, he wrote, "parties are impatient of control and are never manageable except in moments of great public danger" — and he was writing in an age of presidential domination as overweening as in the age of FDR. Tocqueville correctly traced this unmanageability to the dependence of the legislator on his constituents. "A representative," he wrote, "is never sure of his supporters, and, if they foresake him, he is left without a resource." In consequence legislators "think more of their constituents than of their party. . . . But what ought to be said to gratify constituents is not always what ought to be said to serve the party to which representatives profess to belong." [15]

The observation that a legislator's loyalty runs more to his constituents than to his party remains true today; but it is hardly a new truth. And is legislative indiscipline altogether a bad thing? Is the republic better off when legislators give unquestioning obedience to the whips and ask not to reason why? "Reader, suppose you were an idiot," Mark Twain wrote. "And suppose you were a member of Congress. But I repeat myself." [16] Congressional fragmentation in recent times springs in part from the fact that Congress today probably has fewer idiots and more educated, informed and independent-minded legislators than the nation has enjoyed since the early republic. The price democracy pays for independent-minded legislators is precisely their insistence on making up their own minds.

Nor are lobbies a novel phenomenon. The United States has had lobbies as long as it has had Congresses. Those who suppose lobbies to be some horrid invention of the late twentieth century should read *The Gilded Age* (1873), by Mark Twain and Charles Dudley Warner. The twentieth-century innovation is the public-interest lobby; and Common Cause and Ralph Nader somewhat offset the less benign pressures of special-interest lobbies.

The same historical discount must be applied to single-issue movements. Such movements are hardly the terrifying novelty that our contemporaries, intimidated by the feminists, the environmentalists, the right-to-lifers, the gun-lovers, the Moral Majority, the homosexuals and so on, suppose them to be. What, after all, was Madison writing about in November 1787 when he discussed the "mischiefs of faction" in the 10th Federalist?

Single-issue movements have flickered through the political scene from 1787 to the present, whether dedicated to the extirpation of Freemasonry, the abolition of slavery, nativism, issuance of greenbacks or (one of the most alarmingly successful of all) prohibition of drink. American democracy has taken these movements in stride. When the Native American or Know-Nothing party was at its height, Horace Greeley predicted that it was destined "to run its course, and vanish as suddenly as it appeared. . . . It would seem as devoid of the elements of persistence as an anti-cholera or an anti-potato-rot party would be." [17] The Know-Nothing party won far more legislative seats than any single-issue movement of our own day has done. It vanished as Greeley predicted.

IV

Congressional indiscipline, importunate lobbies, single-issue zealots — these are hardly the causes of the plight of the Presidency. Most far-fetched of recent explanations is the notion that the Presidency did itself in when recent Presidents started personalizing the office, appealing over the heads of Congress to the people and arousing expectations beyond hope of fulfillment. Radio and especially television, it is suggested, are responsible for the corruption of what had presumably been up till a few years before an impersonal, decorous, remote office. Personalization, the plebiscitary stance and presidentially induced mass expectations, we are told, began with John Kennedy or, at the earliest, with Franklin Roosevelt.

This notion springs from a curiously foreshortened view of American history. In fact, the Presidency has been a personalized office from the start, both for political reasons — the interests of the President — and for psychological reasons — the emotional needs of the people. The office would not even have taken the form it did "had not," as one member of the constitutional convention wrote, "many members cast their eyes toward General Washington as President; and shaped their ideas of the Powers to be given the President, by their opinions of his Virtue." [18] Washington exploited his advantage and helped create his own myth. The admiring Garry Wills portrays him as "constantly testing public opinion and tailoring his measures to suit it"; and the even more admiring Douglas Southall Freeman found him on occasion "too much the self-conscious national hero." The Father of his Country did not need television in order to personify the nation in the Presidency. Parson Weems (Wills praises his "cinematic vigor") was sufficient. [19]

When Andrew Jackson made his "grand triumphal tour" of the northeastern states in the late spring of 1833, it was "an emotional debauch," as Jackson's most recent biographer describes it; a continuous experience of cheering crowds, booming cannon, popular frenzy. "I have witnessed enthusiasms before," the Hero of New Orleans wrote his son after two days in New York, "but never before have I witnessed such a scene of personal regard as I have today, and ever since I left Washington. I have bowed to upwards of two hundred thousand people to day." [20] When Jackson went on to Boston, "Nothing but one solid mass of heads could be seen," an eyewitness wrote in his journal. ". . . I believe a person could have walked upon the heads and shoulders of the multitude." [21] Every commanding President in the nineteenth century was guilty of personalizing the office and appealing over the heads of Congress to the people, from Old Hickory through Father Abraham to Teddy Roosevelt at the turn of the century, with his bully pulpit and his highly publicized personality and family.

Nor was the backlash against Presidents an innovation of the 1960s. Dickens anticipated Steinbeck by more than a century. "You no sooner set up an idol firmly," he observed of the American people in 1842, "than you are sure to pull it down and dash it into fragments. . . . Any man who attains a high place among you, from the President downwards, may date his downfall from that moment." [22]

Nor is the expectations gap, so widely invoked to explain the troubles of the contemporary Presidency, a novel phenomenon. The Presidency by its very existence excites expectations. It has always been a target of popular hope and supplication. "I am applied to almost daily," Polk wrote in 1846. ". . . The idea seems to prevail with many persons that the President is from his position compelled to contribute to every loafer who applies." [23] When a friend said to Lincoln that he must get tired of shaking hands, Lincoln supposedly replied that "the tug of the hand was much easier to bear than that upon the heartstrings for all manner of favors beyond his power to grant." Benjamin Harrison, who reported this remark, added that letters imploring help "come from every part of the land, and relate to every possible subject. . . . Many people greatly enlarge the powers of the President, and invoke his interference and protection in all their troubles." [24]

William Howard Taft can hardly be accused of seeking to personalize the office or to rouse excessive expectations. But, well before FDR, JFK or television, Taft wrote of the President that "the whole government is so identified in the minds of the people with his personality, that they make him responsible for all the sins of omission and of commission of society at large." Taft complained bitterly of those who "visit the President with responsibility for everything that is done and that is not done," adding that "the President cannot make clouds to rain, he cannot make the corn to grow, he cannot make business to be good." [25] Gabriel has always hovered over the White House.

The expectations-gap thesis rests on the assumption that voters really believe campaign promises and are consequently overcome with astonishment and anger when those promises are not thereafter fulfilled. It assumes, in other words, that the electorate is a pack of fools. But voters are on the whole as intelligent as you or I. They do not take it literally when presidential candidates say they will abolish poverty, guarantee prosperity, and usher in utopia. They regard campaign oratory as campaign oratory — that is, not as a sacred covenant with the people but as a clue to the candidate's values, priorities and character. They are not greatly bothered by "over-promising." They understand with Emerson that "nothing great was ever achieved without enthusiasm."* The situation is one not of voters deluded by excessive expectations but of voters depressed by absence of expectation. Too many think it makes no difference who is President.

As for the idea that overwhelming forces of history conspire against the contemporary Presidency, obviously the substantive problems of the last third of the twentieth century are not easy. But do we really face tougher problems than our forefathers did? Nuclear weapons excepted, the political problems Americans face today are modest compared to the problems that confronted Washington's generation in achieving independence and fashioning a

---

*In "Circles." Valéry Giscard d'Estaing, when President of France, observed sensibly, "A word about optimism. I have to inspire people. . . . It would be quite inconceivable to ask someone to make an effort and then tell him that this effort would be of no avail. . . . Mine is, therefore, not the optimism of illusion but rather the optimism of proposal, which is inherent in the nature of my office." *Paris Match*, September 14, 1979.

free state, or to the problems that confronted Lincoln's generation in bringing the republic through the glare of civil war, or to the problems that confronted Franklin Roosevelt's generation in overcoming the worst depression and winning the greatest war in American history. Let us avoid the fallacy of self-pity that leads every generation to suppose that it is peculiarly persecuted by history. Historical forces have always conspired against the Presidency. The Presidency has survived.

v

The Presidency survives because, whatever its weaknesses and frustrations, the office retains its constitutional and institutional prerogatives. I never had a moment's worry during the times when pundits lamented the fragility of the Presidency. Whatever political scientists, lawyers and journalists may think, historians know that the American Presidency is indestructible.

This is partly so for functional reasons. A governing process based on the separation of powers among three supposedly equal and coordinate branches has an inherent tendency toward stalemate and inertia. One of the three branches must take the initiative if the system is to move. The executive branch alone is structurally capable of taking that initiative. The Founding Fathers intended that it should do so. "Energy in the Executive," said Hamilton in the 70th Federalist, "is a leading character in the definition of good government."

Moreover, the growth of presidential initiative resulted not from presidential rapacity for power but from the necessities of governing an increasingly complex society. As a tiny agricultural country, straggling along the Atlantic seaboard, turned into a mighty continental, industrial and finally world power, problems assailing the national polity increased in size, number and urgency. Most of these problems could not be tackled without vigorous executive leadership. Through American history, a robust Presidency kept the system in motion. The President remains, as Woodrow Wilson said, "the only national voice," the Presidency "the vital place of action in the system." [26]

A further reason for the indestructibility of the Presidency lies in the psychology of mass democracy. Once again Tocqueville provides the text. "Our contemporaries," he wrote, "are constantly excited by two conflicting passions: they want to be led, and they wish to remain free. . . . By this system the people shake off their state of dependency just long enough to select their master and then relapse into it again." [27] Americans have always had considerable ambivalence about the Presidency. One year they denounce presidential power. The next they demand presidential leadership. While they are quite capable of cursing out Presidents, they also have a profound longing to believe in and admire them.

The indestructibility of the Presidency was demonstrated in the very years when political scientists were pronouncing presidential government an illusion. After Nixon resigned, everyone expected a shift in the balance of the system. Congress would now come into its own. Its acquiescence and pusillanimity, which had contributed so much to the rise of the imperial Presidency, would end. Having tasted power and recovered a sense of responsibility, Congress would resume the role of partnership in government the Founding Fathers had intended for it. The press, basking in worldwide congratulations over the intrepidity of its investigative reporting, would be more vigilant than ever as a check on an overweening executive. The voters, now so sadly aware of the infirmity of Presidents, would be less inclined to see the man in the White House as larger than life.

The new President, moreover, was more than any of his predecessors an accidental and therefore especially vulnerable President. He arrived in the White House not through the choice of the voters but through the operations of the 25th Amendment. No one outside of 120,000 people in the Fifth District of Michigan had ever voted for him for any federal office. The Presidency he had inherited was badly damaged by the revulsion against Nixon. Gerald Ford himself was a modest, unassuming conservative politician, a loyal Capitol Hill man, without great appetite for adulation or power. Moreover, by pardoning Nixon, he dissipated in one stroke the confidence that had come to him on his succession and inflicted a wound on his own administration from which it never recovered. Nor did he succeed even in winning the clear backing of his own party — as shown by the challenge mounted against him by Ronald Reagan in 1976. And he became in these years the butt of nightclub comics across the country for his supposed dumbness and clumsiness. Vice President Nelson Rockefeller, it was said, was "a banana peel away from the Presidency."

Gerald Ford had every strike against him in the White House. Yet, for all his political and personal vulnerability, he retained a dominant role in the American polity. This was because the Presidency itself, as an office and institution, confers power on even a weak incumbent. It enabled Ford, for example, to institute a policy of government by veto. The loyal Capitol Hill man such a short time before, Ford vetoed seventy-two acts passed by Congress in a little over two years. It had taken the imperial Nixon nearly six years to veto forty-two bills. The mighty Lyndon Johnson vetoed only thirty in five years. More than four-fifths of Ford's vetoes were sustained.

In foreign policy the resurgent Congress had its way on a number of specific points. Some of its actions — such as the restraint on CIA intervention in Angola and elsewhere, the insistence on human rights, the resistance to arms sales and to nuclear proliferation — were an improvement over what the executive branch would have done on its own. Others — such as the Jackson-Vanik amendment tying Soviet-American trade to the emigration of Russian Jews — were ill-considered initiatives produced by what one senator termed "domestic ethnic politics." [28] Ford complained, in the manner of Presidents, about "impermissible shackles" on his ability to conduct foreign relations. [29] One doubts that his foreign policy would have been greatly better unshackled.

Certainly the War Powers Resolution, the most publicized shackle of all, turned out to be a toy handcuff. The origins of the resolution are described on pages 301–307. When it was enacted over Nixon's veto in 1973, it was acclaimed as a triumph of congressional self-assertion. If it was a triumph of anything, it was of symbol over substance. The resolution began by yielding the President what he had heretofore lacked: statutory authority to begin wars without congressional consent. The resolution's preamble laid down various standards, but the conference report said that the rest of the act was "not dependent" on the preamble, thereby leaving the standards as pious rhetoric rather than binding law. The resolution went on to direct the President to terminate what the Senate-House conferees interestingly called "unauthorized use of the Armed Forces" within sixty days (in practice, ninety days, since the resolution offered the President thirty additional days if he thought it necessary in the interests of disengagement) *unless* Congress explicitly provided otherwise. Congress, moreover, could order the withdrawal of American forces at any point by concurrent resolution, which is, of course, not subject to presidential veto.[30]

This proved from the start a richly ambiguous statute. Legislators argued whether it was an expansion or limitation of presidential war-making power. Some liberals, looking at the early sections of the resolution, denounced it as an unconstitutional delegation of the war-making power to the executive. Senator Thomas Eagleton of Missouri called the resolution "an undated, 90 day declaration of war."[31] Congressman John Culver of Iowa said it would give the President "a blank check to wage war anywhere in the world for any reason of his choosing for a period of 60 to 90 days."[32] Conservatives, looking at the later sections of the resolution, denounced it as an intolerable restriction of presidential authority. Barry Goldwater called it "destructive of America's credibility in any future crisis."[33] Nixon in his veto message said ominously that, since his powers could be altered only by constitutional amendment, "any attempt to make such alterations by legislation alone is clearly without force"[34]—a statement that, taken literally, appeared to serve notice that, because he personally found the law unconstitutional, he would not be bound by it.

Both sides exaggerated the significance of a pretentious and empty statute. Those who felt that it strengthened presidential war-making power probably had the better of the argument. Before the passage of the resolution, unilateral presidential war was a matter of usurpation. Now, at least for the first ninety days, it was a matter of law.

Experience under the resolution has, I fear, justified the skepticism expressed on pages 302–307 of this book. From President Ford's attack on Cambodia after the seizure of the *Mayaguez* in 1975 to President Reagan's attacks on Lebanon, Grenada and Libya in the 1980s, the resolution has had no success in deterring Presidents from sending forces into combat without congressional authorization.

But my skepticism did not go deep enough, for I naively assumed that Presidents would at least make a good-faith effort to honor the resolution. Instead, Presidents have simply ignored it, except for occasional and perfunctory compliance with the reporting requirements. Textual ambiguities in defining those requirements have left uncertain the point at which the sixty-day clock starts ticking and thereby the hope that the resolution would be self-activating and automatic in its operation. And the Supreme Court, when it declared the legislative veto unconstitutional in *Immigration and Naturalization Service v. Chadha* (1983), presumably annulled the congressional power to terminate hostilities through concurrent resolution. Thereafter not a shadow of sanction remained to enforce or even to encourage presidential compliance.

A good deal of the much-vaunted congressional reclamation of power after Watergate similarly turned out to be make-believe. In the Congressional Budget Act of 1974 Congress planned to give itself a legislative budget process comparable to the one it had long before given the President in the Budget and Accounting Act of 1921. Some features of the Act, like the Congressional Budget Office and the control of impoundment, proved useful, though the 1983 Supreme Court decision invalidating the legislative veto probably invalidates the impoundment restrictions too. But the Act itself, as President Reagan demonstrated in 1981, failed in its purpose of assuring Congress a coordinate voice in determining budget priorities. What began as a statute designed by Congress to discipline itself and to retrieve power from the President ended, a careful student of the budget process has written, "as an instrument which enhanced the president's power and allowed him to discipline Congress." [35] By 1986, with the Gramm-Rudman Act, Congress handed over the impoundment authority laboriously reclaimed in 1974 and relinquished some of its constitutional power, bestowed on it by the Founding Fathers, to decide taxing and spending policy.

Nor did Congress in its post-Watergate righteousness take effective action to restrain presidential abuse of executive privilege. The secrecy system, that bulwark of the imperial Presidency, found new sustenance and support. When Frank Snepp, a former CIA officer, published *Decent Interval*, a book about the fall of Saigon, the Carter administration prosecuted and convicted him on the ground that he had violated his CIA contract by failing to submit his manuscript for clearance. No classified information was involved; no allegation was made of injury to national security; no one denied that Snepp's book was of value to the concerned citizen and the future historian. Congress rolled over and did nothing.

"The rise of presidential authority," as Henry Jones Ford wrote in his penetrating book of 1898, *The Rise and Growth of American Politics*, "cannot be accounted for by the intention of presidents: it is the product of political conditions which dominate all the departments of government, so that Congress itself shows an unconscious disposition to aggrandize the presidential office. The existence of a separate responsible authority to which questions of public policy may be resigned opens to Congress an easy way out of difficulty when the exercise of its own jurisdiction would be troublesome." [36] Ford was writing in the fading twilight of congressional government. His words became truer than ever in the high noon of presidential power. Watergate produced much huffing and puffing, but the White House was not blown in. Far from justifying fears or hopes about the resurgence of Congress, the post-Watergate tale illustrates once again the indestructibility of the Presidency.

VI

"In analysing history," Emerson said, "do not be too profound, for often the causes are quite simple." [37] Journalists and political scientists, seeking to understand the troubles of the Presidency in the 1970s, rashly ignored Emerson's dictum. They advanced "profound" explanations — unprecedentedly intractable problems, excessive personalization of the office, excessive expectations in the country, the constitutional separation of powers, the post-Watergate resurgence of Congress, the rise of single-issue movements, the power of lobbies; and they reached a "profound" conclusion — that the fault lay not in the men who occupied the Presidency but in the institution itself and the system to which it responded.

The conditions invoked as explanations were real enough, and they had acquired great salience in the 1970s. But they were far from new; they were indeed recurrent conditions of American politics, and less causes of the presidential dilemma than alibis for it. The commentators got their order wrong. They argued that these conditions accounted for the supposed failure of the Presidency. On closer examination, perhaps the failure of particular Presidents accounted for the salience of the conditions. The absence of effective presidential leadership created a vacuum in the center of the political system. It was this vacuum that Congress, lobbies and single-issue movements rushed to fill. The Presidency was in trouble not because of the fragility of the office or the unworkability of the system nor even because of restrictions imposed in the post-Watergate frenzy. It was in trouble because President Nixon had acted in a manner contrary to his trust as President and subversive of constitutional government, and because of the feebleness of the leadership Presidents Ford and Carter provided and of the remedies they proposed.

Whatever else may be said about Ronald Reagan, he quickly showed that the reports of the death of the Presidency were greatly exaggerated. In short order, he made the lamentations of 1980 seem overwrought and irrelevant. A comparison of Reagan with his immediate predecessor is instructive.

Reagan was obviously no student of public affairs. He did not work nearly so hard as Jimmy Carter nor know nearly so much. But he understood the Presidency as Carter never did. In particular, he understood that an effective President must meet two indispensable requirements. And he was right in supposing that when a President meets these requirements, the fact that he does not command or even comprehend the details of policy need not be of major political consequence.

The first requirement is to point the republic in one or another direction. This can be done only if the man in the White House possesses, or is possessed by, a vision of the ideal America. The President, said Henry Adams, "resembles the commander of a ship at sea. He must have a helm to grasp, a course to steer, a port to seek." [38] After four years of the Carter Presidency, no one knew where Carter wished to steer the country. But no one could doubt that Reagan had a deeply felt and indeed explicitly ideological sense of his destination. No one could doubt either that his personal values dominated his administration or that his subordinates, far from manipulating him, labored to make administrative and policy sense out of his bundle of prejudices.

The second requirement is to explain to the electorate why the direction the President proposes is right for the nation. Reagan-understood, as Carter never did, that politics is ultimately an educational process. Where Carter gave the impression of regarding presidential speeches as disagreeable duties, to be rushed through as perfunctorily as possible, Reagan knew that the speech is the vital weapon of presidential leadership.His best speeches had a structure and an argument. They were well written and superbly delivered. They were potent vehicles for the President's charm, histrionic skill and genius for simplification.

If the President can point the country and persuade the voters that it is the right direction in which to go, and if he can find reasonably competent subordinates to figure out the details, it need not matter so much politically that he himself hardly knows what is going on. Reagan's early success proved that the Presidency, if you can work it, is not all that tough a job. He spent fewer hours at his desk and more on holiday than most readers of this book are accustomed to doing. Yet he effectively dispelled the learned doubts of the late 1970s about the capacity of Presidents to govern and restored national confidence in the workability of the office and the system. The foe of government ironically revived faith in government.

Reagan added to this a talent that was Eisenhower's signal strength — the ability to divorce himself from the actions and consequences of his own administration. He piled up the largest budgetary deficits in American peacetime history. Yet no one continued to denounce deficits with more impassioned eloquence and apparent sincerity. He sent Marines to Lebanon in 1983 and insisted that their continued presence was crucial to America's position in the world. When he withdrew them in 1984, the nation, instead of demanding an accounting for an indefensible fiasco, breathed a sigh of grateful relief. If Carter had been President, Congress and the press would have been merciless. But Carter, by priding himself on his mastery of detail, acquired a responsibility in the public mind that Reagan, by eschewing detail, adroitly escaped.

As John R. Sears, Reagan's first campaign manager in 1980, remarked, "He walks away from more political car crashes than anyone" [39] — walks away and never looks back. When pressed, Reagan genially blamed his troubles on someone else, with Congress usually the favored scapegoat. Voters forgave and forgot.

In the same way, Reagan was indulged in his manifold misstatement of facts and in his endless flow of fable and fantasy. He gave the prime minister of Israel and Simon Wiesenthal, the Nazi hunter, on separate occasions the clear impression that, as a Signal Corps photographer, he had personally filmed Nazi concentration camps toward the end of the war. Of course, he never left the United States during the Second World War.[40] Similarly he told an assembly of winners of the Congressional Medal of Honor about the posthumous award to a B-17 commander who chose to go down in his plane with a wounded soldier. Lars-Erik Nelson of the *New York Daily News* checked all 434 citations of the Medal of Honor winners in the Second World War and could not find the Reagan tale. Eventually Nelson established that the tale came from the April 1944 *Reader's Digest* and from a 1944 movie, *Wing and a Prayer*.[41] Such revelations fell with a dull thud. No one appeared to care about the President's affable fabrications.

Reagan was the President as master illusionist. Many Americans perceived him as the personification of patriotism, of "standing tall" and rushing to the defense of the republic. If asked to compare Reagan with, say, George McGovern, they would of course name Reagan as the exemplary American patriot. Yet, when the nation was in its greatest danger, McGovern was a bomber pilot, flew thirty-five missions, twice brought in planes severely damaged by antiaircraft fire and won the Distinguished Flying Cross, while Reagan fought the Second World War on the film lots of Hollywood, sleeping in his own bed every night. (The young Reaganites of the 1980s continued in this tradition. Many of the fire-eaters of the 1980s so prepared to risk the lives of younger Americans by pushing a hard line against Nicaragua and the Soviet Union—Richard Perle, John Lehman, Richard Cheney, Elliot Abrams, Newt Gingrich, Pat Buchanan, Richard Burt—had managed for one reason or another, when they were themselves of military age in the 1960s, not to fight in Vietnam.*)

Similarly Reagan made himself exceptional among American Presidents in the public zeal with which he advocated and exploited religion. Yet he rarely went to church himself. The proclaimed champion of the family, he was the only divorced man ever elected President, and his relations with his own children were strained. The proclaimed champion of traditional morality, he had spent more of his life in a long Hollywood career in friendly association with adulterers, alcoholics, homosexuals, with people who procured abortions and people who took drugs, than any previous President. The proclaimed champion of law, order

---

*Jane Mayer, "Vietnam Service Isn't on the Resumes of Some Vocal, Middle-Aged Hawks," *Wall Street Journal*, January 11, 1985; Jack Newfield, "Reagan's War Hawks without Wings," *Village Voice*, June 11, 1985. Congressman Andrew Jacobs, a Democrat who served in the Marines in Korea, called these characters "War Wimps." A War Wimp is "one who is all too willing to send others to war, but never gets around to going to war himself."

and virtue, he headed an administration marked at home by the debasement of public ethics and abroad by a determination to make the United States a law unto itself in the world.

Reagan's triumph over anomaly, fantasy and failure was due in part to the serene and contagious optimism with which he walked away from car crashes. Like Franklin Roosevelt, the hero of his youth, he radiated a reassuring confidence that all contradictions would be dissolved and all difficulties overcome. For six years he enjoyed that most useful of political blessings — luck. Optimism and luck, along with an instinct for the levers of presidential effectiveness and a gift for dodging accountability, carried him very far. Even after the Iran-contra scandals, when his luck began to run out, he retained a hold on popular affection.

Reagan's record showed how far instinct in the use of executive resources can go in revitalizing an office over which last rites have been recently pronounced. It is a salutary reminder of the indestructibility of the American Presidency.

VII

Is it also a portent of the revival of the imperial Presidency? The critical tests of the imperial Presidency are threefold: the war-making power; the secrecy system; and the employment against the American people of emergency authority acquired for use against foreign enemies.

In 1973, when I wrote *The Imperial Presidency* and when Congress debated the War Powers Resolution, rhetoric about the war-making power considerably outran knowledge about the way that power had been exercised in American history. The State Department used to vindicate the presidential prerogative in committing troops to combat by putting out lists of the 80 or 125 or 150 times Presidents had done so without congressional authorization; the number escalated like Joe McCarthy's estimate of the number of Communists in the State Department. No one, however, really knew the facts about these incidents until the work begun by Abraham D. Sofaer (see page 51) resulted in two valuable volumes: Sofaer's own *War, Foreign Affairs and Constitutional Power: The Origins* (1976) and the continuation by

Henry Bartholomew Cox, *War, Foreign Affairs and Constitutional Power, 1829–1901* (1984). (Sofaer meanwhile became a
federal judge and then legal adviser for Ronald Reagan's State
Department.)

As Sofaer's researches showed, foreign perplexities tempted,
sometimes forced, Presidents to evade constitutional limitations
from the earliest years of the republic. It now appears that even
Jefferson himself, the apostle of strict construction, sent a naval
squadron to the Mediterranean under secret orders to fight the
Barbary pirates, applied for congressional sanction six months
later and then misled Congress as to the nature of the orders. He
unilaterally authorized the seizure of armed vessels in waters
extending to the Gulf Stream, engaged in rearmament without
congressional appropriations, developed "a system of secrecy
largely immune from legislative check" and invoked the Lockean
doctrine of emergency prerogative to justify presidential action
beyond congressional authorization. The broad discretionary powers
Madison as President obtained from Congress led on to the War
of 1812. Long before there was a Central Intelligence Agency,
Madison secretly sent Joel R. Poinsett as an executive agent to
Latin America and winked at his clandestine revolutionary adventures in Argentina and Chile; Madison's Secretary of State
removed Poinsett's despatches from State Department files lest
Congress request them. The Madison and Monroe administrations
used covert action to facilitate the annexation of Florida.[42]

But did this pattern of unilateral presidential adventurism in
the early republic legalize unilateral war-making by modern Presidents? Sofaer's surmise is that the early Presidents deliberately
selected venturesome agents, deliberately kept their missions secret, deliberately gave them vague instructions, deliberately failed
either to approve or to disapprove their constitutionally questionable plans and deliberately denied Congress and the public
the information to determine whether aggressive acts were
authorized — all because they wanted their men in the field to do
things that they knew lay beyond the constitutional right of Presidents to command. "At no time," Sofaer writes of the classical
period, "did the executive claim 'inherent' power to initiate military actions."[43]

The vital difference between the early republic and the imperial Presidency resides not in what Presidents did but in what Presidents believed they had the inherent right to do. Early Presidents, even while they circumvented the Constitution, had a cautious and vigilant concern for consent in a practical if not a formal sense. They had legislative majorities; they obtained broad delegations of authority; Congress approved their objectives and chose to let them take the lead; they acted in secret only when they had some assurance of support and sympathy if they were found out; and, even when they occasionally withheld essential information, they willingly shared much more than their twentieth-century successors, including such choice items as the instructions given envoys despatched on overseas negotiations. And, when Presidents initiated military action in the nineteenth century, it was typically against brigands, pirates, revolutionaries and other stateless and lawless groups; not, as in the twentieth century, against sovereign states.

In the late twentieth century Presidents made sweeping claims of inherent power, neglected the collection of consent, withheld information *ad libitum* and went to war against sovereign states. In so doing, they departed from the principles, if less from the practice, of the early republic. Reagan, not a close student of the Constitution, warmly embraced latter-day theories of inherent presidential power, including the inflation of the title Commander in Chief into a source of extraconstitutional authority. He sent Marines to their fate in Lebanon and, without congressional authorization, launched sneak military attacks on Grenada and Libya. He brought the CIA back from its season of disgrace, made it once again the President's private army and sent it off, in flagrant violation of congressional restrictions, to overthrow the government of Nicaragua. In the use of the war-making power, Reagan was a stout defender of the "almost royal" prerogatives.

The constitutional defense of unilateral presidential war-making continues to rest on the Supreme Court's *Curtiss-Wright* decision (see pages 100–103). The defenders cannot have read that decision with much care. *Curtiss-Wright* did not involve the war-making power. It involved the commerce power. The decision did not sanction independent executive action. It sanctioned presidential execution of powers delegated to the executive by Congress. As Justice Jackson later summed it up, *Curtiss-Wright* "involved, not the question of the President's right to act without congressional authority, but the question of his right to act under and in accord with an Act of Congress." [44]

But the case was decided a year after a unanimous Court in the *Schechter* case had struck down the National Recovery Act as an unconstitutional and invalid delegation of congressional power to the President. In upholding delegated power in *Curtiss-Wright*, the Court felt obliged to draw a dramatic distinction between delegation in domestic policy and delegation in foreign policy. So Sutherland engaged in his much quoted homily about "the very delicate, plenary and exclusive power of the President as the sole organ of the federal government in the field of international relations." [45] Justice Jackson subsequently dismissed these thoughts as *dicta* — that is, as views aside from the point to be decided and therefore not part of the Court's holding. *Curtiss-Wright* gave the imperial Presidency rhetorical encouragement but not constitutional vindication.

It may well be that the exact allocation of powers over foreign policy as laid down by the Framers for a minor eighteenth-century state does not meet the needs of a twentieth-century superstate. But underneath that allocation lies a deeper principle. With regard to foreign affairs in general and to the war-making power in particular, the Constitution commands above all a partnership between the legislative and executive branches. The terms of the partnership vary according to the pressures, political and geopolitical, of the day. That surely is the way it should be in a democratic polity.

It is a delusion, though one sedulously encouraged by the executive branch, that Presidents are wiser or even better informed than Congress. Sometimes they are; sometimes they aren't. Franklin Roosevelt was wiser and better informed than the isolationist senators William E. Borah and Burton K. Wheeler. But which body made more sense about the Vietnam War in the 1960s or about Central America in the 1980s, the National Security Council or the Senate Foreign Relations Committee?

Presidents in their own self-interest should regard the requirement of congressional collaboration not as a challenge to be evaded or a burden to be rejected but as an opportunity to be embraced — a heaven-sent opportunity to give their policies solid basis in consent. Congressional criticism alerts a President to flaws in his proposals. Congressional support strengthens his hand, increases his authority and spreads his responsibility.

The vital decisions, in foreign policy as elsewhere, must be argued out with Congress and the electorate. The salient question must be the wisdom of the course proposed. But, however the balance may shift, the partnership must endure. Neither branch of government is infallible. Neither has a divine right to prevail over the other. Congress must recognize that it cannot conduct day-to-day foreign policy. The President must recognize that no foreign policy can last that is not founded on public understanding and congressional consent.

VIII

The second test of the imperial Presidency is the secrecy system. Here Reagan devoted particular energy to rebuilding that fortress of the imperial Presidency. In his Executive Order 12356 of April 2, 1982, he discarded the Carter doctrine that the case for secrecy had to be weighed against the "public interest in disclosure." The Reagan order also discarded the standard that required a finding of "identifiable" potential damage to national security before documents can be classified. It eliminated the automatic declassification of government records. It even provided for the reclassification of documents already made public. The message to the bureaucracy was unmistakable: when in doubt, classify. The State Department, for example, after declassifying a minimum of 30 million pages a year in 1973–1981, declassified less than 13 million pages in both 1983 and 1984; the percentage of documents censored after review for declassification increased from 10 percent in 1983 to 75 percent in 1984.[46]

On March 11, 1983, Reagan promulgated National Security Decision Directive 84. This one required all officials with security clearances to sign agreements promising not to disclose classified information. It required them, if called upon, to take lie detector tests, with "adverse consequences" in event of refusal — even though evidence from such tests is too unreliable for admission to federal courts. And, most astonishing of all, it required those with access to "sensitive compartmented intelligence" — i.e., the 120,000 officials who see secret intelligence reports — to submit all their writings to prepublication censorship for the rest of their lives.

Congressional protest caused Reagan to suspend the provision for prepublication review. But a General Accounting Office report in June 1984 showed, in the words of Congressman Jack Brooks of Texas, that the alleged suspension "has, in reality, suspended very little of this administration's censorship and polygraph policies." [47] Over 100,000 government officials, including the Secretary of State and the Attorney General, had signed agreements accepting some form of lifetime prepublication review, and the lie detector program was continuing unabated. On November 1, 1985, a new Reagan national security directive applied the lie detector to "all individuals with access to United States Government sensitive compartmentalized information."

The Reagan administration reasserted claims to unconditional executive privilege. The Freedom of Information Act was subjected to administration restriction and sabotage. The press was forbidden to cover the invasion of Grenada. The release of historical documentation to scholars was gravely slowed down.

The case of Samuel Loring Morison was especially ominous. Having failed to persuade Congress to consider an American Official Secrets Act, the administration decided in 1985 to seek the same result by judicial reinterpretation of the Espionage Act of 1917. Morison was convicted under that act for the delivery of classified photographs to *Jane's Defence Weekly*, a respected English journal. The Morison prosecution came with especially ill grace from a Department of Justice that proclaimed its dedication to "original intent" as the standard for statutory as well as constitutional interpretation, for the original intent of the Espionage Act had been to prevent transfer of information to a foreign enemy, not to prevent leaks to the press; nor had so expansive a reading of the act ever been upheld in the seventy years of its history. Only an "activist" judiciary, of the sort ordinarily condemned by the Reagan Department of Justice, could seek to convert the Espionage Act into an Official Secrets Act.

What in any case was the need for laws punishing leaks to the press — laws that both repudiated the American libertarian tradition and restricted the flow of information indispensable to a democratic polity? The republic had faced the gravest perils of its history — the Civil War, two world wars — without an Official Secrets Act. What mightier emergency demands an intensification of executive secrecy today?

No one questions the state's right to keep certain things secret — weapons technology and deployment, intelligence methods and sources, diplomatic negotiations in progress, military contingency plans and the like. But the target of the Reagan program was not the disclosure of information to enemy governments; it was the disclosure of information to the Congress, press and people.

All Presidents are exasperated by leaks. They are really not, however, against leaks in principle. The selective leak is a familiar tool of government. What enrages Presidents are the leaks they do not ordain themselves — leaks that embarrass, expose or undermine their policies, which is to say leaks that stimulate and fortify national debate.

Presidents like to claim that such leaks do ineffable harm to national security. What they mostly mean is that leaks do harm to the political interests of the administration. The harm to national security through leaks is always exaggerated. We have had leaks from the start of the republic — from the day in 1795 when Senator Mason of Virginia enraged President Washington by giving the secret text of Jay's Treaty to the *Philadelphia Aurora*, or the day in 1844 when Senator Tappan of Ohio enraged President Tyler by giving the secret text of the treaty annexing Texas to the *New York Evening Post*. No one has ever demonstrated that these leaks harmed national security. No one can doubt that the disclosures benefited the democratic process.

The most recent notorious case was the Pentagon Papers prosecution of 1971 (see pages 345–348). It fell to Erwin Griswold,

Solicitor General of the United States and former dean of the Harvard Law School, to make the government's argument that national security required the suppression of the Defense Department's forty-seven-volume secret history of American participation in the Vietnam War. Griswold asked three high officials from the State and Defense Departments and the National Security Administration to go through the volumes and pick out those items that, if disclosed, would constitute threats to the security of the republic. They came up with about forty items. Most of these Griswold dismissed as too trivial for serious argument, thereby reducing the list to eleven items he thought faintly arguable.

The eleven did not impress the Court, and the Pentagon Papers were of course published in their entirety. The republic survived. The threats to national security? Dean Griswold observed eighteen years later, "I have never seen any trace of a threat to the national security from the publication. Indeed, I have never seen it even suggested that there was such an actual threat." He concluded: "It quickly becomes apparent to any person who has had considerable experience with classified material that there is massive overclassification and that the principal concern of the classifiers is not with national security, but rather with governmental embarrassment of one sort or another." [48]

Presidents are not infallible. Six thousand seven hundred bureaucrats (as of 1989) brandishing Top Secret stamps are even more fallible. The prime historic function of the secrecy system has not been to protect national security. In this respect it has done rather badly. As the system expands, too much paper is classified (12 million documents in 1987, 10 percent more than in 1986), too much of this is overclassified, too many people get security clearances (4.2 million) and too many spies slip through the net.

The real function of the secrecy system in practice is to protect the executive branch from accountability for its incompetence

---

*A recent illustration is the censorship by the Central Intelligence Agency of a book by its former director Admiral Stansfield Turner. "Having been

and its venality, its follies, errors and crimes.* "I spent fourteen years on the House Armed Services Committee," Otis Pike has written, "and was eventually and reluctantly forced to the conclusion that the most sensitive matters were those that might embarrass somebody politically." [49] Classified information, Congressman Lee Hamilton has said, is too often designed "to make policy look good, rather than to make good policy." [50] (*Glasnost* has permitted Russians to express similar conclusions. "The preservation of the secrecy cult," according to Vladimir A. Rubanov (of the KGB, no less), ". . . is a way of supporting faith in the infallibility of bureaucratic thinking and a chance for power to be used irresponsibly and uncontrollably in the narrow interests of small groups of people.")[51]

Nicholas P. Trist once expostulated to Andrew Jackson about Old Hickory's indifference to the fact that an unreliable servant had access to his official papers. "They are welcome, sir," Jackson replied, "to anything they can get out of my papers. . . . Let them make the most of it. Our government, sir, is founded upon the intelligence of the people; it has no other basis; upon their capacity to arrive at right conclusions in regard to measures and in regard to men." Trist, who was a professional diplomat, observed that this was all very well if the people had access to the whole truth; but what about partial disclosures and selective quotations? "Well, if they can't know all," said Jackson, "let them know as much as they can. The more they know of matters the better." [52]

This is the tradition that the secrecy system seeks to abolish.

---

responsible for protecting the nation's intelligence secrets for four years," Turner writes in his foreword, "I am well aware what the release of some kinds of information could mean to our national security." Yet the Reagan CIA demanded more than a hundred deletions, ranging, Turner says, "from borderline issues to the ridiculous." They did this, Turner believes, "because they were upset with the book's highly critical view of the Reagan administration's mishandling of our intelligence activities." *Secrecy and Democracy: The CIA in Transition* (Boston, 1985), xi. For cogent reviews of the Reagan record, see Steven L. Katz, *Government Secrecy: Decisions Without Democracy* (Washington, 1987), and Richard O. Curry, ed., *Freedom at Risk: Secrecy, Censorship, and Repression in the 1980s* (Philadelphia, 1988).

"Executive secrecy," John Taylor of Caroline, the philosopher of Jeffersonianism, wrote in 1814, "is one of the monarchical customs, plausibly defended, and certainly fatal to republican government. . . . How can national self government exist without a knowledge of national affairs? or how can legislatures be wise or independent, who legislate in the dark upon the recommendation of one man?" [53]

IX

The secrecy system and the war-making power interlock to create the special problems raised by resort to "covert action" as a major instrument of American foreign policy. For covert action—the use of clandestine means to change policies and regimes in other countries—enables Presidents to escape congressional restraints on conventional military action, and the secrecy system emboldens them to undertake rash and mindless adventures. Conceivably the United States might have been spared various small disasters—the Bay of Pigs, for example, and the Iran-contra affair—had our recent history been marked by fewer secrets and more leaks.

States unquestionably require secret services. The 64th Federalist argued that the power to negotiate treaties gave Presidents authority "to manage the business of intelligence," and the first Congress provided the President unvouchered funds for what it tactfully called "foreign intercourse." Secret agents sent abroad by Presidents to gather information not seldom found themselves involved in covert action. Early Presidents protected secret operations from undue congressional curiosity (see pages 47–48).

But, except in wartime, covert action remained for a century and a half spasmodic, marginal and *ad hoc*. Then the nation plunged into the shadows of the Cold War. Truman rather diffidently founded the CIA, and Eisenhower made it a major foreign policy tool. Reluctant to send regular forces into combat abroad, Eisenhower silently turned the CIA into the secret army of the executive branch (see page 167). Covert action displaced intelligence collection and analysis as the main charge on the CIA budget. CIA spooks tried to influence, alter and overthrow governments around the planet. With secret operations acquiring unprecedented salience, a host of legal and constitutional (not to mention political) complications emerged.

Espionage is in a sense "normal," with an accepted if illegal status in interstate relations. Spies routinely break the law and, when caught, accept the consequences. Except in wartime, most secret services concentrate on gathering information about foreign countries. The CIA's great innovation was to concentrate on covert action. Instead of contenting itself with finding out what is happening, the CIA surpasses other intelligence services in trying to *make* things happen.[54]

Covert action is purposeful intervention in the internal affairs of other nations. It carries a far more drastic threat than old-fashioned espionage to treaty obligations and interstate comity. But the Cold War consensus continued for years to throw a mantle of protection over CIA covert action (see pages 316–319) — a mantle still pretty much in place when *The Imperial Presidency* was first published.

Efforts to establish congressional oversight had been unavailing. Senator Mike Mansfield's proposal in 1956 for a Joint Committee on Central Intelligence was fiercely opposed by Eisenhower, who, we now know, told one congressman that "this kind of bill would be passed over my dead body." [55] Then in 1974 Congress finally bestirred itself and enacted the Hughes-Ryan amendment, requiring Presidents to make a "finding" that each covert operation was important to national security and a "timely" report of each finding to the appropriate congressional committee. The hope was to establish presidential accountability for each operation and to outlaw the favorite intelligence agency pretext for withholding its dark deeds from Presidents and everybody else — the "plausible deniability" dodge.

The next year a Senate select committee to study governmental operations with respect to intelligence activities began its investigations under the chairmanship of Frank Church of Idaho. In 1976 the committee issued a series of very able reports that gave Congress and the people for the first time a systematic understanding of what the CIA had been up to. The Church Committee revelations, including CIA assassination plots against foreign leaders — plots authorized, so far as the committee could discover, by no President — provoked a moment of shock and revulsion and gave new impetus to the movement for congressional oversight. In 1977 each house organized its intelligence committee, and the Intelligence Oversight Act of 1980 regularized the oversight system.

In its early years, however, legislative oversight was polite and rather incurious, especially as to legal implications. The vice chairman of the Senate Select Committee on Intelligence, Daniel Patrick Moynihan of New York, observed in 1983 that, although covert operations almost by their nature violated treaty law, "in six and more years of interminable closed hearings and briefings, I do not ever recall hearing a discussion of legal obligations of any kind." [56] Nor, until the Iran-contra affair burst into public attention in 1986–1987, was there more than sporadic discussion of executive compliance with domestic law.

The contras were a force organized and subsidized by the CIA in 1981 to overthrow the Sandinista regime in Nicaragua. The next year Congress passed the first of several amendments presented by Congressman Edward Boland of Massachusetts intended to prohibit CIA aid to the contras when used to overthrow rather than simply contain the Sandinistas. Reagan then directed his National Security Council staff to hold the contras together "in body and in soul" — an assignment entrusted to the eager hands of Lieutenant Colonel Oliver North.[57]

If Congress would not come along, Reagan told Admiral John Poindexter, his national security adviser, in 1986, "I want to figure out a way to take action unilaterally to provide assistance." As Poindexter continued in a memorandum to North, "He was taken with the examples of Presidential actions in the past without Congressional approval." [58] Poindexter and North then undertook to do what Congress had forbidden the CIA to do — and lied freely to Congress along the way.

The hearings, reports and trials produced by the Iran-contra affair exposed the damage that presidential infatuation with covert

action had done to American constitutional procedures. The secret
National Security Decision Directives issued by Presidents and
denied to Congress amounted, in the words of Congressman Jack
Brooks of Texas, to "secret laws." [59] Intelligence findings, it
turned out, were not always reported in timely fashion to the
congressional oversight committees, as the Intelligence Oversight
Act required, and thus amounted to secret decrees. The finding
of January 17, 1986, in which Reagan "found" that selling arms
to Iran was important to the national security, included this arresting sentence: "I . . . direct the Director of Central Intelligence
to refrain from reporting this Finding to the Congress." [60] In some
cases the claim was made (within the executive branch) that
findings gave the President the power to override duly enacted
statutes. Some covert actions, moreover, were undertaken without any presidential findings at all.

What was notable throughout was the White House indifference
to legal and constitutional standards. When James Baker, then
White House chief of staff, suggested to Reagan that he might
be impeached for permitting the solicitation of other countries
after Congress denied funds for the contras, everyone else in the
inner circle said Baker was wrong, and the matter was dropped.[61]
According to the Tower Commission, appointed by Reagan to
look into the Iran-contra affair, "Throughout the Iran initiative,
significant questions of law do not appear to have been adequately
addressed. . . . There appears to have been . . . little attention,
let alone systematic analysis, devoted to how Presidential actions
would comply with U.S. law." [62] When the President does it,
that means that it is not illegal.

Infatuation with covert action thus gave rise to a body of secret
laws, decrees and actions that increased presidential power, reduced presidential accountability, denied Congress and the people
essential knowledge about public policy and revitalized the imperial Presidency. Clark Clifford, who as an assistant to President
Truman had worked on the legislation setting up the CIA and
who in the 1960s served on the Foreign Intelligence Advisory
Board, called the system "a secret government operating in a
democracy. I don't think that our forefathers had any concept of

anything like that taking place. I know I had no thought at any time of such an organization being formed." [63]

X

I suppose a case could be made for such a system if covert action had proved itself an indispensable way of saving the republic from terrible dangers. As one who served as an intelligence officer in the Office of Strategic Services during the Second World War, I am well aware that covert action has its uses. I am also well aware of its limitations, especially in peacetime, and of the problems it presents to a democracy.

For covert action, far from being the salvation of the state, is in peacetime a marginal and dubious instrument of policy, quite likely to turn in the hands of the user. Its importance in the conduct of foreign affairs is vastly overrated. The very term is a misnomer. "Covert" action is often easy to detect, always hard to control, and in its nature illegal and immune to normal procedures of accountability. Founded as it is on law breaking, deception and lies, it imports bad habits into a democratic polity.

Experience should long since have undermined the cult of covert action. In 1956 Eisenhower established a Board of Consultants on Foreign Intelligence Activities. The Board appointed a panel headed by Robert Lovett, a former Secretary of Defense and Undersecretary of State, and David Bruce, an experienced diplomat who had been a top OSS officer during the war, to take a look at the CIA's covert operations. "Bruce was very much disturbed," Lovett said later. "He approached it from the standpoint of 'what right have we to go barging around into other countries buying newspapers and handing money to opposition parties or supporting a candidate for this, that or the other office?' He felt this was an outrageous interference with friendly countries." [64]

The Lovett-Bruce report heartily condemned the failure to control promiscuous CIA intervention and pleaded with the Eisenhower administration to question "the long-range wisdom of activities which have entailed our virtual abandonment of the international 'golden rule,' and which, if successful to the degree claimed for them, are responsible in a great measure for stirring up the turmoil and raising the doubts about us that exist in many countries of the world today. . . . Where will we be tomorrow?" [65]

Where indeed? Eisenhower rejected his board's recommendations. In its last report to him, the board called for "a total reassessment of our covert action policies." It declared bleakly, "We have been unable to conclude that, on balance, all of the covert action programs undertaken by CIA up to this time have been worth the risk or the great expenditure of manpower, money and other resources involved. In addition, we believe that CIA's concentration on political, psychological and related covert action activities have tended to detract substantially from the execution of its primary intelligence-gathering mission." [66] Clark Clifford, who later headed the board, reached the same conclusion. "I believe," he told the Senate Intelligence Committee in 1988, "that on balance covert activities have harmed this country more than they have helped us. . . . We have reached the point now where we must reassess the very idea of conducting covert activities." [67]

Within a system of law, covert action vanishes into a constitutional black hole. Yet, under proper control and in emergencies, it may be essential to the security of the state. What can a democracy do about it?

The first step in reconciling covert action to the Constitution is, in the words of Robert C. McFarlane, one of Reagan's national security advisers, to end the recent reliance on covert activity as "the core of our policy." [68] Oversight is only part of the answer. The surest way is to reduce the covert action budget, which, among other things, will force the CIA to concentrate on what should be its primary mission — intelligence collection and analysis. If reserved for only the most acute and demonstrable national emergencies, covert action is much less likely to burst the bonds of the Constitution.

The next rule has been well stated by Congressman Lee Hamilton of Indiana: "The U.S. government should not carry out any covert action that a fully informed American public would not support" [69] — a proposition that implies that clandestine activities should be consistent with official policy and with national traditions and ideals (all standards violated in the Iran-contra business). Prudence further enjoins that the operators be required to accompany their submissions to the President with assessments of the consequences of exposure and of failure — a precaution overlooked in the past. The establishment of an independent inspector general with full access to CIA operations and answerable to Congress would be another safeguard.

But these are all pious hopes that an infatuated President may simply ignore. Can anything be done to compel Presidents to restrain their penchant for dirty tricks?

The answer is yes, possibly. Congress might enact legislation requiring that all presidential intelligence findings (and all National Security Decision Directives bearing on intelligence operations) be put in writing and be delivered within forty-eight hours to the chairmen and vice chairmen of the intelligence committees and to the statutory members of the National Security Council. The statute might also impose criminal penalties in case of violation and assure the standing of Congress to bring suits in the courts. Doubtless one reason why the Reagan administration so casually defied the Hughes-Ryan amendment, the Intelligence Oversight Act and the Boland amendments is that violation incurred no punishment.

Oversight cannot be confused with authorization; nor can secret briefing of the chairmen and vice chairmen of the intelligence committees be taken as the equivalent of congressional consent. Nor is any system of oversight foolproof, above all for an agency whose pride is its skill in the arts of deception. Yet one can be reasonably sure that, if the Reagan administration had submitted the Iran-contra schemes to the congressional oversight committees, the reaction would have been swift and scoffing — which of course is why Reagan directed that his great finding not be reported to Congress. In an imperfect world, the best guarantee against covert action follies may well be to arrange for experienced politicians to cast a cold eye on the schemes dreamed up in the vaporous world of intelligence agencies.

XI

Executive war-making power, executive secrecy, executive covert action — these are vital weapons of the imperial Presidency.
Reagan used them all to fend off Congress and the press and to
strengthen executive domination of foreign policy. Unlike Nixon,
however, Reagan did not bring the imperial Presidency into its
final stage — the policy of stigmatizing opponents of the President
as traitors to the republic. In his relaxed way, Reagan accepted
opposition as an unavoidable feature of democracy. One doubts
that he had an Enemies List. There was no McCarthyism in his
administration.

Still, "national security" became for Reagan as for Nixon the
all-purpose alibi when presidential agents ignored or overrode
the law. "If the President, for example, approves something
because of national security," Nixon told David Frost, ". . . then
the President's decision in that instance is one that enables those
who carry it out, to carry it out without violating a law." [70]
National security is the contemporary version of Lockean prerogative.

The very term "national security" was an incantation in the
Nixon White House. Egil Krogh, Jr., wondering in later years
why in the world he had organized the burglary of the office of
Daniel Ellsberg's psychiatrist, said, "The key is the effect that
the term 'national security' had on my judgment. The very words
served to block critical analysis. It seemed at least presumptuous
if not unpatriotic to inquire into just what the significance of
national security was. . . . To suggest that national security was
being improperly invoked . . . appeared to be beyond the scope
and in contravention of the faithful performance of the duties of
my office. . . . Freedom of the President to pursue his planned
course was the ultimate national security objective." [71]

Roscoe Conkling once observed, "When Dr. Johnson defined
patriotism as the last refuge of a scoundrel, he was unconscious
of the then underdeveloped capabilities of the word reform." [72]
Both Dr. Johnson and Senator Conkling would have been edified
by the interpretation of "national security" prevailing in Wash-

ington circa 1970 and again circa 1985. The doctrine that the invocation of national security was an inherent and absolute presidential right, whatever the surrounding circumstances, a right to be exercised in secret at presidential pleasure without accountability to the Congress and the people, represented an extraordinary abuse of presidential power.

Yet no one can doubt that on occasion the law of self-preservation may justify temporary enlargement of executive initiative. Though the question is dealt with in earlier chapters (see especially pages 7–10, 141–50, 161–162, 193, 263–265, 320–324), it might be useful to put in summary form the criteria that alone warrant presidential resort to emergency prerogative. For the danger always remains that power asserted by Presidents during authentic emergencies may create precedents for abuses of power in emergencies that exist only in the hallucinations of the Oval Office and are invisible to most of the nation.

The perennial question is how to distinguish real crises threatening the life of the republic from nightmares troubling the minds of paranoid Presidents. How to distinguish the actions of Lincoln during the Civil War and of the second Roosevelt immediately before the Second World War from Jefferson's actions in face of the Burr conspiracy, Truman's seizure of the steel mills, Nixon's lawlessness in 1972–1973 and the Reagan administration's covert policies toward Iran and the contras?

Lincoln in 1861 and Roosevelt in 1941 did what they did under what appeared to be a popular demand and a public necessity. Both Presidents acted on high and commanding moral grounds, stated in each case in a famous speech — Lincoln in his Gettysburg Address ("that government of the people, by the people, for the people, shall not perish from the earth"), Roosevelt in his annual message of January 6, 1941 ("we look forward to a world founded upon four essential freedoms").

Both Presidents took their actions in light of day to the accompaniment of uninhibited political debate. They did not claim to be exercising routine or inherent presidential power. They threw themselves in the end on the justice of the country and the rectitude of their motives. Whatever Lincoln and Roosevelt felt compelled to do under the pressure of crisis did not corrupt their essential commitment to constitutional ways and democratic processes nor their dedication to higher ideals.

The experience of Lincoln and Roosevelt suggests, I think, the standards that warrant presidential resort to emergency prerogative:

1. There must be a clear, present and broadly perceived danger to the life of the nation and to the ideals for which the nation stands.
2. The President must define and explain to Congress and the people the nature and urgency of the threat.
3. The understanding of the emergency, the judgment that the life of the nation is truly at stake, must be broadly shared by Congress and the people.
4. Time must be of the essence; existing statutory authorizations must be inadequate; and waiting for normal legislative action must constitute an unacceptable risk.
5. The danger must be one that can be met in no other way than by presidential initiative beyond the laws and the Constitution.
6. Secrecy must be strictly confined to the tactical requirements of the emergency. Every question of basic policy must be opened to national debate.
7. The President must report what he has done to Congress, which, along with the Supreme Court and ultimately the people, will serve as the judge of his action.
8. None of the presidential actions can be directed against the domestic political process and rights.

Emergency prerogative, in short, cannot be rightly invoked on presidential say-so alone but only under stringent and persuasive conditions, both of threat and of accountability, with the burden of proof resting on the President. These standards, I believe, sufficiently distinguish what Lincoln did in the spring of 1861 and Roosevelt did in the autumn of 1941 from the actions of Jefferson, Truman, Nixon and Reagan.

Lincoln's policy after Sumter, Roosevelt's in the North Atlantic, at least in the eyes of most Americans at the time and of most scholars in retrospect, represented a necessity—but not a precedent. By declining to use claims of inherent presidential power to justify their actions, Lincoln and Roosevelt took care not to give lesser men precedents to be invoked against lesser dangers. These two Presidents remained faithful to the spirit, if not the letter, of the Constitution: acting on the spirit to save the letter.

"If the people ever let command of the war power fall into irresponsible and unscrupulous hands," Justice Jackson said in dissent in the *Korematsu* case, "the courts wield no power equal to its restraint. The chief restraint upon those who command the physical forces of the country, in the future as in the past, must be their responsibility to the political judgments of their contemporaries and to the moral judgments of history." [73]

XII

When I wrote *The Imperial Presidency*, I expressed surprise (see pages 389 and 392) that Vietnam and Watergate had not led more people to call for changes in the Constitution. Reformers like the young Woodrow Wilson had floated quasi-parliamentary remedies in the last years of the nineteenth century; and it might have seemed that such parliamentary features as the vote of confidence and the question hour could help resolve the contemporary crisis of the American Presidency.

In fact, I spoke too soon. Interest in constitutional reform along parliamentary lines was beginning to revive in the year of the book's publication. At a conference on the Presidency in 1973, for example, eminent foreigners—Gunnar Myrdal of Sweden and Lord Ritchie-Calder of Great Britain—impressed their audience by insisting "that Watergate simply couldn't happen in their countries—or rather that, if something like it did happen, the party in power would be out of office within a matter of hours." [74]

Under this benign light, parliament seemed an idyllic spot

where legislators reveled in the power to oversee, interrogate and dismiss the executive. In the presidential model, the executive is protected by the separation of powers; in the parliamentary model, the executive is drawn from the legislative majority and presumably obedient to it. Would not constitutional revision along parliamentary lines supply the perfect antidote to the imperial Presidency? In 1974 the political scientist Charles M. Hardin offered an elaborate parliamentary blueprint in his book *Presidential Power and Accountability: Toward a New Constitution*. In the same period Richard Lee Strout (TRB of the *New Republic*) argued the advantages of the British and Canadian systems in sprightly columns. Members of Congress advanced less sweeping proposals designed to appropriate the question period and the vote of confidence and insert them into the presidential system.

Then, at the end of the 1970s, the frustrations of the Carter Presidency set off a new cry for constitutional reform. This time, however, the parliamentary model fascinated for opposite reasons—not as a means of restraining executive abuse but as a means for restoring executive authority. For in the parliamentary system the executive can count on the automatic enactment of his program, and the electorate knows where to fix accountability for the result. Lloyd N. Cutler, who as Carter's White House counsel had seen plenty of frustration at first hand, published an influential article in 1980, arguing that the constitutional separation of powers made the national government incoherent and irresponsible and proposing reforms designed to move the political order in a parliamentary direction.[75]

Cutler then joined with Douglas Dillon, a distinguished public servant in the Eisenhower and Kennedy administrations, to set up a committee on the constitutional system. In the call for the committee, Dillon wrote that the "question transcending all immediate issues is whether we can continue to afford the luxury of the separation of power" and whether we should not contemplate "a change to some form of parliamentary government that would eliminate or sharply reduce the present division of authority between the executive and legislative arms."[76] The committee's Basic Problem Statement provided a powerful summary:

The checks and balances inspired by the experience of the Eighteenth Century have led repeatedly, in the Twentieth Century, to government stalemate and deadlock, to an incapacity to make quick and sharp decisions in the face of urgent problems. Rash and impulsive governmental actions have been deterred, and that is a benefit. But it is a benefit often gained at the cost of inability to act at all, or at least to act in a timely and decisive manner. When, after arduous delays, policies are produced, they are liable to be a contradictory hodge-podge that neither the President nor the legislators fully support. No one accepts responsibility, and the people have difficulty holding anyone accountable. The President blames the Congress, members of Congress blame the President and one another, and amid the recriminations people lose confidence in government altogether.[77]

This situation, it is argued, is devastating enough in domestic policy, where it prevents concerted action by the executive and legislative branches to deal with the budget deficit, the trade deficit, the national debt and other public woes. And (as some extend the indictment) it is disastrous in foreign policy. We are engaged in a global struggle (the argument goes) with an unscrupulous adversary. Can we let the Constitution tie our hands and thereby imperil the survival of the republic? Does not national security require the concentration of authority in the hands of the President, since he has the best information and alone can act with the necessary secrecy and despatch? Can we afford congressional meddling with the conduct of foreign affairs? Can we afford 535 Secretaries of State? Does not the very existence of this obsolete system of checks and balances force Presidents into circumvention and illegality (as in the Iran-contra affair) out of a patriotic desire to save the nation?

A British observer sums up the case. The Iran-contra affair, George Urban tells us, has made it "clear yet again that the American constitutional system is an obstacle to the conduct of a successful Western security policy. Most particularly, it deprives U.S. administrations of those unconventional tools which great powers have always had to use in a cruel world. . . . The American system, with duality (or worse) built into the conduct of foreign policy, is unequal to the demands the modern world makes on a world power." [78]

The conclusion is evident. We should retreat from the separation of powers and give our President the authority to do the job—as the Prime Minister has in Great Britain. Thus Lloyd Cutler's program proposed a quasi-parliamentary regime, providing that the President and Congress (both houses) be elected for simultaneous six-year terms and empowering both the President and Congress to break stalemates by dissolving the government and calling for new elections.

Such a program, however, confronted the problem emphasized by that able and irrepressible reformer James MacGregor Burns in *The Power to Lead* in 1984: that the parliamentary model can work only on the foundation of centralized, disciplined parties. Apart from the danger that excessively ideological parties might split the nation irremediably, as they did in 1860, history shows that American parties have always resisted centralization and discipline. They are loose coalitions, open at the joints, filled with internal argument, held together by broad biases and historic memories. When Hardin, for example, proposed to veto the nomination of "persistent mavericks" for Congress and to punish legislators who made "a career of independence,"* he underlined the practical irrelevance of his plan. The systematic exclusion from Congress of all dissent save that of the official opposition is unimaginable in the American political culture. Rigid discipline, the prohibition of free voting, the persecution of mavericks, the abolition of primaries—all such things are against the genius of American politics, and never more so than in the electronic age.

*C. M. Hardin, *Presidential Power and Accountability* (Chicago, 1974), II, 185. I should add that, though this book's essential argument seems to me to lie in the domain of political fantasy, there are many shrewd insights into the American political order along the way.

The decisive fact is that Americans have come to *want* divided government. For half the time since the Second World War, control of the White House has rested in one party and control of one or both houses of Congress in the other party. What Samuel Lubell calls "the deliberate and widespread use of both parties," balancing one off against the other, began in the Eisenhower years.[79] It became thereafter a purposeful technique of self-defense against the imperial Presidency. In 1957, Eisenhower was the first President since Grover Cleveland in 1885 to win an election without carrying both houses of Congress. In five of the next eight presidential elections, the voters gave one party the Presidency and the opposition party one house of Congress. By 1989, George Bush had to deal with a Congress in which *both* houses were controlled by the opposition. Americans, it would seem, have decided to add political checks and balances to the structural checks and balances already ordained by the Constitution.

At a time when political parties can hardly keep afloat in the turbulent sea of voter independence, the idea of making them more cohesive and commanding than ever before in American history is an exercise in fantasy. If a crisis of governmental impotence should arise in the future, a President is not likely to ask the Congress to move toward parliamentary government through the laborious process of constitutional amendment. He is more likely to say, as Franklin Roosevelt said in his first inaugural, "I shall ask the Congress for the one remaining instrument to meet the crisis — broad Executive power to wage a war against the emergency."

XIII

Even if a conversion to parliamentarianism were possible, there is little reason to suppose it would be desirable. The American admiration for the parliamentary model springs from romantic misconceptions about the British system.

Our constitutional reformers yearned after the parliamentary model, as noted, for two contradictory reasons: the post-Watergate reformers because they believed it would assure legislative supremacy; and the post-Carter reformers because they believed it would assure executive supremacy. The second group understood the parliamentary system better. While the parliamentary model formally assumes legislative omnipotence, in practice it produces an almost unassailable dominance of the executive over the legislature.

The British Prime Minister thus appoints people to office without parliamentary confirmation, makes foreign policy without parliamentary participation, declares war without parliamentary authorization, concludes treaties without parliamentary ratification, sets the budget without parliamentary consultation, withholds information without parliamentary recourse and essentially inherits the prerogatives that once belonged to absolute monarchy. As Lloyd George said in 1931, "Parliament has really no control over the Executive; it is a pure fiction." [80] This is the continuing refrain of British politics. "The government controls Parliament," Lord Hailsham said in 1976, "and not Parliament the government. . . . We live under an elective dictatorship, absolute in theory, if hitherto thought tolerable in practice." [81] Nor in the British system does a Supreme Court exist to check executive abuse.

The alleged check on prime ministerial discretion is cabinet government — the theory of collective responsibility for government decisions. "You, Mr. President," Churchill said to Roosevelt during the Second World War, "are concerned to what extent you can act without the approval of Congress. You don't worry about your Cabinet. On the other hand, I never worry about Parliament, but I continuously have to consult and have the support of my Cabinet." [82] No doubt in the age of Bagehot and possibly even in the age of Churchill cabinet government was a reality. But collective decision-making has notably declined in modern times. Many vital decisions — Chamberlain at Munich, Attlee and the building of the British nuclear capacity, Eden and the Suez war — were taken by the Prime Minister and a small inner group. No one in the age of Margaret Thatcher can doubt that cabinet government has given way to prime ministerial government. [83]

American parliamentarists cite dissolution following the loss of a vote of confidence as the legislature's check on prime ministerial discretion. But in practice, the threat of dissolution hands the Prime Minister one more means of whipping recalcitrant MPs into line—lest they be forced to risk their seats in a general election. The vote of confidence is so drastic a resort that it is rarely employed. The last time the loss of a vote of confidence overthrew a government commanding majority support in the House of Commons was a century ago, in 1885. Nor does defeat of a government bill automatically count as a vote of confidence. In the 1970s, British governments suffered a series of defeats without being forced to dissolve Parliament and call a new general election.[84] No doubt the possibility of a no-confidence vote has brought about changes in Prime Ministers, as after Narvik in 1940 and Suez in 1956. But this was done by reshuffling people inside the government, not by going to the electorate and getting a fresh mandate.

In the American system, the dissolution capability would give legislators the power, which they lack under the impeachment clause, to dismiss Presidents on grounds of disagreement over policy. Is this such a good idea? One has only to reflect what might have happened, for example, when John Adams resisted the congressional passion for war with France in 1798 or when Harry Truman faced down an explosion of congressional wrath after firing Douglas MacArthur in 1950. Yet in retrospect those two doughty Presidents never had finer hours. Nor, as Allan Sindler has pointed out, would a brisk no-confidence dismissal of Nixon have been nearly so satisfactory a resolution of the Watergate mess as the "thoroughness, deliberateness, gravity and nonpartisanship of the impeachment inquiry." [85]

It is conceivable that an incident like Watergate might have forced out a British Prime Minister through behind-the-scenes sleight of hand. But that does not mean that Parliament and the electorate would know what had been going on. "Don't think a Watergate couldn't happen here," Woodrow Wyatt, a former member of Parliament and a continuing political commentator, has written. "You just wouldn't hear about it." [86] Nixon might even have escaped unscathed. "If only Mr. Nixon had the blessing of the British system," according to Edward Pearce, the political correspondent of the *London Daily Telegraph*. ". . . Woodward and Bernstein would have been drowned in the usual channels, a D-Notice would have been erected over their evidence, and a properly briefed judge, a figure of outstanding integrity, would have found the essential parts of the tapes to be either not relevant or prejudicial to the national security. The British system of protecting the authorities is almost part of the constitution." [87] The Iran-contra affair? "Can one imagine an Irangate inquiry here?" observed Edward Heath, the former British Prime Minister. "Not for one moment." [88]

The question period is another device much fancied by American parliamentarists. The notion of compelling executive officials to defend policies in face-to-face confrontation has initial appeal as a way to demystify the Presidency. But the device is less fancied by those who use it every week. "What most questions usually reveal," wrote R. H. S. Crossman, "is the capacity of a Minister to evade an issue." [89] Lord Hailsham spoke of "the twice-weekly exhibition of schoolboy humour in the House of Commons," [90] *The Economist* of "an undergraduate pastiche of a White House press conference." [91] Woodrow Wyatt called question time a "useless privilege," a "charade," a "fake instrument of democracy," "a Punch and Judy show"; "when a Minister has something to hide, Question Time has little hope of dragging it into the open." [92] It works no better in Canada. "Anyone who has participated in question period," wrote Professor James Gillies, a former MP, "knows its main purposes are to embarrass the government, to amuse the tourists and TV audiences, and to make life easier for reporters. It is a totally ineffective way to elicit significant information." [93]

Given congressional obsequiousness toward Presidents, one doubts whether a presidential question time would help in the United States. Newspapermen at press conferences are less obsequious, but they rarely elicit significant information. As for cabinet members, they are subject to far more sustained and searching interrogation before congressional committees than they would ever receive in a general question hour.

"It works quite well for us," Sir Oliver Wright, a recent British ambassador to the United States, has written of the parliamentary system. "I doubt it would for you. I'm glad you didn't try. For the parliamentary system of government gives . . . astonishing power to the executive." This is all right for a medium-sized nation like Britain. "But give the executive of a superpower . . . powers of that magnitude, and we all should be in trouble." [94]

XIV

The irony is that British reformers are as dissatisfied with the fusion of powers as American reformers are with the separation of powers. And for many British reformers the model is — the American Congress. "The United States constitutional system has many disadvantages," Edward Heath told the House of Commons in 1988. ". . . But it has one advantage, that Congress is not beholden to the President. . . . Therefore its debates are free and it searches out its information from every quarter. . . . There is a difference between the American open system, with all its faults, and our system. That is what I believe we must move on to." [95]

British reformers want to set Parliament free. They want to increase legislative initiative, legislative scrutiny and executive accountability. They want a Bill of Rights. They want fixed terms for Parliament. (Heath once spoke to me with envy about the American system of midterm elections. "The only means we have between general elections of bringing public opinion to bear on national policies," he said, "is through by-elections, and this depends on a sufficiency of MPs resigning or dying. Luck has been with Mrs. Thatcher, and she has had far less than the average number of by-elections. How much better to give the whole country a chance to express itself every two years!") They want back-bench independence. They want to select parliamentary candidates through primaries. They want the topmost civil service posts to be filled by political appointment. They want to abolish the Official Secrets Act and to enact a Freedom of Information Act. They finally (in 1979) forced the government to accept a system of watchdog committees overseeing major departments, and they want now to increase committee staffs and to gain authority to review pending legislation. They want a select committee to monitor the intelligence services. They want control over government spending through a national audit office solely responsible to Parliament, like the General Accounting Office in Washington. They want, in short, to limit power, in Lord Hailsham's words, "both by law and by a system of checks and balances." [96]

While American parliamentarists envy the centralized and disciplined parties of Britain and Canada, British and Canadian reformers think that centralization and discipline have reduced individual legislators to nonentities. The ordinary back-bencher, observes Woodrow Wyatt, "may be the greatest orator since Demosthenes, the finest administrator since Pericles, the shrewdest judge of men since Napoleon. It will be all to no avail." [97] The situation is no better in Canada. "Cicero and Demosthenes together could not change a vote in the Canadian parliament," writes Professor Gillies. ". . . Few [speeches] are even listened to." [98]

Nothing is more damaging to Parliament, British reformers argue, than the fusion of powers. Confining the selection of ministers to MPs narrows the pool of talent available for governing. It bases appointment on a superficial test — facility in debate — rather than on a serious test — ability in policy and administration. It creates "a conspiracy of common interest" (Wyatt) to keep the executive strong and the legislature weak, for two thirds of the House of Commons either have been or aspire to be ministers and find it personally advantageous to exalt the executive. "The presence of the Prime Minister, Ministers and the machinery of party discipline in the House of Commons results in its members being prisoners in their own House." [99]

Recent British developments — the spread of "cross-voting" (that is, voting against measures advanced by one's own party); the establishment of watchdog committees; the demand to initiate legislation; the defiance of the Official Secrets Act by whistleblowing civil servants and their vindication in the courts[100] —

all represent movement in the American direction. In Great Britain as in the United States party dealignment increases in the electronic age.[101]

Where American constitutional reformers yearn after Parliament, the British reform agenda adopts essential features of the American system. Each country tends to play the defects of its own system against the charms of the one across the seas. "Play" is the word, because constitutional blueprinting is in the end a game. Constitutions, whether written or unwritten, must express deeply imbedded values, habits and folkways of a nation. They cannot be revised mechanically.

XV

The argument thus far has been about the structure of government. But are the difficulties encountered these days in governing really the consequences of defects in structure? After all, the United States has had the separation of powers from the beginning of the republic. The existence of an independent Congress and of an independent Supreme Court has not prevented competent Presidents from acting with decision and despatch.

In practice the separation of powers is a rather flexible and accommodating doctrine. The Founding Fathers were intensely practical men determined to charter a republic that would work and last in a dangerous world. They recognized, as the Supreme Court itself has said, that a "hermetic sealing off of the three branches of Government from one another would preclude the establishment of a Nation capable of governing itself effectively." [102] The system devised at Philadelphia in 1787 did not separate the powers of government into three watertight compartments. The Philadelphia system, as Richard Neustadt has notably said, was rather one of "separated institutions *sharing* powers." [103] Justice Jackson provided the classic statement in the steel seizure case: "While the Constitution diffuses power the better to secure liberty, it also contemplates that the practice will integrate the dispersed powers into a workable government. It enjoins upon its branches separateness but interdependence, autonomy but reciprocity." [104]

The independence of Congress and the courts did not disable Jefferson or Andrew Jackson or Lincoln or Wilson or the two Roosevelts. Of course they all complained on occasion. Theodore Roosevelt once clenched his fist and said to the young Franklin Roosevelt, "Sometimes I wish I could be President and Congress too." FDR added thirty years later, "I suppose if the truth were told, he is not the only President that has had that idea." [105] But they all persevered, and mostly succeeded where they deserved to succeed. The most powerful plea this century for strong national authority — Herbert Croly's *The Promise of American Life* — did not see the separation of powers as an obstacle to effective government. Frank J. Goodnow's *Social Reform and the Constitution*, another classic of the Progressive era, worried far more about federalism, the division of power between national and state governments, as a bar to reform than about the division of power within the national government.

Why are things worse now? It cannot be because of the separation of powers itself; this has been a constant through American history. It cannot be because contemporary problems are worse; this, as noted, is hardly the case. The real difference is that the presidents who operated the system successfully in the past knew what they thought should be done — and were able to persuade Congress and the nation to give their ideas a try. The problem today is not at all that our leaders know what to do and are prevented from doing it by structural gridlock in the system. The problem is that they know not what to do.

Efficient enactment of a poor program is a dubious triumph. A system in which a rubber-stamp legislature delivers whatever the executive requests is only as good as the executive and his requests. If the United States had had a parliamentary system in 1937, Congress would have given Franklin Roosevelt his court-packing plan. If it had had a parliamentary system in the 1980s, Congress would have criminalized abortion, legalized school prayer, ended oversight of the CIA and given Colonel North a global hunting license.

A century ago Bryce in *The American Commonwealth* reported the English view that the separation of powers made it almost impossible for the American polity to settle major national issues.

He also reported the rejoinder by American political leaders. Congress, they told Bryce, had forborne to settle such issues not because of defects in structure,

> but because the division of opinion in the country regarding them has been faithfully reflected in Congress. The majority has not been strong enough to get its way; and this has happened, not only because abundant opportunities for resistance arise from the methods of doing business, but still more because no distinct impulse or mandate towards any particular settlement of these questions has been received from the country. It is not for Congress to go faster than the people. When the country knows and speaks its mind, Congress will not fail to act.[106]

When the country is not sure what ought to be done, it may be that the delay, debate and further consideration enjoined by the separation of powers are not a bad idea. What is the virtue of acting with decision and despatch if you don't know what you are doing? And, when our leadership is sure what to do, it must begin by educating Congress and public opinion—and that is not a bad idea either. A competent President with a sensible policy or even (as in the case of the Reagan tax bill of 1981) a less than sensible policy has the resources under the present Constitution to get his way.

The separation of powers is most deplored in the field of foreign policy. Yet here it is the indispensable engine of consent, and consent is never more indispensable than on questions of peace and war. Both Ford and Carter complained about the Clark amendment of 1976, prohibiting military or paramilitary operations in Angola without express congressional authorization. Had there been no Clark amendment, either President might have sent the CIA or even the Marines into the Angolan civil war. Apart from the question whether armed intervention in Angola made any sense, it obviously could not have been sustained without a clear and formal expression of congressional support.

The separation of powers has caused its share of problems. But in the main it has worked well enough. It has ensured discussion when no consensus exists for action, and it has permitted action when a majority is convinced that the action is right. In short, if the executive has a persuasive remedy, you don't need fundamental constitutional change. If the executive remedy is not persuasive, you don't want fundamental constitutional change.

But the greatest importance of the separation of powers lies precisely in the old theory of the Founding Fathers: to preclude the exercise of arbitrary power. The separation of powers provides the vital mechanism of self-correction in the American system. It is the means of protection against the resurgence of the imperial Presidency. It is the ultimate safeguard of accountability. The Constitution cannot guarantee that wicked men, ambitious of power, with hatred of liberty and contempt of law, may not fill the place once occupied by Washington and Lincoln. But it can, through the separation of powers, guarantee that, when a President abuses power, corrective forces will arise to redress the constitutional balance. As Senator Sam Ervin memorably put it in Watergate days, "One of the great advantages of the three separate branches of government is that it's difficult to corrupt all three at the same time." [107]

XVI

If on balance the separation of powers has justified itself, what about more limited constitutional change designed to improve specific aspects of a less than perfect document? Despairing of root-and-branch transformation, reformers propose a series of discrete amendments: a single six-year presidential term; a presidential item veto; the direct election of the President by popular vote.

The idea of a single six-year term has been around for a long time. The perennial argument for this amendment is that the quest for reelection, in the words of a bipartisan group of former cabinet members in 1985, lies "at the heart of our inability to manage complex, long-term national problems." [108] The prospect of a second term, it is claimed, stains Presidents with partisanship. It makes the nation suspect their motives and tempts them to issue easy promises and to postpone hard decisions. A single six-year term would liberate Presidents from the low business of politics. Instead of urging measures designed to secure their re-election, they would gain the freedom, the time and the public trust to enable them to do only what is best for the country.

The argument, however superficially enticing, is profoundly anti-democratic in its implications. It assumes, as noted on pages 386–389, that Presidents know better than anyone else what is best for the country and that the people are so wrong-headed and ignorant that Presidents should be encouraged to disregard their wishes. It assumes that, the less responsive a President is to popular desires and needs, the better President he will be. It assumes that the democratic process itself is the obstacle to wise decisions.

The theory of American democracy is quite the opposite. It is that the give-and-take of the democratic process is the best guarantee of wise decisions. It is that the President's duty is not to ignore and override popular concerns but to acknowledge and heed them. It is that the President's accountability to the popular will is the best means of ensuring that he will do a decent job.

The Founding Fathers dismissed the single-term idea. The proposal, Hamilton told the Constitutional Convention, would make the President "a Monster elected for seven years, and ineligible afterwards; having great powers . . . & continually tempted by this constitutional disqualification to abuse them." The one-term limitation, said Gouverneur Morris, would "destroy the great motive to good behavior," which is the President's hope of re-election; "it was saying to him, make hay while the sun shines." A President, added Oliver Ellsworth of Connecticut, "should be re-elected if his conduct proved himself worthy of it. And he will be more likely to render himself, worthy of it if he be rewardable with it." [109] Re-eligibility, Hamilton explained in the 72nd Federalist, was essential to give the President "the inclination and the resolution to act his part well" and to give the people "time and leisure to observe the tendency of his measures." The Founders had rejected the single term precisely because it would diminish "the inducements to good behavior."

The opposing argument is that a ban on re-election, by emancipating Presidents from partisanship, would inspire the nation to follow the President as a man above politics. This argument finds no historical sustenance. The second-term records of Presidents elected under the anti–third-term 22nd Amendment (Eisenhower, Nixon, Reagan) show that ineligibility for re-election purifies neither their own performance nor the national attitude toward them. And while the quest for re-election may on occasion cause Presidents to defer hard decisions — for example, Kennedy's refusal to pull out of Vietnam till after the 1964 election — it more often has a salutary impact in increasing sensitivity to public needs and hopes.

A single six-year term would release Presidents from the test of submitting their records to the voters. It would enshrine the "President knows best" myth that has already got us into sufficient trouble as a nation. It would be a mighty blow against presidential accountability. It would be a mighty reinforcement of the imperial Presidency. It would be an impeachment of the democratic process itself. The Founding Fathers were everlastingly right when they turned down this well-intentioned but ill-considered proposal two centuries ago.

If popular government is about anything, it is about the unfettered right of the voters to choose their leaders. This was certainly the way the Founders saw it. The wisdom of the Founders was rejected in 1947 when a conservative Congress carried out an act of retrospective vengeance against Franklin D. Roosevelt and perpetrated the 22nd Amendment. If this amendment was intended as an obstacle to presidential aggrandizement, the subsequent growth of the imperial Presidency showed how ineffective it was. In the meantime, unlike all other constitutional amendments save the 18th, it has narrowed rather than enlarged the power of the people. The 18th Amendment was, thank heavens, repealed. Despite my belief that the practical argument against a President serving more than two terms has great force, I think that the 22nd Amendment should be repealed too. Surely the object of the amending process must be to expand and not to shrink the scope of democratic choice in the national polity.

XVII

"The President," the Constitution reads (Article I, Section 7), "may approve any appropriation and disapprove any other appropriation in the same bill. In such case he shall, on signing the bill, designate the appropriations disapproved; and shall return a copy of such appropriations, with his objections, to the House in which the bill shall have originated."

Actually I am quoting the *Confederate* Constitution. But the idea of an "item" veto — now mysteriously and redundantly known as a "line-item" veto — has enchanted Presidents ever since Appomattox. Ulysses S. Grant, to whom the Confederates surrendered on the battlefield, surrendered himself thereafter to the Confederate theory of the veto; indeed, he proposed to extend its reach beyond appropriations to all congressional statutes. In recent times Franklin D. Roosevelt, Dwight D. Eisenhower, Ronald Reagan and George Bush have all requested an item veto for appropriations bills. Forty-three state governors had a form of item veto in the 1980s.

The late-nineteenth-century argument for the item veto, as advanced especially by Rutherford B. Hayes, was as a presidential defense against riders tacked on to appropriations bills — that is, against objectionable amendments that Presidents could not reject without rejecting the entire bill. The twentieth century added a new argument — that the item veto would enable the executive to check extravagant legislative appropriations. This argument had particular appeal in the era of Reagan's massive budget deficits. Forty-seven senators sponsored an item-veto bill in 1985, and, according to the Gallup poll, two-thirds of the electorate favored it. Armed with the item veto, the argument ran, Presidents would put on their green eye-shades, edit social and pork barrel legislation and strike out all manner of wasteful projects.

The argument that the item veto would bring about a material reduction in government spending proved on examination less than convincing. More than 85 percent of the Reagan deficit was caused by defense, untouchable by presidential decree, and by entitlements, debt service and tax giveaways, immune to the item veto since they do not require appropriation lines. The remaining 15 percent of the budget offered meager opportunities for savings. "Approval of a line item veto," Reagan's own Council of Economic Advisers declared in its annual report in February 1985, "may not have a substantial effect on total federal expenditures," pointing out that per capita spending in the seven states without the item veto was actually lower than in the forty-three states enjoying the supposed blessing. Moreover, Reagan already enjoyed a de facto item veto in the rescission authority granted Presidents by the Budget Act of 1974 — the power not to spend appropriated funds if Congress approves within forty-five days. In 1981 Congress accepted nearly 90 percent of the $16 billion in rescissions requested by Reagan. But, since rescission leaves the decision to a simple congressional majority, the executive prefers the item veto, which would require a two-thirds vote to override. In any event, the item veto campaign of the mid-1980s was largely a function of Reagan's presence in the White House. Few advocates would have been enthusiastic if a different President were set to wield it against the defense budget.

The item veto raises deeper problems. It would empower the President to dictate spending priorities, giving him the unlimited impoundment authority supposedly withheld by the Budget Control Act of 1973. An unscrupulous President could use his life-or-death power over specific projects to blackmail legislators by threatening to kill their pet projects unless they supported unrelated administration measures. The item veto would significantly alter the historic balance between the executive and legislative branches.

At the same time, it would invite congressional irresponsibility. Legislators would be inclined to propitiate importunate lobbies and authorize more spending than ever, trusting to the President to defend the budget. The item veto, moreover, would imperil the complex of compromises that give stability to congressional action, for no legislator could be sure that a deal with a colleague would survive once the bill reached the White House. The subversion of congressional deals by item veto would raise questions of double-cross and undermine confidence in the legislative leadership of the President's own party.

With the item veto, said Senator Mark Hatfield, a Republican, "we will be giving up one of our most important powers — 'the power of the purse.' " [110] A conservative congressman warned his ideological comrades, "Powers delegated to the presidency to be dispensed according to the wisdom and conscience of a Ronald Reagan will remain in place for a time, certain to come, when a Democrat again ascends to that increasingly lofty presidential throne. . . . The acquiescence to the imperial presidency for the immediate short-term gain threatens the foundation of our form of government." [111]

A conservative President who became an even more conservative Chief Justice had summed up the case against the item veto long before. "If it is urged that the President should have the power to veto items in an appropriation bill to restrain Legislative extravagance," said William Howard Taft, "the answer is that this is not the best way." The item veto, Taft said, "would greatly enlarge the influence of the President, already large enough from patronage and party loyalty and other causes. I am inclined to think that it is better to trust to the action of the people in condemning the party which becomes responsible for such riders, than to give, in such a powerful instrument like this, a temptation to its sinister use by a President eager for continued political success." [112]

Failing an item veto, opponents of social spending seek a final solution in a constitutional amendment mandating a balanced budget. This idea violates Justice Holmes's dictum: "A Constitution is not intended to embody a particular economic theory." [113] If rigidly enforced, a balanced budget amendment would make government impossible. Since government must somehow continue, such an amendment would simply challenge the President and Congress to discover creative ways of circumvention, substitution and evasion. The prohibition of deficits, like the prohibition of hard liquor, would end in bootlegging.

XVIII

The Electoral College is the vermiform appendix in the American body politic. It was a last-minute addition to the Constitution. It installs a mystic agency between the electorate and the President. It systematically distorts the popular vote. It is impossible to explain to foreigners. Even Americans don't understand it.

When Jimmy Carter in 1977 proposed a constitutional amendment for the direct popular election of the President, he gave new impetus to a cause that goes back at least to Andrew Jackson. Carter offered only one reason for the abolition of the Electoral College, but it was a powerful one. The amendment, he said, would "ensure that the candidate chosen by the voters actually becomes President. Under the Electoral College, it is always possible that the winner of the popular vote will not be elected." [114] This had already happened, Carter said, in 1824, 1876 and 1888.

Jackson had expounded the deeper rationale a century and a half before. "To the people belongs the right of electing their Chief Magistrate," he told Congress in his first annual message. He mentioned the constitutional provisions for election by the Electoral College or, failing a majority there, by the House of Representatives. "Experience proves," he added, the experience in mind being no doubt that of his defeat in the House of Representatives in 1824 after leading in the popular vote, "that in proportion as agents to execute the will of the people are multiplied there is danger of their wishes being frustrated. . . . It is safer for them to express their own will. . . . A President elected by a minority can not enjoy the confidence necessary to the successful discharge of his duties." [115] The winner of the popular vote, in other words, has the strongest claim to democratic legitimacy.

This line of argument received added force when the Supreme Court in 1963 established the principle of one person, one vote in statewide elections. Under the Electoral College each state casts its total electoral vote for the winner even if the win is by a single vote. This procedure obviously tramples on the one person, one vote principle; as the Court itself noted, the conception of political equality embodied in the Electoral College "belongs to a bygone day." [116] And it does more than disenfranchise those who voted for the loser. The case, as Senator Thomas Hart Benton pointed out in 1824, is not just one "of votes lost, but of votes taken away, added to those of the majority, and given to a person to whom the minority is opposed." [117] In a fair system, surely every voter should have equal weight and every vote count as the voter intended.

By the 1970s many eminent leaders and organizations — Richard Nixon, Gerald Ford, Hubert Humphrey, Edward Kennedy, Henry Jackson, Howard Baker, Robert Dole; the American Bar Association, the League of Women Voters, the AFL/CIO, the Chamber of Commerce — joined Carter in advocating that the people vote directly for the President. Polls showed overwhelming public support for direct presidential elections. The favorite amendment, devised by that indefatigable constitutional reformer Senator Birch Bayh, provides that if no candidate receives more than 40 percent of the vote, the top two candidates would fight it out in a run-off election. This process, the argument goes, would meet the moral criteria of a democracy. It would ensure equal treatment of all votes. It would elect the people's choice. It would reduce the power of sectionalism in politics. It would reinvigorate party competition and combat voter apathy by giving parties an incentive to get out their vote in states in which they are hopeless minorities. The abolition of the Electoral College would also solve the problem of the "faithless elector" — the person who is sent to the Electoral College to vote for one candidate and then votes for another. This has happened a few times in the past, could happen again and might change the result when the electoral vote is closely divided.*

---

*There is a myth, much cherished by nonhistorians, that the Founding Fathers intended the electors to be free agents. As Lucius Wilmerding, Jr., has pointed out, the preponderance of evidence is that the Founding Fathers fully expected the Electoral College to execute the popular will; see Wilmerding, *The Electoral College* (1958; Beacon paperback, 1964), 19–21, 171–174.

All this sounds reasonable enough. But there are countervailing arguments. Let us put aside the problem of the faithless elector. That problem can be easily solved by abolishing the Electoral College while retaining the electoral vote and the unit rule. Let us put aside too the wearisome and inconclusive debate over who benefits from the Electoral College: large states or small states, whites or blacks, urban or rural interests. It was long supposed that the Electoral College gave special weight to large swing states and therefore benefited minorities holding the balance of power in such states. Computer analysis suggests that the Electoral College favors both the largest and the smallest states and disfavors medium-size states. Contrary to traditional belief, it may hurt black voters more than it helps them.[118] Such calculations, however, do not allow for changes wrought in voter dynamics by candidates, issues and external events.

But there are compelling reasons to believe that the abolition of state-by-state electoral votes would hasten the disintegration of the party system. Direct election with a run-off would give single-issue movements, major-party dissidents and free-lance media adventurers an unprecedented incentive to jump into presidential contests. Ecological parties, old folks' parties, women's parties, racial parties, right-to-life parties, Moral Majority parties, prohibitionist parties, homosexual rights parties — for that matter, communist or fascist parties — have a dim future in the Electoral College. Unless third parties have a solid geographical base, like the Populists of 1892 or the Dixiecrats of 1948, they cannot hope to win electoral votes. Millard Fillmore, the Know-Nothing candidate in 1856, received 21.6 percent of the popular vote and only 2 percent of the electoral vote. In 1912, when Theodore Roosevelt's Bull Moose candidacy turned the Republicans into a third party, William Howard Taft carried 23 percent of the popular vote and only 1.5 percent of the Electoral College. But under direct elections ideological parties and personalist movements could drain away enough popular votes, cumulating from state to state, to win the 20 percent necessary to force the presidential contest into a run-off. The encouragement of multiple parties would be a further blow to a party structure already gravely weakened by passage into the electronic age.

Moreover, these ad hoc political raids on the presidential process might well make run-offs the rule rather than the exception. It would also threaten to cloud the ultimate result with a stigma of deals and illegitimacy. For third parties would enter the contest not in order to win but in order to extract concessions from the run-off candidates in exchange for promises of support. In the House of Representatives run-off of 1824, Henry Clay gave his backing to J. Q. Adams and was thereafter pursued by charges of a "corrupt bargain." Direct elections would very likely usher in an age of corrupt bargains.

Direct elections would probably lead in addition to a procession of Presidents who do not get anywhere near a majority of the popular vote. This probability is tacitly recognized by the run-off provision and the 40 percent cut-off. The prospect would be a succession of 41 percent Presidents or else a fatiguing succession of double national elections — in which case the final prize might sometimes go to the person who came in second in the first round. The result in either case would hardly strengthen the sense of legitimacy the presidential election is supposed to provide.

In short, an amendment designed to ensure that the popular-vote winner gains the Presidency may have the paradoxical effect of reducing the proportion of the popular vote required for victory. Far from relieving frustrations in the electorate, this result could weaken the presidential mandate, confirm the conviction that tricky politicians are manipulating the system and intensify mistrust of the political process.

Jimmy Carter's problem remains, however — the possibility that the winner of the popular vote will not be elected. In fact, of Carter's three popular-vote-loser Presidents — J. Q. Adams in 1824, Hayes in 1876, Benjamin Harrison in 1888 — the first two cases had nothing to do with the Electoral College. Eighteen twenty-four is no test, since the present system did not exist. There were no parties, no popular vote in six states and no unit electoral vote in six others. In any event, it was the House of Representatives, not the Electoral College, that put Adams in over Jackson. In 1876 Samuel J. Tilden initially led in the Electoral College; it was a rigged electoral commission that put in Hayes.

This leaves only one occasion in American history where the Electoral College deprived the popular-vote winner of the Presidency. This was in the dead heat election of 1888, when neither candidate received a majority and the gap between them was 95,000 votes. Even here the claim was made, and was widely accepted at the time and by historians since, that over 300,000 black Republican voters in southern states were denied participation in the election.[119] But it is unprofitable to go behind official election figures, and 1888 may be granted as a case of Electoral College misfire.

One instance in two hundred years hardly seems enough to justify a drastic alteration of the system — especially if the proposed alteration is quite likely to produce second-choice Presidents itself. However, there is a simple and effective way to guard against the theoretical possibility that a candidate might come in first in the popular vote but second in the Electoral College. The answer is the National Bonus Plan proposed in 1978 by the Twentieth Century Fund Task Force on Reform of the Presidential Election Process.*

Under the National Bonus Plan, a national pool of 102 electoral votes — two for each state plus the District of Columbia — would be awarded to the winner of the popular vote. The national bonus would balance the existing federal bonus — the two electoral votes conferred by the Constitution on each state regardless of population. This reform would virtually guarantee that the popular-vote winner would also win a majority of electoral votes. At the same time, by retaining state electoral votes on a winner-take-all basis, the National Bonus Plan would preserve both the constitutional and the practical role of the states in the presidential election process, thereby contributing to the vitality of federalism.

---

*See *Winner Take All: Report of the Twentieth Century Fund Task Force on Reform of the Presidential Election Process* (New York, 1978). I must declare an interest: I was a member of the Task Force, and I first proposed the bonus plan in "The Electoral College Conundrum," *Wall Street Journal*, April 4, 1977.

By discouraging the proliferation of presidential candidates, the plan would protect the party system. By encouraging parties to maximize their vote in states they have no hope of winning, it would stimulate turnout, revitalize state parties and enhance voter equality. It would eliminate the faithless elector by abolishing the Electoral College and allocating electoral votes to the popular winner in each state and in the nation as a whole. The National Bonus Plan would, in short, combine the advantages of the historic system with the assurance that the popular-vote winner would also be the electoral-vote winner. It represents a sensible and desirable project of constitutional reform.*

XIX

Another proposal, much discussed in recent years, is that the republic make better use of its ex-Presidents. As I write, four ex-Presidents live among us. At other times — in that dangerous year when the Civil War broke out, for example — five ex-Presidents were alive and reasonably active. Indeed, in nearly two centuries, there have been only four brief interludes, adding up to about sixty months, when the United States lacked a living ex-President.

What unique wisdom ex-Presidents must possess! Only forty-one men have served as President, and the office is sui generis. "Even after passing through the Presidential office, it still remains

---

*In 1979 a majority report of the Senate Judiciary Committee advocating a direct popular election amendment dismissed the National Bonus Plan as "nothing more than a direct election achieved by a highly complicated mechanism." The Committee did this on the ground that under either system candidates would concentrate on winning the greatest number of popular votes nationwide. No doubt they would. But the national bonus amounts to only 16 percent of the total electoral vote. To get the further 35 percent required for a majority, candidates would have to carry particular states — a concern they would not have under direct elections. In this regard the National Bonus Plan respects and the direct election amendment overrides the federal character of American politics. Nor is the national bonus "a highly complicated mechanism." It is a device of elegant simplicity. See Senate Judiciary Committee, *Direct Popular Election of the President and Vice President of the United States: Report*, 96th Cong., 1st Sess. (1979), 40.

a great mystery," wrote the ordinarily prosaic Calvin Coolidge. "... Like the glory of a morning sunrise, it can only be experienced — it cannot be told." [120] Secular life has no equivalent for what these forty-one men learned, no substitute for the ultimate responsibility concentrated in the Oval Office. Yet when this rare education is completed, the President's time is up, and the nation abruptly turns him out to pasture. "The United States has had six presidents and eight secretaries of state since 1960," laments one writer, "but this priceless talent pool is treated by America's throwaway society like any other disposable commodity." [121] Is this not a grave loss to the public? Cannot some way be found to organize their hard-bought knowledge and draw on it through dark days to come?

For a long time Americans did not think so. In 1891 Grover Cleveland observed ironically that the people had no idea what to do with ex-Presidents: "Of course the subject would be relieved of all uncertainty and embarrassment if every President would die at the end of his term." Some citizens "think we should interfere in every political contest. . . . Others still regard it as simply dreadful for us to do these things. . . . Not a few appear to think we should simply exist and be blind, deaf and dumb the remainder of our days." [122] William Howard Taft, another ironist, thought the best solution might be "a dose of chloroform . . . and the reduction of the flesh of the thus quietly departed to ashes in a funeral pyre." [123] Millard Fillmore long before had pleaded in vain for a presidential pension. Many men, he said, "gave up a lucrative profession" for the White House. (The President was then paid $25,000 a year.) "It is a national disgrace that our Presidents, having occupied the highest position in the country should be cast adrift, and, perhaps, be compelled to keep a corner grocery for subsistence." [124]

But cast adrift ex-Presidents were, "wandering among the people like discontented ghosts," as Hamilton predicted in the 72nd Federalist. They themselves were uncertain what their role should be. Monroe thought ex-Presidents should abstain from politics, reserving themselves for emergencies "in which the opinion of those who have had long experience may be useful." [125] Monroe's successor, J. Q. Adams, pointed out that the two-term tradition meant that "ex-Presidents will survive for many years the termination of their offices" [126] and he was not inclined to take the veil for the rest of his life. Adams went on to serve nine embattled terms in the House of Representatives. Van Buren, Fillmore, Cleveland and the first Roosevelt all ran for President again after a period of retirement. John Tyler was elected to the Confederate House of Representatives, but died before he took his seat. Andrew Johnson became a senator. Several ex-Presidents wrote books. None became a grocer.

Harry Truman was the first ex-President to agitate seriously about the fate of what he insisted on calling the "former President." (An otherwise sensible man, Truman perceived a mighty distinction between "ex-President," a usage he abhorred, and "former President," which he declared was alone correct — a metaphysical subtlety invisible to grammarians. If "ex-President" was acceptable to such punctilious fellows as J. Q. Adams and Benjamin Harrison, the author of *Views of an Ex-President*, there seems no reason for the rest of us to renounce it.) When Truman retired in 1953 to Independence, Missouri, one of the first things he thought about, he later wrote, was the question of "how the unique experience and special knowledge that a former President acquires could be put to some use to serve the country. . . . We ought not waste all these assets." He envied the British and their Privy Council, where former prime ministers and cabinet members are available to advise the government in office. If the United States could not establish an equivalent council of state, then why should not ex-Presidents be designated Free Members of the Congress, entitled to sit in either House and take part in debate though not to vote?[127]

The second Charles Francis Adams proposed in 1906 that ex-Presidents be made Senators at Large. At least twenty-five bills to this effect have been introduced in Congress since the Second World War. In 1963 the Bureau of the Budget saw problems in having senators "who would be accountable to no one and who would represent no one," whose views might be "decades behind those of the American consensus or who would be both talkative and senile." [128] The proposal also raised constitutional questions, and the Senate that year decided instead to permit ex-Presidents to address the Senate on their own initiative. Truman and Ford have been the only ex-Presidents thus far to avail themselves of this opportunity. Despite the unique wisdom supposedly confided to ex-Presidents, no one remembers what either of them said.

In the meantime, Congress through the Presidential Libraries Act of 1955 and the Former Presidents Act of 1958 in effect established what John W. Chambers II, the authority on the subject, has called "a quasi-public office, the office of the former president." [129] The theory was that public provender would enable ex-Presidents to live out their lives in dignified retirement, sparing them from the pressure to demean themselves and the office by cashing in on their Presidencies. The result of this institutionalization of the ex-Presidency is that ex-Presidents by the mid-1980s were endowed by the taxpayers with annual pensions of $83,000, office space in federal buildings, free personal staff, free mailing privileges, free telephone privileges, free health care at military hospitals, free subscriptions to newspapers and magazines, travel allowances, Secret Service protection, classified foreign policy briefings, a residence for their Washington visits and the maintenance of libraries for their papers. This largesse did not visibly reduce the determination of the beneficiaries to cash in on their Presidencies. Ex-President Nixon, who used to live over my back fence in New York City, was given in those years to upbraiding the American people as unduly "coddled, pampered, truckled to." [130] My impression, from glances out the window, is that exceedingly few Americans are nearly so coddled, pampered and truckled to as ex-Presidents, even the one who resigned the office in order to escape impeachment.

In 1955 Congress appropriated $64,000 to maintain presidential libraries. Thirty years later the annual bill for ex-Presidents was nearly $30 million. It cost more each year to take care of ex-Presidents than to run the White House for the incumbent President—and it was reported in 1989 that federal protection for ex-President Reagan would probably cost more than the combined protection of all the other living ex-Presidents.[131] Pampering eventually reached the point where it caused serious discomfort in Congress. One senator spoke darkly of the imperial ex-Presidency. [132] Congressional reformers proposed to set limits on ex-presidential expenditures and to prohibit federal employees from helping an ex-President make money or to engage in partisan politics. These are sound proposals.

Some reformers wanted to go further and replace the presidential library system with a central depository for presidential papers. Though library maintenance accounts for half the ex-presidential bill, this proposal seems to me far less sound. The dispersion of presidential libraries around the country has been a stimulus to scholarship, enabling many more students to work in modern political history than would be the case if they had to make expensive trips to Washington. The management of documents by specialists is of inestimable benefits to scholars. And there is value to studying Presidents in their native habitats — Franklin Roosevelt in the Hudson Valley, Kennedy by Massachusetts Bay, Johnson in Texas, Reagan in California.

Institutionalization of the ex-Presidency, if it could be restrained from fiscal improvidence, confers a few benefits. It speeds the opening of presidential papers and changes their legal status. Papers once were private property of Presidents to open, close or burn as they wished; now they belong to the people. But institutionalization does not solve the problem of tapping the accumulated sagacity of these few men with the singular advantage of presidential experience.

Still one wonders whether the Founding Fathers might not have had a point in casting ex-Presidents adrift. For is it correct to suppose that ex-Presidents are automatically blessed with superior wisdom, especially on questions that have emerged since their own days in office? Patriarchy works in traditional societies, where problems remain much the same from one generation to the next. But, with the acceleration of change in modern times, patriarchs swiftly become obsolescent.

Ex-Presidents, like other old folk, tend to live in the past, preoccupied with the issues, remedies and self-justifications of another time. Their excursions into the unfamiliar present — Tyler's chairmanship in 1861 of a peace conference designed to avert the Civil War, for example, or Hoover's impassioned isolationism in 1940–1941 — are often the height of irrelevance. Would the republic have benefited if Lincoln had been compelled by some mechanism of state to listen to the advice of the five living ex-Presidents — Buchanan, Pierce, Fillmore, Tyler, Van Buren? We are alert to superannuation in the private sector. When presidents retire from corporations or from universities, no one wants them hanging around and proffering advice. William Howard Taft proposed chloroforming ex-Presidents precisely in order to "enable the public to pass to new men and new measures." [133]

This is not to say that ex-Presidents should take vows of silence. When they think they have some profound revelation to utter, let them by all means utter it. When a successor calls on them for counsel or for service, let them by all means cooperate. But imposing ex-Presidents on the Senate as daily participants, or assembling them in a council of state, or otherwise giving their ruminations official status would be a superfluity. Why anyone should think it "necessary to add to the discussion in the Senate the lucubrations of ex-presidents," observed Taft, "I am at a loss to say." [134] No one has greater access than ex-Presidents to every forum; no one has greater opportunity to command every channel of public influence. They can write books and articles, deliver speeches, hold interviews, organize conferences, dispense wisdom on television, testify before congressional committees, address the Senate in formal session. The public cannot be said to be deprived of their most vagrant thoughts.

If the four ex-Presidents living in the mid-1980s were really all that wise, they would surely have been better Presidents when they had the chance. People who believe that ex-Presidents are a wasted national asset should turn their energies to repealing the 22nd Amendment, thereby permitting these great oracles to stay on as President. In the meantime, the rest of us must remember that ex-presidential musings must stand or fall on the merits of the argument, not on the sanctity of the source.

XX

Nixon showed the abuses of the Presidency. Carter showed the vulnerabilities of the Presidency. Both abuse and vulnerability provoked structural panaceas. As our most thoughtful foreign visitors have pointed out, Americans attribute excessive importance to structure. "The student of institutions, as well as the lawyer," wrote Bryce, "is apt to overrate the effect of mechanical contrivances in politics." [135] Constitution tinkering is an engaging intellectual diversion. But it is also a flight from the hard question, which is the search for remedy. Structure is an alibi for policy failure. Let us not be beguiled by constitutional reform from the real tasks of statecraft. In the end, politics is the high and noble art of solving substantive problems.

Constitutions and statutes succeed, moreover, only as they express the temper, circumstances, traditions, history — the mores — of a people. "Laws are always unstable," said Tocqueville, "unless they are founded upon the customs of a nation." [136] Changes uncongenial to the mores — the 18th Amendment, for example, and the Volstead Act — will be ejected in time like artificial hearts. Enacted into law, such changes are easily revoked. Engraved in the Constitution, they are harder to efface. So long as they remain in the fundamental charter, they touch off the law of unintended consequences. People zealous to put right the abuse of the fleeting moment are as likely to deform as to reform the constitutional order. In his great opinion in the steel seizure case, Justice Jackson warned against the error "of confounding the permanent executive office with its temporary occupant. The tendency is strong to emphasize transient results . . . and lose sight of enduring consequences upon the balanced power structure of our Republic." [137] There is no fail-safe mechanism guaranteed either to contain or to restore presidential authority. The effort to devise such a mechanism may lead to forms of constitutional or statutory overkill damaging to other national interests, such as liberty. Digging in the foundations of the state, Burke said, is a dangerous adventure.

The Founding Fathers devised a pretty good engine of government in 1787. That engine has chugged along fairly well for two hundred years. It has proved equal to most contingencies. It has enabled strong leaders to meet great crises. It has endured because the separation of powers protects and nourishes the two essential components of free government—consent and accountability—and because power restrained by accountability and consent is more likely than arbitrary and unrestrained power to produce wise policies.

If our democracy is in trouble today, it is not because the constitutional machinery works poorly. It is because our brains work poorly. If we had convincing cures for our ailments, we could make the machinery work. Tinkering with the machinery is no substitute for thinking hard about what to do with it—and it may distract intelligent men and women from confronting the grave substantive problems in all our futures.

The Constitution is a permanent challenge to presidential leadership. It is a test of a President's capacity to persuade Congress and the people that his policies make sense. The salvation of the Presidency lies in the realm of politics, not in that of constitutional reform.

Let us return to where we began: the Founding Fathers. They had two things in mind: fashioning a strong national government and holding that government within a strong system of accountability. The perennial problem is twofold: to preserve the Presidency as the robust office that, despite a bad apple or two, has served the republic nobly and to reinvigorate the system of accountability that checks the abuse of executive power. The challenge is to balance power and accountability without creating a government too strong, in Lincoln's words, for the liberties of the people or too weak to maintain its own existence.

The Constitution gives competent Presidents the authority to govern and competent Congresses the authority to make them accountable. But the Constitution is not self-executing. It requires Presidents, Congresses and citizens who are responsive to constitutional standards. The hope lies in a campaign of national consciousness-raising. The object must be to raise the consciousness of Presidents, so that they will honor the system of accountability; to raise the consciousness of Congresses, so that they will discharge their constitutional responsibilities; and to raise the consciousness of citizens, so that, as they enter the voting booth, they will think about a candidate's openness, integrity and commitment to constitutional values as well as about his program and his charm.

Since Presidents and Congresses are chosen by the electorate, citizens bear a heavy responsibility. They must begin by abandoning the latter-day myth of the President as a man raised above the rest, not to be questioned except at risk of *lèse-majesté*. In 1937 Kingsley Martin, the English editor, wondering how the British throne had gained its sacrosanct character, wrote a book called *The Magic of Monarchy*. In the nineteenth century the crown had been freely criticized. As late as the 1870s Britain had a thriving republican movement. In the twentieth century British republicanism was extinct. Martin concluded that the magic of monarchy emerged with the British Empire when the Queen Empress was systematically glorified as the symbol of imperial grandeur.

As in Britain, the notion of the Presidency as a sacrosanct institution is a comparatively recent development. Washington, Jackson and Lincoln stirred mass emotions, but they excited vituperation as well as worship. There were no nineteenth-century personality cults of Franklin Pierce, say, or Chester A. Arthur. As in Britain, the myth rose in unison with empire. The imperial Presidency began with the first Roosevelt and was nourished by the second Roosevelt. It burst into full splendor in the days after the Second World War. "By the twentieth century," writes George Reedy, a former presidential press secretary, "the presidency had taken on all the regalia of monarchy except ermine robes, a scepter, and a crown." [138]

Presidential magic may well be more potent than the magic of monarchy. For the President is not just the supreme national symbol. He is also the supreme repository of public authority. As the incarnation of power as well as of myth, he appeals to prudential as well as to mystical motives. The word "incarnation" has a religious flavor; perhaps rightly so in this context. Some people behave as if the presidential oath works a miraculous personality change, a kind of transubstantiation. So a run-of-the-mill politician, with whom one had exchanged drinks and jokes a few months before, is transformed by the anointment of the Oval Office into an awe-inspiring being.

Strong men wilt in the august presence. When Walter F. Mondale was Vice President, friends would ask him to take them to see the President, saying, "I'm going to tell him bluntly the mistakes he's making, and he's going to get it raw from me." But when Mondale led them into the Oval Office: " 'Hello, Mr. President. How is Rosalynn and how is Amy? You're doing a wonderful job.' Hawks would become doves, conservatives would become liberals. I did not recognize half my friends when they got in there." [139]

Nixon used to talk a good deal about the importance of "respect for the Presidency" — a curious phrase to fall from the lips of a man who showed such systematic disrespect for the Presidency. Yet perhaps a little disrespect for the office might not be a bad idea on the part of everyone except the President himself. Little is more mischievous than the singular idea that the President has a sacred right to be protected from secular exposure and confrontation; little more damaging than the ghastly neoconservative theory that persons in authority must have respect, whether or not they have done anything to earn it. An American President is entitled to full courtesy, like every other citizen of the land, but only to the respect his words and actions earn him.

The President, after all, is simply a politician luckier than the rest — the one who made it, in Disraeli's phrase, to the top of the greasy pole. Shinnying up the pole does not transform him into a demigod and carry him out of our sight and jurisdiction. He can expect to stay on top only so long as he remains in close touch with the people below and operates within the disciplines of consent. "There is no worse heresy," said Lord Acton, "than that the office sanctifies the holder of it." [140]

It is not required to dig into the foundation of the state. If the political will exists in Congress and the citizenry, structural surgery is not necessary. If the will does not exist, structural surgery will make little difference. The secularization of the Presidency is indispensable for the reassertion of congressional and popular prerogative. And, from a President's viewpoint, consensus secured by consent rather than by command and coercion is far more likely both to supply a solid basis for executive policy and to keep the White House in touch with the reality principle.

XXI

"Power," Henry Adams once said, "is poison. Its effect on presidents had been always tragic." [141] But is this really so? I do not think that power per se removes a President from reality. The achievement of the great Presidents springs precisely from the fact that they had a deeper sense of reality than most of their contemporaries and penetrated to problems their fellow countrymen preferred to ignore.

Power isolates Presidents only to the extent they wish to be isolated (see pages 214–215). If they want to know what is going on, they have better facilities than anyone else in the country for finding out. Mediocre Presidents passively accept information percolating up through official channels. Great Presidents reach out for information not contaminated by self-serving bureaucratic processes. "Men moving only in an official circle," said Lincoln, "are apt to become merely official — not to say arbitrary — in their ideas." Lincoln valued his twice-a-week White House receptions, where ordinary citizens seized his elbow, offered recommendations and aired grievances. "I call these receptions my public-opinion baths . . . and, though they may not be pleasant in all particulars, the effect as a whole is renovating and invigorating to my perceptions of responsibility and duty. It would never do for a President to have guards with drawn sabres at his door, as if he fancied he were, or were trying to be, or were assuming to be, an emperor." [142]

The press conference is the contemporary equivalent of Lincoln's White House receptions, and the White House staff has become the guard with drawn sabres at the presidential door. "A president's most persistent problem in staying in touch with reality," George Reedy says, "lies in his staff." [143] As another ex–White House special assistant, I could not agree more. Nothing has carried recent Presidents away from the reality principle more than the remorseless expansion of the White House staff.

The Government Reorganization Act of 1939 created the modern White House staff. Franklin Roosevelt, the first beneficiary, kept his staff small enough so that he could deal personally with all his special assistants. His executive order setting up the staff specified that the special assistants should have "no authority over anyone in any department or agency" and should "in no event be interposed between the President and the head of any department or agency." [144] FDR served as his own chief of staff. So too did Truman, Kennedy and Johnson. The quantum leap in the White House staff took place under Nixon, thereby demonstrating the law propounded by Woodrow Wilson's biographer, Arthur Link: "The less secure a President is, the larger staff he will want."* Nixon interposed his swollen White House staff between himself and most of the cabinet and Congress, and then interposed an inner circle of palace guards between himself and most of his White House staff.

The concentration of power in the White House enfeebled the cabinet. Once a proud instrument of government containing strong leaders with positions and constituencies of their own, the cabinet under Nixon and his successors became, with few exceptions, a collection of faceless clerks. The concentration of power in the White House also concealed much of the policy process behind the shield of executive secrecy, because White House aides, unlike cabinet ministers, are not ordinarily subject to the call of congressional committees.

Nixon's successors—Ford, Carter, Reagan—all entered office proclaiming their iron determination to combat bureaucracy. None significantly reduced the White House staff. A Carter special assistant reported that many top assistants "don't see the President once a week or speak to him in any substantive way once a month." Try to communicate directly with the President, and irate colleagues accuse you of "circumventing the system." "Feed your advice through the system, and what may have begun as a bold initiative comes out the other end as unrecognizable

---

*Arthur Link, "Enormous White House Staff Weakens the Presidency," *U.S. News & World Report*, August 15, 1983. The number of full-time White House employees increased from 203 in Johnson's last year to 547 in 1971. Hugh Heclo, *Studying the Presidency*, a report to the Ford Foundation, 1977, 36. The number of senior presidential aides increased proportionately.

mush." [145] By the 1980s the President's wife had a larger staff than Roosevelt had when he was fighting the Great Depression; the Vice President, a larger staff than Roosevelt had when he was fighting the Second World War.

Of course a President needs a White House staff. He needs eyes and ears throughout his administration so that he can find out what is going on, introduce a measure of coordination into public policy and make the sprawling executive bureaucracy reasonably responsive to presidential purpose. He needs a few special assistants — but he does not need a sprawling bureaucracy of his own. A small staff, keeping the President up to date on the government and the country, reinforces the presidential link to reality. But the bloated staffs of modern times withdraw the President from the real world.

Far from facilitating presidential control, enlarging his staff beyond a point quickly reached makes the President's problems worse. Consider the testimony of two men who witnessed the inordinate expansion from FDR's small, crack staff to the tumescent White House of modern days. "The larger such a staff gets," said Sam Rosenman, "the more clumsy and inefficient it becomes. It demands more and more time from the President, whereas a staff's basic function should be to leave him more, rather than less, time to concentrate on major policy decisions." Rosenman recalled that, when he served as Roosevelt's counsel in the war years, "I had no assistants at all. The man in that position today has at least four or five. I cannot imagine what they all do." Averell Harriman: "A large staff around a President can waste, rather than save, his time, and its simple existence can lessen, rather than increase, the hours he has for quiet thoughts and independent work." [146]

Moreover, by building a wall of separation between himself and the rest of the government, a President diminishes his direct influence and dilutes the impact of his personal leadership. The larger the staff grows, the more endless meetings the staff calls, the more useless paper the staff generates, the more the President will hunker up behind it; the less he will know what is going on. The staff becomes the shock absorber, shielding the President

against the facts of life. When Presidents find themselves in
difficulties, they must sometimes feel, like Shakespeare's King
John:

> It is the curse of kings to be attended
> By slaves that take their humours for a warrant
> To break within the bloody house of life. . . .
> Hadst thou but shook thy head or made a pause
> When I spoke darkly what I purposed,
> Or turn'd an eye of doubt upon my face,
> As bid me tell my tale in express words,
> Deep shame had struck me dumb, made me break off.[147]

A President needs people around him who will, when necessary,
turn eyes of doubt and shake their heads.

The White House staff should be the personal extension of the
President — and stop there. A large praetorian bureaucracy, filled
with ambitious, possessive, overprotective and often sycophantic
people, makes work and makes trouble. It cuts off the nation
from the President and the President from the nation.

XXII

There is little more typically American than to despair of the
republic. As early as 1802, Hamilton pronounced the Constitution
a "frail and worthless fabric." [148] Seventy years later Henry Adams
declared that "the system of 1789" had "broken down." [149] The
dirges of our own day are hardly novel. But the constitutional
strain imposed by chronic international crisis is new.

Tocqueville's warning lingers. International crisis has given
American Presidents the opportunity to exercise almost royal
prerogatives. Some Presidents have exercised these prerogatives
with circumspection. Others have succumbed to the delusion that
America has been charged by the Almighty with a global mission
to redeem fallen humanity. In *The Imperial Presidency* I doubted
that a messianic foreign policy, America as world savior, was
reconcilable with the American Constitution (see pages 163–166,

206–208, 298). Nearly two decades later, I conclude with the same question.

When an American President conceives himself the appointed guardian of a world in which an eternal foreign threat requires a rapid and incessant deployment of men, weapons and decisions behind a wall of secrecy, the result can only be a radical disruption of the balance of the American Constitution. It is hard to reconcile the separation of powers with a foreign policy driven by an indignant ideology and disposed to intervene unilaterally and secretly everywhere around the planet. The Constitution must buckle under the weight of a vainglorious policy, aiming at the redemption of lesser breeds without the law, relying on secret actions and duplicitous methods, involving the United States in useless wars and grandiose dreams.

This vision of the American role in the world unbalances and overwhelms the American Constitution. If such a foreign policy is essential to the future of the republic, then the constitutional reformers are right and the nation needs a new constitution. It needs to retract the separation of powers and to give decisive authority to the President. But if a messianic foreign policy does indeed burst the limits of the Constitution, then the wisdom of the Framers is even greater than one had supposed. For so vainglorious a foreign policy is hopeless on its merits. It is beyond our wisdom to conceive and beyond our power to execute. It can only bring disaster to the republic.

This is not to say that the Constitution is a mandate for isolationism. It has always sustained the weight of a rational, responsible and discriminating internationalism, addressed to the historic interests of the United States and sensitive to the limitations of American power and American wisdom. The United States can defend itself and play a constructive role in the world without losing its own soul. But as John Quincy Adams famously said on July 4, 1821, forty-five years after the adoption of the Declaration of Independence, if America were to become involved in all the wars that "assume the colors and usurp the standard of freedom . . . the fundamental maxims of her policy would insensibly change from *liberty* to *force*. . . . She might become the dictatress of the world. She would no longer be the ruler of her own spirit." [150] One hundred and seventy years later, America has small chance of becoming dictatress of the world —but every chance, if she continues on the messianic course, of ceasing to be the ruler of her own spirit.

Still the Constitution staggers along, and the republic with it. The political give-and-take invited by a flexible constitutional process offers Presidents ample opportunity to govern and Congress ample opportunity to restrain Presidents. Secularize the Presidency, elect Presidents who understand their business, cut the White House staff in half, revitalize the system of accountability —and forever seek serious solutions to substantive problems. Long live the republic.

But in the end it comes down to the people. Truman's famous sign—"The buck stops here"—tells only half the story. It is on the decision of the voter, not on the desk of the President, that the buck finally stops. "Toute nation," said de Maistre, "a le gouvernement qu'elle mérite." Let us conclude with the ever skeptical, ever hopeful poet of American democracy:

> A great city is that which has the greatest men and
> women . . .
> Where the populace rise at once against the never-
> ending audacity of elected persons,
> Where fierce men and women pour forth as the sea
> to the whistle of death pours its weeping and
> unript waves,
> Where outside authority enters always after the
> precedence of inside authority,
> Where the citizen is always the head and ideal, and
> President, Mayor, Governor and what not, are
> agents for pay. . . .
> There the great city stands. [151]

★★

Notes

Foreword (*Pages vii–x*)

1. Cf. that most eminent of constitutional historians, Charles Howard McIlwain: "There is no medieval doctrine of the separation of powers. . . . It is a figment of the imagination of eighteenth-century doctrinaires who found it in our earlier history only because they were ignorant of the true nature of that history. These political balances were unknown before the eighteenth century, were almost untried before the nineteenth." C. H. McIlwain, *Constitutionalism: Ancient and Modern*, rev. ed. (Ithaca, 1947), 142–43.
2. *Myers v. United States,* 272 U.S. 52, 293 (1926).
3. Woodrow Wilson, *Constitutional Government in the United States* (New York, 1908), 56–57.
4. Madison to Jefferson, May 13, 1798, S. K. Padover, ed., *The Complete Madison* (New York, 1953), 258.

1. What the Founding Fathers Intended (*Pages 1–12*)

1. *McCulloch v. Maryland,* 4 Wheaton 316, 415 (1819).
2. Woodrow Wilson, *Constitutional Government in the United States* (New York, 1908), 192.
3. C. H. McIlwain, *The American Revolution: A Constitutional Interpretation* (Ithaca, 1958), 64. I am indebted to Judge Henry Friendly for reminding me of this apt observation.
4. Felix Gilbert, *The Beginnings of American Foreign Policy: To the Farewell Address* (Harper Torchbook, 1965), 42–43.
5. 69th Federalist.
6. E. S. Corwin, *The President: Office and Powers* (New York, 1940), 154.
7. C. C. Tansill, ed., *Documents Illustrative of the Formation of the Union of the American States* (Washington, 1927), 224.
8. For the Madison-Gerry motion, see Tansill, ed., *Documents,* 562. The indispensable commentary is Charles A. Lofgren, "War-Making Under the Constitution: The Original Understanding," *Yale Law Review,* March 1972 (81 Yale L.J.), 672.

9. Lofgren, "War-Making Under the Constitution," 685.
10. Cf. James Grafton Rogers, *World Policing and the Constitution* (Boston, 1945), 21.
11. 75th Federalist.
12. Madison to Jefferson, April 2, 1798, Madison, *Writings,* Gaillard Hunt, ed. (New York, 1906), VI, 312–13.
13. 73rd Federalist.
14. The quotations are from the 47th, 48th and 75th Federalist Papers.
15. Corwin, *President,* 200.
16. John Locke, *Second Treatise of Government,* Ch. 14.
17. Clinton Rossiter, *Constitutional Dictatorship* (Princeton, 1948), 212.
18. 28th and 41st Federalist Papers.
19. Lucius Wilmerding, Jr., "The President and the Law," *Political Science Quarterly,* September 1952, 324, 338.
20. James Bryce, *The American Commonwealth* (London, 1888), I, 86.
21. Raoul Berger, *Impeachment: The Constitutional Problems* (Cambridge, 1973), 70–71, 86, 162, 299.
22. Monroe in *The People, The Sovereigns* (S. L. Gouverneur, ed., 1867), 48ff., excerpted in A. B. Tourtellot, *The Presidents on the Presidency* (New York, 1964), 198–99.

2. Where The Founding Fathers Disagreed (*Pages 13–34*)

1. Jefferson, April 24, 1790, *The Complete Jefferson,* S. K. Padover, ed. (New York, 1943), 138–39.
2. J. D. Richardson, ed., *Messages and Papers of the Presidents* (New York, 1897), IV, 1485.
3. Madison to Jefferson, May 13, 1798, L. D. White, *The Federalists* (New York, 1948), 65.
4. White, *Federalists,* 62.
5. In a famous statement in the House of Commons in 1742, Pitt the Elder said, "We are called the Grand Inquest of the Nation, and as such it is our duty to inquire into every Step of publick management, either Abroad or at Home, in order to see that nothing has been done amiss." In 1791 James Wilson, by now on the Supreme Court, said in his notable lectures at the College of Philadelphia, "The house of representatives . . . form the grand inquest of the state. They will diligently inquire into grievances, arising both from men and things." For an able discussion, see Telford Taylor, *Grand Inquest,* rev. ed. (New York, 1961), 22–30.
6. Raoul Berger, "Executive Privilege v. Congressional Inquiry," *UCLA Law Review,* XII, 1077 (1965).
7. As recorded by Jefferson in his diary, *The Complete Jefferson,* 1222–23.
8. Richardson, ed., *Messages,* I, 186–88.
9. Berger, "Executive Privilege," *UCLA Law Review,* XII, 1085, 1088.
10. The relevant passages from the Pacificus-Helvidius argument can be

conveniently found in E. S. Corwin, *The President's Control of Foreign Relations* (Princeton, 1917), Ch. 1.

11. Richardson, ed., *Messages,* I, 131.
12. See the citation by J. N. Moore of Maurice, "Hostilities Without Declaration of War" (1883), Senate Foreign Relations Committee, *War Powers Legislation: Hearings,* 92 Cong., 1 Sess., 462–63.
13. Alexander De Conde, *The Quasi-War* (New York, 1966), 18, 90, 108.
14. 4 Dall. 37, 40–43 (1800).
15. 1 Cranch 1, 28 (1801).
16. Richardson, ed., *Messages,* I, 315.
17. "I am not ready to say that he [the President] has any other power than merely to employ ships or convoys, with authority to repel *force* by *force* (but not to capture). . . . Anything beyond this must fall under the idea of *reprisals,* and requires the sanction of that department which is to declare or make war." Raoul Berger, "War-Making by the President," *Pennsylvania Law Review,* November 1972, 62.
18. C. A. Berdahl, *War Powers of the Executive in the United States* (Urbana, 1921), 64.
19. Richardson, ed., *Messages,* I, 377–78.
20. For the relevant documents, see Richard Skolnik, ed., *1803: Jefferson's Decision — The United States Purchases Louisiana* (New York, 1969), 161–70.
21. Richardson, ed., *Messages,* I, 416.
22. Jefferson to W. C. Claiborne, February 3, 1807, to James Brown, October 27, 1808, to J. B. Colvin, September 20, 1810, Jefferson, *Writings,* Memorial ed., XI, 151, XII, 183, 418–22.
23. T. P. Abernethy, *The Burr Conspiracy* (New York, 1954), 274.
24. H. V. Ames, *State Documents on Federal Relations: The States and the United States* (Philadelphia, 1906), 85.
25. Joseph Story, *Commentaries on the Constitution of the United States,* 2nd ed. (Boston, 1851), II, 89–90.
26. Richardson, ed., *Messages,* II, 600–601.
27. J. Q. Adams, *Memoirs,* C. F. Adams, ed. (Philadelphia, 1877), IV, 32, 107–15.
28. Quincy Wright, *The Control of American Foreign Relations* (New York, 1922), 283.
29. R. J. Bartlett, ed., *The Record of American Diplomacy* (New York, 1947), 185–86.
30. S. F. Bemis, *The Latin American Policy of the United States* (New York, 1943), 70.
31. Richardson, ed., *Messages,* III, 1116.
32. Richardson, ed., *Messages,* III, 1325.
33. E. S. Corwin, *The President: Office and Powers, 1787–1957* (New York, 1957), 448.
34. See Irving Brant to Jacob K. Javits, April 2, 1972, in *Congressional Record,* April 10, 1972, S 5756–S 5760.

35. S. F. Bemis, *John Quincy Adams and the Union* (New York, 1956), 313.

36. F. D. Wormuth, "The Vietnam War: The President versus the Constitution," in R. A. Falk, ed., *The Vietnam War and International Law* (Princeton, 1969), II, 782.

37. Richardson, ed., *Messages*, IV, 1485.

38. Irving Brant, *Impeachment: Trials and Errors* (New York, 1972), 30.

39. Adams, *Memoirs*, I, 321–22.

40. Raoul Berger, *Impeachment: The Constitutional Problems* (Cambridge, 1973), Ch. 8.

41. Abernethy thus sums up the precedents established by the Burr trial for the power of courts to summon Presidents: "The prosecution admitted that the court might subpoena the President as well as any other man, but maintained that he was not bound to disclose confidential communications. Marshall held otherwise": Abernethy, *Burr Conspiracy*, 238. Berger's excellent discussion in "Executive Privilege," 1102–10, makes clear how the Burr precedents have been twisted in subsequent discussion, especially by Attorney General William Rogers in his defense of "executive privilege" during the Eisenhower administration. Cf. also M. D. Peterson, *Thomas Jefferson and the New Nation* (New York, 1970), 868–70; E. S. Corwin, *The President: Office and Powers* (New York, 1940), 439.

42. L. W. Levy, *Jefferson and Civil Liberties: The Darker Side* (Cambridge, 1963), 79–81.

43. Thomas Jefferson, *Writings*, P. L. Ford, ed. (New York, 1895), X, 141.

44. Richardson, ed., *Messages*, III, 1288–1312.

3. The Rise of Presidential War (*Pages 35–67*)

1. Story to S. P. Fay, February 18, 1834, W. W. Story, *Life and Letters of Joseph Story* (Boston, 1851), II, 154.

2. J. D. Richardson, ed., *Messages and Papers of the Presidents* (New York, 1897) II, 501.

3. H. V. Ames, *State Documents on Federal Relations: The States and the United States* (Philadelphia, 1906), 56–65, for statements and judicial opinions from Massachusetts, Connecticut, Rhode Island and Vermont.

4. *Martin v. Mott*, 12 Wheat. 19, 32–33 (1827).

5. Ralston Hayden, *The Senate and Treaties, 1789–1817* (New York, 1920), 206.

6. C. A. Berdahl, *War Powers of the Executive in the United States* (Urbana, 1921), 28.

7. My account draws heavily from the magistral analysis in Frederick Merk, *Slavery and the Annexation of Texas* (New York, 1972); the quotation is from page 6.

8. Merk, *Slavery and the Annexation of Texas*, 42.

9. T. H. Benton, *Thirty Years' View* (New York, 1954), II, 642–43.

10. Merk, *Slavery and the Annexation of Texas*, 55–56, 75, 140–45, 269.

11. J. Q. Adams, *Memoirs*, C. F. Adams, ed. (Philadelphia, 1877), XII, 174.

12. Adams to Gallatin, December 26, 1847, S. F. Bemis, *John Quincy Adams and the Union* (New York, 1956), 499.

13. Lincoln to Herndon, February 15, 1848, Abraham Lincoln, *Collected Works*, R. P. Basler, ed. (New Brunswick, 1953), I, 451–52.

14. For Jefferson's message to Congress of January 22, 1807, Richardson, *Messages and Papers*, I, 400; see also J. Russell Wiggins's notable historical inquiry, "Lawyers as Judges of History," printed originally in the *Proceedings of the Massachusetts Historical Society* and reprinted as an appendix in the revised edition of J. R. Wiggins, *Freedom or Secrecy* (New York, 1964). The researches of Mr. Wiggins and of Raoul Berger throw invaluable light on the origins of what came to be known in the 1950s as the doctrine of "executive privilege."

15. Richardson, ed., *Messages*, II, 847; Raoul Berger, "Executive Privilege v. Congressional Inquiry," *UCLA Law Review*, XII, 1093–94 (1965).

16. Richardson, *Messages*, III, 1255, 1351–52; Wiggins, *Freedom or Secrecy*, 261–62.

17. Richardson, ed., *Messages*, V, 2075–77.

18. Berger, "Executive Privilege," 1097.

19. 64th Federalist.

20. Richardson, ed., *Messages*, V, 2281–86.

21. Richardson, ed., *Messages*, V, 2416.

22. Frederick Merk, *The Monroe Doctrine and American Expansionism, 1843–1849* (New York, 1966), 274.

23. J. Q. Adams, *Eulogy on Madison* (Boston, 1836), 47.

24. I have drawn this account from an excellent article by D. F. Long, " 'Martial Thunder': The First Official American Armed Intervention in Asia," *Pacific Historical Review*, May 1973. This is part of a larger study on American armed intervention in Asia in the nineteenth century.

25. The "over 150" estimate comes from Senate Foreign Relations Committee, *War Powers Legislation: Hearings*, 92 Cong., 1 Sess. (1971), 380. For "at least 204," see House Foreign Affairs Committee, National Security Policy Subcommittee, *War Powers: Hearings*, 93 Cong., 1 Sess. (1973), 297. It is not evident, however, that Senator Goldwater had thought very rigorously about his categories. In between these two estimates, he announced the score as "at least 197 foreign military hostilities," of which 192 were "undeclared wars." He then added, a little anticlimactically, "nearly half involved actual fighting"; see B. M. Goldwater, "The President's Ability to Protect America's Freedoms — The Warmaking Power," *Arizona State University Law Journal*, 1971, No. 3, 423, 424.

26. S. E. Morison, *"Old Bruin": Commodore Matthew C. Perry* (Boston, 1967), 282, 290, 416; R. J. Bartlett, ed., *The Record of American Diplomacy* (New York, 1948), 269–70.

27. 135 U.S. 1, 64 (1890).
28. Richardson, ed., *Messages,* VI, 2815.
29. 4 Blatch. 451, 457 (1860).
30. Richardson, ed., *Messages,* VII, 3101.
31. Richardson, ed., *Messages,* VII, 3070, 3101; F. D. Wormuth, "The Vietnam War: The President versus the Constitution," in R. A. Falk, ed., *The Vietnam War and International Law* (Princeton, 1969), II, 786.
32. Dean Sprague, *Freedom Under Lincoln* (Boston, 1965), 159.
33. The standard work is still J. G. Randall, *Constitutional Problems Under Lincoln* (New York, 1926); see also Sprague, *Freedom Under Lincoln.*
34. James Bryce, *The American Commonwealth* (London, 1888), I, 61.
35. Quotations are from Lincoln's Message to Congress, July 4, 1861, and his letter to A. G. Hodges, April 4, 1864, Lincoln, *Collected Works,* IV, 421–41, VII, 281–82.
36. Adams in the House of Representatives, May 25, 1836, Berdahl, *War Powers,* 15; Bemis, *Adams and the Union,* 338, 454.
37. Lincoln to Erastus Corning, et al., June 12, 1863, to A. G. Hodges, April 4, 1864, Lincoln, *Works,* VI, 261–69, VII, 281–82.
38. 2 Cranch 170, 178 (1805).
39. *Fleming v. Page,* 9 Howard 603, 615 (1850).
40. S. P. Huntington, "Civilian Control and the Constitution," *American Political Science Review,* September 1956.
41. Lincoln to J. G. Conkling, August 26, 1863, to M. Birchard, et al., June 29, 1863, Lincoln, *Works,* VI, 406–10.
42. Emancipation Proclamation, January 1, 1863, Lincoln to S. P. Chase, September 2, 1863, Lincoln, *Works,* VI, 29, 428; E. S. Corwin, *The President: Office and Powers* (New York, 1940), 382; Lincoln to Chicago church committee, September 13, 1862, *Works,* V, 421.
43. William Whiting, *War Powers Under the Constitution of the United States,* 43rd ed. (Boston, 1871), 39–40.
44. Prize Cases, 2 Black 635, 648, 668–70 (1863); cf. also the discussion in Corwin, *President* (1940), 158–61.
45. Walter Bagehot, *The English Constitution,* Richard Crossman, ed. (Fontana Books, 1963), 81.
46. Letter to Erastus Corning, et al., Lincoln, *Collected Works,* VI, 267.
47. Abraham Lincoln, *Speeches and Writings,* R. P. Basler, ed. (Cleveland, 1946), 655, 793.

4. Congress Makes a Comeback (*Pages 68–99*)

1. Quincy Wright, *The Control of American Foreign Relations* (New York, 1922), 280; E. S. Corwin, *The President: Office and Powers, 1787–1957* (New York, 1957), 432.
2. 4 Wall. 120–21, 126 (1866).

3. Louis Henkin, *Foreign Affairs and the Constitution* (New York, 1972), 446.

4. E. S. Corwin, *The President: Office and Powers* (New York, 1940), 298.

5. *Mississippi v. Johnson*, 4 Wall. 475, 482, 484, 498, 501 (1867).

6. Cf. William Howard Taft's opinion in *Myers v. United States*, 272 U.S. 52 (1926).

7. Corwin, *President* (1957), 63–64.

8. My account is drawn from two valuable but sharply contrasting analyses: Chapter 9 in Raoul Berger, *Impeachment: The Constitutional Problems* (Cambridge, 1973) and M. L. Benedict, *The Impeachment and Trial of Andrew Johnson* (New York, 1973). While I agree with Berger's conclusions, Benedict's stimulating essay in revisionism is worth careful consideration. His case would, however, have been considerably more convincing if Johnson's sabotage of Reconstruction, which he ably describes, had been listed in the articles of indictment. The Tenure of Office Act, a law of exceedingly dubious wisdom as well as constitutionality, was a feeble excuse for impeachment. There is also a useful account in W. E. Binkley, *President and Congress* (New York, 1962), Ch. 7.

9. Walter Bagehot, *The English Constitution*, Richard Crossman, ed. (Fontana Books, 1963), 79.

10. Woodrow Wilson, *Congressional Government*, 15th ed. (Boston, 1901), 276.

11. James Bryce, *The American Commonwealth* (London, 1888), I, 208.

12. H. J. Ford, "Municipal Corruption," *Political Science Quarterly*, December 1904, 685.

13. Berger, *Impeachment*, 167.

14. Wilson, *Congressional Government*, 45.

15. Wilson, *Congressional Government*, 278, 279, 299, 301, 303.

16. Bernard Schwartz, "A Reply to Mr. Rogers," *American Bar Association Journal*, XLV, 468 (1958).

17. Dorothy Schaffter and D. M. Mathews, "The Powers of the President as Commander in Chief of the Army and Navy of the United States," House Doc. 443, 84 Cong., 2 Sess. (1956), 61; Richardson, ed., *Messages*, IX, 4022.

18. E. S. Corwin, *President* (1957), 137–38.

19. Woodrow Wilson, *Constitutional Government in the United States* (New York, 1908), 138. Wilson was then writing as a political scientist. He was less wise as President; or rather he then reverted to a view he had expressed in 1885 that the President's "only power of compelling compliance on the part of the Senate lies in his initiative in negotiation, which affords him a chance to get the country into such scrapes, so pledged in the view of the world to certain courses of action, that the Senate hesitates to bring about the appearance of dishonor which would follow its refusal to ratify the rash promises" (*Congressional Government*, 233–34).
   It is of interest that Wilson's great antagonist in the fight over the

Versailles Treaty, himself an able historian, believed that the spirit of
the executive council should not have lapsed. Nearly two decades before Versailles, Henry Cabot Lodge pointed to the significant difference in the placement of the "advice and consent" phrases in relation to the nominating power and the treaty power. In the first case
"advice and consent" did not modify the power to nominate, only
the confirmation of the nomination. In the second case "the words
'by and with the advice and consent of' come in after the words
'shall have power' and before the power referred to is defined. The
'advice and consent of the Senate' are therefore coextensive with the
'power' conferred on the President, which is 'to make treaties,' and
apply to the entire process of treaty-making." H. C. Lodge, "The
Treaty-Making Powers of the Senate," in *A Fighting Frigate and
Other Essays and Addresses* (New York, 1902), 231–32.

20. E. S. Corwin, *President* (1957), 209–10.
21. Henry Adams, *Education* (Sentry edition), 375.
22. W. S. Holt, *Treaties Defeated in the Senate* (Baltimore, 1933), 123,
    165.
23. Wilson, *Congressional Government,* 49, 233–34, 50; Hay to Adams,
    May 27, 1898, W. R. Thayer, *Life and Letters of John Hay* (New
    York, 1915), II, 170.
24. Holt, *Treaties,* 159, 178, 179; Adams, *Education,* 393, 422.
25. Preface to fifteenth edition, Wilson, *Congressional Government,*
    xi–xii.
26. 135 U.S. 1, 64, 69 (1890).
27. Theodore Roosevelt, *An Autobiography* (New York, 1913), 357, 464.
28. E. S. Corwin, *President's Control of Foreign Relations* (Princeton,
    1917), 171, 172, 198.
29. Archibald Butt, *Letters* (New York, 1924), 305–6.
30. Executive Order 1062, April 14, 1909, see Library of Congress, "The
    Present Limits of 'Executive Privilege,'" *Congressional Record,*
    March 28, 1973, H2244.
31. Taft, *Our Chief Magistrate and His Powers* (New York, 1916), 129.
32. In the Camillus letters of 1795, quoted by Raoul Berger, "The Presi-
    dential Monopoly of Foreign Relations," *Michigan Law Review,* No-
    vember 1972, 35.
33. Edwin Borchard, "Shall the Executive Agreement Replace the
    Treaty?" *Yale Law Journal,* September 1944, 668.
34. *Holmes v. Jennison,* 14 Peters 540, 572 (1840).
35. S. B. Crandall, *Treaties, Their Making and Enforcement* (New York,
    1904), 85; Wallace McClure, *International Executive Agreements*
    (New York, 1941), 31.
36. I take the statistics from Louis Fisher, *President and Congress* (New
    York, 1972), 45.
37. Roosevelt, *Autobiography,* 510.
38. Tyler Dennett, *Roosevelt and the Russo-Japanese War* (New York,
    1925), 2.
39. *Hamilton v. McLaughry,* 136 Fed. 445 (1905).

40. Theodore Roosevelt to H. C. Lodge, January 28, 1909, Roosevelt, *Letters,* Elting Morison, ed. (Cambridge, 1951–1956), VI, 1497–98.
41. J. Reuben Clark, *The Right to Protect Citizens in Foreign Countries by Landing Troops* (Washington, 1912).
42. Elihu Root, *The Military and Colonial Policies of the United States* (Cambridge, 1916), 157–58.
43. Taft, *Our Chief Magistrate,* 94; R. A. Taft, *A Foreign Policy for Americans* (Garden City, 1951), 28.
44. Wilson, *Constitutional Government,* 77.
45. *Congressional Record,* April 20, 1914, 6908–9.
46. S. F. Bemis, *The Latin American Policy of the United States* (New York, 1943), Chs. 10, 11.
47. E. S. Corwin, *President* (1940), 189.
48. Richardson, ed., *Messages and Papers,* xvii, 8211.
49. E. S. Corwin, *Total War and the Constitution* (New York, 1947), 2.
50. H. K. Beale, *Theodore Roosevelt and the Rise of America to World Power* (Collier), 301.
51. Senate Foreign Relations Committee, "General Arbitration Treaties with Great Britain and France," August 3, 1911.
52. Wilson, *Constitutional Government,* 140.
53. Schaffter and Mathews, "Powers of the President," 67.
54. Schaffter and Mathews, "Powers of the President," 72.
55. I am indebted to an informative Columbia Ph.D. thesis, Rogelio Garcia, "Opposition Within the Senate to the American Military Intervention in Nicaragua, 1926–1933," especially Ch. 7.
56. R. A. Divine, *The Illusion of Neutrality* (Chicago, 1962), Ch. 2.
57. *Franklin D. Roosevelt and Foreign Affairs,* E. B. Nixon, ed. (Cambridge, 1969), II, 377.
58. Divine, *Illusion of Neutrality,* Ch. 4.
59. R. D. Burns and W. A. Dixon, "Foreign Policy and the 'Democratic Myth': The Debate on the Ludlow Amendment," *Mid-America,* January 1965.
60. Walter Lippmann, *U.S. Foreign Policy: Shield of the Republic* (Boston, 1943), 42.

5. The Presidency Resurgent: The Second World War (*Pages 100–126*)

1. W. L. Langer and S. E. Gleason, *The Challenge to Isolation* (New York, 1952), 144. A primary source of Borah's information was the party-line newsletter *The Week* of London. Claud Cockburn, its editor, has since written most entertainingly about his fellow-traveling years.
2. 299 U.S. 304 (1936).
3. He was quoting an unnamed federal judge. I am indebted to Judge Charles Wyzanski for this recollection.
4. 301 U.S. 324, 330–31 (1937).
5. Louis Henkin, *Foreign Affairs and the Constitution* (New York, 1972), 178–79.

6. E. M. Byrd, Jr., *Treaties and Executive Agreements in the United States* (The Hague, 1960), 157 n.

7. S. A. Riesenfeld, "The Power of the Congress and the President in International Relations: Three Recent Supreme Court Decisions," *California Law Review*, September 1937, 674.

8. D. M. Levitan, "The Foreign Relations Power: An Analysis of Mr. Justice Sutherland's Theory," *Yale Law Journal*, April 1946, 493.

9. *Congressional Record*, April 30, 1970, S6331 (Church), April 14, 1971, S4784 (Fulbright).

10. R. H. Jackson, "Acquisition of Naval and Air Bases in Exchange for Over-Age Destroyers," *Official Opinions of the Attorneys General of the United States*, J. T. Fowler, ed. (Washington, 1941), XXXIX, 484–96.

11. The last chapter in W. L. Langer and S. E. Gleason, *The Challenge to Isolation* (New York, 1952) provides an excellent analysis. See also the able work by Philip Goodhart, *Fifty Ships That Saved the World* (New York, 1965). I am indebted to Benjamin V. Cohen for further significant detail on the inner history of the transaction.

12. Langer and Gleason, *Challenge to Isolation*, 539.

13. Again I owe this recollection to Benjamin V. Cohen.

14. E. S. Corwin, *The Constitution and What It Means Today*, Atheneum ed. (1963), 25. I agree with Corwin that Roosevelt was wrong; see chapter 9.

15. Frank Murphy, "Request of the Senate for an Opinion as to the Powers of the President 'In Emergency or State of War,' " *Official Opinions of the Attorneys General*, XXXIX, 344–48.

16. Franklin D. Roosevelt, *Public Papers and Addresses . . . 1941* (New York, 1950), 195.

17. R. A. Taft, *A Foreign Policy for Americans* (Garden City, 1951), 31.

18. J. W. Fulbright, "The Decline — and Possible Fall — of Constitutional Democracy in America," *Congressional Record*, April 14, 1971, S4784.

19. Roosevelt, *Public Papers . . . 1941*, 33, 256, 410; Press Conference No. 770, September 23, 1941.

20. He did invoke his authority as Commander in Chief to justify government seizure in 1941 of plants producing material considered essential for national defense.

21. E. S. Corwin, *Total War and the Constitution* (New York, 1947), 33.

22. *Ex parte Quirin*, 317 U.S. 1, 26 (1942).

23. See the critical discussion in E. S. Corwin, *The President: Office and Powers, 1787–1957* (New York, 1957), 250–52, 562.

24. *Korematsu v. United States*, 323 U.S. 214, 246 (1944).

25. R. H. Jackson, "Position of the Executive Department Regarding Investigative Reports," April 30, 1941, *Official Opinions of the Attorneys General of the United States*, XL, 45–47.

26. A. H. Vandenberg, Jr., ed., *The Private Papers of Senator Vandenberg* (Boston, 1952), 24–25, 67–71.

27. R. A. Divine, *Second Chance: The Triumph of Internationalism in America During World War II* (New York, 1967), 197–98, 222; Vandenberg, *Private Papers*, 116–18.
28. Divine, *Second Chance*, 238–40.
29. Press conference 972, October 13, 1944; S. I. Rosenman, *Working with Roosevelt* (New York, 1952), 481.
30. Franklin D. Roosevelt, *Public Papers and Addresses . . . 1944–1945* (New York, 1950), 350.
31. See, for example, F. D. Wormuth, "The Vietnam War: The President versus the Constitution," in R. A. Falk, ed., *The Vietnam War and International Law* (Princeton, 1969), II, 790.
32. Letter from Vandenberg to Arthur Krock, reprinted in Krock's column, *New York Times*, April 27, 1951.
33. M. J. Pusey, *Charles Evans Hughes* (New York, 1951), 795.
34. Vandenberg, *Private Papers*, 42.
35. Charles E. Bohlen, *Witness to History, 1929–1969* (New York, 1973), 210.
36. Dean Acheson, *Present at the Creation* (New York, 1969), 72, 99–101; Acheson, "A Citizen Looks at Congress" in *Private Thoughts on Public Affairs* (Harvest book, 1967), 42, 44.
37. G. F. Kennan, *Memoirs: 1950–1963* (Boston, 1972), 298, 320, 322.
38. G. F. Kennan, *Realities of American Foreign Policy* (Princeton, 1954), 95–96.
39. Thomas A. Bailey, *The Man in the Street* (New York, 1948), 13.
40. See Mr. Cronin's interesting paper "The Textbook Presidency and Political Science," delivered before the American Political Science Association in September 1970 and reprinted in the *Congressional Record*, October 5, 1970, S17102-S17115.
41. Quoted on back cover of paperback edition of Alexander DeConde, *The American Secretary of State* (New York, 1963).
42. Walter Lippmann, *The Public Philosophy* (Mentor ed.), 23–24, 29, 48.
43. Alexis de Tocqueville, *Democracy in America*, I, Ch. 13.

6. The Presidency Ascendant: Korea *(Pages 127–176)*

1. James T. Patterson, *Mr. Republican: A Biography of Robert A. Taft* (Boston, 1972), 197.
2. The Taft speech was reprinted in the *Congressional Record* twenty years later on the motion of Senator Hatfield of Oregon, May 19, 1971, S7318–S7323.
3. See Arthur Krock's column, *New York Times*, April 15, 1955.
4. A. H. Vandenberg, Jr., ed., *The Private Papers of Senator Vandenberg* (Boston, 1952), 553.
5. Vandenberg, *Private Papers*, 559–60.
6. Dean Acheson, *Present at the Creation*, 415.
7. *New York Times*, April 23, 1948; E. S. Corwin, *The President: Office and Powers, 1787–1957* (New York, 1957), 448.

8. The relevant documents may be found in Glenn Paige, ed., *1950: Truman's Decision–The United States Enters the Korean War* (New York, 1970).

9. Acheson, *Present at the Creation,* 402–15.

10. *Department of State Bulletin,* July 31, 1950.

11. It is sometimes said that Truman violated Section 6 of the UN Participation Act by not securing congressional approval for the use of American forces under United Nations command. This is incorrect. Section 6 applied to special agreements negotiated with the Security Council under Article 43 of the UN Charter. No such special agreements were ever negotiated. The intervention in Korea was undertaken not under Article 43 but under Article 39 of the Charter.

12. *Congressional Record,* July 5, 1950, 9792–94.

13. Vandenberg, *Private Papers,* 572–73.

14. Acheson, *Present at the Creation,* 415.

15. "Powers of the President to Send the Armed Forces Outside the United States" in Dorothy Schaffter and D. M. Mathews, "The Powers of the President as Commander in Chief of the Army and Navy of the United States," House Doc. 443, 84 Cong., 2 Sess. (1956), 47–50.

16. See interview with Coudert by Bert Andrews, *New York Herald Tribune,* January 4, 1951.

17. H. S. Truman, *Public Papers and Messages . . . 1951* (Washington, 1965), 4, 19.

18. F. R. Coudert, Jr., to the Editor, *New York Herald Tribune,* January 10, 1951.

19. E. S. Corwin, *The President: Office and Powers* (New York, 1940), 246; Corwin, "Who Has the Power to Make War?" *New York Times Magazine,* July 31, 1949.

20. *Congressional Record,* May 19, 1971, S7318–S7323.

21. On January 22, 1951, quoted by Senator Allott of Colorado, *Congressional Record,* June 4, 1970, S8419.

22. *Congressional Record,* August 30, 1951, 11075.

23. Robert A. Taft, *A Foreign Policy for Americans* (New York, 1951), 25.

24. Senate Report 797, "National Commitments," 90 Cong., 1 Sess. (1967), 17.

25. Vandenberg, *Private Papers,* 567–72.

26. H. S. Commager, "Presidential Power: The Issue Analyzed," *New York Times Magazine,* January 14, 1951.

27. Letter to the *New York Times,* January 9, 1951.

28. E. S. Corwin, "The President's Power," *New Republic,* January 29, 1951.

29. Taft, *Foreign Policy,* 36.

30. Acheson, *Present at the Creation,* 496.

31. *Woods v. Miller,* 333 U.S. 138, 141, 146 (1948).

32. Harold Stein, "Foreign Policy and the Dispersion of Power," *Public Administration Review,* summer 1953.

33. Harry S. Truman, *Public Papers . . . 1952–1953* (Washington, 1966), 283–85, 301.

34. Truman said later, truthfully but tardily, that the thought of seizing press and radio had never occurred to him. See Truman, *Public Papers . . . 1952–1953*, 250–51, 273, 290–91, 293–94, 301.

35. *Youngstown Sheet & Tube Co. v. Sawyer*, 343 U.S. 579 (1952).

36. For valuable contemporaneous commentaries, see John P. Roche, "Executive Power and Domestic Emergency: The Quest for Prerogative," *Western Political Science Quarterly*, December 1952; P. G. Kauper, "The Steel Seizure Case," *Michigan Law Review*, December 1952; E. S. Corwin, "The Steel Seizure Case: A Judicial Brick Without Straw," *Columbia Law Review*, January 1953; Lucius Wilmerding, Jr., "The President and the Law," *Political Science Quarterly*, September 1952.

37. Dean Acheson, *Private Thoughts on Public Affairs* (New York, 1967), 44.

38. W. F. Buckley, Jr., and L. B. Bozell, *McCarthy and His Enemies* (Chicago, 1954), 335.

39. W. E. Binkley, "The Decline of the Executive," *New Republic*, May 18, 1953.

40. Letter in *New York Herald Tribune*, May 29, 1953.

41. E. S. Corwin, *President*, 113.

42. *Congressional Record*, April 22, 1948, 4783.

43. *St. Louis Post-Dispatch*, May 10, 1948.

44. H. S. Truman, *Public Papers . . . 1950* (Washington, 1965), 241, 510; *Public Papers . . . 1952–1953*, 236.

45. Clark Mollenhoff, "Secrecy in Washington," *Atlantic Monthly*, July 1959.

46. Herman Wolkinson, "Demands of Congressional Committees for Executive Papers," *Federal Bar Journal*, April 1949, 103, 105; October 1949, 340.

47. Mollenhoff, "Secrecy in Washington."

48. Emphasis added. The full text may be found in *U.S. News & World Report*, May 28, 1954.

49. W. P. Rogers, "Constitutional Law: The Papers of the Executive Branch," *American Bar Association Journal*, October 1958, 942.

50. Brownell's rewrite (without credit) of Wolkinson can be found in *U.S. News & World Report*, May 28, 1954.

51. *New York Times*, May 18, 1954; *Washington Post*, May 20, 1954.

52. Telford Taylor, *Grand Inquest* (revised edition, New York, 1961), 155.

53. Raoul Berger, "Executive Privilege v. Congressional Inquiry," *UCLA Law Review*, XII, 1310.

54. Rogers, "Constitutional Law," 1013. Plagiarism is more conspicuous, indeed practically total, in the accompanying memorandum, "The Power of the President to Withhold Information from the Congress," submitted by the Attorney General to the Subcommittee on Constitutional Rights of the Senate Judiciary Committee, 85 Cong., 2 Sess.

(1958). Ironically in 1948–1949 Rogers, as counsel for a Senate investigating committee headed by Homer Ferguson, had guided the attack on the executive branch that led to the preparation of the Wolkinson memorandum.

55. Mollenhoff, "Secrecy in Washington."

56. Emphasis added.

57. Krock in the *New York Times*, January 30, 1955; Lippmann in the *Washington Post*, January 27, 1955. The Formosa documents are conveniently assembled in Schaffter and Mathews, "The Powers of the President."

58. H. S. Truman, *Mr. Citizen* (Popular Library ed., n.d.), 208.

59. *Congressional Record*, February 11, 1957, 1671–72.

60. *Congressional Record*, July 31, 1967, S10488.

61. J. W. Fulbright, "American Foreign Policy in the 20th Century under an 18th Century Constitution," *Cornell Law Quarterly*, fall 1961, reprinted in Senate Foreign Relations Committee, *War Powers Legislation: Hearings*, 92 Cong., 1 Sess. (1971), 46–53.

62. Subcommittee on National Security, Staffing and Operations, Senate Government Operations Committee, *Administration of National Security: Hearings*, 88 Cong., 1 Sess. (1963), 77.

63. Eric Goldman, "The President, the People, and the Power to Make War," in R. A. Falk ed., *The Vietnam War and International Law* (Princeton, 1972), III, 501–2.

64. Arthur M. Schlesinger, Jr., "The Oppenheimer Case," *Atlantic Monthly*, October 1954, reprinted in *The Politics of Hope* (Boston, 1963), 215.

65. Senate Foreign Relations Committee Report No. 797, "National Commitments," 90 Cong., 1 Sess., November 20, 1967, 14.

66. John F. Kennedy, Press Club speech, January 14, 1960.

67. Dean Rusk, "The President," *Foreign Affairs*, April 1960, in H. F. Armstrong, ed., *Fifty Years of Foreign Affairs* (New York, 1972), 306.

68. Fulbright, "American Foreign Policy . . . Under an 18th Century Constitution," 47, 50.

69. In the *New York Times Magazine*, January 3, 1965.

70. *Congressional Record*, October 3, 1967, S14058.

71. Letter to *Washington Post*, June 7, 1973; *Congressional Record*, April 26, 1971, S5639.

72. H. L. Trewhitt, *McNamara: His Ordeal in the Pentagon* (New York, 1971), 92–93.

73. Berger, "Executive Privilege," 1045; Subcommittee on Separation of Powers, Senate Judiciary Committee, *Executive Privilege: The Withholding of Information by the Executive: Hearing*, 92 Cong., 1 Sess. (1971), 346.

74. Berger, "Executive Privilege," 1045, 1051.

75. Arthur M. Schlesinger, Jr., *A Thousand Days* (Boston, 1965), 164.

76. I am aware of the line of thought that says this was not a genuine emergency and there was no need for the United States to have done anything about the Soviet nuclearization of Cuba. I have no doubt

myself that American acceptance of so drastic a shift in the political and military balance would have meant a different, and considerably more dangerous, world in the years after 1962. It is sufficient for our purposes here to note that the attempted nuclearization of Cuba was seen as an emergency by the President, Congress and most of the American people.

77. The story, heretofore unknown to me, is told in Max Frankel, "A Washington Education," *Columbia Forum,* winter 1973.
78. J. W. Fulbright, *The Arrogance of Power* (New York, 1966), 48.
79. T. C. Sorensen, *Kennedy* (New York, 1965), 702.

7. The Presidency Rampant: Vietnam (*Pages 177–207*)

1. Speech at Omaha, June 30, 1966.
2. P. L. Geyelin, *Lyndon B. Johnson and the World* (New York, 1966), 238.
3. Arthur M. Schlesinger, Jr., *A Thousand Days* (Boston, 1965), 992.
4. Senate Foreign Relations Committee, *War Powers Legislation: Hearings,* 92 Cong., 1 Sess. (1971), 552.
5. The phrase is from Johnson's own account in a press conference of August 18, 1967. *New York Times,* August 19, 1967.
6. M. J. Pusey, *The Way We Go to War* (Boston, 1969), 143.
7. *Congressional Record,* May 18, 1970, S7334.
8. *New York Times,* August 19, 1967.
9. Lyndon B. Johnson, *The Vantage Point* (New York, 1971), 116.
10. George Reedy, *The Twilight of the Presidency* (New York, 1970), 80.
11. Senate Report No. 91–129, "National Commitments," 91 Cong., 1 Sess. (April 16, 1969), 25.
12. Subcommittee on Separation of Powers, Senate Judiciary Committee, *Executive Privilege: The Withholding of Information by the Executive: Hearing,* 92 Cong., 1 Sess. (1971), 23.
13. Senate Foreign Relations Committee, *U.S. Commitments to Foreign Powers: Hearings,* 90 Cong., 1 Sess. (1967), 82, 141.
14. *Congressional Record,* June 24, 1969, S7083.
15. Lodge's remark was in *U.S. News & World Report,* February 15, 1965; Leonard C. Meeker wrote Arthur Larson on April 3, 1965, that there were no legal obligations toward Vietnam, Arthur Larson, *The Eisenhower I Knew* (Popular Library edition, 1968), 171; Krock's column was in the *New York Times,* March 6, 1966. I am indebted to a letter from J. H. Crown and W. L. Standard published in the *Times,* September 1, 1972. Johnson, however, did mention SEATO in his message to Congress of May 4, 1965.
16. Leonard C. Meeker, "The Legality of United States Participation in the Defense of South Viet-Nam," March 4, 1966, reprinted in J. N. Moore, *Law and the Indo-China War* (Princeton, 1972), 603–32.
17. J. A. Schumpeter, *Imperialism and Social Classes* (New York, 1955), 51.

18. Subcommittee on the Separation of Powers, *Executive Privilege*, 466.
19. Townsend Hoopes, *The Limits of Intervention* (New York, 1969), 145.
20. Cf. letter from the Acting Secretary of State to Senator Fulbright, May 30, 1970: "In his letter to you of March 12, 1970, Mr. [Horace] Torbert [Deputy Secretary for Congressionl Relations] stated that the Administration does not depend on the Tonkin Gulf Resolution as legal or constitutional authority for its present conduct of foreign relations, or its contingency plans." *Congressional Record*, April 2, 1973, S6287.
21. Richard M. Nixon, *A New Road For America: Major Policy Statements, March 1970 to October 1971* (New York, 1972), 38, 675, 683.
22. *Congressional Record*, April 26, 1971, S5640. Cf. Senator Goldwater in another mood (1964): "Some of the current worship of powerful executives may come from those who admire strength and accomplishment of any sort. Others hail the display of Presidential strength . . . simply because they approve of the *result* reached by the use of power. . . . If ever there was a philosophy of government totally at war with that of the Founding Fathers, it is this one"; Marcus Cunliffe, *American Presidents and the Presidency* (London, 1969), 112.
23. Nixon, *New Road For America*, 39, 687.
24. Afterword by R. E. Neustadt and Graham Allison in Norton paperback edition of Robert F. Kennedy, *Thirteen Days* (New York, 1971), 118–19.
25. *New York Times*, June 30, 1970.
26. *The Exchange v. McFaddon*, 7 Cranch 116, 140–41 (1812). I owe this quotation to the excellent article by F. D. Wormuth, "The Nixon Theory of the War Power: A Critique," *California Law Review*, May 1972, 650.
27. W. H. Rehnquist, "The President and Cambodia: His Constitutional Authority," *New York Law Journal*, June 8–9, 1970, reprinted in Senate Foreign Relations Committee, *War Powers Legislation*, 827–32.
28. *Congressional Record*, May 5, 1972, S7386.
29. Interview with Howard K. Smith, March 22, 1971. Emphasis added.
30. Interview with Marvin Kalb, *The Listener*, March 1, 1973.
31. Elliot Richardson to J. W. Fulbright, May 30, 1970, *Congressional Record*, April 2, 1973, S6287.
32. Section 6 of the Supplementary Foreign Assistance Act of 1970.
33. *Congressional Record*, May 17, 1973, S9371.
34. *New York Times*, May 1, 1973.
35. It also had at least one passage of notable dishonesty. The Rogers memorandum claimed that the decision of the United States Court of Appeals in *Mitchell v. Laird* "makes it clear that the President has the constitutional power" to bomb Cambodia for the purpose of bringing the military conflict to an end. "In the words of Judge Wy-

zanski the President properly acted 'with a profound concern for the durable interests of the nation — its defense, its honor, its morality.' " Wyzanski made no such judgment. What he said was very different: "President Nixon's duty did not go beyond trying to bring the war to an end as promptly as was consistent with a profound concern for the durable interests of the nation — its defense, its honor, its morality. *Whether President Nixon did so proceed is a question which at this stage in history a court is incompetent to answer.*" (Emphasis added.) *Congressional Record*, May 16, 1973, S9259.

36. Library of Congress, "Congress and the Termination of the Vietnam War," Senate Foreign Relations Committee Print, 93 Cong., 1 Sess. (1973), 10.

37. *New York Times*, March 28, 1973; *Washington Post*, March 30, 1973.

38. Tocqueville, *Democracy in America*, II, Third Book, Chs. 22–23.

39. Cf. the interview with John Frankenheimer, who directed *Seven Days in May:* "Those were the days of General Walker and so on. . . . President Kennedy wanted *Seven Days in May* made. Pierre Salinger conveyed this to us. The Pentagon didn't want it done. Kennedy said that when we wanted to shoot at the White House he would conveniently go to Hyannis Port that weekend." Charles Higham and Joel Greenberg, *The Celluloid Muse: Hollywood Directors Speak* (Signet Books, 1972), 92.

40. *Congressional Record*, July 31, 1967, S10503.

41. CBS News Special Report, April 19, 1966.

42. Indestructible, that is, except by the Israeli government itself; the commitment was considerably damaged when the Israeli government mounted a blatant and unprecedented ambassadorial intervention into the internal politics of the United States during the 1972 presidential campaign.

43. The Symington Committee hearings were published in twelve volumes (with frequent deletions for security reasons), 1969–1970; see particularly the Committee Report, "Security Agreements and Commitments Abroad," 91 Cong., 2 Sess., December 21, 1970, and the article by Senator Symington, "Congress Right to Know," *New York Times Magazine*, August 9, 1970. Two useful books sum up the findings: M. J. Pusey, *The U.S.A. Astride the Globe* (Boston, 1971) and R. A. Paul, *American Military Commitments Abroad* (New Brunswick, New Jersey, 1973). Mr. Paul was chief counsel to the Committee.

44. Separation of Powers Subcommittee. *Congressional Oversight of Executive Agreements*, 92 Cong., 2 Sess. (1972), 138.

45. Pusey, *U.S.A. Astride the Globe*, 129.

46. Paul, *American Military Commitments*, Ch. 8; *Department of State Bulletin*, March 14, 1966.

47. Symington Committee, "Security Agreements," 5, 17, 26; Paul, *American Military Commitments*, 78.

48. Symington Committee, "Security Agreements," 9–10, 24.

49. Symington Committee, "Security Agreements," 11–12; Pusey, *U.S.A. Astride the Globe,* 137–41.
50. Symington Committee, "Security Agreements," 12–13, 18–19; Stuart Symington "Where Are Our Nuclear Weapons?" *New York Times,* July 30, 1972.
51. Symington Committee, "Security Agreements," 17, 19.
52. Separation of Powers Subcommittee. *Congressional Oversight of Executive Agreements,* 93 Cong., 1 Sess. (1973), 1, 3.

8. The Revolutionary Presidency: Washington (*Pages 208–277*)

1. E. S. Corwin, *Total War and the Constitution* (New York, 1947), 172.
2. In this analysis I have shamelessly appropriated insights from Samuel Lubell's original and arresting book *The Future While It Happened* (New York, 1973). Mr. Lubell developed some of his points further in an important five-part series released by the *New York Times* Special Features (though, oddly, not printed in the *New York Times*), June 3–7, 1973.
3. Lubell, *Future While It Happened,* 13.
4. Clark Clifford, "The Presidency As I Have Seen It," in Emmet Hughes, *The Living Presidency* (New York, 1973), 315.
5. T. C. Smith, *Life and Letters of James A. Garfield* (New Haven, 1925), II, 1044.
6. I take this formulation from a mimeographed paper (1966), "Problems of Isolation in the Presidency," prepared by Mr. Reedy for a conference at the Center for the Study of Democratic Institutions.
7. George E. Reedy, *The Twilight of the Presidency* (New York, 1970), 90–93.
8. The word "awesome" should be banished from all discussions of the American Presidency.
9. Kennedy's introduction to Theodore C. Sorensen, *Decision-Making in the White House* (New York, 1963), xiii.
10. Reedy, *Twilight,* 96.
11. Richard M. Nixon, *Six Crises* (New York, 1962), 317.
12. Arthur M. Schlesinger, Jr., *Kennedy or Nixon: Does It Make Any Difference?* (New York, 1960), 10.
13. An incident in Nixon's 1962 campaign for the governorship of California has received too little notice. His campaign manager was H. Robert Haldeman. In the last weeks of the campaign a group calling itself the Committee for the Preservation of the Democratic Party in California became suddenly active against Nixon's opponent, the Democratic governor, until a restraining order obtained by a suspicious Democratic State Committee forced it to cease and desist. In 1964 a decision by the California Superior Court described a postcard "poll" sent out by the phony committee as "reviewed, amended and finally approved by Mr. Nixon personally." The judge added,

"Mr. Nixon and Mr. Haldeman approved the plan and project . . . and agreed that the Nixon campaign committee would finance the project." This involved, the decision said, "the largest single item of expenditure for payment of personnel" reported by the Nixon organization. The decision by Judge Byron Arnold in the case of *Democratic State Central Committee v. Committee for the Preservation of the Democratic Party in California* in the California Superior Court, October 30, 1964, is reprinted in the *Congressional Record*, May 7, 1973, S8377–S8383.

14. Huston, writing in the conservative magazine *The Alternative*, as quoted in Lou Cannon, "The Siege Psychology and How It Grew," *Washington Post*, July 29, 1973.

15. No one could gainsay the need for full presidential protection after the murders of the 1960s. But the fortification of Camp David went far indeed. Cf. the account by Simon Winchester of the *Manchester Guardian:* "It is just like Berlin. There are in fact three fences. One, tall and silvery new, tipped with barbed coils. Another, smaller, with porcelain insulators on the supporting stanchion. . . . Behind that another taller, mesh fence, and more barbed wire. And in the trees on Nixon's side of the final wall a figure moves swiftly into cover; a rifle swings up, there is a glint of sun on telescopic sight as a camouflaged Marine surveys you, charts your every move and telephones your presence to some mystery controller in the mountain depths. . . . To Mr. Nixon, Camp David seems to have become less a Shangri-La, more a Berchtesgaden, less a Walden, more a prison." Reprinted in *Washington Post*, June 26, 1973.

16. The interview quotations are from Saul Pett, *Washington Post*, January 14, 1973.

17. This seems to have been another Nixon first. Truman used to stay in a Coast Guard station in Key West. Roosevelt, Eisenhower, Kennedy and Johnson had their holiday residences but did not use federal money for their improvement. It was characteristic too that the Nixon administration, as late as May 26, 1973, admitted the spending of only $39,525 in federal money at San Clemente. Later the total expended on the President's various retreats was conceded to be at least $10 million. One mercifully slides over the complex financial arrangements that enabled Mr. Nixon to buy his San Clemente estate with a minimal outlay of his own money.

18. Machiavelli, *The Prince*, Chs. 22, 23.

19. Richard M. Nixon, "The Nature of the Presidency," radio speech, September 19, 1968.

20. *London Times*, May 11, 1973.

21. For a discussion of the tension between the presidential government and the permanent government, see Arthur M. Schlesinger, Jr., *A Thousand Days* (Boston, 1965), 680–89.

22. President's Committee on Administrative Management, *Report* (Washington, 1937), 5.

23. Library of Congress, "The Development of the White House Staff,"

Congressional Record, June 20, 1972, H5818–H5820. See also T. E. Cronin, "The Swelling of the Presidency," *Saturday Review of the Society,* February 1973, and Lou Cannon, "White House Staff," *Washington Post,* January 7, 1973.

24. Testimony before the Watergate committee by John W. Dean III, *New York Times,* June 29, 1973; Haldeman in an interview with the *New York Daily News,* September 14, 1971, reprinted in the *News,* July 29, 1973.

25. Subcommittee on the Separation of Powers, *Executive Privilege,* 17.

26. Interview with Jeremy Campbell, *London Evening Standard,* May 18, 1973.

27. Louis Heren, "Watergate," *London Times,* May 11, 1973.

28. Caesar: Who is it in the press that calls on me? I hear a tongue shriller than all the music. . . — *Julius Caesar,* Act I, Scene ii.

29. Franklin D. Roosevelt, Press Conference No. 1, March 8, 1933.

30. H. S. Truman, "My View of the Presidency," *Look,* November 11, 1958.

31. See Douglass Cater, "The President and the Press" in "The Office of the American Presidency," *Annals of the American Academy,* September 1956, 55–65.

32. Clinton Rossiter, *The American Presidency,* 2nd ed. (New York, 1960), 114–18.

33. J. MacG. Burns, *Presidential Government* (Boston, 1966), 199.

34. Rossiter, *American Presidency,* 118.

35. In a press conference in Omaha, June 1972, quoted by Elmer W. Lower, "Freedom of the Press and Our Right to Know," May 3, 1973.

36. Arthur M. Schlesinger, Jr., *The Coming of the New Deal* (Boston, 1958), 562.

37. *New York Times,* May 1, 1973.

38. Adams, "Dissertation on the Canon and Feudal Law," *Works* (Boston, 1856), III, 457.

39. Tocqueville, *Democracy in America,* vol. I, Ch. 12.

40. Theodore Roosevelt, *An Autobiography* (New York, 1913), 354.

41. "Conversation with President Kennedy," December 17, 1962, J. F. Kennedy, *Public Papers and Addresses . . . 1962* (Washington, 1963), 891.

42. Quoted by Francis Williams, "Stay on the Outside," *Progressive,* July 1967. The contemporary *Times* (London) appears, alas, to have abandoned these bracing views. The *Times* leader, "Due Process of Law," June 5, 1973, was accurately described by William Shawcross, a correspondent for the *Sunday Times* (London — a separate newspaper), in these terms: "The idea that the press should censor news that the law allows it to publish because that news is damaging to a politician is an extraordinary one for a paper ever to advocate. When it is applied to a politician who has, for twelve months, allowed himself and his employees to do all they can to discredit and mislead the press, it becomes grotesquely irresponsible. . . . The views expressed in the *Times* editorial seem to be more suited to a govern-

ment information service than to a newspaper." *Washington Post,*
June 25, 1973.

43. *New York Times,* October 17, 1972.

44. Interview with Garnett D. Horner, *Washington Star-News,* reprinted
New York Times, November 10, 1972.

45. "The Press Covers Government: the Nixon Years from 1969 to Watergate," study by Department of Communications, American University, for the National Press Club, with conclusions and recommendations by the Professional Relations Committee of the National Press
Club, *Congressional Record,* June 13, 1973. S11058–S11071.

46. *Washington Post,* January 14, 1973.

47. For a useful summary, see Representative Moorhead's speech before
the Pennsylvania Society of Newspaper Editors, *Congressional Record,* E945–E946, February 21, 1973. The speech by Clay Whitehead of the Office of Telecommunications was reprinted in the *New
York Times,* December 31, 1972.

48. *Branzburg v. Hayes, Supreme Court Reporter,* July 15, 1972, at 2671.

49. Sam Ervin, "Constitutional Casualties in the War on Crime," *Denver
Law Journal,* 1971, *Congressional Record,* October 12, 1972, S17591–
S17596.

50. "That Elitist Conspiracy," *New Republic,* February 10, 1973; see
also James McCartney, "The Washington 'Post' and Watergate," *Columbia Journalism Review,* July/August 1973.

51. *Congressional Record,* July 26, 1973, S14767.

52. Lubell, *Future While It Happened,* 36.

53. Lubell, *Future While It Happened,* 132.

54. Lubell, *Future While It Happened,* 12.

55. Jefferson, annual messages of October 17, 1803, and November 8,
1804, J. D. Richardson, *Messages and Papers of the Presidents* (New
York, 1897), 348, 360. For the Nixon administration's use of the
Jefferson example, see, for example, the statement of Deputy Attor-
ney General Joseph T. Sneed on "Presidential Authority to Impound
Appropriated Funds" before the Subcommittee on Separation of
Powers, February 6, 1973, mimeograph, 4–5.

56. Merrill Jensen, *Thomas Jefferson and the New Nation* (New York,
1970), 839.

57. Richardson, *Messages,* IX, 4331.

58. Senate Appropriations Committee, *First Supplemental National Defense Appropriation . . . Hearings,* 78 Cong., 1 Sess. (1944), 739.

59. See the decision by the Eighth Circuit Court, April 2, 1973, in the
case of *State Highway Commission v. Volpe and Weinberger* on the
question of the applicability of the Anti-Deficiency Acts: "The legislative history is emphatic in noting that this power to withhold funds
cannot be used if it would jeopardize the policy of the statute." The
opinion is reprinted in the *Congressional Record,* April 5, 1973,
S6791–S6799.

60. John F. Kennedy, *Public Papers . . . 1963* (Washington, 1964), 333,
347.

61. Emphasis added. Rehnquist to the Deputy Counsel to the President,

December 19, 1969, quoted in *Congressional Record,* October 13, 1972, S18055.

62. *Congressional Record,* February 20, 1973, S2873.
63. *Congressional Record,* March 26, 1973, E1835–E1836.
64. Library of Congress, "Presidential Impoundment of Funds," *Congressional Record,* March 15, 1973, E1586–E1587.
65. *Congressional Record,* January 16, 1973, S636–S637.
66. Sneed, "Presidential Authority," 11–12, 23.
67. Press Conference, January 31, 1973, *New York Times,* February 1, 1973.
68. Corwin, *Total War and the Constitution,* 77; Corwin, *The President: Office and Powers, 1787–1957* (New York, 1957), 252.
69. Decision of Judge William B. Jones in the United States District Court for the District of Columbia in the case of *Local 2677 et al. v. Phillips* (1973), *Congressional Record,* April 12, 1973, S7333–S7340. Subsequently the same court found that the Acting Director of OEO, whose name Nixon had declined to submit to the Senate even though the Senate was in session continuously from the moment of his appointment, had held his position "unlawfully and illegally." See the decision in *Williams et al. v. Phillips* (1973), *Congressional Record,* June 14, 1973, S11151–S11154.
70. *Okanogan Indians v. U.S.,* 279 U.S. 655 (1929).
71. 302 U.S. 583 (1938).
72. James Madison, *Writings,* Gaillard Hunt, ed. (New York, 1906), IX, 515. I have drawn heavily in this discussion on the cogent plaintiff's brief in the case of *Kennedy v. Sampson and Jones* before the United States District Court of the District of Columbia, 1973. Quotations are from 63, 77, 90.
73. *New York Times,* April 2, 1970.
74. Theodore Roosevelt, *An Autobiography* (New York, 1913), 358.
75. See TRB in *New Republic,* March 10, 1973; and Louis Fisher, "Big Government, Conservative Style," *Progressive,* March 1973.
76. For Ervin's analysis, along with the texts of the opinions in *U.S. v. Gravel* and *U.S. v. Brewster, Congressional Record,* August 16, 1972, S13610–S13636.
77. See the Library of Congress study, "The Present Limits of 'Executive Privilege,'" *Congressional Record,* March 28, 1973, H2242–H2246.
78. See the statement by Deputy Comptroller General R. F. Keller, *Congressional Record,* May 18, 1972, E5506–E5508.
79. Senate Subcommittee on the Separation of Powers, *Executive Privilege,* 30 (Fulbright), 220 (Symington).
80. Kleindienst's prepared statement can be found in the *Congressional Record,* April 10, 1973, S6692–S6695; see also *New York Times,* April 11, 1973. For Richardson, *Washington Post,* June 27, 1973.
81. J. W. Bishop, Jr., "The Executive's Right of Privacy," *Yale Law Journal,* February 1957, 487–88.
82. For a stimulating discussion, see Lord Balogh's essay, "The Apotheosis of the Dilettante" in Hugh Thomas, ed., *The Establishment* (London, 1959), especially 111–12.

83. Raoul Berger, "Executive Privilege v. Congressional Inquiry," *UCLA Law Review*, XII, 1328–29 (1965).

84. Senate Foreign Relations Committee, *War Powers Legislation: Hearings*, 92 Cong., 1 Sess. (1971), 792–93.

85. Senate Subcommittee on the Separation of Powers, *Executive Privilege: The Withholding of Information from the Executive, Hearing* (1971), 359.

86. Letter of April 20, 1972, to Jeremy J. Stone, director of the Federation of American Scientists, *Washington Post*, March 26, 1973.

87. Emphasis added. Statement in *New York Times*, March 13, 1973; *Boston Globe*, May 5, 1973.

88. In this analysis — and for many other insights through the years — I am especially indebted to the column signed TRB, and written, if I may disclose what is hardly a secret any longer, by Richard Lee Strout, in the *New Republic*. For illuminating discussions of the problems involved here, see "Contempt of Congress" and "Speaking of Reform" in the *New Republic* for April 21 and May 26, 1973.

89. Kevin Phillips, "Our Obsolete System," *Newsweek*, April 23, 1973.

90. Robert Michels, *Political Parties* (Collier Books, 1962), 212–14.

91. In *The Rise and Growth of American Politics* (1898), quoted by Corwin, *President* (1957), 28.

92. *New York Times*, July 25, 31, 1973; *Washington Post*, August 14, 1973.

93. *New York Times*, May 23, 1973.

94. Quoted by Tom Braden, "A Chance to Restore Law and Order," *Washington Post*, May 12, 1973.

95. *Congressional Record*, June 18, 1973, S11306.

96. *United States v. U.S. District Court, Supreme Court Reporter*, July 15, 1972, at 2145.

97. Arthur J. Goldberg, "The Legality of Wiretapping the National Security Staff," *Washington Post*, June 1, 1973.

98. *New York Times*, June 26, 1973.

99. *New York Times*, June 28, 1973. I must of course declare an interest. I was myself on the List, along with such noted Americans as Hans Morgenthau, former federal attorney in New York City, Joe Namath of the New York Giants and former Secretary of Defense Clark Gifford.

100. *New York Times*, July 4, 1973.

101. *The Report of the President's Commission on Campus Unrest* (Washington, 1970), 1, 53.

102. *New York Times*, May 23, 1973 (Nixon); *New York Times*, May 25, 1973 (CIA). One CIA officer who participated in the studies told Seymour M. Hersh of the *New York Times*, "We tried to show that the radical movements were home-grown, indigenous responses to perceived grievances and problems that had been growing for years. We said the radicals were clean and that we couldn't find anything. But all it turned out to be was another nail in Helms's coffin." Richard Helms was then the CIA director.

103. *New York Times*, August 2, 1973.

104. *Washington Post,* June 26, 1973 (Dean).
105. For a review of some of these activities, see the article by Senator Ervin, "Constitutional Casualties in the War on Crime," *Congressional Record,* October 12, 1972, S17591–S17596.
106. The Huston memoranda were published in the *New York Times,* June 7, 1973. President Nixon had already acknowledged the existence of the plan in his statement of May 22. It is not clear whether he would ever have disclosed the plan had not John Dean delivered the incriminating memoranda to the Ervin Committee. The Dulles quote is from A. W. Dulles, *The Craft of Intelligence* (New York, 1963), 245.
107. More so than I knew when I wrote *A Thousand Days.*
108. *New York Times,* September 17, 1971.
109. *New York Times,* August 16, 1973.
110. Richard M. Nixon, *A New Road to America* (New York, 1972), 370.
111. T. P. Abernethy, *The Burr Conspiracy* (New York, 1954), 42, 65.
112. His Secretary of Commerce, the defendant in *Youngstown Sheet & Tube v. Sawyer,* was an Ohio Democrat named Charles E. Sawyer. Though Sawyer had been unhappy about the steel seizure, he evidently reconciled himself in later years to the imperial Presidency. In the spring of 1973, he was one of very few Democrats to make a forthright defense of Nixon over Watergate; see his letter to the *Cincinnati Enquirer,* June 13, 1973.
113. Michels, *Political Parties,* 214.
114. *New York Times,* July 25, 1973.
115. Diplomatic historians will, and perhaps rightly, make a different judgment.
116. *Olmstead v. U.S.,* 277 U.S. 438, 470 (1928).
117. James Wechsler, "When It All Began," *New York Post,* April 25, 1973.
118. Cf. Arthur M. Schlesinger, Jr., "Law and Order: Where Are You Now?" *Wall Street Journal,* October 25, 1972.
119. Richard Crossman, "The Wartime Tactics that Led to Watergate," *London Times,* May 16, 1973.
120. Stewart Alsop, "War, Not Politics," *Newsweek,* May 14, 1973.
121. Commencement Address at Notre Dame University, May 20, 1973, *Congressional Record,* May 29, 1973, H4046.
122. *New York Times,* May 18, 1973.
123. Locke, *Second Treatise on Civil Government,* Ch. XIX.
124. Truman's letter of November 12, 1953, to Chairman Harold Velde of the House Un-American Activities Committee was enclosed by Nixon with his own letter of July 7, 1973, to Senator Ervin.
125. For the presidential zigzag on this question, see his various letters as reprinted in the *New York Times,* July 8, 24, 27, 1973.
126. Leonard Garment, et al., "Brief in Opposition," August 7, 1973, 2, 4, 21, 23, 24, 29; the last sentence is from a second document filed on August 17; see *Washington Post,* August 18, 1973.
127. Archibald Cox, et al., "Memorandum in Support," August 13, 1973, 12, 19, 20, 21, 31, 44.

128. *New York Times,* August 16, 1973.
129. *Wall Street Journal,* August 17, 1973.
130. Garment, "Brief in Opposition," 6.
131. *Clark v. United States,* 289 U.S. 1, 15 (1933).
132. Woodrow Wilson, *Constitutional Government in the United States* (New York, 1908), 19.
133. The Internal Revenue Service also deserves credit for being, in the words of a John Dean memorandum, "unresponsive and insensitive" when the White House tried to use it for political purposes.
134. *New York Times,* June 7, 1973.
135. The quotation is from Nixon's statement of May 22, 1973. In this statement the President used the phrase "national security" 24 times and the word "security" in one or another context 13 additional times. Security was thus invoked on the average of once every hundred words. "Many a bum show," George M. Cohan used to say, "has been saved by the flag."
136. See Walters memoranda of July 6, July 13, 1972, *New York Times,* June 4, 1973.
137. In a conversation on June 21, 1973.
138. Hugh Trevor-Roper, "Nixon — America's Charles I?", *Spectator,* August 11, 1973.

9. Democracy and Foreign Policy *(Pages 278–330)*

1. Walter Bagehot, *The English Constitution* (Fontana edition, 1963), 220.
2. There was also, of course, the District of Columbia.
3. "In our country, it is the collective that works, and herein lies our strength. If one makes a mistake, others set him right" — Kosygin, quoted in *Life,* February 2, 1968. No doubt the process by which the maker of mistakes is set right in the Soviet Union can be a trifle drastic. Nevertheless, it seems likely that Soviet leadership in the past few years has been more collegial on questions of war and peace than American leadership has been.
4. Winston S. Churchill, *The Grand Alliance* (Boston, 1950), Book 2, Ch. 12.
5. I am much indebted for my understanding of British practice to a memorandum from John Palmer of the Library of the House of Commons, made available to me through the kindness of the Rt. Hon. Roy Jenkins.
6. Max Beloff, *Foreign Policy and the Democratic Process* (Johns Hopkins paperback, 1965), 22–24.
7. James Bryce, *Modern Democracies* (New York, 1921), II, Ch. 61.
8. I am aware that Daniel Ellsberg has opposed this view with force and elegance. But I continue to find unconvincing the argument that, instead of the quagmire image of leaders blundering into what, to their surprise, turned out to be quicksand, we must accept Mr. Ells-

berg's counter-image of "repeatedly, a leader striding with his eyes open into what he *sees* as quicksand." This argument that the system worked is based in the main on CIA National Intelligence Estimates, which were often sound but also were often ambiguous and were generally canceled out by more optimistic assessments from a host of other sources. In any case, there is little evidence that the people who made the decisions ever read the NIEs. The Pentagon Papers, in my judgment, reinforce the view that the system failed wretchedly and that the Vietnam adventure was marked far more by ignorance, muddle and a profound and chronic absence of foreknowledge than by foresight, awareness and calculation. For Ellsberg's original statement, see "The Quagmire Myth and the Stalemate Machine," *Public Policy*, spring 1971; for a response, Arthur M. Schlesinger, Jr., "Eyeless in Indochina," *New York Review of Books*, October 21, 1971. There are further reflections on the debate in Daniel Ellsberg, *Papers on the War* (New York, 1972).

9. *Missouri v. Holland*, 252 U.S. 416, 433 (1920).
10. J. Q. Adams, *Eulogy on Madison* (Boston, 1836), 47.
11. Hans Morgenthau, "Congress and Foreign Policy," *New Republic*, June 14, 1969.
12. I. F. Stone, "Impeachment," *New York Review of Books*, June 28, 1973.
13. *Chicago and S. Airlines v. Waterman S. S. Corp.*, 333 U.S. 103, 111 (1948).
14. *Marbury v. Madison*, 1 Cranch 137, 165 (1803); *Foster v. Neilson*, 2 Peters 253 (1829).
15. Learned Hand, *The Bill of Rights* (Atheneum paperback, 1964), 15.
16. *Baker v. Carr*, 369 U.S. 186, 211, 217, 226 (1962).
17. *Baker v. Carr*, 267.
18. Alexander Bickel, *The Least Dangerous Branch* (Indianapolis, 1962), Ch. 4; Herbert Wechsler, "Toward Neutral Principles of Constitutional Law," *Harvard Law Review*, November 1959, 9. For an able general discussion, see M. E. Tigar, "Judicial Power, the 'Political Question Doctrine,' and Foreign Relations," *UCLA Law Review* (1970), XVII, 1135–79.
19. For much valuable material, see Leon Friedman and Burt Neuborne, *Unquestioning Obedience to the President* (New York, 1972); *Luftig v. McNamara* is mentioned on 26.
20. *Mora v. McNamara*, 389 U.S. 934 (1967).
21. The quotations are from Judge Dooling in *Orlando v. Laird*, Friedman and Neuborne, *Unquestioning Obedience*, 110 and Judge Coffin, *Massachusetts v. Laird*, *Congressional Record*, November 16, 1971, E12248.
22. It might be noted that the Supreme Court in 1942 had in a sense disclaimed the *Curtiss-Wright* theory, though when Chief Justice Stone said, "Congress and the President, like the courts, possess no power not derived from the Constitution," he was, like Sutherland before him, indulging in dictum. *Ex parte Quirin*, 317 U.S. 1, 25 (1942).

23. Judge Dooling said of the resolution in his opinion in the District Court in the case of *Orlando v. Laird*, "Its importance no doubt lay in its practical effect on the presidential initiative rather than its constitutional meaning." On the other hand, Judge Judd said in *Berk v. Laird* that the resolution gave "authority to prevent aggression against Southeast Asia peoples who were protecting their freedom." Friedman and Neuborne, *Unquestioning Obedience*, 115, 121.

24. Friedman and Neuborne, *Unquestioning Obedience*, 115, 222, 249.

25. J. N. Moore, *Law and the Indo-China War* (Princeton, 1972), 629.

26. *Ex parte Endo* 323 U.S. 283, 303 (1944).

27. Frederick Merk, "Dissent in the Mexican War," in Merk, S. E. Morison and Frank Freidel, *Dissent in Three American Wars* (Cambridge, 1970), 46.

28. Lincoln to Herndon, February 1, 1848, Abraham Lincoln, *Collected Works*, R. P. Basler, ed. (New Brunswick, 1953), I, 447.

29. S. F. Bemis, *John Quincy Adams and the Union* (New York, 1956), 498.

30. John Rothchild, "Cooing Down the War: The Senate's Lame Doves," *Washington Monthly*, August 1971, 13.

31. *Congressional Record*, June 11, 1968, H4824. For a multitude of similar congressional disclaimers, see Friedman and Neuborne, *Unquestioning Obedience*, 86–109.

32. The quotations are from Judge Dooling in *Orlando* and Judge Judd in *Berk;* Friedman and Neuborne, *Unquestioning Obedience*, 115, 123.

33. District of Columbia Court of Appeals, *Mitchell v. Laird, Congressional Record*, May 16, 1973, S9259. Wyzanski expressed his earlier view in *United States v. Sisson*, 295 F. Supp. 511 (D. Mass. 1968). In *Mitchell* he concluded that, while legislation could not be construed "as a valid assent" to the war, the issue was nonetheless a political question and beyond the court's jurisdiction.

34. *Congressional Record*, July 29, 1971, S12446, S12448. See also the valuable article, heretofore cited by John Rothchild in the *Washington Monthly*, August 1971.

35. U.S. Court of Appeals for the First Circuit, *Massachusetts v. Laird* (1971), reprinted in *Congressional Record*, November 16, 1971, E12247–E12249.

36. Judd's decision in *Holtzman et al. v. Schlesinger* may be found in the *Congressional Record*, July 30, 1973, H6907–H6911. The Schlesinger involved, it need hardly be said, was the Secretary of Defense.

37. Marshall's ruling is in the *Congressional Record*, August 1, 1973, H7194–H7196.

38. *New York Times*, August 5, 1973.

39. United States Court of Appeals for the Second Circuit, *Holtzman et al. v. Schlesinger*, September Term, 1972, 4957, 4963. The majority opinion made a somewhat opaque effort to distinguish this case from earlier affirmations of justiciability by the same court in

Berk and *Orlando*. The dissenting opinion by Judge James Oakes added the point at 4976–77 that, if congressional appropriations were to imply authorization of an otherwise unauthorized executive policy, "the congressional action must be based on a knowledge of the facts," and that the concealment of the American air war against Cambodia in 1969–1970 therefore invalidated any implied authorization.

40. *Korematsu v. U.S.*, 323 U.S. 214, 248 (1944).
41. J. D. Richardson, *Messages and Papers of the Presidents* (New York, 1897), VI, 2515, 2517.
42. Adolf Berle, "The President and Foreign Policy," *New Leader*, July 28, 1952.
43. Senate Foreign Relations Committee, *War Powers Legislation: Hearings*, 92 Cong., 1 Sess. (1971), 395.
44. J. W. Fulbright, "American Foreign Policy in the 20th Century under an 18th-Century Constitution," *Cornell Law Quarterly*, fall 1961.
45. Senate Foreign Relations Committee, *War Powers Legislation*, 530.
46. Wechsler, "Toward Neutral Principles," especially 15, 19.
47. *Congressional Record*, June 19, 1969, S6831.
48. John Quincy Adams, Address, July 4, 1821. This passage had also been quoted during the isolationist-interventionist debate of 1939–1941. Oddly some of the isolationist argument of that period, so totally misdirected when the United States confronted threats, as it did then, in areas of direct and vital interest, applied rather more accurately to the indiscriminate globalism that culminated in the Indochina War.
49. The quotation is apocryphal. It was a favorite of Dean Acheson's who, alas, did not always follow the injunction himself. See Dean Acheson, *Present at the Creation* (New York, 1969), 199.
50. Joseph A. Schumpeter, *Imperialism and Social Classes* (Meridian Books, 1955), 25.
51. *Congressional Record*, April 1, 1971, H2409–H2410.
52. Marcus Raskin, "The Erosion of Congressional Power," *Congressional Record*, February 27, 1973, H1192.
53. For the text of the bill and explanatory remarks by Senators Javits, Eagleton, Humphrey, Muskie and others, see *Congressional Record*, January 18, 1973, S870–S894. I am indebted to a perceptive memorandum on the bill by Benjamin V. Cohen, June 7, 1971.
54. *Congressional Record*, April 22, 1971, S5425.
55. *Congressional Record*, July 20, 1973, S14161 (Abourezk), S14202–S14203 (Fulbright).
56. E. S. Corwin, *The Constitution and What It Means Today* (Atheneum, 1963), 24–25; cf. also E. S. Corwin, *Total War and the Constitution* (New York, 1947), 45–47.
57. See Moore's testimony, Senate Foreign Relations Committee, *War Powers Legislation*, 465; J. N. Moore, *Law and the Indo-China War* (Princeton, 1972), 545; Quincy Wright, "The Power of the Executive

to Use Military Forces Abroad," *Virginia Journal of International Law*, X, 49 (1969).

58. W. W. Willoughby, *The Constitutional Law of the United States*, 2nd ed. (New York, 1929), III, 1567.
59. Alexander M. Bickel, "Sharing Responsibility for War," *New Republic*, September 25, 1971.
60. Theodore Roosevelt, *An Autobiography* (New York, 1913), 552–53.
61. For this and other useful items, see J. T. Emerson, "War Powers Legislation," *West Virginia Law Review*, LXXIV, 53–119, reprinted in *Congressional Record*, February 15, 1972, especially S1720.
62. Richardson, *Messages*, I, 317.
63. Raoul Berger, "War-Making by the President," *University of Pennsylvania Law Review*, November 1972, 78–81.
64. Symington Committee, "Security Agreements and Commitments Abroad," 91 Cong., 2 Sess., December 21, 1970, 28.
65. Committee for Economic Development, *Military Manpower and National Security* (New York, 1972). I am indebted to Professor Thomas Schelling, the project director, for further illumination on various points in the proposal.
66. *Reid v. Covert*, 354 U.S. 1 (1957).
67. Senate Foreign Relations Committee, *War Powers Legislation*, 778.
68. Subcommittee on Separation of Powers, Senate Judiciary Committee, *Congressional Oversight of Executive Agreements: Hearing*, 92 Cong., 2 Sess. (1972), 249. The problem of the definition of an executive agreement is by no means simple. "Every time we open a new privy," John Foster Dulles said in 1953, "we have to have an executive agreement," claiming about 10,000 minor agreements in relation to NATO alone. However, he was arguing against the Bricker Amendment and was no doubt tempted into exaggeration. Cf. Louis Henkin, *Foreign Affairs and the Constitution* (New York, 1972), 420.
69. Subcommittee on Separation of Powers, *Congressional Oversight*, 3, 249.
70. Subcommittee on Separation of Powers, *Congressional Oversight*, 53, 54.
71. *Congressional Record*, June 19, 1972, S9641.
72. *Congressional Record*, June 14, 1973, S1178.
73. Senate Report 91–129, "National Commitments," 91 Cong., 1 Sess., April 16, 1969, 28.
74. *Congressional Record*, June 14, 1973, S1174–S1175.
75. Subcommittee on Separation of Powers, *Congressional Oversight*, 241.
76. *Congressional Record*, March 10, 1954, 2811–14.
77. For a valuable summary of congressional attempts to deal with CIA, see Gary Sperling, "Central Intelligence and its Control," *Congressional Record*, July 14, 1966, 15041–50.
78. Harry S. Truman, "Limit CIA Role to Intelligence," *Washington Star*, December 29, 1963.
79. *Congressional Record*, November 23, 1971, S19523.
80. *Congressional Record*, May 8, 1973, H3450.

81. *Congressional Record,* November 23, 1971, S19528.
82. For a useful resumé, see Laurence Stern, "A Sense of Déjà Vu at CIA," *Washington Post,* July 10, 1973.
83. *Congressional Record,* July 20, 1973, S14188.
84. Or so at least it seems to a mere historian. Legal scholarship is not especially helpful on this point. Neither "emergency" nor "national emergency" appear, for example, in the index to Corwin's *The President: Office and Powers* or Henkin's *Foreign Affairs and the Constitution* or even Corwin's monumental *The Constitution of the United States of America: Analysis and Interpretation* (Washington, 1952), though see 142.
85. Cited in Corwin, *The Constitution,* 142. Cf. Chief Justice Hughes's famous and enigmatic statement in the Minnesota mortgage-moratorium case: "While emergency does not create power, emergency may furnish the occasion for the exercise of power." *Home Building and Loan Association v. Blaisdell,* 290 U.S. 398, 426 (1934).
86. For useful suggestions, see Clinton Rossiter, *Constitutional Dictatorship* (Princeton, 1948), 310–11; J. M. Smith and C. P. Cotter, *Powers of the President During Crises* (Washington, 1960), 144–45.
87. Machiavelli, *The Discourses,* Book 1, Ch. 34, in *The Prince and the Discourses* (Modern Library, 1940), 203; Rousseau, *Social Contract,* Book 4, Ch. 6 (World's Classics), 415–16; Mill, *Considerations on Representative Government,* Marshall Cohen ed., *The Philosophy of John Stuart Mill* (Modern Library, 1961), 407.
88. William Howard Taft, *Our Chief Magistrate and His Powers* (New York, 1916), 156.
89. *Paradise Lost,* Book IV, lines 393–94. Had he written three centuries later, the operative term would have been "national security."
90. I am indebted to Benjamin V. Cohen for this general formulation of the problem.
91. Woodrow Wilson, *Constitutional Government in the United States* (New York, 1908), 140.
92. Subcommittee on Separation of Powers, Senate Judiciary Committee, *Executive Privilege: The Withholding of Information by the Executive: Hearing,* 92 Cong., 1 Sess. (1971), 360.
93. The constitutional dimensions of interdependence are cogently laid out in L. G. Ratner, "The Coordinated Warmaking Power — Legislative, Executive, and Judicial Roles," *Southern California Law Review,* XLIV, 461–89 (1971).
94. In 1973 the Senate Foreign Relations Committee included Fulbright, Mansfield, Church, Symington, McGovern, Muskie, Humphrey, Pell, McGee, Aiken, Case, Percy, Pearson, Javits and Scott. Could anyone conceivably claim that Nixon's National Security Council represented men of higher intelligence or wider experience?
95. Benjamin V. Cohen, "The Evolving Role of Congress in Foreign Affairs," *Proceedings of the American Philosophical Society,* October 1948, 213, 214.
96. Wilson, *Constitutional Government,* 141.

97. *Congressional Record*, July 31, 1967, S10488.
98. Senate Foreign Relations Committee, "National Commitments," Report 91–129, 91 Cong., 1 Sess. (1969), 26.
99. I take these examples from Francis O. Wilcox, *Congress, the Executive, and Foreign Policy* (New York, 1971), 42, 47.
100. *Congressional Record*, April 11, 1973, S7082–S7084.
101. For Rusk, see Subcommittee on Separation of Powers, *Executive Privilege*, 344; also personal letter, September 29, 1972; for Cohen, see his war-powers bill memorandum, June 7, 1971; for Wilcox (who would, I think unwisely, have the President himself on the commission), *Congress, the Executive, and Foreign Policy*, 157–58.

10. The Secrecy System (*Pages 331–376*)

1. C. C. Tansill, ed., *Documents Illustrative of the Formation of the Union of the American States* (Washington, 1927), 740, 744–45.
2. He did so, Andrew Jackson explained on his behalf in 1836, because "motives of personal kindness and delicacy" impelled him to postpone disclosure until the other participants were dead. Dolley Madison had written Jackson: "However prevailing the restraint which veiled during the life of Mr. Madison this record of the creation of our Constitution, the grave, which has closed over all those who participated in its formation, has separated their acts from all that is personal to him or to them. His anxiety for their early publicity after this was removed may be inferred from his having them transcribed and revised by himself." Dolley Madison to Jackson, November 15, 1836. J. D. Richardson, *Messages and Papers of the Presidents* (New York, 1897), IV, 1480, 1482.
3. Madison to W. T. Barry, August 4, 1822, S. K. Padover, ed., *The Complete Madison* (New York, 1953), 346.
4. J. C. Miller, *Crisis in Freedom: The Alien and Sedition Acts* (Boston, 1951), 63–85.
5. Jefferson himself did not fully espouse the new theory. He continued to read the First Amendment, as he had when he wrote the Kentucky Resolution in 1798, not as guaranteeing freedom of expression but rather as reserving to state governments the right the Constitution denied Congress "of judging how far the licentiousness of speech, and of the press, may be abridged." When as President himself he fell under newspaper attack, he wrote the governor of Pennsylvania that he had "long thought that a few [state] prosecutions of the most prominent offenders would have a wholesome effect in restoring the integrity of the presses." Cf. Leonard W. Levy, *Jefferson and Civil Liberties* (Cambridge, 1963), 56, 59.
6. Robert V. Remini, "Election of 1832" in Arthur M. Schlesinger, Jr., and F. L. Israel, eds., *History of American Presidential Elections 1789–1968* (New York, 1971), I, 531, 535.
7. National Archives, "Origin of Defense-Information Markings in the

Army and Former War Department" (mimeograph, Washington, 1972), 44.

8. Bertram Wyatt-Brown, *Lewis Tappan and the Evangelical War Against Slavery* (New York, 1971), 277.

9. Richardson, *Messages,* V, 2283.

10. J. G. Randall, *Constitutional Problems Under Lincoln* (New York, 1926), 484–508.

11. W. M. Franklin, "The Availability of Department of State Records," *Department of State Bulletin,* January 29, 1973.

12. W. M. Franklin, "The Future of the 'Foreign Relations' Series," *Department of State Bulletin,* September 15, 1969, 250. This is not to suggest that an Italian government would react to a similar disclosure with comparable equanimity a century later.

13. F. R. Black, "The United States Senate and the Treaty Power," *Rocky Mountain Law Review* (1931), reprinted in *Congressional Record,* July 26, 1971, especially S12065.

14. Woodrow Wilson, "Committee or Cabinet Government?" *Overland Monthly,* January 1884, in *Papers,* A. S. Link, ed. (Princeton, 1966), II, 629.

15. Woodrow Wilson, *The New Freedom* (Englewood Cliffs, 1961), 76.

16. H. H. Gerth and C. Wright Mills, eds., *From Max Weber: Essays in Sociology* (New York, 1946), 233–34.

17. Thorstein Veblen, *Absentee Ownership* (New York, 1954), 444. Thank you, Marcus Cunliffe.

18. I take this description, and some of the subsequent discussion, from various pieces by Harold Nicolson, "An Open Look at Secret Diplomacy," *New York Times Magazine,* September 13, 1953; "The Faults of American Diplomacy," *Harper's,* January 1955; and *Peacemaking 1919* (Universal Library, 1965), 334–37.

19. National Archives, "Origin of Defense-Information Markings," 3, 9, 12–14.

20. Justice Marshall reprinted this provision in his opinion in the Pentagon Papers case; *New York Times Co. v. U.S.,* 403 U.S. 713, 744 (1971).

21. *Gorin v. United States,* 312 U.S. 19, 32 (1941).

22. Robert Murphy, *Diplomat Among Warriors* (New York, 1964), 452.

23. House Government Operations Committee, "Executive Classification of Information," Report 93–221, 93 Cong., 1 Sess. (1973), 6–7.

24. Franklin D. Roosevelt, Press Conference 720, February 21, 1941.

25. Interview with Allen Dulles, *U.S. News & World Report,* March 19, 1954.

26. House Government Operations Committee, "Executive Classification," 8–9.

27. House Government Operations Committee, "Executive Classification," 20, 16.

28. In one of those coincidences that would have rejoiced Anthony Powell, Hennings's son-in-law for a time was John W. Dean III, later of the Nixon White House.

29. All this is well described in the useful book by David Wise, *The Politics of Lying* (New York, 1973), 67–68.
30. House Foreign Operations and Government Information Subcommittee, *U.S. Government Information Policies,* Part 4, 92 Cong., 1 Sess. (1972), 1011.
31. In 1947 Eisenhower as Army Chief of Staff said in an official instruction: "The Army possesses no inherent right to conceal the history of its affairs behind a cloak of secrecy. . . . The historical record of the Army's operations as well as the manner in which these were accomplished are public property, and except where the security of the Nation may be jeopardized, the right of the citizens to the full story is unquestioned. . . . The foregoing directive will be interpreted in the most liberal sense with no reservations as to whether or not the evidence of history places the Army in a favorable light." "Policy Concerning Release of Information from Historical Documents of the Army — with Special Reference to the Events of World War II," November 20, 1947. This admirable order had, alas, little perceptible effect.
32. John F. Kennedy, *Public Papers . . . 1961* (Washington, 1962), 336–38.
33. Douglass Cater, "News and the Nation's Security," *Reporter,* July 6, 1961.
34. *New York Times,* May 10, 1961.
35. See the speech by Clifton Daniel, "The Press and National Security," reprinted as an appendix in William McGaffin and Erwin Knoll, *Anything but the Truth* (New York, 1968), especially 205.
36. Executive Order 10964, September 20, 1961.
37. House Government Operation Committee, "Executive Classification," 26, 17.
38. Wise, *Politics of Lying,* 59–62.
39. Interview with Marvin Kalb, June 17, 1971, *Congressional Record,* June 24, 1971, E6627.
40. House Government Operations Committee, "Executive Classification," 50–51.
41. Foreign Operations and Government Information Subcommittee, House Government Operations Committee, *U.S. Government Information Policies and Practices . . . Hearings,* Part 1, 92 Cong., 1 Sess. (1971), 97–101.
42. I do not suggest that if Ellsberg had acted against the Kennedy administration or Otepka against the Nixon administration there would have been no presidential wrath.
43. *New York Times,* June 16, 1971.
44. Cf. "The Pentagon Papers Revisited," *Washington Post,* June 22, 1972.
45. *New York Times,* May 23, 1973.
46. Nixon himself described the impact in his statement of May 22, 1973, and former members of the White House staff testified to this effect in the Watergate hearings. Nixon was further disturbed by a

New York Times story that, he asserted in 1973, "seriously compromised the United States negotiating position in the SALT talks" *(New York Times,* May 23, 1973). This story, by William Beecher, whom Nixon later made Deputy Assistant Secretary of Defense for Public Affairs, appeared in the *Times* on July 23, 1971. Once again, the presidential agitation seemed excessive. It is unlikely that the story was of much benefit to the Russians, who had been hearing the United States expound its position for the previous fortnight in Helsinki. "The indications are," Herbert Scoville, Jr., subsequently wrote, "that it was not the Russians but the American people that the President wished to keep ignorant of our negotiating stand." Scoville, who had been a deputy director of CIA as well as assistant director of the Arms Control and Disarmament Agency, added that there was "no evidence . . . that the leak caused any actual harm." See Herbert Scoville, Jr., "Are the 'Plumbers' Worse Trouble than the Leaks?" *New York Times,* June 3, 1973.

47. *New York Times Co. v. U.S.,* 403 U.S. 713.
48. Wise, *Politics of Lying,* 154.
49. House Government Operations Committee, "Executive Classification," 31, 54.
50. House Government Information Subcommittee, *U.S. Government Information Policies,* Part 7, 2693.
51. For this analysis of the Nixon order, *Congressional Record,* March 21, 1972, H2774–H2787; see also the cogent discussion by William G. Florence, *Federal Times,* March 29, 1972.
52. *New York Times,* May 25, 1973.
53. For a discussion of this legislation, see the speech by Senator Muskie and accompanying memorandum, *Congressional Record,* April 2, 1973, S6329–S6333; for defense and explanation by the Department of Justice, *Congressional Record,* May 8, 1973, S8508–S8514.
54. Lord Franks, Chairman, *Departmental Committee on Section 2 of the Official Secrets Act 1911 . . . Volume 1 Report of the Committee* (London, 1972), 120.
55. Jonathan Aitken in *Officially Secret* (London, 1971), quoted by Charles Wintour in a trenchant survey of the problem in his excellent book *Pressures on the Press* (London, 1972), 157.
56. Wintour, *Pressures on the Press,* 158, 164.
57. Brian Roberts, "Secrets: The Breaking of the Law," *London Sunday Telegraph,* September 26, 1971.
58. For British reactions to the Franks Commission, *London Daily Telegraph,* September 30, 1972, and Brian Roberts, "Secrets: Mandarins Win a Round," *London Sunday Telegraph,* July 1, 1973.
59. June 11, 1948; quoted by Ben H. Brown, Jr., "Congress and the Department of State," *Annals of the American Academy of Political and Social Science,* September 1953, 107.
60. In his speech of January 5, 1951, reprinted in *Congressional Record,* May 19, 1971, especially S7319.
61. Nicolson, "Open Look at Secret Diplomacy," 17.

62. See Frank Church's Christian A. Herter lecture at Johns Hopkins, "American Foreign Policy in Transition," *Congressional Record,* February 17, 1972, especially S2009. The emphasis is Senator Church's.

63. Dulles, *Craft of Intelligence,* 237.

64. Max Frankel, "The 'State Secrets' Myth," *Columbia Journalism Review,* September/October 1971, 24.

65. April 22, 1951; quoted in *Parade,* September 26, 1971.

66. *New York Times,* July 25, 31, 1973; Richard M. Nixon, *A New Road for America* (New York, 1972), 35.

67. In a letter to the Senate Armed Services Committee, *New York Times,* July 24, 1973.

68. The documents, rescued by Jack Anderson, appeared in the *New York Times,* January 6 and 15, 1972. Publication was much criticized at the time on the ground that the secret minutes displayed the United States government as pettish and deceitful. But, if this was the kind of government the United States had, did not the American people have a right to know it? It was hardly the function of a secrecy system to shield public officials from accountability for their tantrums or to deny Congress the opportunity to discuss Nixon's pro-Pakistan policy on its merits.

69. Phil G. Goulding, *Confirm or Deny* (New York, 1970), 117.

70. George McGovern, "The Pentagon Papers," *Political Science Quarterly,* June 1972, 182.

71. Watergate hearings *passim.*

72. This, I fear, is the kind of statement that drives quantitative historians, as Mr. Nixon would put it, up the wall. But of what other time in American history would it even occur to anyone to make such a statement? For those who derive consolation from public opinion polls, I might mention that Lloyd A. Free and Hadley Cantril, asking a sample in 1964 to rate their confidence in government on a scale of 1 to 10, came out with a thumping 7.43 rating for the executive branch; see Free and Cantril, *The Political Beliefs of Americans* (New Brunswick, 1967), 118. In 1966 the Louis Harris poll reported that 41 percent of respondents professed "a great deal of confidence" in the executive branch. In 1971 this had fallen to 23 percent (*New York Post,* November 13, 1972), and it sank even lower after Watergate.

73. *New York Times Company v. U.S.,* 403 U.S. 713, 729. Emphasis added.

74. Subcommittee on Separation of Powers, Senate Judiciary Committee, *Executive Privilege: The Withholding of Information by the Executive: Hearing,* 92 Cong., 1 Sess. (1971), 347.

75. Bryce, *Modern Democracies,* II, 371.

76. I owe this example to Clayton Fritchey, who has written a number of fine columns on this general theme; see especially his column of July 3, 1972.

77. Edward Teller, "How Many Secrecies?" *New York Times,* December

1, 1971; Teller, "Kicking the Secrecy Habit," *New York Times,* May 27, 1973; *New York Post,* April 25, 1973.

78. The text of the Final Task Force Report is in *Congressional Record,* May 23, 1972, E5675–E5678.

79. Herbert Feis, "The Other Secrets," *New York Times,* July 30, 1971.

80. *Environmental Protection Agency v. Mink,* decided by the Supreme Court on January 22, 1973, 41 U.S.L.W. 4201. *Mink* was directed at the procedures prescribed under the Freedom of Information Act. In the case of *Committee for Nuclear Responsibility* v. *Seaborg,* where the Act was not involved and where the Atomic Energy Commission claimed executive privilege, the Court of Appeals in the District of Columbia sustained a district judge in his ruling that documents concerning the nuclear test be submitted to him for *in camera* inspection.

81. House Government Information Subcommittee, *U.S. Government Information Policies,* Part 5, 92 Cong., 2 Sess. (1972), 1443. The Commission on National Security — the Wright Commission — recognized this right in its 1957 report when it said, *"In the absence of any law to the contrary,* there is an adequate constitutional and statutory basis upon which to predicate the Presidential authority" (emphasis added). Legislative Reference Service, "Security Classification," 5.

82. Wise, *Politics of Lying,* 351.

83. Nicolson, "Open Look at Secret Diplomacy," 17.

84. Kennedy to Rusk, September 6, 1961, *John F. Kennedy, Public Papers . . . 1961* (Washington, 1962), 591–92.

85. Nixon to Rogers, March 8, 1972.

86. I owe this quotation and much of the information on other countries to a paper by W. Kaye Lamb, "Liberalization of Restrictions on Access to Archives: General Survey," written for the International Council on Archives Congress, 1966. For a useful survey of the American situation, see the Twentieth Century Fund study, Carol M. Barker and Matthew H. Fox, *Classified Files: The Yellowing Pages* (New York, 1972).

87. But Truman, despite his lively interest in and professed indebtedness to history, kept his most significant foreign policy papers closed to scholars throughout his life.

88. I have in mind, of course, Sherman Adams, Emmet Hughes, Arthur Larson, Theodore C. Sorensen, Pierre Salinger, Kenneth O'Donnell, Harry McPherson and Eric Goldman.

89. Herbert Feis, "The Shackled Historian," *Foreign Affairs,* January 1967, and *From Trust to Terror: The Onset of the Cold War, 1945–1950* (New York, 1970), 375.

90. Julius Epstein, "A Case for Suppression," *New York Times,* December 18, 1970.

91. See the White House transcript of the joint press conference of John Erlichman and John Dean, still comrades then, explaining the presidential order, August 12, 1971, 4.

92. *New York Times,* November 22, 1972.

93. Not, heaven help us, the thermonuclear Herman Kahn. See Herman Kahn the historian's illuminating article, "Who Shall Have Access?" *Yale Alumni Review*, March 1972.

94. Acheson to Matthew H. Fox, September 1, 1971, Barker and Fox, *Classified Files*, 107.

95. W. L. Langer, "The Historian's Right to See," *New York Times Book Review*, December 20, 1970.

96. James MacGregor Burns, "The Historian's Right to See," *New York Times Book Review*, November 8, 1970.

97. David Kahn is the author of *The Codebreakers*, the standard work on the subject. The quotation is from his article "Does the Enemy Care About Those Papers Because They Unlock Secret U.S. Codes?" *Newsday*, June 25, 1971.

98. Herbert Feis, "Unpublic Public Papers," *New York Times Book Review*, April 21, 1968. The real danger in opening the files is not that the nation would be betrayed but that the historians would be suffocated. "While I was Secretary of State," said Dean Rusk, "two million, one hundred thousand cables went out of the Department of State. I doubt that any single historian will be able to see as many as 1% of them — because the historian, too, is mortal and can't live forever." Rusk to Matthew H. Fox, August 24, 1971, Barker and Fox, *Classified Files*, 111.

99. A. H. Vandenberg, Jr., ed., *The Private Papers of Senator Vandenberg* (Boston, 1952), 2, 22. Adolf Berle: "Vandenberg once stated to me that, in the light of hindsight, from the spring of 1940 on, it was perfectly clear that war with Japan was a pressing danger; he complained that more information would have made the danger clear. A great number of his colleagues, however, were asserting that President Roosevelt's warnings were intended to frighten the country for political purposes." Adolf A. Berle, Jr., "The President and Foreign Policy," *New Leader*, July 28, 1952.

100. Senate Judiciary Committee, *Executive Privilege*, 346.

101. House Government Information Subcommittee, *U.S. Government Information Policies*, Part 7, 92 Cong., 2 Sess. (1972), 2557.

102. *New York Times*, April 9, 14, 1961, September 6, 1963; see the excellent article by Henry Fairlie, "We Knew What We Were Doing When We Went Into Vietnam," *Washington Monthly*, May 1973.

103. Richard Harwood, "Few 'Revelations' for Those Who Had Been Listening," *Washington Post*, June 29, 1971; Peter Arnett, "The Pentagon Papers — Opening Government to the Public," released by Associated Press, June 27, 1971, reprinted *Congressional Record*, June 29, 1971, S10218–S10220.

104. Woodrow Wilson, *Congressional Government*, 15th ed. (Boston, 1901), 303.

105. *Congressional Record*, August 6, 1971, S13743–S13745.

11. The Future of the Presidency (*Pages 377–419*)

1. Jefferson to Madison, March 15, 1789, quoted by Alexis de Tocqueville, *Democracy in America*, I, Ch. 15.
2. James Bryce, *Modern Democracies* (New York, 1921), II, 73.
3. *Ex Parte Milligan*, 4 Wall 2, 125 (1866).
4. "A President Unfit to Rule," *Spectator*, June 9, 1973.
5. *New York Times*, August 16, 1973.
6. *New York Times*, May 1, 1973.
7. Interview in *New York Times*, May 18, 1973.
8. *New York Times*, June 15, 1973; interview with Charles Wheeler, *Listener*, July 26, 1973.
9. Mary McGrory, "A Talk with John Dean," *New York Post*, June 18, 1973.
10. Lou Cannon, "The Siege Psychology and How It Grew," *Washington Post*, July 29, 1973.
11. Interview in *New York Times*, August 5, 1973.
12. *New York Times*, July 24, 1973.
13. C. C. Thach, *The Creation of the Presidency, 1775–1789* (Baltimore, 1969), 147.
14. Woodrow Wilson, *Constitutional Government in the United States* (New York, 1908), 79–80.
15. See, for example, his speech in Milwaukee, March 23, 1968.
16. Barbara Tuchman, "Should We Abolish the Presidency?" *New York Times*, February 13, 1973; Max Lerner, "Presidential Watchmen," *New York Post*, June 11, 1972.
17. They also had been brought up recurrently thereafter — as by August B. Woodward, *Considerations on the Executive Government of the United States* (1809); John C. Calhoun, *Discourse on the Constitution* (1851); Henry C. Lockwood, *The Abolition of the Presidency* (1884); C. Perry Paterson, *Presidential Government in the United States* (1947); Charles S. Hyneman, *Bureaucracy in a Democracy* (1950); Herman Finer, *The Presidency: Crisis and Regeneration* (1960); Rexford G. Tugwell, *The Enlargement of the Presidency* (1960). Two valuable recent books on the Presidency — Marcus Cunliffe, *American Presidents and the Presidency* (London, 1969) and James MacGregor Burns, *Presidential Government: The Crucible of Leadership* (Boston, 1966) — contain useful discussions.
18. C. C. Tansill, ed., *Documents Illustrative of the Formation of the Union of the American States* (Washington, 1927), 131–33, 567, 595, 686–87.
19. 70th Federalist.
20. Jefferson to Destutt de Tracy, January 26, 1811, *The Complete Jefferson*, S. K. Padover, ed. (New York, 1943), 310–12.
21. George Reedy, *The Twilight of the Presidency* (New York, 1970), 20–26. He continues: "Lyndon Johnson looked forward with horror to the long weekends in which there was really nothing to do. The

result was usually a Saturday afternoon spent in lengthy conferences with individual newspapermen who would be hastily summoned from their homes and would spend hours with him while he expounded the thesis that his days were so taken up with the nation's business that he had no time to devote to friends."

22. Thach, *Creation of the Presidency*, 125.

23. Thach, *Creation of the Presidency*, 174.

24. House Judiciary Committee, *Single Six-Year Term for President: Hearing*, 92 Cong., 1 Sess. (1972), 3, 33. The argument advanced by Mansfield and Aiken would appear to be the major source of support for the amendment. It should be noted that Joseph Califano, former Special Assistant to President Johnson, disclaimed the Mansfield-Aiken line but advanced a more sophisticated argument: that the contemporary budget process, by requiring a new President to operate for 18 months under his predecessor's budget, gave him little chance to get things done in so short a time as four years. This would seem to me an argument for shortening the budget process (which need not, in any case, be all that inflexible) rather than for lengthening the presidential term. I have not gone into the question of the lame-duck effect as an argument against the single six-year term because lame-duckery seems to me a very minor element in presidential ineffectiveness.

25. Senate Judiciary Committee, *Single Six-Year Term*, 113.

26. Senate Judiciary Committee, *Single Six-Year Term*, 63.

27. Senate Judiciary Committee, *Single Six-Year Term*, 16.

28. Washington to Lafayette, April 28, 1788, Washington, *Writings*, P. L. Ford, ed. (New York, 1891), XI, 257–58.

29. Wilson to A. Mitchell Palmer, February 5, 1913, Senate Judiciary Committee, *Six-Year Term*, 240–41.

30. E. S. Corwin, *The President: Office and Powers* (New York, 1957), 296.

31. W. H. Taft, *Our Chief Magistrate and His Powers* (New York, 1916), 31–32.

32. See his articles on "Cabinet Government in the United States," *International Review*, August 1879, and "Committee or Cabinet Government?" *Overland Monthly*, January 1884, reprinted in A. S. Link, ed., *The Papers of Woodrow Wilson* (Princeton, 1966), I, 493 ff.; II, 618 ff.; the quotation is from II, 627. Wilson proposed to overcome the constitutional problem by adding four words to Article I, Section 6, to make it read: "and no Person holding *other than a Cabinet* Office under the United States shall be a Member of either House during his Continuance in Office."

33. Wilson to Palmer, Senate Judiciary Committee, *Six-Year Term*, 240.

34. E. S. Corwin, *The President: Office and Powers* (New York, 1940), 304.

35. Thomas K. Finletter, *Can Representative Government Do the Job?* (New York, 1945); cf. also E. S. Corwin, *The President: Office and Powers, 1787–1957* (New York, 1957), 297–98, 489–90. The adop-

tion of a parliamentary system is discussed in such books as William Macdonald, *A New Constitution for America* (1921) and Henry Hazlitt, *A New Constitution Now* (1942).

36. Cf. Don K. Price's prescient article, "The Parliamentary and Presidential Systems," *Public Administration Review*, autumn 1943; and Richard Crossman's introduction to Walter Bagehot, *The English Constitution* (Fontana Books, 1963), especially 51.

37. *Congressional Record*, June 4, 1973, S10235–S10236.

38. Harold Laski thought that it would "transform the president into a person more akin to the president of the French Republic [he was writing at the time of the Third Republic] than to that of the United States"; cf. his thoughtful critique in *The American Presidency* (New York, 1940), 96–110.

39. *Congressional Record*, May 10, 1973, S8839.

40. *Congressional Record*, March 8, 1973, S4204.

41. See pages 314–15.

42. Press conference, March 15, 1973, *New York Times*, March 16, 1973.

43. This was, however, dictum and uttered in dissent; *U.S. v. Gravel*, opinion reprinted in *Congressional Record*, August 16, 1972, at S13630.

44. *U.S. v. Reynolds et al.*, 345 U.S. 1, 8, 9 (1953).

45. *Committee for Nuclear Responsibility, Inc., v. Seaborg.* 436 F. 2d 788, 794 (1971).

46. Ralph Nader had sued the government, charging corruption in connection with the decision to raise milk prices. The judge was William B. Jones.

47. For the Senate debate on this question, with Frank Church's understandable incredulity and ample documentation on both sides, see *Congressional Record*, June 14, 1973, S11183–S11202; the State Department complaints — also understandable but what else did they expect? — are recorded in the *New York Times*, July 29, 1973, and the *Washington Post*, August 7, 1973.

48. *Congressional Record*, February 15, 1973, S2527; for Ervin's resolution, *Congressional Record*, March 8, 1973, S4204–S4205.

49. The judges were Robert R. Merhige, Jr., in a case involving the Environmental Protection Agency and Charles Richey in a case involving the Department of Housing and Urban Development; see *Congressional Record*, June 12, 1973, S10935, and July 26, 1973, E5121.

50. *Congressional Record*, May 10, 1973, S8838.

51. Woodrow Wilson, *Congressional Government*, 15th ed. (Boston, 1901), 180.

52. House Ways and Means Committee, *Revenue Revision — 1939 . . . Hearings*, 76 Cong., 1 Sess. (1939), 3.

53. Joint Study Committee on Budget Control, Interim Report, *Improving Congressional Control over Budgetary Outlay and Receipt Totals*, House Report 93-17, 93 Cong., 1 Sess. (1973). The report rec-

ommended the establishment in each house of a committee of the budget, empowered to collaborate in fixing spending and appropriations ceilings on behalf of Congress as a whole. Two thirds of the members of the new budget committees would be drawn from the appropriations and tax committees, which had become after 1938 the fortress of the conservative coalition of Republicans and southern Democrats. A so-called "rule of consistency" — that is, that the ceilings recommended by the budget committees could not be amended unless the amendment matched an increase in one part of the budget with a cut somewhere else or with an equivalent tax increase — would make it almost impossible for Congress thereafter to alter the priorities determined by the committees. The Joint Study Committee's proposals seemed likely to result in the concentration of power over the budget in a small conservative group, generally hostile to social and urban interests and peculiarly susceptible to presidential persuasion and manipulation. Senator Ervin had his own version of the bill, which would have made the new budget committee a good deal less unrepresentative.

A better approach, advocated by Senator Humphrey, was simply to establish a well-staffed congressional Office of Budget Analysis under the Joint Economic Committee. In addition, Congress would be well advised to try again to pass the bill, vetoed by Nixon in 1973, requiring senatorial confirmation for the director of the Office of Management and Budget. Since the director of OMB had far more power than most cabinet members, ambassadors and other officers on whose qualifications the Senate regularly passed, it seemed reasonable enough that it should pass on his qualifications too. A law requiring senatorial confirmation for the director of the FBI had fully justified itself during the hearings on J. Edgar Hoover's successor.

54. *Congressional Record,* February 28, 1973, S3539–S3560. In a quite unprecedented expression of no confidence in a President, Congress before its August recess in 1973 empowered the congressional leadership to call Congress back into session; this was designed to intercept any effort by Nixon to pocket-veto bills during the summer adjournment. *Congressional Record,* July 28, 1973, S14941. Judge Joseph C. Waddy's decision in the case of *Kennedy v. Sampson and Jones* is reprinted in the *Congressional Record,* September 11, 1973, S16293.

55. Senate Judiciary Committee, *Congressional Oversight of Executive Agreements: Hearing,* 92 Cong., 1 Sess. (1972), 6; report, 93 Cong., 1 Sess. (1973), 9.

56. Authoritative observers argue about the idea of the two Presidencies. I note the following in the fascinating appendix "The Presidency As I Have Seen It" in Emmet Hughes's valuable book *The Living Presidency* (New York, 1973), 312–68. On one side: Averell Harriman ("All talk of 'two Presidencies' — one foreign and one domestic — is nonsense"); Clark Clifford ("I do not find .the distinction valid"); Benjamin V. Cohen ("I do not accept the doctrine that the powers of the President are more limited in domestic affairs than in foreign af-

fairs"). On the other: Abe Fortas ("There is obviously a broad difference between the range of Presidential power and initiative in domestic and in foreign affairs"); Theodore Sorensen ("There is a clear difference"); Bryce Harlow ("It is incontestably true"). There may be a confusion in this question between the constitutional accountability of the President to Congress and the people, which is the same in foreign as in domestic affairs, and the President's operating scope, which for a generation after the Second World War was obviously much greater in foreign affairs. That the years 1941–1966 saw the existence of the two Presidencies is effectively demonstrated by Aaron Wildavsky, "The Two Presidencies" in Wildavsky, ed., *The Presidency* (Boston, 1969), 230–48.

57. Louis Fisher, *President and Congress* (New York, 1972), 173.
58. Arthur M. Schlesinger, Jr., *The Coming of the New Deal* (Boston, 1958), 254.
59. Woodrow Wilson, *The New Freedom* (Englewood Cliffs, 1961), 164.
60. Calvin Coolidge, "The President Lives Under a Multitude of Eyes," *American Magazine,* August 1929.
61. Charles L. Black, Jr., to Congressman Bob Eckhardt, *Congressional Record,* August 1, 1973, E5321; also "Mr. Nixon, the Tapes and Common Sense," *New York Times,* August 3, 1971.
62. Wilson, *Constitutional Government,* 11, 12.
63. Harriman, "The Presidency As I Have Seen It," in Hughes, *Living Presidency,* 249.
64. Lincoln to H. L. Pierce et al., April 6, 1859, Lincoln, *Collected Works,* R. P. Basler, ed. (New Brunswick, 1953), III, 375. Lincoln was amused by the fact that the Democrats of his day had stopped mentioning Jefferson while the Republicans constantly invoked him. "If the two leading parties of this day are really identical with the two in the days of Jefferson and Adams, they have performed about the same feat as the two drunken men."
65. Wilson, *New Freedom,* 50, 72.
66. In "Song of the Broad-Axe" (*Leaves of Grass*).
67. In his press conference of August 22, 1973, Nixon said: "The President doesn't pick up the phone and call the Attorney General every time something comes up on a matter. He depends on his counsel, or whoever he's done the job to — or given the assignment to — to do the job." This really carries the royal theory of the Presidency to extraordinary lengths. One wonders where in the world Nixon got the singular idea that Presidents don't make phone calls. Johnson, Kennedy, Truman, Roosevelt never hesitated for an instant to pick up the phone when they wanted to find something out. Even the telephone may serve as a link to reality.
68 Though my testimony on this point may well be suspect, I am sure that among FDR's successors John F. Kennedy had far the clearest understanding of the need to fashion a Presidency that would be at once strong and open. He thought FDR went a little far in encouraging dissension within his administration, and he himself went a little

far in trying to grab hold of decisions at too early a stage; but he understood the problem. For an illuminating comparison of the administrative methods of FDR and JFK, see the observations of Ben Cohen and Tom Corcoran quoted in Arthur M. Schlesinger, Jr., *A Thousand Days* (Boston, 1965), 686.

69. Samuel Lubell, *The Future While it Happened* (New York, 1973), 42.
70. J. D. Richardson, *Messages and Papers of the Presidents* (New York, 1897), III, 1290.
71. Roosevelt to Lodge, July 19, 1908, *Selections from the Correspondence of Theodore Roosevelt and Henry Cabot Lodge* (New York, 1925), II, 304.
72. The quotation is from a Moynihan memorandum to Nixon, January 3, 1969, *New York Times*, March 11, 1970. The doctrine that authority deserves automatic respect has been expounded by Henry Kissinger, Irving Kristol, Robert Nisbet, Edward Shils and others. In this connection it may be well to recall that on October 15, 1972, nearly four months after Nixon's plumbers organized the Watergate break-in, the following full-page advertisement appeared in the *New York Times:* "Of the two major candidates for the Presidency of the United States, we believe that Richard Nixon has demonstrated the superior capacity for prudent and responsible leadership. Consequently, we intend to vote for President Nixon on November 7th and we urge our fellow citizens to do the same." Kristol, Nisbet and Shils signed this touching testimonial along with such other eminent if addled scholars as Oscar Handlin, George Homans, W. V. Quine, Edward O. Banfield, Sidney Hook, Milton Friedman, Paul Seabury, Morton Keller, Samuel E. Thorne, Ithiel de Sola Pool, Bertram D. Wolfe and Donald Fleming. The last line explained in type of microscopic size that the advertisement had been "published and paid for by the Finance Committee to Re-elect the President. M. H. Stans, Chairman."
73. See page 36.
74. Clark Clifford, "A Government of National Unity," *New York Times*, June 4, 1973.
75. I owe this quotation to Rebecca West, "The Hoover Frame of Mind," *Atlantic Monthly*, June 1943.
76. For Bingham's proposal, *Congressional Record*, May 8, 1973, H3413, and May 21, H3816–H3817; for Mrs. Green's variation, *Congressional Record*, July 17, 1973, H6213.
77. The classic argument was made by William Yandell Elliott in *The Need for Constitutional Reform* (New York, 1935), 234–35.
78. Finletter, *Representative Government*, 110.
79. Bill Archer of Texas, *Congressional Record*, July 17, 1973, H6214.
80. Tansill, ed., *Formation of the Union*, 417–19.
81. Tansill, ed., *Formation of the Union*, 691.
82. *New York Times*, August 16, 1973.
83. See page 53.
84. *New York Times*, August 2, 1973.

85. "Indeed, in some respects, the separation of powers requires stronger executive leadership than does the parliamentary and cabinet system," Harry S. Truman, *New York Times*, May 9, 1954.

86. "The only way to attack crime in America is the way crime attacks our people — without pity," Richard M. Nixon in his special message to Congress on crime, *New York Times*, March 11, 1973.

87. I adapt here a phrase of Reed Powell's in his review of Zechariah Chafee's *Freedom of Speech* (1920), quoted in Chafee's introduction to the second edition of his *Freedom of Speech in the United States* (Atheneum paperback, 1969), Ch. 14.

88. 48th Federalist.

89. Walt Whitman, "Notes for Lecturers on Democracy and 'Adhesiveness,'" C. J. Furness, *Walt Whitman's Workshop* (Cambridge, 1928), 58.

Epilogue (*Pages 420–499*)

1. Alexis de Tocqueville, *Democracy in America*, I, Ch. 8.

2. Television interview with David Frost, May 19, 1977.

3. Richard M. Nixon, *Memoirs* (New York, 1978), 763.

4. Thomas E. Cronin, "A Resurgent Congress and the Imperial Presidency," *Political Science Quarterly*, summer 1980, 210.

5. Theodore Lowi, *The Personal President* (Ithaca, 1985), 151.

6. T. D. Schellhardt, "Do We Expect Too Much?" *Wall Street Journal*, July 10, 1979.

7. Robert Shogan, *None of the Above* (New York), 1982, 3–4.

8. Godfrey Hodgson, *All Things to All Men: The False Promise of the Modern American Presidency* (1980; Touchstone paperback, 1981), 49.

9. Ibid., 13.

10. Hugh Heclo, "The Presidential Illusion," in H. Heclo and L. M. Salamon, eds., *The Illusion of Presidential Government* (Boulder, 1981), 1.

11. Gerald R. Ford, "Imperiled, Not Imperial," *Time*, November 10, 1980.

12. Jonathan Daniels, *Frontier on the Potomac* (New York, 1946), 31.

13. Richard Neustadt, *Presidential Power: The Politics of Leadership* (1960; rev. ed., New York, 1976), 77.

14. Woodrow Wilson, *Congressional Government* (Boston, 1885), 92, 98–99.

15. Tocqueville, *Democracy*, II, First Book, Ch. 21.

16. Janet Smith, ed., *Mark Twain and the Damned Human Race* (New York, 1962), 105.

17. E. M. Stanwood, *A History of the Presidency* (Boston, 1898), 260.

18. Pierce Butler of South Carolina; D. S. Freeman, *George Washington* (New York, 1954), VI, 117.

19. Garry Wills, *Cincinnatus: George Washington and the Enlightenment* (Garden City, N.Y., 1984), 47, 103; Freeman, *Washington*, VI, 86.

Samuel Eliot Morison wrote of Washington: "No other subsequent President of the United States has lived in such a glare of publicity." *Oxford History of the American People* (New York, 1965), 318.

20. Robert V. Remini, *Andrew Jackson and the Course of American Democracy, 1833–1845* (New York, 1984), 73.

21. Benjamin Brown French, in D. B. Cole and J. J. McDonough, eds., *Witness to the Young Republic: A Yankee's Journal, 1828–1870* (Hanover, N.H., 1989), 30.

22. Charles Dickens, *American Notes*, Ch. 18.

23. James K. Polk, *Diary*, M. M. Quaife, ed. (Chicago, 1910), II, 28.

24. Benjamin Harrison, *This Country of Ours* (New York, 1897), 163–64, 180.

25. William Howard Taft, *The Presidency* (New York, 1916), 47–48, 50.

26. Woodrow Wilson, *Constitutional Government in the United States* (New York, 1908), 68, 73.

27. Tocqueville, *Democracy*, II, Fourth Book, Ch. 6.

28. Senator Robert Griffin of Michigan, quoted by James L. Sundquist, *The Decline and Resurgence of Congress* (Washington, 1981), 292.

29. *New York Times*, September 2, 1976.

30. The quoted observations are from the Conference Report, *Congressional Record*, October 4, 1973, H8657 (daily ed.), and "Statement of War Powers Conferees," October 4, 1973, mimeographed, 2.

31. Eagleton cogently developed this theme in his *War and Presidential Power: A Chronicle of Congressional Surrender* (New York, 1974).

32. *Congressional Record*, November 7, 1973, H9661 (daily ed.).

33. Letter in *Washington Post*, December 6, 1973.

34. Veto message, *Congressional Record*, October 25, 1973, H9400 (daily ed.).

35. Howard E. Shuman, *Politics and the Budget: The Struggle Between the President and the Congress* (Englewood Cliffs, N.J., 1984) 246.

36. Henry Jones Ford, *The Rise and Growth of American Politics* (New York, 1898), 284.

37. Ralph Waldo Emerson, *Journals*, E. W. Emerson and W. E. Forbes, eds. (Boston, 1909–1914), IV, 160.

38. Henry Adams, "The Session, 1869–1870," in G. E. Hochfield, ed., *The Great Secession Winter of 1860–61 and Other Essays* (New York, 1958), 197.

39. Quoted by David Broder, *Washington Post*, February 9, 1984.

40. Lou Cannon, "Dramatic Account of Film of Nazi Death Camps Questioned," *Washington Post*, March 5, 1984.

41. Lars-Erik Nelson in *New York Daily News*, December 16, 1983, December 28, 1983, January 11, 1984.

42. Abraham D. Sofaer, *War, Foreign Affairs and Constitutional Power: The Origins* (Cambridge, Mass., 1976), 225–227, 265, 377–379.

43. Ibid., 377–379.

44. *Youngstown Sheet and Tube Co. v. Sawyer*, 343 U.S. 574, 635 (1952).

45. *United States v. Curtiss-Wright Export Corporation*, 299 U.S. 304, 319–320 (1936).

46. "Resolution on the 1984 Annual Report of the Information Security Office," adopted by the Council of the American Historical Association, December 27, 1985.
47. *Congressional Record*, June 18, 1984, H6021 (daily ed.).
48. Erwin N. Griswold, "Secrets Not Worth Keeping," *Washington Post National Weekly Edition*, February 20–26, 1989.
49. Otis Pike, "Top Secret? Spell It E-m-b-a-r-r-a-s-s-i-n-g," *Newsday*, March 20, 1988.
50. Lee Hamilton, "Washington Report, February 8, 1989.
51. Rubanov's article appeared in the September issue of *Kommunist*; see report by Philip Taubman, *New York Times*, September 8, 1988.
52. James Parton, *Life of Andrew Jackson* (Boston, 1860), III, 607.
53. John Taylor of Caroline, *An Inquiry into the Principles and Policy of the Government of the United States* (1814; New Haven, 1950), 194.
54. On this important point, see R. W. Johnson, "Making Things Happen," *London Review of Books*, September 6–19, 1984, and H. S. Ferns, "This Spy Business," *Encounter*, May 1985.
55. Stephen E. Ambrose, *Eisenhower the President* (New York, 1984), 135.
56. Daniel Patrick Moynihan, "The Role of Law in World Affairs," *Bulletin of the American Academy of Arts and Sciences*, November 1983.
57. Congressional Committees Investigating the Iran-Contra Affair, *Report*, 100 Cong. 1 Sess. (1987), 37.
58. The computer note of May 2, 1986, from Poindexter and North to other members of the national security staff is reproduced photographically in the *New York Times*, July 11, 1987.
59. Steven L. Katz, *Government Secrecy: Decisions Without Democracy* (Washington, 1987), 5.
60. *The Tower Commission Report* (Bantam paperback, 1987), 217.
61. *Newsday*, March 11, 1989; *New York Times*, April 14, 1989.
62. *Tower Commission Report*, 78.
63. Clark Clifford interviewed by Philip Geyelin, "The Workings of the National Security System: Past, Present, and Future," *SAIS Review*, winter/spring 1988.
64. Robert A. Lovett in testimony before the Cuba Study Group, May 19, 1961, in Arthur M. Schlesinger, Jr., *Robert Kennedy and His Times* (Boston, 1978), 455.
65. David Bruce and Robert A. Lovett, "Covert Operations," report to President's Board of Consultants on Foreign Intelligence Activities [1956], in Schlesinger, *Robert Kennedy*, 456.
66. President's Board of Consultants on Foreign Intelligence Activities, report to President Eisenhower, January 5, 1961, in Schlesinger, *Robert Kennedy*, 457–58.
67. Clark Clifford testimony quoted by Senator Patrick Leahy. *Congressional Record*, March 4, 1988, S1935 (daily ed.).
68. "It was clearly unwise to rely on covert activity as the core of our policy." McFarlane's statement to the investigating committees, *New York Times*, May 12, 1987.

69. Lee Hamilton, "The Trouble with Covert Action," *Washington Post*, August 17, 1986.

70. Television interview with David Frost, May 19, 1977.

71. *New York Times*, January 25, 1974.

72. Clifton Fadiman, ed., *The American Treasury 1455–1955* (New York, 1955), 342–43.

73. *Korematsu v. U.S.*, 323 U.S. 14 (1944). For an extended discussion of the issues of emergency prerogative, see Arthur M. Schlesinger, Jr., *War and the Constitution: Abraham Lincoln and Franklin D. Roosevelt*. 27th Annual Fortenbaugh Lecture (Gettysburg, Pa., 1988); also in the *Gettysburg Review*, winter 1989.

74. The conference was sponsored by the Center for the Study of Democratic Institutions and held in December 1973. The quotation is from a report on the conference by Mortimer Adler to Joseph Slater of the Aspen Institute, December 23, 1973.

75. Lloyd N. Cutler, "To Form a Government," *Foreign Affairs*, fall 1980.

76. Douglas Dillon, "The Challenge of Modern Governance," in *Reforming American Government: The Bicentennial Papers of the Committee on the Constitutional System*, D. L. Robinson, ed. (Boulder, Col., 1985), 28–29.

77. "After Two Centuries: Our Eighteenth Century Constitution in Today's Complex World," Committee on the Constitutional System Basic Policy Statement, February 1, 1983, 3.

78. George Urban in *Encounter*, April 1987.

79. Samuel Lubell, *The Hidden Crisis in American Politics* (New York, 1970), 43. See also James L. Sundquist, "Needed: A Political Theory for the New Era of Coalition Government in the United States," *Political Science Quarterly*, winter 1988–89.

80. Don K. Price, "The Parliamentary and Presidential Systems," *Public Administration Review*, autumn 1943, 320.

81. Lord Hailsham, "Elective Dictatorship," *Listener*, October 21, 1976.

82. As told by FDR to Benjamin V. Cohen; see Cohen's May 23, 1974, Royer Lecture at the University of California, "Presidential Responsibility and American Democracy," 13.

83. See R. H. S. Crossman's introduction to Walter Bagehot, *The English Constitution* (London, Fontanta paperback, 1963), and his Godkin Lectures, *The Myths of Cabinet Government* (Cambridge, Mass., 1972).

84. See Philip Norton, "The Norton View," in *The Politics of Parliamentary Reform*, David Judge, ed. (Cranbury, N.J., 1984), esp. 62–65; and Norton, *The Constitution in Flux* (Oxford, 1982).

85. Allan Sindler, "A Critique of the Reuss Proposal," in Robinson, ed., *Reforming American Government*, 324.

86. Woodrow Wyatt, *Turn Again, Westminster* (London, 1973). The quoted sentiment is from the author's inscription in my copy of the book.

87. Edward Pearce, "London Commentary," *Encounter*, September-October 1982, 36.

88. *Hansard*, January 15, 1988, 612 (daily ed.).

89. Crossman, *Myths of Cabinet Government*, 1.
90. Lord Hailsham, "Wilson the Conservative," *Listener*, October 28, 1976.
91. "House of Cards," *Economist*, August 4, 1984.
92. Wyatt, *Turn Again, Westminster*, 17, 28–31.
93. James Gillies, "The Parliamentary Imperative," *Saturday Night*, June 1984, 55.
94. Oliver Wright, "The British View," *American Heritage*, May/June 1987.
95. *Hansard*, January 15, 1988, 611–12 (daily ed.).
96. Hailsham, "Elective Dictatorship."
97. Wyatt, *Turn Again, Westminster*, 50.
98. Gillies, "Parliamentary Imperative," 55.
99. Wyatt, *Turn Again, Westminster*, 57.
100. See Clive Ponting, *The Right to Know* (London, 1985), and Tam Dalyell, "Ponting Bites Back," *London Review of Books*, April 4, 1985.
101. Cf. Samuel H. Beer, *Britain Against Itself: The Political Contradictions of Collectivism* (New York, 1982), 189–92.
102. *Buckley v. Valeo*, 424 U.S. 1 (1976).
103. Neustadt, *Presidential Power*, 101.
104. *Youngstown Sheet and Tube Co. v. Sawyer*, 343 U.S. 579, 635 (1952).
105. In Dallas, June 12, 1936; Franklin D. Roosevelt, *Public Papers* . . . *1936* (New York, 1938), 215.
106. James Bryce, *The American Commonwealth* (London, 1988), I, 147–48.
107. J. M. Blum, et al., *The National Experience*, 7th ed. (San Diego, 1989), 792.
108. Griffin Bell, Herbert Brownell, William Simon and Cyrus Vance (the national co-chairmen of the Committee for a Single Six-Year Presidential Term), "For a One-Term, Six-Year Presidency," *New York Times*, December 31, 1985.
109. C. C. Tansill, ed., *Documents Illustrative of the Formation of the Union of the American States* (Washington, 1927), 675, 396, 444.
110. *Congressional Record*, February 5, 1985, S 1004 (daily ed.).
111. Mickey Edwards, "A Conservative's Case Against the Line Item Veto," *Washington Post*, February 8, 1984.
112. William Howard Taft, *Our Chief Magistrate and His Powers* (New York, 1916), 27–28.
113. *Lochner v. New York*, 198 U.S. 45, 75.
114. *New York Times*, March 23, 1977.
115. Andrew Jackson, first annual message, December 8, 1829.
116. *Gray v. Sanders*, 372 U.S. 368 (1963).
117. Neal R. Peirce, *The People's President: The Electoral College in American History and the Direct-Vote Alternative* (New York, 1968), 152.

118. J. H. Yunker and L. D. Longley, *The Electoral College: Its Biases Newly Measured for the 1960s and 1970s* (Beverly Hills, Calif., 1976), 37.

119. See the Library of Congress study by Joseph Gorman, "The Election of 1888"; *Congressional Record*, June 13, 1979, S 7604–7615 (daily ed.).

120. Calvin Coolidge, *Autobiography* (New York, 1929), 234, 194.

121. Lincoln P. Bloomfield, "What's Wrong with Transitions," *Foreign Policy*, Summer 1984, 35.

122. Grover Cleveland, address at Sandwich, Mass., July 25, 1891, *Letters and Addresses*, A. E. Bergh, ed. (New York, 1909), 234.

123. Henry F. Pringle, *The Life and Times of William Howard Taft* (New York, 1939), II, 845.

124. Millard Fillmore, *Papers*, F. H. Severance, ed. (Buffalo, 1907), II, 139, quoted in A. B. Tourtellot's valuable compendium, *The Presidents on the Presidency* (New York, 1964), 384.

125. James Monroe, *Writings*, S. M. Hamilton, ed. (New York, 1898–1903), VII, 54, quoted in Tourtellot, *Presidents*, 378.

126. J. Q. Adams, *Memoirs*, C. F. Adams, ed. (Philadelphia, 1874–1877), VIII, 245.

127. Harry S. Truman, *Mr. Citizen* (1960; Popular Library paperback, n.d.), 78–79, 85, 91.

128. Bureau of the Budget Staff Memorandum, "Utilization of Former Presidents," April 3, 1963, transmitted by William Carey to Lawrence O'Brien, April 8, 1963, John F. Kennedy Library.

129. John W. Chambers II, "Transformation of the Ex-Presidency," prospectus (1981), 2.

130. Richard M. Nixon, *The Real War* (New York, 1980), 243.

131. See Saul Friedman's story in *Newsday*, April 4, 1989.

132. Senator William V. Roth, Jr., "Ex-presidential Perks Are Way out of Hand," *USA Today*, March 28, 1984.

133. Pringle, *Taft*, II, 845–846.

134. Ibid., 846.

135. Bryce, *American Commonwealth*, I, 349.

136. Tocqueville, *Democracy*, I, Ch. 16.

137. *Youngstown Sheet and Tube Co. v. Sawyer*, 343 U.S. 579, 634 (1952).

138. George Reedy, *The Twilight of the Presidency* (New York, 1970), 9.

139. Walter F. Mondale, "The Institution of the Vice Presidency," lecture at the University of Minnesota, February 18, 1981, mimeograph, 3.

140. In his letter to Bishop Mandell Creighton, April 5, 1887.

141. Henry Adams, *The Education of Henry Adams*, ch. xxviii.

142. Lincoln in conversation with Major Charles Halpine, reported in Halpine's *Baked Meats of the Funeral* and quoted in *The Face of Lincoln*, James Mellon, ed. (New York, 1979).

143. Reedy, *Twilight*, 85.
144. Franklin D. Roosevelt, *Public Papers . . . 1939* (New York, 1941), 492.
145. Greg Schneiders, "Goodbye to All That," *Newsweek*, September 24, 1979.
146. Rosenman and Harriman in interviews with Emmet J. Hughes, *The Living Presidency* (New York, 1973), 348, 362.
147. *King John*, Act IV, scene ii.
148. Hamilton to Gouverneur Morris, February 27, 1802, Hamilton, *Works*, H. C. Lodge, ed. (New York, 1904), VII, 591.
149. Adams, *Education*, Ch. 28.
150. John Quincy Adams, Address, July 4, 1821.
151. Walt Whitman, "Song of the Broad-Axe," *Leaves of Grass*.

★ ★

Index

Abernethy, Thomas Perkins, 25, 503, 504, 524

Abolition, 38

Abourezk, James, 304

Abrams, Elliot, 440

Accountability, presidential, 325, 386, 407, 410, 420, 451, 475, 491; and parliamentary system, 390; and cabinet role, 390–391; and secrecy system, 448–449

Acheson, Dean, 107, 123, 134, 325; and Truman, 131; and Korea, 131–134; and debate *re* commitment of troops abroad, 138–140; 308; and congressional agitation over presidential agreements, 151; and Nixon, 217; in Truman cabinet, 219; and government secrecy system, 370, 371; cited, 511, 512, 513, 528, 537

Acton, Lord, 493

Adams, Charles Francis, 503, 505, 549

Adams, Charles Francis, II, 486

Adams, Henry, xiv, 80, 81, 438, 494, 497, 545, 549, 550

Adams, John, 17, 21, 31, 62, 196, 319, 334, 466, 520; and transmission of information to Congress, 44; and treaty-making process, 79; on freedom of press, 228

Adams, John Quincy, 26, 28, 29, 36, 37–38, 49, 482, 485–486; and annexation of Cuba, xxii; and annexation of Texas, 41; on congressional recognition of Mexican War (1847), 41; on presidential war-making, 51, 286; on "peace power" vs. "war power," 60; and treaty-making process, 81; and

executive agreements, 86; and congressional appropriations for troops, 291; his warnings against globalism, 299; and secrecy, 334; on foreign policy, 498–499; cited, 503, 504, 505, 526, 528, 549, 550

Adams, Sherman, 536

Adams v. Richardson, 241

Adler, Mortimer, 547

Afghanistan, prisoners from, xix–xx

Africa, 51, 204

Agency for International Development, 395–396

Agnew, Spiro T., 226, 230, 413

Aid. *See* Foreign aid

Aiken, George, 386–389, 530, 539

Air Force, U.S., 130; and bombing of Cambodia, 294

Aitken, Jonathan, 353, 534

Alaska purchase, xxii

Algeria, 26, 160, 192

Alliance for Progress, 151

Allison, Graham, 516

Allott, Gordon, 512

Al-Qaeda, xvi, xix–xx

Alsop, Joseph, 218

Alsop, Stewart, 268, 524

Ambrose, Stephen E., 546

Amchitka Island, Alaska, 365

American Civil Liberties Union (ACLU), xviii–xix

American Empire, xxi–xxiv

American Historical Association, xxi, 371

American Newspaper Publishers Association, 342

Ames, H. V., 503, 504

Anderson, Jack, 358, 366, 535
Andrews, Bert, 512
Angola, 433, 472
Annexation efforts, xxi–xxiii
Anti-Deficiency Acts (1905, 1906), 236, 521
Anti-Masonic party, 334, 345
Appointments, Nixon's interpretation of his power in, 245, 252
Appropriations, legislative, 150, 248, 476–478; congressional duties in, 3, 234–235; for armed forces, 6, 290–291; and war in Vietnam, 194, 290–291; and international commitments made by President, 202, 205–206; and impoundment, 235–240 passim, 252, 266, 378, 395–400; and Cambodia, 293; and the CIA, 318–319; as congressional threat to Nixon administration, 396–397. See also Impoundment
Arbitration treaties, 93
Archer, William, 543
Argentina, 15, 28
Armaments, embargo on, 100; and FDR (1933), 96, 101
Armed forces, U.S.: and Congress, 3; constitutional assurances of civilian control, 6; appropriations for, 6, 290–291; volunteer professional (Nixon administration), 198–200, 324–325. See also Troop deployment
Arms Control and Disarmament Agency, 396
Arms limitation, 168, 301
Armstrong, H. F., 514
Army Appropriation Act, 78
Arnett, Peter, 374, 537
Arnold, Byron, 519
Articles of Confederation, 2, 384
Ashcroft, John, xvii–xviii
Asia, American military action in, 51–52, 505. See also Indochina War; Vietnam War
Asquith, Henry H., 352
Associated Press, 230
Atlantic Charter (Pact), 112, 140, 315

Atomic energy, 355, 362; testing of, 365. See also Nuclear age
Atomic Energy Act, 365
Atomic Energy Commission, 365, 375, 536
Attlee, Clement, 151
Attorneys general, xvii–xviii
Austin, Warren, 403
Australia, 138
Avon, Lord. See Eden, Anthony

Babcock, General Orville, 270
Bache, Benjamin Franklin, 333
Bachrach, Judy, xvii
Bacon, Augustus O., 84, 90
Bagehot, Walter, 60, 75, 278, 322, 414, 465; cited, 506, 507, 525, 540, 547
Bagot, Charles, 86
Bahrain, 314
Bailey, Thomas A., 124, 511
Baker, James, 453
Baker, Newton D., 219
Baker v. Carr, 526
Ball, George, 185, 220, 370
Ball, Joseph, 119–122
Balogh, Lord, 522
Banfield, Edward O., 543
Bank of the United States, 53, 72; Second, 411
Barbary War, xii
Barker, Carol M., 536, 537
Barr, Bob, xix
Barry, W. T., 531
Bartlett, R. J., 503, 505
Easier, R. P., 505, 506, 527, 542
Bas v. Tingy, 21–22, 30
Batista, Fulgencio, 168
Bayh, Birch, 480
Bay of Pigs, 172, 174, 215; and government secrecy, 342, 343, 356, 362, 450
Beale, H. K., 509
Beecher, William, 534
Beer, Samuel H., 548
Belair, Felix, Jr., 370
Bell, Griffin, 548
Beloff, Max, 302, 525
Bemis, S. F., 449, 503, 504, 505, 509, 527

Benedict, M. L., 507
Benton, Thomas Hart, 38, 39–40, 480, 504
Berdahl, C. A., 503, 504, 506
Berger, Raoul, II, 30, 172, 249, 394; and control of international troop deployment, 308, 309; cited, 502, 503, 504, 505, 507, 508, 513, 514, 523, 529
Berk v. Laird, 290, 293, 527, 528
Berle, Adolf, 296, 528, 537
Berlin crisis, 173
Beschloss, Michael, ix
Bickel, Alexander, 179, 289, 308, 526, 529
Biddle, Francis, xvii, 219
Bierce, Ambrose, 268
Bill of Rights, 404. *See also* Constitution, U.S.
Bin Laden, Osama, xvii
Bingham, Hiram, 95
Bingham, Jonathan, 413, 543
Binkley, Wilfred E., 152, 507, 513
Bipartisanship, and foreign affairs, 128–129. *See also* Foreign affairs
Bishop, J. W., Jr., 249, 522
Black, Charles L., Jr., 542
Black, F. R., 532
Black, Hugo, 144–145, 147, 148; and Pentagon Papers, 347; destruction of his "bench notes," 370
Black, Jeremiah, 80
Black Panthers, 257, 264
Blackstone, Sir William, 3
Blaine, James G., 74, 80, 94–95, 390
Blair, Montgomery, 219
Blair, Tony, xx
Bloomfield, Lincoln P., 549
Blount, William, 30
Blum, J. M., et al., 548
Boer War, 281
Bohlen, Charles E., 123, 511
Boland, Edward, 452
Boland amendments, 452, 456
Bolívar, Simón, 38
Bolivia, sale of arms to (1934), 101
Borah, William E., 94, 95, 100, 308, 326, 373, 444, 509

Borchard, Edwin, 508
Bourne, Randolph, 82
Boxer Rebellion, 89, 90
Braden, Tom, 523
Brandeis, Louis D., 132, 266
Brant, Irving, 503, 504
Branzburg v. Hayes, 231, 521
Brazil, 313
Brennan, William J., 288; and Pentagon Papers, 347
Bretton Woods conference, 119
Brewster, Daniel, 246
Brezhnev, Leonid, 151, 191, 279
Bricker Amendment, 151–152, 311–312, 529
Brill, Steven, xvii
Brinkmanship, 165–166
Britain, 128; and destroyer deal (1940), 105–109; and Lend-Lease, 109–110; immunity of civil servants, 249; and war-making and treaty-making powers, 279–280; Official Secrets Act, 346, 352–354; availability of government documents in, 368, 369, 398; as model for constitutional reform, 389–392, 460–468; parliamentary reform in, 468–470; role of Privy Council, 486; republican movement in, 492
British Empire, xxi
Broder, David, 545
Brooks, Jack, 446, 453
Brown, Ben H., Jr., 534
Brown, General George S., 357
Brown, James, 503
Brownell, Herbert, 157–158, 248, 513, 548
Brownlow, Louis, 225, 227
Bruce, David, 454–455, 546
Bryan, William Jennings, 219
Bryant, William Cullen, 334
Bryce, James, II, 59, 281–282, 319, 327, 471–472, 490, 548, 549; on American colonial ambitions, xxi; view of impeachment process, 75; on secrecy in diplomacy, 362; on Presidents' faithfulness to their trust, 378; cited, 502, 506, 507, 525, 535, 538

Buchanan, James, 56, 58, 160, 297; on Congress's power to declare war, 57
Buchanan, Pat, 440
Buckley, William F., Jr., 152, 513
Buckley v. Valeo, 548
Budget, 539, 540–541; presidential manipulation of, 211, 212, 398–399; FDR press conferences on, 226–227; and Nixon, 233, 300; and defense, 310; deficits under Reagan, 476–477
Budget Act of 1974, 423, 435–436, 477
Budget and Accounting Act of 1921, 158, 399, 435
Budget Control Act of 1973, 477
Bureau of Corporations, U.S., 84
Burger, Warren E., 289, 294
Burgess, Guy, 369
Burke, Edmund, 10, 414, 490
Burns, James MacGregor, 225, 371, 463, 520, 537, 538
Burns, R. D., 431
Burr (Aaron) conspiracy, 25, 31, 44, 60, 71, 114, 148, 264, 335, 348; precedents established by, 504
Burt, Richard, 440
Burton, Harold H., 119, 147
Bush, George H. W., xvi, 232, 464
Bush, George W., ix; Patriot Act (2001), xviii–xix; Patriot Act II, xix; handling of Guantánamo Bay prisoners, xix–xx; secrecy of administration, xx; Executive Order 13223, xxi
Butler, Benjamin F., 73, 74, 219
Butler, Pierce, 544
Butt, Archibald, 508
Byrd, E. M., Jr., 510
Byrne, W. Matthew, Jr., 259, 348, 380
Byrnes, James F., 80, 219, 250, 329

Cabinet, 219–220, 390–391, 408–409; FDR's, 215, 219–221, 407–408; Nixon's, 220, 225, 252
Calhoun, John C., 26, 46; and Texas, 40
Califano, Joseph, 461
California 1962 Nixon campaign, 518–519
Cambodia, 113, 187, 189–190, 304, 421, 425, 516, 528; and Nixon's and John-

son's theories of presidential war power, xv, 193–196; Nixon compares to Cuban missile crisis, 189; Nixon's constitutional defense of his actions in, 190–193, 417; Congress's denial of funds for, 193–197; bombing of (1973), 195–196, 378; congressional dilemma *re* constitutionality of Nixon's bombing of, 195–197; and Paris Agreement, 196–198; leaks concerning "secret" raids over, 256; and campus riots, 257–260; and the judiciary, 293–295; and congressional appropriations, 293; and government secrecy system, 357, 362
Campbell, Jeremy, 520
Camp David, Nixon's retreat, 218, 519
Canada, xxii
Canham, Erwin D., 225
Cannon, Lou, 519, 520, 538, 545
Cantril, Hadley, 535
Cardozo, Benjamin N., 101, 273
Carey, William, 549
Carswell, G. Harrold, 245
Carter, Jimmy, 424, 493; and weakness of presidency, xvi; compared with Reagan, 438–439; proposes direct popular election, 479, 480; White House staff of, 495
Case, Clifford, 530; bill, 312, 313–314, 315
Casement, Sir Roger, 368
Cass, Lewis, 219
Castlereagh, Viscount (Robert Stewart), 352
Castro, Fidel, 167, 172
Cater, Douglass, 343, 520, 533
Catledge, Turner, 343
Caulfield, Justice, of Britain, 353
Cavour, Camillo, 367
Censorship, 335. *See also* Secrecy
Censure, 33; as alternative to impeachment, 411; and Jackson, 411–412
Central America, 57, 92
Central Intelligence (Agency) Act, 167, 316
Central Intelligence Agency (CIA), 172, 347, 352, 362, 371, 436, 450–454;

and Eisenhower administration, 167, 318, 356; and Nixon's view of internal security problems (1970s), 259, 260, 261, 267, 301, 317–318; and Watergate, 274–275; and Congress, 316–319, 423, 451–454; inaccessibility of documents to historians, 368; and dissemination of intelligence analyses, 375; intervention in Angola, 433; under Reagan, 443; censorship by, 448–449 (note); and Eisenhower, 450; covert action by, 450–453; congressional oversight of, 451–454; and Iran-contra affair, 452

Chafee, Zechariah, 544

Chambers, John W., II, 487, 549

Chapin, Dwight, 381

Charles I, of England, Nixon compared to, 275–276

Chase, Salmon P., 72, 219, 506

Chase, Samuel, 22, 31; impeachment of, 30

Cheney, Richard, xviii, 440

Cherokee land frauds (1843), 46

Chesapeake, U.S. frigate, 24

Chiang Kai-shek, 130, 168

Chicago and S. Airlines v. Waterman S. S. Corp., 526

China, 15; U.S. armed force in (1900), 88–89; and Truman, 130; Nixon visit to (1972), 217, 226, 315; and Soviet Union, 300

Church, Frank, 105, 108, 194, 313, 451–452, 530, 535, 540

Churchill, Winston S., 105–106, 355; and Yalta, 151; on Crown's war-making power, 279; and Official Secrets Act, 352; on role of Parliament and Cabinet, 465; cited, 525

CIA. *See* Central Intelligence Agency

Civil liberties, xvii–xix, 258, 274

Civil Rights Act (1964), 236–237; and Nixon's selective enforcement of law, 240–241

Civil Rights Commission, 237

Civil War, U.S., 57–67 *passim,* 82, 94, 114, 116, 398, 458; Lincoln's constitutional justification for his actions in,
61; Congress's repudiation of Lincoln following, 127; as precedent, 188; and British public opinion, 281; as genuine emergency, 323–324; basic lack of government secrecy in conduct of, 335–336

Claiborne, W. C., 503

Clark, J. Reuben, 89; and distinction between "interposition" and "intervention" with armed force, 89; cited, 509

Clark, Ramsey, 220

Clark, Thomas C., 147–148

Clark, William A., 84

Clark amendment (1976), 472

Clark v. United States, 447

Classification, government documents. *See* Secrecy

Classification Review Commission, 366

Clay, Henry, 27, 28, 326, 482

Clemenceau, Georges, 337

Cleveland, Grover, 77, 78, 320, 485, 549

Clifford, Clark, 186, 220, 381, 387; description of executive branch, 212; and resignation of a President, 412; on secret government, 453–454; on covert activities, 455; cited, 518, 523, 541, 543, 546

Clinton, Bill, ix

Cockburn, Claud, 509

Coffin, Frank, 292, 526

Cohan, George M., 525

Cohen, Benjamin V., 106, 107, 326, 510, 528, 530, 541, 543, 547; and means for intergovernmental consultation, 329

Cohen, Marshall, 530

Cohn, Roy, 371

Cold War, 126, 153, 164, 188, 348, 450; and curtailment of congressional war-making power, xv–xvi; and national-security intelligence, 168; and global intervention policy, 300; and treaty-making powers, 311; and rise of executive agreement, 311–312; and secrecy, 339–340, 363

Cole, D. B., 545

Collective security, 120–122

Colombia, 27

Colson, Charles, 262

Colvin, J. B., 503

Commager, Henry Steele, 139, 286, 512

Commander in Chief, President as, 86,
114–115, 144, 192–193, 198; and
Constitution, 5–6, 61–63, 319; and
Supreme Court, 62, 114–115, 143–
144; and Lincoln, 63–67, 187–188;
and cease-fire and armistice agreements, 86; and FDR, 113–115, 122;
and troop deployment, 90–92, 307;
and Truman, 131–140, 143–144; Vandenberg's view, 139; and Eisenhower,
159–163; and Nixon, 187–193; and
impoundment, 236; and Javits's war-
powers bill, 301–304; and secrecy,
339

Commerce, 2–3, 103. See also Trade

Commission on Campus Unrest, Nixon
administration, 258–259

Commission on Federal Election Reform, Nixon administration, 386

Commission on Government Security,
341

Commitments, unilateral presidential,
85–86, 88; and Eisenhower, 165,
202–203; and Congress, 200–206,
311–319. See also Executive agreements

Committee for Economic Development, Research and Policy Committee of, 310, 529

Committee for Nuclear Responsibility v.
Seaborg, 536, 540

Committee for the Preservation of the
Democratic Party in California, 518

Committee for the Re-election of the
President (1972), 227, 233, 254–255

Committee on Foreign Relations. See
Senate Foreign Relations Committee

Committee on the Conduct of the War.
See Congress, U.S.

Committee to Defend America by Aiding the Allies, 107

Common Cause, 427

Communications, privileged, 155–159

Communications media, and exaltation
of Presidency, 209–210. See also
Press

Communism, international, 161, 163,
208; and U.S. containment policy,
164–165; and secrecy system, 339,
341

Condon, Edward U., 153

Confederate Constitution, 386, 390

Confidentiality: and press news sources,
231; and Nixon tapes, 270–273

Congress, U.S., 213, 377, 419, 421–422;
and Jefferson, xi–xii, 23–26; post–
Civil War reclamation of lost authority, xiv, 76–81 passim; and war-making powers, xv, 4–5, 18–23, 26–29, 35,
37–38, 41–42, 50–51, 77–78, 190,
200–201, 279, 393; response to Executive Order 13223, xxi; and Founding Fathers, 2–3, 8, 188; and separation of powers, 2, 252–255, 266, 277,
295–298, 398; and regulation of commerce, 3; and appropriations, 3, 6,
194, 202, 205, 234–235, 240–241,
290–293, 398–399; and treaty-making
process, 3, 18, 78, 150–151; and conduct of foreign affairs, 3, 13–15, 95,
102–103, 122–124, 166, 200–201, 208,
283–284, 294–298, 319–320; and
President's emergency prerogative,
9; and impeachment, 10–12, 70–76;
deference to executive branch, 14;
and executive control of information, 15–18, 43–46, 49, 76–77, 83–84,
102, 117–118, 153–159, 246–252,
331–332; and neutrality prerogative,
18–20; and Monroe, 27; and Monroe
Doctrine, 27; and President's right to
wage limited war, 28; and annexation
of Texas, 41; and Mexican War
(1847), 41–42; and executive control
of foreign intelligence operations,
47; distinction between foreign and
domestic policy information, 49; and
presidential extension of theory of
defensive war, 50–58; and Civil War,
58–67 passim; Committee on the
Conduct of the War, 68; retaliation
for Lincoln's expanded presidential

initiative, 68–69; and Andrew Johnson, 71–75; power of military deployments, 78, 135–140, 307–311; and Spanish-American War, 82; joint resolution and treaty veto, 85; and presidential commitment of armed forces overseas, 88–93; constraints on foreign policy (1919–1939), 93–99; and FDR, 95–99, 105–126 *passim,* 206, 213, 339; Second World War, 100; and FDR's destroyer deal with Britain (1940), 105–109; and Lend-Lease to Britain, 110; and internment of Japanese-Americans (World War II), 116; and access to information concerning internal security, 117–118,152–155, 347–348; and military and diplomatic reins of World War II, 118–119; role in making of peace, 119; and postwar international organization (UN), 119–122, 133; and domestic affairs, 123, 233–234; and Truman's domestic program, 127; 22nd Amendment, 127, 389; and the Cold War, 127–128; and Truman's foreign policy, 128–130; 80th Congress, 129; and China, 130; and defense budget (1948), 130; and Korea, 130–135; and Truman's seizure of steel industry (1952), 141–143, 150; attempts to reclaim abandoned authority, 150, 422–423; and foreign-aid appropriations, 150–151, and executive agreements, 151–152, 285–287, 311–319, 328–330, 393; Bricker Amendment, 151–152; and "uncontrolled discretion" (executive privilege), 155–159, 405 *(see also* Executive privilege); and Eisenhower, 159–163, 167, 206; and Formosa Resolution (1955), 159–160; and CIA, 167; and delegation of war-making power in nuclear age, 166–170, 175–176, 278; and Cuban missile crisis, 173–176; and U.S. "advisers" in Vietnam, 177; and LBJ, 177–182, 206, 216, 303–304; and Vietnam War, 177–182, 194–195, 196–197, 290–292; and Tonkin Gulf resolution, 179–181, 187; and Cambodia, 189,193–194, 208, 293, 378; and funding of Indochina War, 194–195, 290–292; and Nixon's theories on presidential powers, 195–196, 216; and Paris agreement, 196–197; and security agreements and commitments abroad, 200–205; and placement of nuclear weapons abroad, 205; self-abasement in post–World War II foreign affairs, 206–207; and the economy, 212; and Nixon's White House staff, 222; and Nixon's trade bill, 234; and impoundment, 235–240 *passim,* 397–400; and President's veto power, 241–242, 243; and pocket veto, 243, 400; and Nixon's executive order *re* Subversive Activities Control Board, 245–246; Nixon's control of information to, 246–252; 20th-century failures of, 252–253; and government investigative agencies, 261–262, 264–265; and Watergate, 269–273, 277, 405; assumption of superior virtue of, 395–398; reassertion of its role in constitutional scheme, 299–300; attempts to restrain presidential war, 300–307; and war-power bills, 301–307, 310, 318, 434–435, 441; and CIA-organized military and political operations, 316–319; Joint Committee on Atomic Energy, 317, 375; proposed Joint Committee on Central Intelligence, 317, 451; Armed Services Committee, 318; and restoration of balance in federal system, 319–328; and executive emergency prerogative, 319–323 *passim;* restoration of partnership in foreign affairs, 325–330; individualism of members, 326–327; and secrecy system, 338, 339, 341, 344, 345, 349, 352, 356, 359–360, 364–365, 372–376; and Pentagon Papers, 347–348; and Freedom of Information Act, 349, 364–365; and executive leaks of

Congress, U.S. (*cont.*)
information, 356; and executive's power to lie, 356–357; and security-classification statute, 365–366; preference for ignorance in foreign policy matters, 372–376; proposals *re* Cabinet members' answerability, 391–392; schemes to restrain Nixon Presidency, 392–405; normal disunity in, 399; and emergency economic powers for President, 402–403; and future Presidents, 409–410; and alternatives to impeachment, 411–414; and congressional government, 426; oversight function of, 421–422, 456; dependence of legislators on constituents, 426–427; post-Watergate, 432, 433–436; and War Powers Resolution, 434–435, 441; and control of budget, 435–436; scapegoating of, by Reagan, 439; collaboration with President, 444–445. *See also* House of Representatives, U.S.; Senate, U.S.

Congress of Vienna, 352

Conkling, J. G., 506

Conkling, Roscoe, 457

Connally, John, 220

Connally, Tom, 138, 329

Connally Resolution, U.S. Senate, 119

Constitution, Confederate, 476

Constitution, U.S., 364, 418, 490–492, 498; and conduct of foreign affairs, ix–x, 3–7, 13–15, 33, 279, 282–284, 444; Articles I and II, x; 22nd Amendment, xv, 127, 389, 475; Marshall on, 1; Wilson on, 1; intent of Founding Fathers, 1–12; and commerce clause, 3, 285; and presidential prerogative, 8–10; and impeachment, 10–12, 416; and Washington, 13–17; and President's duty *re* control of information, 15–18; and war- and treaty-making powers, 18–23, 40–41, 421, 444; strict constructionists, 23, 58, 87, 94; Lincoln's view, 59–60; and President's function as Commander in Chief, 61–63; and Lincoln's theory

of war power, 63–64, 69–70; and executive compact, 85–86, 315; and Truman, 142–150 *passim;* post–Korean War vision of globalism, 168–169, 184, 298–299; and separation of powers, 168–169, 278, 286, 324, 421; and freedom of press, 227–228, 231–232; and congressional appropriations power, 234–235, 239–240, 398; and President's veto power, 241, 242; and Supreme Court judges, 245; and legislative privilege, 246; judicial interpretation, 284; and Congress's voice in troop deployment, 306; restoration of balances in, 324–326; assumption of possibility of democratic control of foreign policy, 330; secrecy provisions, 332, 364; faithfulness of early Presidents to, 377–378; reform modeled on parliamentarianism, 389–392, 460–468; and Senator Ervin, 393, 398, 400–401, 403; and impoundment, 398; and impeachment, 414–416, 466; and legislative indiscipline, 426; and constitutional reform, 460–470, 490–492; proposed amendments to, 473–476

Constitutional Convention, 9, 10, 13, 18, 36–37, 41, 87, 191, 414; closed to press and citizenry, 332; and proposals for collegial Presidency, 382

Containment, U.S. policy of, 164

Contras, aid to, 452. *See also* Iran-contra affair

Coolidge, Calvin, 94, 117, 308, 404–405, 484–485, 542, 549

Coolidge, Charles A., 341

Cooper, John Sherman, 180, 319, 326, 375

Cooper, Thomas, 31

Corcoran, Thomas, 387

Corning, Erastus, 506

Corporation for Public Broadcasting, 231

Corwin, Edward S., 7, 70, 92, 108, 285; on FDR's use of presidential power, 113; and commitment of troops abroad, 137, 139–140, 308; and "high-flying" theses of presidential prerogative, 169; on centralization of President's control, 210; and FDR's threatened use of selective enforcement of law, 241; on means by which Congress could recover powers, 306; and proposal that cabinet members be accountable to Congress, 390, 391; cited, 501, 502, 503, 504, 506, 507, 508, 509, 510, 511, 512, 513, 518, 522, 523, 528, 530, 539

Cotter, C. P., 530

Coudert, Frederic R., Jr., 135–137, 139, 160, 286; cited, 512

Council of Foreign Ministers, 329

Court of Appeals, District of Columbia, 289, 395, 536

Courts. See Judiciary; Supreme Court, U.S.

Covert operations, 450–456; by early Presidents, 442–443; in Iran-contra affair, 452–453

Cox, Archibald, 270, 272, 524

Cox, Henry Bartholomew, 442

Crandall, S. B., 508

Credibility, President's, 359–361

Creighton, Bishop Mandell, 549

Crime Control and Safe Streets Act of 1968, 256–257, 265

Crisis, sustained, and the Imperial Presidency, xiv, xv, xxiii–xiv; American obsession with, 168, 208; and Nixon, 216–218, 256–260; and emergency prerogative, 321–324; and executive secrecy, 331

Croly, Herbert, 471

Cromwell, Oliver, Lincoln compared to, 59

Cronin, Thomas E., 124, 511, 520, 544

Crossman, Richard, 467, 506, 507, 524, 540, 547, 548

Crown, J. H., 515

Cuba, 15, 50, 90; Guantánamo Bay naval base, xix–xx, 313; support for annexation of, xxi–xxii; CIA activity in, 167; and Kennedy administration, 172–173; missile crisis, 173–176, 179, 182, 185, 189, 215, 283, 324, 385,

414–415; Nixon compares to Cambodian situation, 189

Culver, John, 434

Cunliffe, Marcus, 532, 538

Curry, Richard O., 449 (note)

Curtis, Benjamin R., 59

Curtiss-Wright case. See U.S. v. Curtiss-Wright Corporation et al.

Curtiss-Wright Corporation, 100

Cutler, Lloyd N., 461, 463, 547

Dalyell, Tam, 548

Daniel, Clifton, 533

Daniels, Jonathan, 425, 544

Daniels, Josephus, 219

Davis, David, 378

Davis, John W., 120

Dean, John W., III, 223, 251, 520, 524, 525, 532, 536; on secrecy of George W. Bush administration, xx; and Nixon's obsession with internal security, 258–260; on moral atmosphere of White House, 380

Death penalty, 350

Declaration of Independence, 34, 102

Declaration of the International Conference on Vietnam, 195, 197

Declassification, government documents. See Secrecy

De Conde, Alexander, 503, 511

Defense Department, U.S., 341–342; and publication of Pentagon Papers, 347–348; and bombing of Cambodia, 357. See also Pentagon

Defense Procurement Authorization Act, 194

Defense Science Board, Task Force on Secrecy, 363–364

De Gaulle, General Charles, 197, 226, 254–255

Delane, John T., 229

Democratic State Central Committee v. Committee for the Preservation of the Democratic Party in California, 519

Dennett, Tyler, 88, 508

Dependent states, xxiii

Depression (1930s), 95, 210

Derby, Lord, 229

De Tracy, Destutt, 538
Detainees, xix–xx
Dewey, Thomas E., 120–121
Dickens, Charles, 429, 545
Diem, Ngo Dinh, 168, 262
Dillon, Douglas, 220, 461, 547
Diplomacy, 41; and the Presidency, 6–7,
    14–15, 33, 35; and the Senate, 37; and
    Eisenhower administration, 166; and
    secrecy, 332, 340, 361–362, 363, 367
Dirksen, Everett, 170
Disclosure, 332–333, 344, 359, 361; and
    popular opinion, 334; and Congress,
    348; and Nixon administration re-
    form of secrecy system, 350–351;
    and Freedom of Information Act,
    349–350; and congressional statute,
    365–366
Disraeli, Benjamin, 493
Dissent, 257–258
Divine, R. A., 509, 511
Dixon, James, 74
Dixon, W. A., 509
Dixon-Yates case, 249
Domestic affairs, 2, 49, 211, 541–542;
    and T. Roosevelt, 84; and FDR, 95,
    101, 104, 146–147; and Congress,
    122–123, 401; and Truman, 127, 129,
    141–148; and Kennedy, 170–171; cen-
    tralization of executive powers in,
    208–212; and spillover from Viet-
    nam, 208–209; and Nixon, 233, 237–
    240; and impoundment, 236–241;
    and secrecy, 340–341; and congres-
    sional revolt against presidential
    power (1970s), 401–402
Domestic security, plan of 1970,
    259–260, 274, 301. See also Internal
    security system
Dominican Republic, 175, 178, 179,
    182, 308
Donovan, Robert J., 370, 372
Dooling, John, 290–291, 526, 527
Douglas, Helen Gahagan, 217
Douglas, Paul H., 133, 138
Douglas, William O., 141, 147, 394; and
    wiretapping, 257; and justifiability of
    presidential war, 289; and retroactive
    legislative ratification of executive
    initiative, 291; and bombing of Cam-
    bodia, 294; and Pentagon Papers,
    347; and *Mink* case, 365; and accessi-
    bility of classified documents to his-
    torians, 369
Douglas-Home, Sir Alec, 368
Downes, Captain John, 52–53
Dred Scott v. Sanford (1857), xiv, 59
Due process, George W. Bush adminis-
    tration suspension of, xix–xx
Dulles, Allen, 260, 339; and security-in-
    formation leaks, 355; cited, 524, 529,
    532, 535
Dulles, John Foster, 80, 129, 325; and
    brinkmanship, 165; and international
    commitments, 202; and Nixon, 217;
    and leaking of government informa-
    tion, 355
Dumbarton Oaks conference (1944),
    119
Durand v. Hollins, 191, 285

Eagleton, Thomas F., 318, 434, 528, 545
East Africa, 204. *See also* Africa
Eckhardt, Robert, 542
Economy, national, 82, 210–212, 402;
    and Nixon, 233–234
Eden, Anthony, 353
Edmunds, George F., 77
Education, federal aid to, 236, 240–241
Edwards, Mickey, 548
Egypt, 167
Ehrlichman, John, 222, 251, 380, 536;
    and White House plumbers,
    261–262; and burglary of Ellsberg's
    psychiatrist's office, 265; and Water-
    gate, 275; as model aide, 380
Eisenhower, Dwight D., 152–153, 156,
    177, 178, 425, 439, 519, 533; and pre-
    rogative, 153; his view of Presidency,
    156–157, 162–163, 171, 206, 210–211,
    214; and executive privilege and con-
    trol of information, 156–159, 171–
    172, 247–250, 252, 426; and foreign
    affairs, 159–167, 172; and Congress,
    159–163, 167, 206; and expansion of
    international commitments, 165, 202,

203, 356; and use of CIA, 167, 318, 356; and decline of party system, 209; and presidential authority, 216, 340; his White House assistants, 221; and presidential press conference, 224; and prime-time television addresses, 226; and item veto, 239; and executive agreements, 312; and secrecy system, 340, 342, 356; and Executive Order 10501, 340, 343, 344, 345, 348–349; moral atmosphere of his White House, 381; and burdens of office, 384; and economic management, 402; and CIA, 450, 451, 454–455; and Board of Consultants on Foreign Intelligence Activities, 454; and 1957 election, 464

Electoral College, 378; proposed abolition of, 479–484; and "faithless elector," 480, 484

Electorate, 377; and proposals for 6-year presidential term, 386–387

Elliott, William Yandell, 543

Ellsberg, Daniel, 259, 261–263, 264, 268, 366, 372; burglary of his psychiatrist's office, 265, 348, 457; and government secrecy, 345; and Pentagon Papers case, 347–348, 351, 353, 355; cited, 525–526, 533

Ellsworth, Oliver, 474

Emergency authority, presidential, xii, 423, 441. *See also* Prerogative, presidential

Emancipation Proclamation, 63, 313, 506

Emergency Price Control Act, 110, 115

Emerson, J. T., 451

Emerson, Ralph Waldo, 430, 437, 545

Empire, American versus European, xxi–xiv; defined, xxiii

Employment (unemployment), 211–212, 402

Employment Act (1946), 236

Enemies List (1971), xvi, 258, 263

Environmental Protection Agency v. Mink. See Mink, Patsy

Epstein, Julius, 369, 536

Ervin, Sam, 180, 187, 473; and Subcommittee on Separation of Powers, 207; and Nixon's harassment of press, 231; on Nixon's impoundment of appropriations, 238; and funds for Subversive Activities Control Board, 245; and Nixon's use of executive privilege, 246–247, 248, 251, 396; on motives for Watergate, 268; and Watergate proceedings, 270–271, 274–275; proposal to veto executive agreements, 314, 315; as author of congressional attacks on presidential supremacy (1970s), 392–393, 406; and the Constitution, 393, 398, 400–401, 403; and establishment of new balance of constitutional power, 393, 397–401, 406; Fulbright bill *re* executive privilege, 396; and restoration of congressional control over power of the purse, 397–398; on Nixon's use of impoundment, 397–400; and prevention of presidential use of pocket veto, 400; and presidential subordination scheme, 401, 406; his view of presidential power, 401, 403–404; and President's domestic powers, 403–404; cited, 521, 522, 524

Espionage, 338, 451; and British Official Secrets Act, 352; and information leaks, 355, 362. *See also* Central Intelligence Agency

Espionage Act, 335, 338, 347, 351, 446–447

"Establishment," eastern, 258

Estes, Billie Sol, 249

Ethiopia, 203, 313

Europe: Truman's commitment of troops to (1951), 135–136, 140; U.S. nuclear warheads in, 205

Evarts, W. M., 80

Exchange v. McFaddon, 516

Executive agreements (compacts), 7, 85–88, 93; and international law, 86; and Supreme Court, 103–104; and FDR, 105–109, 141; and Congress, 151, 285, 310–319, 331, 393; and Nixon, 151, 285, 312–313, 397;

Executive agreements (*cont.*)
and military commitments, 201–206;
and congressional campaign to re-
gain control over commitments,
311–316; and Senator Ervin's pro-
posals, 393
Executive branch, U.S. government.
See Presidency
Executive Order 1062, 508
Executive Order 10501, on government
secrecy, 340, 343, 344, 345, 348–349
Executive Order 10964, 533
Executive Order 11652, on secrecy,
248–350; and declassification of
World War II documents, 369–370
Executive Order 12356, 445
Executive Order 13223, xxi
Executive privilege, 155–159, 404, 505;
and Nixon, xv, 246–253, 266,
349–350, 378, 393–396, 416, 422; and
secrecy system, xv, 331–332; during
Kennedy and Johnson administrations, 247, 248, 249; covering President's conversations with key aides,
250, 426; and Watergate proceedings,
270–271; and Nixon's Watergate
tapes, 271–272; Senator Ervin's proposals concerning, 393; and the judiciary, 393–395; congressional retaliation for Nixon's use of, 396–397;
post-Watergate, 436; and Reagan,
446–447. *See also* Information, executive control of
Ex pane Endo, 527
Ex pane Milligan, xiv, 69, 287, 320, 322,
378, 401, 538
Ex pane Quirin, 510
Ex-Presidents, role of, 484–489

Fadiman, Clifton, 547
Fairlie, Henry, 537
Falk, R. A., 506
Family Practice of Medicine Act
(1970), 244, 400
Fay, S. P., 504
Federal Bureau of Investigation (FBI),
260, 261, 262; under Ashcroft, xviii;
and Watergate, 274–275

Federal Criminal Code, 350; proposed
revision of (1973), 350–351
Federalists, 26, 34, 284–285, 426, 471;
and executive secrecy, 332
Feingold, Russ, xviii
Feis, Herbert, 364, 368, 371, 372, 536,
537
Ferguson, Homer, 312, 514
Ferns, H. S., 546
Fiji Islands, 51
Fillmore, Millard, 54, 56–57, 481, 485,
549
Finch, Robert, 220
Findley, Paul, 317
Finer, Herman, 538
Finletter, Thomas K., 391, 413, 539, 543
First Gulf War, xvi
First War Powers Act, 110
First World War, 92, 127; and Versailles
Treaty, 94; and excessive presidential
discretion in foreign affairs, xiv, 95
Fiscal policy, 233. *See also* Budget
Fisher, Louis, 508, 522, 542
Fleming, Donald, 543
Fleming v. Page, 506
Florence, William G., 344, 534
Florida, annexation of, xii, 442; Jack-
son's invasion of, 26–27, 51, 285
Ford, Gerald, 431–432; on "imperiled
presidency," xvi, 425; his presidency,
424, 432–433; pardon of Nixon by,
432–433; and government by veto,
433; cited, 544
Ford, Henry Jones, 75, 255, 436, 507,
545
Ford, P. L., 539
Foreign affairs, 3–7, 212, 498–499;
threat to constitutional balance, ix;
and separation of powers, ix–x, 472;
ambivalence about annexation,
xxi–xxiii; since Vietnam War,
xxiii–xxiv; congressional duties in, 2;
disagreements concerning conduct
of, 13–15; and control of information, 15–18, 43–49; Washington's testing of executive function, 18–20;
Hamilton's view (1793), 18–19;
House of Representative attempts to

intrude itself in, 68–69; and strengthening of Presidency, 82–84, 208; and executive compact, 85–88, 95; congressional restraints on (1919–1939), 93–99; and Presidency as object of congressional mistrust, 95; and FDR, 95–98, 113; and Ludlow Amendment, 97–98; and Supreme Court (1930s), 101–104; Congress's subordination to domestic politics, 122–125; and democracy, 124–126; following Second World War, 127–128; and bipartisanship, 128–130; and Truman, 128–140,144; Congress's attempts to reclaim authority in, 150, 423, 433; and Eisenhower, 159–167; and fear of communism, 163–164; and brinkmanship, 166; and globalism, 169, 206–207; in nuclear age, 169–170; and Kennedy, 170; and executive initiative and commitments, 201–206; self-abasement of Congress in, 206–207; and traditional separation of powers in, 208, 279–280; in Britain, 279–281; and judicial interpretation, 287–290, 294–295; assumption of presidential or congressional superiority in, 295–298; and congressional war-powers bills, 304–307; and executive's exclusion of Congress by use of CIA, 316–319; and ways to end presidential war-making, 324; and restoration of State Department primacy in, 325; and restoration of congressional partnership in, 325–330; and secrecy, 333, 336, 345–346, 353, 355–356, 359, 363, 372–376; inaccessibility of documents to historians, 368–372; and congressional revolt against presidential powers (1970s), 401; executive power and, 420–421; and Ford, 433–435; covert action and, 450

Foreign aid, 150, 171; and executive initiative, 201–203, 313–314

Foreign Intelligence Advisory Board, 371

Foreign Policy Association, 121

Foreign Relations Committee. See Senate Foreign Relations Committee

Foreign Relations of the United States, State Department publication, 335, 367, 368

Former Presidents Act of 1958, 487

Formosa, 138, 159–161, 302, 514

Forrestal, James, 220

Fortas, Abe, 542

Foster v. Neilson, 526

Founding Fathers, 1–2, 183–185, 391, 393, 490, 491; and war-making powers, x–xi, 3–5, 35, 37, 125, 279, 302; and questions of prerogative, xiii, 8–10, 323; and fashioning of Presidency, 2–3, 319–320, 431; and Commander in Chief clause, 6, 61–62, 188; and conduct of foreign affairs, 6–7, 13–15, 295, 298, 319–320; and impeachment, 10–11, 414, and "Rebellion or Invasion" exception, and habeas corpus, 61, 146; and treaty-making process, 79, 313; question of emergency powers, 143, 146, 148; and freedom of speech and press, 227–228; and secrecy, 332–333; and collegial Presidency, 382–383; and fixing of accountability, 386; and congressional powers of taxing and spending, 436; and separation of powers, 470, 473; and term of office of President, 474–475; on ex-Presidents, 488. See also Constitution, U.S.

Fourteen Points, Wilson, 93, 315; and theory of impropriety of secrecy, 336

Fowler, J. T., 510

Fox, Matthew H., 536, 537

France, 14, 21–22, 28, 333; French Empire, xxi; during World War II, 109; as Nixon's model for plebiscitary Presidency, 254; availability of government documents in, 367–368

Franco, Francisco, 130, 168, 205

Frankel, Max, 174; on government information leaks, 355–356; cited, 515, 517

Frankenheimer, John, 439
Frankfurter, Felix, 132, 147, 196, 289;
   his definition of democratic govern-
   ment, 395
Franklin, Benjamin, 332, 383; and im-
   peachment, 414–415
Franklin, William M., 336, 532
Franks, Lord (Oliver), 353, 534
Free, Lloyd A., 535
Freedom of Information Act, 349–350,
   364–365, 423; under George W.
   Bush, xx–xxi; and the historian,
   369; under Reagan, 446
Freeman, Douglas Southall, 428, 544
Freeman, Orville, 220, 249–250
French, Benjamin Brown, 545
Friedel, Frank, 527
Friedman, Leon, 526, 527
Friedman, Milton, 543
Friedman, Saul, 549
Friendly, Henry, 501
Friendship, seized and looted in Suma-
   tra, 52–53
Fritchey, Clayton, 535
Frost, David, 457, 544, 547
Fulbright, J. William, 105, 108, 112, 119,
   138; and abdication by Congress of
   war-making power, 161–163; and
   presidential responsibility for military decision in nuclear war, 166,
   169–170; and Kennedy, 173, 329; and
   Cuban missile crisis, 175; and Vietnam, 180, 201; and executive-initi-
   ated international agreements, 205,
   313–314; and Nixon's use of executive privilege, 247–248; belief re
   President's authority in foreign affairs, 285–286, 297; and cut-off of
   funds for war in Cambodia, 293; and
   globalist policy, 298–299; and Javits's
   war-powers bill, 304, 310; distinction
   between kinds of power in shaping
   foreign policy, 327–328; -Ervin bill re
   executive privilege, 396–397; cited,
   510, 514, 515, 516, 528, 530
Fulbright Resolution, 119
Furness, C. J., 544

Gallatin, Albert, 29, 40–41, 41–42, 334,
   335, 505
Gallup Poll, 267
Garcia, Rogelio, 509
Gardner, John, 220
Garfield, James A., 213, 390
Garment, Leonard, 524, 525
Garrison, Lindley M., 219
General Accounting Office, 247, 344
Genet, Edmond (Citizen), 14
Geneva Accords (1954), 197
Gentlemen's Agreement (1907), with
   Japan, 88
George III, of England, 279
Gerry, Elbridge, 4
Gerth, H. H., 532
Geyelin, P. L., 515, 546
Giddings, Joshua, 291
Gilbert, Felix, 423
Giles, William B., 30
Gillette, Guy, 104
Gillies, James, 467, 469, 548
Gingrich, Newt, 440
Giscard d'Estaing, Valéry, 430 (note)
Glasnost, 449
Glass, Carter, 219
Gleason, S. E., 109, 372, cited, 509, 510
Globalism, 169, 298–301, 528; and the
   Constitution, 299–300
Goldberg, Arthur J., 185, 220, 250; on
   legality of wiretapping, 257; and gov-
   ernment secrecy, 365; cited, 523
Goldman, Eric, 166, 514, 536
Goldwater, Barry, 53–54, 170, 188, 286,
   505, 516; and Vietnam, 292; on supe-
   rior virtue of President in war-mak-
   ing, 296; and Senate war-powers bill,
   304; and control of troop deploy-
   ment, 304; on War Powers Resolu-
   tion, 434
Goodhart, Philip, 510
Good Neighbor Policy, 151
Goodnow, Frank J., 471
Gorin v. United States, 338, 350–351,
   532
Gorman, Joseph, 549
Goulding, Phil, 358, 534

Gouverneur, S. L., 502
Government Reorganization Act (1939), 220–221, 494–495
Graham, Katharine, 232, 274, 275
Gramm-Rudman Act, 436
Grant, Ulysses S., 74, 75, 77–78, 270, 335; and control of transmission of information to Congress, 77–78; and impoundment, 236; and item veto, 239, 476; scandals in administration of, 268
Gravel, Mike, 246; and government secrecy, 344, 370, 373
Gray, L. Patrick, 294–295, 380
Gray v. Sanders, 548
Greece, 128
Greek-Turkish Aid program (Truman Doctrine), 128
Greeley, Horace, 427–428
Green, Edith, 413, 414, 543
Greenberg, Joel, 517
Greenland, U.S. World War II bases in, 110
Grenada, invasion, xvi, 435, 443
Grey, Sir Edward, 93
Greytown, Nicaragua, 55–56, 65
Griffin, Robert, 545
Griswold, Erwin N., 447–448, 546
Grotius, Hugo, 21
Gruening, Ernest, 177, 179, 181; and Vietnam appropriations, 291
Guantánamo Bay prisoners, xix–xx
Guatemala, 167; Cuban Brigade in, 172
Gulf of Tonkin resolution. See Tonkin Gulf resolution
Gulf War. See First Gulf War; Second Gulf War

Habeas corpus, xiii, 9, 61, 335
Hagerty, James, 342
Hague Convention (1899), 27
Hailsham, Lord, 465, 467, 469, 547, 548
Haiti, 78, 308
Haldeman, H. R. (Bob), 220, 222, 251, 518–519, 520, 442; and student protest of the seventies, 259; and Watergate, 275; Nixon's admiration for, 380

Halpine, Charles, 549
Hamilton, Alexander, 2, 3, 34, 200, 283, 404, 485, 497, 550; and presidential treaty- and war-making power, xi, 18–23 passim, 28, 160, 302; and executive centralization, 3, 7, 10; and problems of national security, 5, 9; and President's power as Commander in Chief, 6; and impeachment, II; his view of the Presidency, 13, 431; on treaty-making provision of Constitution, 85; and Congress's voice in troop deployment, 309; and collegial Presidency, 383–384, 385; and presidential re-eligibility, 388, 474–475; on term of office for President, 474–475
Hamilton, Lee, 449, 455–456, 546, 547
Hamilton, S. M., 549
Hamilton v. McLaughry, 508
Hammond, George, British minister, 15
Hand, Learned, 288, 526
Handlin, Oscar, 543
Hardin, Charles M., 461, 463 and note
Harding, Warren G., 159, 378; scandals in administration of, 268
Hardy, Porter, 171
Harlan, John Marshall, 347
Harlow, Bryce, 542
Harriman, Averell, 153, 219, 220, 250, 406, 541, 542, 550; and restoration of congressional partnership in foreign relations, 325; on size of White House staff, 496
Harris (Louis) Poll, 267, 535
Harrison, Benjamin, 210, 429, 482, 486, 545
Harrison, William Henry, 39
Hartford Convention, 26
Harwood, Richard, 374, 537
Hatch, Carl, 119
Hatfield, Mark, 478, 533
Hawaii, xxii–xxiii, 85
Hay, John, 80, 81, 87, 93, 311, 315
Hayden, Ralston, 504
Hayes, Rutherford B., 78, 210, 387, 476, 482
Heath, Edward, 353, 368, 467, 468

Heclo, Hugh, 495 (note), 544
Helms, Richard, 523
Henkin, Louis, 70, 104, 507, 509, 529, 530
Hennings, Thomas C., Jr., 341, 342, 532
Heren, Louis, 520
Herndon, W. H., 42, 192, 505, 527
Hersh, Seymour M., 523
Hickel, Walter, 220
Higham, Charles, 517
Hill, Lister, 106, 119
Hiss, Alger, 339–340
Hitler, Adolf, 129, 193, 323
Hitler-Stalin pact, 339
Hodges, A. G., 506
Hodgson, Godfrey, 544
Holmes, Oliver Wendell, 284–285, 478
Holmes v. Jennison, 509
Holt, W. S., 509
Holtzman et al. v. Schlesinger, 527
Homans, George, 543
Home Building and Loan Association v. Blaisdell, 530
Honolulu conference (1966), 201
Hook, Sidney, 543
Hoopes, Townsend, 186, 516
Hoover, Herbert, 117, 220, 384, 541; and press conferences, 223–224
Hoover, J. Edgar, 260, 261, 265, 274, 380
Hopkins, Harry, 219, 226
Horner, Garnett, 229, 521
House of Commons, Britain, 279–280, 502; and Official Secrets Act, 352–353
House of Representatives, U.S., 47–48, 502; and power of impeachment, 10; and executive control of information, 16–18, 47; and treaty-making, 41; and executive control of secret funds, 47–48; and recognition of Maximilian regime in Mexico (1864), 68–69; and impeachment of Johnson, 71; Un-American Activities Committee, 153-154, 270; Government Information subcommittee, 172, 341–343, 344; Armed Services Committee, 237; war-powers bill (1973),

305, 310; and executive agreements, 312; and government secrecy system, 364; Ways and Means Committee, 398–399; Appropriations Committee, 398–399; and anti-impoundment legislation, 400; and call for new presidential election if necessary, 413; and initiation of impeachment, 416, 422; Judiciary Committee, 416. See also Congress, U.S.
Houston, David F., 219
Huerta, Victoriano, 91–92
Hughes, Charles Evans, 93, 101, 122, 243, 530
Hughes, Emmet, 518, 536, 541
Hughes-Ryan Amendment, 451, 456
Hull, Cordell, 80, 97, 114, 119–120, 128–129; and FDR cabinet, 219
Humphrey, Hubert H., 201, 202, 216, 232, 528, 530, 541; on Nixon's "policy impoundment," 238; and proposed Joint Committee on National Security, 329
Hunt, E. Howard, 262
Hunt, Gaillard, 501, 502
Huntington, Samuel P., 62, 506
Huston, Tom Charles, 218, 260, 274; on atmosphere of Nixon White House, 380–381; cited, 519, 526
Hyde Park Aide-Memoire, 355
Hydrogen bomb, 362. See also Nuclear age
Hyneman, Charles S., 538

Iceland, American troops in, World War II, 111, 112, 308
Ickes, Harold, 213, 219
Ikenberry, G. John, xxiii
Immigration, 3; and decline of party system, 209
Immigration and Naturalization Service v. Chadha, 435
Immunity, presidential, 157; and White House staff, 248; and presidential papers, 248–249
Impeachment, 10–12, 29–33, 248, 277, 418; and Justice Marshall, 31–33,

48–49; Folk's statement on, 49; and Congress's attempt to bridle Presidency (1860s), 70–76; and Andrew Johnson, 70–71, 72–75, 127, 378–379, 507; of federal district judges, 75; and President's responsibility for White House ethos, 381; Madison's statement on, 412; and Nixon, 410–411, 416, 422; alternatives to, 411–414; and Founding Fathers, 415; as weapon of last resort, 415–418; legal problems of, 415–416

Import quotas, 233

Impoundment, 235–240; and Jefferson, 235–236, 238, 239; and Grant, 236; and FDR, 236, 238, 239; and Truman, 236; and Kennedy, 236–237; and LBJ, 236; Anti-Deficiency Acts, 236; and Nixon, 235–240, 252, 266, 378, 397–400; and attempts to restore congressional control over funds, 397–400; and Senator Ervin, 398, 400; and separation of powers, 398; and congressional legislation, 399–400; restriction of presidential (by Congress), 423, 435; and Gramm-Rudman Act, 436

Indians, American, 50, 78

India-Pakistan war (1971), 358, 535

Indochina War, 124, 135–136, 190–191, 197, 199, 297; funding of military operations in, 194; and executive agreements, 200–201; and Nixon, 226; and question of justiciability of presidential war, 289; and concept of "unavoidable military necessity," 303; and need for shared control in foreign policy, 330; and secret agreements, 355; and government secrecy, 356–358. *See also* Vietnam War

Indonesia, 167

Information, executive control of, 7, 15–18, 43–50, 77, 83–84, 331–332, 397; Wilson's view, 76–77; and Supreme Court, 102, 394–395; and internal security system, 117–118, 153, 155–156; and Truman, 153–156;

and Nixon, 154, 246–252, 392–397; and Eisenhower, 156, 159–160; and confidentiality, 157–159. *See also* Executive privilege

In re Debs, 83

In re Neagle, 55, 82

Intelligence, domestic, xviii–xix, 317–318; and Nixon, 259–260; and Intelligence Evaluation Committee, 260–261; and secrecy, 339, 340, 348–349. *See also* Central Intelligence Agency

Intelligence, foreign, 167; executive control of information concerning, 47–48; and CIA, 167; and secrecy, 332, 371–372. *See also* Espionage

Intelligence Evaluation Committee, 260–261

Intelligence Oversight Act of 1980, 452, 453, 456

Interagency Committee on Internal Security (ICIS), 340

Interior, U.S. Department of, 158

Internal Revenue Service, 525

Internal security system: World War II, 117–118; and Truman, 152–155; and Eisenhower, 167; and Nixon, 256–266, 317–318

International affairs. *See* Foreign affairs

International agreements, 200–202. *See also* Executive agreements

International crisis and presidential imperialism, xiv, xv. *See also* Foreign affairs

International Telephone and Telegraph Corporation (ITT), 233

Intervention, policy of, 167–169, 208; and military establishment, 300

Iran, 167

Iran-contra affair, 441, 450, 452–453, 462–463, 467

Iraq invasion, xvi, xxiii–xxiv

Isolationism, 95–96, 168, 528

Israel, 192, 439; and executive declarations that become national commitments, 201, 315

Italy, 367
Item veto, 236, 473, 476–478; and Nixon, 240

Jackson, Andrew, 15, 26–27, 51, 160. 193–194, 214, 239, 405, 428–429, 503, 548; and presidential authority, 28, 28–29, 35, 72, 285; and general principles of impeachment, 33; and Texan independence, 38; and transmission of information to Congress, 45–46, 83, 117; and seizure and looting of the *Friendship* in Sumatra, 52–53; and privileged information within executive branch, 156, 250; and his advisers, 219; and pocket veto, 242; limits on President's term of office, 387; and presidential accountability, 410; Senate censure of, 411, 415; on right of the people to know, 449; favors direct popular election, 479
Jackson, Robert H., 107–108, 113, 157, 210, 309, 444, 460, 470, 490; and internment of Japanese-Americans (World War II), 116, 295; and congressional requests for internal-security information, 117–118; and presidential war power, 141, 143, 287–288; and Truman's seizure of steel industry (1952), 144–147; definition of separation of powers, 145–147, 149–150; and "law of emergency," 147, 321; in FDR's cabinet, 219; and doctrine of "political questions," 288, 295; cited, 510
Jackson-Vanik amendment, 433
Jacobs, Andrew, 440 (note)
Japan, 54–55, 88
Japanese-Americans, internment of (1940s), 116, 295
Javits, Jacob, 503, 528, 530; his war-powers bill, 244, 301–307, 310; and troop deployment, 301–302; 30-day deadline for presidential war, 303; effect of bill, 303–304; and Eagleton amendment, 318
Jay, John, 18, 283, 332, 337

Jay Treaty, 16–17, 41, 79, 102, 447; secrecy of negotiations, 333, 361
Jefferson, Thomas, 5, 27, 87, 147, 271, 283, 284, 348, 403; unilateral use of troops, xi–xii; on Cuba, xxi–xxii; view of Presidency, 13, 34; and conduct of foreign affairs, 14, 296, 319, 442; and control of information, 15, 44, 83, 117, 154, 335; and war- and treaty-making power, 19, 22–23, 28, 36, 60; view of executive emergency power, 23–25, 148–149, 161, 263–264, 324; and principles of impeachment, 30–33; and treaty-making process, 79; as Lockean, 113–114, 321; on freedom of press, 228, 453; and impoundment, 235–236, 238; view of congressional power, 296; and congressional power in troop deployment, 309; on legislative and executive tyranny, 377; and proposals to decentralize Presidency, 384, 385, 404; and limits on President's term of office, 388; evasion of constitutional limitations by, 442; cited, 502, 504, 505, 521, 531
Jenkins, Roy, 525
Jensen, Merrill, 521
Johnson, Andrew, 70–71, 486; and impeachment, xiv, 71, 73–75, 127, 379, 415, 507; and Tenure of Office Act, 72–73, 378–379; and pocket veto, 242–243; and limits on President's term of office, 387
Johnson, Louis A., 220
Johnson, Lyndon B., 160, 166, 170, 198, 219, 424, 433, 519; and Vietnam, xv, 178–187, 193, 215–216, 290, 303, 356, 386, 421; and Tonkin Gulf resolution, xv, 179–180; view of Presidency, 177–178, 214; and Dominican Republic, 178; and Congress, 177–182, 206, 216, 303–304; conception of presidential prerogative, 180–181, 187, 290; and SEATO treaty, 182–183; shrunken-world theory of defensive war, 184–185, 195; and executive consultation, 185–187; theo-

ries of presidential war power, 193; and executive initiatives and commitments, 200–203; and trend toward veneration of the President, 210; his Presidency, 214, 215–216, 218; and Reedy's *Twilight of the Presidency*, 214–215, 538–539; his cabinet advisers, 220; his White House assistants, 221; his prime-time television addresses, 226; and impoundment, 236, 238; and OEO, 241; and pocket veto, 243; and executive privilege, 247, 248, 249; and Mansfield proposal for Joint Committee on Central Intelligence, 317; and secrecy, 355–356, 361; atmosphere of his White House, 381; strains of office, 384–385; and proposal for 6-year term, 386; cited, 515, 542

Johnson, R. W., 546

Joint Atomic Energy Committee. *See* Congress, U.S.

Joint Chiefs of Staff, 368

Joint Committee on National Security, proposed, 329

Joint Congressional Committee on War Cooperation, proposed (World War II), 118

Joint Economic Committee, 541

Jones, Jesse, 219

Jones, William B., 527, 540

Judd, Orrin, 290–291; and presidential war in Cambodia, 293–294

Judiciary, 273, 277, 418; and executive control of information, xv, 394–395; and interpretation of war-making power in Constitution, 284–287; and doctrine of "political questions," 288–289, 294; and Vietnam War, 290–293; and Cambodia, 293–295; and control of overseas troop deployment, 308; and Pentagon Papers, 346–347; and Nixon efforts to consolidate legal controls of secrecy system, 349–351; and refereeing disputes between executive and legislative branches, 394–395; and impoundment policy, 397; and im-

peachment, 416. *See also* Supreme Court, U.S.

Justice, U.S. Department of, 230; and student protest of the seventies, 259; and test of mutual participation in war-making, 294; and secrecy, 350–351

Kahn, David, 372

Kahn, Herman, 537

Kalb, Marvin, 516, 533

Katz, Steven L., 449 (note), 546

Katzenbach, Nicholas, 182, 220; on executive secret agreements, 316

Kauper, P. G., 513

Keene, David, xix

Kefauver, Estes, 391, 392

Keller, Morton, 543

Keller, R. F., 522

Kellogg, Frank B., 80

Kellogg Pact, 163

Kendall, Amos, 219

Kennan, George, 123, 511

Kennedy, Edward M., 244, 400

Kennedy, John F., 151, 169, 185, 189, 372, 401, 519; his view of Presidency, 170–171, 211, 214; and invocation of executive privilege, 171–173, 247, 248, 249; and Eisenhower's foreign policy views, 172; and Bay of Pigs, 172, 174, 329, 356; his Executive (303) Committee, 173, 175, 185, 189, 385; and Cuban missile crisis, 173–176, 185, 329, 385; and Congress, 174–175, 206; and Vietnam, 177–178, 310, 361, 374, 475; and SEATO treaty, 183; and professional army, 200; commitment to Spain, 204–205; and Imperial Presidency, 214–215, 217; debunking of myth of presidential loneliness, 214–215; his cabinet advisers, 220; his White House assistants, 221, 222; and presidential press conference, 224; prime-time television addresses, 226; respect for freedom of press, 229; and impoundment, 236–237; and Diem assassination, 262; and Mansfield bill pro-

Kennedy, John F., (*cont.*)
   posing Joint Committee on Central
   Intelligence, 317; and consultation
   with Congress on foreign affairs, 329;
   and government secrecy system,
   342–345, 356, 362; on currency of
   publication of government documents, 367; moral atmosphere of his
   White House, 381; and burdens of
   office, 384; and political issues, 388;
   and economic management, 402;
   cited, 514, 518, 520, 521, 533, 536,
   542–543
Kennedy, Joseph P., 185–186
Kennedy, Robert F., 171, 219, 516
Kennedy v. Sampson and Jones, 522
Keynes, John Maynard (Keynesian-
   ism), 211–212
Khrushchev, Nikita S., 173, 372
King, Rufus, 37, 332
Kissinger, Henry A., 190, 195, 198, 325,
   543; power of, in Nixon White
   House, 222; as spokesman for Nixon,
   226; and Nixon's extension of ex-
   ecutive privilege, 251; and India-
   Pakistan war, 357
Kleindienst, Richard G., 248, 522
Knoll, Erwin, 533
Knowland, William, 132, 312
Know-Nothing party, 427–428
Knox, Frank, 219
Knox, Philander C., 80
Koenig, Louis W., 170
Korea (Korean War), 88, 131–132, 169,
   179, 283, 421; Truman's unilateral
   deployment of troops, xv; and Tru-
   man's theory of presidential power,
   131–136, 140–141, 264, 512; congres-
   sional debate on issue of troop deployment, 135–140, 179; and U.S.
   military establishment, 165; and con-
   stitutional separation of powers, 168;
   secret agreement with, 355
Korematsu v. *United States,* 460, 510,
   528, 547
Kosygin, Alexei, 525
Koszta, Martin, 55, 336

Kristol, Irving, 543
Krock, Arthur, 161, 183; description of
   presidential press conference, 225;
   cited, 511, 514, 515
Krogh, Egil, Jr., 261–262, 457
Ky, Nguyen Cao, 201

Laboulaye, Edouard de, 254
Lafayette, Marquis de, 539
Laird, Melvin, 220, 256
Lamb, W. Kaye, 536
Langer, William L., 109, 371, 372; cited,
   509, 510, 537
Lansing-Ishii Agreement (1917), 88
Laos, 167, 192, 193–194, 304, 362; exec-
   utive initiatives and commitments
   with, 203
Larson, Arthur, 515, 536
Laski, Harold, 540
Latin America, 27–28, 37–38, 120, 135;
   and foreign aid, 150–151
League of Nations, 96, 119, 120, 127, 311
Leahy, Admiral William D., 226
Lebanon, 162, 435; Marines sent to by
   Reagan, 439, 443
Lee, General Robert E., 335
Legislative branch, U.S. government.
   See Congress, U.S.
Legislative privilege, 246–247
Lehman, Herbert, 138
Lehman, John, 440
Lend-Lease, 110, 113; Act (1941), xiii,
   306
Lerner, Max, 382, 538
Levitan, D. M., 510
Levy, L. W., 504, 531
Lewis, Flora, 205
Library of Congress, Congressional
   Research Service, 375
Libya, 435, 443
Liddy, G. Gordon, 261, 262
Lie, Trygve, 131–132
Lincoln, Abraham, 81, 92, 114, 134, 142,
   147, 157, 187, 429, 458–459; and war-
   making power, xii–xiii, 42–43, 58–63,
   64–66, 192, 279, 285; and Congress,
   58–59, 68–70, 108–109, 193, 198; view

of the Constitution, 59, 149, 178; and executive prerogative, 60–61, 146, 263, 264, 321, 322; innovations *re* executive war power, 60–68; and Commander in Chief as locus of war power, 62–64, 188; Emancipation Proclamation, 63, 315; and blockade of Confederacy (1861), 64; and appointment of Stanton, 72; and size of armed forces, 165; and public opinion, 213; his advisers, 219; and freedom of press, 228; appearance before Congress, 269–270; and congressional war appropriations, 291; lack of secrecy in administration of, 335; and Gettysburg Address, 458; and emergency prerogative, 458–460; White House receptions of, 494; cited, 505, 506, 527, 542, 549

Lindsay, John V., 160

Link, A. S., 495 and note

Lippmann, Walter, 98, 99, 161, 279, 280, 319; his *The Public Philosophy,* 125; on Watergate scandal, 275; and cabinet members' answerability to Congress, 391; cited, 509, 511, 514

Little v. Barreme, 62, 140, 309

Livingston, Edward, 219

Lloyd George, David, 337, 352, 465

Lobbies, 427. *See also* Single-issue movements

Local 2677 et al. v. Phillips, 522

Lochner v. New York, 548

Locke, John, 8–9, 10, 23, 25, 35–36, 60, 263; and emergency prerogative, xii, xiv, 321, 322; and FDR, 113–114; and Truman, 143, 147; on political corruption, 269; cited, 502, 524

Lockwood, Henry C., 538

Lodge, Henry Cabot, 94, 119, 307–308, 326, 508, 509, 543

Lodge, Henry Cabot, Jr., xxii, 183, 308; cited, 515

Lofgren, Charles A., 4, 501, 502

London *Times,* 352

Long, D. F., 505

Longley, L. D., 549

Lon Nol, 196

Louderback, Harold, 75–76

Louisiana Purchase, 23–24, 79, 235; compared to FDR's destroyer deal (1940), 108

Louis Napoleon, 254

Lovett, Robert, 454–455, 546

Lovett-Bruce report, 454–455

Lower, Elmer W., 520

Lowi, Theodore, 423, 544

Lubell, Samuel, 212, 464, 518, 521, 543, 547; on Nixon's economic priorities, 233; on nature of an activist President, 409

Ludlow (Louis) Amendment, 105, 301

Luftig v. McNamara, 448

McAdoo, William G., 219

MacArthur, General Douglas, 188, 356, 372, 466

McCarthy, Eugene, 187; on depersonalization and decentralization of Presidency, 382

McCarthy, Joseph (McCarthyism), 152–153, 370, 397, 441; and Eisenhower's assertion of presidential prerogative, 153; and Eisenhower's assertion of right to withhold information from Congress, 156, 157–158, 248, 349–350

McCartney, James, 521

McClellan, John L., 245–246

McClure, Wallace, 508

McCulloch v. Maryland, 501

Macdonald, William, 540

McDonough, J. J., 545

McFarlane, Robert C., 455, 546

McGaffin, William, 533

McGee, Gale, 530

McGovern, George S., 177, 196, 216, 440, 530, 535; and the press, 230; and 1972 campaign, 259; and Watergate, 269; and government secrecy, 358

McGrory, Mary, 538

Machiavelli, 452; his *The Prince,* 219, 519; and emergency prerogative, 321–322

McIlwain, C. H., I, 501

Mackenzie, Compton, 353

McKinley, William, 80; and executive compact, 85, 87; and commitment of armed forces to China, 88; and public opinion, 213

MacLean, Donald, 369

Macmillan, Harold, 380

McNamara, Robert S., 171, 220; and security-classification system, 343, 344

McNary, Charles L., 106–107

McPherson, Harry, 536

McReynolds, James Clark, 101

Madison, Dolley, 29, 531

Madison, James, 4, 5, 27, 30, 87, 200, 377, 394, 418, 427, 512, 531; on impact of foreign threats on freedom, xi; covert foreign policy missions, xii; and war- and treaty-making powers, 7, 18–20, 26, 29, 79, 160; and presidential prerogative, 9, 34, 442; on management of foreign relations, 15, 296; and executive control of information, 17, 44; and theory of defense, 36; and veto power, 263–264; view of congressional power, 296; and secrecy system, 332–333, 334; and responsibility of President to remove government officials, 381; and proposals for decentralized Presidency, 383, 404; and impeachment, 410, 415; cited, 522

Magruder, Jeb Stuart, 380

Mahon, George, 291

Malay peninsula, 138

Mansfield, Mike, 316, 530, 539; proposal for Joint Committee on Central Intelligence, 317, 318, 451; and 6-year presidential term, 386–389

Mao Tse-tung, 130, 279

Marbury v. Madison, 271, 288, 526

Marlborough, Duke of, 6

Marquesa Islands, 52

Marsh, George P., 55, 336

Marshall, General George C., 219, 325, 385, 396

Marshall, John, I, 22, 140, 271, 273, 309; and general principle for impeachment, 30–32, 48, 70; his rule re invasion of neutral country, 191–192; and doctrine of "political questions," 288; and Burr trial, 504

Marshall, Thurgood, 394, 527, 532; and Pentagon Papers, 347

Marshall Plan, 128, 130, 164

Martin, Kingsley, 492

Martin v. Mott, 36, 504

Mason, A. T., 370

Mason, George, 4, 383, 414, 415

Mason, Stevens Thomson, 333

Massachusetts, 278

Massachusetts v. Laird, 292, 526, 527

Mathews, D. M., 507, 509, 512, 514

Mathias, Charles, 222–223

Maximilian, Emperor, 68–69

Mayaguez incident, 435

Mayer, Jane, 440 (note)

Meeker, Leonard C., 515

Mendès-France, Pierre, 197

Merhige, Robert R., Jr., 540

Merk, Frederick, 38, 504, 505, 527

Mexican War (1847), xiii, xxii, 41–43, 285, 291

Mexico, 38–41, 49; and Folk's deployment of troops to Texas (1846), 41; Wilson's deployment of troops to (1914), 91–92

Michels, Robert, 254, 264, 523, 524

Middle East, 161–162, 302, 304

Military agreements, by executive initiative: with Thailand, 202–203; with Laos, 203; with Ethiopia, 203–204, 313; with Spain, 204–205, 313; with Morocco and Cuba, 313; with Bahrain and Portugal, 314

Military establishment, 165, 300; civilian control of, 6; in nuclear age, 169–170; and Nixon, 301; and secrecy, 338–340

Military power, limits of, xxiii–xxiv

Militia Act (1795), 36

Mill, John Stuart, 322, 530

Miller, J. C., 531

Mills, C. Wright, 532

Mink, Patsy, 365, 369, 535

Mississippi, 70, 237

Mississippi v. Johnson, 70–71, 273, 507
Missouri v. Holland, 526
Mitchell, John, xvii, 231–232, 256–257, 380
Mitchell v. Laird, 292, 516, 527
Mollenhoff, Clark, 155, 156, 159, 513, 514
Mondale, Walter, 392, 424, 493, 549
Monroe, James, 12, 80, 485, 549; covert foreign policy actions, xii; and executive war-making power, 26; his diplomatic initiative, 27, 37; and transmission of information to Congress, 44, 117; and executive agreements, 86–87, 151; and foreign aid, 150
Monroe Doctrine, 27–28, 37, 86, 150, 315, 316
Moore, John Bassett, 89, 336
Moore, John Norton, 307, 425, 437, 449, 450
Moorhead, William, 344, 370, 521; Committee, 348–349, 365, 366
Moos, Malcolm, 268
Mora v. McNamara, 526
Morgenthau, Hans, 309, 523, 526
Morgenthau, Henry, Jr., 219, 399
Morison, S. E., 505, 527, 545
Morison, Samuel Loring, 446–447
Morocco, 313
Morris, Gouverneur, 386, 474, 550
Morse, Wayne, 138, 174, 177; and Vietnam, 179, 181, 291
Moss, John E., 172, 247, 349; and Government Information Subcommittee, 341–342, 343, 344; and document classification period, 370
Moynihan, Daniel Patrick, 410–411, 452, 543, 546
Mundt-Nixon bill of 1948, 245
Murphy, Frank, 510
Murphy, Robert, 339, 532
Muskie, Edmund, 251, 267, 528, 530, 534; opponent of Nixon's attempted revision of security system, 351; and congressional classification statute 366; and document classification period, 370
Myers v. United States, 501, 507

My Lai massacre, 356
Myrdal, Gunnar, 460

Nader, Ralph, 427, 462, 540
Namath, Joe, 523
Napoleon II, 254, 264
National Bonus Plan, 483–484
National Conference on the Judiciary (1972), 263
National Emergencies Act of 1976, 423
National Intelligencer, 53
National Press Club, 230, 521
National Recovery Act, 444
National security, 4–6, 207; and President as Commander in Chief, 5–6; and Reagan's National Security Decision Directive 84, 445–446; expenditures, and Truman, 165; and Eisenhower administration, 167; and Nixon, 255–266, 267; Ehrlichman's justification for Nixon's actions in, 265; and secrecy, 331–376; invocation of, 422, 457–458; and secrecy system, 445–451; and "leaks," 447–448
National Security Act of 1947, 167
National Security Agency, 260
National Security Council, 167, 185–186, 456, 530; Nixon's order to tap phones of members of (1969–1971), 256; and Vietnam, 282; documents of, inaccessible to historians, 368
National Security Decision Directives, 445–446, 453
Native American (Know-Nothing) party, 427–428
NATO (North Atlantic Treaty Organization), 128, 164, 368–369
Naturalization, 3
Naval Appropriations bill (1940), 105–106
Navy Department, U.S., 50–51
Nelson, Gaylord, 179, 291
Nelson, Lars-Erik, 439–440, 545
Nelson, Samuel, 56, 65, 191, 285
Neuborne, Burt, 526, 527
Neustadt, Richard, ix, 166, 189, 438, 470, 516, 544, 548

Neutrality, 95–97, 297; and Congress, 7, 97, 100, 282–283; and George Washington, 18–20, 98; amendment of laws (1941), 112

New Deal, 100, 113, 115, 127, 208, 210, 426; and delegated congressional power, 146–147; and decline of party politics, 209

New Left, 258

New York Herald Tribune, 136, 229

New York Times, 157–158, 169; and Cuban missile crisis, 174; and Pentagon Papers, 260–261, 345, 346–347, 355, 374; and Vietnam, 374

New Zealand, 137–138

Nicaragua, 94, 308; CIA and, 443, 452

Nicolson, Harold, 355, 366–367, 532, 534, 536

Nisbet, Robert, 543

Nixon, E. B., 509

Nixon, Richard M., 42, 140, 320, 425, 437, 487, 493, 518–519; and executive privilege, xv, 246, 247–252, 266, 348, 378, 393–397, 417; role in creating Imperial Presidency, xv–xvi; his inflation of presidential authority, xv–xvi, 187, 269–270, 275, 377, 397, 401, 406, 421–422; and Cambodia, xv, 187–188, 189–192, 293–295, 356, 378, 417, 421, 517; possibility of impeachment, xvi, 411, 416–419, 422; papers of, ownership debate, xx–xxi; and executive agreements, 151, 201–207, 285, 311–313, 397; and control of transmission of information to Congress, 154, 246–252, 395; and Vietnam, 187–207 *passim,* 290, 358, 378; as Commander in Chief, 187–193; and Congress, 189, 192–194, 195–198, 206, 393–403; and State Department, 189–190; and the Constitution, 190–191; theory of presidential war power, 193–198, 290; and Paris Agreement, 197–198; view of central role of the Congress, 198; and professional volunteer army, 199–200; and trend toward veneration of the President, 210; his reconstruction of

Presidency, 213, 216–218, 254–255; his view of perpetual crisis, 216–218, 256–260; and controlled environment of decision, 216–218; China visit (1972), 217, 226, 315; his monarchical yearnings, 218–219; and banishing of challenge from presidential environment, 219–222, 226, 380–381; his cabinet, 220, 225, 252; centralization of powers of government in White House, 220–222, 232–252; his White House assistants, 221–222, 252; withdrawal from external reality, 222–223; disdain for presidential press conference, 225–227; preference for television address, 226; dislike of the press, 227, 229–230, 252; delusions of persecution, 230, 256, 267, 346; harassment of press by, 230–232; and public opinion, 232, 267, 377; and foreign criticism, 232; and domestic affairs, 233, 237–240, 401–402; and economy, 233–235; and impoundment, 235, 237–240, 252, 266, 378, 397–400; and item veto, 239–240; and selective enforcement of the law, 241–246; use of pocket veto, 242–245, 252, 266, 541; and Supreme Court appointments, 245, 252; and Subversive Activities Control Board, 245–246; and rule by presidential decree, 245–246, 542; and legislative privilege, 246–247; view of presidential supremacy over Congress, 252–253; view of plebiscitary Presidency, 254–255, 264–265, 266–267, 377, 422; his 1972 election "mandate," 255; and leaks of government information, 256–257, 261–262, 355–356, 362 *(see also* and government secrecy system, *below);* and wiretapping, 256–257; and internal security, 256–266, 317; and the "eastern establishment," 258; and CIA, 259–260, 261, 267–268, 301, 316–317; and Pentagon Papers, 260–261, 345–346, 348, 353, 359, 380; and the White House "plumbers," 261–263,

267, 346, 348, 380; and forgery of cable implicating JFK in Diem's assassination, 262; and presidential prerogative, 263–266; 269–270, 321–324; justification for his government's lawless actions, 264–266; and burglary of Ellsberg's psychiatrist's office, 265, 348; revolution against traditional separation of powers, 266–267, 278; and Watergate, 266–277, 351, 380, 405, 416–418, 466–467; and withholding of tapes from Watergate Committee, 271–273, 405, 416; compared to Charles I of England (by Trevor-Roper), 275–277; and foreign policy, 276–277; and judicial interpretation of war-making power, 284–295 passim; vacillation on issues (1951–1971), 285; and Sino-Soviet rift, 300; and concept of "unavoidable military necessity," 303; and control of overseas military deployments, 307–308; and government secrecy system, 343, 344–345, 346, 348–351, 356, 359, 360–361, 362–363; and overture to Ellsberg trial judge, 348, 380; Executive Order 11652, 348–350, 369–370, 372; and currency of publication of government documents, 367; and declassification of government documents, 369–370, 371–372; constitutional offenses of administration, 378; potential criminal charges against his administration, 379; denies knowledge of appointees' crimes and cover-ups, 379; responsibility for moral atmosphere of official family, 379–382; and the burdens of office, 385; and proposal for 6-year term, 386; inevitability of showdown with Congress, 394; and inducing congressional unity, 399; as opposition critic of presidential presumption (pre-1968), 406; his theme of maintenance of respect for the Presidency, 401–411, 543; lack of understanding of the sickness of his

Presidency, 416–417; pardon of, 432–433; veto of War Powers Resolution, 433, 434; White House staff of, 495; cited, 516, 518–519, 522, 524, 525, 533–534, 536, 542, 544, 549
Nixon Doctrine, 300
No-confidence vote, 466
Non-intercourse Act of 1799, 62
Norquist, Grover, xix
Norris, George W., 94
North, Oliver, and Iran-contra affair, 452, 546
North Africa, 138. See also Africa
North Atlantic Treaty Organization. See NATO
North Korea, 131, 173. See also Korea
North Vietnam, 113, 179, 356, 374; Nixon's justification for use of air-power in, 195. See also Vietnam War
Norton, Philip, 547
Nuclear age, 166; and expansion of executive prerogative, 169–170; and unilateral presidential decision, 172–173; and Soviet missiles in Cuba, 173–176; congressional checks and balances in, 189–190; and traditional separation of powers, 278; and executive control of foreign relations, 282–284
Nuclear test ban, 168
Nuclear warheads, placement of, in foreign countries, 205

Oakes, James, 528
O'Brien, Lawrence, 549
O'Donnell, John, 228
O'Donnell, Kenneth, 536
Office of Budget Analysis, proposed, 541
Office of Economic Opportunity, 241
Office of Emergency Management, Second World War, 115
Office of Management and Budget, 541
Office of Price Administration, Second World War, 115
Office of Strategic Services (OSS), 267, 371

Official Secrets Act, 346–347, 350, 447; British, 345, 352–354, 468, 469
Okanogan Indians v. U.S., 522
Olmstead v. U.S., 524
Olney, Richard, 81, 311, 315
Open Door policy, 87, 88
Operation Keelhaul, 369
Oppenheimer, J. Robert, 168, 362
Organization of American States, 175
Orlando v. Laird, 290, 526, 527, 528
Ostend Manifesto, xxii, 50
Otepka, Otto, 345, 533
Oversight power, congressional, 421–422, 456

Padover, S. K., 501, 502, 538
Paige, Glenn, 512
Paine, Thomas, 2
Palestine, 131. *See also* Israel
Palmer, Alexander Mitchell, xvii, 219, 539
Palmer, John, 525
Panama, xvi, 38, 89
Paraguay, sale of arms to (1934), 101
Paris Agreement (on Ending the War and Restoring Peace in Vietnam), 195; and cease-fire in Cambodia, 196–197
Parliament, Britain, 279–280, 465; as model for U.S. constitutional reform, 389–390, 401, 414, 460–470
Parton, James, 546
Party system, 378, 423; decay of, 209–210, 212; and exaltation of President, 210; and Nixon, 254; and dependence of legislators on constituents, 426–427; and third parties, 427, 481–482; and party dealignment, 470
Paterson, C. Perry, 538
Patriot Act (2001), xviii–xix
Patriot Act II, xix
Patterson, James T., 511
Patterson, Robert P., 220
Peace and Freedom Party, California, 258
Peace-keeping, post–World War II, 119–122

Peace of Portsmouth, 89
Pearce, Edward, 547, 567
Pearl Harbor, 98, 114, 115, 122
Pearson, James B., 530
Peirce, Neal R., 548
Pell, Claiborne, 312, 530
Pendleton, George H., 390, 391, 392
Pensions, presidential, 485, 487
Pentagon, 186, 206, 262; under George W. Bush, xix; and military bases overseas, 312; and secrecy classification, 344; Task Force on Secrecy, 363–364
Pentagon Papers, 230, 246, 260, 262, 265, 345–346, 363, 372; and Supreme Court, 347–348; Nixon's interference in trial, 348; issue of leaking of government information, 355–356, 447–448; overclassification of, 368–369; and dangers of premature declassification, 371; availability of information concerning, 374–375; and national security, 447–448
People Power Over War Amendment, 301
Pepper, Claude D., 106
Percy, Charles, 530
Perkins, Frances, 219
Perle, Richard, 440
Perry, Commodore Matthew C., 54
Pershing, General John J., 338
Pescadores, 160, 161
Peterson, M. D., 504
Peterson, Peter G., 220
Pett, Saul, 519
Phillips, Kevin, 253, 392, 523
Phillips, Wendell, 59
Pierce, Franklin, 50, 54–55; and Greytown, Nicaragua, 56, 65, 191
Pierce, H. L., 542
Pike, Otis, 449, 546
Pinckney, Charles, 383
Piracy, 50–52, 65
Pitt, William (the Elder), 502
"Plausible deniability," 451
Pocket veto, 241–245; and Nixon, 241–245 *passim*, 252, 266, 541; defined, 242; and Andrew Johnson,

242; and Truman, 243; and Supreme Court, 242–243; and Lyndon Johnson, 243; and Congress, 242–243, 400; case of 1929, 243

Poindexter, John, xix, 452, 546

Poinsett, Joel R., xii, 442

"Political questions," doctrine of, 288–290

Polk, James K., 41–43, 49, 62, 70, 142, 285, 405, 545; and Mexican War, xiii, xxii; and executive use of secret funds, 48; and control of flow of information to Congress, 83, 156; and Congress, 296; secrecy in administration of, 335; death of, 384; and impeachment, 416; on expectations of President, 429

Ponting, Clive, 548

Pool, Ithiel de Sola, 543

Porter, Captain David, 52

Porter, Herbert, 380

Portugal, 314

Post Office Department, U.S., 259

Powell, Anthony, 532

Powell, Thomas Reed, 103, 544

Prerogative, presidential, 8–10, 421, 425, 441, 450, 458–459, 497–498; versus usurpation of power, xii–xiii; and Jefferson, xiv, 23–25, 148–149, 161, 263–265, 322, 323, 442–443; and Lincoln, xiv, 60–61, 146, 263; and FDR, xiv, 115–116, 263; and George W. Bush, xxiii–xiv; and Truman, 141–150, 263, 320, 324; and Eisenhower, 152–153; and policy of globalism, 169; and Lyndon Johnson, 180–181; and Nixon, 263–266, 269–270, 321–324; and Watergate, 271–272; emergency, 321–324. See also Executive privilege

Presidency, 2–3, 425, 464; imperial, definition of, ix–x; and emergency prerogative, xii–xv, 8–10, 458–459; and the Cold War, xv, 127–128; and Reagan, xvi, 435, 437–441, 443, 457; and Carter, xvi, 438–439; strengthening of, by terrorism, xxiii–xiv; and domestic affairs, 2, 49–50, 84, 95, 101, 104, 122–123, 127, 129, 141–147, 170–171, 208–209; and treaty- and war-making powers, 3–5, 18–20, 41–42, 159–163, 450; role as Commander in Chief, 5–6, 61–64, 86, 114–115, 144, 187–193, 198; and conduct of diplomacy and foreign affairs, 6–7, 14–15, 33–34, 35; and impeachment, 10–12, 29–33, 70–71, 412–416; and diplomatic recognition, 14–15; and control of information, 15–18, 43–46, 49–50, 83; and public opinion, 33–34, 39, 208, 209; and military action not directed against sovereign states, 50; and involvement of nation in war without congressional authorization, 50–67; Congress's attempts to bridle powers of, 68–81; resurgence and rehabilitation of, 82, 88; and international compacts, 85–88; and commitment of armed forces to combat, 88–95; and arbitration treaties, 93; resurgency of, Second World War, 100–126; and United Nations, 118–122; postwar exalted conception of power of, 122–126; and Truman, 127–151; and commitment of troops abroad, 135–140; and use of domestic emergency power, 141–150; and foreign-aid appropriations, 150–151; and doctrine of presidential secrecy, 153–159; and war-making in nuclear age, 166–170; and Kennedy, 170–173; and LBJ, 177–187; and Nixon, 187–207, 377–381, 416–418; and conclusion of international agreements, 200–205; and deployment of nuclear weapons, 205; and decline of the party system, 209–210; exalted by media, 209–210; and 20th-century economic changes, 210–212; chameleon-like quality of, 212–214; historical relationship with Congress, 213; and myth of loneliness and isolation, 214–215, 494; and impoundment, 235–238, 397–398; and item veto, 240, 476–478; and assumption of superiority of Congress,

Presidency (*cont.*)
295–298; and Senate war-powers bill, 301–307; and congressional termination of executive emergency proclamations, 319–320; and restoration of balance in federal system, 322–328; and secrecy system, 341–342, 354–359, 363–364, 365; credibility of, 359–361; future of, 377–419; proposals for reconstruction of institution of, 382; psychological strains of office, 382, 385; and Founding Fathers, 382–386, 431; physical strains of office, 384–385; advantages of single over plural executive, 385–386; and Council of State, 385; and fixing of accountability, 386; and proposals concerning term of office, 386–389, 473–476, 538; proposals concerning accountability and answerability to Congress, 389–392; Congress's efforts to restrain (1970s), 392–405; and authority in economic management, 402; and Watergate, 405–406; effective external checks on, 409–410; and censure, 412; and resignation, 413; and dissolution of an election, 413–414; and Ford, 424, 432–433; plight of, 424–437; personalization of, 428–431; and expectations gap, 429–430; indestructibility of, 431–436; and War Powers Resolution, 434–435; and American parliamentarists, 466–468; and direct popular election, 473, 479–484; and role of ex-Presidents, 484–489; as sacrosanct institution, 492–493

Presidential Libraries Act of 1955, 487–488
Presidential Records Act (1978), xxi
Press, 174, 208; and LBJ, 215; and Nixon, 227, 229–231, 252, 351; traditional emphasis on freedom of, 227–228, 334, 347; role of, and Presidency, 228–229; Kennedy's attitude toward, 229; as restraint on Presidency, 273, 277, 410, 418; and government secrecy system, 331–334, 342–343, 361, 366; and Pentagon Papers, 346–247; British, 352; post-Watergate, 432; and question period, 460, 467–468

Press conference, presidential, 223–227, 326, 494; as two-way form of communication, 224–225; under Nixon, 225–227; and vitality of Presidency, 227
Price, Don K., 540, 547
Price controls, 233, 234
Prime Minister, British, 465, 466
Pringle, Henry F., 549
Privilege. *See* Executive privilege; Legislative privilege
Prize Cases, 65, 91, 191, 285; cited, 506
Project Cannikin, 365, 373
Protest, and Nixon administration, 257–260. *See also* Dissent
Public-interest lobby, 427
Public opinion, 213, 387; and conduct of foreign affairs, xiii, 208, 279, 281; as restraint on President, 33–34, 39, 410, 418; and Nixon, 232, 267, 378; and Watergate, 269; and government secrecy, 332–335, 339, 344–345
Public works, 402, 403
Pusey, Merlo, 205, 511, 515, 517

Question period, 460, 467–468
Quine, W. V., 543

Randall, J. G., 335, 506, 532
Randolph, Edmund, 383
Rarick, John, 301
Raskin, Marcus, 301, 528
Ratner, L. G., 530
Rayburn, Sam, 160
Reagan, Ronald, 433, 435, 439, 440; war against Grenada, xvi; and foreign policy, 433, 435, 439; his Presidency, 435, 437–441, 443, 457; compared with Carter, 437–439; and presidential prerogative, 443, 456; and secrecy system, 445–446; and Iran-contra affair, 452–453; budget deficits under, 476–477; Council of Eco-

nomic Advisers, 477; as ex-President, 487

Recognition, diplomatic, 7, 14–15, 86, 319. *See also* Foreign affairs

Reconstruction, post–Civil War, 70–71, 73, 78, 127, 507

Reed, James A., 94

Reedy, George, 181, 186, 408, 492, 494, 549; his *Twilight of the Presidency,* 214–215, 515, 518, 538; and myth of presidential workload, 384; cited, 518

Rehnquist, William, 190–192, 239, 257, 286, 516, 521; on impoundment, 237; and legitimacy of wiretapping, 257; and Nixon's committee to reform security classification system, 348

Reid v. Covert, 529

Remini, Robert V., 531, 545

Reorganization Act of 1949, 306

Republican Party, 254–255. *See also* Party system

Reston, James, 125

Revenue sharing, 233

Revolutionary War, 2

Reynaud, Paul, 109

Ribicoff, Abraham, 220

Richardson, Elliot, 196, 248, 516

Richardson, J. D., 502, 503, 504, 505, 506, 507, 509, 521, 528, 529, 531, 532, 543

Richey, Charles, 540

Riesenfeld, S. A., 510

Riots, 257–260

Ritchie-Calder, Lord, 460

Rives, William C., 41

Roberts, Brian, 534

Roche, John P., 513

Rockefeller, Nelson, 433

Rogers, James Grafton, 501

Rogers, William P., 158–159, 196–197, 201; defense of executive privilege, 504; cited, 513, 514, 516, 536

Roman Empire, xxi

Romney, George, 220

Roosevelt, Franklin D., 95–98, 122–123, 127, 134, 138, 141, 142, 157, 179, 190, 220, 425, 426, 444, 471, 519; and Lend-Lease, xiii, 110, 112; use of doctrine of prerogative, xiii–xiv, 115–116, 263, 264; and domestic policy, 95–96, 101, 104, 146, 208, 271; and Congress, 95–99, 105–126 *passim,* 206, 213, 270, 320, 339, 396; and neutrality legislation, 96; and Supreme Court, 100–101; and destroyer deal (1940), 105–109, 141; his innate caution, 109, 146–147; and "unlimited national emergency" concept, 110–111, 308; constitutional dilemma (1941), 111; and Lockeanism, 113–114, 321; as Commander in Chief, 114–115, 122, 432; his approach to presidential powers, 115, 193, 206, 208, 303; and transmission of information to Congress, 117; and military and diplomatic reins of war, 118; and congressional role in making peace, 119, 198, 298; and United Nations, 120–122; repudiated by Congress's recommendation of 22nd Amendment, 127; and bipartisanship, 128; his Good Neighbor Policy, 150–151; and treaty power, 151; Eisenhower's view of, 152; as "model President," 210, 410; and public opinion, 213; his effect on White House, 214; his advisers, 215, 219, 220, 221, 408–409; his White House assistants, 221–223; and press conferences, 223–224, 226, 228; and impoundment, 236, 238, 239; and item veto, 239; and selective enforcement of law, 241; and pocket veto, 243; and troop deployment overseas, 308; and executive agreement, 315; and military secrecy-classification system, 338, 355; and establishment of presidential library, 368, 370; moral atmosphere of his White House, 381; strains of the Presidency on, 385; and economic management, 402; and national authority embodied in Presidency, 404; and emergency prerogative, 458–460; first inaugural, 464; staff of, 494–495; cited 510, 511, 520, 542, 543, 548, 550. *See also* New Deal

Roosevelt, Theodore, 93, 95, 150, 157, 321, 404, 471, 481; and flow of information to Congress, 83–84, 117; and executive agreement, 85, 87; and commitment of armed forces overseas, 88–89, 308; as "model President," 210; and public opinion, 213; and presidential press conferences, 223; and the press, 228; and Supreme Court appointments, 245; his philosophy about Presidency, 410; cited, 508, 509, 520, 522, 529, 532

Root, Elihu, 90, 96, 137, 326; and question of troop deployment, 307; cited, 509

Root-Takahiri Agreement (1908), 88

Rosenman, Samuel, 121, 433, 496, 511, 550

Rossiter, Clinton, 9, 152, 502, 520, 530; and presidential press conference, 225, 226

Rostow, Walt W., 226, 345

Roth, William V., Jr., 549

Rothchild, John, 527

Rousseau, Jean Jacques, 322, 323, 530

Rubanov, Vladimir A., 449, 546

Rush, Richard, 86

Rush-Bagot agreement, 87

Rusk, Dean, 169, 172, 183, 202; as Kennedy-Johnson adviser, 220; and means for intergovernmental consultation, 329; and government secrecy, 361, 370; and Congress, 373; cited, 514, 531, 536, 537

Russell, Richard, 174, 175, 329

Russo-Japanese War, 88

Russo-Turkish war, 281

St. Clair, General Arthur, 16

St. Louis Post-Dispatch, 154

Safire, William, xviii

Salinger, Pierre, 517, 536

SALT talks, 534

Samoa, 90

San Clemente, California, 519

Sandinistas, 542. See also Iran-contra affair

Santo Domingo, xxii, 78, 87–88

Sawyer, Charles E., 524

Saxbe, William B., 245

Schaffter, Dorothy, 507, 509, 512, 514

Schechter case, 444

Schellhardt, T. D., 544

Schelling, Thomas, 529

Schlesinger, Arthur M., Jr., 139, 372, 454, 514, 515, 518, 519, 520, 524, 526, 542, 543

Schneiders, Greg, 550

Schumpeter, Joseph, 184, 300, 515, 528

Schwartz, Bernard, 507

Scott, Dred. See Dred Scott v. Sanford (1857)

Scott, Hugh, 530

Scoville, Herbert, Jr., 534

Scranton, William, 259

Seabury, Paul, 543

Sears, John R., 439

SEATO (Southeast Asia Treaty Organization), 180, 182–183, 201, 202; and Nixon, 187–188, 195; and Cambodia, 196

Second Bank of the United States. See Bank of the United States

Second Gulf War, xxiii–xiv

Second War Powers Act, 115

Second World War, xv, 97–98, 127, 153, 191, 206, 323; and resurgence of presidential power, 100–126, 188, 208, 213; and FDR's destroyer deal, 105–109; and FDR's emergency powers, 115–116; military and diplomatic reins of, 118–119; postwar international organization, 119–122; and size of military forces, 165; and techniques and habits of centralized control, 210; declassification of documents of, 369

Secrecy (security classification system), 331–376, 441, 445–450; of George W. Bush administration, xix–xx; and "leaks" of government information, 256–257, 260–263, 355–356, 447–448; and the press, 331–334, 342–343; and Constitutional Convention, 332; and the early Presidents, 332–335; and foreign affairs, 333, 336, 344–346,

354–356, 358, 363–364; and bureaucratic complexity, 337–341; and war, 338–340; and Congress, 338–339, 341, 343, 345, 349, 351, 364–366, 372–376; and Cold War, 339; and Eisenhower (Executive Order 10501), 340, 342–344, 345, 348–349; lack of control over system, 340–341, 344; system's objectives, 340–345; legal limitations of system, 341–342; Congress's investigations into, 341–342; and Kennedy, 343–345; cost to taxpayer, 344; and Pentagon Papers, 346–349; and Supreme Court, 347, 358–360, 365; and Nixon administration, 348–351, 355, 359, 361, 362, 422; and Executive Order 11652 (Nixon), 349, 369; and Freedom of Information Act, 349, 364; in Britain, 352–354; and executive's power to withhold knowledge from public, 354–356; and executive's power to lie, 356–358; and falsification of information directed to the President, 358; effects of, 358–359; and re-establishing balance with disclosure, 359–362; public loss of confidence in integrity of system, 359–361; proposed abolition of, 362–367; Pentagon Task Force on, 362–364; congressional classification statute, 365–366; and the people, 366; and duration of classification period, 367–372; and reporters' observations, 374–375; in post-Watergate era, 436; and declassification of documents, 445; and Reagan (Executive Order 12356), 445–446; and overclassification, 448. *See also* Information, executive control of

Secret Services, 261

Security agreements, 201–202. *See also* Executive agreements

Security system. *See* Internal security system; Secrecy

Sedition Act, 334, 335, 346–347

Seitz, Frederick, 363, 364

Selassie, Haile, 203–204

Selective Service Act of 1940, 308

Senate, U.S., 3, 393–394; and war powers, 3–4, 28; and impeachments, 10–12, 33, 415–416; and President's conduct of foreign transactions, 14, 102; and Monroe Doctrine, 27; voice in diplomacy, 37; and annexation of Texas, 40–41; and executive control of information, 45, 395–396; and House's attempt to intrude itself in foreign policy, 68–69; and treaty-making power, 78–81, 85, 93–94, 103; and executive compacts, 85–87, 103–104; and President's deployment of troops overseas, 90–92, 136–140; and arbitration treaties, 93; and FDR, 95–96, 98, 105–107, 111, 122; and Bricker Amendment, 151–152; and Cambodia, 196, 356–357; Atomic Energy Committee, 201; Armed Services Committee, 201, 205, 357; and executive agreements and commitments, 200–206, 312–319 *passim;* and Kennedy agreement with Spain, 204–205; Judiciary Committee, 207, 387–388; Subcommittee on Separation of Powers, 207; and Supreme Court appointments, 245; and Nixon's executive order *re* Subversive Activities Board, 245–246; and Nixon's use of executive privilege, 248; Subcommittee on Constitutional Rights, 257, 341; and Javits's war-powers bill, 301–305, 310; Naval Affairs Committee, 308; and termination of executive emergency proclamations, 319–321; Special Committee on Termination of the National Emergency, 321; Internal Security Committee, 345; and secrecy, 364; proposal concerning cabinet members' answerability to, 392; Finance Committee, 398; Appropriations Committee, 398–399; Banking and Currency Committee, 398; anti-impoundment legislation, 399–400; and censure of Andrew Jackson, 411–412; and intelligence activities,

Senate, U.S. (*cont.*)
  451–452; Select Committee on Intelligence, 452, 455; ex-President as
  Senator at Large, 486–487, 489. *See
  also* Congress, U.S.
Senate Foreign Relations Committee,
  173, 182, 326; debut of, 37; and arbitration treaties, 93; and FDR, 96, 98;
  and Truman, 140; and Eisenhower,
  162; and cult of executive expertise,
  168; and Cambodia, 196; and Vietnam, 201, 282; and security agreements and commitments abroad,
  202; and military agreements,
  203–204; and deployment of nuclear
  weapons, 205; and executive agreements, 311–315; and "commitment
  by accretion," 328; and secrecy system, 344–345, 355, 357, 364–365, 395
Separation of powers, 501; and George
  W. Bush administration, ix, xvii–xxi,
  xxiii–xiv; and Congress, 2, 252–255,
  266, 277, 295–298, 398, 431, 461,
  470–473, 498; and Constitution, 168,
  278, 286–287, 324; and Korea, 168;
  Senate subcommittee on, 207; and
  foreign affairs, 208, 279–281; and
  Nixon, 252–253, 266–267, 278; in nu-
  clear age, 278; and impoundment,
  398; and executive branch, 426, 431;
  retreat from, 461, 463; and British fu-
  sion of powers, 468–470
Seven Days in May (film), 200, 517
Seward, William H., 57, 58, 68, 219, 285,
  326
Shawcross, William, 520
Sherman, John, 80
Sherman, Roger, 4
Sherman, General William T., 335
Shils, Edward, 543
Shogan, Robert, 544
Shuman, Howard E., 545
Siberia, 93
Simon, William, 548
Sindler, Allan, 466, 547
Singapore, 138
Single-issue movements, 423, 427–428,
  481

Sirica, John, 271, 274, 275
Skolnik, Richard, 503
Slater, Joseph, 547
Slavery, 39
Sloan, Hugh, 380
Smith, Denis Mack, 367
Smith, H. Alexander, 132
Smith, Howard K., 516
Smith, J. M., 530
Smith, Janet, 544
Smith, T. C., 518
Sneed, Joseph T., 521, 522
Snep, Frank, 436
Sofaer, Abraham D., xii, 51, 441–443,
  545
Somali Republic, 203
Sorensen, Theodore, 175, 372,515, 518,
  536, 542
Southeast Asia, 173, 179; and executive
  initiatives, 202–203; troop with-
  drawal from, 293. *See also* Indochina
  War; Vietnam War
Southeast Asia resolution. *See* Tonkin
  Gulf resolution
South Korea, 131, 134, 159, 165, 173.
  See also Korea
South Vietnam, 177, 183, 192; executive
  agreements with, 201. *See also* Vietnam War
Soviet Union, 103, 164; and nuclearization of Cuba, 173–176; and African
  nations, 203–204; Nixon visit (1972),
  217; Nixon grain deals with, 233; and
  China, 300; and arms-limitation
  agreements, 301; government secrecy in, 367
Spain, 80, 88; and Latin America, 38;
  and Truman foreign policy, 130; U.S.
  bases in, 204, 313; Kennedy agreement with (1963), 204–206
Spanish-American War, 82; executive
  strength during, xiv; annexations following, xxii–xiii; attrition of congressional power following, 83–84; and
  executive agreements, 87
Special-interest lobbies, 427
Spectator, London, 379
Sperling, Gary, 529

Spooner, J. C., 84
Sprague, Dean, 506
Stabilization Act, 110
Stalin, Joseph, 129; and Yalta, 151
Stanbery, Henry, 70
Standard, W. L., 515
Stans, Maurice H., 543
Stanton, Edwin M., 71, 219, 415
Stanwood, E. M., 544
Stassen, Harold, 129
State Department, U.S. 49–50,104,262, 325; and treaty-making process, 80–81; former senators as Secretary, 80; Advisory Committee on Postwar Foreign Policy, 119; and exalted conception of presidential power, 122–123; and Korean conflict, 132–133; and Kennedy administration, 171–172; and Cuban missile crisis, 174–175; and Tonkin Gulf resolution, 182–183; and Nixon, 189–190; and secret executive agreements and commitments overseas, 203–204; need for restoration of primacy of, 325; and consultation with other departments, 328–329; and secrecy, 335–336, 338–339, 357, 367, 368; Historical Office, 336; and declassification of World War II papers, 369–370; and transmission of information to Congress, 395; and presidential prerogative, 441; and declassification of documents, 445
State Highway Commission v. Volpe and Weinberger, 521
Steel industry, Truman's seizure of (1952), 141–148, 188, 208, 263–264, 271, 294; and Supreme Court, 143–150, 289, 347, 359, 395
Stein, Harold, 141, 512
Steinbeck, John, 424
Stennis, John, 171, 317, 318
Stern, Laurence, 530
Stevens, Thaddeus, 73
Stevenson, Adlai, 217
Stewart, Potter, 231, 289; and Pentagon Papers, 347, 359–360; and Mink case, 365

Steyn, Lord, xx
Stimson, Henry L., 109, 123, 219; and secret classification of documents, 338
Stone, Harlan Fiske, 114, 370, 526
Stone, I. F., 526
Stone, Jeremy J., 523
Story, Joseph, 16, 26, 39; on A. Jackson's imperiousness, 35; on presidential authority to determine exigency, 36; and proposal that cabinet members be available for congressional debate, 390–392; cited, 503, 504
Story, W. W., 504
Strachan, Gordon, 381
Strout, Richard Lee ("TRB"), 461, 523
Subsidies, 233
Subversive Activities Control Board, 245–246
Suez Canal, 138
Sumatra, 51, 52
Summers, Hatton, 76
Sumner, Charles, 78, 326
Sunday Telegraph, London, 353
Sundquist, James L., 545
Supreme Court, U.S., 11, 21, 25, 210, 435. 479; and Lincoln's theory of war power, xiv, 64–65, 69–70; and presidential authority to declare exigency, 36, 320; in re Neagle, 55, 82–83; and President's role as Commander in Chief, 62, 114–115, 143–145; and efforts to bridle Presidency, 69; and impeachment, 70–71; and Tenure of Office Act, 72; and in re Debs (presidential intervention in labor disputes), 83; and FDR, 100–101, 114–115; and distinction between President's power in domestic and foreign matters, 101–102; and executive control of information, 102, 394; doctrine of inherent presidential authority in foreign affairs, 102–103; and constitutional validity of executive agreement, 103; and internment of Japanese-Americans (World War II), 116; and Truman administration, 140–141, 143, 149–150, 289, 347, 359,

Supreme Court, U.S. (*cont.*)
395; and pocket veto, 242–243; and
Carswell nomination, 245; and legislative privilege, 246; and wiretapping, 257, 265; and Watergate case
tapes, 271; and President's war-making power, 287; and doctrine of "political questions," 288–290; and
retroactive legislative ratification of
executive initiative, 291; and constitutionality of operations in Cambodia, 294–295; and treaty power, 311;
and Espionage Act, 338; and the
Pentagon Papers, 347, 359–360; and
Mink case, 365, 369; and *Curtiss-
Wright,* 443–444; and *Schechter* case,
444
Surveillance, electronic, 260. *See also*
Wiretapping
Sutherland, George, 101–104, 151, 444.
526
Sweden, 232
Symington, Stuart, 247, 375, 517, 518,
529, 530; his committee to investigate secret military agreements,
201–206, 355; and deployment of nuclear weapons, 206; and control of
troop deployment, 307–308, 310;
and control of CIA operations, 317

Taft, Alphonso, 286
Taft, Robert A., 111, 129, 160; and
American intervention in Korea,
132, 134; and debate concerning
President's commitment of troops
abroad (1951), 137–138, 139, 140,
179, 286, 307; and secrecy in foreign
affairs, 354–355; cited, 510, 511, 512
Taft, William Howard, 84, 429–430, 481;
and commitment of armed forces
overseas, 89–91, 137, 286, 308; and
arbitration treaties, 93; and executive emergency prerogative, 322; and
length of President's term of office,
387; and cabinet members and Congress, 389–392; on item veto, 478; on
role of ex-Presidents, 485, 489; cited,
507, 508, 509, 530, 539, 545, 548

Talbot v. Seeman, 22
Talleyrand, Charles, 333
Tampico, 92
Taney, Roger B., 61, 65, 72, 219; on defi-
nitions of "treaty" and "agreement,"
85
Tansill, C. C., 501, 531, 538, 543, 548
Tappan, Benjamin, 334, 345
Tappan, Lewis, 334, 345
Tariffs, 3; and Nixon, 233–234; and
FDR, 402
Taubman, Philip, 546
Taxation, 251, 402–403
Taylor, John, 450, 546
Taylor, General Maxwell, 344
Taylor, Telford, 158, 502, 513
Taylor, Zachary, 42
Teapot Dome scandal, 154, 159
Technology, 166
Television, 209, 229; and presidential
addresses, 226
Teller, Edward, 362, 367, 535–536
Tenure of Office Act, 71–72, 379, 507
Terrorism, xviii, xix–xx, xxiii–xxiv
Texas, recognition and attempted an-
nexation of, xxii, 15, 29, 38–39; Polk's
deployment of troops (1846), 41, 43;
and Senate's treaty veto, 85; secrecy
in negotiations over acquisition of,
334, 361
Thach, C. C., 538, 539
Thatcher, Margaret, 465, 468
Thailand, 194, 328; and U.S. joint con-
tingency plan, 202–203
Third parties, 427, 481–482
Thomas, Hugh, 522
Thorne, Samuel E., 543
Tigar, M. E., 526
Tilden, Samuel J., 482
Tocqueville, Alexis de, 126, 199, 279,
281, 284, 319; on foreign relations, x;
on freedom of press, 228; on executive power, 420–421; on legislators'
dependence on constituents, 426; on
mass democracy, 432; on laws and
customs, 490; cited, 511, 517, 520,
538, 544, 545, 549
Tonkin Gulf incident, 343, 356

Tonkin Gulf resolution, 162, 177–182, 292, 516; and Nixon, 187, 190, 194, 378; repeal of, 187, 195, 378; and Supreme Court, 290; as precedent, 306

Torbert, Horace, 516

Total Information Awareness Project, xix

Tourtellot, H. B., 502, 549

Tower Commission, 453

Trade, foreign: and Nixon, 234; and FDR, 402

Trading with the Enemy Act (1917), 320

Treasury, U.S. Department of, 259

Treaty-making power, 3–5, 17–20, 41, 266, 311, 450; and Congress, 3, 150–151; and Senate, 78–80, 85, 93–94, 103; and Eisenhower, 165, 202, 203–204, 356. See also Executive agreement

Treaty of Ghent, 79

Treaty of Versailles, xv, 94, 118, 123, 283, 297, 337, 508

Trevor-Roper, Hugh, 275–277, 525

Trewhitt, H. L., 514

Tripolitanian War, 22–23, 160; attacked by French (1957), 192

Trist, Nicholas P., 449

Troop deployment, 41–42, 78, 88–94, 137–139; and Tyler, 39–41; and Lincoln, 42–43; and Commander in Chief clause, 89–91; and Congress, 90–91, 135–140, 306, 311; and Wilson, 91–93; and Korea, 135–140, 179; and LBJ, 178–187; and Nixon, 187–193, 285; and globalist policy, 298; and Congress's war-powers bills, 301–302, 305–306; and presidential discretion, 306–310; and Congress's campaign against executive agreement, 306–311

Truman, Harry S., 23, 118, 128–150, 159, 177, 320, 384, 425, 450, 466, 499, 519; and Imperial Presidency, xv, 213, 216, 217; and domestic policy, 127, 129, 208; and Congress, 127–129, 131, 142–143, 150, 206, 270, 320; and cen-

tralization of foreign policy, 128–129; bipartisanship in foreign policy, 128–129; and China policy, 130; and Korea, 131–135, 160, 179, 421; as Commander in Chief, 132–140, 143–144, 512; and commitment of troops abroad (1951), 135–140, 179, 307–308; his theory of presidential power, 140–145, 188, 210; and emergency prerogative, 142–150, 263, 320–321, 323; and seizure of steel mills (1952), 142–150, 188, 208, 263, 264, 271, 289, 294; and the Supreme Court, 143–150, 271; Eisenhower's view of, 152; and internal-security information, 153–155; and national-security expenditures, 165; his advisers, 219; his White House assistants, 221; and presidential press conference, 224–225; his attitude toward the press, 230; and impoundment, 236, 239; and pocket veto, 243; and control of CIA, 316–317; and government secrecy, 340; moral atmosphere of his White House, 381; as former President, 487; cited, 512, 513, 514, 520, 524, 529, 536, 542, 544

Truman Doctrine, 128

Tuchman, Barbara, 382, 538

Tugwell, Rexford G., 538

Turkey, 128

Turner, Stansfield, 448–449 (note)

Twain, Mark, 427

Twentieth Century Fund Task Force on Reform of the Presidential Election Process, 483

Tyler, John, 39–41, 54, 77, 142, 447, 486; and Texas, xii; constitutional views, 39; and congressional war-making power, 41; and control of information, 46–47, 47–48, 83; secrecy in administration of, 334–335

Udall, Morris, 413, 414

Udall, Stewart, 220

Unemployment. See Employment

Union Congress (1864), 390

United Nations, 119–122, 136, 183; General Assembly, 119, 329; Security Council, 120, 121, 131; charter, 121, 133; peace-keeping force in Palestine (1948), 131; and Korea, 131–135, 138, 179, 434; Nixon's contempt for, 232

United Nations Participation Act, 121, 133, 512

United Nations Relief and Rehabilitation Administration, 118

United States Information Agency (USIA), 395–396

United States Steel Corporation, 84

United States v. Belmont, 103–104

United States v. Sisson, 527

United States v. U.S. District Court, 523

Upshur, Abel P., 39–40, 80

Urban, George, 462–463, 547

U.S. v. Brewster, 522

U.S. v. Curtiss-Wright Corporation et al., 100–103, 104, 107, 401–402, 443–444, 545; cited in debate *re* commitment of troops abroad, 138; cited, 526

U.S. v. Gravel, 540

U.S. v. Reynolds, et al., 540

U.S.A. Patriot Act. *See* Patriot Act (2001)

Usurpation of power, versus the Imperial Presidency, xii–xiii

Van Buren, Martin, 38, 219; constraint of public opinion on, 39

Vance, Cyrus, 548

Vandenberg, Arthur H., 118, 120, 122, 326, 329, 373; and Truman's foreign policy, 128; and bipartisanship in foreign policy, 129; and China, 130; and President's defense prerogative, 131; and Korea, 132–134; debate *re* commitment of troops abroad, 139; and secrecy in foreign affairs, 354–355; delegation of economic power to President, 402–403; cited, 510, 511, 512, 537

Vattel, Emmerich von, 85, 87, 107

Veblen, Thorstein, 337, 532

Velde, Harold, 524

Venezuela, 78

Vera Cruz, 92, 134

Versailles, Treaty of, 94, 118, 123, 297, 508; and congressional control of foreign relations, 283; and Wilson's dream of open diplomacy, 337

Veto, 305; item (or line item), 236, 473, 476–478; and funds for war in Cambodia, 293; government by, 433; legislative, 435. *See also* Item veto; Pocket veto

Victor Emmanuel 11, of Italy, 367

Vietnam War, 175, 177–207, 356, 421; and Tonkin Gulf resolution, xv, 179–181, 190, 378; lack of congressional consultation in presidential decisions, xv, 180–182; Ashcroft's and Cheney's deferments during, xviii; and Kennedy, 177–178, 310, 361; and Congress, 178–182, 194, 196, 290–292, 293; and Johnson, 177–187, 193, 215–216, 290, 303–304, 356, 385–386; and SEATO, 182–183; official justification of constitutionality, 183; and enlargement of doctrine of defensive war, 184; debate with LBJ surrounding involvement and escalation, 185–187; and Nixon, 187–207 *passim,* 232, 290, 357, 379; and centralization of presidential authority, 208; foreign criticism of, 232; and LBJ's impoundment of appropriations, 236; Nixon-ordered history of events related to, 262–263; discrediting of theory of executive control of foreign relations, 282–284, 297; and the judiciary, 284–290; and congressional appropriations, 290–292; cease-fire, 293; and congressional war-powers bills, 301–307 *passim;* and controversy *re* executive agreements, 311; and government secrecy, 356–357, 361–362, 448; availability of information concerning, 374

Villa, Pancho, 92

Vinson, Carl, 207, 237

Vinson, Fred, 23, 148; in Truman cabinet, 219

Virgin Islands, xxii
Voorhis, Jerry, 217
Vote of confidence, 460, 466 (loss of)

Waddy, Joseph C., 541
Wade, Benjamin F., 74
Walker, General Edwin A., 517
Wallace, Henry A., 219, 409
Wall Street Journal, 272
Walters, General Vernon, 274, 525
War Department, U.S., 338. *See also*
   Pentagon
War Hawks of 1812, 296
War Investigating Committee, Second
   World War, 118
War Labor Disputes Act, 110
War-making power, 2, 35–43, 98,
   282–284, 441–445, 460, 503; and LBJ,
   xv, 177–187, 193–195; and Nixon, xv,
   187–195, 252, 266; and Congress, 3–5,
   18–23, 26–29, 35, 37–38, 41, 50,
   55–56, 77–78, 189, 200, 401, 421, 423;
   and President as Commander in
   Chief, 5–6; testing of executive
   power, 18–23; intent of Founding Fathers, 21, 35; and Jefferson, 22–25,
   28; and Madison, 26, 28–29; and
   J. Q. Adams, 26–27; and Monroe,
   27; and Jackson, 28, 29, 52–54; and
   Lincoln, 42–43, 58–63, 64–67,
   192–193; and Buchanan, 56; and
   Supreme Court (1930s), 102–103;
   and Grant, 77–78; and Hayes, 78;
   and Cold War, 168–170; in Britain,
   279–280; and popular control,
   283–284, 301; judicial interpretation,
   284–290, 292–295; assumptions of
   congressional or presidential superiority in, 295–298; congressional attempts to restrain presidential,
   301–307; war-powers bills, 301–307;
   attempts to restore constitutional
   balance, 324–326; and restoration of
   congressional-presidential partnership in, 325, 393–394; and War Powers Resolution, 433–435; and Reagan, 443
Warner, Charles Dudley, 427

War of 1812, 26, 33, 36, 52, 442; secrecy
   in, 334
War Powers Acts: First, 110; Second,
   115
War-powers bills, 301–307, 310, 318;
   and troop deployment, 301–302;
   deadline for presidential war, 303,
   305; effect of Senate bill, 303–304;
   effect of House bill, 305; and concurrent resolution, 306; precedents for,
   306
War Powers Resolution of 1973, 423,
   433–435, 441; origins of, 301–307. *See
   also* War-powers bills
Washburne, Elihu, 80
Washington, Bushrod, 21–22
Washington, George, 2, 6, 34, 41, 49,
   102, 377, 384, 428, 447, 545; and foreign relations, 3, 319; on presidential
   prerogative, 10; and application of
   Constitution, 13–15; and precedent
   on control of information, 15–18, 43,
   83, 117, 156; testing of foreign-policy
   function, 18–20, 98; and treaty-making process, 79; appearance before
   Congress, 269; and secrecy system,
   333; on re-eligibility of the President,
   388; cited, 539
Washington Post, 158, 169, 198, 231,
   374; and Pentagon Papers, 346–347
Watergate, 227, 262, 266–277, 278, 350,
   356, 377, 416, 436, 466–467; and the
   Washington Post, 231–232; Alsop on,
   268; and Nixon's refusal to release
   tapes of presidential conversations,
   270–273, 405; and leaks to newspapers, 275; importance of, 275–276;
   and Nixon's attempted reforms of security-classification system, 351; and
   complexity and size of Presidency,
   382; and the institution of Presidency, 405; as deterrent to future
   presidential abuse, 417–418; and
   "national security," 457; cited,
   533–534
Water Pollution Control Act, 240
Weathermen, 257, 264
Weber, Max, 337

Webster, Daniel, 40, 47, 285, 326; and
Perry's mission to Japan, 54
Webster-Ashburton Treaty (1842),
47–48
Wechster, Herbert, 289, 297–298, 526,
528
Wechsler, James, 524
Weimar Republic, 323
Welles, Gideon, 219
Wellington, Duke of (Sir Arthur
Wellesley), 352
West, Rebecca, 543
Wheeler, Burton K., 444
Wheeler, Charles, 538
Wheeler, General Earl, 204–205
Wherry, Kenneth, 132
White, Alexander, 9
White, Byron R., 347
White, L. D., 502
White, William Allen, 107
Whitehead, Clay, 521
White House Office of Telecommuni-
cations, 231, 521
White House staff: and Nixon's exten-
sion of executive privilege, 250–252;
future reduction of, 408; expansion
of, 494–497
Whiting, William, 63–64, 506
Whitman, Walt, xxii, 407, 419, 499, 542,
544, 550
Wiggins, J. Russell, 505
Wilcox, Francis O., 329, 531
Wildavsky, Aaron, 542
Wilkinson, General James, 30–31, 32
Williams, Francis, 520
Williams et al. v. Phillips, 522
Willkie, Wendell, 107
Willoughby, W. W., 308, 529
Wills, Frank, 269, 275
Wills, Garry, 428, 544
Wilmerding, Lucius, Jr., 10, 148–149,
480 (note); distinction between
abuse and usurpation of power, 149;
cited, 502, 513
Wilson, Harold, 249, 353, 368
Wilson, James, 4, 43, 383, 386, 502
Wilson, Woodrow, 1, 92–93, 95, 97, 117,

134, 389, 431; and congressional government, xiv, 76, 406, 407, 426; and
World War I, xiv, 92; choice of attorney general, xvii; view of impeachment process, 75; and treaty-making
process, 79, 80, 93–94; and balance of
power in federal system, 82, 324, 326;
and presidential power over troop
deployment, 91–92; and peace organization, 298; and FDR, 109, 115,
118; Congress's repudiation of, following World War I, 127; as "model
President," 210; and public opinion,
213; his advisers, 219; and presidential press conferences, 223; meetings
with congressional committees, 270;
on culpability of government officers, 273; and government secrecy,
336, 337, 355, 366; and Congress's informing function, 375; and strains of
office, 382, 385; and cabinet members and Congress, 391; on U.S. financial policy, 398; and national authority embodied in Presidency, 404;
and constitutional reform, 460; cited,
501, 507–508, 509, 525, 530, 532, 537,
538, 539, 540, 542, 544, 545
Winchester, Simon, 519
Wintour, Charles, 534
Wiretapping, 230, 256–257, 265
Wirtz, Willard, 220
Wise, David, 533, 534, 536
Wolfe, Bertram D., 543
Wolkinson, Herman, 155–156, 159, 248,
513
Woodbury, Levi, 52–53, 219
Woods v. Miller (1948), 141, 512
Woodward, August B., 538
World Almanac, xviii
World Court treaty (1935), 96
World War I. See First World War
World War II. See Second World War
Wormuth, F. D., 504, 506, 511, 516
Wright, Loyd, 341, 348, 352
Wright, Oliver, 468, 548
Wright, Quincy, 307, 308, 503, 506, 528
Wright v. United States, 243

Wyatt, Woodrow, 466, 467, 469, 547,
 548
Wyatt-Brown, Bertram, 532
Wyzanski, Charles, 292, 509, 516–517,
 527

Yalta Conference, 151, 315
Young, David, 348
*Youngstown Sheet & Tube Co. v.
 Sawyer,* 513, 524, 545, 548, 549
Yunker, J. H., 549

ARTHUR M. SCHLESINGER, JR., the author of eighteen books, is a renowned historian, public intellectual, and political activist. He served as special assistant to President John F. Kennedy and won two Pulitzer Prizes, in 1946 for *The Age of Jackson* and in 1966 for *A Thousand Days*. He also won the National Book Award twice, for *A Thousand Days* and for *Robert Kennedy and His Times* in 1979. In 1998 he was awarded the prestigious National Humanities Medal. He lives in New York City.